Rushden
08

C000196772

STREET ~~ATLAS~~

Denbighshire
Flintshire Wrexham

ATLAS STRYDOEDD Sir Ddinbych, Sir Y Fflint, Wrecsam

First published 2004 by

Philip's, a division of
Octopus Publishing Group Ltd
2-4 Heron Quays, London E14 4JP

First edition 2004
First impression 2004

ISBN 0-540-08589-8 (spiral)

© Philip's 2004

OS Ordnance Survey®

This product includes mapping data licensed from Ordnance Survey® with the permission of the Controller of Her Majesty's Stationery Office. © Crown copyright 2004. All rights reserved. Licence number 100011710.

Printed and bound in Italy by Rotolito

Contents

II **Key to map pages**

IV **Route planning**

VI **Key to map symbols**

VIII **Administrative and Postcode boundaries**

1 **Street maps** at 3½ inches to 1 mile

116 **Street maps** at 1¾ inches to 1 mile

140 **Street maps** at 3½ inches to 1 mile

144 **Street maps of centres of Chester and Wrexham** at 7 inches to 1 mile

146 **Index** of towns and villages

148 **Index** of streets, hospitals, industrial estates, railway stations, schools, shopping centres, universities and places of interest

Digital Data

The exceptionally high-quality mapping found in this atlas is available as digital data in TIFF format, which is easily convertible to other bitmapped (raster) image formats.

The index is also available in digital form as a standard database table. It contains all the details found in the printed index together with the National Grid reference for the map square in which each entry is named.

For further information and to discuss your requirements, please contact Philip's on 020 7644 6932 or james.mann@philips-maps.co.uk

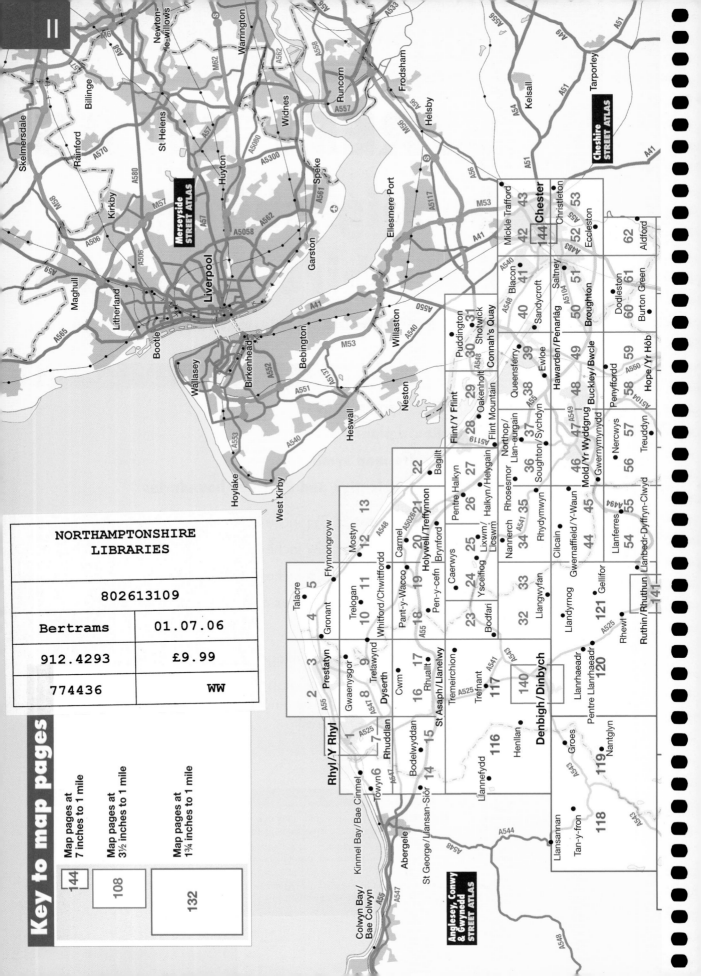

Key to map pages

Map pages at
7 inches to 1 mile
144

Map pages at
3½ inches to 1 mile
108

Map pages at
1¾ inches to 1 mile
132

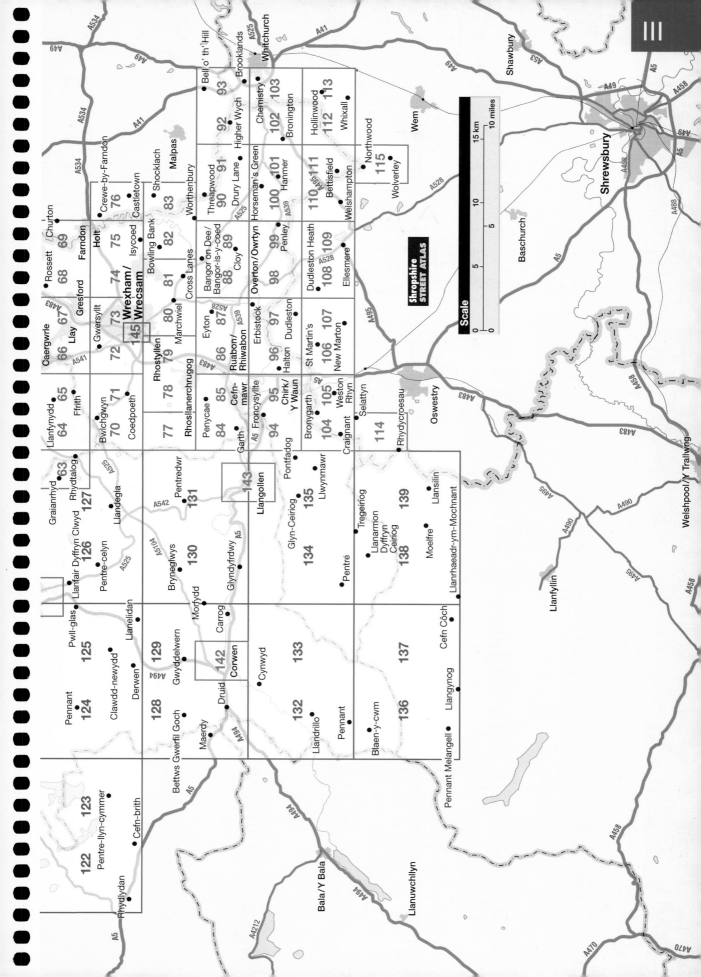

Shropshire STREET ATLAS

Scale

15 km
10 miles

Shrewsbury

Shawbury

Baschurch

Welshpool / Y Trallwng

Oswestry

Llanfyllin

Whitchurch

Bello'th'Hill **93**

Brooklands

Higher Wych **92**

Chemistry **103**
Bronington **102**

Hollinwood **113**
Whixall **112**

Northwood **115**
Wolverley

Crewe-by-Farndon
Shocklach **76**
Castletown
Malpas **83**
Shocklach **82**
Worthenbury

Threapwood **91**
Drury Lane **90**
Horseman's Green **101**
Hanmer **100**
Penley **99**
Welshampton

Bettisfield **111**
Dudleston Heath **110**
Ellesmere **109**

Churton **69**
Rossett **68**
Farndon
Holt **75**
Isycoed **74**
Bowling Bank **81**
Cross Lanes

Bangor on Dee / Bangor-is-y-coed **89**
Cloy **88**
Overton/Owrtyn **98**
Penley **97**

St Martin's **107**
New Marton **106**

Caergwrle **66**
Llay **67**
Gresford **73**
Wrexham / Wrecsam **145**
Rhostyllen **80**
Marchwiel **79**
Eyton **87**
Ruabon / Rhiwabon **86**
Erbistock **96**
Dudleston **95**
Halton

Selattyn **114**
Rhydycroesau

Llanfynydd **65**
Ffrith **64**
Bwlchgwyn **71**
Coedpoeth **70**
Rhosllanerchrugog **78**
Penycae **85**
Cefn-mawr **84**
Froncysyllte **94**
Chirk / Y Waun **105**
Bronygarth **104**
Craignant
Weston Rhyn

Graianrhyd **63**
Rhydtalog **127**
Llandegla
Pentredwr **131**
Llangollen **143**

Glyn-Ceiriog **135**
Llwynmawr
Tregeiriog **139**
Llansilin
Llanrhaeadr-ym-Mochnant

Llanfair Dyffryn Clwyd **126**
Pentre-celyn
Bryneglwys **130**
Glyndyfrdwy

Llanarmon Dyffryn Ceiriog **138**
Moelfre
Pentre **134**

Pwll-glas **125**
Llanelidan
Morfydd
Carrog **142**
Corwen
Cynwyd **133**
Llangynog
Cefn Côch **137**

Pennant **124**
Clawdd-newydd
Derwen **128**
Gwyddelwern **129**
Druid
Maerdy

Llandrillo **132**
Pennant
Blaen-y-cwm **136**
Pennant Melangell

Bettws Gwerfil Goch

Pentre-llyn-cymmer **123**
Cefn-brith
Rhydlydan **122**

Bala / Y Bala
Llanuwchllyn

I R I S H   S E A

HOYLAKE

West Hoyle Bank
Hilbre Island
West Kirby

rmes Head /
-y-Gogarth
Toll
Point of Ayr
Talacre
Mostyn Bank

LLANDUDNO
Little Ormes Head
Penrhyn Bay
Penrhyn-side
Llanrhos
Tywyn
Llandudno Junction
Mochdre
Llansanffraid Glan Conwy
Bryn-y-maen
Pentrefelin
A470

RHYL/Y RHYL   PRESTATYN
A548
Gronant
Gwespyr
Pen-y-ffordd
Flynnongroyw
Meliden
Gwaenysgor
Llanasa
Mostyn
Trelogan
Glan-y-don

COLWYN BAY/BAE COLWYN
Abergele Roads
Rhôs-on-Sea
Llandrillo-yn-Rhos
Old Colwyn
Llanelian-yn-Rhos
Llyslaen
Rhyd-y-foel
Dolwen
Betws-yn-Rhos

Kinmel Bay
Towyn
Pensarn
ABERGELE
Gwrych Castle
St George
Glascoed
A547
Pengwern
Bodelwyddan
A55

Rhuddlan
Dyserth
Moel Hiraddug
Cwm
Rhuallt

Gop Hill
Trelawnyd
Whitford
Downing
Carmel
Greenfield
Gorsedd
HOLYWELL/TREFFYNNON
Brynford
Milwr
Babell
Yscelfiog
Lixwm
Pentre Halkyn

St Asaph/Llanelwy
Llannerch Hall
Tremeirchion
Caerwys
Graig
Bodfari
Afon-wen
Nannerch
Rhosesmor
Hendre
Rhydymwyn
Cilcain
Gwernaffield-y-Waun

Dawn
Trofarth
Moelfre Uchaf
Mynydd Bodrochwyn
Moelfre Isaf
Llanefydd
Bont-newydd
Trefnant
Llangwyfan
Llandyrnog
Llangynhafal
Moel Famau
Jubilee Tower
Gellifor
Tafarn-y-Gelyn
Cadole
Maeshafn
Llanferres

Graig
Eglwysbach
Gell
Mwdwl Eithin
Rhos-y-mawn
Llanfair Talhaiarn
Cefn Berain
Henllan
DENBIGH/DINBYCH
Groes
Pentre
Llanrhaeadr
Pentre-Llanrhaeadr
Llanynys
Rhewl
Llanbedr-Dyffryn-Clwyd
RUTHIN/RHUTHUN
Eryrys
Llanarmon-yn-Ial
Llanfair Dyffryn Clwyd
Graig-fechan
Pentre-celyn
Llandegla
Pen-y-stryt

Tai-y-cafn
Llanddoged
A548
Pandy Tudur
Llangernyw
Llansannan
Tan-y-fron
Bylchau
Nantglyn
Gorsedd Bran
Saron
Prion
Pentre-Llanrhaeadr
Cyffylliog
Llanrhaeadr
Bontuchel
Llanfwrog
Efenechtyd
Pwll-glas
Nantclwyd Hall
Clawdd-newydd
Llanelidan

Pentre-tafarn-y-fedw
LLANRWST
Melin-y-coed
Pennant
Gwytherin
Aled Isaf Reservoir
Bryn Trillyn
Llyn Bran
Llyn Aled
Moel Seisiog
Llyn Aled
Moel Llyn
Llyn Alwen
Mynydd Hiraethog
Llyn Brenig
Nilig
Cefn Du
Clocaenog
Clocaenog Forest
Derwen

BETWS-Y-COED
Oaklands
Nebo
Capel Garmon
Fairy Glen
Conwy Falls
Glan Conwy
Penmachno
Ysbyty Ifan
Hafod-Dinbych
Alwen Reservoir
Pentrefoelas
Rhydlydan
Glasfryn
Cerrigydrudion
Garn Prys
Ty Mawr Cwm
Pentre-llyn-cymmer
Lianfihangel Glyn Myfyr
Melin-y-Wig
Bettws Gwerfil Goch
Gwyddelwern
A5104
Bryneglwys
Moe Morfydd
Llantysilio Mountain
Rhewl
Pentredwr
A542

Gellioedd
Ty-nant
Llangwm
Maerdy
A5
Glan-yr-afon
Druid
Carrog
River Dee/Afon Dyfrdwy
Corwen
Glyndyfrdwy
Berwyn
LLANGOLLEN

Carnedd y Filiast
A4212
Glan-yr-afon
Wenallt
Foel Goch
Cynwyd
Moel Fferna
Glyn Ceiriog
Plas Nantyr

Arenig Fach
Llyn Celyn
Frongoch
Sarnau
Cefn-ddwysarn
Rhiwlas
BALA/Y BALA
Llanfor
Llanycil
Pale
Cefn Coch
Llandrillo
Bryn Du
Pandy
Pentre
Tregeiriog
Llanarmon Dyffryn Ceiriog
Rhiwlas
B4500

Craig y Hyrddod
Arenig Fawr
Rhyd-uchaf
Rhos-y-gwaliau
Dinam
Foel Wen
Mynydd Tarw
Tyn-y-ffridd
Llangower
Pont Cwm Pydew
Moel Sych
Mynydd Mawr
Moelfre
Tai-bach

Mynydd Bryn-llech
Llanuwchllyn
Rhosdylluan
Dyrysgol
Foel Figenau
Foel y Geifr
Pennant Melangell
Llangynog
Pencraig
Craig Rhiwarth
Y Clogydd
Llanrhaeadr-yn-Mochnant

Rhobell Fawr
Aran Benllyn
Cwm Cynllwyd
Cedig
Alltforgan
Hirnant
Penybontfawr
Pennant
Pengarnedd
B4396
Efail-rhyd
Llangedwyn
A494

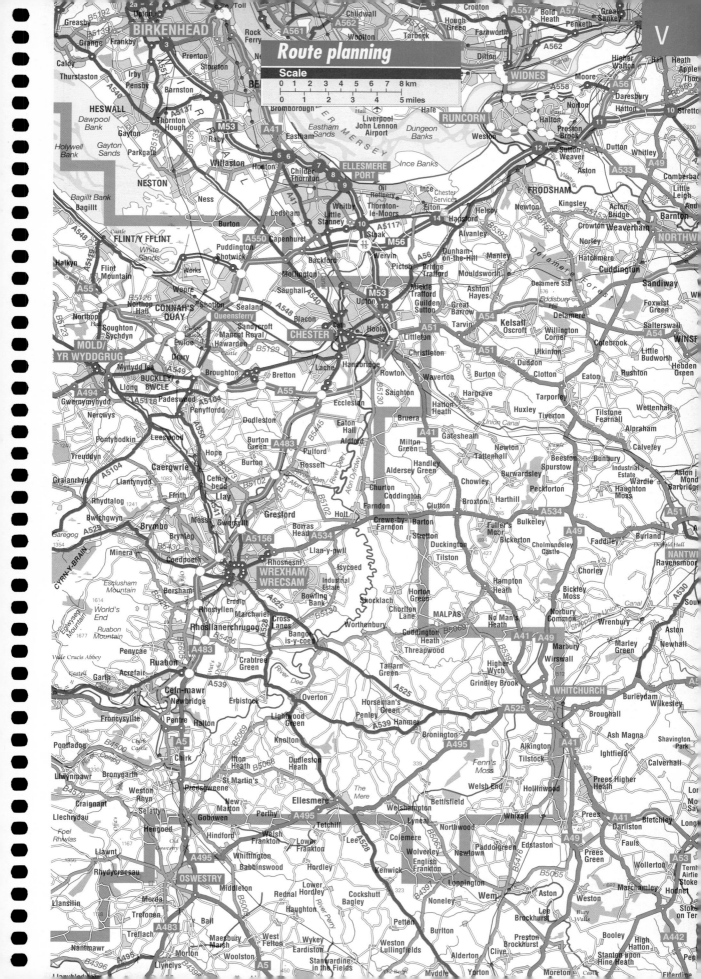

Allwedd i symbolau'r map

Symbol	Description
	Traffordd gyda rhif y gyffordd
	Prif dramwyfeydd – ffordd ddeuol/un lôn
	Ffordd A – ffordd ddeuol/un lôn
	Ffordd B – ffordd ddeuol/un lôn
	Ffyrdd bychan – ffordd ddeuol/un lôn
	Ffyrdd bychan eraill – ffordd ddeuol/un lôn
	Ffordd yn cael ei hadeiladu
	Twnnel, ffordd dan orchudd
	Trac gwledig, ffordd breifat, neu ffordd mewn ardal ddinesig
	Llidiart neu rhwystr i draffig (gall fod cyfyngiadau ddim yn ddilys ar gyfer bob amser neu i bob drafnidiaeth)
	Llwybr, llwybr march, cilffordd yn agored i bob trafnidiaeth, ffordd a ddefnyddir yn lwybr cyhoeddus
	Mân cerddwyr
DY7	**Ffiniau codau-post**
	Ffiniau Sir ac awdurdod unedol
	Rheilffordd, twnnel, rheilffordd yn cael ei hadeiladu
	Tramffordd, tramffordd yn cael ei hadeiladu
	Rheilffordd ar raddfa fychan
Walsall	**Gorsaf rheilffordd**
	Gorsaf rheilffordd breifat
South Shields	**Gorsaf metro**
	Atalfa tram, atalfa tram yn cael ei hadeiladu
	Gorsaf fysiau

Symbol	Description
	Gorsaf ambiwlans
	Gorsaf gwylwyr y glannau
	Gorsaf Dân
	Swyddfa'r heddlu
	Mynedfa damwain ac argyfwng i'r ysbyty
H	**Ysbyty**
	Lle o addoliad
i	**Canolfan gwybodaeth** (a'r agor drwy'r flwyddyn)
P	**Parcio**
P&R	**Parcio a chludo**
PO	**Swyddfa'r post**
	Safle gwersylla
	Safle carafan
	Cwrs golff
	Safle picnic
Prim Sch	**Adeiladau pwysig, ysgolion, colegau, prifysgolion ac ysbytai**
River Medway	**Enw dŵr**
	Afon, cored, nant
	Camlas, loc, twnnel
	Dŵr
	Dŵr llanw
	Coed
	Ardal adeiledig
Church	**Hynafiaeth anrhufeinig**
ROMAN FORT	**Hynafiaeth rhufeinig**
44 / 145	**Arwyddion dalennau cyfagos a bandiau gorymylon** Y mae lliw y saeth â'r band yn dynodi gradd y ddalen gyfagos â'r ddalen gorymyl (gwelwch y graddau islaw)

■ Y mae'r rhifau bach o gwmpas ochrau'r mapiau yn dynodi llinelli grid cenedlaethol 1 cilomedr
■ Mae'r ffin llwyd tywyll ar ochr fewn rhai tudalennau yn dynodi nad yw'r mapio yn canlyn ymlaen i'r tudalen gyffiniol

Acad	**Academi**	IRB Sta	**Gorsaf bad achub y glannau**	Pal	**Palas brenhinol**
Allot Gdns	**Gerddi ar osod**			PH	**Tŷ tafarn**
Cemy	**Mynwent**	Inst	**Institiwt**	Recn Gd	**Maes chwaraeon**
C Ctr	**Canolfan ddinesig**	Ct	**Llys cyfraith**	Resr	**Cronfa ddŵr**
		L Ctr	**Canolfan hamdden**	Ret Pk	**Parc adwerthu**
CH	**Tŷ Clwb**			Sch	**Ysgol**
Coll	**Coleg**	LC	**Croesfan wastad**	Sh Ctr	**Canolfan Siopa**
Crem	**Amlosgfa**			TH	**Neuadd y dref**
Ent	**Menter**	Liby	**Llyfrgell**	Trad Est	**Ystad Fasnachol**
Ex H	**Neuadd Arddangos**	Mkt	**Marchnad**	Univ	**Prifysgol**
		Meml	**Coffa**	W Twr	**Tŵrdŵr**
Ind Est	**Ystad ddiwydiannol**	Mon	**Cofgolofn**	Wks	**Gwaith**
		Mus	**Amgueddfa**	YH	**Hostel ieuenctid**
		Obsy	**Arsylffa**		

	Scale
Gradd y mapiau ar y dalennau gyda rhifau glas yw 5.52 cm i 1 km • 3½ modfedd i 1 filltir • 1: 18103	0 — ¼ — ½ — ¾ — 1 milltir / 0 — 250 m — 500 m — 750 m — 1 km
Gradd y mapiau ar y dalennau gyda rhifau gwyrdd yw 2.76 cm i 1 km • 1¾ modfedd i 1 filltir • 1: 36206	0 — ¼ — ½ — ¾ — 1 milltir / 0 — 250m — 500m — 750m — 1 km
Gradd y mapiau ar y dalennau gyda rhifau coch yw 11.04 cm i 1 km • 7 modfedd i 1 filltir • 1: 9051.4	0 — 220 yards — 440 yards — 660 yards — ½ milltir / 0 — 125 m — 250 m — 375 m — ½ km

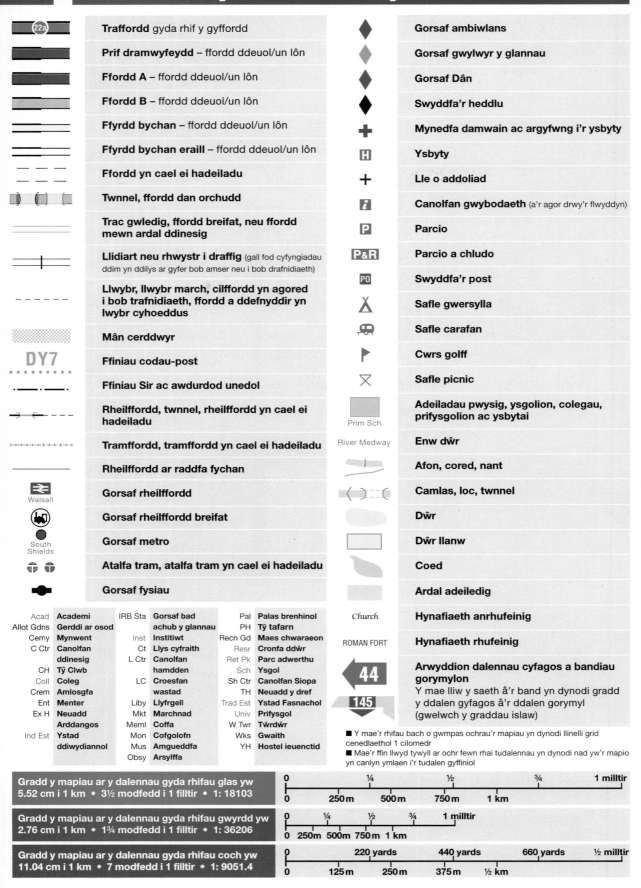

22a	**Motorway** with junction number
	Primary route – dual/single carriageway
	A road – dual/single carriageway
	B road – dual/single carriageway
	Minor road – dual/single carriageway
	Other minor road – dual/single carriageway
	Road under construction
	Tunnel, covered road
	Rural track, private road or narrow road in urban area
	Gate or obstruction to traffic (restrictions may not apply at all times or to all vehicles)
	Path, bridleway, byway open to all traffic, road used as a public path
	Pedestrianised area
DY7	**Postcode boundaries**
	County and unitary authority boundaries
	Railway, tunnel, railway under construction
	Tramway, tramway under construction
	Miniature railway
Walsall	**Railway station**
	Private railway station
South Shields	**Metro station**
	Tram stop, tram stop under construction
	Bus, coach station

◆	**Ambulance station**
◇	**Coastguard station**
◆	**Fire station**
◆	**Police station**
✚	**Accident and Emergency entrance to hospital**
H	**Hospital**
+	**Place of worship**
i	**Information Centre** (open all year)
P	**Parking**
P&R	**Park and Ride**
PO	**Post Office**
Å	**Camping site**
⚐	**Caravan site**
▶	**Golf course**
⋈	**Picnic site**
Prim Sch	**Important buildings, schools, colleges, universities and hospitals**
River Medway	**Water name**
	River, weir, stream
	Canal, lock, tunnel
	Water
	Tidal water
	Woods
	Built up area
Church	**Non-Roman antiquity**
ROMAN FORT	**Roman antiquity**
44 / 145	**Adjoining page indicators and overlap bands** The colour of the arrow and the band indicates the scale of the adjoining or overlapping page (see scales below)

Abbr	Full	Abbr	Full	Abbr	Full
Acad	**Academy**	Inst	**Institute**	Recn Gd	**Recreation Ground**
Allot Gdns	**Allotments**	Ct	**Law Court**		
Cemy	**Cemetery**	L Ctr	**Leisure Centre**	Resr	**Reservoir**
C Ctr	**Civic Centre**	LC	**Level Crossing**	Ret Pk	**Retail Park**
CH	**Club House**	Liby	**Library**	Sch	**School**
Coll	**College**	Mkt	**Market**	Sh Ctr	**Shopping Centre**
Crem	**Crematorium**	Meml	**Memorial**	TH	**Town Hall/House**
Ent	**Enterprise**	Mon	**Monument**	Trad Est	**Trading Estate**
Ex H	**Exhibition Hall**	Mus	**Museum**	Univ	**University**
Ind Est	**Industrial Estate**	Obsy	**Observatory**	W Twr	**Water Tower**
IRB Sta	**Inshore Rescue Boat Station**	Pal	**Royal Palace**	Wks	**Works**
		PH	**Public House**	YH	**Youth Hostel**

■ The small numbers around the edges of the maps identify the 1 kilometre National Grid lines

■ The dark grey border on the inside edge of some pages indicates that the mapping does not continue onto the adjacent page

The scale of the maps on the pages numbered in blue is 5.52 cm to 1 km • 3½ inches to 1 mile • 1: 18103

0 — ¼ — ½ — ¾ — 1 mile
0 — 250 m — 500 m — 750 m — 1 kilometre

The scale of the maps on pages numbered in green is 2.76 cm to 1 km • 1¾ inches to 1 mile • 1: 36206

0 — ¼ — ½ — ¾ — 1 mile
0 — 250m 500m 750m 1 kilometre

The scale of the maps on pages numbered in red is 11.04 cm to 1 km • 7 inches to 1 mile • 1: 9051.4

0 — 220 yards — 440 yards — 660 yards — ½ mile
0 — 125 m — 250 m — 375 m — ½ kilometre

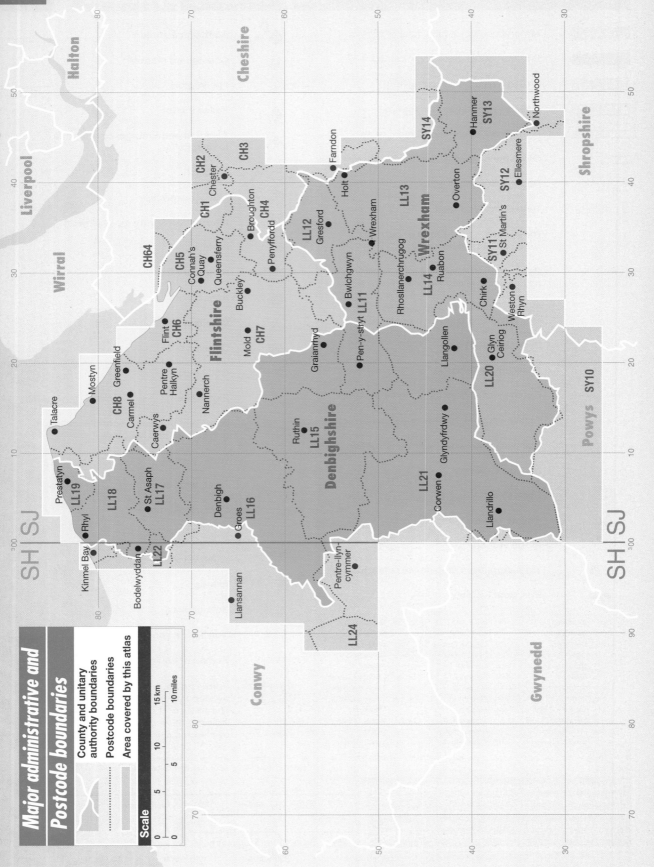

Major administrative and Postcode boundaries

County and unitary authority boundaries

Postcode boundaries

Area covered by this atlas

Scale

| 0 | 5 | 10 | 15 km |
| 0 | 5 | 10 miles |

A   B   C   D   E   F

8

7

85

6

5

84

4

Prestatyn
Nova Ctr

3

Traeth Ffnth/
Ffrith Beach

LLYS MYMBR
LLYS LLYDAW   LLYS VYRNWY
FFORDD IDWAL

LLYS ALED   LLYS BRAN
RHODA TEYRN   FFORDD IDWAL
RHODA PADARN   LLYS OGWEN

BERWYN CRES

GROSVENOR RD
WINDERMERE

A548
VICTORIA RD

LIDO BEACH
CVN PK

THIRD AVE
SECOND AVE
BEACH RD W
FIRST AVE

THE MALL

SEA RD
WENT CL
DEE

CHAPEL
TYWYN
ISAF

Festival
Gardens

Caravan
Park

PURBECK AVE

GLANDWR

SEABANK DR

PEN TYWYN
GLAN-Y-GORS

83

Holiday
Camp

KYNASTON RD
GREEN LANES

METHVEN DR

SANDIWAY

OLD DALE RD

BRIE-Y-DON

VICTORIA RD W

CERI AVE

MORGAN RD

MORRIS AVE
RUSSELL CR

PENLEY AVE

BEVERLEY DR

OVERTON AVE

MILMOR WAY

MONMOUTH
GR

1 VICTORIA LA
2 FFORDD FFRITH
3 POPLAR GR
4 SUSAN GR
5 CLOS GWAUN DEAU/
   SOUTH MEADOW CL
6 CLOS PRY COPYN
7 MIN Y MORFA
8 Tai Tywyn Bsns Pk
9 TYWYN GANOL
10 VICTORIA PARK AVE

2

WEST CL

EAST CL

JACLYN CL

EARLSWOOD AVE

VERNIC CL

ROY AVE

STEPHEN RD

RENE AVE

ADELE AVE

MARION RD

CATHERINE AVE

FFORDD PENRHWYLFA

PETER CL

LLANDAF DR

THE BROADWAY

THE WEALS

DURLSTON DR

STIRLING DR

LL18

RHYL COAST RD

A548

BROCKLANDS
CAMP

TERFYN PELLA AVE

SHENWOOD AVE

ARFON AVE

GARNETT DR

FRANKLYN AVE

CHARLESTON

THE BOULEVARD

LL19

TOWYN CL

MORFA CL

YORK CL

FFORDD PENRHWYLFA

WINCHESTER
CL

CHESTER
CL

DURHAM
DR

WORCESTER DR

ROCHESTER
DR

CHICHESTER
DR

BANGOR
CRES

ST
JAMES
DR
TIP LA

1

LYONS
HOLIDAY PK

ROBIN HOOD
HOLIDAY CAMP

TERFYN
PELLA
CAMP

CHRISTINA
AVE

Caravan
Site

LON TALIESIN 1
LON CYNAN 2

LON GWYNON

CRUD YR
AWEL

FFORDD PANT
Y CELYN
LON

FFORDD Y DYFFRYN

SALISBURY DR

CANTERBURY DR

82

FFORDD MAES YR HAF

03   A   04   B   C   D   05   E   F

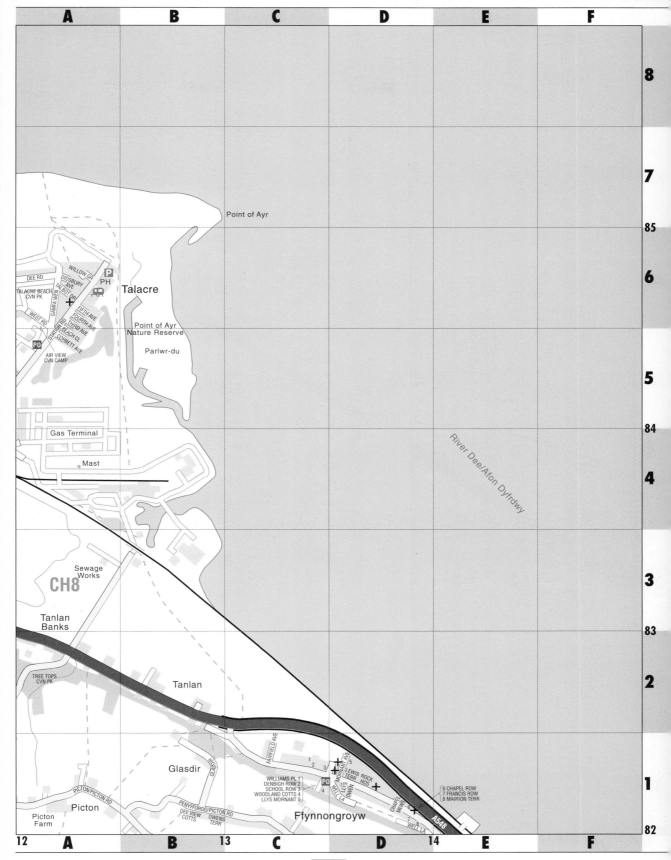

	A	B	C	D	E	F

8

7

85

Point of Ayr

6

WILLOW DR
DEE RD
DIDSBURY AVE
TALACRE BEACH CVN PK
GARN WEN
TALBOT DR
FIFTH AVE
WEST RD
FOURTH AVE
THIRD AVE
STATION RD
BEACH CL
CORBETT AVE
PH
P
Talacre

Point of Ayr
Nature Reserve

Parlwr-du

PO
AIR VIEW
CVN CAMP

5

84

Gas Terminal

River Dee/Afon Dyfrdwy

Mast

4

Sewage
Works

CH8

3

83

Tanlan
Banks

2

TREE TOPS
CVN PK

Tanlan

FAIRFIELD AVE

Glasdir

1

WILLIAMS PL 1
DENBIGH ROW 2
SCHOOL ROW 3
WOODLAND COTTS 4
LLYS MORNANT 5

GLASDIR

MORGAN AVE
LEWIS ROCK TERR
LLYS OWEN
WELL LA
PO

LEWIS ROCK
HOS

6 CHAPEL ROW
7 FRANCIS ROW
8 MAIRION TERR

PICTON/PICTON RD

PENYFFORDD/PICTON RD
DEE VIEW COTTS
OWENS TERR

Ffynnongroyw

CHAPEL MEWS

A548

WELL LA

Picton

Picton
Farm

82

12	A		B	13	C		D	14	E		F

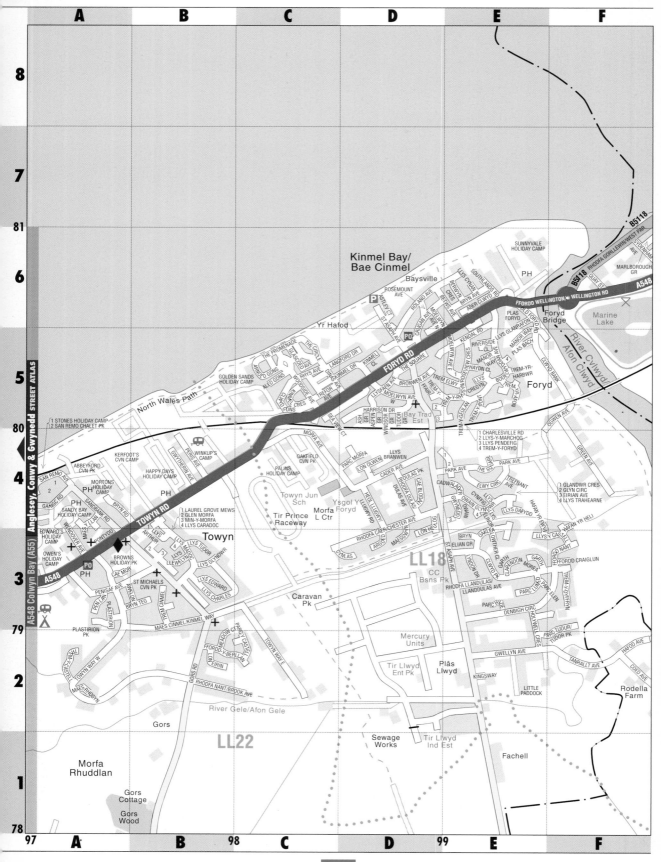

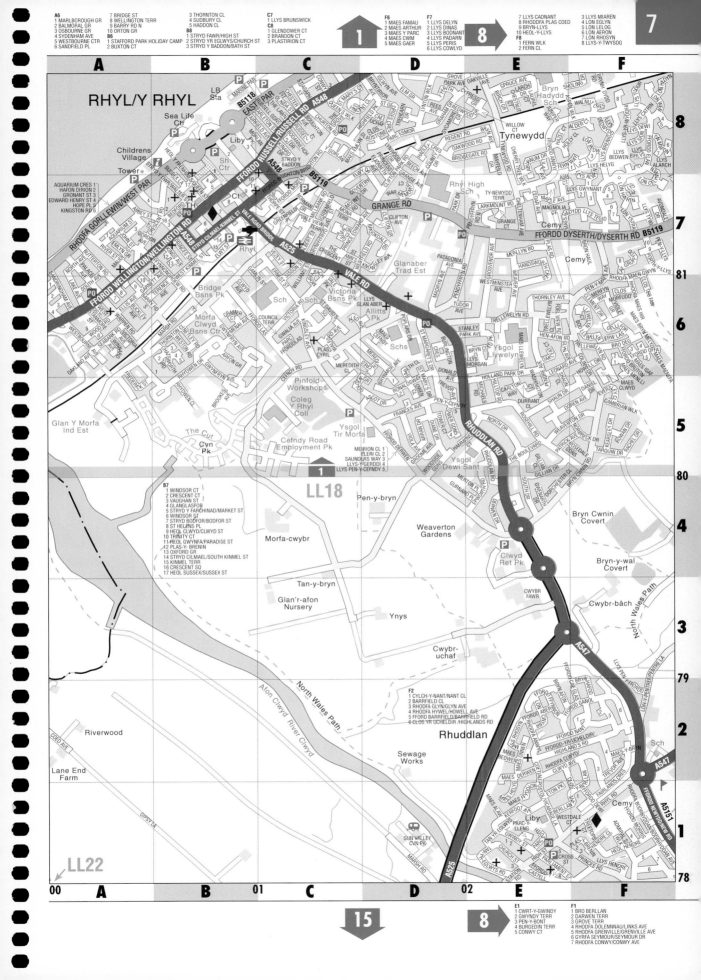

A6
1 MARLBOROUGH GR
2 BALMORAL GR
3 OSBOURNE GR
4 SYDENHAM AVE
5 WESTBOURNE CTR
6 SANDFIELD PL

7 BRIDGE ST
8 WELLINGTON TERR
9 BARRY RD N
10 ORTON GR

B6
1 STAFFORD PARK HOLIDAY CAMP
2 BUXTON CT

3 THORNTON CL
4 SUDBURY CL
5 HADDON CL

B8
1 STRYD FAWR/HIGH ST
2 STRYD YR EGLWYS/CHURCH ST
3 STRYD Y BADDON/BATH ST

C7
1 LLYS BRUNSWICK
C8
1 GLENDOWER CT
2 BRANDON CT
3 PLASTIRION CT

F6
1 MAES FAMAU
2 MAES ARTHUR
3 MAES Y PARC
4 MAES CWM
5 MAES GAER

F7
1 LLYS DELYN
2 LLYS DINAS
3 LLYS BODNANT
4 LLYS PADARN
5 LLYS PERIS
6 LLYS COWLYD

7 LLYS CADNANT
8 RHODDFA PLAS COED
9 BRYN-LLYS
10 HEOL-Y-LLYS

F8
1 FERN WLK
2 FERN CL

F1
1 LLYS MIAREN
2 LON EGLYN
3 LON LELOG
4 LON AERON
6 LON RHOSYN
8 LLYS-Y-TWYSOG

7

RHYL/Y RHYL

AQUARIUM CRES 1
HAFON DIRION 2
GRONANT ST 3
EDWARD HENRY ST 4
HOPE PL 5
KINGSTON RD 6

B7
1 WINDSOR CT
2 CRESCENT CT
3 VAUGHAN ST
4 GLANGLASFOR
5 STRYD Y FARCHINAD/MARKET ST
6 WINDSOR ST
7 STRYD BODFOR/BODFOR ST
8 ST HELENS PL
9 HEOL CLWYD/CLWYD ST
10 TRINITY CT
11 HEOL GWYNFA/PARADISE ST
12 PLAS-Y-BRENIN
13 OXFORD GR
14 STRYD CILMAEL/SOUTH KIMMEL ST
15 KINMEL TERR
16 CRESCENT SQ
17 HEOL SUSSEX/SUSSEX ST

LL18

LL22

F2
1 CYLCH-Y-NANT/NANT CL
2 BARRFIELD CL
3 RHODFA GLYN/GLYN AVE
4 RHODFA HYWEL/HOWELL AVE
5 FFORD BARRFIELD/BARRFIELD RD
6 CLOS YR UCHELDIR/HIGHLANDS RD

Rhuddlan

E1
1 CWRT-Y-GWINDY
2 GWYNDY TERR
3 PEN-Y-BONT
4 BURGEDIN TERR
5 CONWY CT

F1
1 BRO BERLLAN
2 DARWEN TERR
3 GROVE TERR
4 RHODFA DOLENNNAU/LINKS AVE
5 RHODFA GRENVILLE/GRENVILLE AVE
6 GYRFA SEYMOUR/SEYMOUR DR
7 RHODFA CONWY/CONWY AVE

15

8

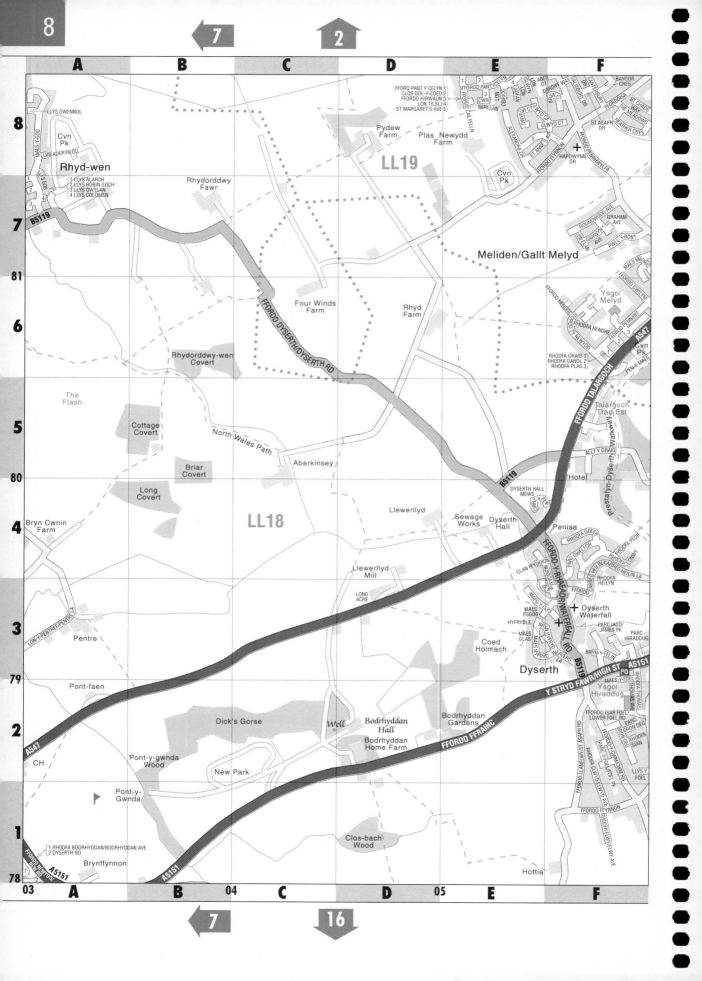

A **B** **C** **D** **E** **F**

8

LLYS GWENNOL
MAES-Y-GOG
Cvn
Pk
LLYS ADERYN DU
Rhyd-wen
1 LLYS ALARCH
2 LLYS ROBIN GOCH
3 LLYS GWYLAN
4 LLYS COLOMEN
LLYS EOS

Rhydorddwy
Fawr

FFORD PANT Y CELYN 1
CLOS DOL-Y-COED 2
FFORDD HIRWAUN 3
LON TILSLI 4
ST MARGARET'S AVE 5

Pydew
Farm

Plas Newydd
Farm

St Asaph
Dr
The Meadows

St Chads
Way

Bangor
Cres

Fforddisa

Heather Cres

Hardwynn Dr

Alexandra Dr

Canterbury

Cardiff Way
Salisbury Dr

Cwrt
Berllan

LL19

Cvn
Pk

Ffordd Ffynnon
Ffordd Fairwylfa

7
B5119

Roundwood Ave
Lon Eilwen Ave
Graham Ave

Pwll-y-Bont

Maes Me

Meliden/Gallt Melyd

Ffordd Gwilym

81

6

Four Winds
Farm

Rhyd
Farm

Ffordd Hendre
Ffordd Ty Newydd
Rhodfa Hendre

Ffordd Pennant

Ysgol
Melyd

A547

Rhydorddwy-wen
Covert

RHODFA GRAIG 1
RHODFA GANOL 2
RHODFA PLAS 3

Pen-y-Maes
Cvn
Pk

Ffordd Talargoch

Talargoch
Trad Est

The
Flash

North Wales Path

Cottage
Covert

Briar
Covert

Aberkinsey

Allt Y Graig

Prestatyn-Dyserth Walkway

5

80

Long
Covert

Llewerllyd

Sewage
Works

Dyserth
Hall

Hotel

B5119

Dyserth Hall
Mews

Penisa

4

Bryn Cwnin
Farm

LL18

Llewerllyd
Mill

Long
Acre

Glan Rhyddion

Ffordd-y-Rhaeadr/Waterfall Rd

Rhodfa Gofer
Rhodfa Pedh
Rhodfa Cinwy

Carreg Heilin
Carreg Heilin La
Rhodfa
Heilyn

Maes Teilys
Maes
Esgob

Dyserth
Waterfall

3

Pentre

LON-Y-PENTRE/PENTRE LA

Maes
Glas

Hyfrydle

Maes Hyfryd

Bryn Hyfryd
Weavers Ave

Bryn-y-Felin

PARC IAGO
James Pk

Parc
Hiraddug

Parc-y-felin

Coed
Holmach

Dyserth

B5119

A5151

79

Pont-faen

Maes-y-Foel

Ysgol
Hiraddug

Maes-Y-Foel

Ffordd Thomas

2

A547

Dick's Gorse

Well

Bodrhyddan
Hall

Bodrhyddan
Gardens

Ffordd Ffrainc

Bodrhyddan
Home Farm

Y Stryd Fawr/High St

PO

Ffordd Isar Foel
Lower Foel Rd

Bron Deg

Rhodfa
Sian

Pont-y-gwnda
Wood

New Park

Ffordd Llanelwy/St Asaph Rd

Rhodfa Clwyd/Clwyd Ave
Rhodfa-y-foel/Foel Pk

Ffordd-y-Conwy/Conwy Rd

Parc
Bron Deg

CH

1

1 RHODFA BODRHYDDAN/BODRHYDDAN AVE
2 DYSERTH RD

Pont-y-
Gwnda

Clos-bach
Wood

Ffordd Ffynnon

Rhodfa Elwy/Elwy Ave

Llys Y
Foel

78

Brynffynnon

A5151

Hottia

03 **A** **B** **04** **C** **D** **05** **E** **F**

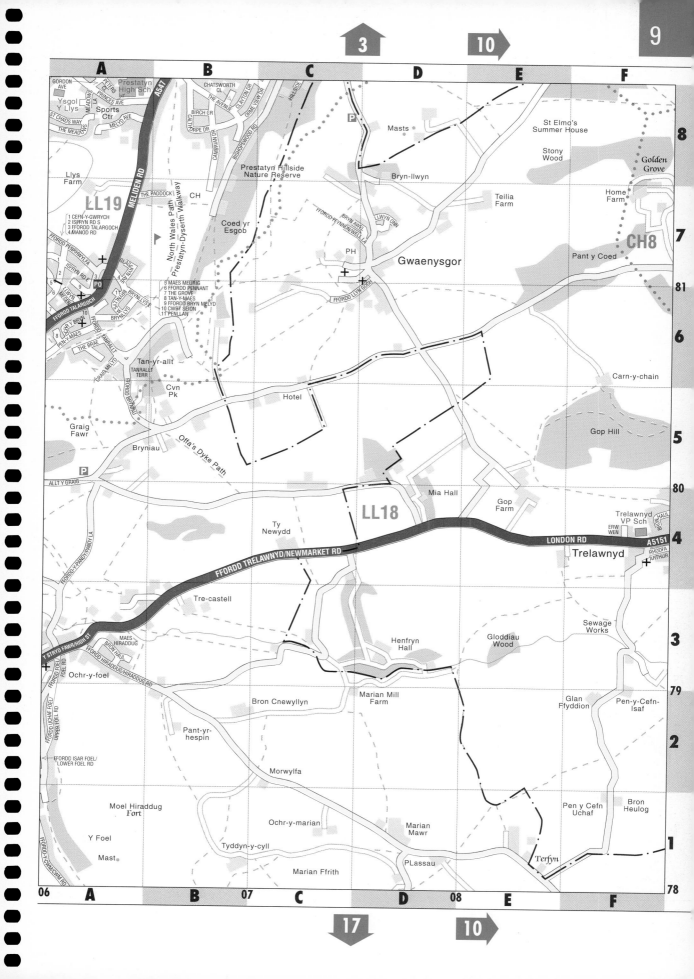

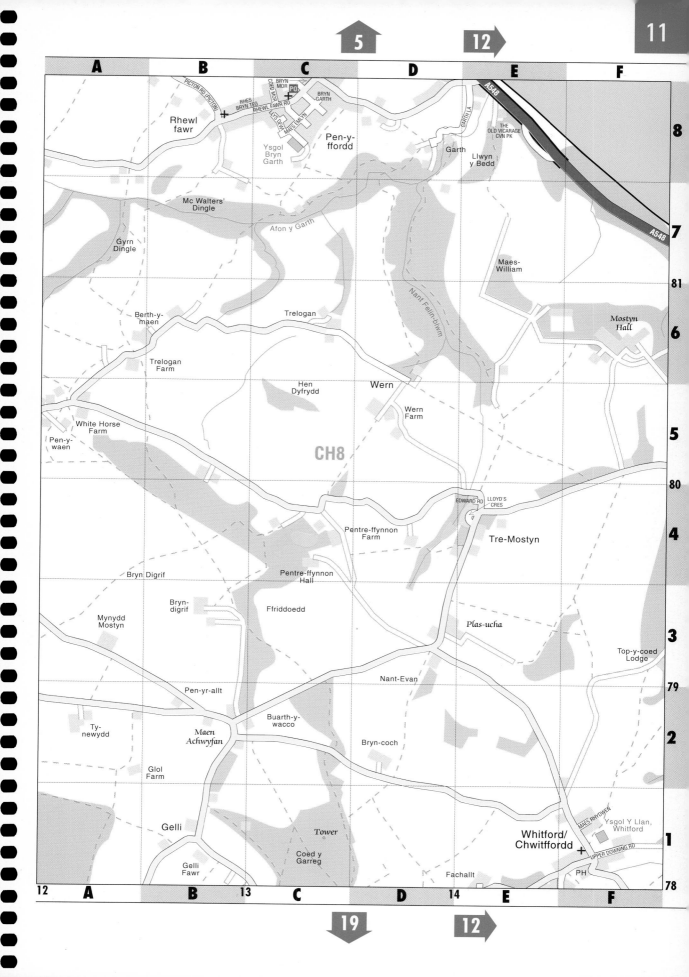

A   B   C   D   E   F

8

7

81

6

A548

PH

Mostyn
Quay

River Dee/Afon Dyfrdwy

Mostyn
Park

MIRRAL
VIEW

GLODDAETH
CRES

BRYN TIRION

Mostyn

5

PH

ALARCH

PO

Y NANT

PH

Sewage
Works

Rhewl-Mostyn

RED ST

80

BODHYFRYD

FFORDD
YSGUBOR

Bychton
Hall

FFORDD-Y-
FLYNNON

FFORDD AER

FFORDD AER

FFORDD DYFRDWY

Y OREFLAN

FFORDD HIRAETHOG

FFORDD PANDARUS

YSGOROI

GARDEN PONT

4

Ysgol
Bryn Pennant

PO

FFORDD PENNANT

Maes
Pennant

PH

Glan-y-don

Whitford
Wood

Caeau
Gwylltion

CH8

HAFOD-Y-
DDOL

3

Coed-isa

Gwibnant

HAFOD-Y-DDOL RD

Works

PH

Llannerch-y-
môr

P

79

Plas
Tirion

Gwibnant
Farm

Bryn-
Caesar

A548

2

LLYS-Y-WENNOL

Mertyn
Downing

Plás-tirion
Wood

CH

Hotel

Downing

Coed
Mertyn

Kennels
Farm

Mertyn
Isaf

Upper Downing
Hall

Mertryn-
Crewe

Pentre

1

Cae-côch

Bryn-y-baw

Llŷyn Ifor

LLWYN IFOR LK

ISGLAN RD

Afon Marsiandwr

78

15   A   B   16   C   D   17   E   F

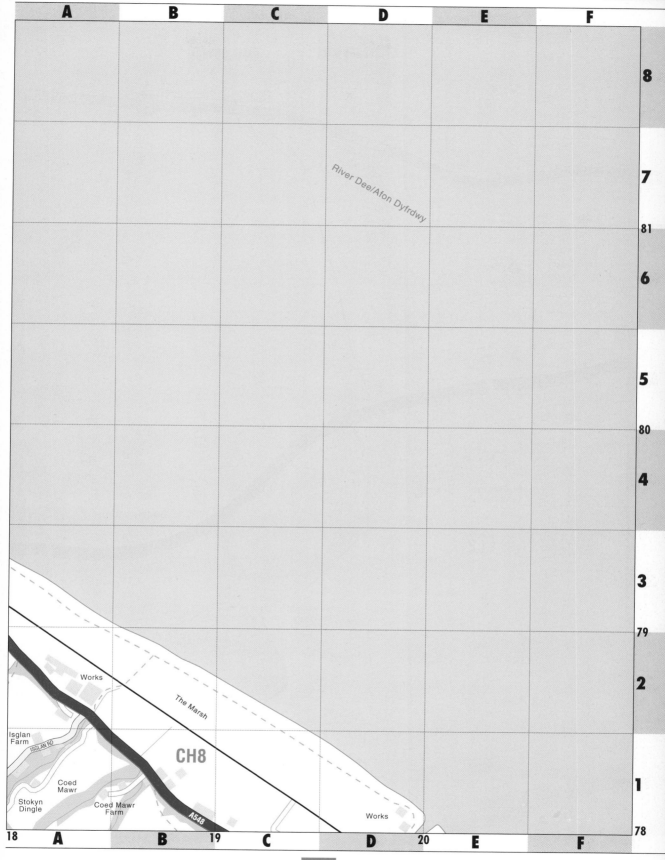

River Dee/Afon Dyfrdwy

Works

The Marsh

Isglan
Farm

ISGLAN RD

CH8

Coed
Mawr

Stokyn
Dingle

Coed Mawr
Farm

A548

Works

18   19   20

78   79   80   81

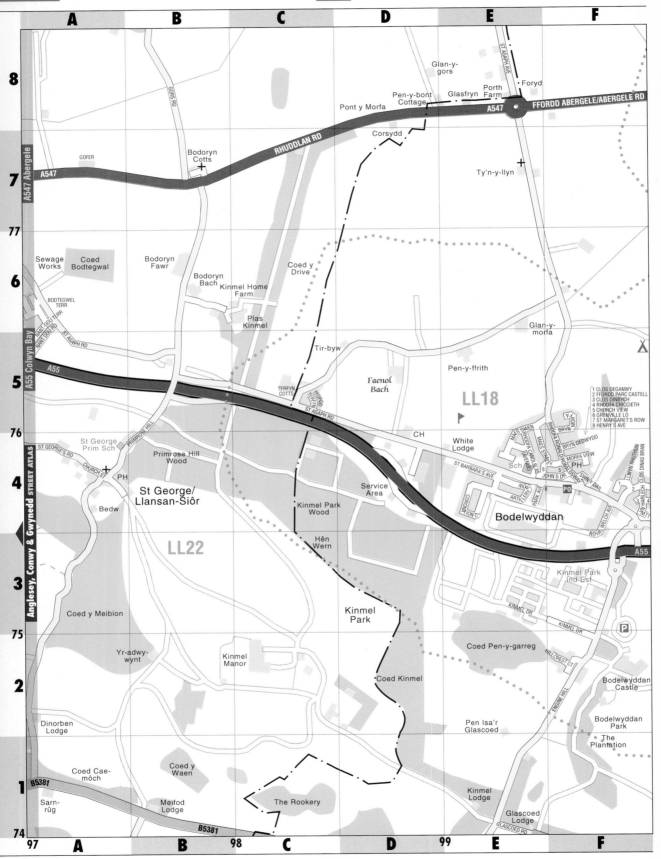

A B C D E F

8

7

77

6

5

76

4

3

75

2

1

74

97 A B 98 C D 99 E F

A547 Abergele

A55 Colwyn Bay

Anglesey, Conwy & Gwynedd STREET ATLAS

GORS RD

RHUDDLAN RD

A547

A547

Bodoryn Cotts

GOFER

Sewage Works

Coed Bodtegwal

Bodoryn Fawr

Bodoryn Bach

BODTEGWEL TERR

NANT DDU TERR

NANT DINORBEN

ST ASAPH RD

Kinmel Home Farm

Plas Kinmel

Coed y Drive

Pont y Morfa

Corsydd

Pen-y-bont Cottage

Glan-y-gors

Glasfryn

Porth Farm

Foryd

FFORDD ABERGELE/ABERGELE RD

A547

Ty'n-y-llyn

Tir-byw

TERFYN COTTS

FFORDD TERFYN

ST ASAPH RD

Faenol Bach

Pen-y-ffrith

Glan-y-morfa

LL18

A55

St George Prim Sch

ST GEORGE'S RD

PRIMROSE HILL

Primrose Hill Wood

CHURCH ST

PH

Bedw

St George/ Llansan-Siôr

CH

White Lodge

Sch

ST BARBARA'S AVE

MAES OWEN

RHODFA CANOL

MAES ESGOB

MAES STANLEY

RHODFA RONALL

RHODFA DONALL OSWALD

BRYN DEDWYDD

BRYN -Y-

JOHN'S DR

MORFA VIEW

SWYN DYFI

PH

PO

LLWYN RHUTHUN

CLOS DINAS BRAN

LLWY HARLECH

1 CLOS DEGANWY
2 FFORDD PARC CASTELL
3 CLOS DINBYCH
4 RHODFA CRICCIETH
5 CHURCH VIEW
6 GRENVILLE LO
7 ST MARGARET'S ROW
8 HENRY S AVE

LL22

Service Area

Kinmel Park Wood

Hên Wern

Kinmel Park

MOR- ARTR

PARK AVE

CRIMION C

ROYAL

WELCH AVE

Bodelwyddan

Kinmel Park Ind Est

KINMEL DR

KINMEL DR

HILLCREST CT

Coed Pen-y-garreg

P

Coed y Meibion

Yr-adwy-wynt

Kinmel Manor

Coed Kinmel

Pen Isa'r Glascoed

ENGINE HILL

Bodelwyddan Castle

Bodelwyddan Park

The Plantation

Dinorben Lodge

Coed Cae-môch

Coed y Waen

The Rookery

Kinmel Lodge

B5381

Sarn-rûg

Meifod Lodge

B5381

Glascoed Lodge

GLASCOED RD

7
16
116
16

A B C D E F

Hadfod-llwyn

HTM
Bsns Pk

A547

Pont
Robin

FFORDD ABERGELE/ABERGELE RD

MARSH RD

STATION RD

PH

A525

A525

Rhuddlan
Castle

DYSERTH RD

LON HYLAS/HYLAS LA

PRINCE'S PARADING AVE

BRYN CRES

WYNNE CL

Rhuddlan

Ysgol y
Castell

Twt
Hill

PLEASANT VIEW
CAMP

ABBEY RD

Abbey
Farm

River Clwyd (Afon Clwyd)

Ty-gwyn

8

Tytywyrch

Meadow Brook
Farm

7

LL22

Fferm

77

Bryn-carrog
Farm

Ty-isaf

ST ASAPH RD

Bryn Gwyn
Farm

6

LL18

Pengwern Hall
Coll

Faenol Fawr
(Hotel)

Sarn

Hall Farm
Park

Sarn Wood

Pengwern
Farm

Aber

Ysbyty
Glan Clwyd

Erw'-gaseg

Little
Pengwern

Glyn Derw
Farm

5

A525

76

FFORDD PARC CASTELL

RHODFA CRICCIETH

LOWTHER CL

CILGANT EGLWYS

RHES CL

THE
VILLAGE

Coed
Tŷ-mawr

NANT-Y-FAENOL RD

4

MARBLE CHURCH RD

VICARAGE
CL

Marble Church

Tŷ-mawr

Tyddan
Isaf

Gwernigron
Farm

Plas-coch

3

Trout
Fishery

Prince's
Gorse

75

Bodelwyddan
Park

Faenol-
broper

LL17

A55

2

PANT GLAS

TAN-Y-BRYN

Coed y
Gors

Green Gates
Farm

Pen-y-Bryn
Boderw

LL22

St Asaph
Bsns Pk

FFORDD WILLIAM MORGAN

CWTTIR LA

HEOL ESGOB

1

LLYS EDMUND PRYS

Works

74

00 A B 01 C D 02 E F

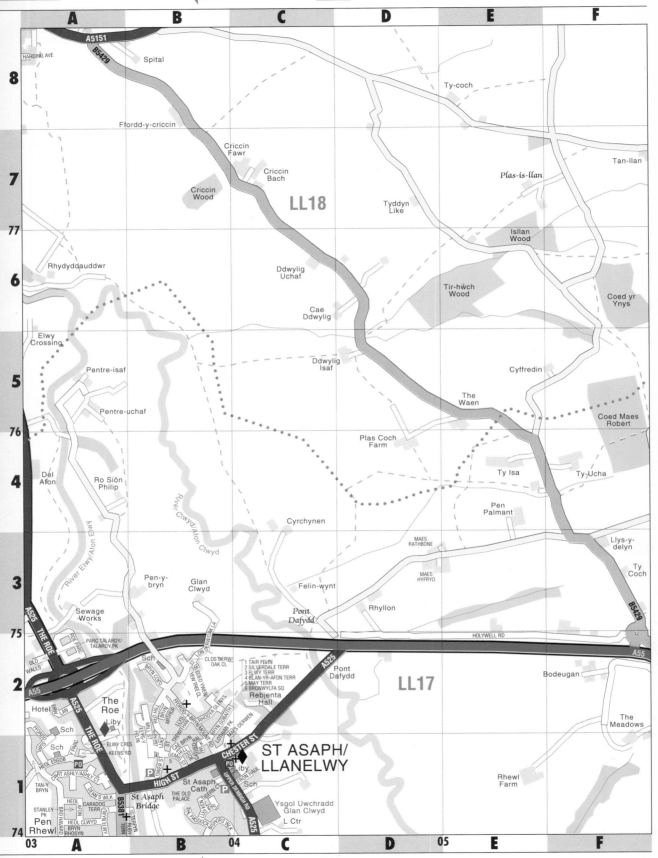

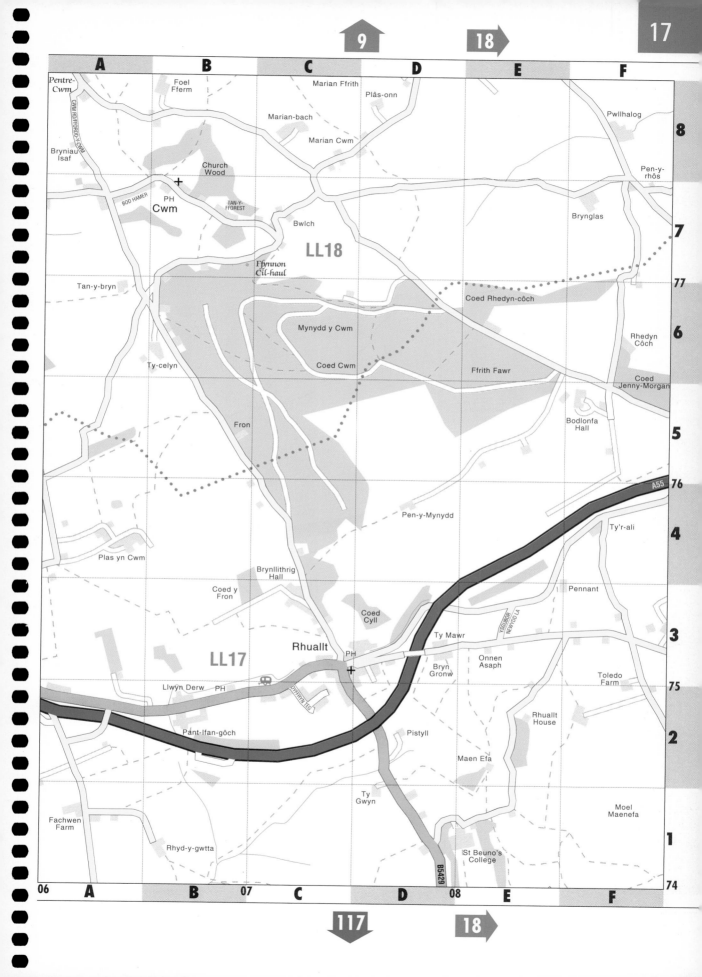

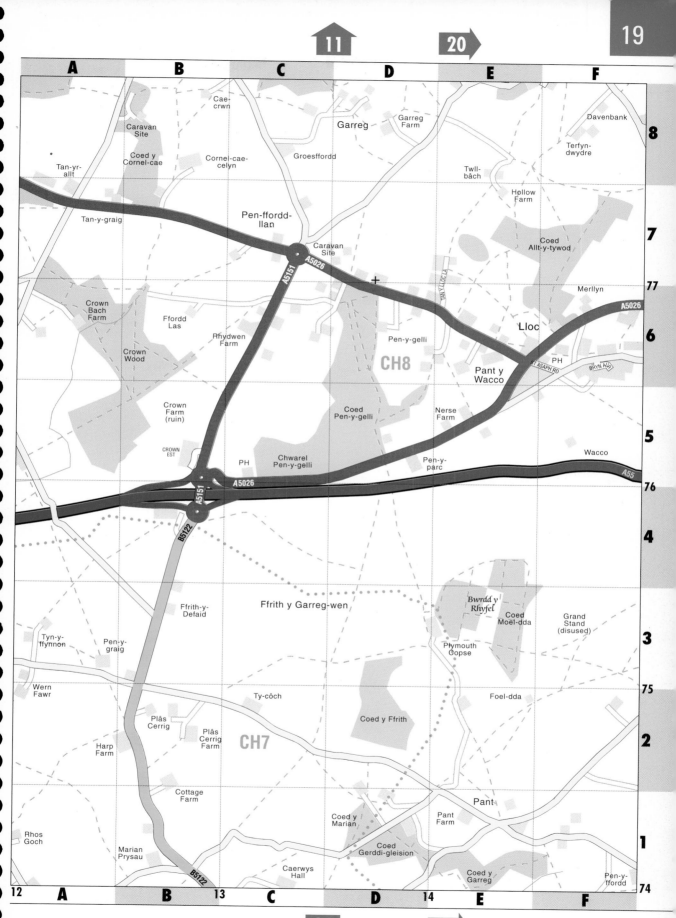

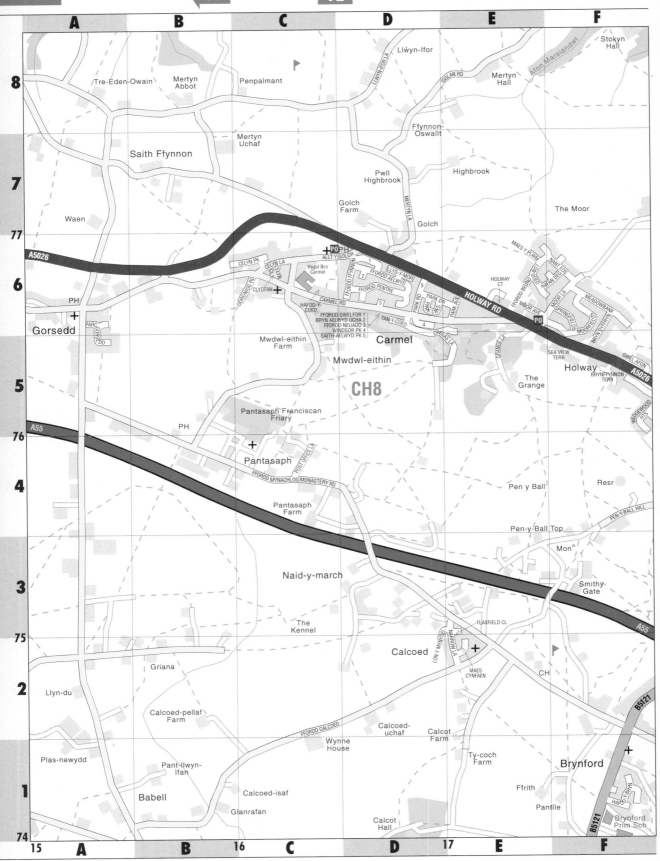

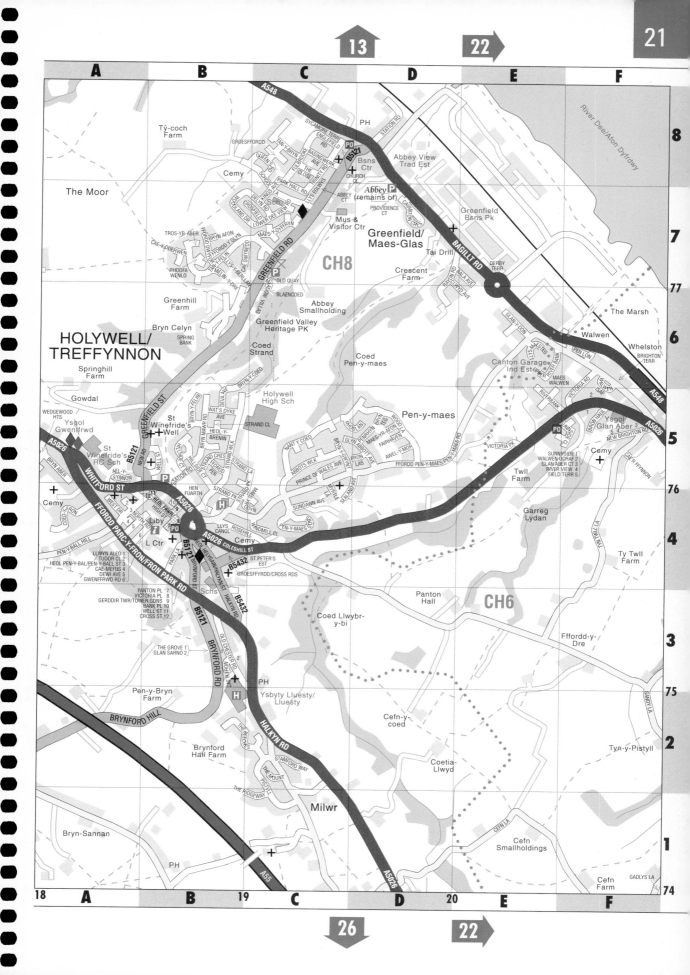

21

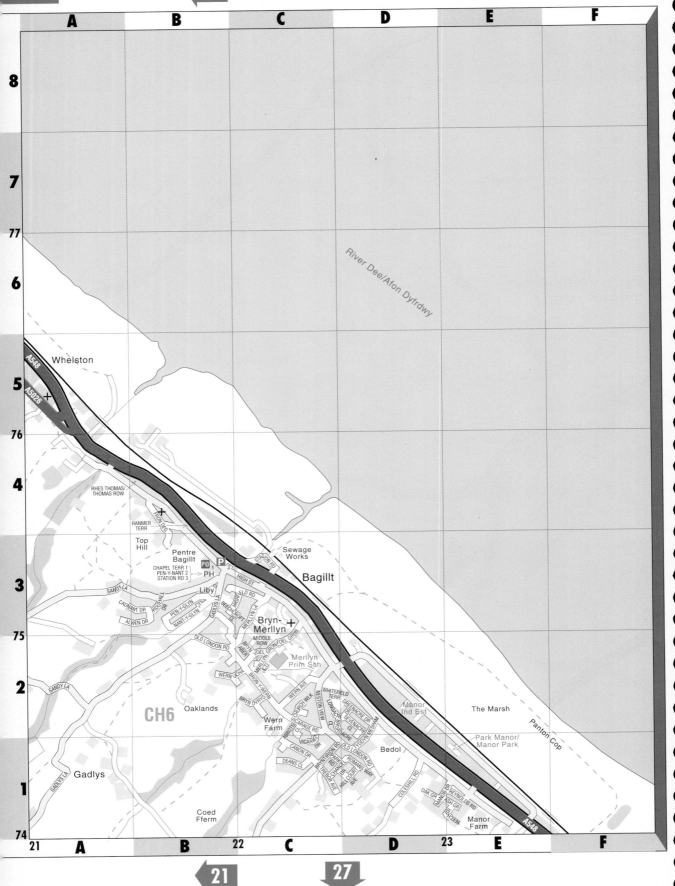

21 27

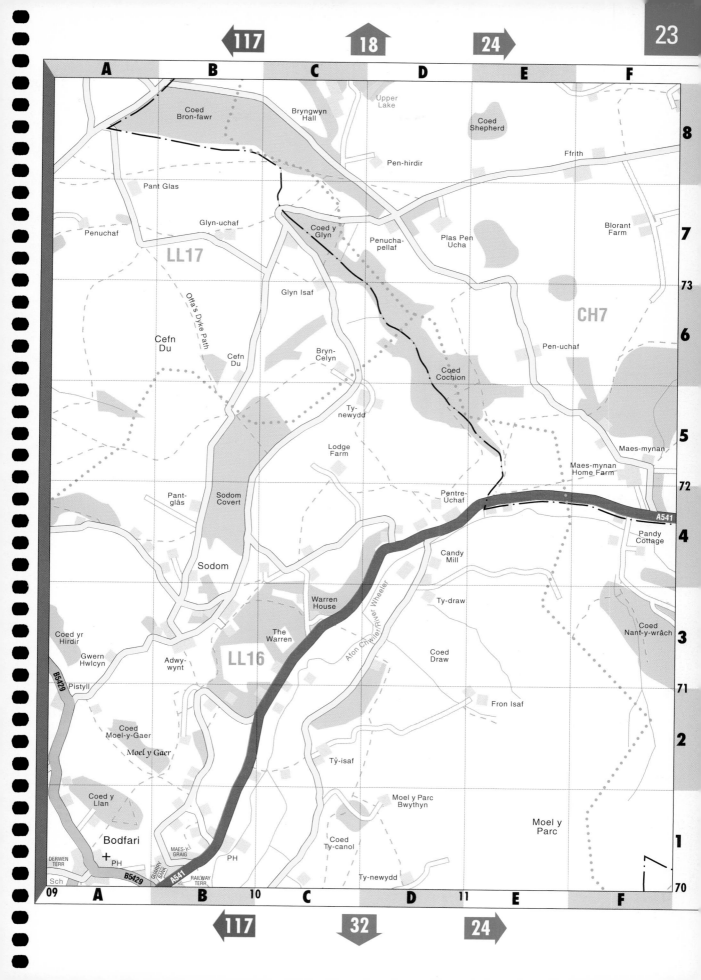

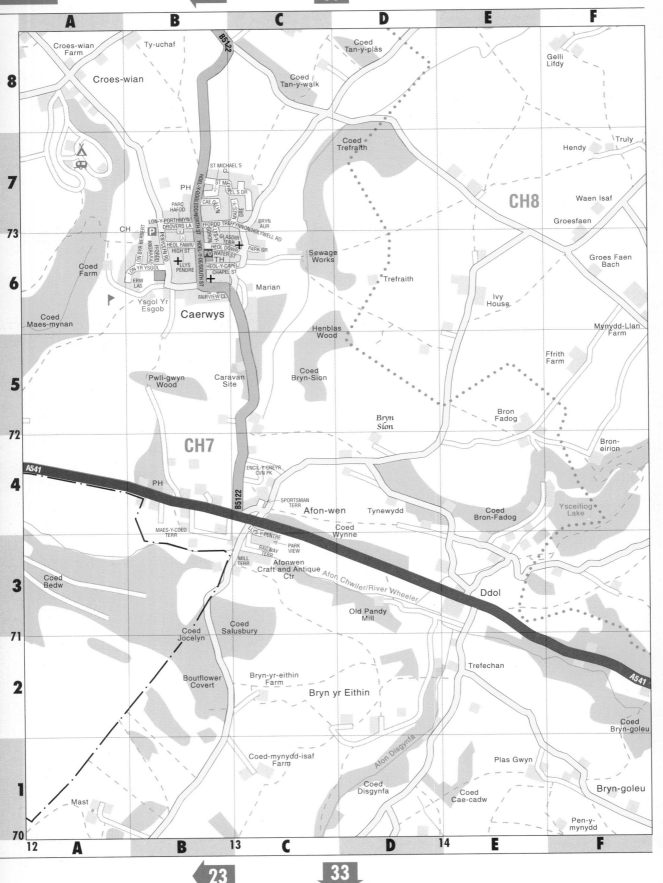

A B C D E F

8

7

73

6

5

72

4

3

71

2

1

70

12 A B 13 C D 14 E F

Croes-wian Farm
Ty-uchaf
Croes-wian
Coed Tan-y-plâs
Coed Tan-y-walk
Gelli Lifdy
Hendy
Truly

Coed Trefraith

CH8

Waen Isaf
Groesfaen

St MICHAEL'S CL
ST MA
PH
EL'S DR
St MA
PARC HAFOD
CAE GLYN
BRYN AUR
LON-Y-PORTHMYN/DROVERS LA
HEOL-Y-GOGLEDD/NORTH ST
FFORDD TREFFYNNON/HOLYWELL RD
LLYS Y GORON
GLASDIR TERR
PARK GR
CH
P
PENYCEFN RD
FFORDD ANGHARAD
LON SYR HERBERT
HEOL FAWR/HIGH ST
HEOL-Y-DE/SOUTH ST
WATER ST
HEOL DDWR
HEOL-Y-CAPEL
CHAPEL ST
P
TH
Sewage Works
Groes Faen Bach

ERW LAS
LLYS PENDRE
FAIRVIEW CL
Marian
Trefraith
Ivy House
Mynydd-Llan Farm

LON YR YSGOL
Ysgol Yr Esgob
Caerwys
Henblas Wood
Ffrith Farm

Coed Farm
Coed Maes-mynan

Pwll-gwyn Wood
Caravan Site
Coed Bryn-Sion
Bryn Sion
Bron Fadog
Bron-eirion

CH7
ENCIL-Y-GREYR CWM PK
SPORTSMAN TERR
Afon-wen
Tynewydd
Coed Bron-Fadog
Ysceifiog Lake

A541
PH
MAES-Y-COED TERR
LLYS-Y-PENTRE
PARK VIEW
RAILWAY TERR
MILL TERR
B5122
Coed Wynne
Afonwen Craft and Antique Ctr
Afon Chwiler/River Wheeler

Coed Bedw
Coed Jocelyn
Coed Salusbury
Old Pandy Mill
Ddol
A541

Boutflower Covert
Bryn-yr-eithin Farm
Bryn yr Eithin
Trefechan
Coed Bryn-goleu

Coed-mynydd-isaf Farm
Afon Disgynfa
Plas Gwyn
Mast
Coed Disgynfa
Coed Cae-cadw
Bryn-goleu
Pen-y-mynydd

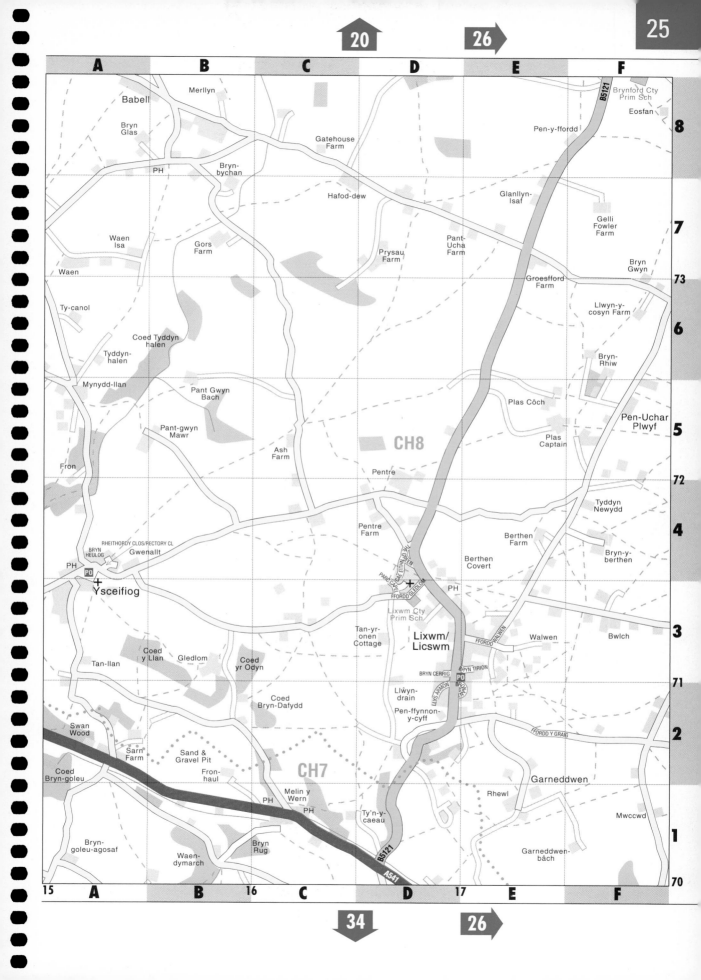

A B C D E F

8

Pwll-clai

Pen-yr-hwylfa Farm

PH

Dolphin

Fron Dudur

Wat's Dyke

Graig

CEFN LA

GADLYS LA

CH6

Holywell Common

Pen-yr-Hwylfa

Llongley

Bryn Mawr

7

Pant y Pydew

Waen-brodlas

Henblas

Lygan-y-wern

73

Bryn-y-Grug

Pen yr Henblas

Caeau

Pystyll Isa

6

Pant-y-groes

Pentre Halkyn

MAES GWELFOR

LLYS DEGANS

WILLINFIELD

BRYNFORD RD

CAE HELIG

BRYN ELIN

LA DERW

TEMLE

CAER ONNEN

ALLT-Y-PANS

BRYN

BUXTON LA

K MASARN

MAES LYGAN

PO

UWCH-Y-MOR

BRYN EITHIN

HALKYN HALL

B5123

Springfield Hotel

Hafod

A5026

5

Nant-y-fuwch

The Billins

HAFOD DR

FFORDD FRON

LLON-Y-FRON

LLYS-Y-NANT

BRYN-Y-GWYNT

A55

72

Linden Farm

CH8

Fron

4

Pwll-melyn

Mast

Windmill

PENTRE RD

3

The Gables

Halkyn Mountain

Old Hall

Waen-trochwaed

Rhes-y-cae Sch

BRYN RODYN

Halkyn Castle

71

CHURCH TERR

OCHR-Y-BRYN

Liby

2

PH

TRE'M-Y-FOEL

Rhes-y-cae

Catch

PO

Tyddyn-isaf

Halkyn/ Helygain

FFORDD Y GRAIG

Cefn-y-gildia

Mast

Wireless Station

JUBILEE DR

PH

1

Tan-y-Foel

Lilly Farm

Bryn Siriol

B5123

Ffagnallt

70

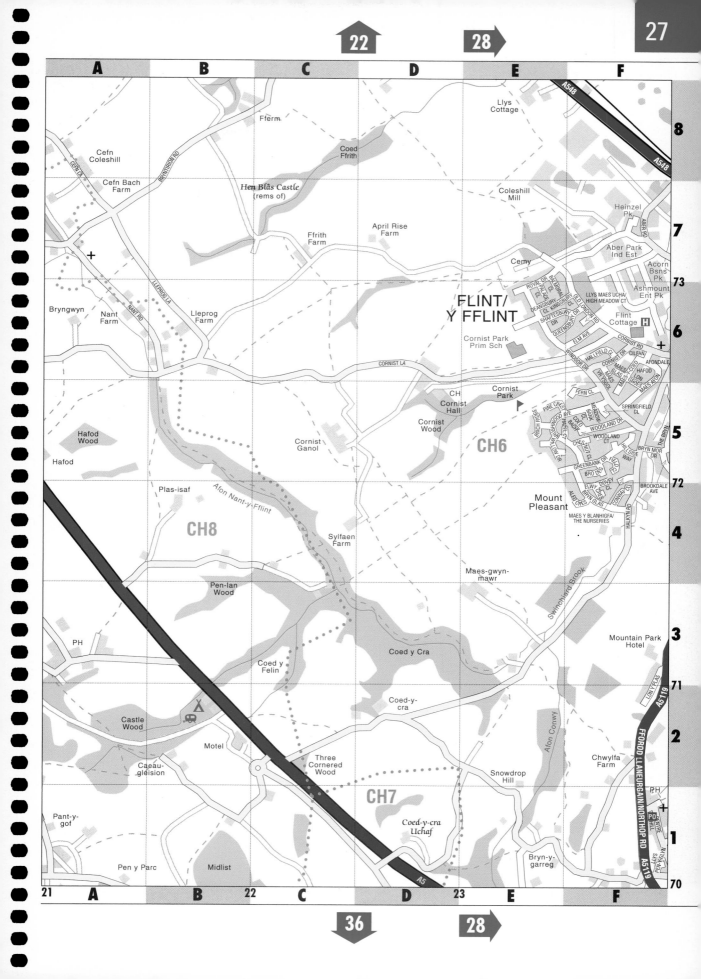

27

A6
1 LON Y CAPEL/CHAPEL ST
2 PERRINS WLK
3 MUMFORTH WLK
4 SWAN WLK
5 DUKE WLK
6 ROSEMARY WLK
7 MUSPRATT WLK
8 MOUNT WLK

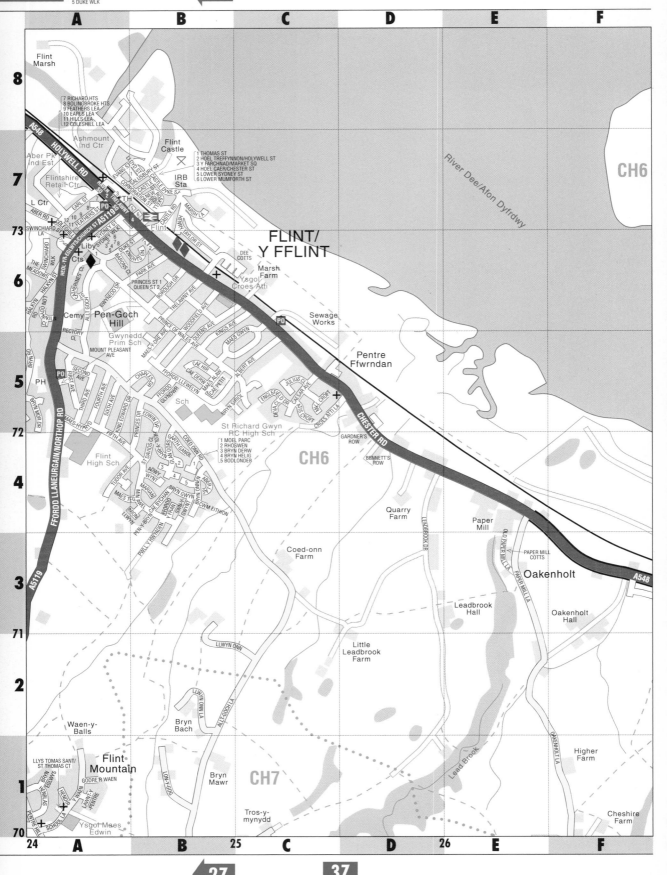

7 RICHARD HTS
8 BOLINGBROKE HTS
9 FEATHERS LEA
10 EARLS LEA
11 HILLS LEA
12 COLESHILL LEA

1 THOMAS ST
2 HOEL TREFFYNNON/HOLYWELL ST
3 Y FARCHNAD/MARKET SQ
4 HOEL CAER/CHESTER ST
5 LOWER SYDNEY ST
6 LOWER MUMFORTH ST

Flint
Marsh

Ashmount
Ind Ctr

Flint
Castle

CH6

Aber PK
Ind Est

Flintshire
Retail Ctr

River Dee/Afon Dyfrdwy

IRB
Sta

L Ctr

FLINT/
Y FFLINT

Marsh
Farm

Ysgol
Croes Atti

Pen-Goch
Hill

Cemy

Sewage
Works

Gwynedd
Prim Sch

Pentre
Ffwrndan

Mount Pleasant
Ave

CH6

PH

Sch

St Richard Gwyn
RC High Sch

1 MOEL PARC
2 RHOSWEN
3 BRYN DERW
4 BRYN HELIG
5 BODLONDEB

Flint
High Sch

Gardner's
Row

Bennett's
Row

Quarry
Farm

Paper
Mill

PAPER MILL
COTTS

Oakenholt

Coed-onn
Farm

Leadbrook
Hall

Oakenholt
Hall

A548

Little
Leadbrook
Farm

Llwyn Onn

Higher
Farm

Waen-y-
Balls

Bryn
Bach

Llys Tomas Sant/
St Thomas Ct

Flint
Mountain

Godre'r Waen

Bryn
Mawr

CH7

Lead Brook

Cheshire
Farm

Ysgol Maes
Edwin

Tros-y-
mynydd

Cheshire STREET ATLAS

A B C D E F

8

CH64

DANGER AREA

CH6

7

DANGER AREA

73

6

DANGER AREA

CH6

White
Sands

5

CH5

A548
WEIGHBRIDGE RD

72

4

WEIGHBRIDGE
RD

Power
Sta

CHESTER RD

Nature Study
Ctr

River Dee/
Afon Dyfrdwy

KELSTERTON RD

3

Power
Sta

Beacon

BUCKLEY LA

B5129

Kelsterton
Farm

71

Kelsterton

2

NORTH RD

CH5

COATINGS
TWO

RING RD

COATINGS BY-PASS RD

CH6

KELSTERTON LA

KELSTERTON RD

Park
Farm

Golftyn

RIVER RD

Coleg Glannau
Dyfrdwy/
Deeside Coll of
F Ed

1 COLEHILL PL
2 CLIFTON PARK AVE
3 TALFYN CL
4 QUEEN'S AVE
5 ROCK COTTS
6 KINGS CROFT
7 KINGS RD
8 WILLOW CT
9 ROCK RD

1

CONNAH'S
QUAY

Sports
Ctr

CHURCH ST

PO

GOLFTYN LA

COLLEGE VIEW DR

CEDAR AVE

ROWAN GR

YORK RD

COOPER'S LA

JAMES ST

LANSDOWNE
RD

DURBAN CL

LOWER BROOK ST

HAMILTON
RD

DEE VIEW RD

B5129

Top-y-fron

KELSTERTON LA

FARM DR

GOLFTYN DR

HAFOD
CL

HOLLY
CL

Connah's Quay
High Sch

70

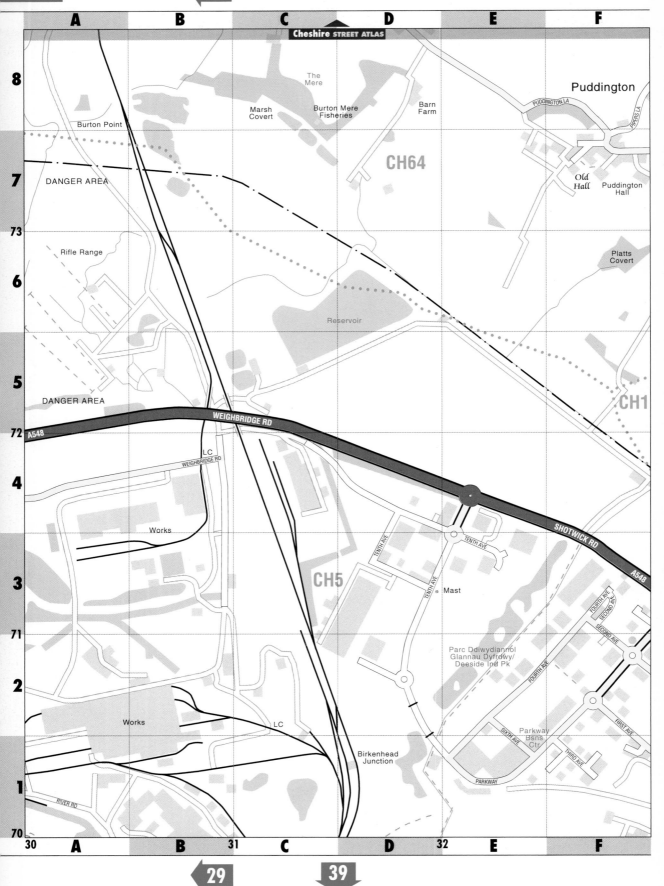

Cheshire STREET ATLAS

A B C D E F

8

The Mere

Puddington

Marsh Covert

Burton Mere Fisheries

Barn Farm

PUDDINGTON LA

PIPERS LA

CH64

Burton Point

Old Hall

Puddington Hall

7

DANGER AREA

73

Rifle Range

Platts Covert

6

Reservoir

CH1

5

DANGER AREA

72

A548

WEIGHBRIDGE RD

SHOTWICK RD

LC

WEIGHBRIDGE RD

4

Works

A548

TENTH AVE

TENTH AVE

TENTH AVE

Mast

3

CH5

FOURTH AVE

SECOND AVE

SECOND AVE

71

Parc Ddiwydiannol Glannau Dyfrdwy/ Deeside Ind Pk

FOURTH AVE

FIRST AVE

2

Works

LC

SIXTH AVE

Parkway Bsns Ctr

THIRD AVE

Birkenhead Junction

1

RIVER RD

PARKWAY

70

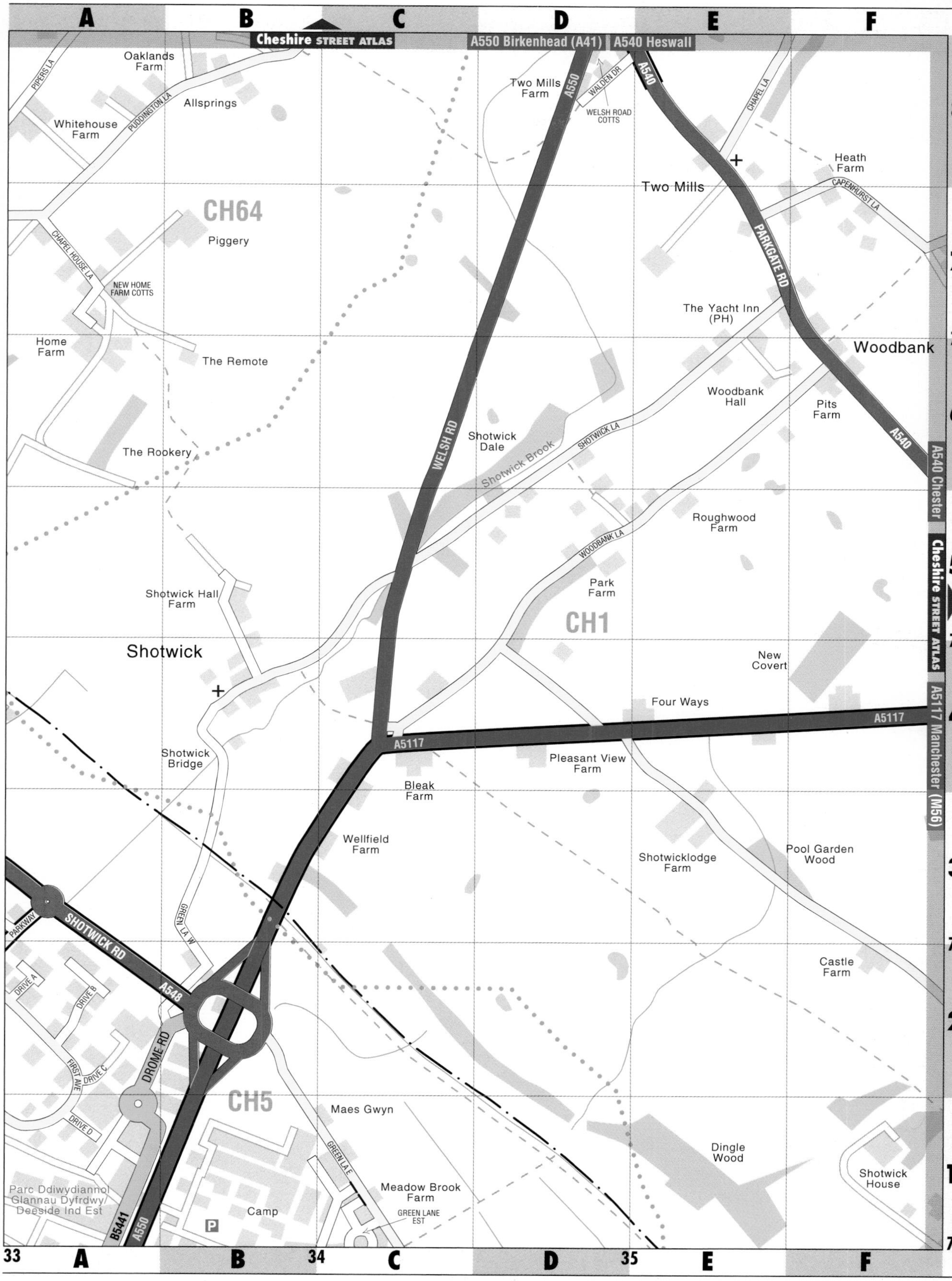
A
B
C
D
E
F
Cheshire STREET ATLAS
A550 Birkenhead (A41)
A540 Heswall
Oaklands Farm
PIPERS LA
PUDDINGTON LA
Allsprings
Whitehouse Farm
Two Mills Farm
A550
WALDEN DR
WELSH ROAD COTTS
A540
CHAPEL LA
Heath Farm
Two Mills
CAPENHURST LA
CH64
Piggery
CHAPEL HOUSE LA
NEW HOME FARM COTTS
PARKGATE RD
The Yacht Inn (PH)
Home Farm
The Remote
Woodbank
Woodbank Hall
Pits Farm
The Rookery
WELSH RD
Shotwick Dale
Shotwick Brook
SHOTWICK LA
A540
A540 Chester
Roughwood Farm
WOODBANK LA
Cheshire STREET ATLAS
Shotwick Hall Farm
Park Farm
CH1
Shotwick
New Covert
Four Ways
A5117
A5117 Manchester (M56)
Shotwick Bridge
A5117
Pleasant View Farm
Bleak Farm
Wellfield Farm
Shotwicklodge Farm
Pool Garden Wood
PARKWAY
SHOTWICK RD
GREEN LA W
Castle Farm
DRIVE A
DRIVE B
A548
DROME RD
FIRST AVE
DRIVE C
DRIVE D
CH5
Maes Gwyn
Dingle Wood
GREEN LA E
Shotwick House
Meadow Brook Farm
Parc Ddiwydiannol Glannau Dyfrdwy/ Deeside Ind Est
Camp
GREEN LANE EST
B5441
A550
8
7
73
6
5
72
4
3
71
2
1
70
33
34
35

117
23

A **B** **C** **D** **E** **F**

CH7

Sch

Geinas Farm

A541

8 Geinas Farm

Berllan

The Grove Hall

Grove Hall Farm

B5429

Geinas

7 Sewage Works

Waen Aberwheeler

Glan Clwyd Farm

Ty'n-y-celyn Cottage

Offa's Dyke Path

Fron Haul Aifft

Aifft

Ty Newydd

69

6 Maes-siêd

Castell

Berth Farm

Bwlch

Cil Llwyn

Glan Clwyd Isa

Glan-Clwyd

Dregoch Ucha

Dre-gôch Ganol

Wern-fawr

Gelli

5 Glan Clwyd Ganol

Dre-gôch

Finger Cottage

68

LL16

Plâs Ashpool

Fron Banadl

Garn Clwyd Bella

4 Cae'r Fedwen

Fron-vox

Cyn-y-Cornel

Pont Ashpool

Nant-Lewis-Alyn

Pont-garreg

Fron-gelyn

3 Wern

Pen Llwyn

67

Pentre-mawr

Ty Brazier

Penrhyn

2 Pentre-bach

Erw Vran

Bancar

Y Gilfach

1 Glan-y-wern Farm

B5429

Cross Keys

Llangwyfan Farm

66

River Clwyd/Afon Clwyd

Glan-y-wern Hall

09 **A** 10 **B** **C** 10 **D** 11 **E** **F**

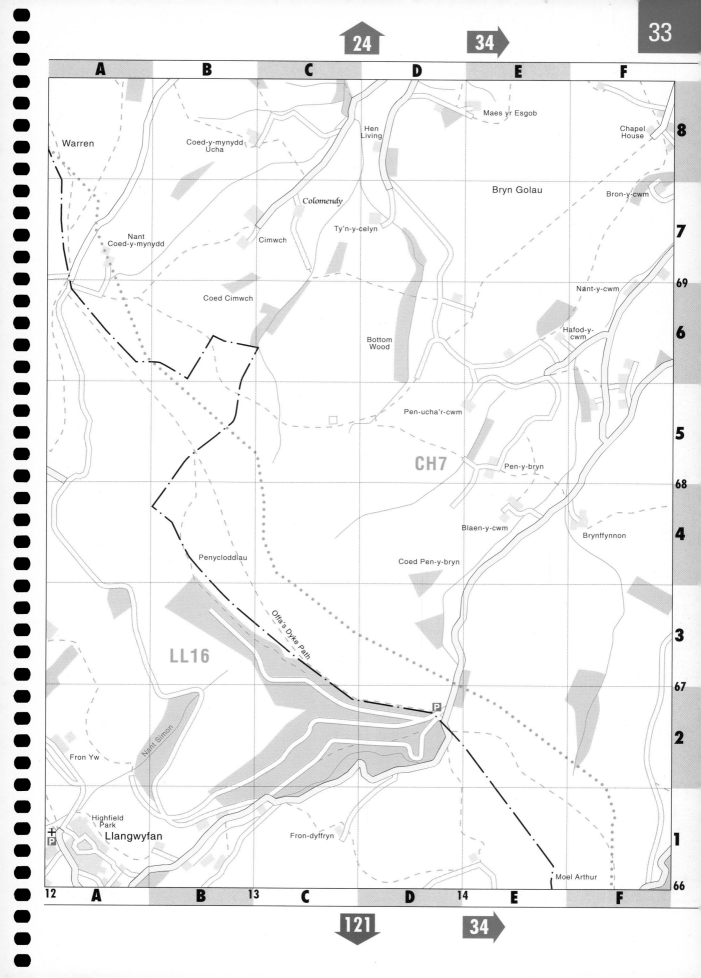

A   B   C   D   E   F

8

Warren

Coed-y-mynydd
Ucha

Maes yr Esgob

Chapel
House

Bryn Golau

Bron-y-cwm

Colomendy

7

Nant
Coed-y-mynydd

Cimwch

Ty'n-y-celyn

69

Coed Cimwch

Nant-y-cwm

Hafod-y-
cwm

6

Bottom
Wood

Pen-ucha'r-cwm

5

CH7

Pen-y-bryn

68

Blaen-y-cwm

Brynffynnon

4

Penycloddiau

Coed Pen-y-bryn

3

Offa's Dyke Path

67

LL16

P

2

Nant Simon

Fron Yw

Highfield
Park

Fron-dyffryn

1

Llangwyfan

Moel Arthur

66

12   A   B   13   C   D   14   E   F

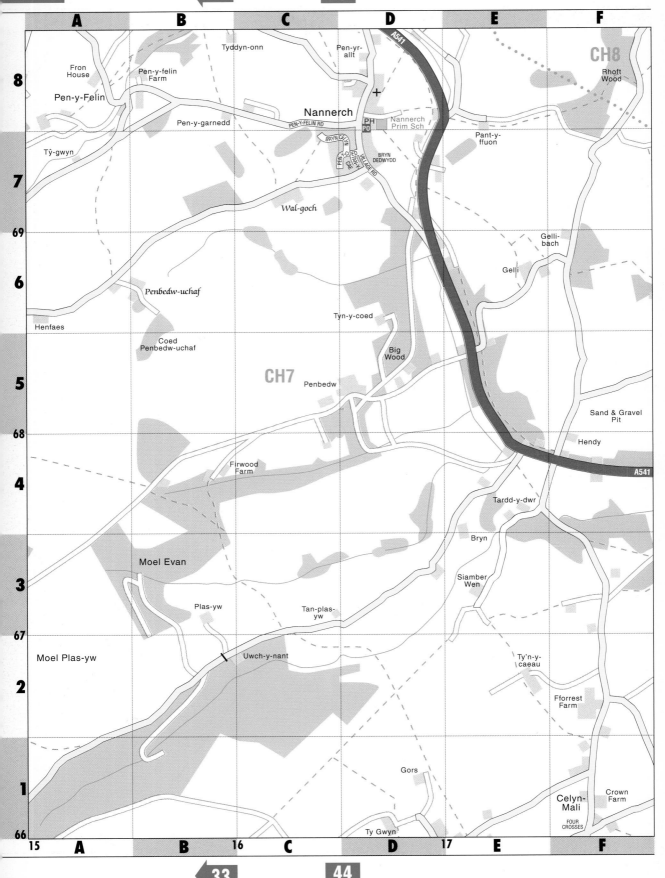

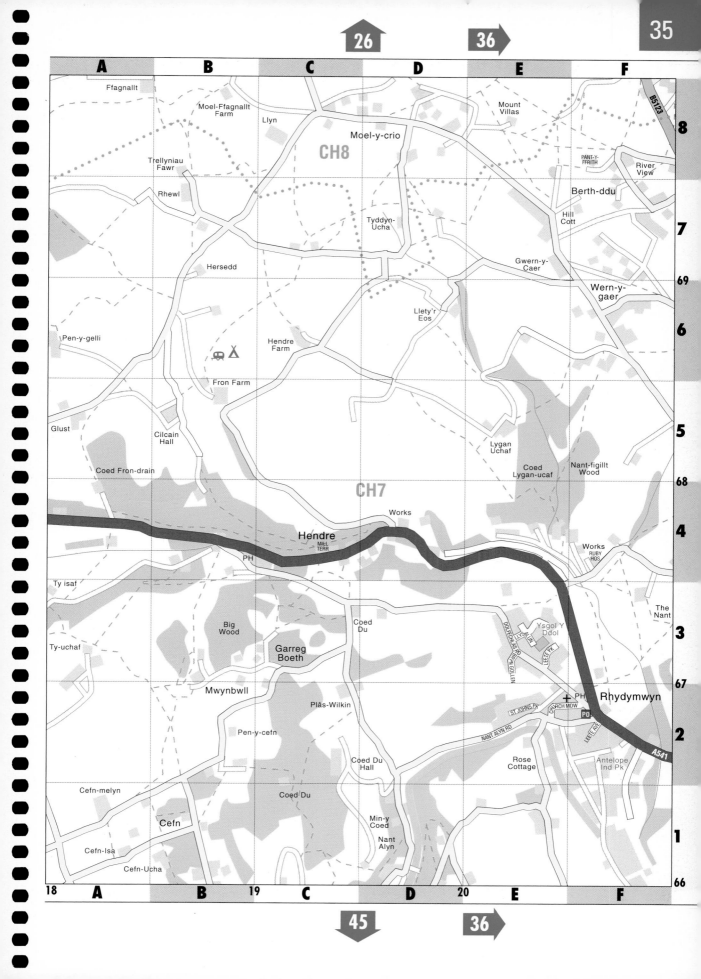

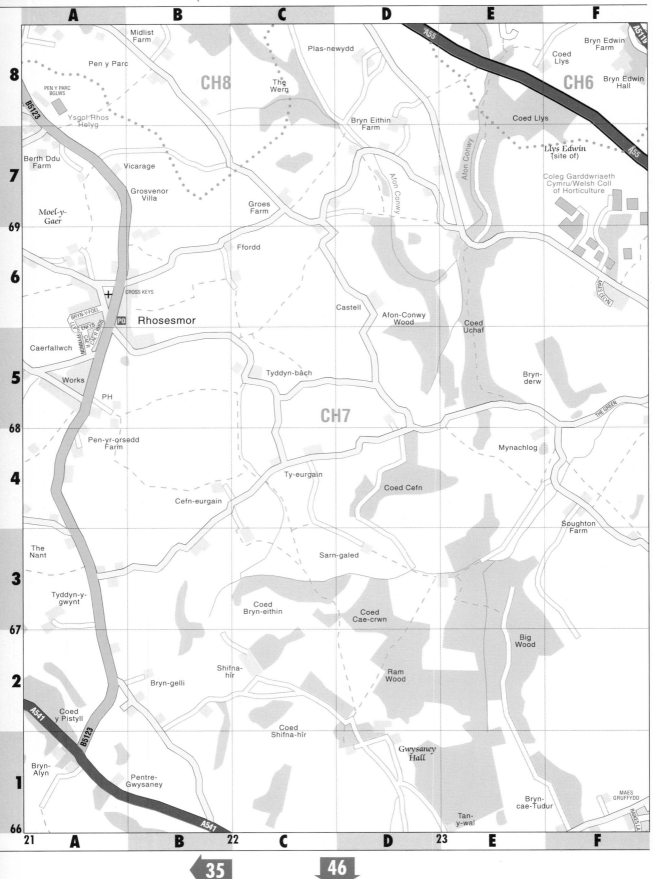

A B C D E F

8

CH8

Midlist Farm

Pen y Parc

PEN Y PARC BGLWS

Ysgol Rhos Helyg

Plas-newydd

The Wern

Bryn Eithin Farm

A55

Bryn Edwin Farm

Coed Llys

CH6

Bryn Edwin Hall

Coed Llys

A5119

7

B5123

Berth Ddu Farm

Vicarage

Grosvenor Villa

Groes Farm

Afon Conwy

Afon Conwy

Llys Edwin (site of)

Coleg Garddwriaeth Cymru/Welsh Coll of Horticulture

69

Moel-y-Gaer

Ffordd

6

CROSS KEYS

BRYN-Y-FOEL

ENEYS

LLYS FFYNNON

CAER

CREF RHOS

PO

Rhosesmor

Castell

Afon-Conwy Wood

Coed Uchaf

MAES CELYN

Caerfallwch

Tyddyn-bâch

Brynderw

5

Works

CH7

THE GREEN

PH

68

Pen-yr-orsedd Farm

Mynachlog

4

Ty-eurgain

Coed Cefn

Cefn-eurgain

Soughton Farm

The Nant

Sarn-galed

3

Tyddyn-y-gwynt

67

Coed Bryn-eithin

Coed Cae-crwn

Big Wood

2

A541

Bryn-gelli

Shifna-hîr

Ram Wood

Coed y Pistyll

B5123

Coed Shifna-hîr

Gwysaney Hall

1

Bryn-Alyn

Pentre-Gwysaney

Tan-y-wal

Bryn-cae-Tudur

MAES GRUFFYDD

PARKES LA

A541

66

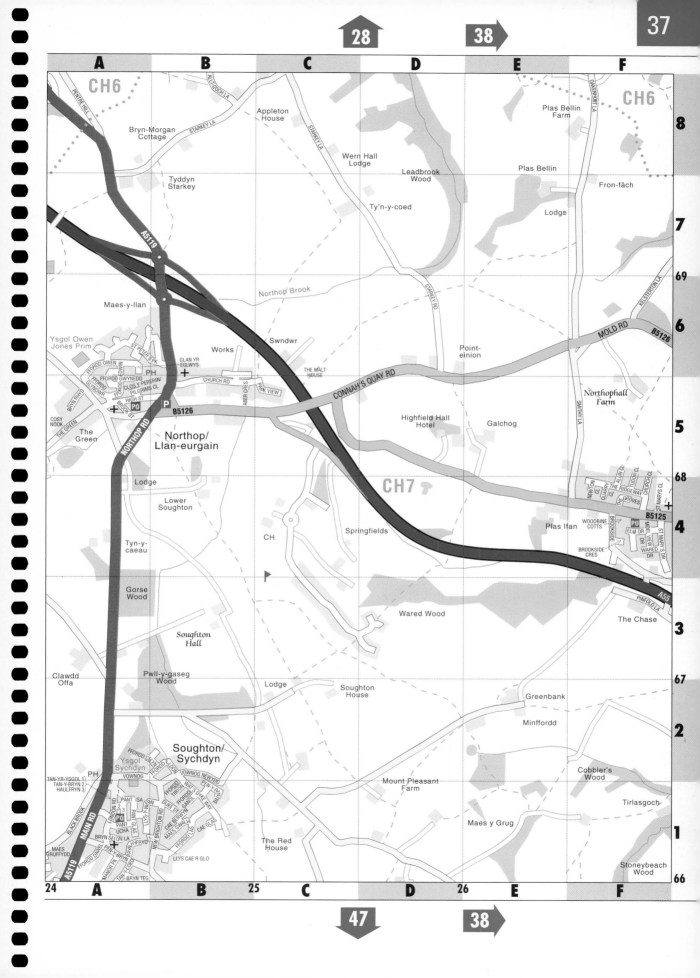

CH6

CH6

Plas Bellin Farm

Plas Bellin

Fron-fâch

Lodge

Bryn-Morgan Cottage

Appleton House

Wern Hall Lodge

Leadbrook Wood

Tyddyn Starkey

Ty'n-y-coed

A5119

Northop Brook

Maes-y-llan

Swndwr

Point-einion

MOLD RD

B5126

Ysgol Owen Jones Prim

Works

THE MALT HOUSE

CONNAH'S QUAY RD

Northophall Farm

CHURCH RD

Northop/ Llan-eurgain

B5126

Highfield Hall Hotel

Galchog

SMITHY LA

NORTHOP RD

The Green

CH7

Lodge

Plas Ifan

B5125

Lower Soughton

Springfields

Tyn-y-caeau

CH

WOODBINE COTTS

BROOKSIDE CRES

Gorse Wood

Wared Wood

A55

PINFOLD LA

The Chase

Soughton Hall

Clawdd Offa

Pwll-y-gaseg Wood

Lodge

Soughton House

Greenbank

Minffordd

Soughton/ Sychdyn

Cobbler's Wood

Ysgol Sychdyn

Mount Pleasant Farm

Tirlasgoch

MAIN RD

A5119

BLACK BROOK

PO

Maes y Grug

The Red House

Stoneybeach Wood

MAES GRUFFYDD

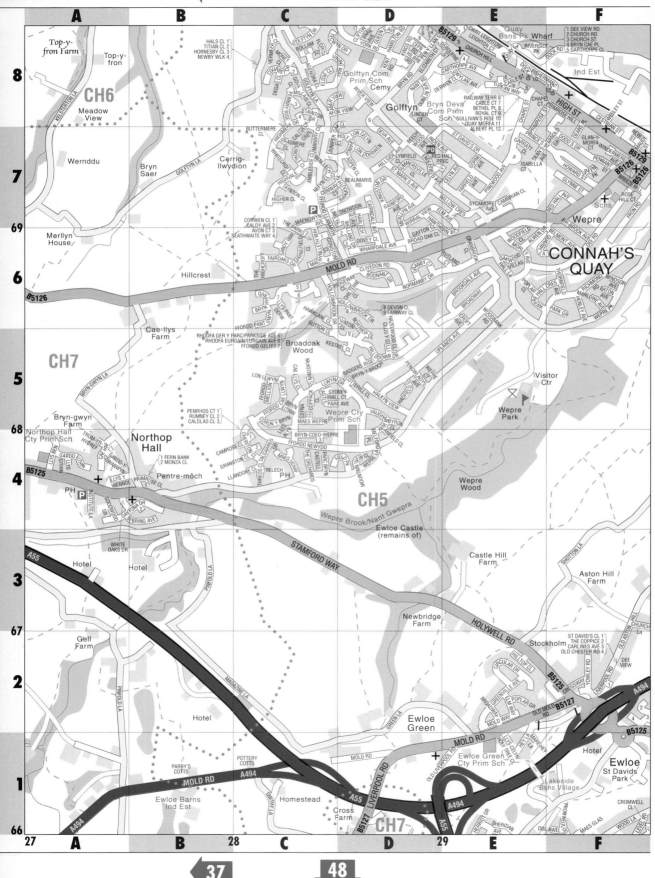

D8
1 HAFOD PK
2 IVY CT
3 FERN CT
4 CEDAR CT
5 HOLLY CT

6 BIRCH CT
7 CHESTNUT CT
8 NEW UNION ST
9 UPPER BRYN RD

Connah's Quay / Northop Hall / Ewloe area map

Top-y-fron Farm
Top-y-fron
Meadow View
CH6
Wernddu
Bryn Saer
Cerrig-llwydion
Merllyn House
Hillcrest
Cae-llys Farm
CH7
Bryn-gwyn Farm
Northop Hall Cty Prim Sch
Northop Hall
Pentre-môch
B5125
PH
White Oaks Dr
Hotel
Hotel
A55
Gell Farm
Hotel
Parry's Cotts
Pottery Cotts
Ewloe Barns Ind Est
Homestead
Cross Farm
CH7
Mold Rd
A494

HALS CL 1
TITIAN CL 2
HORNESBY CL 3
NEWBY WLK 4

Buttermere Cl
Golftyn Com Prim Sch
Cemy
Golftyn
Bryn Deva Com Prim Sch
Quay Bsns Pk Wharf
Riverside Pk
Ind Est
Church Hill
B5129

1 DEE VIEW RD
2 CHURCH RD
3 CHURCH ST
4 BRYN CAE PL
5 GARTHORPE CL

High St
B5129
B5126
B5126
Wepre
Rose Hill Cl
Schs

RAILWAY TERR 6
CABLE CT 7
CABLE CT 9
SULLIVAN'S RISE 10
QUAY MORFA 11
ALBERT PL 12

CONNAH'S QUAY

Visitor Ctr
Wepre Park
Wepre Wood

Maengwyn
Mold Rd
The Parks
Fairoaks
The Highfield
Broadoak Wood

CORWEN CL 1
CALDY AVE 2
AVON CT 3
SEATHWAITE WAY 4

RHODFA GER Y PARC/PARKSIDE AVE 5
RHODFA EURGAIN/EURGAIN AVE 6
FFORDD GELFFT 7

8 DEVON CL
9 FAIRWAY CL

PENRHOS CT 1
RUMNEY CL 2
CALDLAS CL 3

Wepre Cty Prim Sch

1 FERN BANK
2 MONZA CL

CH5

Wepre Brook/Nant Gwepra
Ewloe Castle (remains of)
Stamford Way

Castle Hill Farm
Aston Hill Farm
Shotton La
Newbridge Farm
Holywell Rd
Stockholm
Dee View

ST DAVID'S CL 1
THE COPPICE 2
CARLINES AVE 3
OLD CHESTER RD 4

B5125
B5127
Ewloe Green
Ewloe Green Cty Prim Sch
Old Mold Rd
B5125
A494
Lakeside Bsns Village
Ewloe St Davids Park
Hotel

Magazine La
Pinfold La

Maes Glas
Dol Awel
Sheridan Ave
Herriot Gr
Cromwell Cl
Wood La
Level Rd

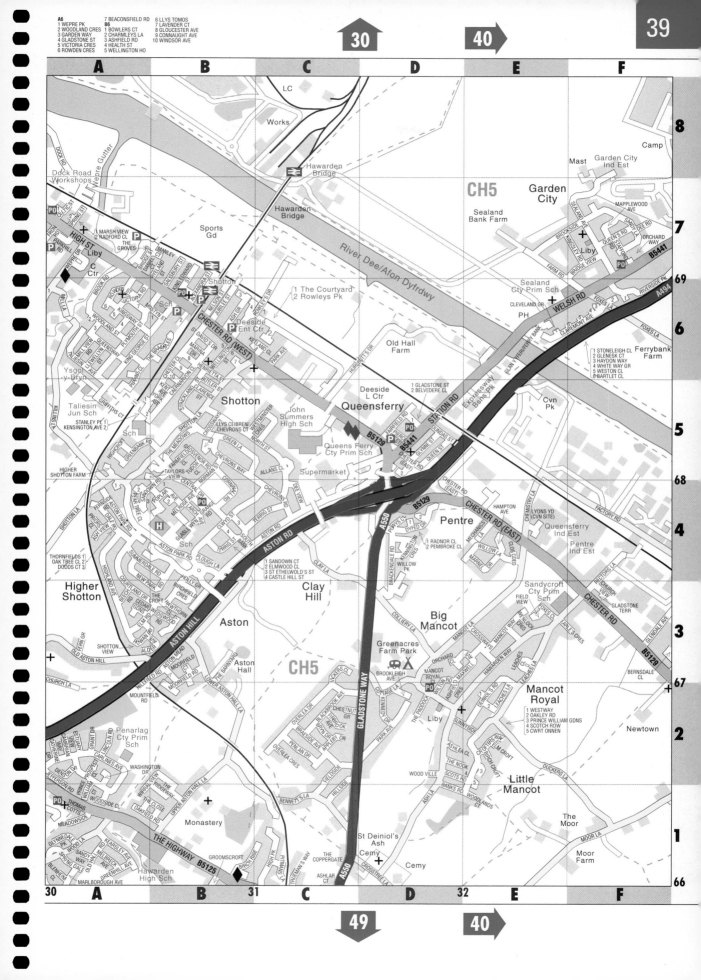

A B C D E F

8 Camp
Old Marsh Farm
GREEN LANE EST
Bridge Farm
FERNLEA CT
FOX LEA

HAWTHORN VIEW
CEDAR AVE
Deva Bsns Pk
SEAHILL RD
CROFTERS WAY
Seahill Farm

CEDAR CL
7
B5441
A548
Brookfield Farm
GREEN LAE
STATION COTTS

69
A494
RIVERSIDE PK
VILLA RD
Willow Farm
Brook Farm
BARTHOLOMEWS ST

Home Farm
SEALAND RD

6
MANOR RD
The Owl Ind Est
Waterloo Farm
Sealand

MEADOW VIEW
SOUTH GN
NORTH GN
PERRY CT
EAST GN

FOX'S DR
CH5
DEESIDE CRES
Church Farm
A548

Sealand Manor

5 Shooting School
CH1

68 Deeside Cottages

4 Engineer Pk
River Row Cottages
Deeside House
DEESIDE LA
THE BOWERY
Sealand Nursery

GLENDALE AVE
BABBAGE RD
St Ives Pk
WHITLE
FACTORY RD
ALVIS RD
Works
OLD FARM COTTS

Glendale Bsns Pk
ST IVES WAY

BERNSDALE CL
Glendale Pk
CLAIR AVE
CROFTERS PK
RAILWAY
ASIATIC COTTS
PRINCE WILLIAM AVE
River Dee/Afon Dyfrdwy
Wood Farm

3
HAMILTON AVE
HARRISON CT
QUEEN'S AVE

EVANSLEIGH
PHOENIX ST
NORTH ST

67
AMREDALE ST
FAIRWAY
MARWIN ST
PHILIP ST
STATION RD
Sandycroft

B5129
WOOD ST
CH5

2 Bridge Inn (PH)
CHESTER RD
The Beeches
CH4

MOOR LA
ROSSLYN CL
CH4

1
Cop House Farm

66
RAKE LA
B5129
B5129

33 A B 34 C D 35 E F

39 50

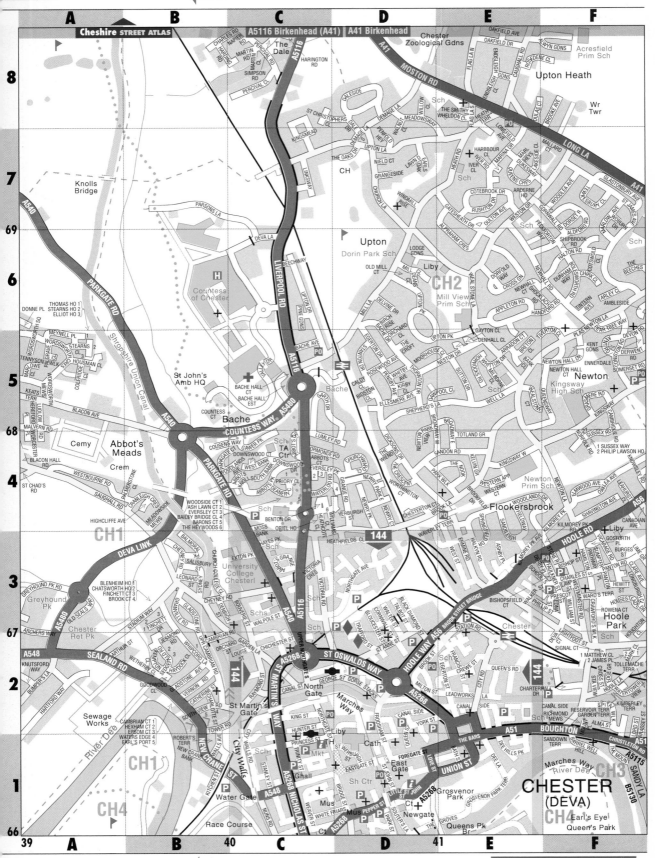

Cheshire STREET ATLAS

For full street detail of the highlighted area see page 144.

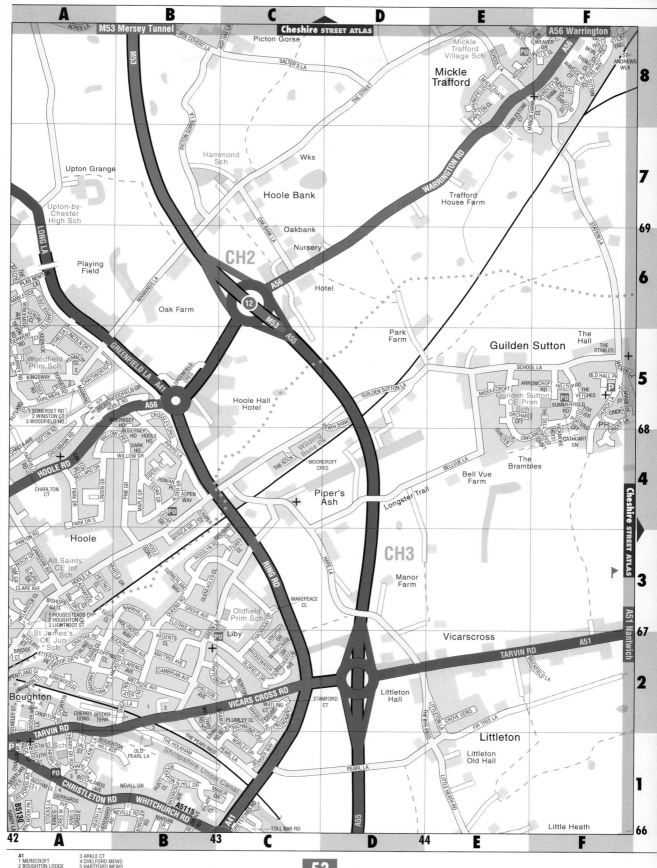

A1
1 MERECROFT
2 BOUGHTON LODGE
3 ORCHARD CT
4 KING EDWARD BLDGS
5 STOCKS AVE
6 WESTWARD RD
B2
1 MARLBOROUGH CT
2 VICARS CROSS CT

3 ARKLE CT
4 CHELFORD MEWS
5 HARTFORD MEWS

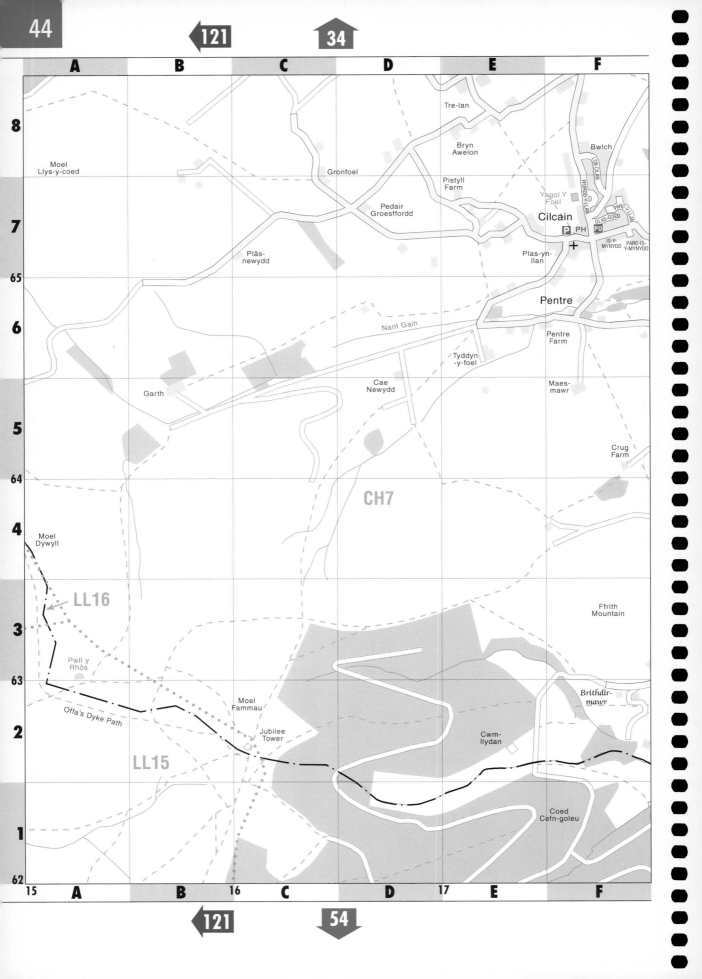

A   B   C   D   E   F

8

Moel
Llys-y-coed

Tre-lan

Bryn
Awelon

Gronfoel

Pistyll
Farm

Pedair
Groesffordd

Ysgol Y
Foel

Cilcain

7

Plâs-
newydd

P PH PO

IS-Y-
MYNYDD

PARC-IS-
Y-MYNYDD

Plas-yn-
llan

65

Pentre

6

Nant Gain

Pentre
Farm

Tyddyn
-y-foel

Maes-
mawr

Garth

Cae
Newydd

CH7

5

Crug
Farm

64

4

Moel
Dywyll

Ffrith
Mountain

LL16

3

Pwll y
Rhôs

63

Brithdir-
mawr

Moel
Fammau

2

Offa's Dyke Path

Jubilee
Tower

Cwm-
llydan

LL15

1

Coed
Cefn-goleu

62

15   A   B   16   C   D   17   E   F

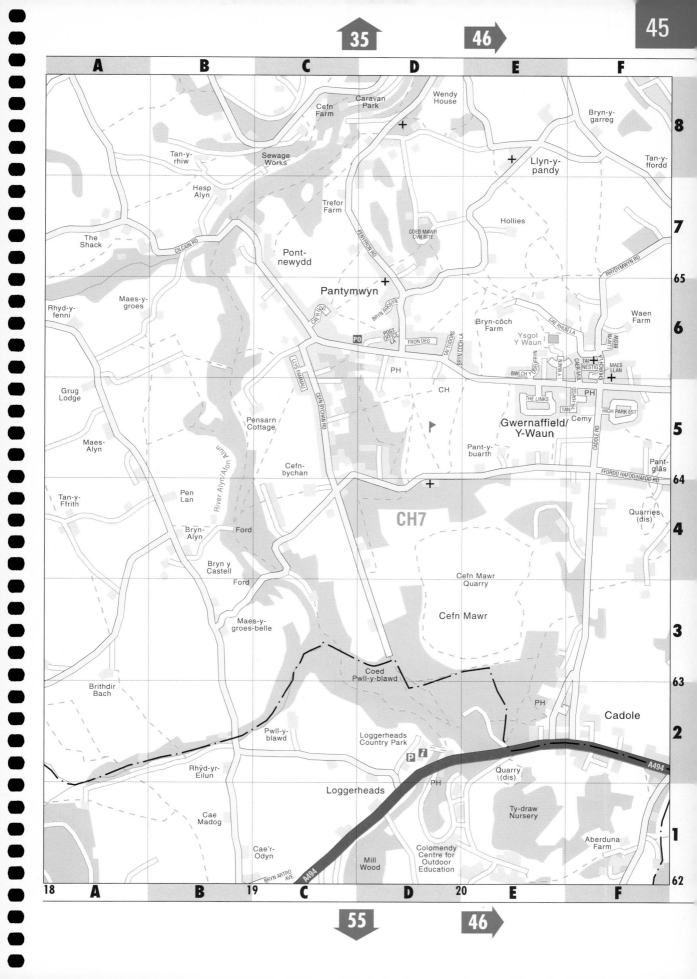

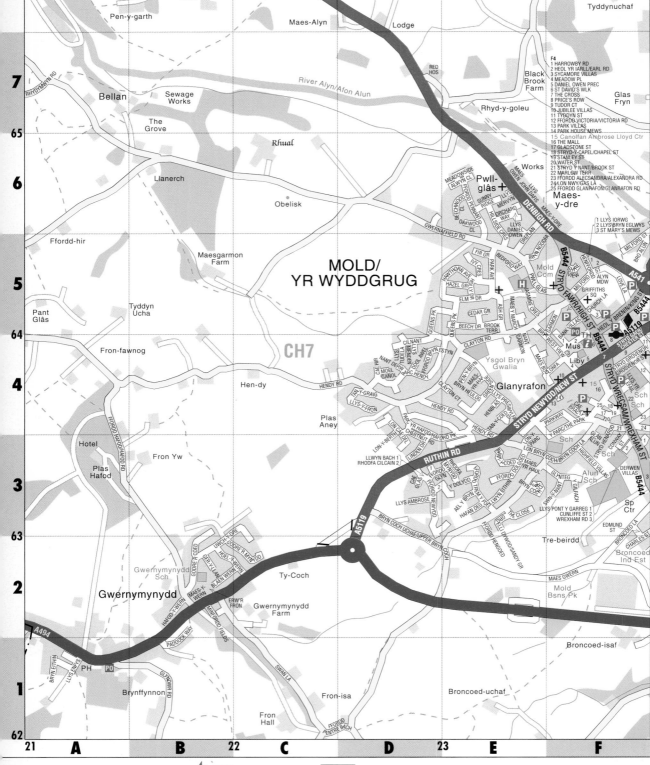

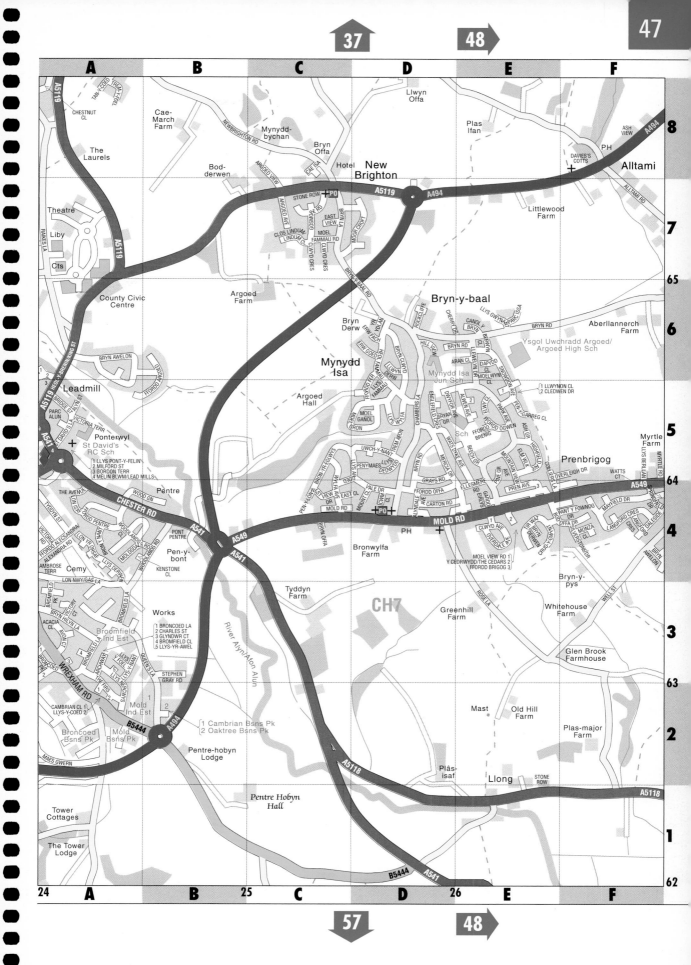

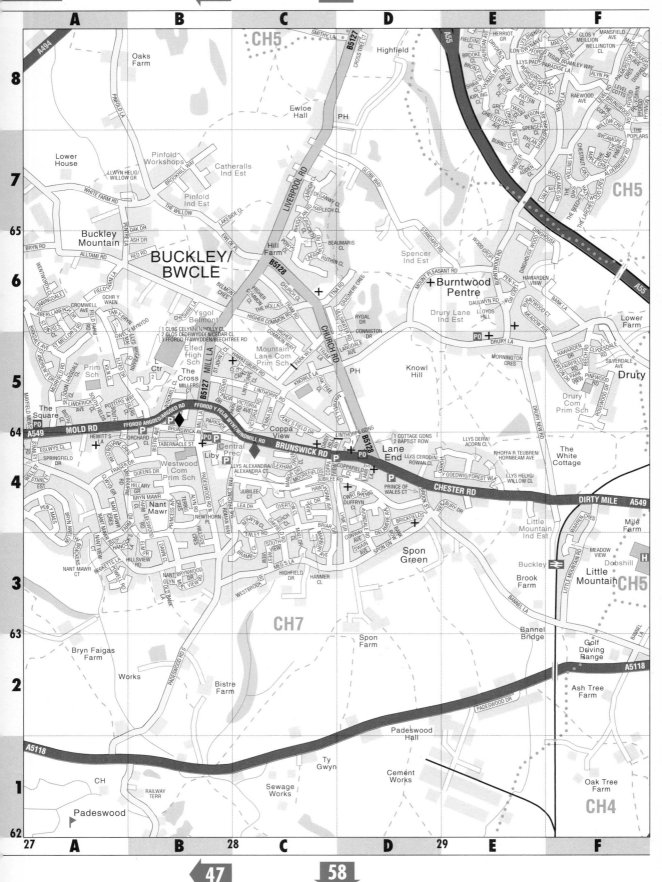

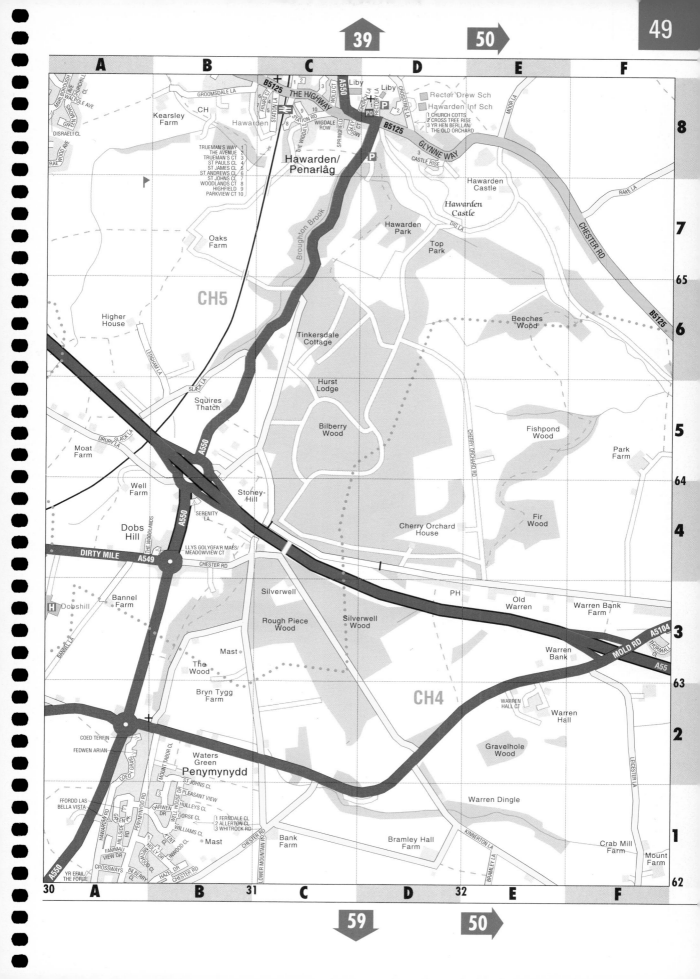

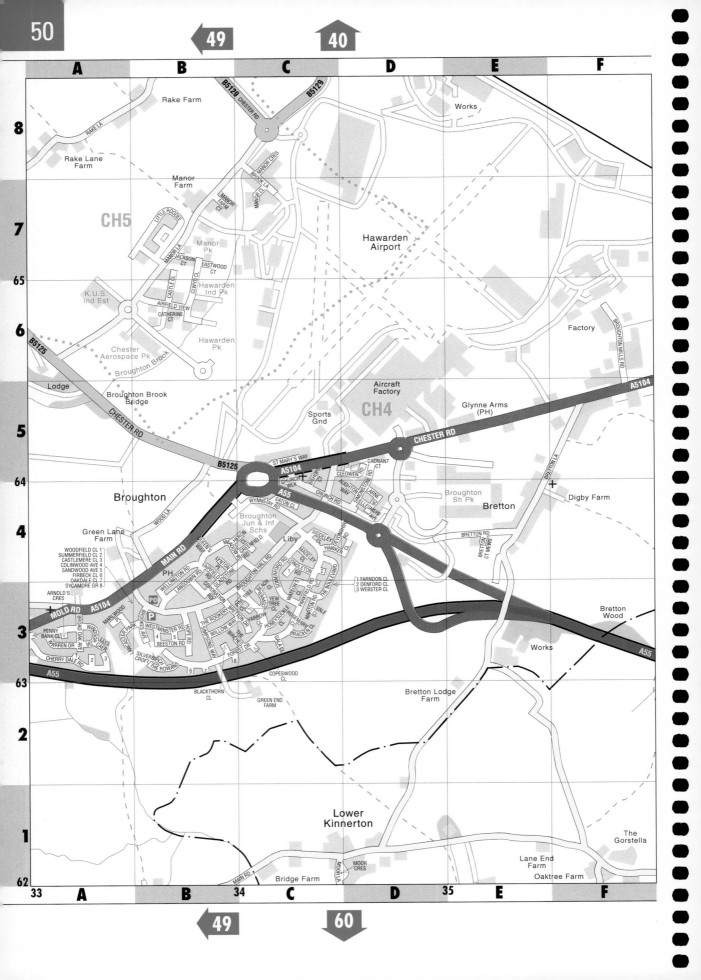

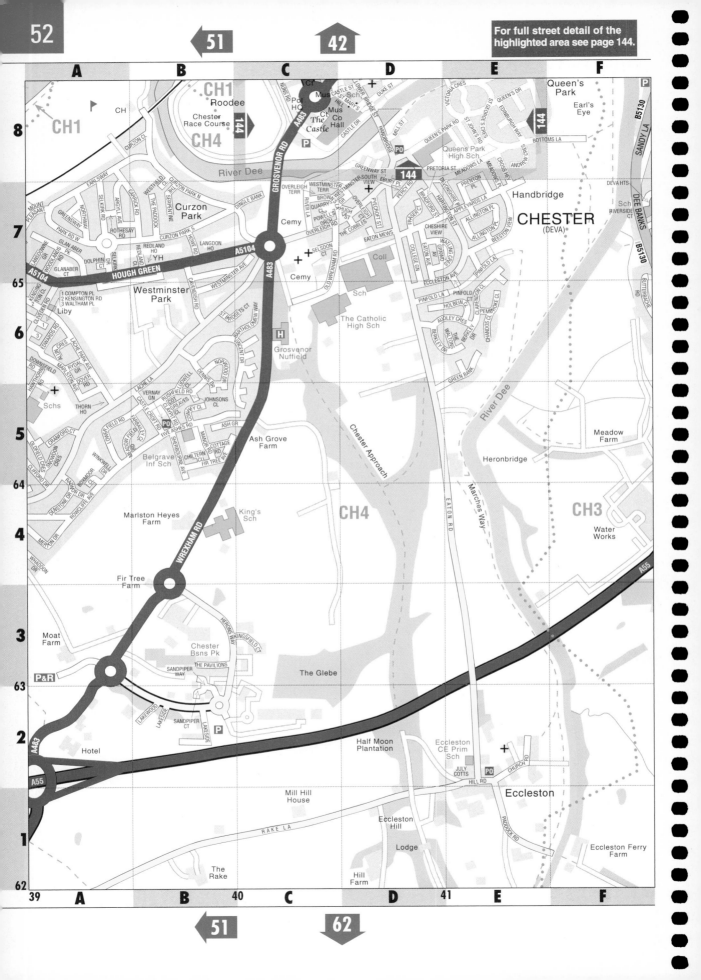

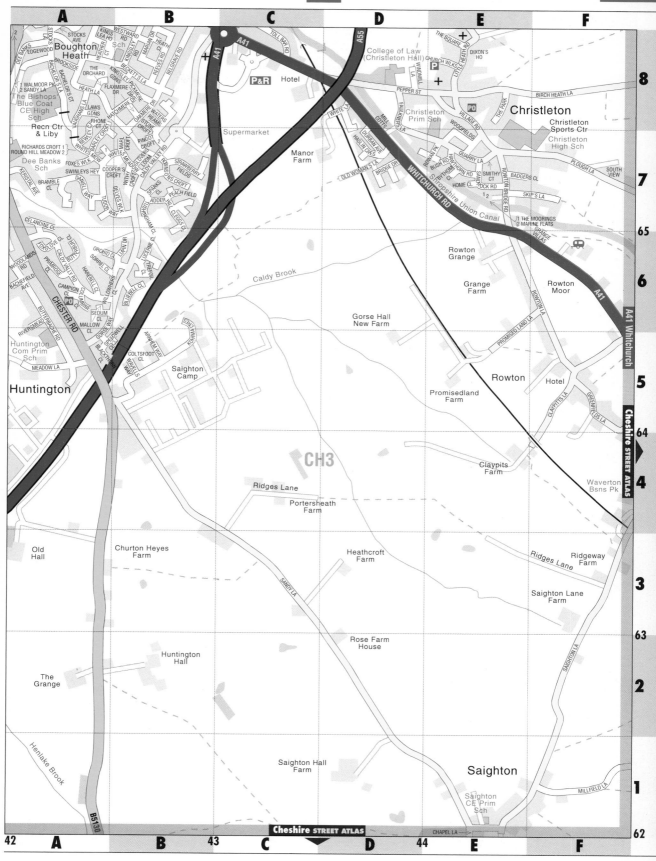

A B C D E F

Boughton Heath

Christleton
Christleton Sports Ctr
Christleton High Sch

College of Law (Christleton Hall)

The Bishops' Blue Coat CE High Sch

Recn Ctr & Liby

Dee Banks Sch

Supermarket

Manor Farm

WHITCHURCH RD

Shropshire Union Canal

Caldy Brook

Rowton Grange

Grange Farm

Rowton Moor

Gorse Hall New Farm

Rowton

Hotel

Huntington Com Prim Sch

Huntington

Saighton Camp

Promisedland Farm

Claypits Farm

CH3

Waverton Bsns Pk

Ridges Lane

Portersheath Farm

Heathcroft Farm

Ridges Lane

Ridgeway Farm

Old Hall

Churton Heyes Farm

Saighton Lane Farm

Rose Farm House

Huntington Hall

The Grange

Saighton Hall Farm

Saighton

Saighton CE Prim Sch

Henlake Brook

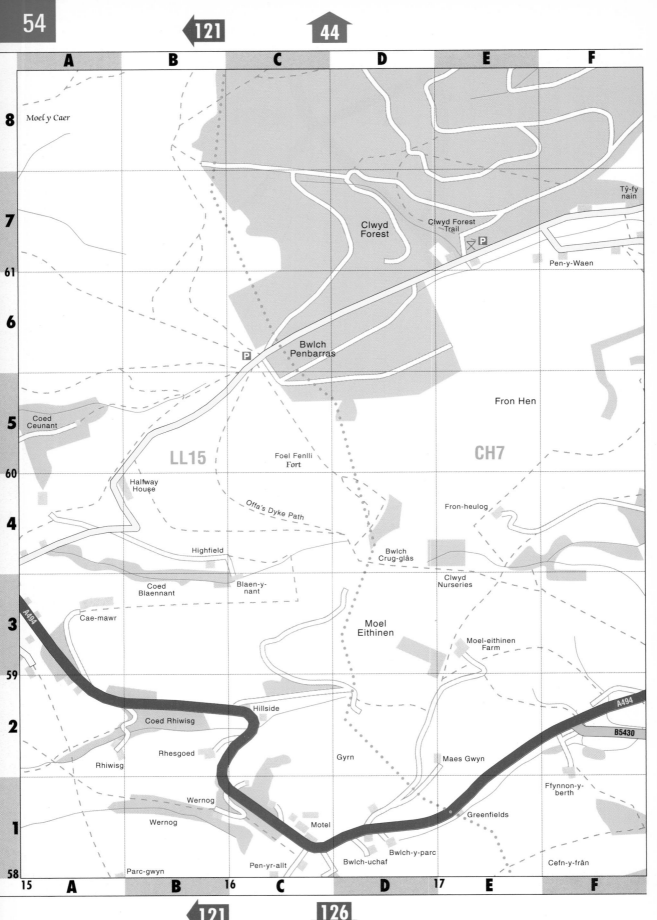

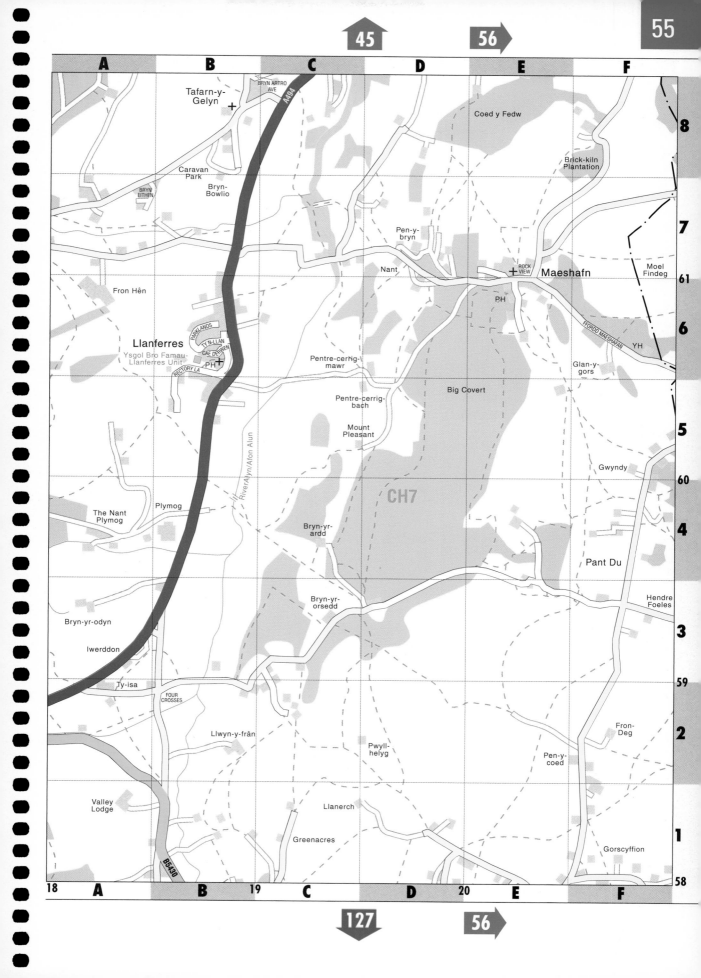

45
56

A B C D E F

8

7

61

6

5

60

4

3

59

2

1

58

18 A B 19 C D 20 E F

127
56

Tafarn-y-Gelyn

BRYN ARTRO AVE

A494

Caravan Park

BRYN EITHEN

Bryn-Bowlio

Coed y Fedw

Brick-kiln Plantation

Pen-y-bryn

Nant

ROCK VIEW

Maeshafn

Moel Findeg

Fron Hèn

PH

FFORDD MAESHAFAN

YH

PARKLANDS

TY N-LLAN

CAE DERWEN

Llanferres

Ysgol Bro Famau-
Llanferres Unit

PH

RECTORY LA

Pentre-cerrig-mawr

Big Covert

Glan-y-gors

River Alyn/Afon Alun

Pentre-cerrig-bach

Mount Pleasant

Gwyndy

CH7

The Nant Plymog

Plymog

Bryn-yr-ardd

Pant Du

Bryn-yr-odyn

Bryn-yr-orsedd

Hendre Foeles

Iwerddon

Ty-isa

FOUR CROSSES

Fron-Deg

Llwyn-y-frân

Pwyll-helyg

Pen-y-coed

Valley Lodge

B5430

Llanerch

Greenacres

Gorscyffion

55
46

A   B   C   D   E   F

8

Bryngwyn

Fron
Ucha

Pentre-bâch

GLYNDWR RD

Tower Wood

Hendre Isa

Ty Gwernen

Plâs-Onn

7

Bryngwyn
Farm

FFORDD PENTRE BÂCH

Hendre
Ucha

Fron

FRON
HEULOG
TERR

Owain Glyhdwr
Inn
(PH)

61

Moel
Findeg

America Farm

Penrallt
Farm

FFORDD GLYNDWR

Bryn-
Goleu

TAN-Y-RHOS

FFORDD Y PENTRE

Rhos
Ithel

AEL-Y-BRYN

GER-Y-PISTYLL

Nercwys

6

FFORDD PEN Y BRYN

Nercwys
Prim Sch

SCHOOL
TERR

PH

FFORDD MAESHAFAN

Pant-y-Bettws

PH

PH

5

Tir-y-coed
Farm

Freezland

CH7

HENFFORDD

60

Gelli

FFORDD LLEWELYN

Llewelyn

4

Tir y Coed

Ty'n-yr-ynn

Tŷ-coch

Ty-melyn

Hendre
Foelas

FFORDD CAE NEWYDD

Woodland
Cottage

Trefrwd

FFORDD PLAS UCHA

Plas
Ucha

Glan
Terrig

3

59

Coed
Gwern-rhiw

Plas Nant-y-Glyn

FFORDD TALWYRN

2

Nercwys Mountain

Talwrn

River Terrig

Pwll Farm

Gwern Rhiw

Ddadau
Farm

1

Graig Goch
Ucha

Erw-goed

Ty-draw

58

21   A   B   22   C   D   23   E   F

55
63

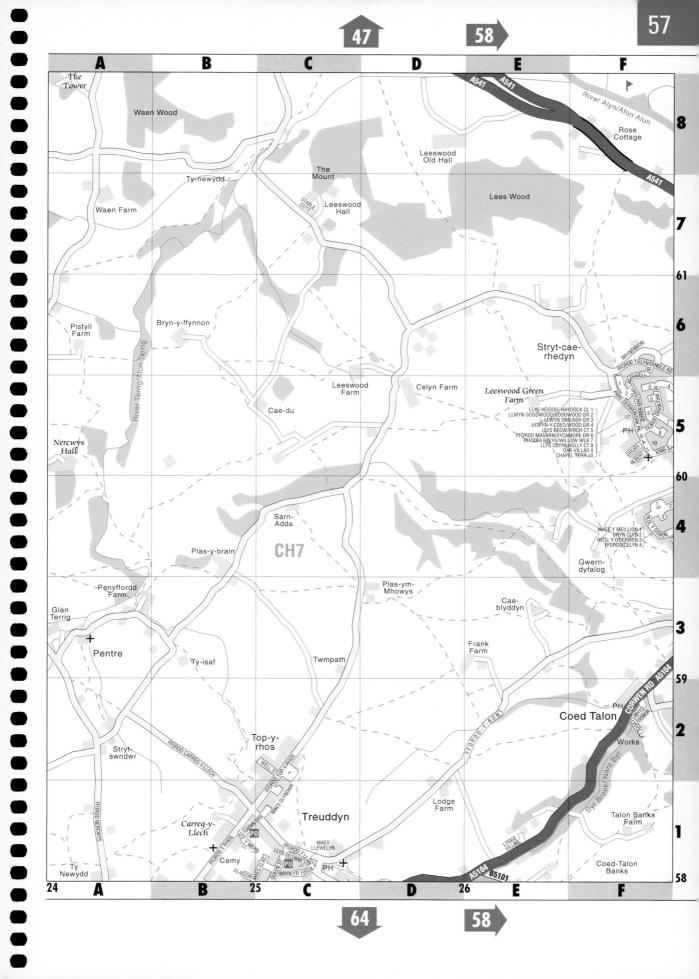

47
58

The Tower

A B C D E F

Waen Wood

Ty-newydd

The Mount

Leeswood Old Hall

River Alyn/Afon Alun

Rose Cottage

A541 A541

8

Waen Farm

Stable Cott

Leeswood Hall

Lees Wood

7

Pistyll Farm

Bryn-y-ffynnon

61

6

Stryt-cae-rhedyn

BRYNTIRION

Nercwys Hall

Cae-du

Leeswood Farm

Celyn Farm

Leeswood Green Farm

FFORDD Y GLYN/DINGLE RD
PARC DERWEN/OAK PK
MAXWELL
FFORDD DRWOIM DR

LLYS HEIDOG/HAYDOCK CL 1
LLWYN GOODWOOD/GOODWOOD GR 2
LLWYN ONN/ASH GR 3
LLWYN-Y-COED/WOOD GR 4
LLYS BEDW/BIRCH CT 5
FFORDD MASARN/SYCAMORE DR 6
RHODFA HELYG/WILLOW WLK 7
LLYS CELYN/HOLLY CT 8
OAK VILLAS 9
CHAPEL TERR 10

PH

DRURY LA
ALBERT ST
KINGS ST

5

60

Sarn-Adda

CH7

Plas-y-brain

Gwern-dyfalog

MAES Y MEILLION 1
BRYN CLYD 2
HEOL-Y-DDERWEN 3
FFORDD CELYN 4

HEOL Y GORON

4

Penyffordd Farm

Plas-ym-Mhowys

Cae-blyddyn

Glan Terrig

Pentre

Ty-isaf

Twmpath

Frank Farm

FFORDD-Y-BONT

Coed Talon

CORWEN RD A5104

PH

SCHOOL LA
OSSBR
HINTO

59

3

2

Strytswndwr

FFORDD CARREG-Y-LLECH

Top-y-rhos

FFORDD TOP-Y-RHOS
WELL ST

FFORDD TOP-Y-RHOS

MAES GLYNDWR

Lodge Farm

Works

Byr Brook/ Nant Byr

Talon Banks Farm

Carreg-y-Llech

FFORDD Y RHOS
FFHAM-HEG
LLYS Y WERN
PO

MAES LLEWELYN

LODGE VILLAS

FFORDD NERCWYS

Ty Newydd

Cemy

MAES GLASI
GLASDIR
QUEEN ST
FFORDD Y LLAN
LLYS DEGWM
BRYN YR YSGOL
PO
PH

Treuddyn

A5104 B5101

Coed-Talon Banks

24 A B 25 C D 26 E F 58

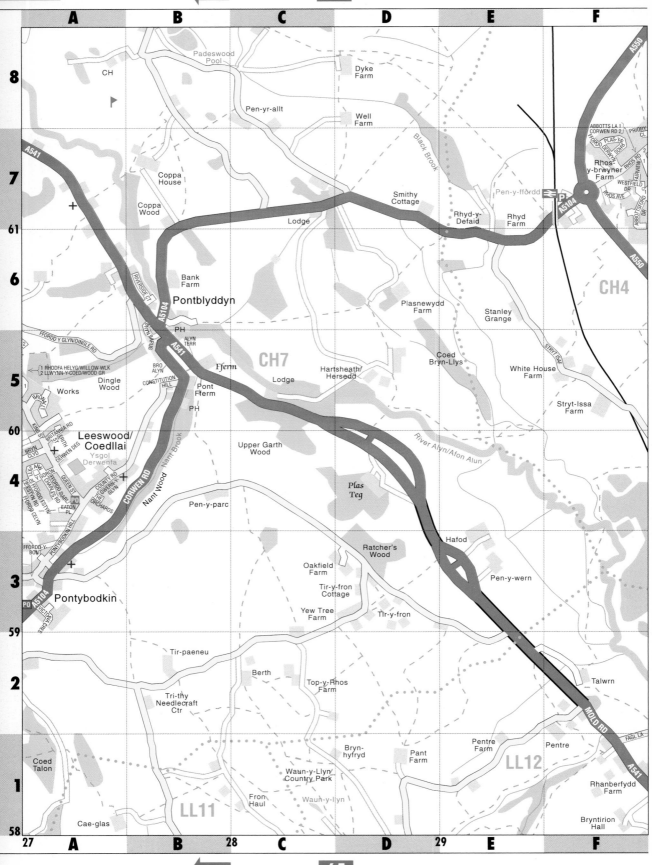

A B C D E F

8
7
61
6
5
60
4
3
59
2
1
58

CH

Padeswood Pool

Dyke Farm

Pen-yr-allt

Well Farm

Coppa House

Black Brook

A541

Coppa Wood

Smithy Cottage

Pen-y-ffordd

A5104

Rhos-y-brwyner Farm

ABBOTTS LA 1
CORWEN RD 2
PLAS-YN-
FFORDD-DERWN RD
PRIORY CL

WESTFIELD DR

RHOS AVE

ABBOTTSFORD DR

CH4

RIVERSIDE CT

Lodge

Rhyd-y-Defaid

Rhyd Farm

A5104

Bank Farm

Pontblyddyn

Plasnewydd Farm

Stanley Grange

STRYT ISAF

BETHEL PARUG

PH

ALYN TERR

CH7

Hartsheath/ Hersedd

Coed Bryn-Llys

White House Farm

BRO ALYN

Fferm

Lodge

A541

CONSTITUTION HILL

Pont Fferm

PH

Stryt-Issa Farm

1 RHODFA HELYG/WILLOW WLK
2 LLWYNN-Y-COED/WOOD GR

Dingle Wood

Works

1

BROMLEY

Upper Garth Wood

River Alyn/Afon Alun

FFORDD Y GLYN/DINGLE RD

Nant Wood

Nant Brook

Leeswood/ Coedllai

Ysgol Derwenfa

BRITANNIA RD

BRYN CLYD

DERWEN DEG

KING ST

1 GORON
2 GORON
GWERN-Y-
GLYN

Plas Teg

Hafod

CORWEN RD

COUNTY RD

Pen-y-parc

Pen-y-wern

HEOL Y
GORON

THE ORCHARDS

CHARLES RD

QUEEN'S RD

FFORDD ESTYN

FFORDD SELYN

EATON PL

Ratcher's Wood

PO

PONTYBODKIN HILL

Oakfield Farm

Tir-y-fron Cottage

Tir-y-fron

FFORDD-Y- BONT

Yew Tree Farm

PO

A5104

Pontybodkin

VICTORIA CRES

Tir-paeneu

Berth

Top-y-Rhos Farm

Talwrn

Tri-thy Needlecraft Ctr

MOLD RD

Pentre Farm

Pentre

A541

Coed Talon

Bryn-hyfryd

Pant Farm

LL12

Waun-y-Llyn Country Park

Fron Haul

Waun-y-llyn

Rhanberfydd Farm

LL11

Cae-glas

Bryntirion Hall

A550

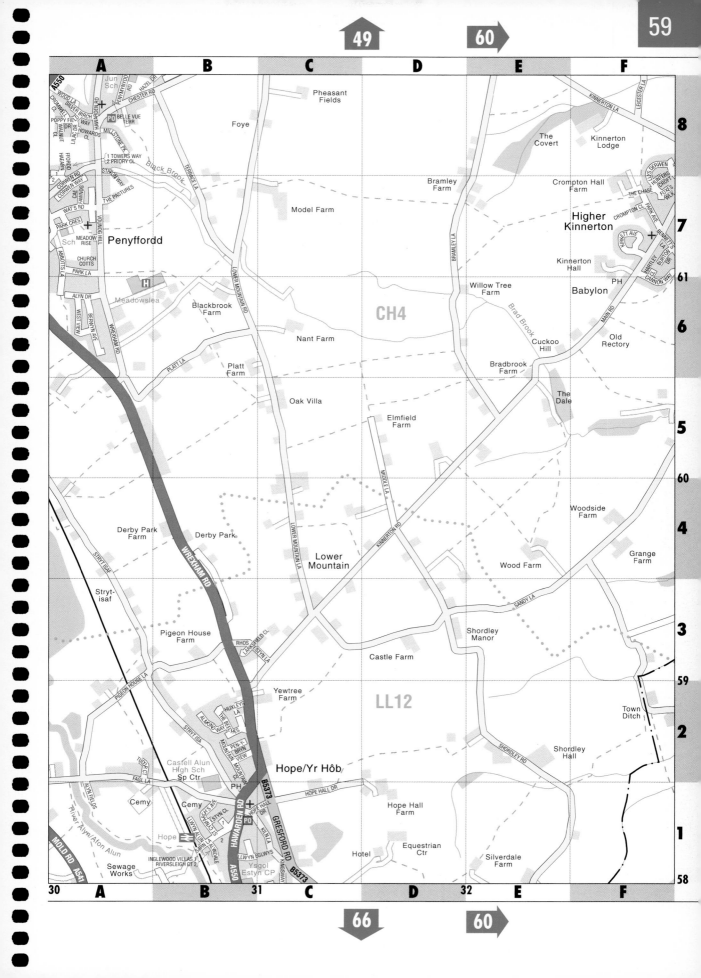

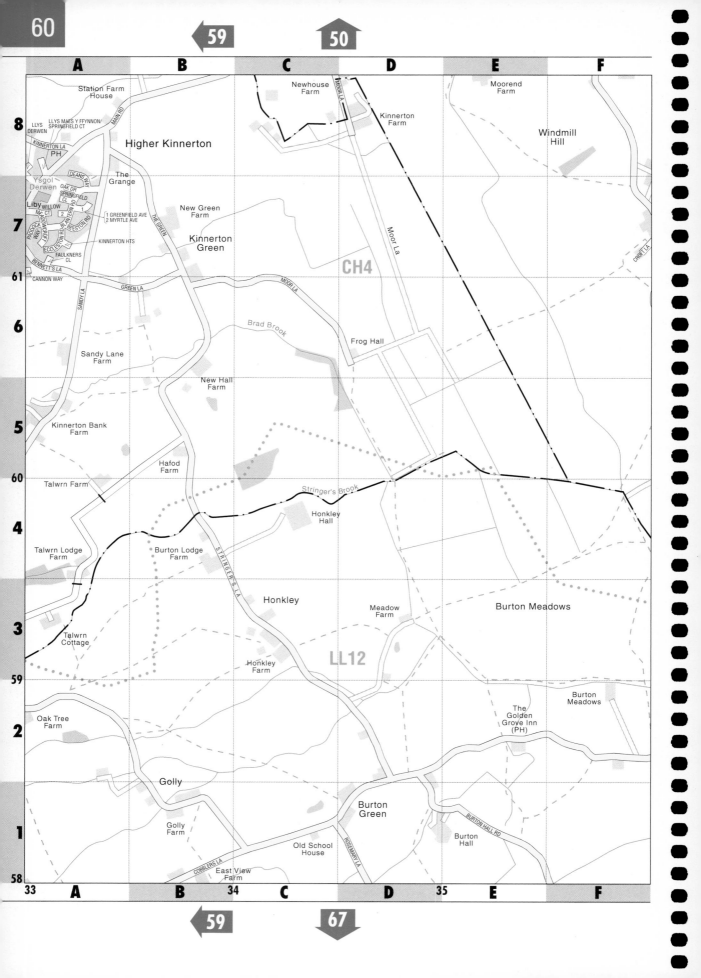

A B C D E F

8

Station Farm House
Newhouse Farm
Moorend Farm
Kinnerton Farm
MOOR LA
Windmill Hill
LLYS MAES Y FFYNNON/ SPRINGFIELD CT
LLYS DERWEN
KINNERTON LA
PH
Higher Kinnerton
Ysgol Derwen
DEANS WAY
The Grange
OAK DR
SPRINGFIELD CL
Liby
WILLOW
McCT
2
THE GREEN
BEESTON RD
LANTERN RD
1 GREENFIELD AVE
2 MYRTLE AVE
New Green Farm

7

MEADOWCROFT
PADDOCK
KINNERTON HTS
FAULKNERS CL
Kinnerton Green
ECCLESTON RD
BENNETT'S LA
61
CANNON WAY
SANDY LA
GREEN LA
MOOR LA
CH4
Moor La

6

Brad Brook
Frog Hall
Sandy Lane Farm

5

New Hall Farm
Kinnerton Bank Farm
Hafod Farm
60
Talwrn Farm
Stringer's Brook

4

Honkley Hall
Talwrn Lodge Farm
Burton Lodge Farm
STRINGER'S LA

3

Honkley
Meadow Farm
Burton Meadows
Talwrn Cottage
LL12

59
Honkley Farm
Burton Meadows

2

Oak Tree Farm
The Golden Grove Inn (PH)

1

Golly
Golly Farm
Burton Green
Burton Hall
BURTON HALL RD
ROSEMARY LA

58
Old School House
COBBLERS LA
East View Farm
Burton Hall

33 A B 34 C D 35 E F

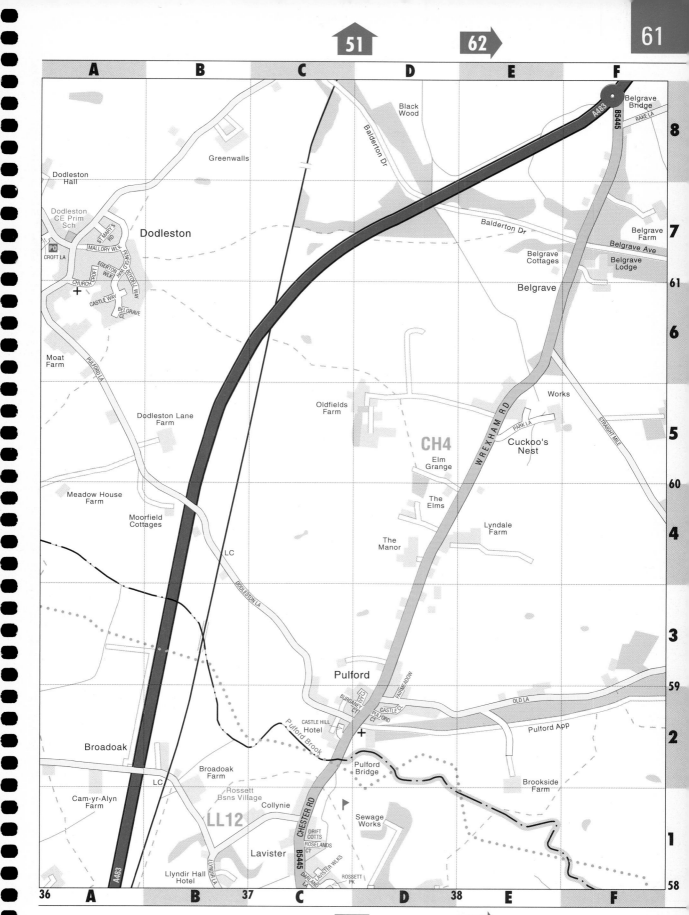

A B C D E F

8
7
61
6
5
60
4
3
59
2
1
58

Belgrave Bridge
RAKE LA
A483
B5445
Belgrave Farm
Belgrave Ave
Belgrave Cottages
Belgrave Lodge
Belgrave
Black Wood
Balderton Dr
Balderton Dr
Greenwalls
Dodleston Hall
Dodleston CE Prim Sch
ST MARY'S RD
Dodleston
MALLORY WLK
PO
CROFT LA
CHURCH
CROFT
PENFOLD ROYDELL WAY
EGERTON WLK
CASTLE WAY
BELGRAVE CL
Moat Farm
PULFORD LA
Dodleston Lane Farm
Meadow House Farm
Moorfield Cottages
LC
DODLESTON LA
Oldfields Farm
CH4
Elm Grange
The Elms
The Manor
WREXHAM RD
Cuckoo's Nest
PARK LA
Works
STRAIGHT MILE
Lyndale Farm
Pulford
BURGANE CT
PULFORD CT
FAIRMEADOW
CASTLE CL
OLD LA
Pulford App
Brookside Farm
Broadoak
Castle Hill Hotel
Pulford Brook
Pulford Bridge
Sewage Works
LC
Broadoak Farm
Rossett Bsns Village
Collynie
LL12
CHESTER RD
DRIFT COTTS
ROSELANDS CT
Cam-yr-Alyn Farm
Lavister
B5445
Llyndir Hall Hotel
LLYNDIR LA
DARLAND LA
LAVISTER WLKS
ROSSETT PK
A483

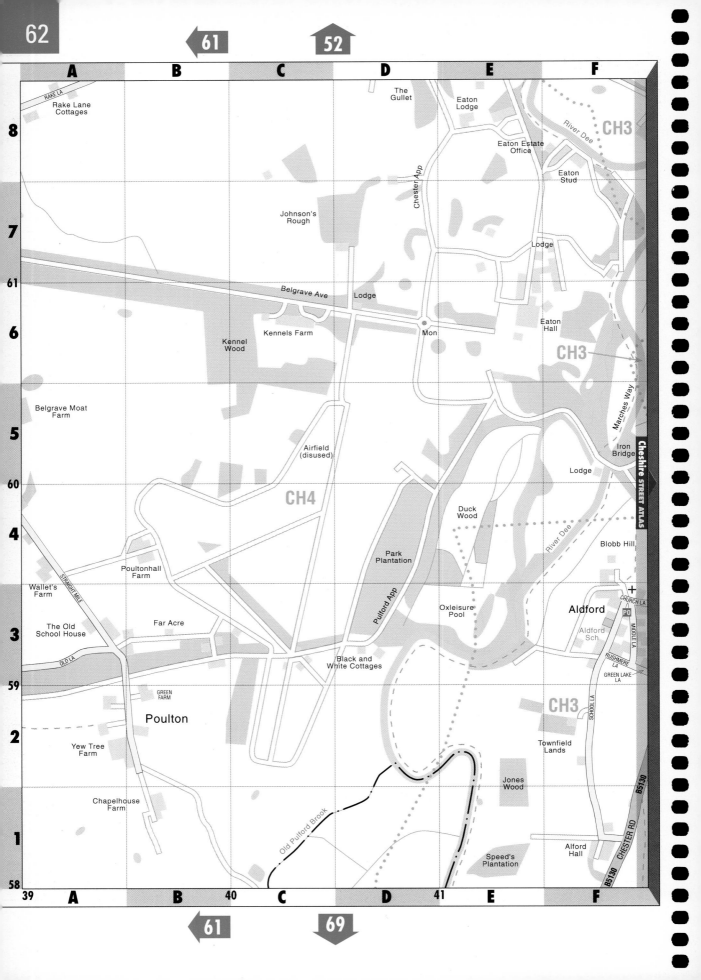

61
52

A B C D E F

8
7
61
6
5
60
4
3
59
2
1
58

RAKE LA
Rake Lane
Cottages

The Gullet

Eaton
Lodge

River Dee

CH3

Eaton Estate
Office

Eaton
Stud

Chester App

Johnson's
Rough

Lodge

Belgrave Ave

Lodge

Eaton
Hall

CH3

Kennels Farm

Mon

Kennel
Wood

Marches Way

Belgrave Moat
Farm

Iron
Bridge

Cheshire STREET ATLAS

Airfield
(disused)

Lodge

CH4

Duck
Wood

Park
Plantation

River Dee

Blobb Hill

Poultonhall
Farm

Wallet's
Farm

Pulford App

Oxleisure
Pool

Aldford

CHURCH LA
PO

Far Acre

Aldford
Sch

MIDDLE LA

The Old
School House

OLD LA

Black and
White Cottages

RUSHMERE
LA

GREEN LAKE
LA

GREEN
FARM

59

CH3

STRAIGHT MILE

Poulton

SCHOOL LA

Yew Tree
Farm

Townfield
Lands

Jones
Wood

B5130

Chapelhouse
Farm

Old Pulford Brook

Speed's
Plantation

Alford
Hall

CHESTER RD

B5130

39 A B 40 C D 41 E F

61
69

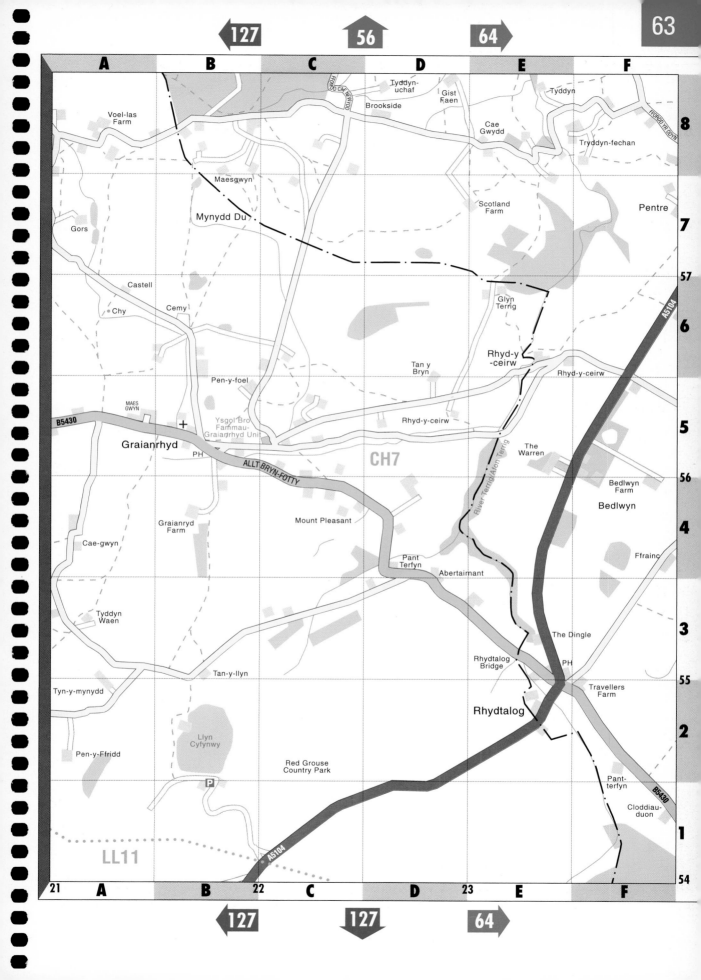

63
57

A   B   C   D   E   F

8

Tyn Rhos
Pen-y-stryt
Ddau Gae Farm
RHOS HELYG
LLYS GWYDDFID
QUEEN ST
ERW FFYNNON
HERITAGE SQ.
FFORDD Y GILRHOS
FFORDD NERCWYS
FFORDD YR ODYN
FFORDD Y RHOS
Ysgol Terrig
Ysgol Parc Y Llan
CAE MYNACH
ERW'R LLAN
FFORDD Y LLAN
A5104
Ffrith Farm
B5101
FFORDD LLAN-Y-NYDD
Tan-llan
B5101

7
Cae Mawr
Pant-y-ffordd
FFORDD PANT-Y-FFORDD
A5104
Tree Tops (Outdoor Activity Ctr)

57
Allandale
Ffrith-bâch
River Cegidog/Afon Cegidog

6
Tryddyn Cottage
Rhos-uchaf (Riding School)
Ty-draw
Tithe Barn

5
CH7
Cae Hic
Cae-glâs
Heulog Farm
Bryn Common

56
Blaenau Road Farm
Old Smithy
Cae-rheinallt Farm
LL11

4
Cae Hic Bach
Cae-grugog
Cae Rheinallt
Cae-rheinallt-isaf
Mount Farm
FFORDD Y BLAENAU

3
Ty Capel
Blaenau
Bryn-hafod
Hafod-y-swch
Rabbit Warren

55
Gwernto
Talwrn-glas

2
Gwernto Plantation
Gwernto-bâch
Werngate Farm
Mount Wood
Pen-Llan-y-gwr
Nant y Ffrith

1
B5430
Gwern
Tyddyn Llwyd
Wern Ganol
Nant y Ffrith
Darnau Wood
GLASCOED RD

54
24   A   B   25   C   D   26   E   F

63
70

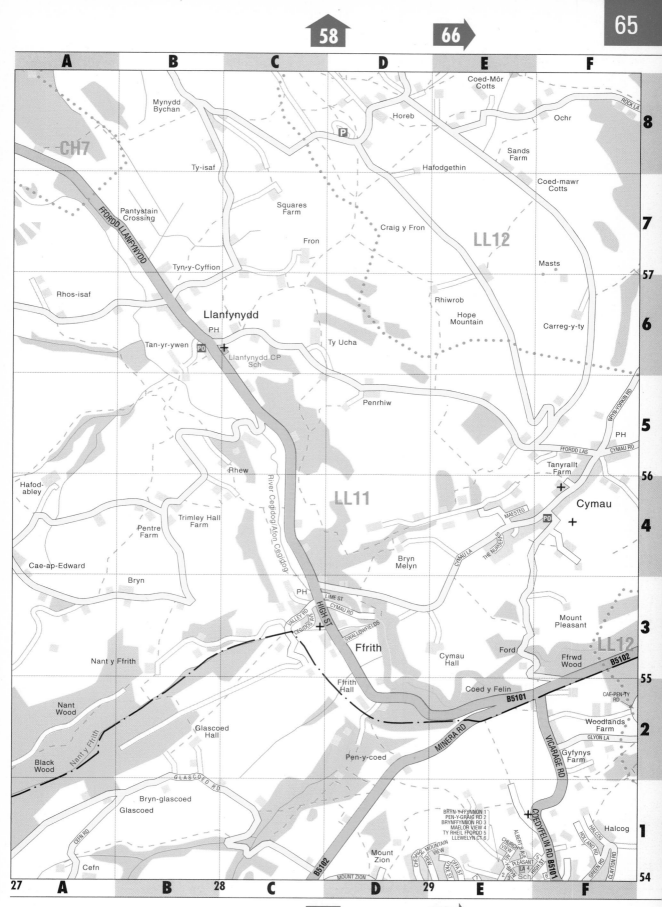

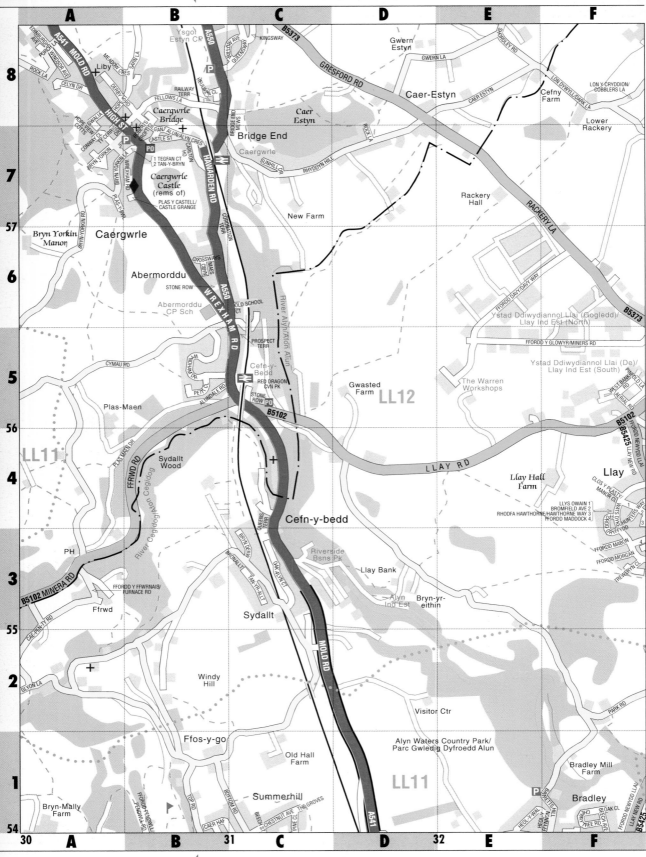

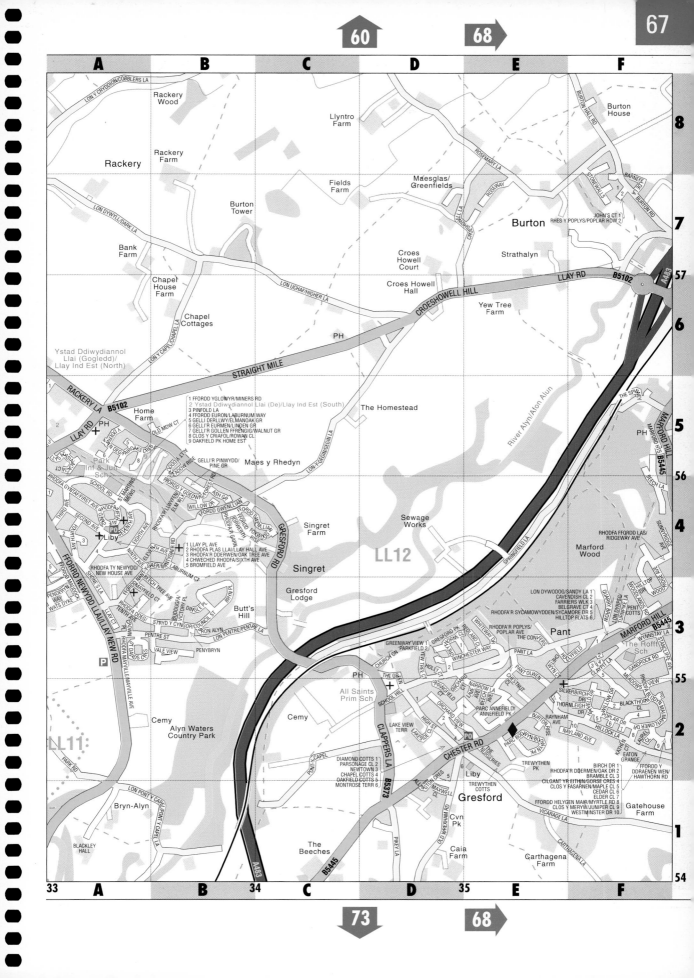

A B C D E F

8

7

6

5

4

3

2

1

Rackery
Wood

Llyntro
Farm

Burton
House

Rackery
Farm

Fields
Farm

Maesglas/
Greenfields

Rackery

Burton
Tower

Rhes y Poplys/Poplar Row 2
John's Ct 1

Burton

Bank
Farm

Croes
Howell
Court

Strathalyn

Chapel
House
Farm

LON UCHAF/HIGHER LA

Croes Howell
Hall

CROESHOWELL HILL

LLAY RD

B5102

A483

57

Chapel
Cottages

Yew Tree
Farm

MARFORD HTS

Ystad Ddiwydiannol
Llai (Gogledd)/
Llay Ind Est (North)

PH

STRAIGHT MILE

RACKERY LA

B5102

Home
Farm

OLD MDW CT

1 FFORDD YGLOWYR/MINERS RD
2 Ystad Ddiwydiannol Llai (De)/Llay Ind Est (South)
3 PINFOLD LA
4 FFORDD EURON/LABURNUM WAY
5 GELLI DERLLWY/ELMANOAK GR
6 GELLI'R EURMEN/LINDEN GR
7 GELLI'R GOLLEN FFRENGIG/WALNUT GR
8 CLOS Y CRIAFOL/ROWAN CL
9 OAKFIELD PK HOME EST

The Homestead

River Alyn/Afon Alun

PH

B5445

LLAY RD

PH

Park
Inf & Jun
Sch

Gelli'r Pinwydd/
Pine Gr

Maes y Rhedyn

GRESFORD RD

Singret
Farm

Sewage
Works

LL12

Rhodfa Ffordd Las/
Ridgeway Ave

Marford
Wood

56

Liby

1 LLAY PL AVE
2 RHODFA PLAS LLAI/LLAY HALL AVE
3 RHODFA'R DDERWEN/OAK TREE AVE
4 CHWECHED RHODFA/SIXTH AVE
5 BROMFIELD AVE

Singret

Singret

FFORDD NEWYDD LAI/LLAY NEW RD

P

Butt's
Hill

Gresford
Lodge

LON DYWODOG/SANDY LA 1
CAVENDISH CL 2
FARRIERS WLK 3
BEL GRAVE CT 4
RHODFA'R SYCAMWYDDEN/SYCAMORE DR 5
HILLTOP FLATS 6

Pant

MARFORD HILL

B5445

The Rofft
Sch

PENYBRYN

PH

Greenway View 1
Parkfield 2

55

P

Cemy

Cemy

All Saints
Prim Sch

SCHOOL HILL

CHURCH GN

THE GN

CLAPPERS LA

B5373

LAKE VIEW
TERR

Parc Annefield/
Annefield Pk

Silverbirches

Alyn Waters
Country Park

CHESTER RD

Liby

PO

Trewythen
Cotts

Birch Dr 1
Rhodfa'r Ddermen/Oak Dr 2
Bramble Cl 3
Cilgant yr Eithin/Gorse Cres 4
Clos y Fasarnen/Maple Cl 5
Cedar Cl 6
Elder Cl 7
Ffordd Helygen Mair/Myrtle Rd 8
Clos y Meryw/Juniper Cl 9
Westminster Dr 10

LL11

Bryn-Alyn

Trewythen
Cotts

Gresford

Eaton
Grange

Ffordd y
Ddraenen Wen/
Hawthorn Rd

DIAMOND COTTS 1
PARSONAGE CL 2
NEWTOWN 3
CHAPEL COTTS 4
OAKFIELD COTTS 5
MONTROSE TERR 6

Gatehouse
Farm

BLACKLEY
HALL

Cvn
Pk

VICARAGE LA

CARTHAGENA LA

The
Beeches

B5445

A483

Caia
Farm

Carthagena
Farm

54

A **B** **C** **D** **E** **F**

Pulford Brook

CH4

A483

Cam-yr-Alyn

8

Darland Cottage Cl
ROSSETT PK
DARLAND CL
DARLAND COTTAGE CL
Darland Hall
The Darland

B5445

Sports Ctr
Darland High Sch
Darland

THE SMITHY
PARK VIEW
WAVERLEY CRES
CROMAR CRES
DARLAND VIEW
St Peters CW Prim Sch
DARLAND LA

Hotel
THE ORCHARD
THE LIMES
CHAPEL LA
FFORDD HOLT/HOLT RD
TREVALYN HALL VIEW

GAMFORD LA

Gamford House

DARLAND LA

The Darland

Rossett
WILLIAMS WAY
PH

SUNNY VILLAS

B5102

1 MOSS GN
2 RODENS CL

Trevalyn Farm

7

ELM CT
BURTON CL
THE CORSE
PARK CT

EATON CL
WEST WAY

NARROW LA

A483

STATION RD

P PO

CHESTER RD
HALKYN TERR
ALYN ST
NOOK BR
CAMPBELL CL
BROGS
OAK DR
ALYN DR

Lane Farm

57

Marford Mill

HARWOOD'S LA

MOUNTAIN VIEW
HARWOODS CL

Trevalyn
PH

+

Meadow Farm

B5102

Trevalyn Hall

MAUDI LA

BROAD LA

6

Cooksbridge Farm

ROSSETT RD

River Alyn/Afon Alun

B5445

H

Trevalyn

Cooks Bridge

5

THE OLD CARRIAGE YD

LL12

B5445

VILLAGE WALKS

DAISY LA

56

Marford Hall

Crabmill Farm

MARFORD HILL

Allington Farm

Hem House

4

Marford

Pistyll House Farm

Cox Wood

Coxwood Farm

SUNNYRIDGE AVE

B5445

Moorside Farm

Corner House

PISTYLL HILL

Parkside

Lower Parks Farm

3

STANCLIFFE AVE
MARELLAN AVE

HOSELEY LA

Wavertree Farm

55

HUDSONS HILL

PARK LA

Park Leigh Farm

Parkside Farm

B5102

2

HILLOCK LA
WYNNSTAY LA

Hoseley House

VICARAGE LA

Horsley Gorse

Lodge Farm

1

LL13

The Elms

Hoseley Bank Farm

The Parks

54

36 **A** **B** **37** **C** **D** **38** **E** **F**

62

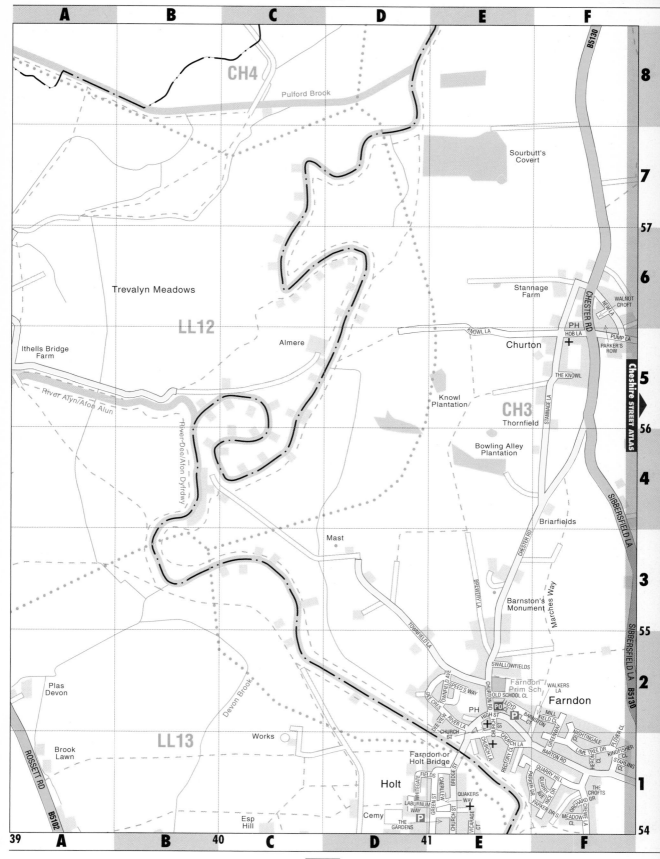

75

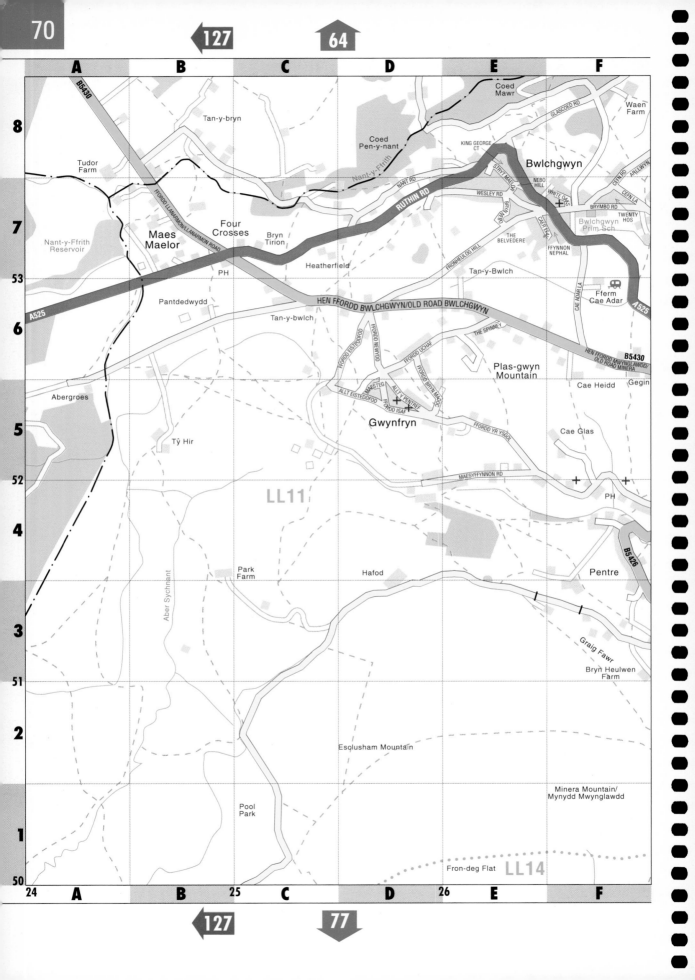

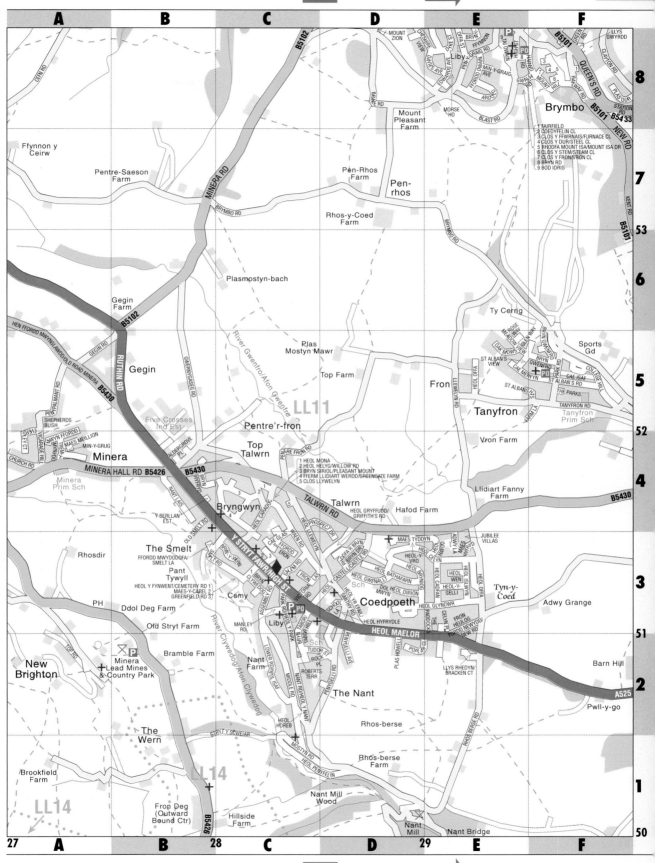

← 71

D6
1 FFORDD Y BANNAU/BEACON RD
2 CLOS Y GWEUNDIA/HEATHWOOD CL
3 ERW HEULOG/SUNNYACRE
4 WILLOW LEA CL
5 CLYWEDOG CL
6 FERNDALE RISE

66 ↑

D7
1 BRYN AWEL CT
2 GREENWOOD AVE
3 TAI CAPEL
4 AURELIUS HO
5 LLYS YR ORSAF/STATION CT
6 ROSEBINE VIEW

D8
1 GREENFIELD TERR
2 CLAREMONT COTTS
3 CLOS Y RHAGLAW/REGENT CL
4 LON CARLTON/CARLTON DR
5 FFORDD MENAI/MENAI WAY
6 MAESTAG

7 RHODFA GELE/GELE AVE

Map of area including Moss, Pentre Broughton, Summer Hill, Gwersyllt, Bradley, New Rhosrobin, Old Rhosrobin, Lower Stansty, Brynteg, Coed Efa, New Broughton, Southsea, Rhosrhedyn, Caego, Higher Berse Bridge, Berse Drelincourt, Plas Coch, Wrexham. Postcode districts LL11, LL13.

← 71

79 ↓

A4
1 CHAPEL CT
2 ZION COTTS
3 BRIDGE CT
4 GWENFRA COTTS
5 NELSON TERR
6 WESTERN VILLAS

B4
1 CORONATION COTTS
2 VULCAN COTTS
3 GLADWYN TERR
4 STURGES WLK
5 THE BRAMBLES
6 SCHOOL LA

C3
1 GORPHWYSFA
2 CORONATION TERR
3 IMPERIAL TERR
4 GREENFIELD TERR
5 CLEMENT HO
6 ALEXANDER HO
7 SOAR CHAPEL
8 WESTON VIEW
9 LABURNUS GR

C3
10 WILSON HO
11 GERDDI'R BERSE/BERSE GDNS
12 PLEASANT VILLAS
13 DUNALE VILLAS

For full street detail of the highlighted area see page 145.

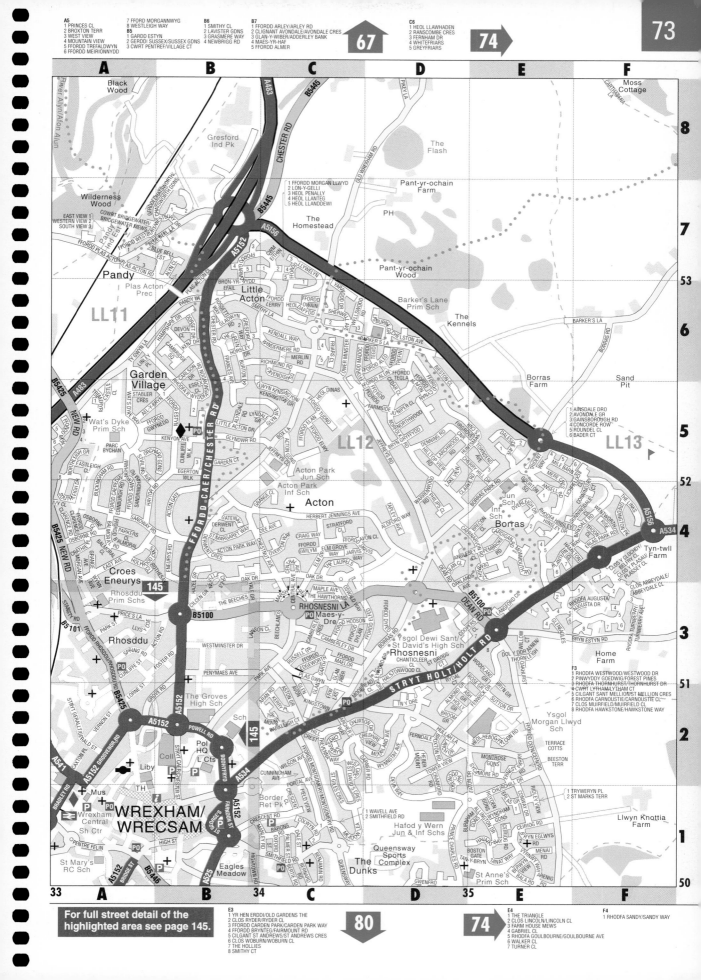

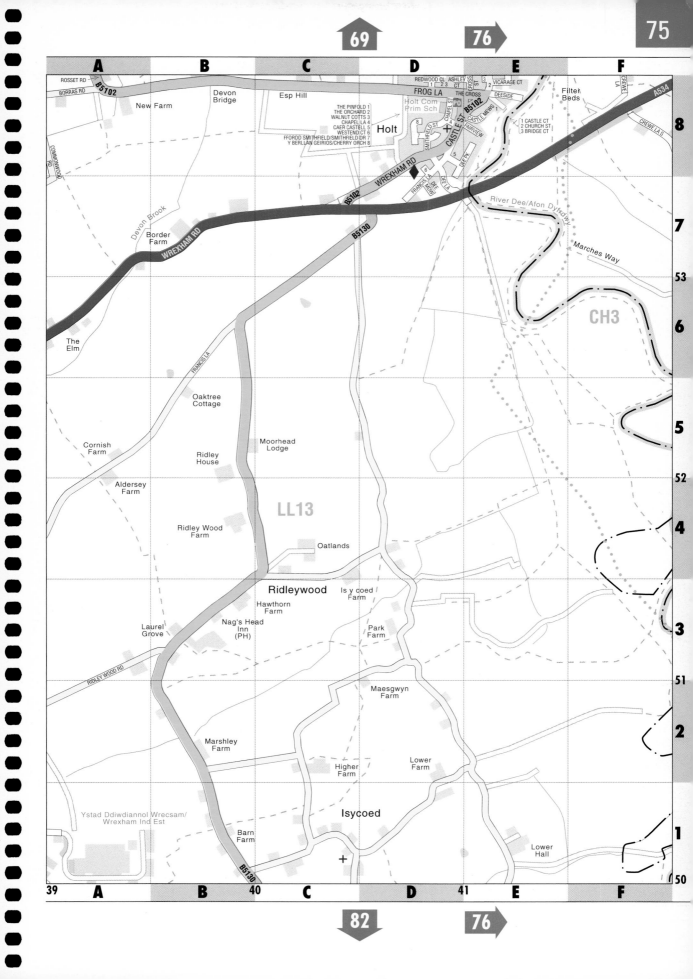

75

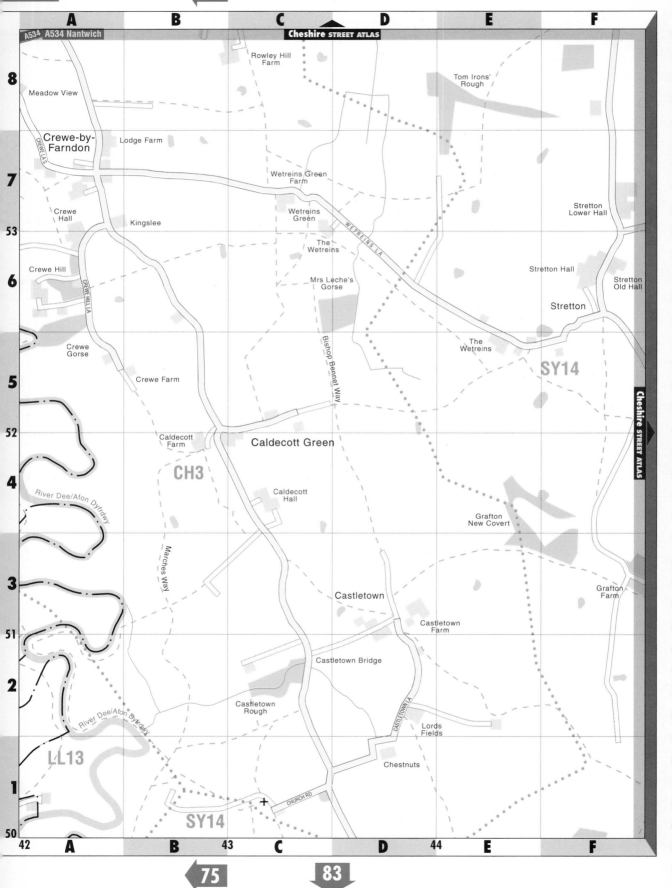

A   B   C   D   E   F

A534   A534 Nantwich

Cheshire STREET ATLAS

8   Meadow View
Rowley Hill Farm
Tom Irons' Rough

Crewe-by-Farndon
Lodge Farm
Wetreins Green Farm

7   CREWE LAS
Stretton Lower Hall

Crewe Hall
Kingslee
Wetreins Green

53   The Wetreins
Stretton Hall

6   Crewe Hill
CREWE HILL LA
Mrs Leche's Gorse
Stretton
Stretton Old Hall

Crewe Gorse
The Wetreins
WETREINS LA

5   Crewe Farm
SY14
Bishop Bennet Way

52   Caldecott Farm
Caldecott Green

4   CH3
Caldecott Hall
River Dee/Afon Dyfrdwy
Grafton New Covert

3   Marches Way
Castletown
Grafton Farm

51   Castletown Farm
Castletown Bridge

2   Castletown Rough
River Dee/Afon Dyfrdwy
CASTLETOWN LA
Lords Fields

Chestnuts

1   LL13
CHURCH RD

50   SY14

42   A   B   43   C   D   44   E   F

75   83

Cheshire STREET ATLAS

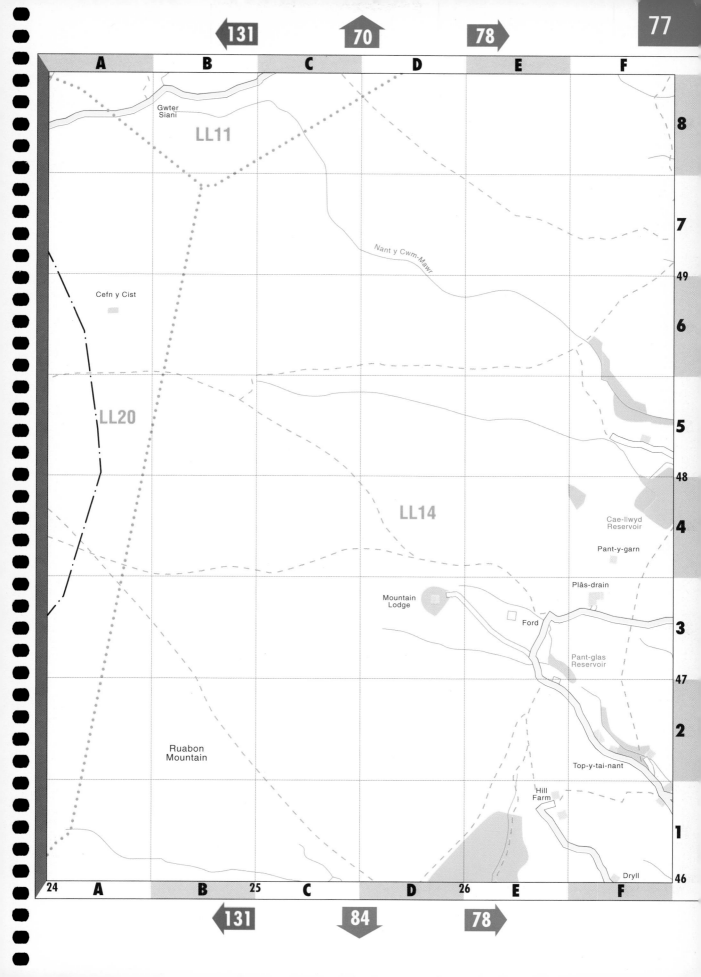

A B C D E F

Gwter
Siani

LL11

8

7

49

Cefn y Cist

6

Nant y Cwm-Mawr

LL20

5

48

LL14

Cae-llwyd
Reservoir

4

Pant-y-garn

Plâs-drain

Mountain
Lodge

Ford

3

Pant-glas
Reservoir

47

Ruabon
Mountain

2

Top-y-tai-nant

Hill
Farm

1

Dryll

46

24   A   B   25   C   D   26   E   F

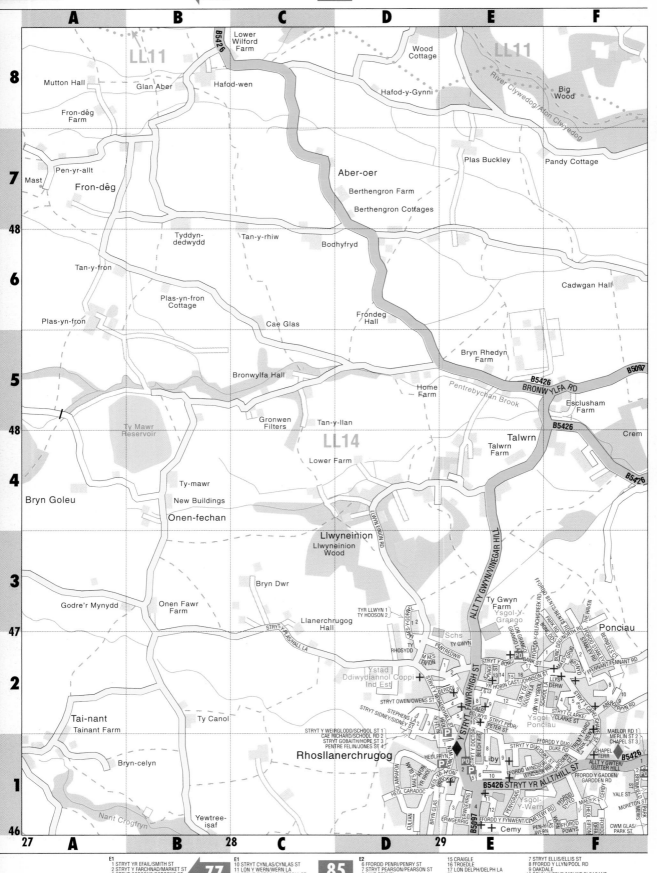

LL11
Lower Wilford Farm
B5426
Mutton Hall
Glan Aber
Hafod-wen
Wood Cottage
Hafod-y-Gynni
LL11
River Clywedog/Afon Clwyedog
Big Wood

Fron-dêg Farm
8

Pen-yr-allt
Plas Buckley
Pandy Cottage
7
Aber-oer
Mast
Fron-dêg
Berthengron Farm
Berthengron Cottages

48
Tyddyn-dedwydd
Tan-y-rhiw
Bodhyfryd

6
Tan-y-fron
Cadwgan Hall

Plas-yn-fron Cottage
Cae Glas
Frôndeg Hall

Plas-yn-fron
Bryn Rhedyn Farm

5
Bronwylfa Hall
Home Farm
Pentrebychan Brook
B5426 BRONWYLFA RD
B5097
Esclusham Farm

48
Gronwen Filters
Tan-y-llan
B5426
Crem

Lower Farm
LL14
Talwrn Farm
Talwrn

4
Bryn Goleu
Ty-mawr
New Buildings
Onen-fechan
B5426

Llwyneinion
Llwyneinion Wood
Llwyn Einion Rd

3
Godre'r Mynydd
Onen Fawr Farm
Bryn Dwr
Allt Ty Gwyn/Vinegar Hill
Ty Gwyn Farm
Ysgol-Y-Grango
Ponciau

47
Llanerchrugog Hall
Stryt Plas-Hall La
TYR LLWYN 1
TY HOOSON 2
Schs
PO

2
Ystad Ddiwydiannol Coppi Ind Est
Stryt Yr Allt/High St

Tai-nant
Tainant Farm
Ty Canol
STRYT Y WEIRGLODD/SCHOOL ST 1
CAE RICHARD/SCHOOL RD 2
STRYT GOBAITH/HOPE ST 3
PENTRE FELIN/JONES ST 4
Libry

Bryn-celyn
Rhosllanerchrugog
B5426 STRYT YR ALLT/HILL ST

1
Ysgol-Y-Wern
Yewtree-isaf
B5097

Nant Crogfryn
Cemy

46

27   28   29

E1
1 STRYT YR EFAIL/SMITH ST
2 STRYT Y FARCHNAD/MARKET ST
3 STRYT OSBORNE/OSBORNE ST
4 STRYT Y GOF/CHURCH ST
5 RHES Y CIGYDD/BUTCHERS ROW
6 STRYT Y BRENIN/KING ST
7 FFORDD Y TYWYSOB/PRINCES RD
8 RHODFA'R POPLYS/POPLAR AVE
9 STRYT Y FRENHINES/QUEEN ST

E1
10 STRYT CYNLAS/CYNLAS ST
11 LON Y WERN/WERN LA
12 STRYT FICTORIA/VICTORIA ST
E2
1 LLWYDIARTH
2 HEOL-Y-MYNYDD/MOUNTAIN ST
3 STRYT Y CAMBELIAID/CAMPBELL ST
4 STRYT YR ALARCH/SWAN ST
5 STRYT FECHAN/ROBERTS LA

E2
6 FFORDD PENRI/PENRY ST
7 STRYT PEARSON/PEARSON ST
8 LLYS PENUEL
9 STRYT NEWYDD/NEW ST
10 STRYT Y CIGYDD/BUTCHER ST
11 STRYT LYDAN/BROAD ST
12 STRYT Y BEDYDDWYR/BAPTIST ST
13 TY WESLEY
14 HEOL AWSTRALIA/AUSTRALIA ST

15 CRAIGLE
16 TROEDLE
17 LON DELPH/DELPH LA
F2
1 YR ERW/HAND LA
2 FFORDD Y DDERWEN/OAK RD
3 CAERNARVON TERR
4 STRYT Y CASTELL/CASTLE ST
5 LON WALKER/WALKERS LA
6 STRYT WILLIAM/WILLIAM ST

7 STRYT ELLIS/ELLIS RD
8 FFORDD Y LLYN/POOL RD
9 OAKDALE
10 BRYN HYFRYD/MOUNT PLEASANT

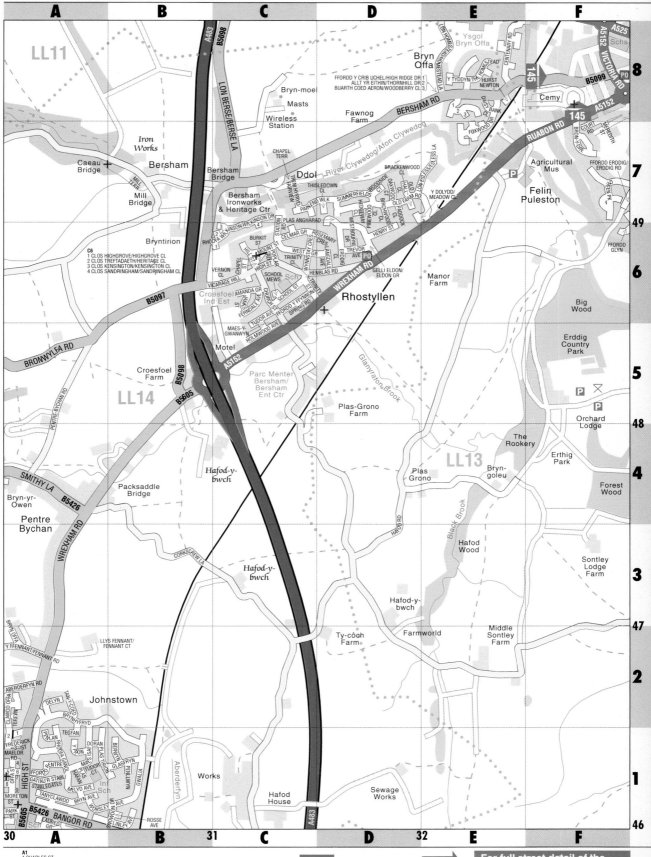

LL11

Iron Works

Caeau Bridge

Bersham

Mill Tehr

Mill Bridge

Bryntirion

C6
1 CLOS HIGHGROVE/HIGHGROVE CL
2 CLOS TREFTADAETH/HERITAGE CL
3 CLOS KENSINGTON/KENSINGTON CL
4 CLOS SANDRINGHAM/SANDRINGHAM CL

Bersham Bridge

Bersham Ironworks & Heritage Ctr

CHAPEL TERR

Ddol

THISLEDOWN CL

Bryn-moel

Masts

Wireless Station

Fawnog Farm

BERSHAM RD

River Clywedog/Afon Clywedog

BRACKENWOOD CL

Ysgol Bryn Offa

Bryn Offa

FFORDD Y CRIB UCHEL/HIGH RIDGE DR 1
ALLT YR EITHIN/THORNHILL DR 2
BUARTH COED AERON/WOODBERRY CL 3

Y TYDDYN TY

HURST NEWTON

CENTENARY RD

LON HOMESTEAD/HOMESTEAD LA

DAISY BANK

FOXWOOD DR

145

RUABON RD

Cemy

A525
A5152 VICTORIA RD

Schs

B5099

A5152

145

BRYN YORK

COURT RD

MEREDITH

OPEN PK

FFORDD ERDDIG/ERDDIG RD

Agricultural Mus

Felin Puleston

FFORDD GLYN

49

8

7

WOODSIDE

SUMMERFIELDS

OAKWOOD DR

HALL RD

OLD FARM RD

LON FELIN/FELIN LA

Y DOLYDD/MEADOW CL

B5097

JASON WILKINSON DR

RHODA WY

BURKIT ST

MOUNT ST

POPLAR

STATION RD

CELMAR GR

PARFND WLK

HEDGEWAY

BROOMHILL DR

ODDWAY

OLD PADDOCK

Manor Farm

Big Wood

VERNON CL

CHAPEL

HIGH ST

WEST ST GR

ROSEMARY CRES

ERDDIG DR

TREVOR AVE

HENRY ST

GELLI ELDON/ELDON GR

Erddig Country Park

6

VICARAGE HILL

SCHOOL MEWS

TRINITY CL

HENBLAS RD

P.O

Rhostyllen

Croesfoel Ind Est

AMANDA GR

FERNDALE AVE

CHURCH ST

SCHOOL LA

FFORDD Y FFYNNON

SPRING RD

WREXHAM RD

MAES-Y-GWANWYN

HOLMWOOD AVE

Motel

A5152

B5098

Croesfoel Farm

LL14

PENTRE-BYCHAN RD

B5605

Parc Menter Bersham/Bersham Ent Ctr

Plas-Grono Farm

Glanyafon Brook

P

P

Erddig Park

The Rookery

Orchard Lodge

5

48

BRONWYLFA RD

Hafod-y-bwch

Plas Grono

LL13

Bryn-goleu

Erthig Park

Forest Wood

4

SMITHY LA

Bryn-yr-Owen

B5426

Packsaddle Bridge

Black Brook

HAFOD RD

Hafod Wood

Sontley Lodge Farm

Pentre Bychan

WREXHAM RD

CORKSCREW LA

Hafod-y-bwch

Hafod-y-bwch

Middle Sontley Farm

3

47

BRYN OFFA

Y FFENNANT/FENNANT RD

LLYS FENNANT/FENNANT CT

Ty-côch Farm

Farmworld

2

CLAWDD OFFA

ABERDERFYN RD

TAN-Y-COED

DELYN

BRYNHYFRYD

TEGFAN

Johnstown

BERWYN

Y PON

GLASFRYN

PLAS TIRION

FERNLWYN

GWALIA

Aberderfyn

Sewage Works

FREDERICK ST

MAELOR RD

OFFA

HIGH ST

RHODA DANOL

MAES SAF

TUDOR RD

STABLEGATES

MELYD AVE

BRYN AVE

TANYCLAWDD

WORSLEY ST

TUDOR AVE

LINLEY AVE

Inf Sch

Works

Hafod House

1

MORETON ST

PARK

B5605

B5426

BANGOR RD

ROSSE AVE

A483

Sewage Works

46

A1
1 CHARLES ST
2 VICTORIA AVE
3 HAFOD-Y-GLYN
4 OFFA CT
5 MERLIN ST
6 LLYS HAFOD
7 MERLIN CT
8 YALE ST
9 MILLARS CT

For full street detail of the highlighted area see page 145.

79 73

D7
1 RHODFA GWDIG/GOODWICK DR
2 RHODFA CEINEWYDD/NEWQUAY DR
3 GELLE GOODWOOD/GOODWOOD GR
4 CLOS CARTMEL/CARTMEL CL

For full street detail of the highlighted area see page 145.

A B C D E F

8

RUTHIN RD
RUABON RD
A525
PEN-Y-BRYN
A5152
B5152
B5446
SALOP RD A525
SALISBURY RD
B5100
ST GILES WAY
Ind Est
POYSER ST
EDWARD ST
FFORDD Y TYLWYTH TEG/FAIRY RD
POPLAR RD
TALBOT RD
HAIG RD
Schs
PO
145
HIGHTOWN
RIVULET RD
GREENBANK RD
BENJAMIN RD
CAIA GDNS
QUEENSWAY TERR
PONT WEN
RUTLAND RD
NEWTON ST
WHITEGATE RD
HAMPSON AVE
GWENFRO
PRINCE CHARLES RD
GLAN GORS
ANTHONY EDEN DR
COED ABEN
Y WERN
QUEENSWAY
PO
BOD HAFOD
CERNANT
CEFNDRE
Cefn Park

7
145
BENNIONS RD
MAES TOMOS
LONGUEVILLE
FFORDD FFRIDD
HILLBURY RD
DERWEN
FFORDD TUDOR
NORMAN RD
HANOVER WAY
STUART WAY
STUART WAY
BEECHLEY RD
BRYN-Y-CABANAU RD
St Joseph's RC High Sch
St Christophers Sch/ Ysgol Sant Christopher
Ysgol Bodhyfryd
Barracks Hightown
NELSON ST
WARING RD
KINGSMILLS RD
ST JOHN'S CT
CLWYD AVE
COLLINS CT
SYLVESTER CT
SHIELDS CT
THOMAS CT
HACKETT CT
WARWICK AVE
CARTER ROAD
OAK CT
OAKFIELD
WINDRUSH CL
WEALD CT
RIVER CL
MILLRISE RD
THE ORCHARDS
King's Mill Visitor Ctr
Kings Mills
Whitegate Ind Complex
Queensway Ind Est
Gwenfro Jun & Inf Sch
COED-Y-BRYN
PENTRE CWM
NEWPORT CL
ABENBURY RD
WESTFIELD CT
HIGHMORE RD
MILLBROOK RD
TAN-Y-COED
WHITLAND WAY
WESTFIELD RD
Frog Hall
Llwyn Onn Hall Hotel
BEVERLEY CL
KEMPTON CL
CLOS ASCOT
RHODDA TAUNTON
Llwyn-Onn

49
TREM-YR-EGLWYS
FFYNNON
MAES CELYN
FFORDD GLYN
COED-Y-NANT
TREM CLWYD
COEDFFORDD CWM
BRON-Y-COED
FFORDD HENDRE
ITHENS WAY
STRETTON CL
FFORDD BERWYN
VALLEY WAY
RANGE RD
FRONHEULOG
COBHAM CT
Coed-y-glyn Wood
WREXHAM/ WRECSAM
1 CWRT AFALLON/AVALON CT
2 CLOS Y PREN AFAL/APPLEWOOD CL
3 CWRT BEDWYR/BEDWYR CT
4 CWRT PENDRAGON/PENDRAGON CT
5 RIDLEY WOOD CL
6 BARTON CL
RED LION COTTS
FFORDD EPSOM
EPSOM WAY
GREEN-WAYS
RIVERDALE
BROOK CL
RHIW NEWMARKET
NEWMARKET RISE
CLOS NEWBURY
NEWBURY CL
CLOS SEDGEFIELD
SEDGEFIELD CT
1 OCHR Y BRYN/BRAESIDE
2 EASTFIELD CT
3 FAIRCROFT CT
4 CLOS KELSO/KELSO CL
5 CLOS FONTWELL/FONTWELL CL
6 CLOS EFROG/YORK CL

6
Bryn-y-cabanau Wood
Bryn-y-cabanau
Marchwiel Resr
River Clywedog Afon Clywedog
BRYN-Y-GROG
Bryn-newydd Farm
Mill Wood

5
Sontley Bridge
Sontley Hill
New Sontley
Erddig Country Park
Bryn-y-grog Farm
Bryn-y-grog Hall
Croes-y-mab
LL13
BELLS WAY
YORKE AVE
GROVE TERR
BRECK CL
TALFRYN CL
DANESWOOD
ELWYN DR
THE GLEN
THE GROVE
MALLOR CT
VIEW
SCOTS CL
STATION RD
CHURCH VIEW
THE RIDGEWAY
YSNIOL AV

48
Lodge
Crabmill
Mill Pool Covert
Marchwiel Hall
Lodge
Pen-y-llan
PENRHYN
BERWYN CL
PIERCY AVE
WREXHAM RD
PO
Sch

4
Plâs Noble
Berthengron
Plâs Noble Bridge
Reynold's Grave
SONTLEY RD
Gefeiliau Brook
Bentley's Farm
The Old Rectory
Marchwiel
SMITHY COTTS 1
SCHOOL COTTS 2
CHURCH VIEW
PH
BANGOR RD A525
A528

3
Old Hall Farm
Marchwiel Hall Cottage
WOODHOUSE LA
Highfield Farm

47
Sontley
Stryt-yr-hwch Farm
Ford
Old Hall Cottages
Pont-y-ffrwd

2
Kiln Farm
Wood House
Pont-y-ffrwd

1
Old Sontley Farm
Clay Pits Farm
Stryt-yr-hwch
Oakley House
BWGAN-DDU LA
COCK BANK LA
Pentre Mailyn
A528
B5130

46

33 A 34 B C 35 D E F

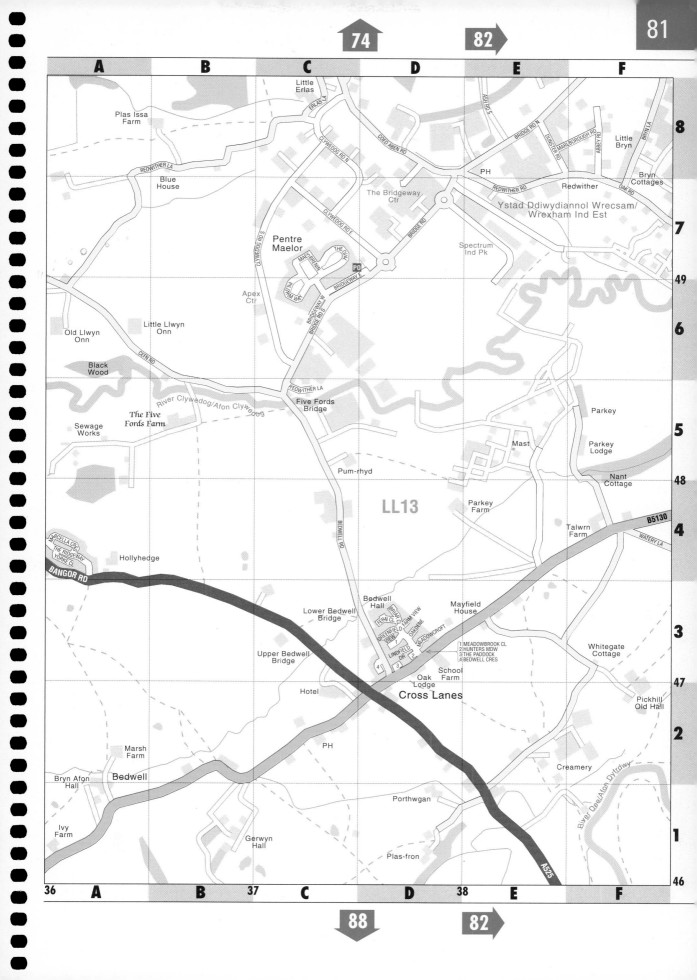

A   **B**   **C**   **D**   **E**   **F**

St Paul's
Prim Sch

B5130

School
Farm

8

Higher
Hall

Old
Farm

Ystad Ddiwydiannol Wrecsam/
Wrexham Ind Est

Bryn
Villa

Sutton
Lodge

Cobham
Farm

7

49

OAK RD

Lower
Oak

Bowling Bank
Farm

Roden's
Hall

6

Higher
Oak

Bowling
Bank

Suttongreen Fox
Covert

Mill
Wood

Pickhill
Bridge

SUN LA

River Clywedog/Afon Clwedog

5

Pickhill Bridge
Farm

Fingerpost
Cottage

Sutton
Green

48

Willow
Farm

4

B5130

Pickhill
Farm

Pickhill
Cottages

LL13

Wern

WATERY LA

Pickhill
Lower Farm

Pickhill
Hall

3

River Dee/Afon Dyfrdwy

Upper
Wern

47

2

Pickhill
Meadows

Brook
Farm

Dongray
Hall

1

Dungrey
Bridge

Worthenbury

CHURCH RD

Dolennion
Farm

B5069

46

The Graig

Elks
Wood

PH

39   **A**   **B**   **40**   **C**   **D**   **41**   **E**   **F**

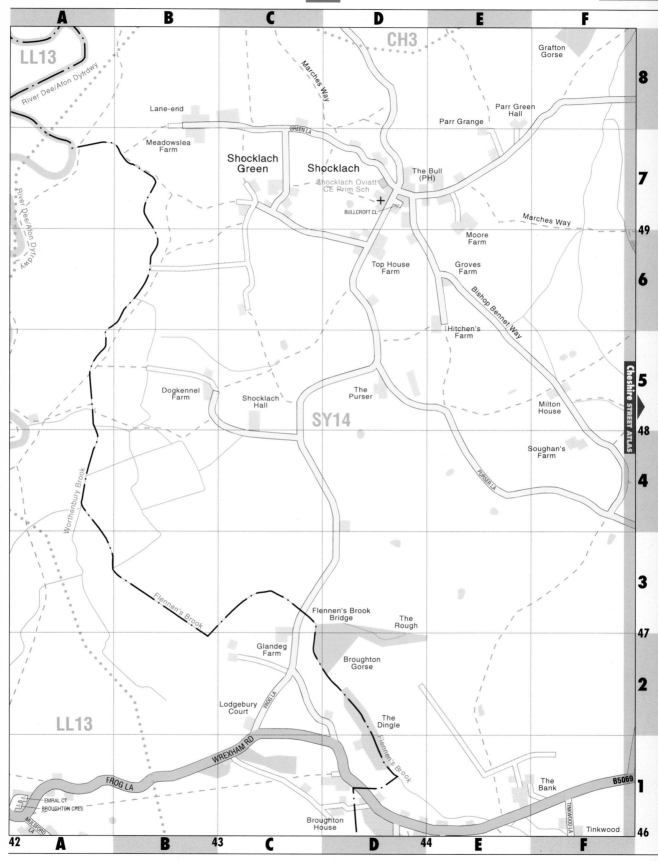

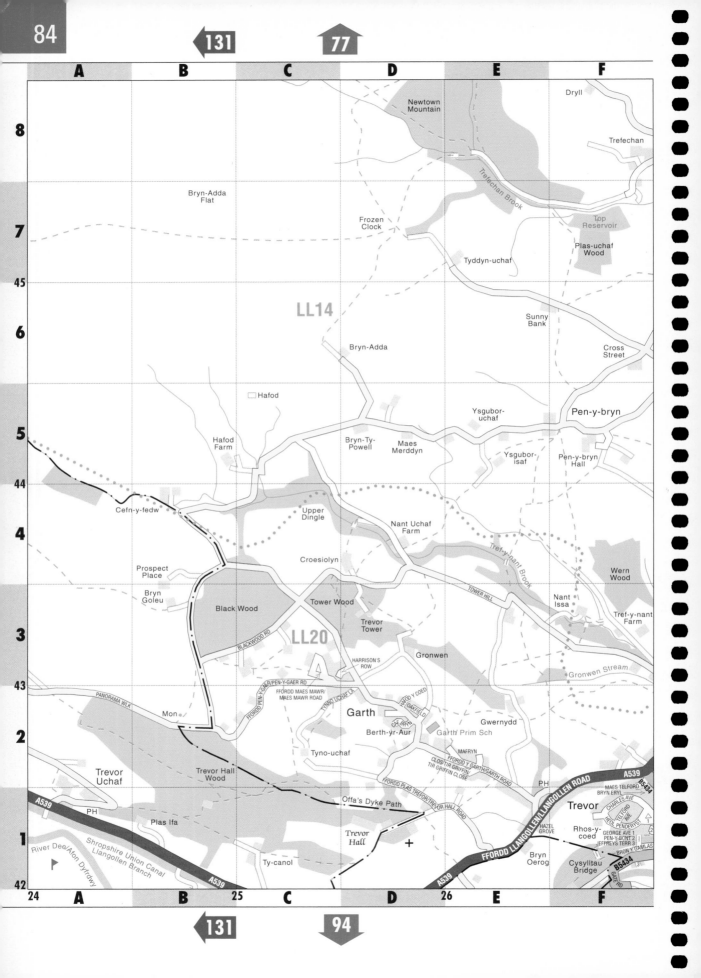

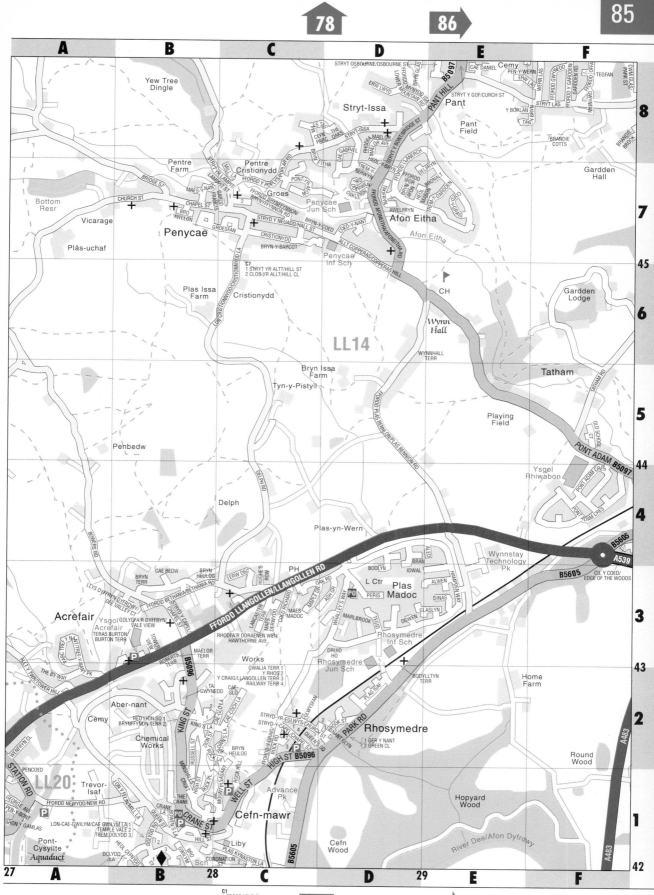

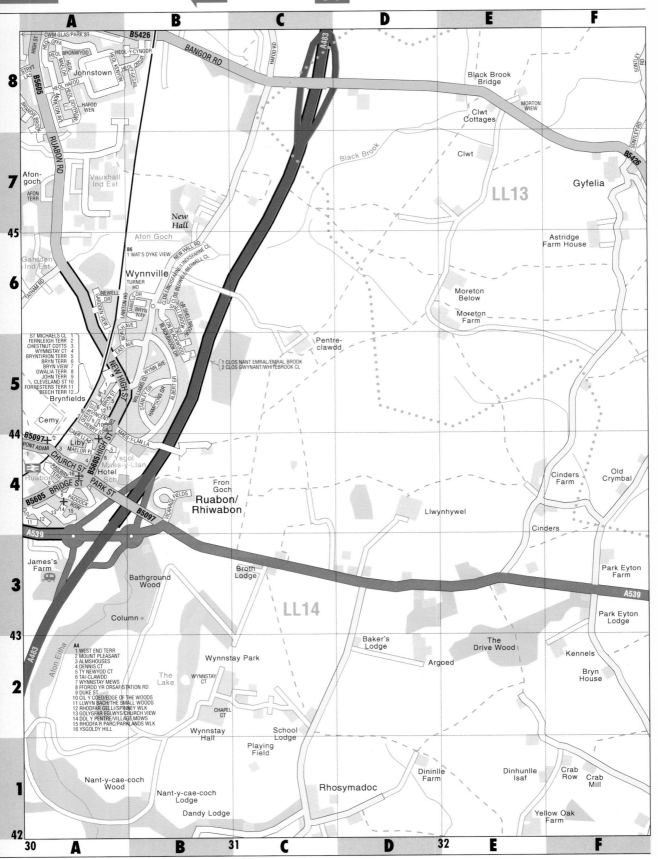

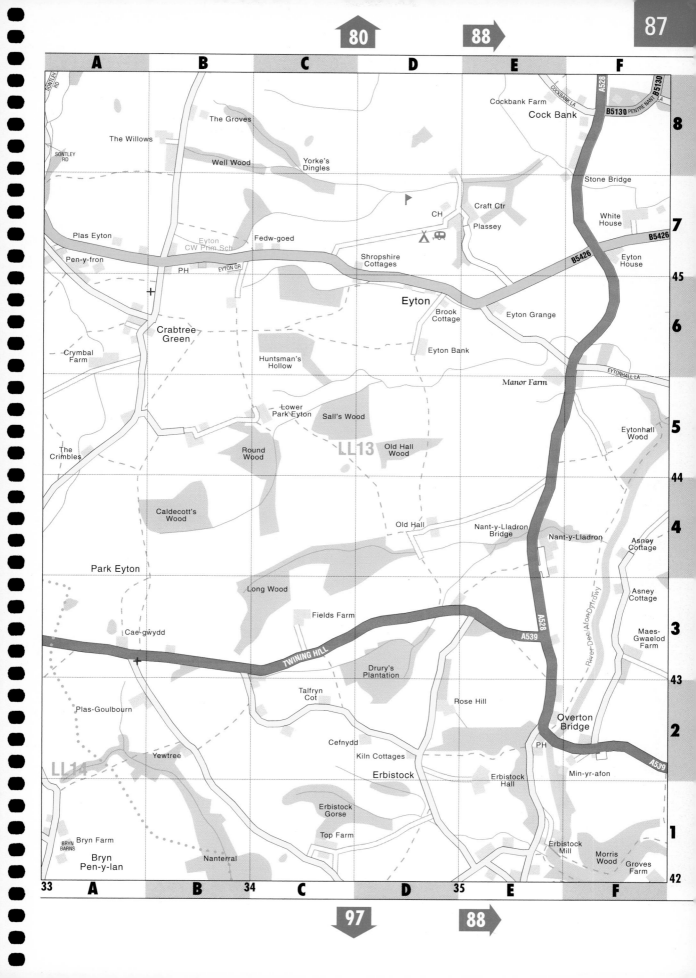

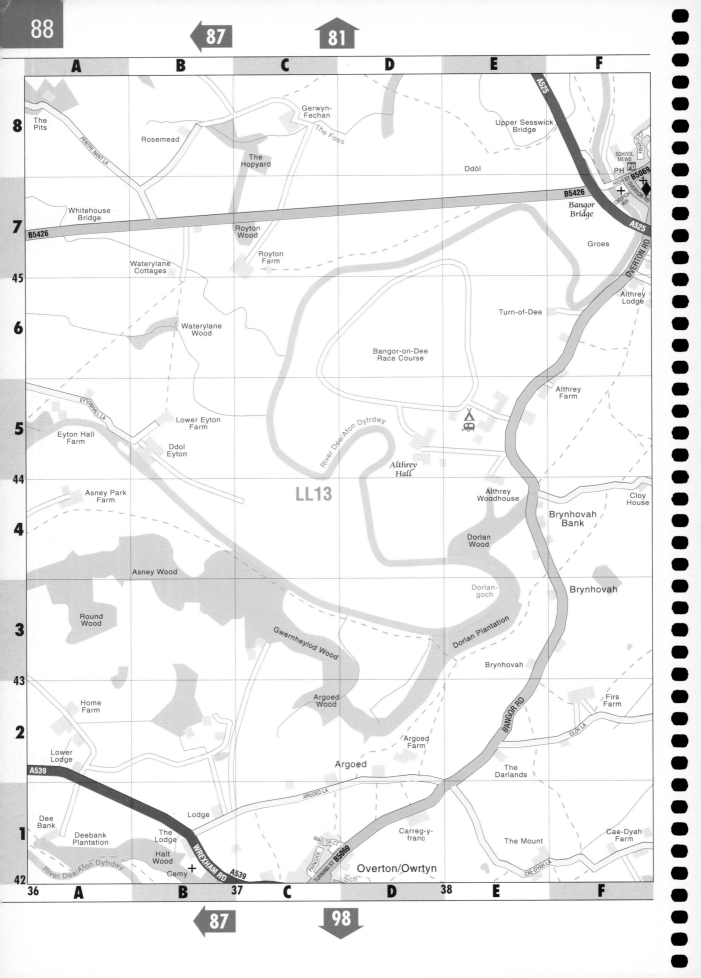

87
81

A B C D E F

8 The Pits

Gerwyn-Fechan

Rosemead

The Foss

Upper Sesswick Bridge

The Hopyard

Ddôl

A525

SCHOOL MEWS

PH PO

B5069

HIGH ST

B5426

Bangor Bridge

OVERTON RD

CHURCH AVE

Whitehouse Bridge

7 B5426

Royton Wood

Groes

Waterylane Cottages

Royton Farm

45

Althrey Lodge

A525

6 Waterylane Wood

Turn-of-Dee

Bangor-on-Dee Race Course

Althrey Farm

EYTON HALL LA

5 Eyton Hall Farm

Lower Eyton Farm

River Dee/Afon Dyfrdwy

Althrey Hall

Althrey Woodhouse

Cloy House

Ddol Eyton

44

LL13

Brynhovah Bank

4 Asney Park Farm

Dorlan Wood

Asney Wood

Brynhovah

Round Wood

Dorlan-goch

3 Gwernheylod Wood

Dorlan Plantation

43

Home Farm

Argoed Wood

Brynhovah

Firs Farm

2 Argoed Farm

BANGOR RD

CLOY LA

Lower Lodge

Argoed

The Darlands

A539

Argoed La

1 Dee Bank

Lodge

MAELOR CT

Carreg-y-franc

The Mount

Cae-Dyah Farm

Deebank Plantation

The Lodge

WREXHAM RD

PARKSIDE

B5069

Halt Wood Cemy

A539

TURNING ST

Overton/Owrtyn

CAE-DYAH LA

42 River Dee/Afon Dyfrdwy

Sch

36 A B 37 C D 38 E F

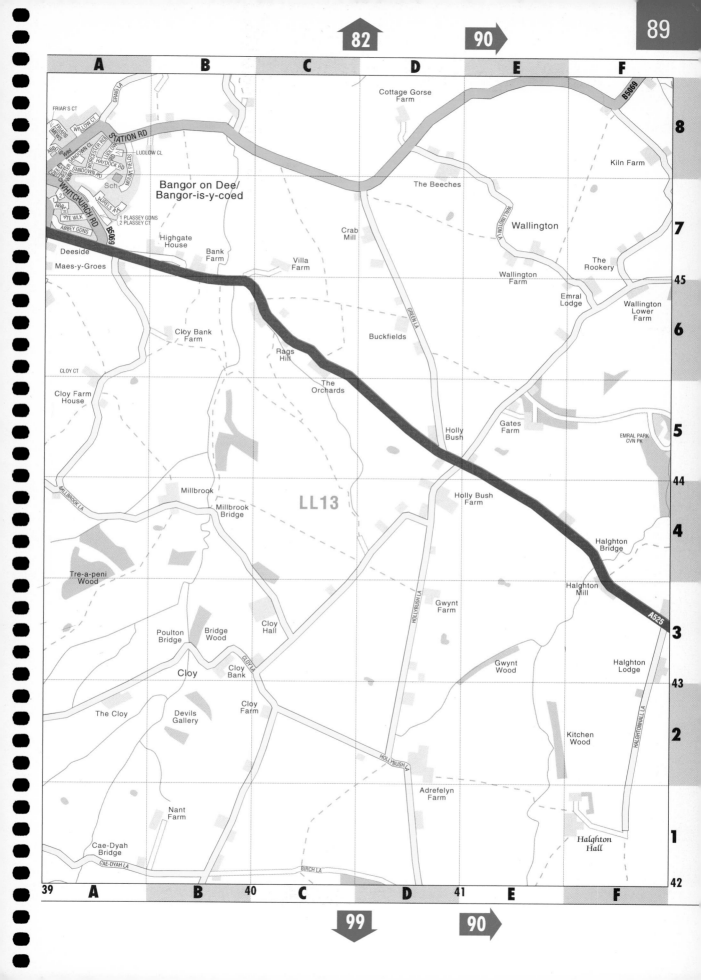

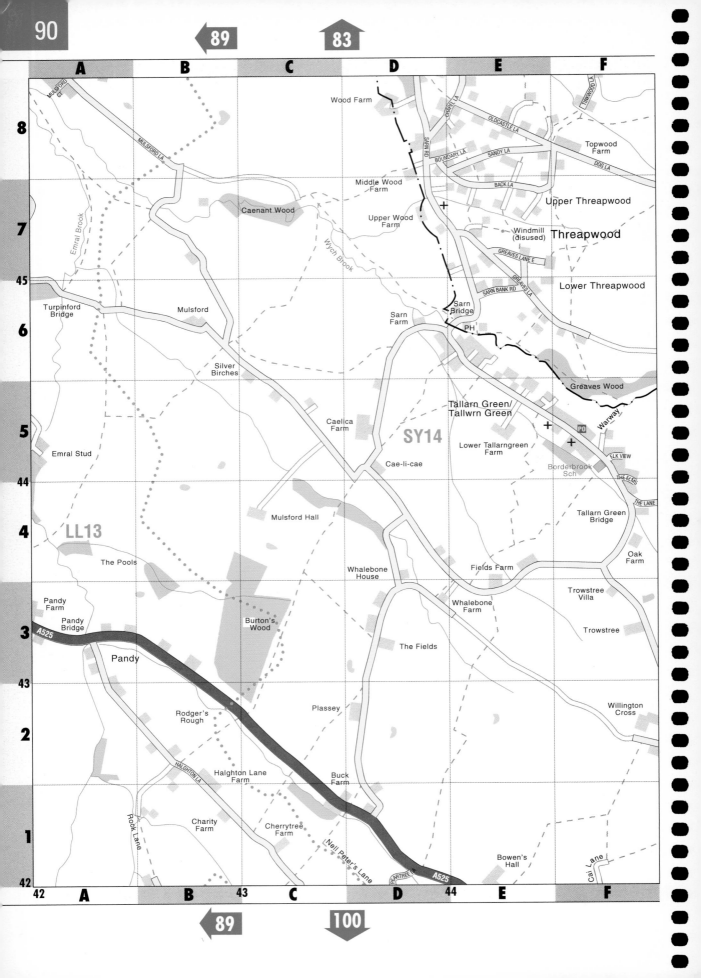

89
83

A   B   C   D   E   F

8

7

45

6

5

SY14

44

4

LL13

3

A525

43

Pandy

2

1

42

42   A   B   43   C   D   44   E   F

Mulsford Ct

Mulsford La

Emral Brook

Wych Brook

Wood Farm

Caenant Wood

Middle Wood Farm

Upper Wood Farm

Chapel La

Sarn Rd

Boundary La

Oldcastle La

Sandy La

Back La

Tinkwood La

Dog La

Topwood Farm

Upper Threapwood

Windmill (disused)   Threapwood

Greaves Lane E

Greaves La

Lower Threapwood

Turpinford Bridge

Mulsford

Silver Birches

Sarn Farm

Sarn Bank Rd

Sarn Bridge

PH

Emral Stud

Caelica Farm

Cae-li-cae

Tallarn Green/ Tallwrn Green

Lower Tallarngreen Farm

Greaves Wood

Warway

PO

ELK VIEW

Borderbrook Sch

THE ELMS

The Pools

Mulsford Hall

Whalebone House

Fields Farm

Tallarn Green Bridge

THE LANE

Oak Farm

Trowstree Villa

Trowstree

Pandy Farm

Pandy Bridge

Burton's Wood

Whalebone Farm

The Fields

Rodger's Rough

Plassey

Willington Cross

Halghton La

Halghton Lane Farm

Buck Farm

Rock Lane

Charity Farm

Cherrytree Farm

Nell Peter's Lane

Pear Tree Ln

A525

Bowen's Hall

Cai Lane

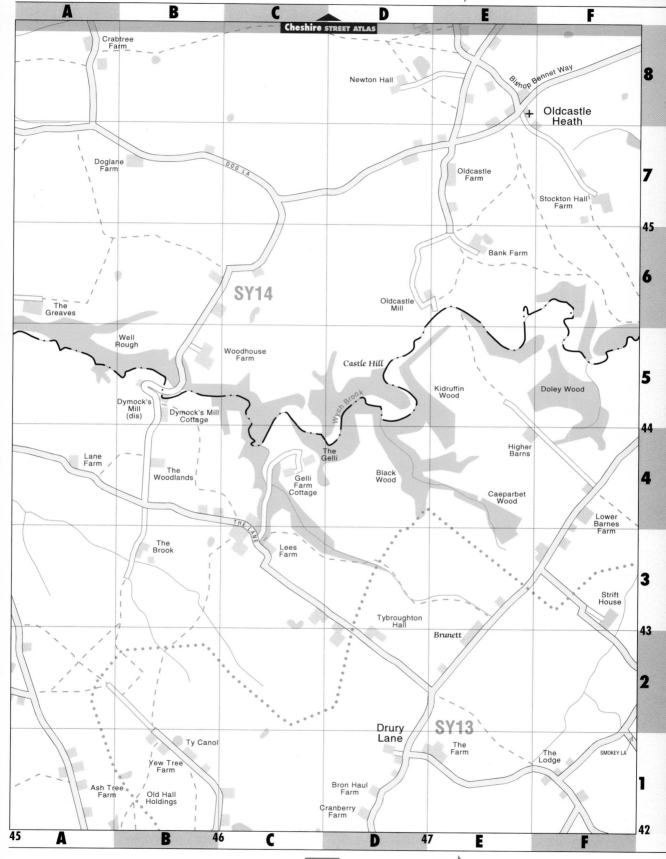

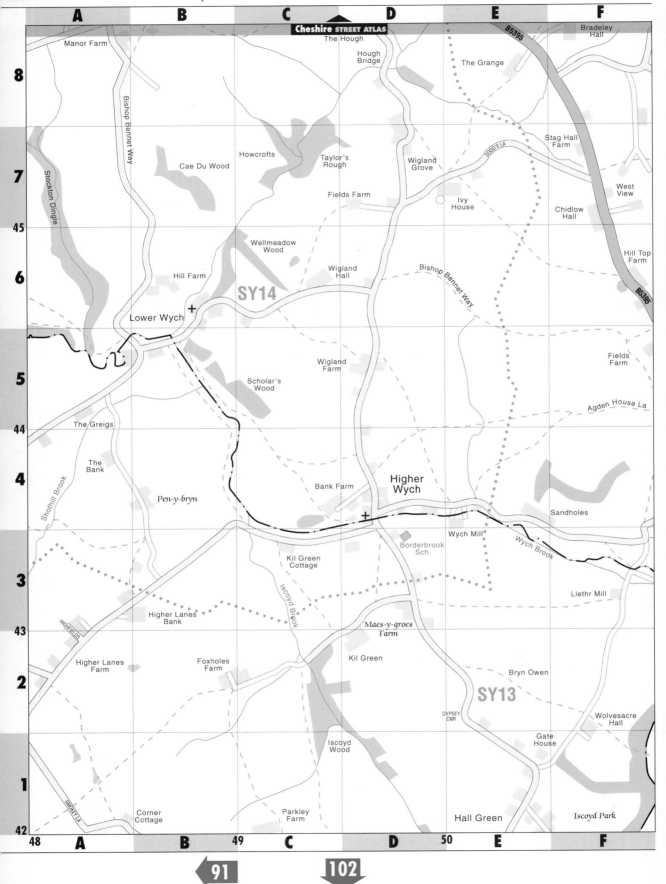

91

Cheshire STREET ATLAS

A **B** **C** **D** **E** **F**

Manor Farm
The Hough
Hough Bridge
The Grange
B5395
Bradeley Hall

8

Bishop Bennet Way
Cae Du Wood
Howcrofts
Taylor's Rough
Wigland Grove
DODD'S LA
Stag Hall Farm

7

Stockton Dingle
Fields Farm
Ivy House
West View
Chidlow Hall

45

Wellmeadow Wood
Hill Farm
Wigland Hall
Bishop Bennet Way
Hill Top Farm

6

SY14
Lower Wych
B5395

Scholar's Wood
Wigland Farm
Fields Farm

5

The Greigs
Agden House La

44

The Bank
Pen-y-bryn
Bank Farm
Higher Wych
Sandholes

4

Shothill Brook
Kil Green Cottage
Borderbrook Sch
Wych Mill
Wych Brook
Llethr Mill

3

HIGHFIELDS
Higher Lanes Bank
Iscoyd Brook
Maes-y-groes Farm
Kil Green

43

Higher Lanes Farm
Foxholes Farm
Bryn Owen
SY13
Wolvesacre Hall

2

GYPSEY CNR
Gate House

Iscoyd Wood

1

SMOKEY LA
Corner Cottage
Parkley Farm
Hall Green
Iscoyd Park

42

48 **A** **B** 49 **C** **D** 50 **E** **F**

91
102

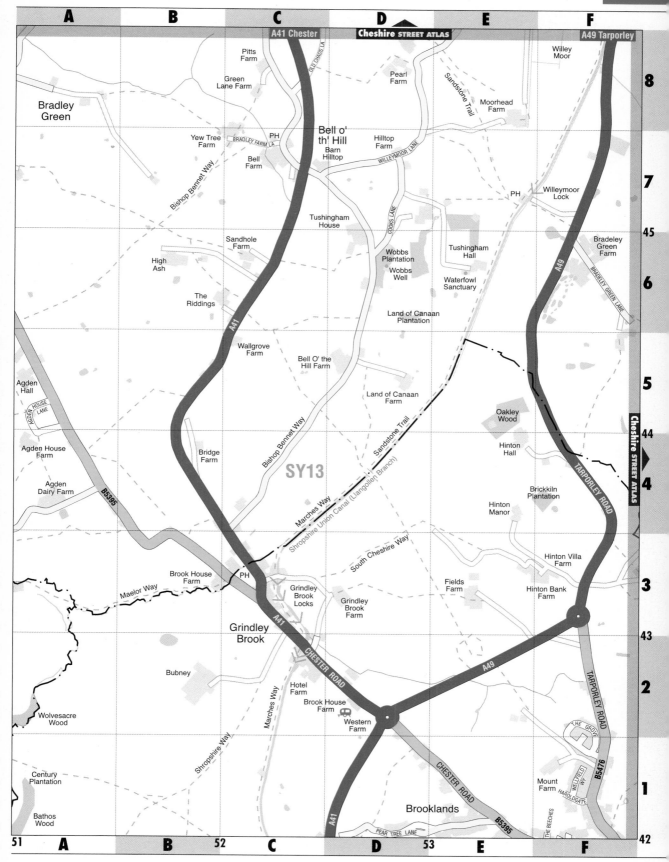

A41 Chester

A49 Tarporley

A B C D E F

Willey Moor

8

Pitts Farm

Pearl Farm

Sandstone Trail

Green Lane Farm

Moorhead Farm

Bradley Green

Bell o' th' Hill

7

Yew Tree Farm

PH

BRADLEY FARM LA

Bell Farm

Hilltop Farm

WILLEYMOOR LANE

PH

Willeymoor Lock

Barn Hilltop

45

Bishop Bennet Way

Tushingham House

COOKS LANE

Bradeley Green Farm

Sandhole Farm

Wobbs Plantation

Tushingham Hall

High Ash

Wobbs Well

A49

6

Waterfowl Sanctuary

BRADLEY GREEN LANE

The Riddings

Land of Canaan Plantation

Wallgrove Farm

Bell O' the Hill Farm

A41

5

Land of Canaan Farm

Oakley Wood

Agden Hall

AGDEN HOUSE LANE

Sandstone Trail

Bishop Bennet Way

Hinton Hall

44

Cheshire STREET ATLAS

Agden House Farm

Bridge Farm

SY13

Brickkiln Plantation

TARPORLEY ROAD

4

Marches Way

Shropshire Union Canal (Llangollen Branch)

Hinton Manor

Agden Dairy Farm

B5395

South Cheshire Way

Hinton Villa Farm

Brook House Farm

PH

Fields Farm

Hinton Bank Farm

3

Maelor Way

Grindley Brook Locks

Grindley Brook Farm

A41

43

Grindley Brook

A49

Bubney

Marches Way

CHESTER ROAD

THE GROVE

2

Hotel Farm

TARPORLEY ROAD

Brook House Farm

Western Farm

WELLFIELD WY

B5476

Shropshire Way

Wolvesacre Wood

CHESTER ROAD

HAROLDGATE

Mount Farm

1

Century Plantation

A41

Brooklands

THE BEECHES

Bathos Wood

PEAR TREE LANE

B5395

42

A B C D E F

51 52 53

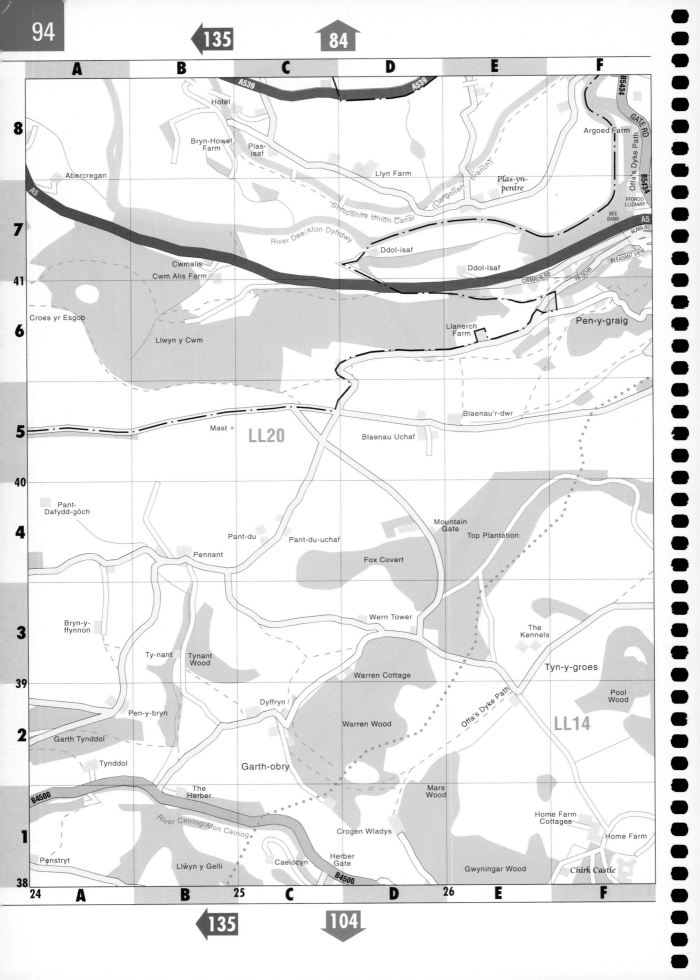

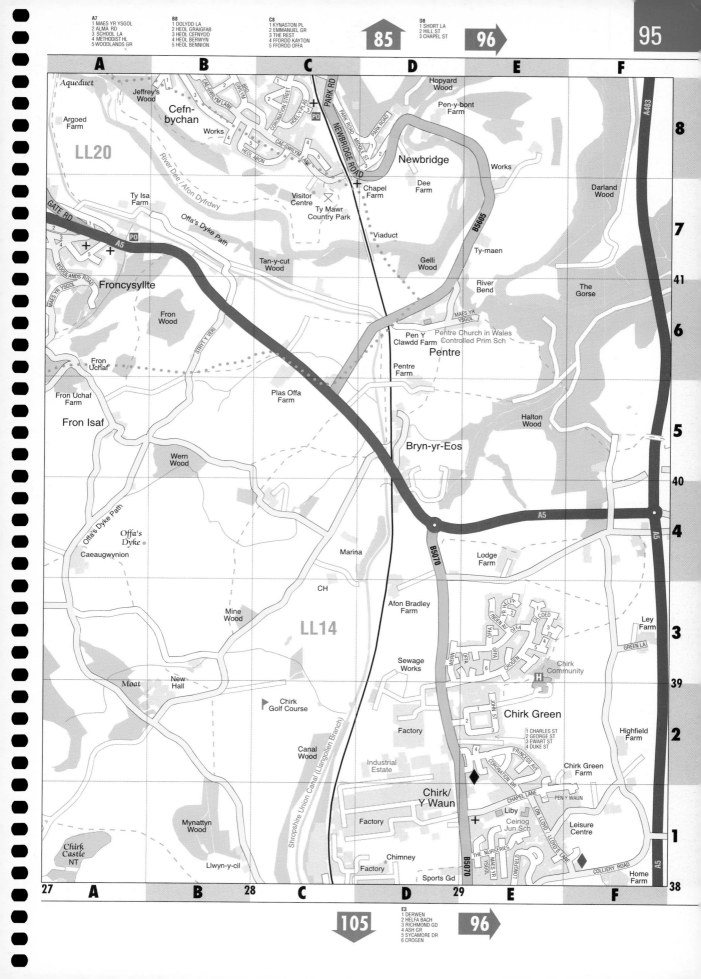

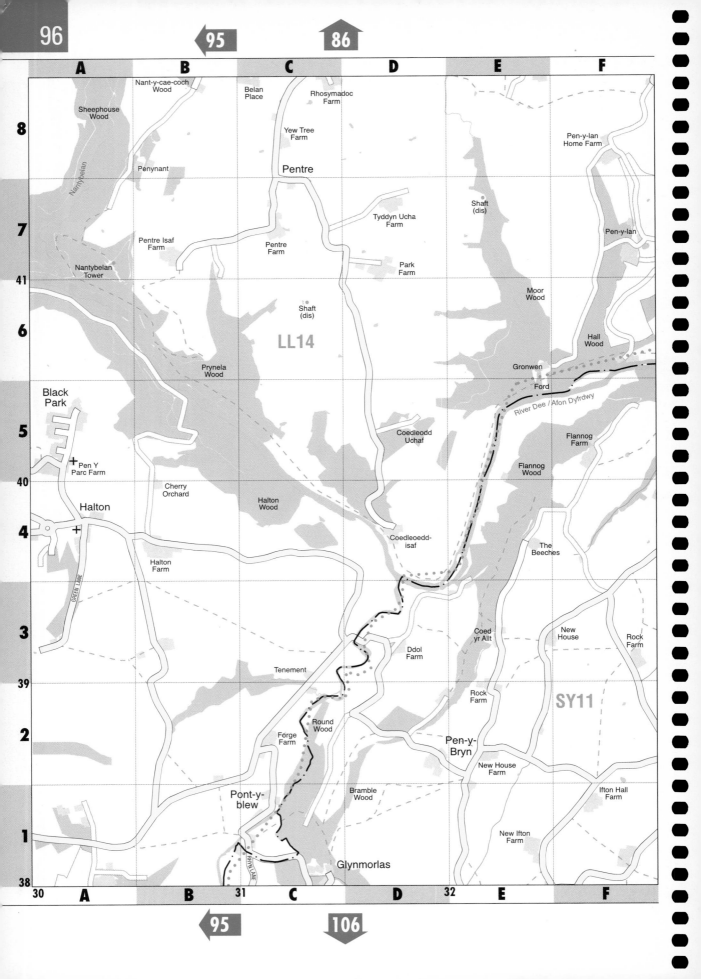

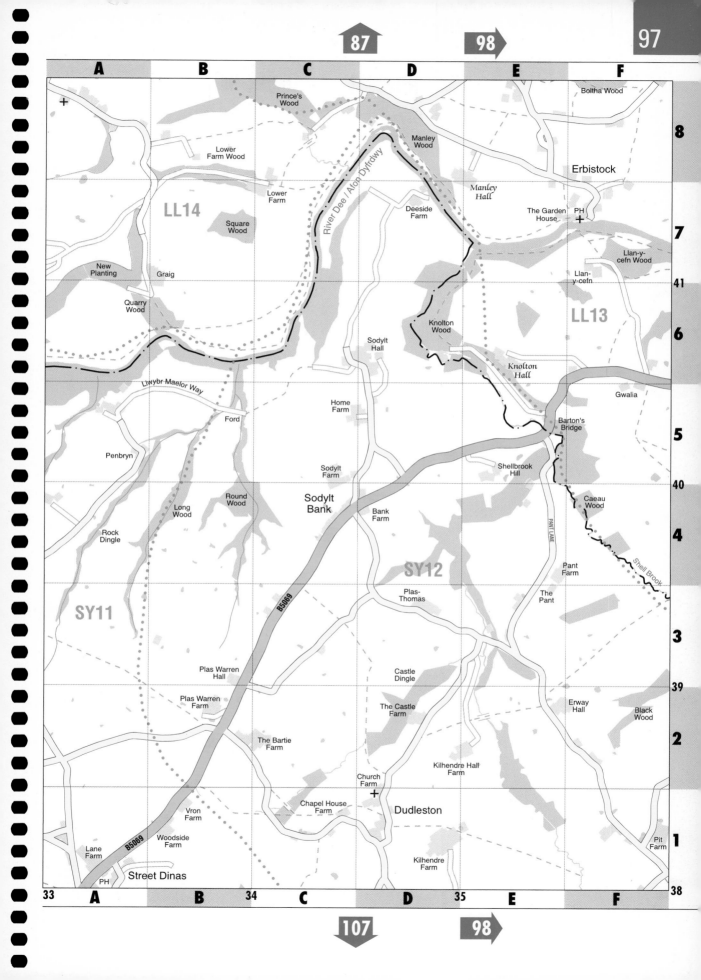

87

98

A B C D E F

8

Boltha Wood

Erbistock

Prince's
Wood

Manley
Wood

Lower
Farm Wood

7

LL14

Lower
Farm

Manley
Hall

The Garden
House

PH

Square
Wood

Deeside
Farm

Llan-y-
cefn Wood

River Dee / Afon Dyfrdwy

41

Llan-
y-cefn

New
Planting

Graig

LL13

Knolton
Wood

6

Quarry
Wood

Sodylt
Hall

Knolton
Hall

Gwalia

Llwybr Maelor Way

Home
Farm

Barton's
Bridge

Ford

Shellbrook
Hill

5

Penbryn

Sodylt
Farm

Caeau
Wood

40

Round
Wood

Sodylt
Bank

Bank
Farm

PANT LANE

Long
Wood

Pant
Farm

Shell Brook

4

Rock
Dingle

SY12

Plas-
Thomas

The Pant

SY11

B5069

3

Plas Warren
Hall

Castle
Dingle

39

Plas Warren
Farm

The Castle
Farm

Erway
Hall

Black
Wood

2

The Bartie
Farm

Kilhendre Hall
Farm

Church
Farm

Vron
Farm

Chapel House
Farm

Dudleston

1

Woodside
Farm

B5069

Kilhendre
Farm

Pit
Farm

Lane
Farm

PH

Street Dinas

97
88

C8
1 OLD SCHOOL MS
2 PLAS MADOC
3 DARK LA
4 SUNDORNE
5 PEEL CL
6 HANMER CL
7 MILL CT
8 CWRT BRYN Y PYS
9 MILLWOOD RI

A　B　C　D　E　F

8

WREXHAM ROAD
Overton/
Owrtyn
WILLOW ST
PO
Helt
Wood
P
St MARY'S AV
Cemy
Plas yn
Coed
HIGH ST
SCHOOL LA
PEN-Y-LLAN STREET
Little
Overton
Farm
Groves
Plantation
Tan House
Farm
STATION ROAD
Mill
Wood
SPRINGFIELD PK
Little
Overton
7
Llwybr Maelor Way
Neile's
Wood
SALOP ROAD
Corner
Farm
Hill
Farm
River Dee / Afon Dyfrdwy
Blake's
Wood
Moat
41
Lightwood
Green Farm
A539
A528
Lightwood
Hall
6
Knolton
Farm
B5069
The Grange
Farm
Musley
Farm
Lightwood
Green
MUSLEY LANE
CLWY LA
Gwalia
Farm
LL13
5
Queensbridge
Queensbridge
Hall Farm
Lightwood
Plantation
40
Rhewl
4
Model
Farm
Rhewl
Farm
Hollyberry
Farm
Deans
Farm
Crab Mill
Farm
A528
Old Post
Office Farm
Knolton Villa
Farm
3
Knolton
Bryn
Trench
Farm
RED HALL LANE
39
Bryn
Wood
Knolton
2
PH
Nantclimbers
Wood
Blackthorn
Farm
Goblindale
Plantation
EASTWICK LANE
1
Pentrecoed
Farm
Lower
Farm
SY12
Goblindale
Farm
A528
38

36　A　37　B　C　37　D　38　E　F

97
108

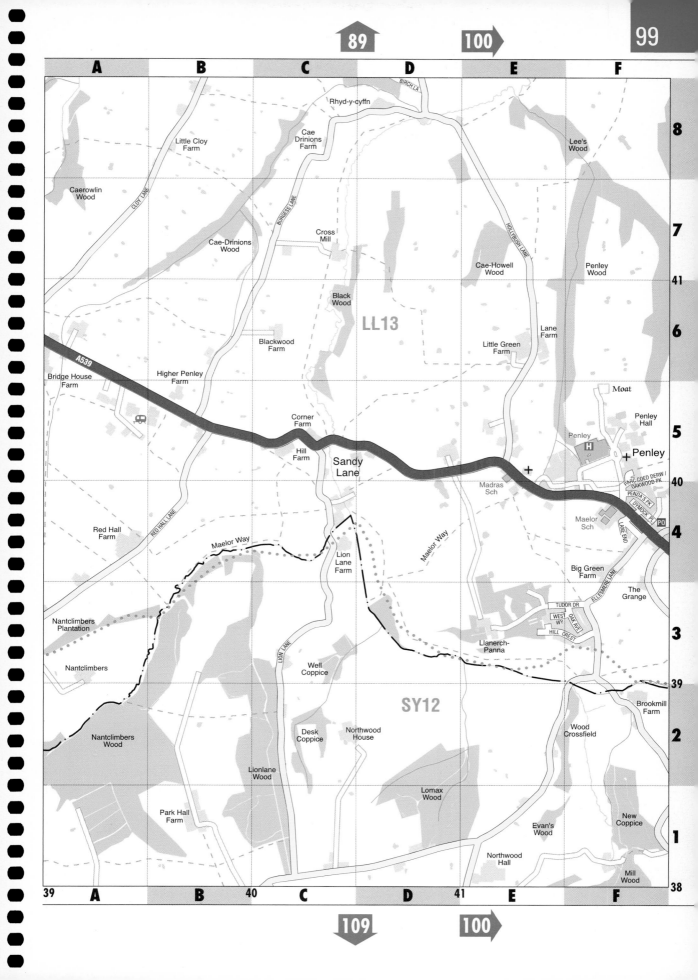

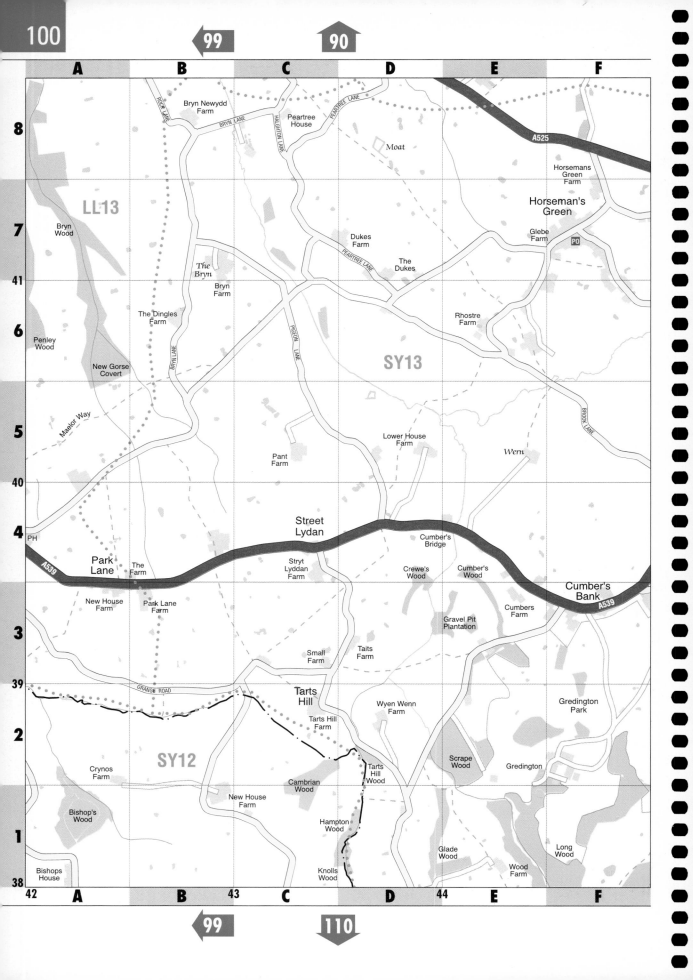

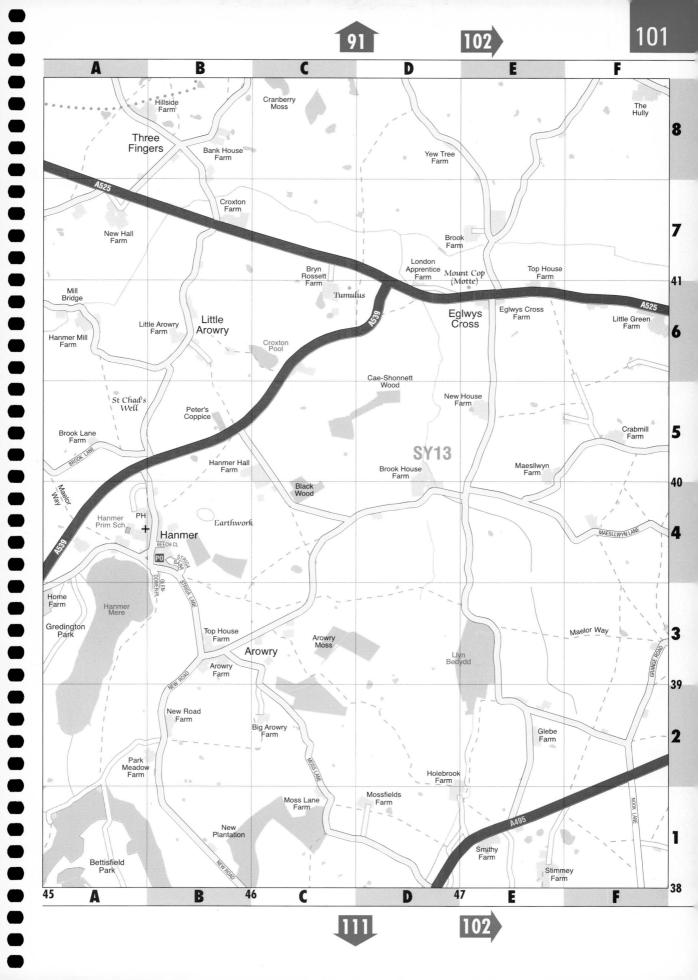

91
102
111
102

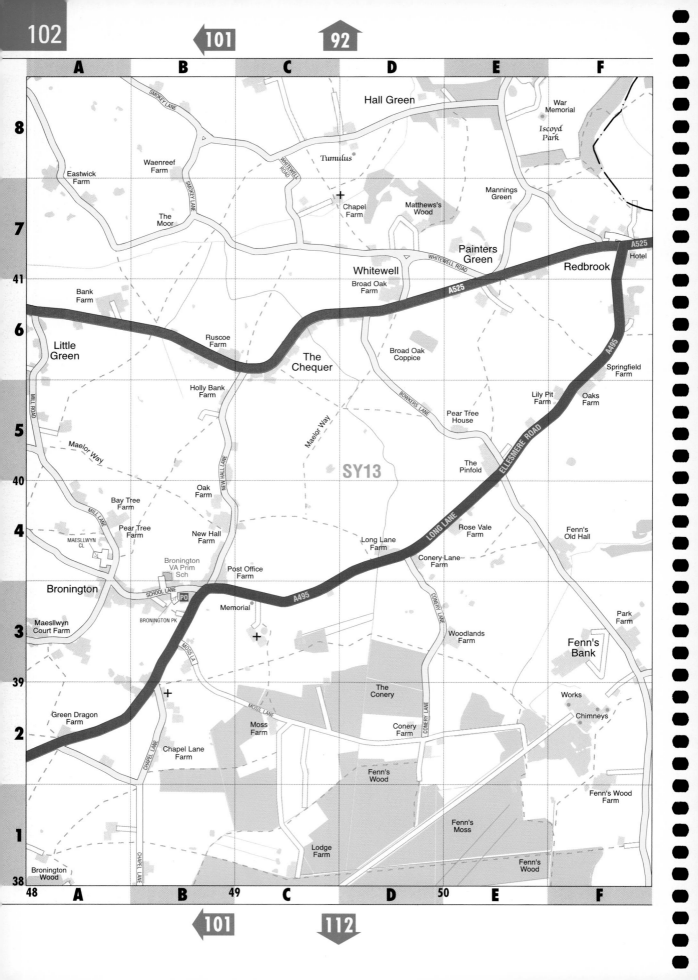

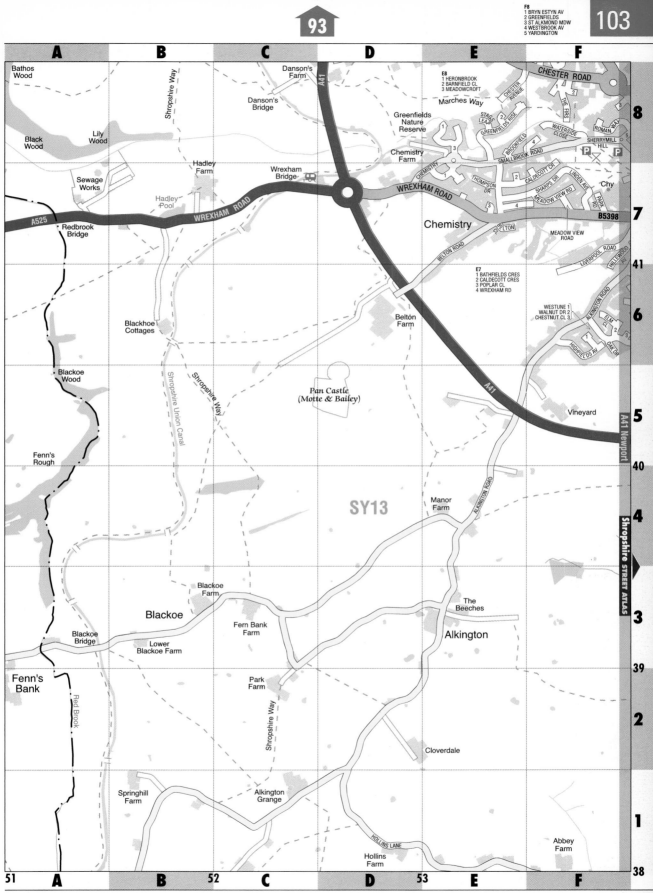

Bathos Wood

Black Wood

Lily Wood

Shropshire Way

Danson's Farm

Danson's Bridge

E8
1 HERONBROOK
2 BARNFIELD CL
3 MEADOWCROFT

CHESTER ROAD

Marches Way

Greenfields Nature Reserve

CHESTER AVENUE

STAGS LEAP

GREENFIELDS RISE

THE FIRS

WATERSIDE CLOSE

ROMAN WAY

Sewage Works

Hadley Farm

Wrexham Bridge

Chemistry Farm

BROOKFIELD

SMALLBROOK ROAD

SHERRYMILL HILL

Hadley Pool

WREXHAM ROAD

WREXHAM ROAD

THOMPSON DR

CALDECOTT CR

SHARPS DR

LINDEN AVE

PARK PROD

Chy

A525

Redbrook Bridge

MEADOW VIEW RD

Chemistry

CHEMISTRY

CILTON

B5398

MEADOW VIEW ROAD

BELTON ROAD

LIVERPOOL ROAD

HILLWOOD AV

E7
1 BATHFIELDS CRES
2 CALDECOTT CRES
3 POPLAR CL
4 WREXHAM RD

Blackhoe Cottages

Belton Farm

WESTUNE 1
WALNUT DR 2
CHESTNUT CL 3

ALKINGTON ROAD

ELM CL

OAK CR

Blackoe Wood

HIGHFIELDS AV

Shropshire Way

Shropshire Union Canal

Pan Castle
(Motte & Bailey)

A41

Vineyard

Fenn's Rough

A41 Newport

SY13

Manor Farm

ALKINGTON ROAD

Shropshire STREET ATLAS

Blackoe Farm

The Beeches

Blackoe

Fern Bank Farm

Alkington

Blackoe Bridge

Lower Blackoe Farm

Fenn's Bank

Red Brook

Park Farm

Shropshire Way

Cloverdale

Springhill Farm

Alkington Grange

HOLLINS LANE

Hollins Farm

Abbey Farm

51   52   53

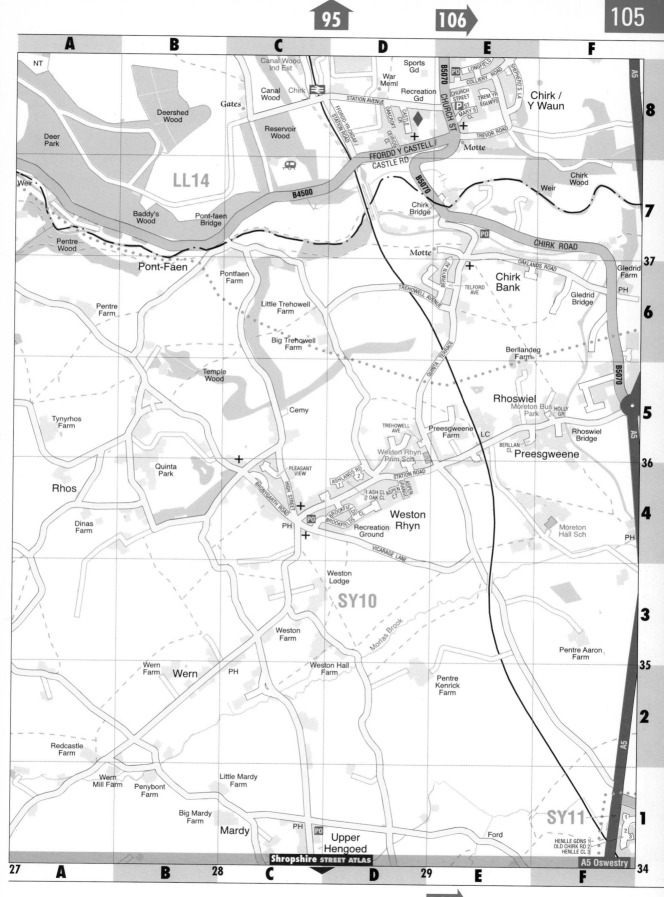

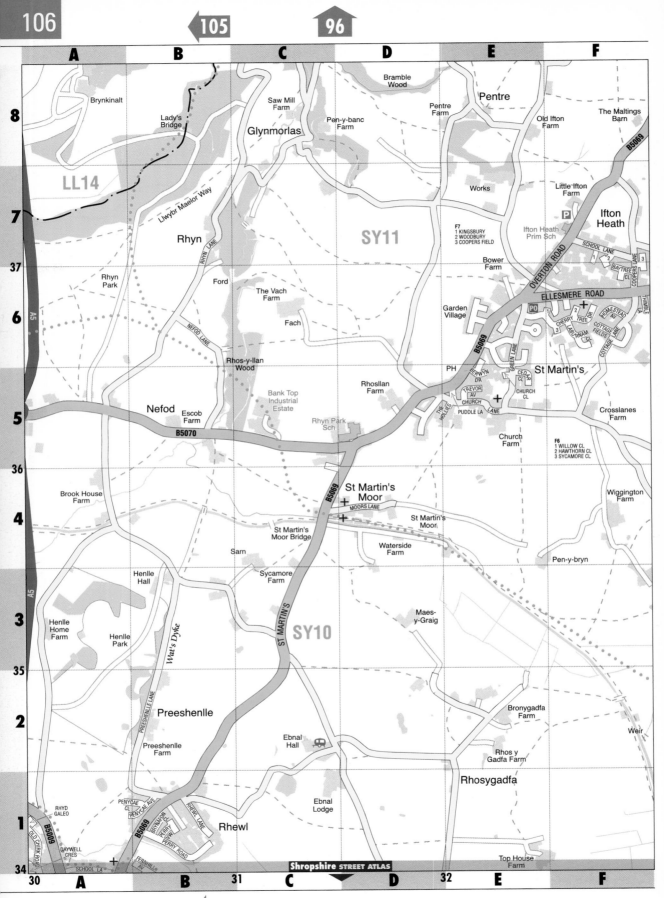

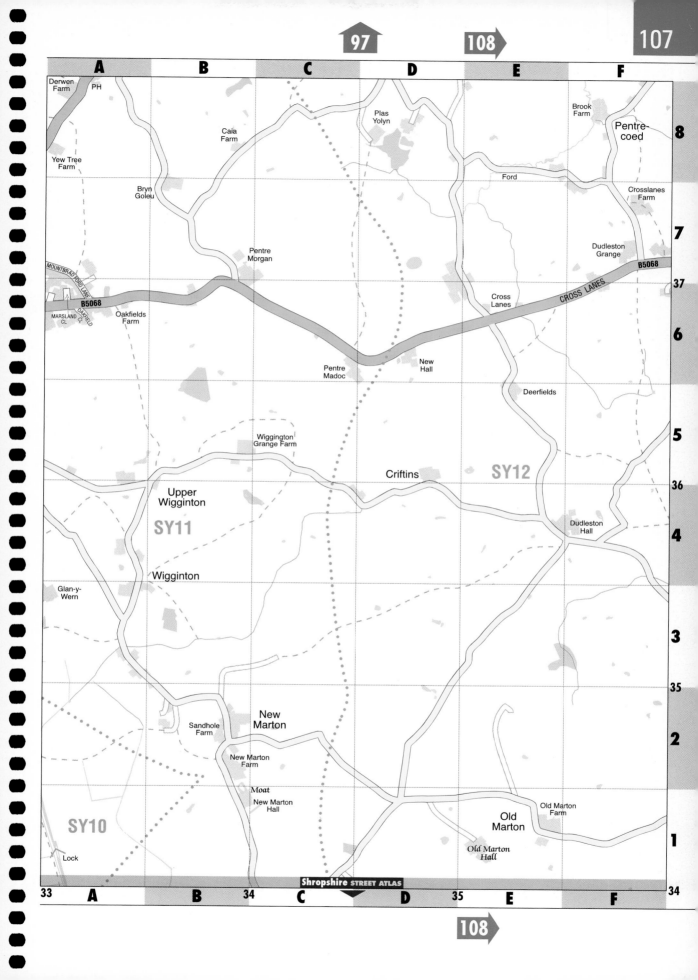

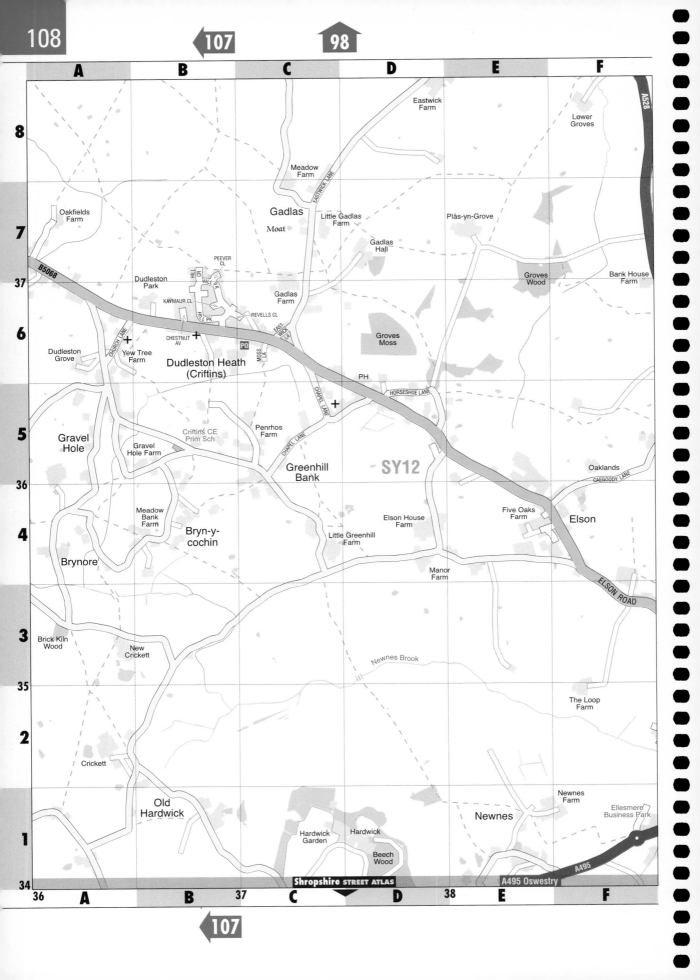

A   B   C   D   E   F

8

7

37

6

5

36

4

3

35

2

1

34

Oakfields Farm

B5068

Dudleston Park

PEEVER CL

HILL CR

HILL PK

KAYMAUR CL

REVELLS CL

CHESTNUT AV

Dudleston Grove

Yew Tree Farm

CHURCH LANE

PO

MOSS LA

Dudleston Heath
(Criftins)

Gravel Hole

Gravel Hole Farm

Criftins CE Prim Sch

Meadow Bank Farm

Bryn-y-cochin

Brynore

Brick Kiln Wood

New Crickett

Crickett

Old Hardwick

Meadow Farm

Gadlas

Moat

Little Gadlas Farm

Gadlas Farm

EAST-WICK LA

CHAPEL LANE

Penrhos Farm

Greenhill Bank

Little Greenhill Farm

Newnes Brook

Hardwick Garden

Hardwick

Beech Wood

Eastwick Farm

Gadlas Hall

Groves Moss

PH

HORSESHOE LANE

SY12

Elson House Farm

Manor Farm

Newnes

Plâs-yn-Grove

Groves Wood

Five Oaks Farm

Oaklands

CAEGOODY LANE

Elson

ELSON ROAD

The Loop Farm

Newnes Farm

Lower Groves

Bank House Farm

A528

A495

Ellesmere Business Park

A495 Oswestry

36   A   B   37   C   D   38   E   F

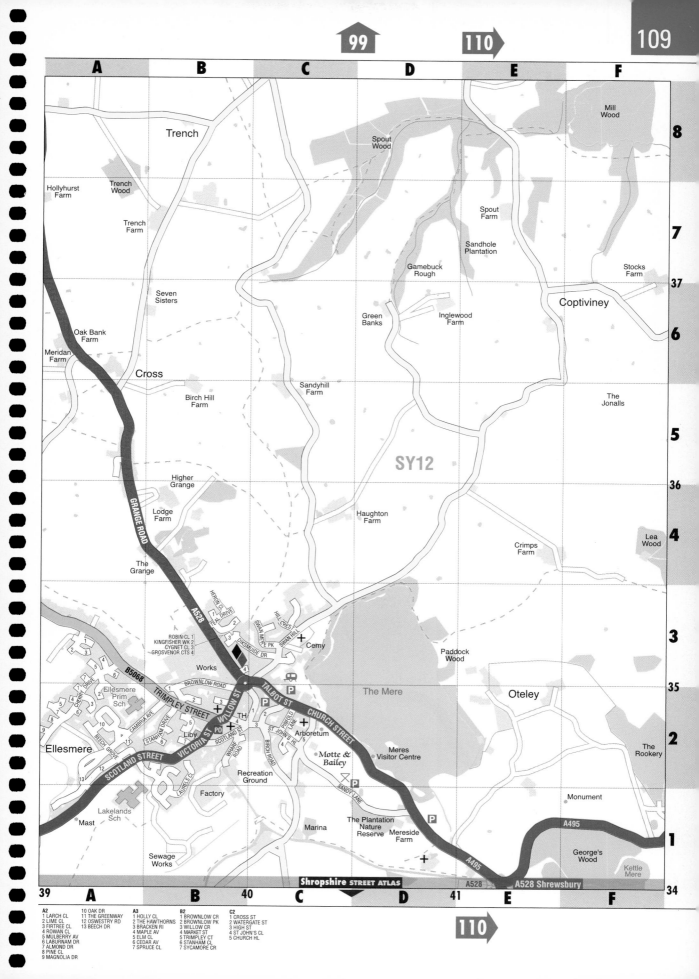

	A	B	C	D	E	F	

Mill Wood

Trench

Spout Wood

Hollyhurst Farm

Trench Wood

Spout Farm

8

Trench Farm

Sandhole Plantation

7

Seven Sisters

Gamebuck Rough

Stocks Farm

37

Coptiviney

6

Oak Bank Farm

Green Banks

Inglewood Farm

Meridan Farm

Cross

Birch Hill Farm

Sandyhill Farm

The Jonalls

5

SY12

Higher Grange

36

Lodge Farm

Haughton Farm

4

Crimps Farm

Lea Wood

The Grange

GRANGE ROAD

A528

HERON CL 7
TEAL DRIVE

HILL CRES

SWAN MEWS PK

SWANTHILL

Cemy

3

Paddock Wood

ROBIN CL 1
KINGFISHER WK 2
CYGNET CL 3
GROSVENOR CTS 4

DIKSMUIDE DR

Works

Oteley

35

BROWNLOW ROAD

TALBOT ST

Ellesmere Prim Sch

B5068

TRIMPLEY STREET

WILLOW ST

CHURCH STREET

CHERRY DRIVE

CAMBRIA AVE

BEECH GROVE

STANHAM DRIVE

Liby

TH

PO

ST JOHN'S HL

PINFOLD LANE

BIRCH ROAD

St John's CL

Arboretum

2

Ellesmere

Meres Visitor Centre

The Rookery

SCOTLAND STREET

VICTORIA ST

LAURELS CL

WHARF ROAD

SCOTLAND ST

Recreation Ground

Motte & Bailey

Factory

Lakelands Sch

Mast

Sandy Lane

Monument

The Plantation Nature Reserve

A495

1

Sewage Works

Marina

Mereside Farm

George's Wood

A495

Kettle Mere

A2
1 LARCH CL
2 LIME CL
3 FIRTREE CL
4 ROWAN CL
5 MULBERRY AV
6 LABURNAM DR
7 ALMOND DR
8 PINE CL
9 MAGNOLIA DR
10 OAK DR
11 THE GREENWAY
12 OSWESTRY RD
13 BEECH DR

A3
1 HOLLY CL
2 THE HAWTHORNS
3 BRACKEN RI
4 MAPLE AV
5 ELM CL
6 CEDAR AV
7 SPRUCE CL

B2
1 BROWNLOW CR
2 BROWNLOW PK
3 WILLOW CR
4 MARKET ST
5 TRIMPLEY CT
6 STANHAM CL
7 SYCAMORE CR

C2
1 CROSS ST
2 WATERGATE ST
3 HIGH ST
4 ST JOHN'S CL
5 CHURCH HL

A	B	C	D	E	F

8

Hampton Wood

Hampton Wood

Hampton Wood Hall

Woodside Farm

Long Wood

Hill Farm

SY13

7

Brook House Farm

Lewis's Wood

37

Brookhouse Wood

Ashes Farm

6

The Stocks

Bank Farm

Lower Farm

Breaden Heath

Old Hall Farm

A495

5

36

SY12

The Fields Farm

Corner Farm

4

Lea Wood

RONE LANE

3

Hampton House Farm

COPES LANE

PH

B5063

35

Welshampton CE Prim Sch

Old Shop Farm

Tumulus

Hampton Grove

Balmer

Balmer Heath

2

Cathay's Moss

St MICHAEL'S GN 1
St MICHAELS CL 2

Welshampton

LYNEAL LANE

Hampton Bank Farm

Newton Farm

Newton

Hampton Moss

Towery Moss

Hampton Wood

1

A495

Newton Mere

Clarepool Moss

Lyneal Coppice

The Moss

Lyneal Moss

34

| 42 | A | | B | 43 | C | | D | 44 | E | | F |

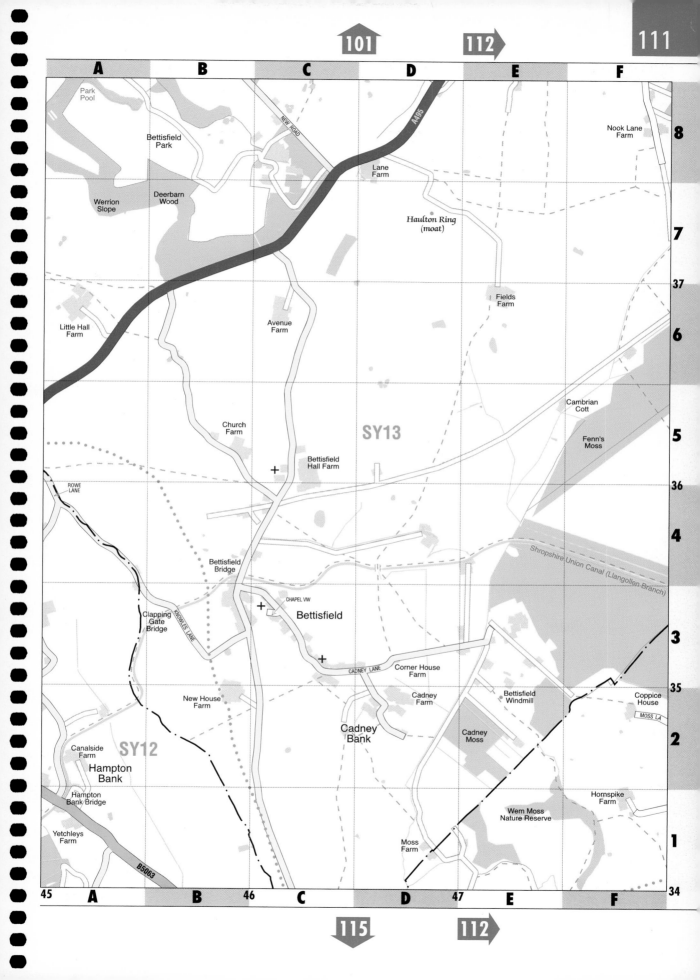

A B C D E F

8

Park
Pool

Bettisfield
Park

NEW ROAD

A495

Nook Lane
Farm

Lane
Farm

7

Werrion
Slope

Deerbarn
Wood

Haulton Ring
(moat)

37

Little Hall
Farm

Avenue
Farm

Fields
Farm

6

Cambrian
Cott

SY13

Church
Farm

Fenn's
Moss

5

+

Bettisfield
Hall Farm

ROWE
LANE

36

Shropshire Union Canal (Llangollen Branch)

4

Bettisfield
Bridge

KNOWLES LANE

Clapping
Gate
Bridge

CHAPEL VW

+

Bettisfield

3

+

CADNEY LANE

Corner House
Farm

35

New House
Farm

Cadney
Farm

Bettisfield
Windmill

Coppice
House

MOSS LA

Canalside
Farm

SY12

Cadney
Bank

Cadney
Moss

2

Hampton
Bank

Hampton
Bank Bridge

Wem Moss
Nature Reserve

Hornspike
Farm

Yetchleys
Farm

B5063

Moss
Farm

1

45 A B 46 C D 47 E F 34

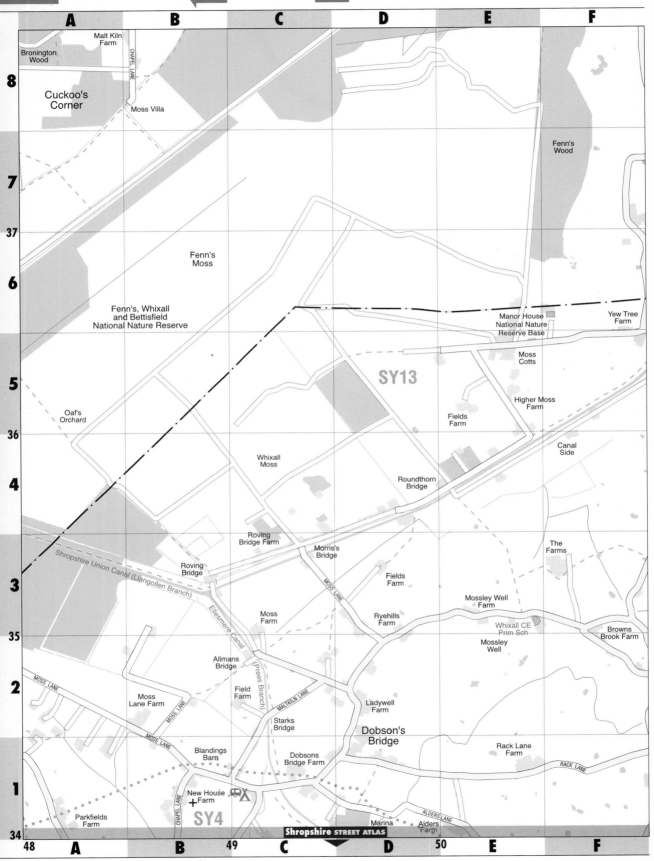

Bronington Wood
Malt Kiln Farm
CHAPEL LANE
8
Cuckoo's Corner
Moss Villa
7
37
Fenn's Moss
6
Fenn's, Whixall and Bettisfield National Nature Reserve
Manor House National Nature Reserve Base
Yew Tree Farm
Fenn's Wood
Moss Cotts
5
SY13
Higher Moss Farm
Oaf's Orchard
Fields Farm
36
Canal Side
4
Whixall Moss
Roundthorn Bridge
Roving Bridge Farm
Morris's Bridge
The Farms
Shropshire Union Canal (Llangollen Branch)
Roving Bridge
Fields Farm
3
MOSS LANE
Mossley Well Farm
35
Moss Farm
Ryehills Farm
Whixall CE Prim Sch
Browns Brook Farm
Ellesmere Canal
Mossley Well
Allmans Bridge
2
MOSS LANE
(Prees Branch)
Field Farm
Ladywell Farm
Moss Lane Farm
MOSS LANE
MALTKILN LANE
Starks Bridge
Dobson's Bridge
Rack Lane Farm
Blandings Barn
Dobsons Bridge Farm
RACK LANE
1
New House Farm
CHAPEL LANE
SY4
Parkfields Farm
Marina
ALDERS LANE
Alders Farm
34

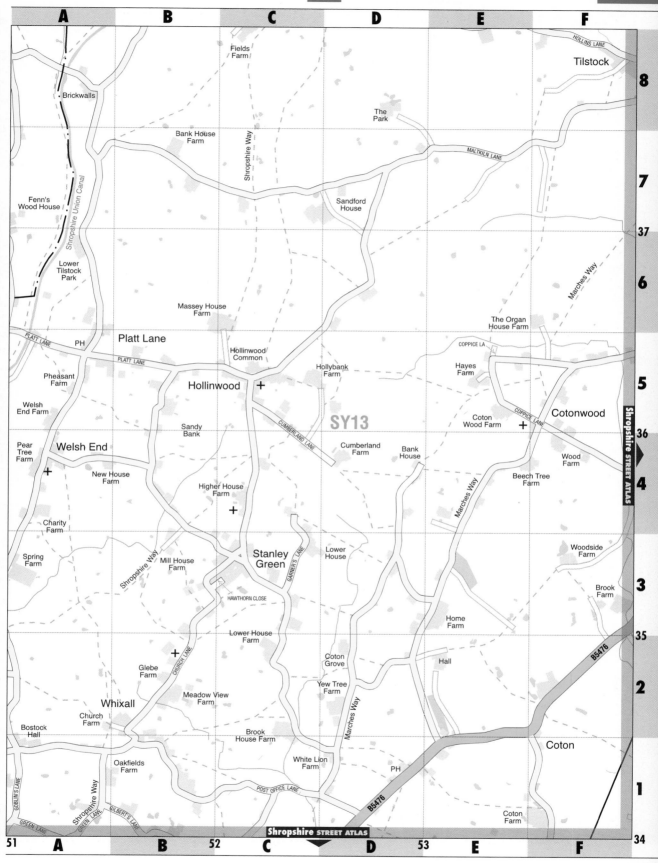

139

104

A B C D E F

8

7

33

6

5

32

4

3

31

2

1

30

Quarry (dis)

Orseddwen

Holly Farm

Brookhouse Farm

B4579

PH
Selattyn CE Prim Sch
Selattyn

Gyrn

Gyrn Farm

Bank Coppice

The Springs

The Palace Farm

Crown House

Lawr-y-pant

Offa's Dyke Path

Higher Vron Farm

Tyn y Drain Farm

River Morda
Afon Morda

Carreg-y-big

SY10

Foel Wood

Quarry (dis)

Rhosfach

Rhos-fach Wood

Mast

Black Wood

Offa's Dyke

Baker's Hill

Coppice Farm

Racecourse (dis)

Glopa Wood

Rock Plantation

Coppice House Farm

Llawnt

Racecourse Common

Radio Masts

Underhill Farm

B4580

B4580

Quarry (dis)

PO

Rhydycroesau

Derwent Grange

Underhill

Llawnt Wood

Standing Stone

Viewpoint

Parc Uchaf

Offa's Dyke Path

Racecourse Wood

Middle Cynonion Farm

24 A B 25 C D 26 E F

139

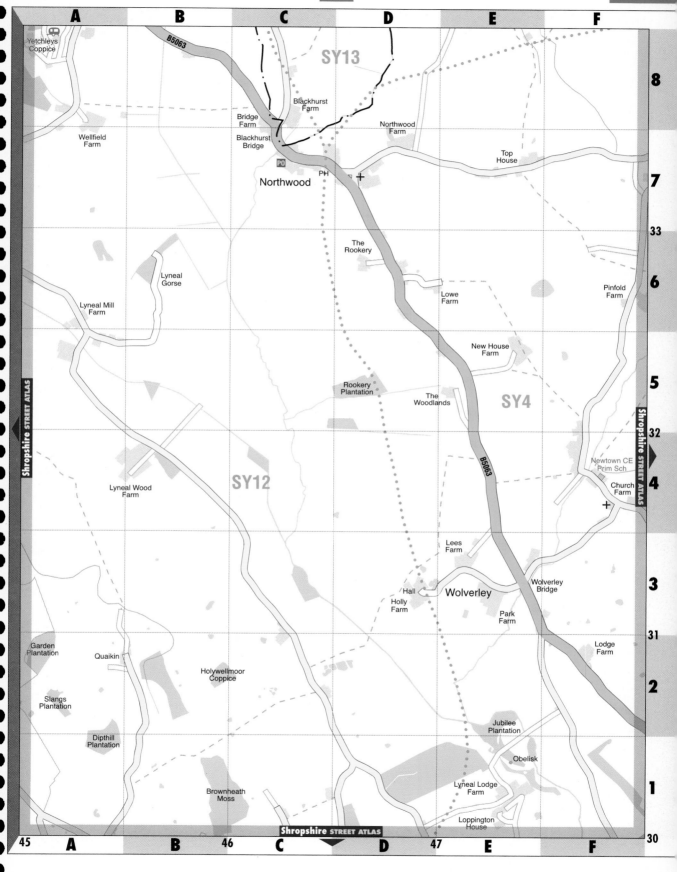

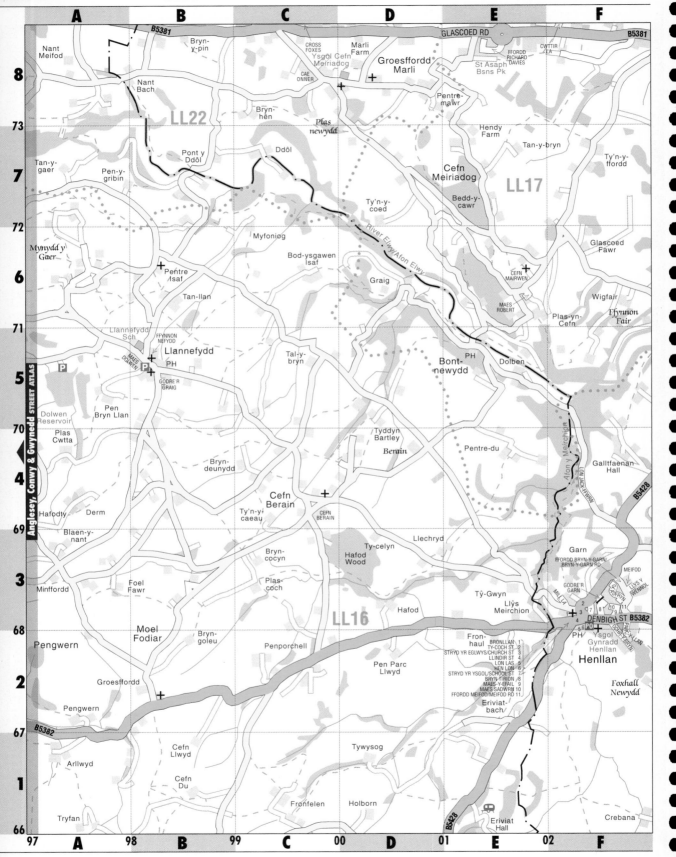

Scale: 1¾ inches to 1 mile
0   ¼   ½ mile
0   250m 500m 750m 1 km

A   B   C   D   E   F

GLASCOED RD
B5381   B5381

Nant
Meifod
Bryn-
y-pin   CROSS
FOXES   Marli
Farm   Groesffordd
Ysgol Cefn   Marli
CAE   Meiriadog   FFORDD
ONNER   RICHARD   CWTTIR
DAVIES   LA
Nant
Bach   St Asaph
LL22   Bryn-   Bsns Pk
hên   Plas   Pentre-
newydd   mawr
Tan-y-   Pont y   Hendy
gaer   Pen-y-   Ddôl   Ddôl   Farm   Tan-y-bryn   Ty'n-y-
gribin   ffordd
Cefn
Ty'n-y-   Meiriadog
coed   LL17
Bedd-y-
Myfoniog   cawr   Glascoed
Mynydd y   Bod-ysgawen   Fawr
Gaer   Isaf   CEFN
Pentre   Graig   MAIRWEN   Plas-yn-   Ffynnon
Isaf   MAES   Cefn   Wigfair   Fair
Tan-llan   ROBERT
Ffynnon
Nefydd   Llannefydd   PH
Llannefydd Sch   Tal-y-   Bont-   Dolben
MAES   bryn   newydd
DOLWEN   PH
P   GODRE'R   Afon y Meirchion
GRAIG   LON MCK-Y-FFRYN
Pen   Tyddyn
Dolwen   Bryn Llan   Bartley   Galltfaenan
Reservoir   Berain   Pentre-du   Hall
B5428
Plas   Bryn-
Cwtta   deunydd
Hafodty   Derm   Cefn   CEFN
Berain   BERAIN
Blaen-y-   Ty'n-y-   Llechryd   Garn
nant   caeau   FFORDD BRYN-Y-GARN
BRYN-Y-GARN RD
Bryn-   Ty-celyn   GODRE'R
Hafodty   cocyn   GARN   MEIFOD
Minffordd   Foel   Plas-   Hafod   Tŷ-Gwyn   MILL LA   LLYS Y
Fawr   coch   Wood   Llŷs   IWENNOL
Moel   Bryn-   Meirchion   DENBIGH ST   B5382
Fodiar   goleu   Penporchell   PH   PO
Pengwern   Pen Parc   Fron-   BRONLLAN   1   Ysgol
Llwyd   haul   TY-COCH ST   2   Gynradd
STRYD YR EGLWYS/CHURCH ST 3   Henllan   Henllan
Groesffordd   LLINDIR ST   4
LÔN LAS   5
Pengwern   HEN LÔN   6   Foxhall
STRYD YR YSGOL/SCHOOL ST 7   Newydd
BRYN-TIRION 8
MAES-Y-FFAIL 9
B5382   Eriviat-   MAES SADWRN 10
Cefn   bach   FFORDD MEIFOD/MEIFOD RD 11
Arllwyd   Llwyd   Tywysog
Cefn   Crebana
Du   Fronfelen   Holborn   Eriviat
Tryfan   B5428   Hall

97   A   98   B   99   C   00   D   01   E   02   F

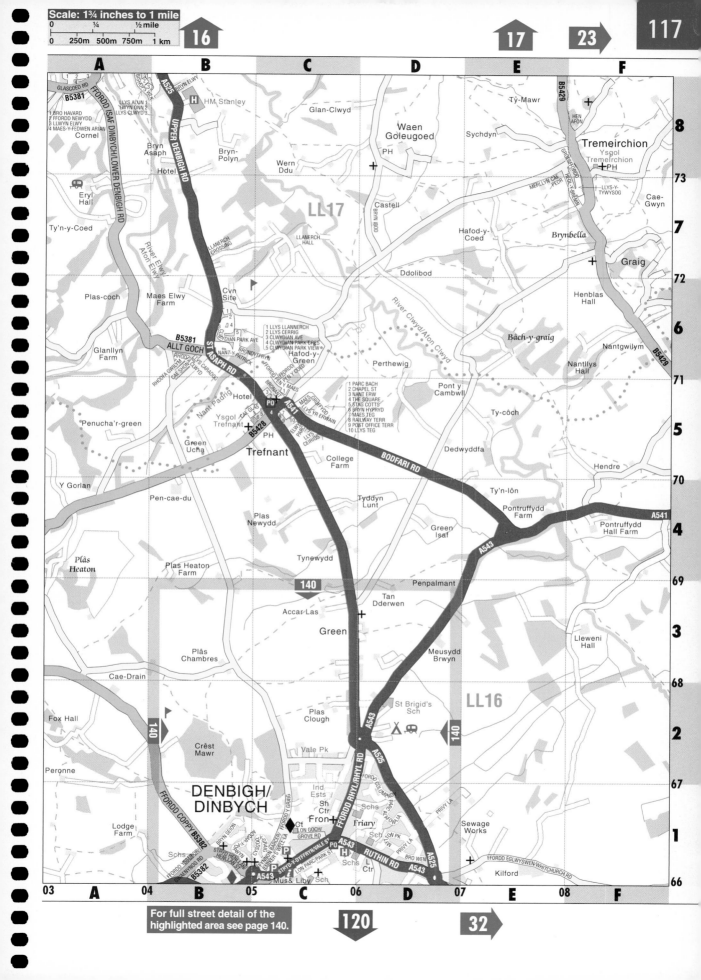

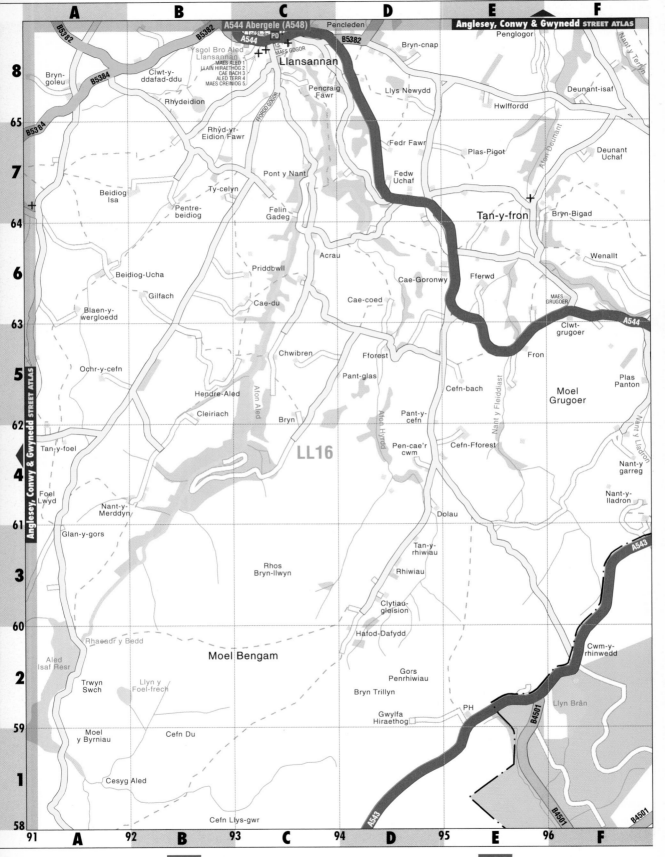

Anglesey, Conwy & Gwynedd STREET ATLAS

A544 Abergele (A548)

Pencleden

A544

B5382

Bryn-cnap

Penglogor

Nant y Terfin

B5382

Ysgol Bro Aled
Llansannan
MAES ALED 1
LLAIN HIRAETHOG 2
CAE BACH 3
ALED TERR 4
MAES CREINIOG 5.

PO

MAES GOGOR

Llansannan

Clwt-y-ddafad-ddu

Bryn-goleu

B5384

Rhydeidion

Pencraig Fawr

Llys Newydd

Hwlffordd

Deunant-isaf

B5384

Rhŷd-yr-Eidion Fawr

FFORDD GOGOR

Fedr Fawr

Plas-Pigot

Afon Deunant

Deunant Uchaf

Pont y Nant

Beidiog Isa

Ty-celyn

Fedw Uchaf

Pentre-beidiog

Felin Gadeg

Tan-y-fron

Bryn-Bigad

Acrau

Beidiog-Ucha

Priddbwll

Cae-Goronwy

Fferwd

Wenallt

Gilfach

Cae-du

Cae-coed

MAES GRUGOER

Blaen-y-wergloedd

Clwt-grugoer

A544

Ochr-y-cefn

Chwibren

Fforest

Fron

Plas Panton

Hendre-Aled

Pant-glas

Cefn-bach

Moel Grugoer

Cleiriach

Bryn

Afon Aled

Pant-y-cefn

Nant y Fleiddiast

Cefn-Fforest

Nant y Lladron

Tan-y-foel

LL16

Afon Hyddu

Pen-cae'r cwm

Nant-y-garreg

Foel Lwyd

Nant-y-Merddyn

Nant-y-lladron

Glan-y-gors

Dolau

A543

Rhaeadr y Bedd

Rhos Bryn-llwyn

Tan-y-rhiwiau

Rhiwiau

Moel Bengam

Clytiau-gleision

Cwm-y-rhinwedd

Aled Isaf Resr

Hafod-Dafydd

Llyn Brân

Trwyn Swch

Llyn y Foel-frech

Gors Penrhiwiau

B4501

Moel y Byrniau

Cefn Du

Bryn Trillyn

PH

Gwylfa Hiraethog

Cesyg Aled

A543

B4501

B4501

Cefn Llys-gwr

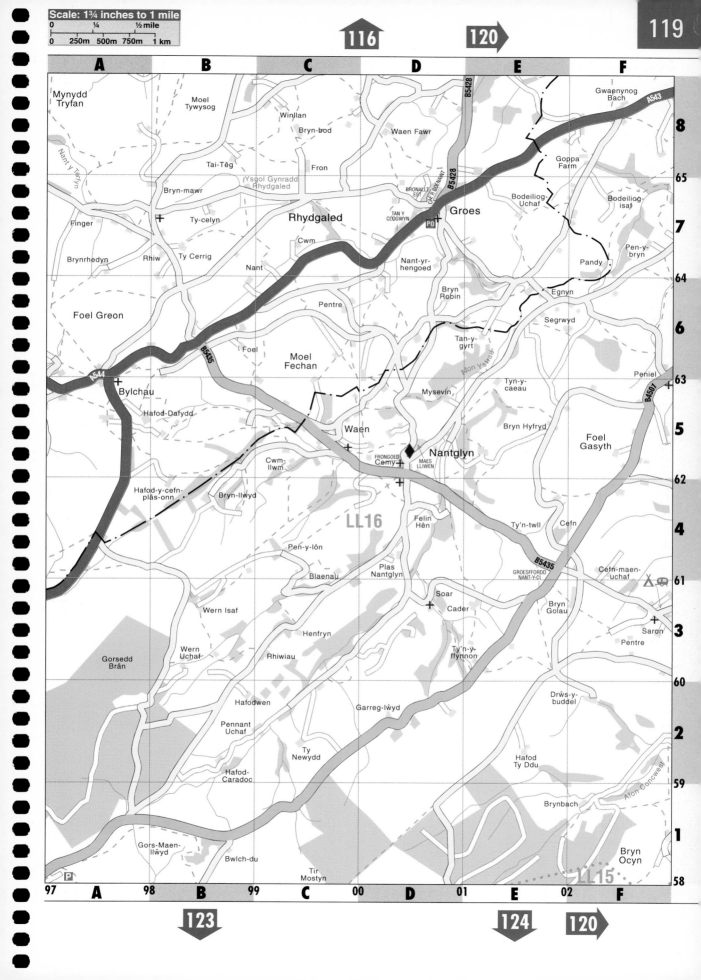

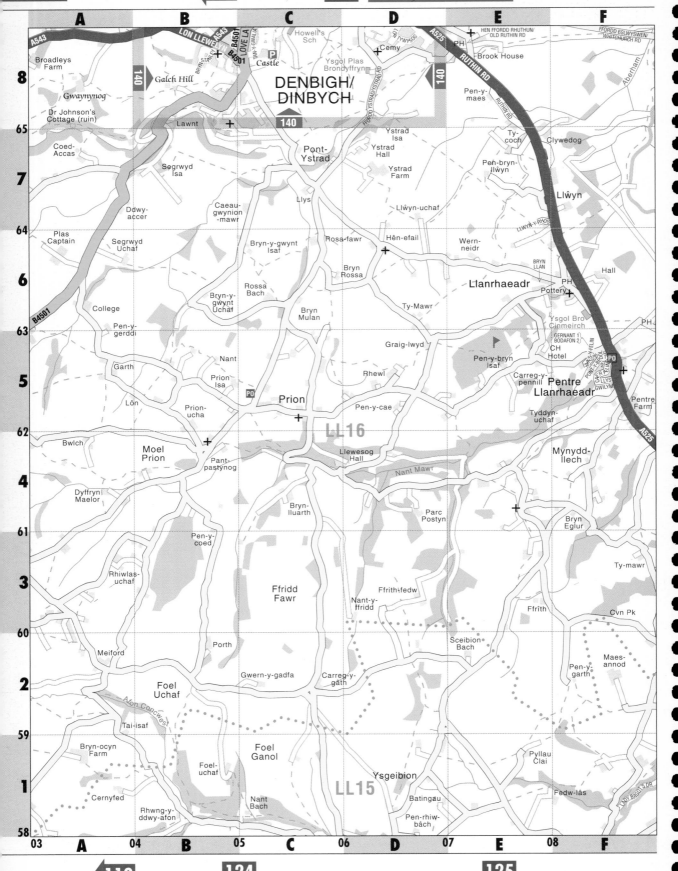

119

117

For full street detail of the highlighted area see page 140.

Scale: 1¾ inches to 1 mile

0   ¼   ½ mile
0   250m 500m 750m 1 km

A   B   C   D   E   F

A543
LON LLEWELYN
B4501
LOVE LA
TAN-Y-GWALIA
BRYN STABLE
Castle
P
Howell's Sch
Ysgol Plas Brondyffryn
FFORDD Y TWYSOG
Cefny
PH
Brook House
HEN FFORDD RHUTHUN/ OLD RUTHIN RD
FFORDD EGLWYSWEN/ WHITCHURCH RD

Broadleys Farm
140
Galch Hill
DENBIGH/ DINBYCH
A525
RUTHIN RD
140
Pen-y-maes
Aberham

8

Gwaynynog
Lawnt
140
Ystrad Isa
Ty-coch
Clywedog

Dr Johnson's Cottage (ruin)
65
Pont-Ystrad
Ystrad Hall
Pen-bryn-llwyn

Coed-Accas
Segrwyd Isa
Llys
Ystrad Farm
Llwyn-uchaf
Llŵyn

7

64
Ddwy-accer
Caeau-gwynion-mawr
Bryn-y-gwynt Isaf
Rosa-fawr
Hên-efail
Wern-neidr
LLWYN-Y-RHOS
BRYN LLAN

Plas Captain
Segrwyd Uchaf
Bryn Rossa
Llanrhaeadr
Hall
PH

6

College
Bryn-y-gwynt Uchaf
Rossa Bach
Bryn Mulan
Ty-Mawr
Pottery
PH
Ysgol Bro Cinmeirch
PH

63
Pen-y-gerddi
Nant
Graig-lwyd
GERNANT 1 BODAFON 2
CH Hotel
MAES-FELIN
PONT-Y-PRIOL
CAER Y LLYN

Garth
Prion Isa
Rhewl
Pen-y-bryn Isaf
Carreg-y-pennill
Pentre Llanrhaeadr
CLER Y GWILYM

5

Lôn
Prion-ucha
Prion
Pen-y-cae
Pentre Farm

62
Bwlch
Moel Prion
Pant-pastynog
LL16
Tyddyn-uchaf
Mynydd-llech

Llewesog Hall
Nant Mawr
A525

4
Dyffryn Maelor
Bryn-lluarth
Parc Postyn
Bryn Eglur

Pen-y-coed
61

Rhiwlas-uchaf
Ty-mawr

3
Ffridd Fawr
Ffrith-fedw
Nant-y-ffridd
Ffrith
Cvn Pk

60
Meiford
Porth
Sceibion Bach
Maes-annod

2
Foel Uchaf
Gwern-y-gadfa
Carreg-y-gâth
Pen-y-garth

Afon Concwest
Tai-isaf
59

Bryn-ocyn Farm
Foel Ganol
Pyllau Clai
LADY BAGOT'S DR

1
Foel-uchaf
Ysgeibion
Batingau
Fedw-lâs

Cernyfed
LL15
Pen-rhiw-bâch

58
Rhwng-y-ddwy-afon
Nant Bach

03   A   04   B   05   C   06   D   07   E   08   F

119

124

125

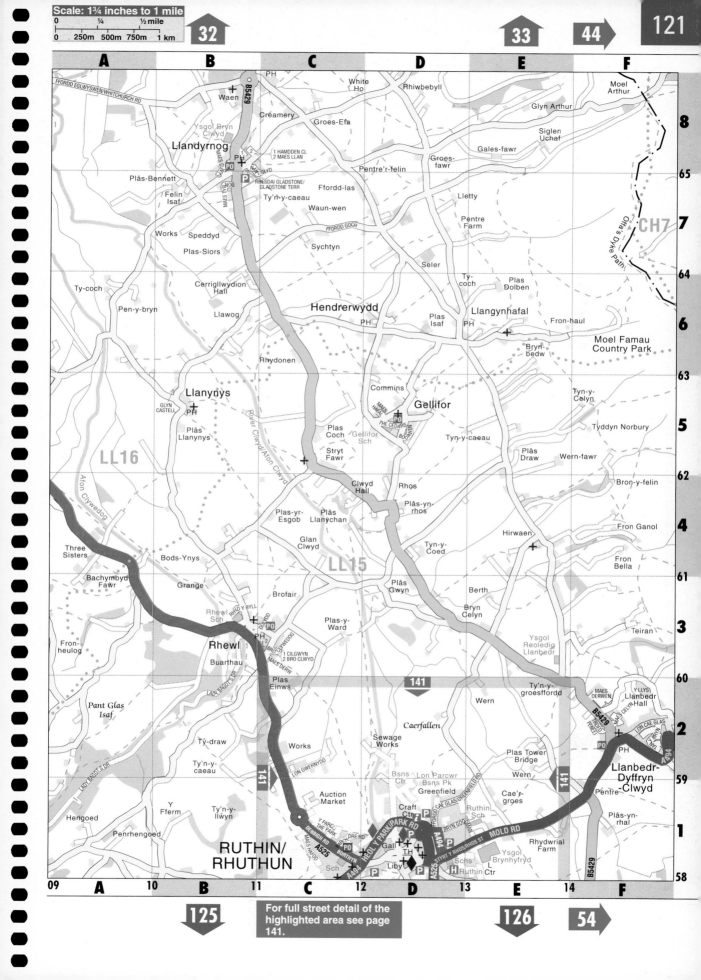

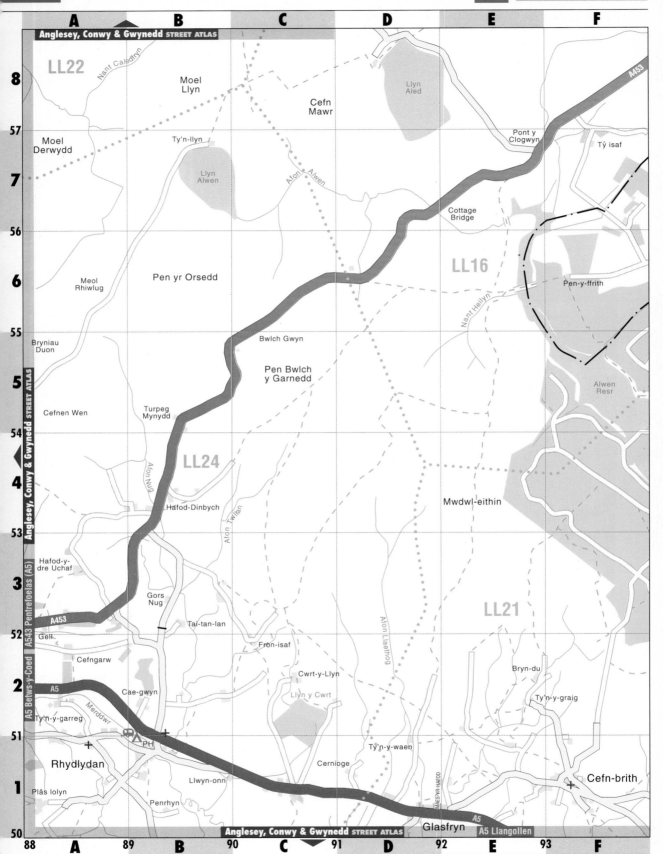

Anglesey, Conwy & Gwynedd STREET ATLAS

LL22

Moel Llyn

Moel Derwydd

Nant Caledfryn

Ty'n-llyn

Cefn Mawr

Llyn Aled

Pont y Clogwyn

Tŷ isaf

A453

Llyn Alwen

Afon Alwen

Cottage Bridge

LL16

Pen-y-ffrith

Meol Rhiwlug

Pen yr Orsedd

Nant Hellyn

Bryniau Duon

Bwlch Gwyn

Alwen Resr

Cefnen Wen

Pen Bwlch y Garnedd

Turpeg Mynydd

Afon Nug

LL24

Mwdwl-eithin

Hafod-Dinbych

Afon Twllan

Hafod-y-dre Uchaf

Gors Nug

Afon Llaethog

LL21

A453 Pentrefoelas (A5)

A453

Gell

Tai-tan-lan

Fron-isaf

Bryn-du

Cefngarw

Cwrt-y-Llyn

A5 Betws-y-Coed

A5

Cae-gwyn

Llyn y Cwrt

Ty'n-y-graig

Merddwr

Ty'n-y-garreg

PH

Ty'n-y-waen

Cerniog

MAESYR-HAFOD

Cefn-brith

Rhydlydan

Llwyn-onn

Plâs Iolyn

Penrhyn

Glasfryn

A5

A5 Llangollen

Anglesey, Conwy & Gwynedd STREET ATLAS

88   89   90   91   92   93
A   B   C   D   E   F

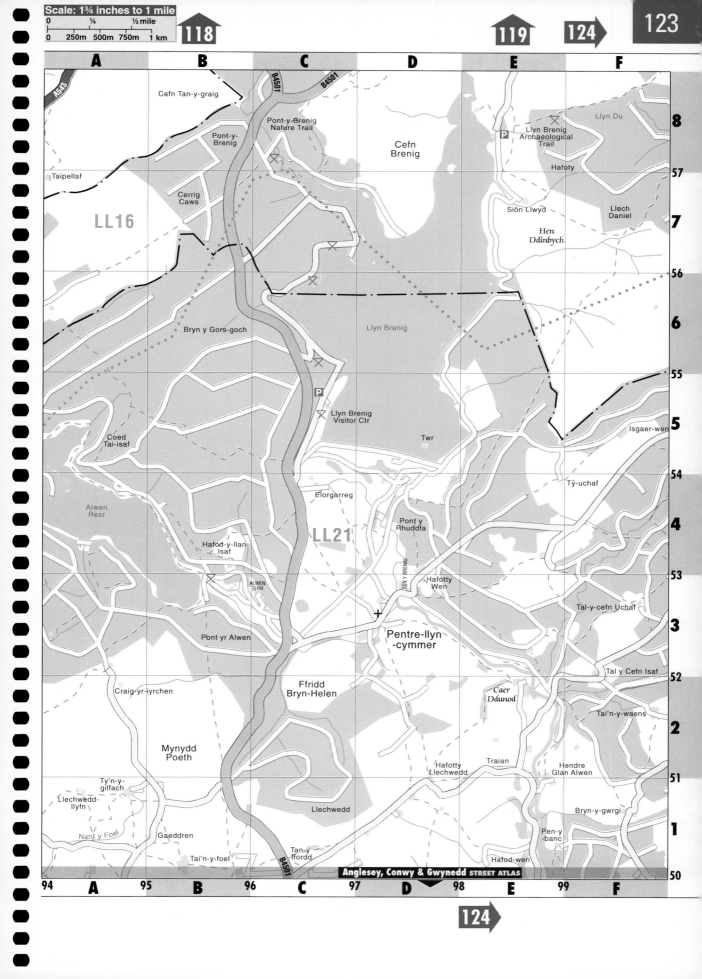

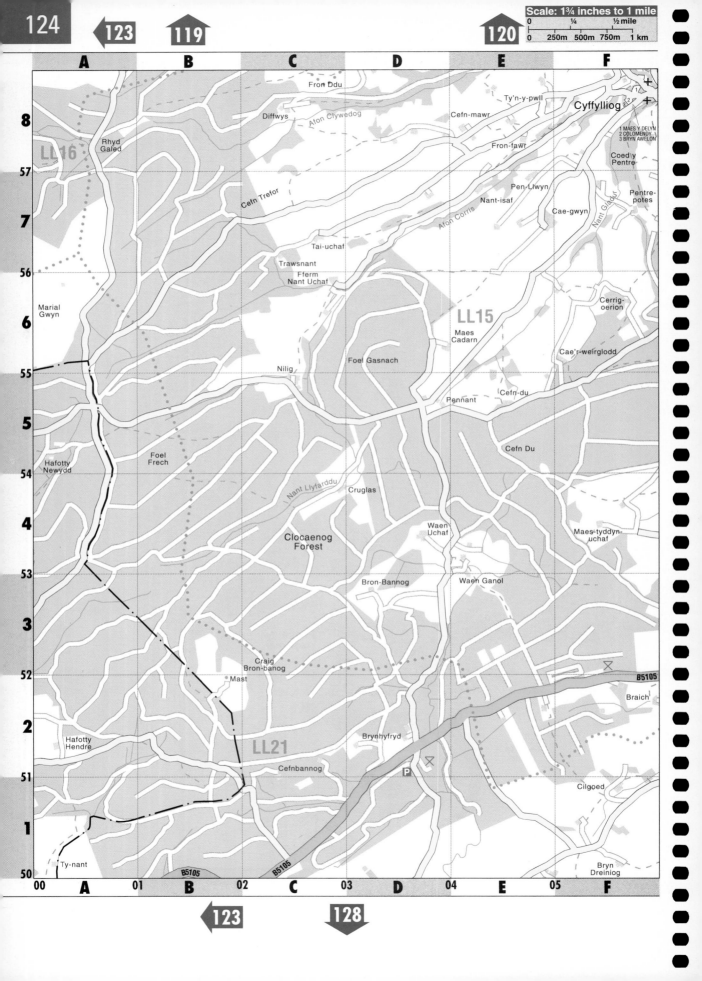

Scale: 1¾ inches to 1 mile

0   ¼   ½ mile
0 250m 500m 750m 1 km

LL16

8

57

7

56

6

55

5

54

4

53

3

52

2

51

1

50

Rhyd Galed

Diffwys

Fron Ddu

Afon Clywedog

Ty'n-y-pwll

Cefn-mawr

Cyffylliog

1 MAES Y DELYN
2 COLOMENDY
3 BRYN AWELON

Fron-fawr

Coed y Pentre

Cefn Trefor

Afon Corris

Pen-Llwyn

Nant-isaf

Cae-gwyn

Pentre-potes

Tai-uchaf

Trawsnant

Fferm Nant Uchaf

Nant Gladur

Cerrig-oerion

Marial Gwyn

LL15

Maes Cadarn

Cae'r-weirglodd

Nilig

Foel Gasnach

Pennant

Cefn-du

Hafotty Newydd

Foel Frech

Cefn Du

Nant Llyfarddu

Cruglas

Waen Uchaf

Maes-tyddyn-uchaf

Clocaenog Forest

Bron-Bannog

Waen Ganol

Craig Bron-banog

Mast

B5105

Braich

LL21

Brynhyfryd

Hafotty Hendre

Cefnbannog

P

Cilgoed

Ty-nant

B5105

B5105

Bryn Dreiniog

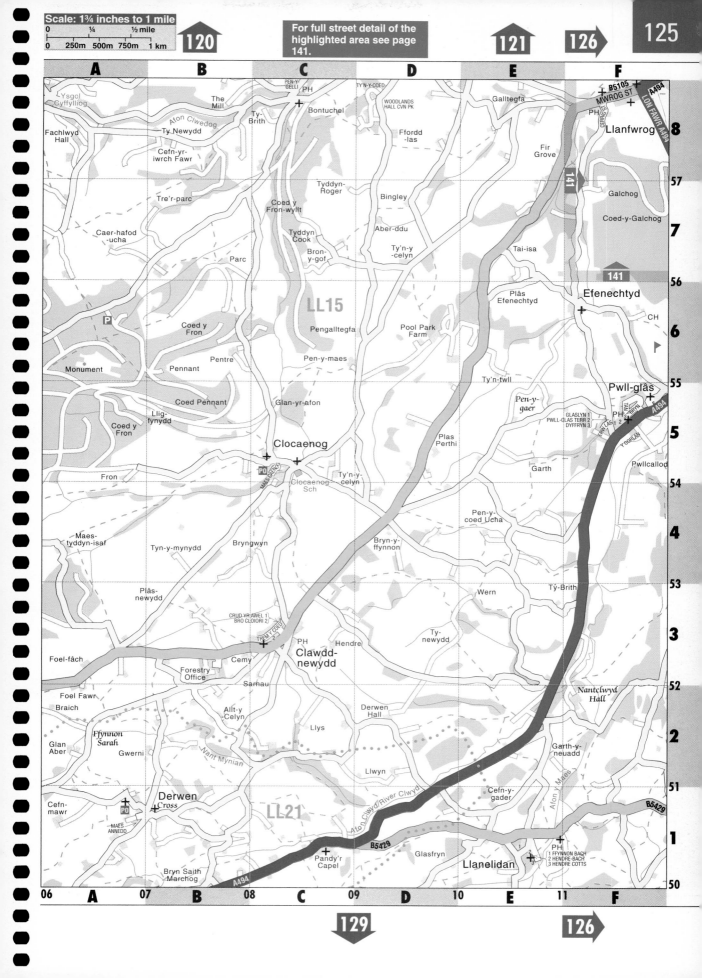

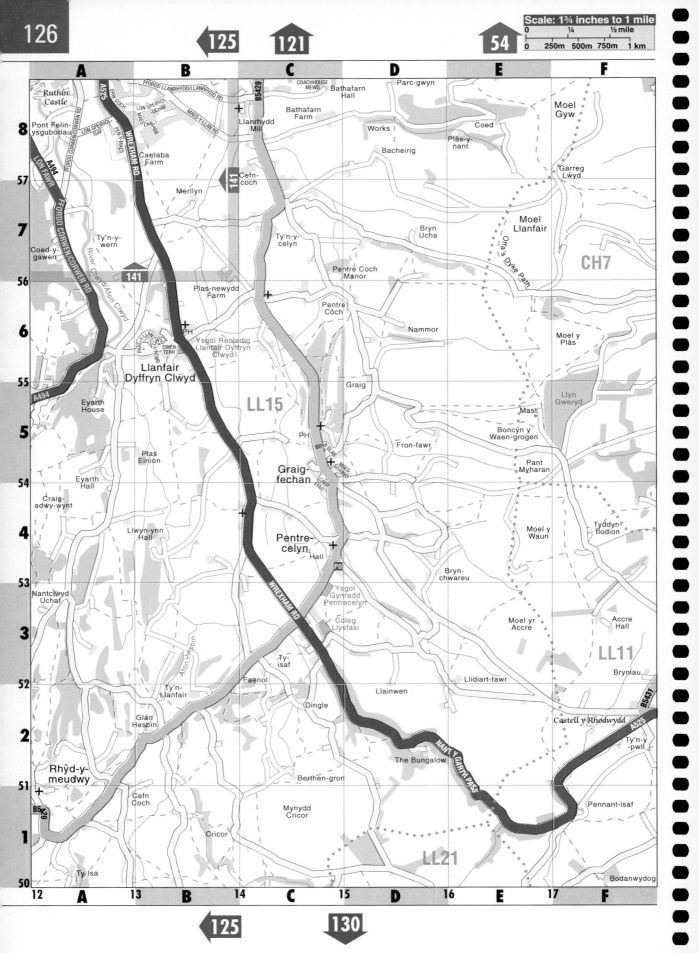

Scale: 1¾ inches to 1 mile
0   ¼   ½ mile
0   250m 500m 750m 1 km

A   B   C   D   E   F

8
57
7
56
6
55
5
54
4
53
3
52
2
51
1
50

Ruthin Castle
Pont Felin-ysguboriau
Coed-y-gawen
A494 LON FAWR
FFORDD CORWEN/CORWEN RD
River Clwyd/Afon Clwyd
A525
ERW GOCH
FFORDD LLANRHYDD/LLANRHYDD RD
LON SPEIRIOL UCHAF
MAES CYMLA
LON SPEIRIOL ISAF
PEN-Y-MAES
WREXHAM RD
Cantaba Farm
Merllyn
Maes-y-llan Rd
B5429
Llanrhydd Mill
COACHHOUSE MEWS
Bathafarn Hall
Bathafarn Farm
Parc-gwyn
Works
Bacheirig
Coed
Plâs-y-nant
Moel Gyw
Garreg Lŵyd
Cefn-coch
141
Ty'n-y-wern
Ty'n-y-celyn
Bryn Ucha
Moel Llanfair
Offa's Dyke Path
CH7
141
Plas-newydd Farm
Pentre Coch Manor
Nammor
Moel y Plâs
PH
Ysgol Reoledig Llanfair Dyffryn Clwyd
Pentre Côch
OWEN TERR
PARC GLAS
BRON...
Llanfair Dyffryn Clwyd
Graig
Llyn Gweryd
LL15
Eyarth House
A494
Mast
Boncyn y Waen-grogen
PH
Fron-fawr
Pant Myharan
Plas Einion
BRYN GLAS
MAES HYFRYD
CAER EFAIL
Graig-fechan
Eyarth Hall
Craig-adwy-wynt
Llwyn-ynn Hall
Moel y Waun
Tyddyn Tlodion
Pentre-celyn
Hall
PO
Brynchwareu
Afon Hesbin
Ysgol Gynradd Pentrecelyn
Coleg Llysfasi
Moel yr Accre
Accre Hall
LL11
Nantclwyd Uchaf
WREXHAM RD
Ty-isaf
Llidiart-fawr
Bryniau
Faenol
Llainwen
B5431
Ty'n-llanfair
Dingle
Berthen-gron
Glân Hesbin
The Bungalow
NANT Y GARTH PASS
Castell y Rhodwydd
A525
Ty'n-y-pwll
Rhŷd-y-meudwy
Cefn Coch
Mynydd Cricor
Pennant-isaf
B5
Cricor
LL21
Ty Isa
Bodanwydog

12   A   13   B   14   C   15   D   16   E   17   F

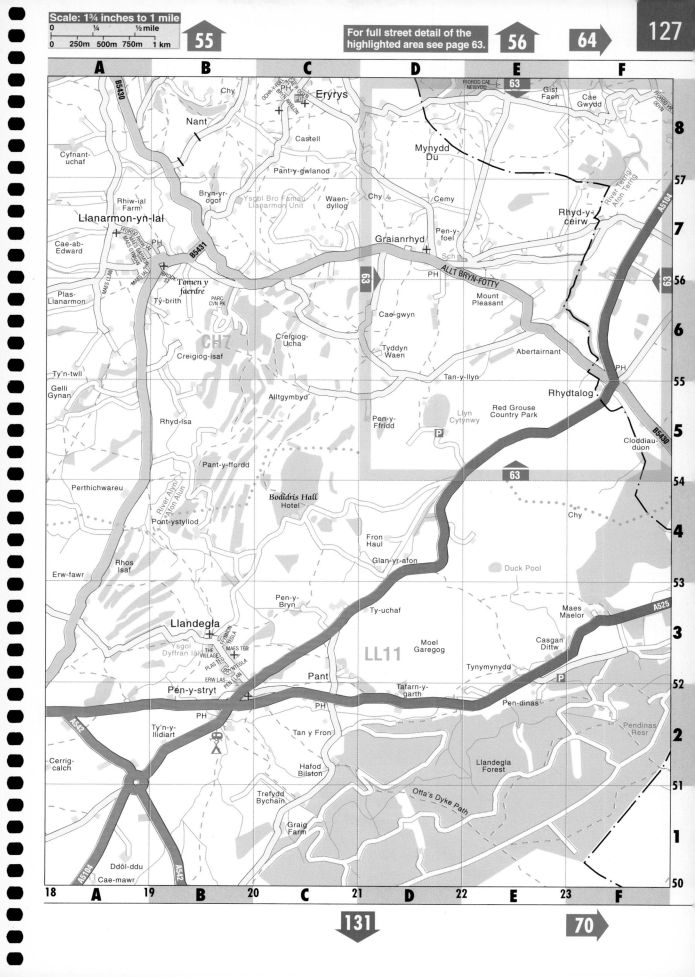

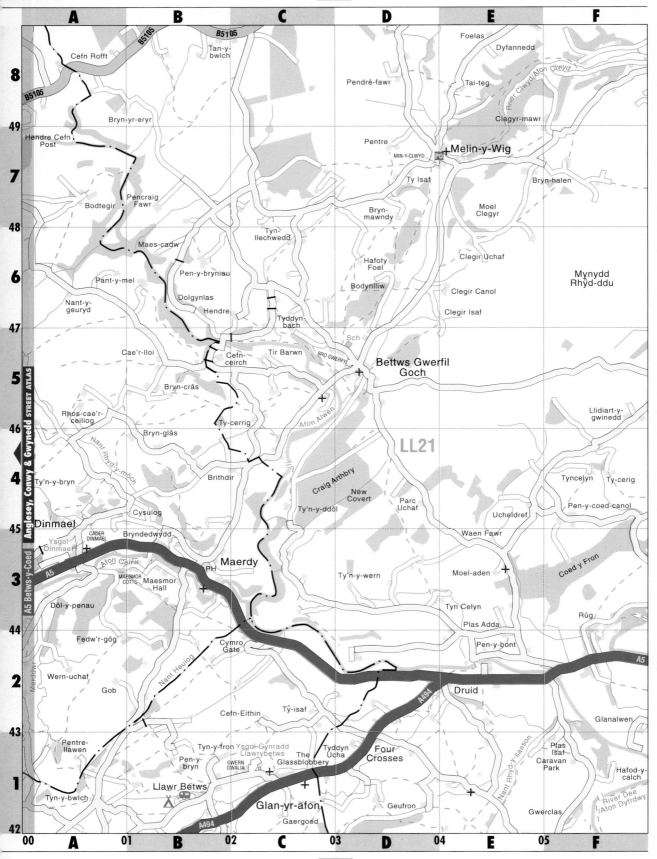

124

Scale: 1¾ inches to 1 mile

0   ¼   ½ mile

0   250m   500m   750m   1 km

A **B** **C** **D** **E** **F**

8

Cefn Rofft

Tan-y-bwlch

B5105

B5105

Foelas

Dyfannedd

Pendrê-fawr

Tai-teg

River Clwyd / Afon Clwyd

49

Bryn-yr-eryr

Hendre Cefn Post

Pentre

Clegyr-mawr

7

Bodtegir

Pencraig Fawr

MIN-Y-CLWYD PO

Melin-y-Wig

Ty Isaf

Bryn-halen

Moel Clegyr

48

Maes-cadw

Tyn-llechwedd

Bryn-mawndy

Clegir Uchaf

6

Pant-y-mel

Pen-y-bryniau

Hafoty Foel

Clegir Canol

Mynydd Rhŷd-ddu

Nant-y-geuryd

Dolgynlas

Hendre

Bodynlliw

Clegir Isaf

47

Cae'r-lloi

Tyddyn-bach

Sch

Cefn-ceirch

Tir Barwn

BRO GWERFYL

Bryn-crâs

5

Rhos-cae'r-ceiliog

Ty-cerrig

Afon Alwen

Bettws Gwerfil Goch

Llidiart-y-gwinedd

Bryn-glâs

46

Nant Rhyd-y-môch

LL21

4

Ty'n-y-bryn

Brithdir

Craig Arthbry

New Covert

Parc Uchaf

Tyncelyn

Ty-cerig

Pen-y-coed-canol

Cysulog

Ty'n-y-ddôl

Ucheldref

45

Dinmael

CADER DINMAEL

Bryndedwydd

Waen Fawr

Ysgol Dinmael

A5 Betws-y-Coed **Anglesey, Conwy & Gwynedd STREET ATLAS**

Afon Ceirw

Maesmor Hall

MAESMOR COTTS

Maerdy

PH

Ty'n-y-wern

Moel-aden

Coed y Fron

3

A5

Dôl-y-penau

Tyn Celyn

Rûg

44

Fedw'r-gôg

Cymro Gate

Plas Adda

Pen-y-bont

A5

Nant Heulog

2

Wern-uchaf

Gob

Druid

A494

Cefn-Eithin

Tŷ-isaf

Glanalwen

43

Pentre-llawen

Tyn-y-fron

Ysgol Gynradd Llawrybetws

Tyddyn Ucha

Four Crosses

Plas Isaf

Hafod-y-calch

Pen-y-bryn

GWERN GWALIA

The Glassblobbery

Nant Rhyd-y-saeson

Caravan Park

1

Llawr Betws

Glan-yr-afon

Geufron

Gwerclas

River Dee / Afon Dyfrdwy

Tyn-y-bwlch

Gaergoed

A494

42

00 **A** **01** **B** **02** **C** **03** **D** **04** **E** **05** **F**

132

Scale: 1¾ inches to 1 mile

0   ¼   ½ mile
0   250m   500m   750m   1 km

125

130

129

A   B   C   D   E   F

Meyarth Hall
River Clwyd
Afon Clwyd
Pen-y-banc
Merllyn

8

Hendre-isa
Hafotty-boeth
Ty-newydd
Pentre

LL 15

49

Plasau
Ty-ucha'r-llyn
Gwndir
Gwrych-bedw
Cefn-griolen

7

Maerdy-uchaf
Cefn-maen-llwyd
Cwm

Wern-ddu
Hendre
Bryn-du
Moel Truan

48

Siambar Wen
Oror
Llyn Oror
Maes Truan

6

Bryn Gwenallt
Maerdy-mawr
Bryn-ysguboriau

Tyn-llechwedd
DEUNANT
PH
Saw Mill
PO
MAES YR EFAIL
Bryn Elwern
LL 21
Hafotty Wen
Bryn Tangor

Moel Truan

Ysgol Gynradd Gwyddelwern
Lletty
Highgate
Cae-du
A5104

5

Gwyddelwern
Ty-nant
142
Caenog
Moel Fodig
Hendre Bryn Cyffo
Ty'n-y-rhos
B5436
Apon Morwynion

46

Groes-lwyd
Foel Fodig
Cae-Einion
Morfydd

4

Tyddyn-Angharad
Berth-ddu
Foel Isaf
Fron-newydd
Pont-swil
Ty-mawr

45

Clawdd Poncen
A5104
B5437
Ystad Ddiwydianol Corwen
Nant Fawr
Tan-y-coed
Ty-newydd

Ty'n-y-llidian Ind Est
Bwlch Coch

3

CLAWDD PONCEN
Sch
Cemy
MAESAFALLEN
Caer Drewyn
Mast
Fedw
B5436

FFORDD TY CERRIG
Trewyn
142
Rhagatt Hall
Ysgol Gynradd Carrog
PH

Chapel
A494
Afon Dyfrdwy/River Dee
Y LON LAS GREEN
PO
P
Unedau Busnes Llys Edeyrnion Bsns Units
MAES-Y-LLAN
PO
Carrog
A5

44

Ty'n-y-cefn
STRYD Y BONT/BRIDGE ST
PEN Y BRYN
MILL HILL
HEOL LLUNDAIN/LONDON RD
Bonwm-uchaf
MAES-Y-WAEN
Cemy
GLYNDWR TERR
GWYLFA TERR
B5437
PARC TERR
SCRYN ST

2

B4401
PEN Y BRYN
Coleg Y Groes (The College)
Mast
Carrog

Corwen
Penarth

43

Bryn Saint
Nant Cawrddu
Nant Llechog

1

B4401
142

42

06   A   07   B   08   C   09   D   10   E   11   F

For full street detail of the highlighted area see page 142.

133

130

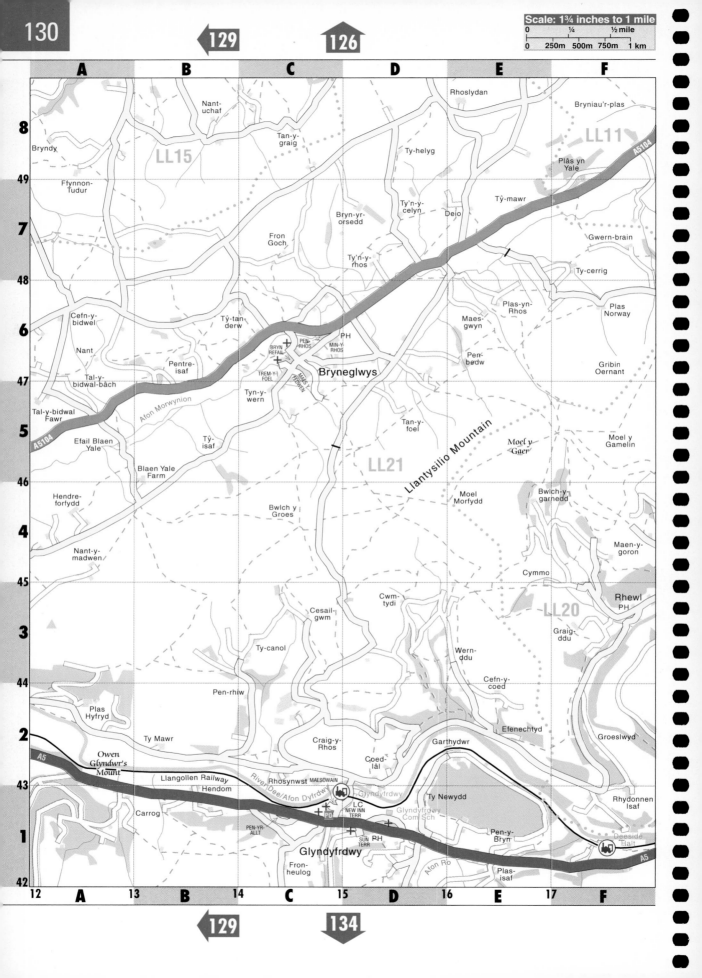

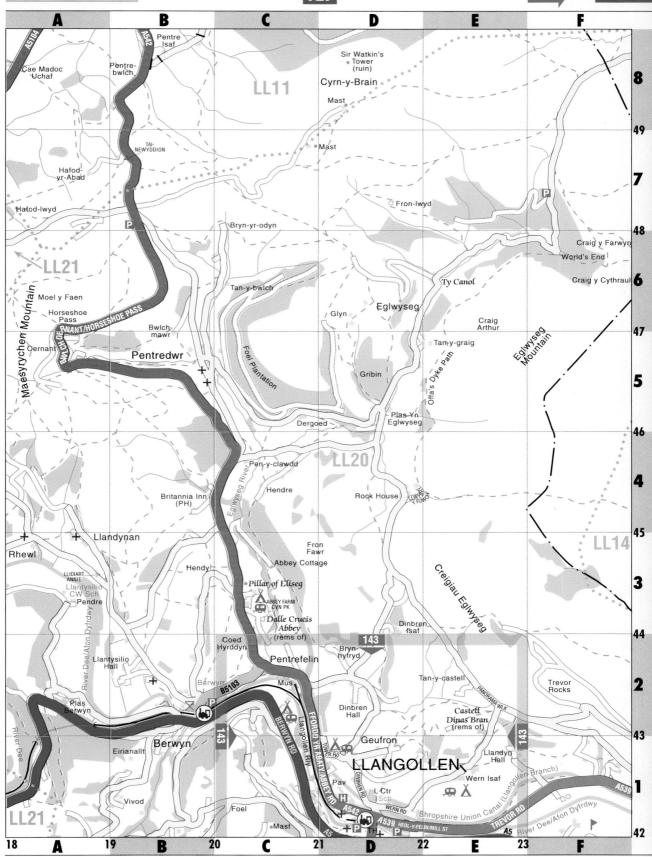

LL11

Sir Watkin's Tower (ruin)

Cyrn-y-Brain

Cae Madoc Uchaf

Pentre Isaf

Pentre-bwlch

Mast

Mast

TAI-NEWYDDION

Hafod-yr-Abad

Fron-lwyd

P

Hafod-lwyd

Bryn-yr-odyn

Craig y Farwyn

World's End

LL21

Maesyrychen Mountain

Moel y Faen

Horseshoe Pass

BWLCH OERNANT/HORSESHOE PASS

Oernant

Bwlch-mawr

Pentredwr

Tan-y-bwlch

Glyn

Eglwyseg

Ty Canol

Craig y Cythraul

Craig Arthur

Tan-y-graig

Offa's Dyke Path

Eglwyseg Mountain

Foel Plantation

Eglwyseg River

Gribin

Plas Yn Eglwyseg

Dergoed

LL20

Pen-y-clawdd

Rook House

Hendre

LLWYN-Y-FUWCH

LL14

Britannia Inn (PH)

Fron Fawr

Abbey Cottage

Creigiau Eglwyseg

Llandynan

River Dee/Afon Dyfrdwy

Rhewl

Hendy

LLIDIART ANNIE

Llantysilio CW Sch

Pendre

Pillar of Eliseg

ABBEY FARM CVN PK

Dinbren Isaf

143

Valle Crucis Abbey (rems of)

Bryn-hyfryd

Coed Hyrddyn

Pentrefelin

Tan-y-castell

Trevor Rocks

Llantysilio Hall

Berwyn

B5103

Mus

Dinbren Hall

Castell Dinas Bran (rems of)

PANORAMA WLK

143

River Dee

Plas Berwyn

P

143

BERWYN RD

FFORDDD YR ABATY/ABBEY RD

Llangollen Riv

TŴR RD

Geufron

LLANGOLLEN

Llandyn Hall

Wern Isaf

A539

Eirianallt

Berwyn

Pav

DINBREN RD

L Ctr

Llangollen Branch)

TREVOR RD

A5

Shropshire Union Canal (Llangollen Branch)

Vivod

Foel

H

A542

WERN RD

A539 HEOL-Y-FELIN/MILL ST

P

TH

P

A5

River Dee/Afon Dyfrdwy

A539

LL21

Mast

135

For full street detail of the highlighted area see page 143.

84

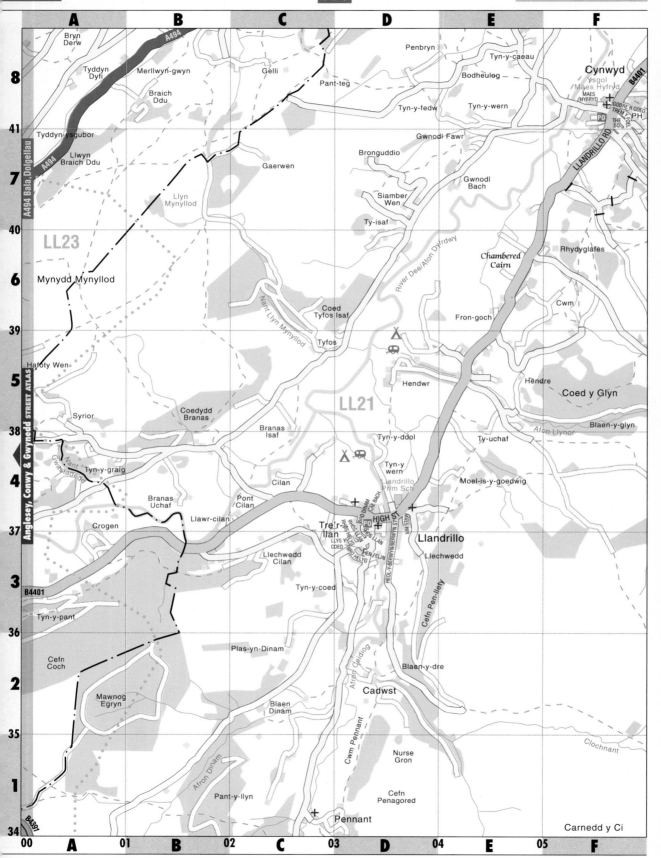

128

Scale: 1¾ inches to 1 mile
0   ¼   ½ mile
0   250m   500m   750m   1 km

A   B   C   D   E   F

8

41

7

40

6

39

5

38

4

37

3

36

2

35

1

34

Anglesey, Conwy & Gwynedd STREET ATLAS

A494 Bala, Dolgellau

Bryn Derw
Tyddyn Dyfi
Merllwyn-gwyn
Braich Ddu
Gelli
Pant-teg
Penbryn
Tyn-y-caeau
Bodheulog
Cynwyd
ysgol
Maes Hyfryd
MAES HYFRYD
GODRE'R COED
TREM Y FOEL
PH
PO
THE SQ

Tyddyn-ysgubor
Llwyn Braich Ddu
Gaerwen
Tyn-y-fedw
Tyn-y-wern
Gwnodl Fawr
LLANDRILLO RD

LL23
Llyn Mynyllod
Bronguddio
Gwnodl Bach
Rhydyglafes

Mynydd Mynyllod
Siamber Wen
Ty-isaf
Chambered Cairn
Cwm

Coed Tyfos Isaf
Fron-goch

Hafoty Wen
Tyfos
Hendwr
Hendre
Coed y Glyn

Syrior
Coedydd Branas
Branas Isaf
Tyn-y-ddol
Ty-uchaf
Afon Llynor
Blaen-y-glyn

Nant Gwastadedd
Tyn-y-graig
Cilan
Tyn-y-wern
Llandrillo Prim Sch
Moel-is-y-goedwig

Branas Uchaf
Pont Cilan
Llawr-cilan
BFRO DINAM
CAE BACH
HIGH ST
PO
Tre'r-llan
Llandrillo

Crogen
Llechwedd Cilan
RHOS LLAN
RHOS HELYG
HEOL-Y-BERWYN
BERWYN ST
MAES HIR
Llechwedd
Cefn Pen-lletty

B4401
Tyn-y-coed
Tyn-y-pant

Cefn Coch
Plas-yn-Dinam
Afon Ceidiog
Blaen-y-dre

Mawnog Egryn
Blaen Dinam
Cadwst
Cwm Pennant
Nurse Gron

Afon Dinam
Pant-y-llyn
Cefn Penagored
Pennant
Carnedd y Ci
B4401

00   A   01   B   02   C   03   D   04   E   05   F

River Dee/Afon Dyfrdwy
Nant Llyn Mynyllod
LL21
Clochnant

136

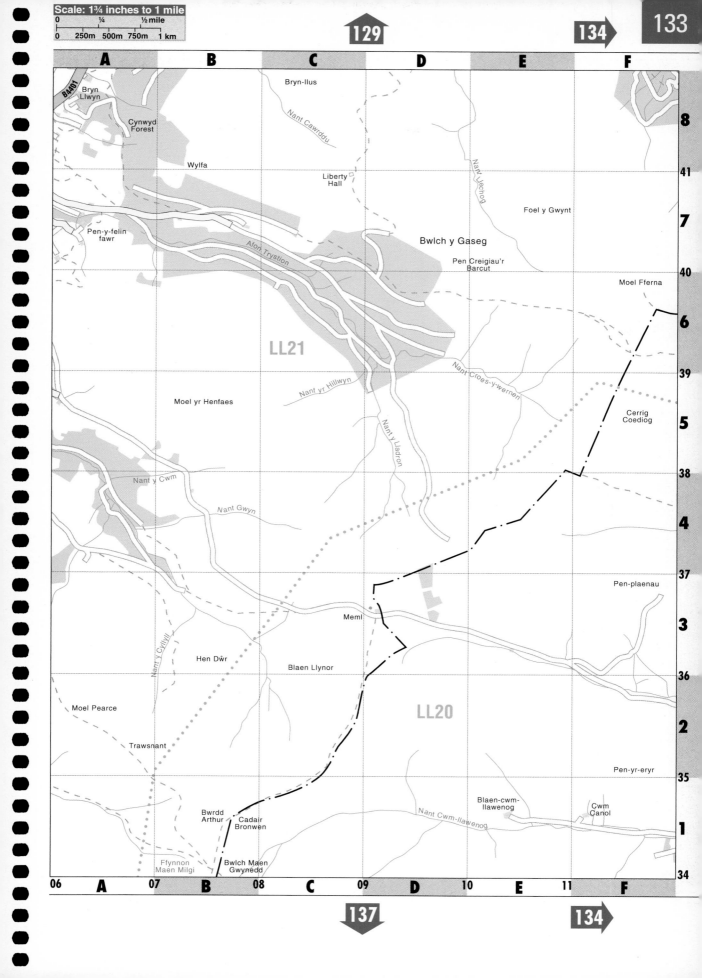

Scale: 1¾ inches to 1 mile

0   ¼   ½ mile
0   250m 500m 750m 1 km

A   B   C   D   E   F

Bryn Llwyn

B4401

Cynwyd Forest

Bryn-llus

Nant Cawrddu

Wylfa

Liberty Hall

Nant Uechog

Foel y Gwynt

Pen-y-felin fawr

Afon Trystion

Bwlch y Gaseg

Pen Creigiau'r Barcut

Moel Fferna

LL21

Nant Croes-y-wernen

Cerrig Coediog

Moel yr Henfaes

Nant yr Hillwyn

Nant y Lladron

Nant y Cwm

Nant Gwyn

Pen-plaenau

Meml

Nant y Cyllyll

Hen Dŵr

Blaen Llynor

LL20

Moel Pearce

Pen-yr-eryr

Trawsnant

Blaen-cwm-llawenog

Cwm Canol

Bwrdd Arthur

Cadair Bronwen

Nant Cwm-llawenog

Ffynnon Maen Milgi

Bwlch Maen Gwynedd

06   A   07   B   08   C   09   D   10   E   11   F

8
41
7
40
6
39
5
38
4
37
3
36
2
35
1
34

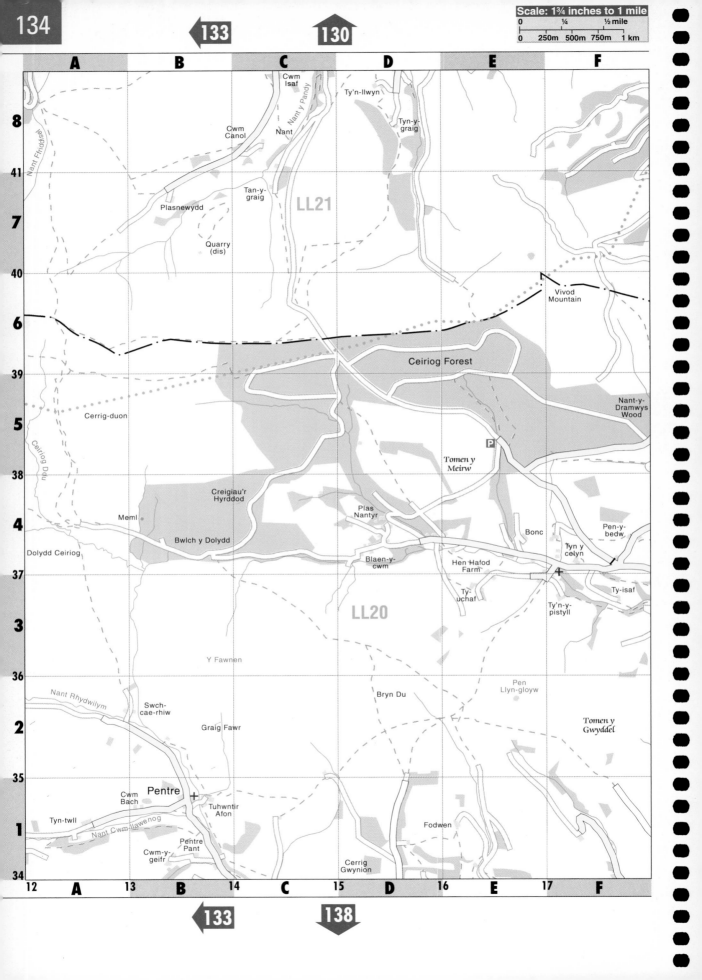

A   B   C   D   E   F

8

41

7

Nant Ffridsa

LL21

Plasnewydd

Tan-y-graig

Cwm Canol

Cwm Isaf

Nant y Pandy

Nant

Ty'n-llwyn

Tyn-y-graig

Quarry (dis)

40

6

Vivod Mountain

39

Ceiriog Forest

Cerrig-duon

Nant-y-Dramwys Wood

5

Ceiriog Ddu

P

Tomen y Meirw

38

Creigiau'r Hyrddod

Meml

Plas Nantyr

Bonc

Pen-y-bedw

4

Bwlch y Dolydd

Dolydd Ceiriog

Blaen-y-cwm

Hen Hafod Farm

Ty-uchaf

Tyn y celyn

Ty'n-y-pistyll

Ty-isaf

37

LL20

3

Y Fawnen

Bryn Du

Pen Llyn-gloyw

36

Nant Rhydwilym

Swch-cae-rhiw

Tomen y Gwyddel

2

Graig Fawr

35

Pentre

Cwm Bach

Tuhwntir Afon

Fodwen

1

Tyn-twll

Nant Cwm-llawenog

Pentre Pant

Cwm-y-geifr

Cerrig Gwynion

34

12   A   13   B   14   C   15   D   16   E   17   F

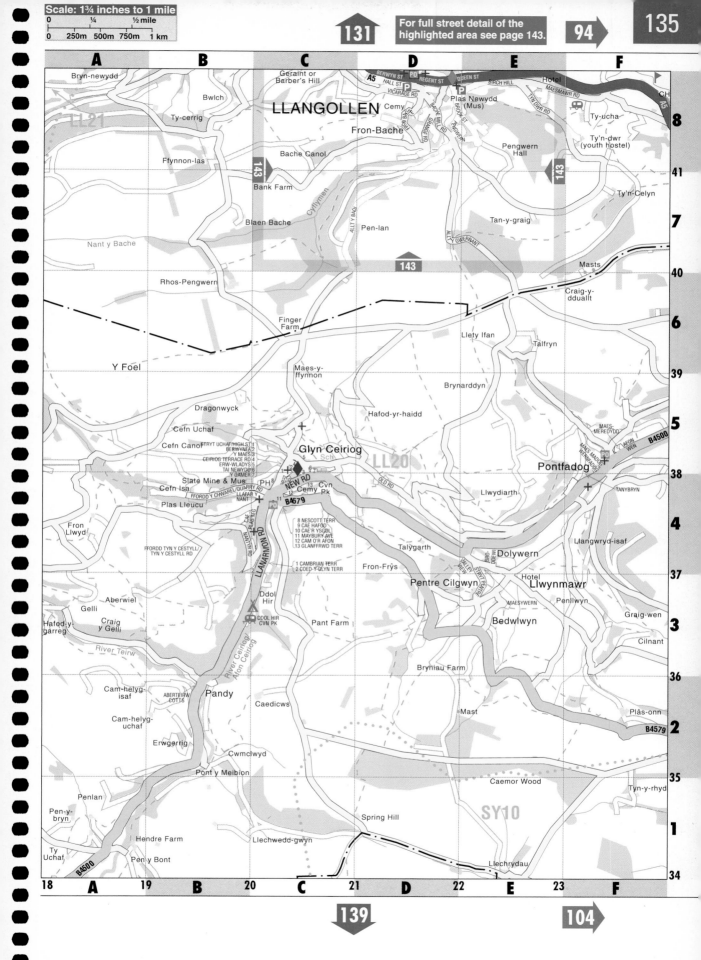

Scale: 1¾ inches to 1 mile

0   ¼   ½ mile
0 250m 500m 750m 1 km

131

For full street detail of the highlighted area see page 143.

94

135

A   B   C   D   E   F

Bryn-newydd

Geraint or Barber's Hill

BERWYN ST
A5   HALL ST   REGENT ST   QUEEN ST   BIRCH HILL   Hotel
VICARAGE RD   MAESMAWR RD   CH

Bwlch

Ty-cerrig

LLANGOLLEN   Cemy   Plas Newydd (Mus)

Ty-ucha

8

Ffynnon-las

Fron-Bache

Pengwern Hall   Ty'n-dwr (youth hostel)

Bache Canol

143

143

Ty'n-Celyn

41

Bank Farm

Cyflymen   ALLT Y BADI   Pen-lan

Tan-y-graig

7

Blaen Bache

ALLT Y GWERNANT

Nant y Bache

Masts

40

Rhos-Pengwern

Craig-y-dduallt

6

Finger Farm

Llety Ifan   Talfryn

39

Y Foel

Maes-y-ffynnon

Brynarddyn

Dragonwyck

Hafod-yr-haidd

MAES-MEREDYDD   B4500

5

Cefn Uchaf

Cefn Canol   STRYT UCHAF/HIGH ST 1
BERWYN TERR 2
Y MAES 3
CEIRIOG TERRACE RD 4
ERW-WLADYS 5
TAI NEWYDD 6
Y GAMER 7

Glyn Ceiriog   Sch   LL20

MAES MADOG   AFON WEN   VERNFORDD

Pontfadog

38

PH 8   Slate Mine & Mus   NEW RD   QUARRY RD   Cvn Pk
Cefn Isa   FFORDD Y CHWAREL   LLAFAR Y NANT
Plas Lleucu   B4579   OLD RD

Llwydiarth   TANYBRYN

Fron Llwyd

8 NESCOTT TERR
9 CAE HAFOD
10 CAE'R YSGOL
11 MAYBURY AVE
12 CAM O'R AFON
13 GLANFFRWD TERR

Llangwryd-isaf

4

FFORDD TYN Y CESTYLL
TYN Y CESTYLL RD

Talygarth

Dolywern

1 CAMBRIAN TERR
2 COED-Y-GLYN TERR

Fron-Frŷs   DALL EY   STRYT FECHT   Hotel   Llwynmawr

37

Aberwiel   Ddol Hir   Pentre Cilgwyn   Penllwyn

Gelli

Craig y Gelli   DDOL HIR CVN PK   Pant Farm   MAESYWERN   Bedwlwyn   Graig-wen

Hafod-y-garreg

River Teirw   Plas-onn   Cilnant

3

Cam-helyg-isaf

ABERTEIRW COTTS   Pandy   Caedicws   Bryniau Farm

36

Cam-helyg-uchaf

River Ceiriog   Afon Ceiriog   Mast   B4579

2

Erwgerrig

Cwmclwyd

Penlan   Pont y Meibion   Caemor Wood   Tyn-y-rhyd

35

Pen-y-bryn   Spring Hill   SY10

1

Ty Uchaf   Hendre Farm   Pen y Bont   Llechwedd-gwyn   Llechrydau

B4500

34

18   A   19   B   20   C   21   D   22   E   23   F

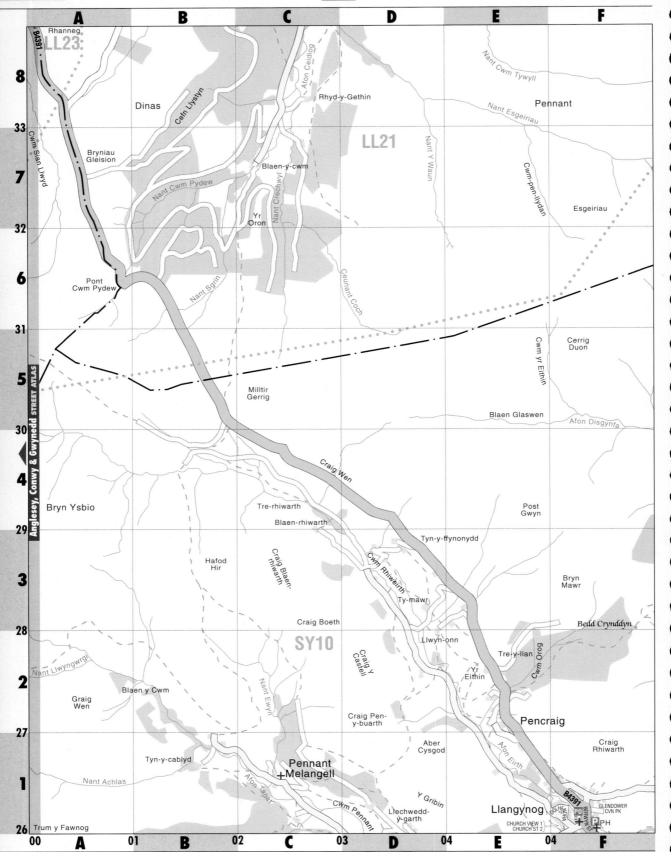

B4391
Rhanneg
LL23

Cwm Sian Llwyd

Dinas

Cefn Llystyn

Bryniau
Gleision

Nant Cwm Pydew

Blaen-y-cwm

Nant Crechwyl

Yr
Oron

Pont
Cwm Pydew

Nant Sgrin

Aton Ceidiog

Rhyd-y-Gethin

LL21

Nant Cwm Tywyll

Pennant

Nant Esgeiriau

Nant Y Waun

Cwm-pen-llydan

Esgeiriau

Nant Yr Wydd

Ceunant Coch

Cwm yr Eithin

Cerrig
Duon

Milltir
Gerrig

Blaen Glaswen

Afon Disgynfa

Craig Wen

Bryn Ysbio

Tre-rhiwarth

Blaen-rhiwarth

Hafod
Hir

Craig Blaen-
rhiwarth

Cwm Rhiweirth

Tyn-y-ffynonydd

Post
Gwyn

Ty-mawr

Craig Boeth

SY10

Nant Ewyn

Craig y
Castell

Llwyn-onn

Yr
Eithin

Tre-y-llan

Cwm Orog

Bryn
Mawr

Bedd Crynddyn

Nant Llwyngwrgi

Graig
Wen

Blaen y Cwm

Tyn-y-cablyd

Craig Pen-
y-buarth

Aber
Cysgod

Afon Eirth

Pencraig

Craig
Rhiwarth

Nant Achlas

Afon Tapat

Pennant
Melangell

Cwm Pennant

Y Gribin

Llechwedd-
y-garth

Llangynog

DOL HENDRA
PO
BERWYN ST
GLENDOWER
CVN PK
P PH

Trum y Fawnog

CHURCH VIEW 1
CHURCH ST 2

B4391

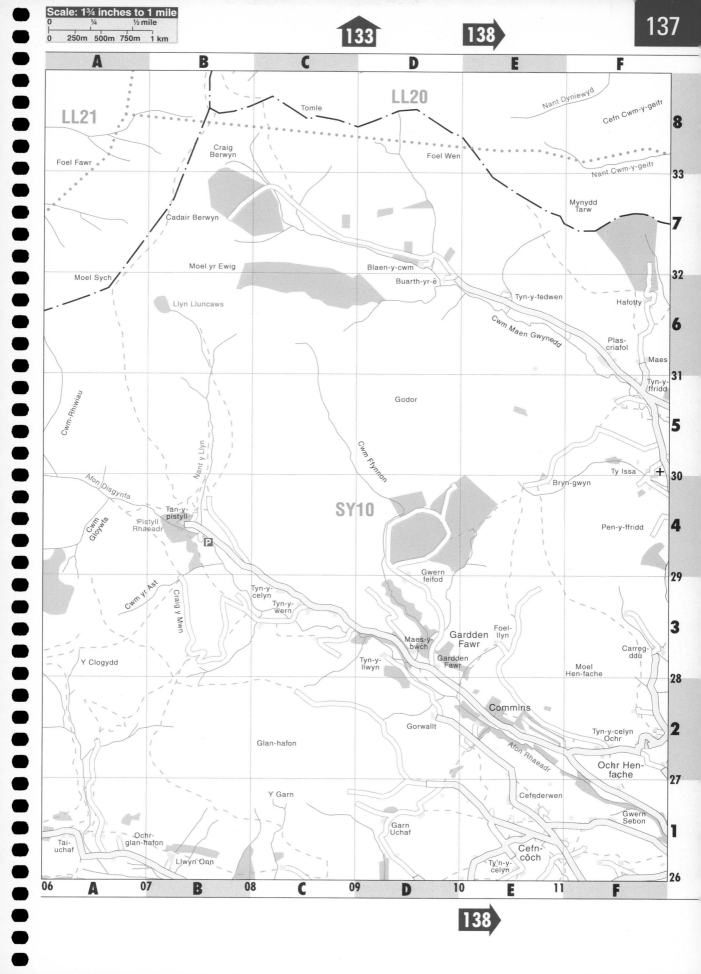

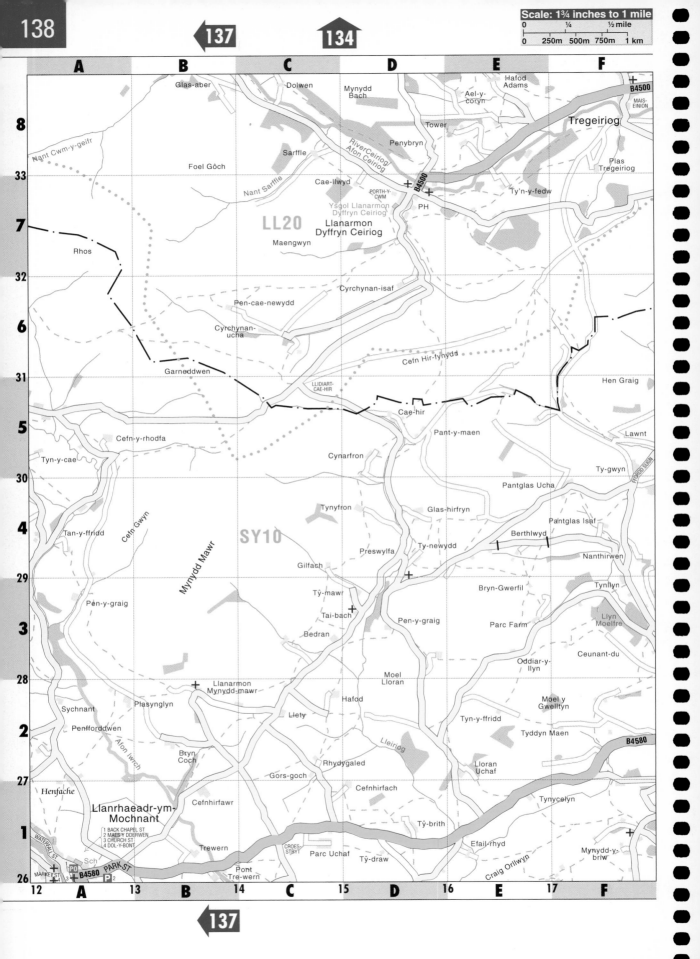

Scale: 1¾ inches to 1 mile

0   ¼   ½ mile

0   250m   500m 750m   1 km

A   B   C   D   E   F

Glas-aber

Dolwen

Mynydd Bach

Hafod Adams

B4500

MAIS-EINION

Nant Cwm-y-geifr

8

Sarffle

River Ceiriog
Afon Ceiriog

Penybryn

Tower

Ael-y-coryn

Tregeiriog

33

Foel Gôch

Nant Sarffle

Cae-llwyd

PORTH-Y-CWM

B4500

Ty'n-y-fedw

Plas Tregeiriog

Ysgol Llanarmon Dyffryn Ceiriog

LL20

PH

7

Rhos

Llanarmon Dyffryn Ceiriog

Maengwyn

32

Cyrchynan-isaf

6

Pen-cae-newydd

Cyrchynan-ucha

Cefn Hir-fynydd

Hen Graig

31

Garneddwen

LLIDIART-CAE-HIR

Cae-hir

5

Cefn-y-rhodfa

Pant-y-maen

Lawnt

Tyn-y-cae

Cynarfron

Ty-gwyn

FFORDD-SYCH

30

Pantglas Ucha

4

Tan-y-ffridd

Cefn Gwyn

SY10

Tynyfron

Glas-hirfryn

Ty-newydd

Pantglas Isaf

Berthlwyd

Nanthirwen

Preswylfa

Mynydd Mawr

Gilfach

29

Pen-y-graig

Tý-mawr

Bryn-Gwerfil

Tynllyn

Llyn Moelfre

3

Tai-bach

Pen-y-graig

Parc Farm

Bedran

Ceunant-du

28

Moel Lloran

Oddiar-y-llyn

Llanarmon Mynydd-mawr

Moel y Gwelltyn

2

Sychnant

Plasynglyn

Llety

Hafod

Tyn-y-ffridd

Tyddyn Maen

B4580

Penfforddwen

Afon Iwrch

Lleiriog

Lloran Uchaf

27

Bryn Coch

Rhydygaled

Cefnhirfach

Tynycelyn

Henfache

Gors-goch

Cefnhirfawr

Tý-brith

1

Llanrhaeadr-ym-Mochnant

1 BACK CHAPEL ST
2 MAES Y DDERWEN
3 CHURCH ST
4 DOL-Y-BONT

CROES-STRYT

Parc Uchaf

Efail-rhyd

Mynydd-y-briw

WATERFALL ST

Trewern

Tý-draw

Craig Orllwyn

26

MARKET ST

PO

Sch

PARK ST

B4580

P

Pont Tre-wern

12   A   13   B   14   C   15   D   16   E   17   F

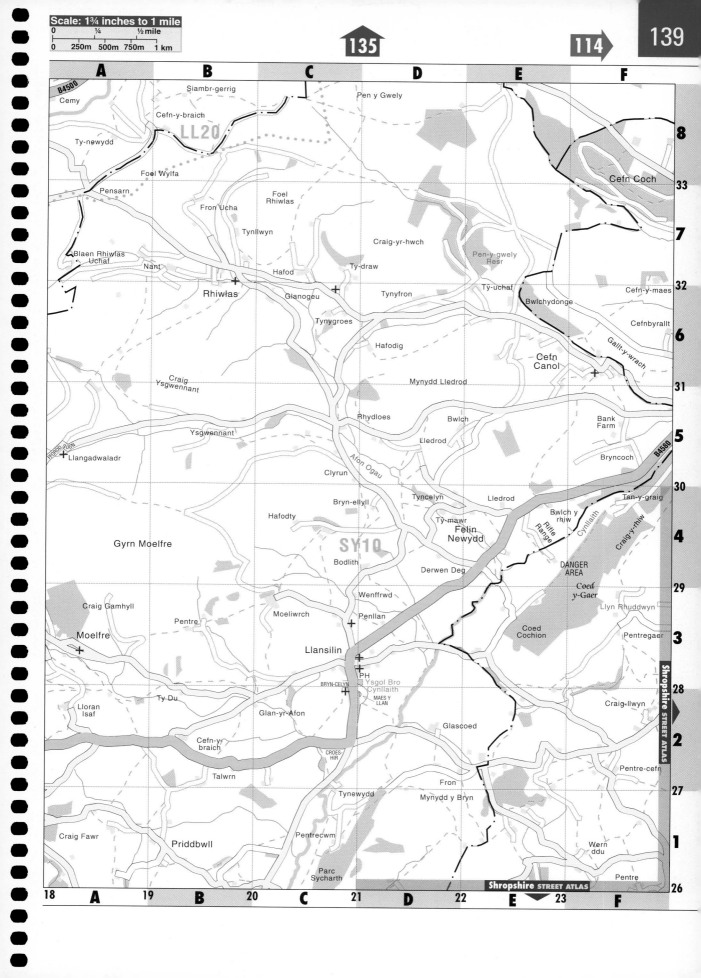

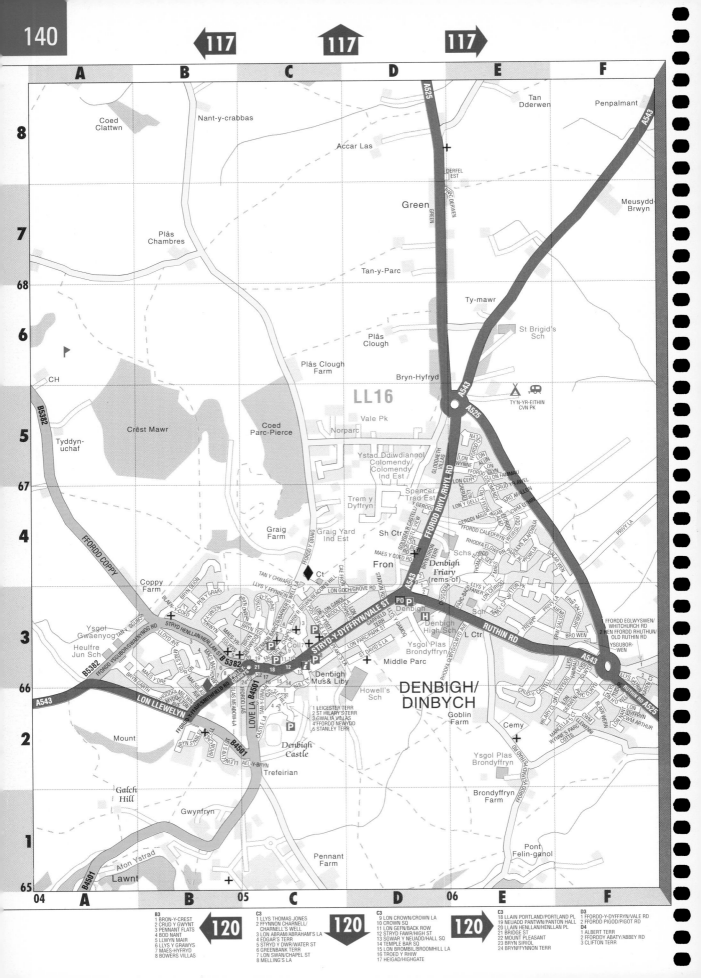

117 117 117

LL16

DENBIGH/
DINBYCH

B3
1 BRON-Y-CREST
2 CRUD Y GWYNT
3 PENNANT FLATS
4 BOD NANT
5 LLWYN MAIR
6 LLYS Y GRAWYS
7 MAES-HYFRYD
8 BOWERS VILLAS

120

C3
1 LLYS THOMAS JONES
2 FFYNNON CHARNELL/
  CHARNELL'S WELL
3 LON ABRAM/ABRAHAM'S LA
4 EDGAR'S TERR
5 STRYD Y DWR/WATER ST
6 GREENBANK TERR
7 LON SWAN/CHAPEL ST
8 MELLING'S LA

120

C3
9 LON CROWN/CROWN LA
10 CROWN SQ
11 LON GEFN/BACK ROW
12 STRYD FAWR/HIGH ST
13 SGWAR Y NEUADD/HALL SQ
14 TEMPLE BAR SQ
15 LON BROMBIL/BROOMHILL LA
16 TROED Y RHIW
17 HEIGAD/HIGHGATE

120

C3
18 LLAIN PORTLAND/PORTLAND PL
19 NEUADD PANTWN/PANTON HALL
20 LLAIN HENLLAN/HENLLAN PL
21 BRIDGE ST
22 MOUNT PLEASANT
23 BRYN SIRIOL
24 BRYNFFYNNON TERR

D3
1 FFORDD-Y-DYFFRYN/VALE RD
2 FFORDD PIGOD/PIGOT RD
D4
1 ALBERT TERR
2 FFORDDY ABATY/ABBEY RD
3 CLIFTON TERR

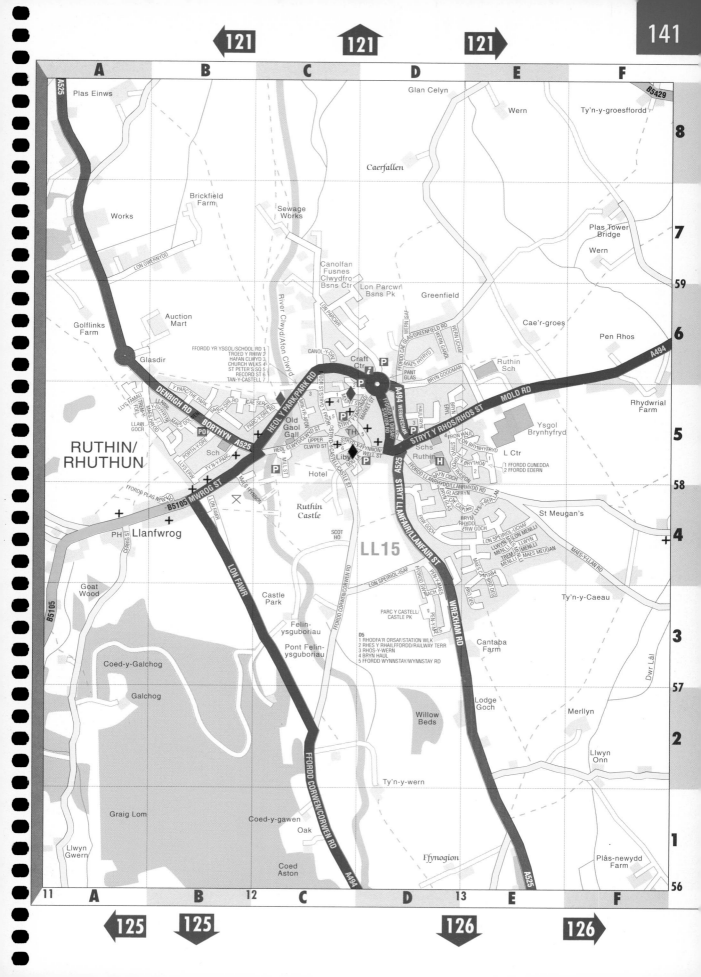

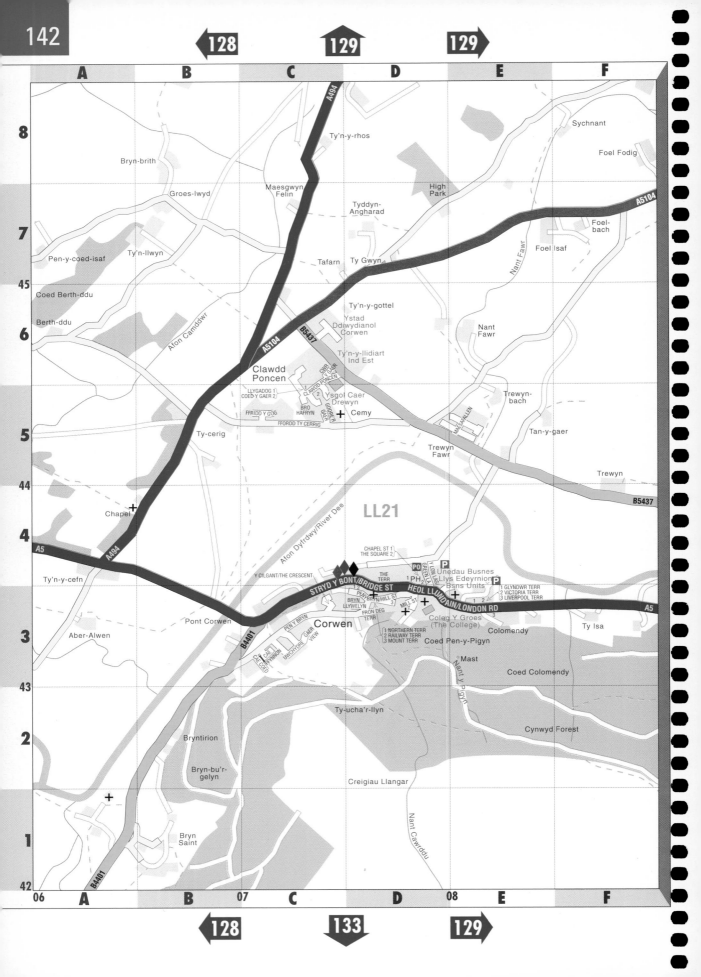

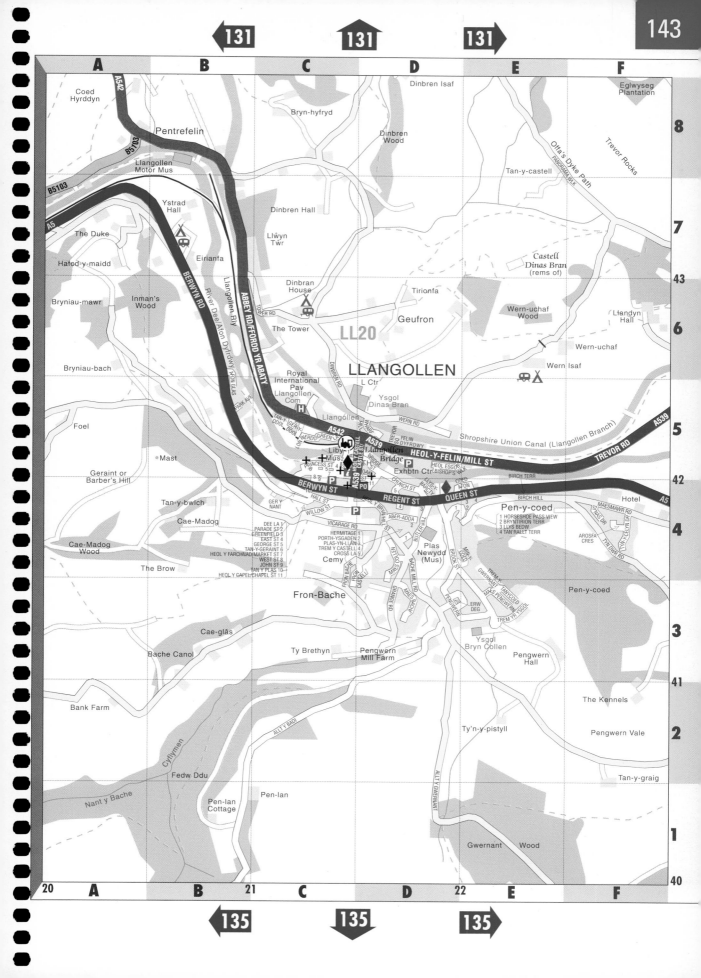

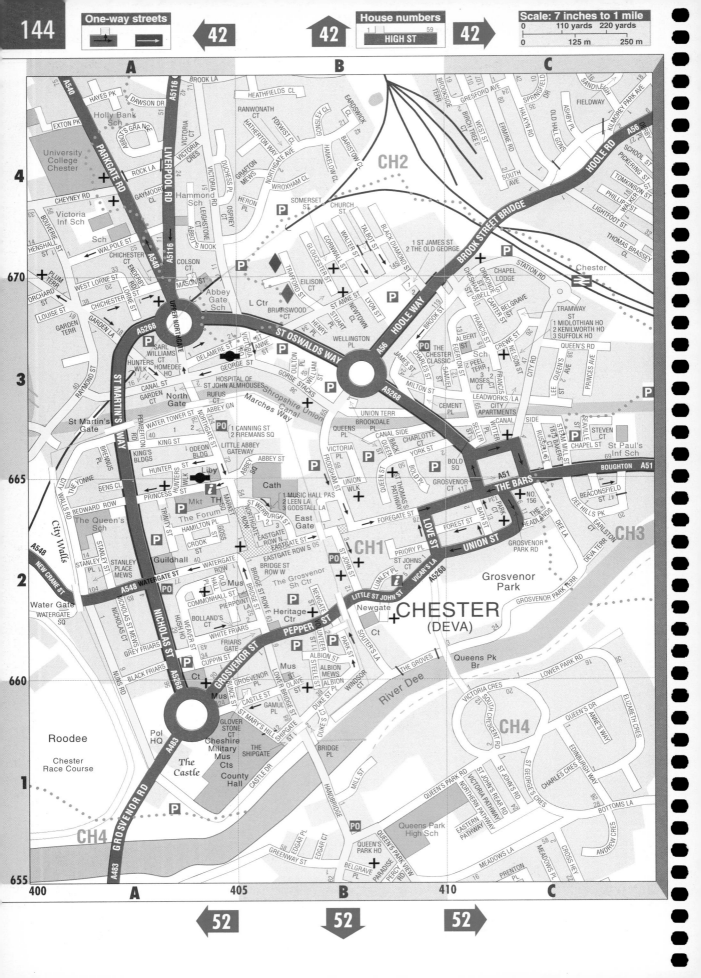

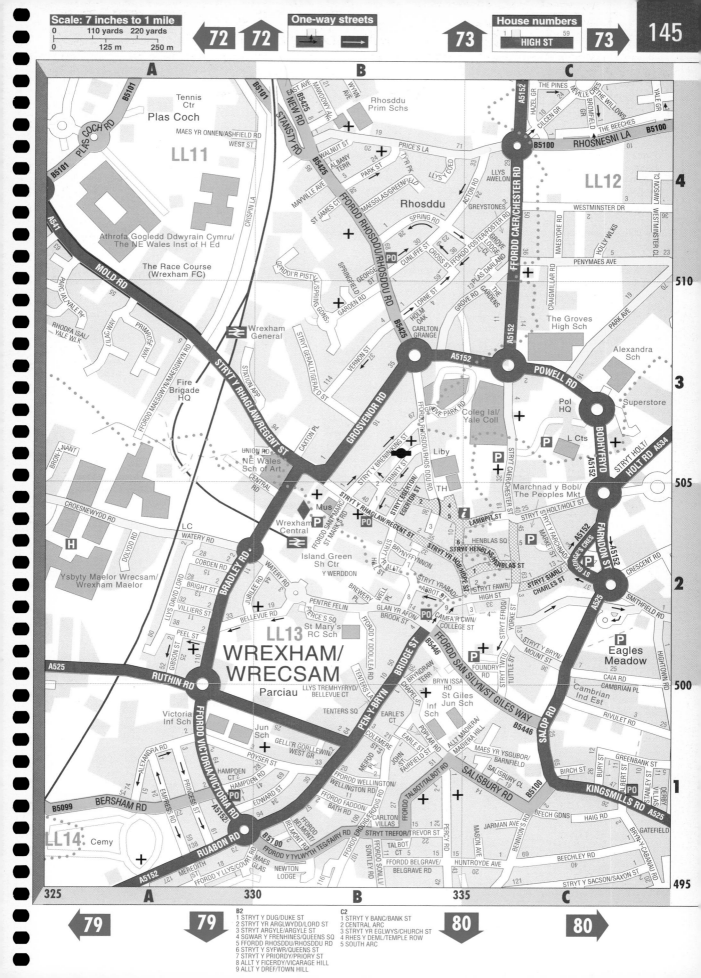

146

Index

Church Rd **6** Beckenham BR2..........**53** C6

Place name
May be abbreviated on the map

Location number
Present when a number indicates the place's position in a crowded area of mapping

Locality, town or village
Shown when more than one place has the same name

Postcode district
District for the indexed place

Page and grid square
Page number and grid reference for the standard mapping

Public and commercial buildings are highlighted in **magenta**   **Places of interest** are highlighted in **blue** with a star★

Abbreviations used in the index

Acad	Academy	Comm	Common	Gd	Ground	L	Leisure	Prom	Prom
App	Approach	Cott	Cottage	Gdn	Garden	La	Lane	Rd	Road
Arc	Arcade	Cres	Crescent	Gn	Green	Liby	Library	Recn	Recreation
Ave	Avenue	Cswy	Causeway	Gr	Grove	Mdw	Meadow	Ret	Retail
Bglw	Bungalow	Ct	Court	H	Hall	Meml	Memorial	Sh	Shopping
Bldg	Building	Ctr	Centre	Ho	House	Mkt	Market	Sq	Square
Bsns, Bus	Business	Ctry	Country	Hospl	Hospital	Mus	Museum	St	Street
Bvd	Boulevard	Cty	County	HQ	Headquarters	Orch	Orchard	Sta	Station
Cath	Cathedral	Dr	Drive	Hts	Heights	Pal	Palace	Terr	Terrace
Cir	Circus	Dro	Drove	Ind	Industrial	Par	Parade	TH	Town Hall
Cl	Close	Ed	Education	Inst	Institute	Pas	Passage	Univ	University
Cnr	Corner	Emb	Embankment	Int	International	Pk	Park	Wk, Wlk	Walk
Coll	College	Est	Estate	Intc	Interchange	Pl	Place	Wr	Water
Com	Community	Ex	Exhibition	Junc	Junction	Prec	Precinct	Yd	Yard

Translations Welsh – English

Aber	Estuary, confluence	Cwrt	Court	Maes	Open area, field, square	Rhodfa	Avenue
Afon	River	Dinas	City			Sgwar	Square
Amgueddfa	Museum	Dôl	Meadow	Môr	Sea	Stryd	Street
Bro	Area, district	Eglwys	Church	Mynydd	Mountain	Swyddfa post	Post office
Bryn	Hill	Felin	Mill	Oriel	Gallery	Tref, Tre	Town
Cae	Field	Fferm	Farm	Parc	Park	Tŷ	House
Caer	Fort	Ffordd	Road, way	Parc busnes	Business park	Uchaf	Upper
Canolfan	Centre	Gelli	Grove	Pen	Top, end	Ysbyty	Hospital
Capel	Chapel	Gerddi	Gardens	Pentref	Village	Ysgol	School
Castell	Castle	Heol	Road	Plas	Mansion, place	Ystad, stad	Estate
Cilgant	Crescent	Isaf	Lower	Pont	Bridge	Ystad ddiwydiannol	Industrial estate
Clòs	Close	Llan	Church, parish	Prifysgol	University		
Coed	Wood	Llyn	Lake	Rhaeadr	Waterfall	Ystrad	Vale
Coleg	College	Lôn	Lane	Rhes	Terrace, row		
Cwm	Valley			Rhiw	Hill, incline		

Translations English – Welsh

Avenue	Rhodfa	Estuary	Aber	Lower	Isaf	Square	Sgwâr, maes
Bridge	Pont	Farm	Fferm	Mansion	Plas	Street	Stryd
Business Park	Parc busnes	Field	Cae	Meadow	Dôl	Terrace	Rhes
Castle	Castell	Fort	Caer	Mill	Felin	Top, end	Pen
Centre	Canolfan	Gallery	Oriel	Mountain	Mynydd	Town	Tref, tre
Chapel	Capel	Gardens	Gerddi	Museum	Amgueddfa	University	Prifysgol
Church	Eglwys	Grove	Gelli	Parish	Llan, plwyf, eglwys	Upper	Uchaf
City	Dinas	Hill	Bryn, rhiw	Park	Parc	Vale	Ystrad, glyn, dyffryn
Close	Clòs	Hospital	Ysbyty	Place	Plas, maes	Valley	Cwm
College	Coleg	House	Tŷ	Post office	Swyddfa post	Village	Pentref
Court	Cwrt	Industrial estate	Ystad ddiwydiannol	River	Afon	Waterfall	Rhaeadr
Crescent	Cilgant	Lake	Llyn	Road	Heol	Way	Ffordd
District	Bro	Lane	Lôn	School	Ysgol	Wood	Coed
Estate	Ystad, stad			Sea	Môr		

Index of localities, towns and villages

A

Abbot's Meads 42 B4
Abermorddu 66 B6
Aber-oer 78 D7
Acrefair 85 A3
Acton 73 C4
Afon Eitha 85 D7
Afon-gôch 10 E5
Afon-wen 24 C4
Aldford 62 F3
Alkington 103 E3
Alltami 47 F8
Arowry 101 C3
Aston 39 B3

B

Babell 20 B1
Babylon 59 F6
Bache 42 C5
Bagillt 22 C3
Balderton 51 C1
Balmer 110 E2
Balmer Heath 110 F2
Bangor on Dee /
Bangor-is-y-coed ..89 B7
Bedwell 81 A2
Bedwlwyn 135 E3
Belgrave 61 E6
Bellan 46 A7
Bell o' th' Hill 93 C7
Bersham 79 D7
Berth-ddu 35 F7
Berthengam 10 F4
Berwyn 131 B1
Bettisfield 111 C3
Bettws Gwerfil Goch .128 D5
Big Mancot 39 D3
Blackoe 103 B3
Black Park 96 A5
Blacon 41 F3
Blaenau 64 B3
Bodelwyddan 14 E4
Bodfari 23 A1
Bont-newydd 116 E5
Borras 73 E4
Boughton 43 A2
Boughton Heath 53 A8
Bowling Bank 82 B6
Bradley 72 F8
Bradley Green 93 A8
Breaden Heath 110 E6
Bretton 50 E4
Bridge End 66 C7
Broadoak 61 A2
Bronington 102 A3
Bronygarth 104 F7
Brooklands 93 E1
Broughton 50 B4
Brymbo 71 F8
Bryn Common 64 F5
Bryneglwys 130 C6
Brynford 20 F1
Bryn-goleu 24 F1
Bryngwyn 71 C4
Brynhovah Bank 88 F4
Bryn-Merllyn 22 C3
Bryn Offa 79 E8
Brynore 108 A4
Bryn-Pen-y-lan 87 A1
Brynteg 72 A6
Bryn-y-baal 47 D6
Bryn-y-cochin 108 B4
Bryn yr Eithin 24 C2
Bryn-yr-Eos 95 D5
Buckley / Bwcle 48 B6
Buckley Mountain 48 A6
Burntwood Pentre 48 E6
Burton 67 F7
Burton Green 60 D1
Bwlchgwyn 70 F8
Bylchau 119 A5

C

Cadney Bank 111 C2
Cadole 45 F2
Cadwst 132 D2
Caego 72 D3
Caer-Estyn 66 D8
Caergwrle 66 A6
Caerwys 24 B6
Calcoed 20 D2
Caldecott Green 76 C4
Carmel 20 D5

Carrog 129 F2
Castletown 76 C3
Cefn 35 B1
Cefn Berain 116 C4
Cefn-brith 122 F1
Cefn-bychan 95 B8
Cefn Canol 139 E6
Cefn-côch 137 E1
Cefn-mawr 85 C1
Celyn-Mali 34 F1
Chemistry 103 E7
Chester 144 B2
Chirk Bank 105 E6
Chirk Green 95 E2
Chirk / Y Waun 105 E8
Christleton 53 F8
Churton 69 E5
Cilcain 44 F7
Clawdd-newydd 125 C3
Clawdd Poncen 142 C6
Clocaenog 125 C5
Cloy 89 B3
Cock Bank 87 E8
Coed Efa 72 B4
Coedpoeth 71 D3
Coed Talon 57 F2
Connah's Quay 38 F6
Corwen 142 C3
Coton 113 F1
Cotonwood 113 F5
Craignant 104 D3
Crewe-by-Farndon 76 A7
Croes Eneurys 73 A4
Croes-wian 24 A8
Cross 109 A6
Cross Lanes 81 D2
Cuckoo's Nest 61 E5
Cumber's Bank 100 F3
Curzon Park 52 B7
Cwm 17 B7
Cyffylliog 124 F8
Cymau 65 F4
Cynwyd 132 F4

D

Darland 68 D3
Ddol CH7 ....24 D8
Ddol LL14 ....79 C7
Denbigh / Dinbych 140 D2
Derwen 125 B1
Dinmael 128 A4
Dobs Hill 49 A4
Dobson's Bridge 112 D2
Dodleston 61 B7
Dolphin 26 D8
Dolywern 135 E4
Dre-gôch 32 C5
Druid 128 E2
Drury 48 F5
Drury Lane 91 D1
Dudleston 97 D1
Dudleston Heath
(Criftins) 108 B6
Dyserth 8 E3

E

Eagles Meadow 145 C2
Eccleston 52 E1
Efenechtyd 125 F6
Eglwys Cross 101 E6
Eglwyseg 131 D6
Ellesmere 109 A2
Elson 108 F4
Erbistock 97 F8
Eryrys 127 C8
Ewloe 38 F1
Ewloe Green 38 F7
Eyton 87 D6

F

Farndon 69 F2
Felin Puleston 79 F7
Fenn's Bank 102 F3
Ffos-y-go 66 B1
Ffrith 65 D3
Ffynnongroyw 5 C1
Flint Mountain 28 A1
Flint / Y Fflint 28 C6
Flookersbrook 42 E4
Foryd 6 E5
Four Crosses LL11 .....70 B7
Four Crosses LL21 ....128 D1

Fron 104 F4
Fron-Bache 143 C5
Froncysyllte 95 A6
Fron-dêg 78 A7
Fron Isaf 95 A5

G

Gadlas 108 C7
Gadlys 22 A1
Garden City 39 E7
Garden Village 73 A6
Garneddwen 25 E2
Garreg 19 D8
Garth 84 D2
Gegin 71 B5
Geinas 32 B8
Gelli 11 B1
Gellifor 121 D5
Geufron 143 D6
Glan-y-don 12 D4
Glanyrafon CH7 ....45 F4
Glan-yr-afon CH8 ....10 F8
Glan-yr-afon LL21 ....128 C1
Glasdir 5 B1
Glasfryn 122 E1
Glyn Ceiriog 135 C5
Glyndyfrdwy 130 C1
Glynmorlas 106 C8
Golftyn 38 D8
Gorsedd 20 A6
Graianrhyd 63 B5
Graig 117 F2
Graig-fechan 126 C5
Gravel Hole 108 A5
Green 140 D7
Greenfield / Maes-Glas 21 D7
Greenhill Bank 108 C5
Gresford 67 E1
Grindley Brook 93 C3
Groes 119 D7
Groesffordd Marli 116 D8
Gronant 4 A3
Guilden Sutton 43 E5
Gwaenysgor 9 D7
Gwernaffield / Y-Waun .45 E5
Gwernymynydd 46 B2
Gwersyllt 72 E7
Gwersyllt Hill 72 C7
Gwespyr 4 D3
Gwibnant 12 D3
Gwyddelwern 129 B5
Gwynfryn 70 D5
Gyfelia 86 F7

H

Halkyn / Helygain 26 C1
Hall Green 102 D8
Halton 96 A4
Hampton Bank 111 A2
Hampton Wood 110 B8
Handbridge 52 E7
Hanmer 101 B4
Hawarden / Penarlâg .49 C8
Hendre 35 C4
Hendrerwydd 121 C6
Henllan 116 F3
Higher Kinnerton 59 F7
Higher Shotton 39 A3
Higher Wych 92 D4
Hightown 80 C7
Hollinwood 113 C5
Holt 69 D1
Holway 20 F5
Holywell / Treffynnon .21 A6
Honkley 60 C3
Hoole 43 A3
Hoole Bank 43 C7
Hoole Park 42 F3
Hope / Yr Hôb 59 C2
Horseman's Green 100 F1
Huntington 53 A5

I

Ifton Heath 106 F7
Isycoed 75 C1

J

Johnstown 79 B2

K

Kelsterton 29 B2
King's Mills 80 D7
Kinmel Bay / Bae Cinmel 6 D6
Kinnerton Green 60 B7
Knolton 98 D2
Knolton Bryn 98 C3

L

Lache 51 F5
Lane End 48 D4
Lavister 61 C1
Lawnt 140 A1
Leadmill 47 A5
Leeswood / Coedllai 58 A4
Lightwood Green 98 F6
Little Acton 73 B6
Little Arowry 101 B6
Little Green 102 A6
Little Mancot 48 F3
Little Mountain 48 A6
Little Overton 98 D7
Littleton 43 E1
Lixwm / Licswm 25 D3
Llanarmon Dyffryn
Ceiriog 138 D7
Llanarmon-Yn-Ial 127 A7
Llanasa 10 C8
Llanbedr Dyffryn Clwyd 121 F2
Llandegla 127 B3
Llandrillo 132 D3
Llandynan 131 B3
Llandyrnog 121 B8
Llanelidan 125 E1
Llanfair Dyffryn Clwyd .126 B6
Llanferres 55 B6
Llanfwrog 141 A4
Llanfynydd 65 B6
Llangollen 143 D6
Llangwyfan 33 A1
Llangynhafal 121 E6
Llangynog 136 E1
Llannefydd 116 B5
Llannerch-y-môr 12 F3
Llanrhaeadr 120 E6
Llanrhaeadr-ym-
Mochnant 138 A1
Llansannan 118 C8
Llansilin 139 C3
Llanynys 121 5
Llan-y-pwll 74 C4
Llawndy 4 F4
Llawnt 114 C2
Llawr Betws 128 B1
Llay 66 F4
Lloc 19 E6
Llong 47 E2
Llwyneinion 78 D3
Llwynmawr 135 E3
Llwyn-Onn 80 F7
Llyn-y-pandy 45 E8
Loggerheads 45 D1
Lower Kinnerton 50 D1
Lower Mountain 59 C4
Lower Threapwood 90 F6
Lower Wych 92 B6

M

Maerdy 128 B3
Maeshafn 55 E7
Maes Maelor 70 B7
Maes Pennant 12 C4
Mancot Royal 39 E2
Marchwiel 80 E4
Mardy 105 C1
Marford 68 A4
Marian 10 B4
Meliden / Gallt Melyd .8 E7
Melin-y-Wig 128 E7
Mickle Trafford 43 E8
Milwr 21 C1
Minera 71 A4
Moel-y-crio 35 D8
Mold / Yr Wyddgrug .46 F4
Morfa Rhuddlan 6 A1
Morfydd 129 F4
Moss 72 A8
Mostyn 12 B5
Mount Pleasant 27 E4
Mwdwl-eithin 20 D5
Mwynbwll 35 B2
Mynydd Isa 47 C6

N

Naid-y-march 20 C3
Nannerch 34 C8
Nant 104 F2
Nantglyn 119 D5
Nefod 106 B5
Nercwys 56 F6
Newbridge 95 D8
New Brighton CH7 ....47 C8
New Brighton LL11 ....71 A2
New Broughton 72 C4
New Marton 107 C2
Newnes 108 E1
New Rhosrobin 72 F7
Newton CH2 ....42 F5
Newton SY12 ....110 A1
Northop Hall 38 B4
Northop / Llan-eurgain 37 B5
Northwood 115 C7

O

Oakenholt 28 E3
Ochr Hen-fache 137 F2
Oldcastle Heath 91 F8
Old Hardwick 108 B1
Old Marton 107 E1
Old Rhosrobin 72 F6
Onen-fechan 78 B4
Oteley 109 E2
Overton Bridge 87 F2
Overton / Owrtyn 98 D8

P

Padeswood 48 A1
Painters Green 102 E7
Pandy LL11 ....73 A7
Pandy LL13 ....90 A3
Pandy LL20 ....135 B2
Pant CH8 ....19 E1
Pant LL12 ....67 E3
Pant LL14 ....85 E8
Pantasaph 20 C4
Pant-y-ffordd 64 A7
Pantymwyn 45 C6
Pant y Wacco 19 E6
Park Lane 100 A4
Pencraig 136 E2
Pen-ffordd-llan 19 C7
Pen-Goch Hill 28 A6
Penley 99 F5
Pennant 132 D1
Pennant Melangell 136 C1
Pen Rhewl 16 A1
Pen-rhos 71 D7
Pentre CH5 ....39 D4
Pentre CH7 ....43 F6
Pentre CH7 ....57 A3
Pentre LL11 ....70 F4
Pentre LL14 ....95 D6
Pentre LL14 ....96 C8
Pentre LL20 ....134 B1
Pentre SY11 ....106 E8
Pentre-bâch 56 D8
Pentre Broughton 72 A7
Pentre Bychan 79 A3
Pentre-celyn 126 C4
Pentre Cilgwyn 135 D3
Pentre-coed 107 E8
Pentre-dwr 131 B5
Pentrefelin 143 B8
Pentre Ffwrndan 28 D5
Pentre Halkyn 26 D6
Pentre Llanrhaeadr 120 F5
Pentre-llyn-cymmer 123 D3
Pentre Maelor 81 C7
Pentre-newydd 104 F6
Pen-Uchar Plwyf 25 F5
Pen-y-bryn LL14 ....84 F5
Pen-y-Bryn SY11 ....96 E2
Penycae 85 B7
Pen-y-cefn 18 E3
Pen-y-coed 143 E4
Pen-y-Felin 34 A8
Penyffordd CH4 ....59 A7
Pen-y-ffordd CH8 ....11 E8
Pen-y-graig 94 F6
Pen-y-maes 21 D5
Penymynydd 49 B2
Pen yr Henblas 26 B6
Pen-y-stryt 127 B2
Picton 5 A1
Piper's Ash 43 C4
Pistyll Rhaeadr 137 B4

Plas Coch 145 A4
Plas Madoc 85 D3
Platt Lane 113 B5
Ponciau 78 F3
Pontblyddyn 58 B6
Pont-Cysyllte 85 A1
Pontfadog 135 E5
Pont-Faen 105 B6
Pont-y-blew 96 C1
Pontybodkin 58 A3
Pont-Ystrad 120 C7
Poulton 62 B2
Preesgweene 105 F5
Preeshenlle 106 B2
Prenbrigog 47 F5
Prestatyn 3 C4
Prion 120 C5
Puddington 30 F8
Pulford 61 C3
Pwll-clai 26 B8
Pwll-glâs CH7 ....45 E6
Pwll-glâs LL15 ....125 F5

Q
Queensferry 39 C5

R
Redbrook 102 F7
Rhes-y-cae 26 B2
Rhewl LL13 ....98 B4
Rhewl LL15 ....121 B3
Rhewl SY10 ....106 B1
Rhewl fawr 11 B8
Rhewl-Mostyn 12 A5
Rhiwlas 139 B6
Rhos CH7 ....18 F1

Rhos SY10 ....105 A4
Rhosddu 145 B4
Rhosesmor 36 B6
Rhosllanerchrugog 78 D1
Rhosnesni 73 D3
Rhosrhedyn 72 B4
Rhostyllen 79 D6
Rhoswiel 105 E5
Rhosymadoc 86 C1
Rhosymedre 85 D2
Rhuallt 17 C3
Rhuddlan 7 D2
Rhydgaled 119 C7
Rhydlydan 122 A1
Rhydtalog 63 E2
Rhyd-wen 8 A8
Rhyd-y-ceirw 63 E6
Rhydycroesau 114 A2
Rhyd-y-meudwy 126 A2
Rhydymwyn 35 F2
Rhyl / Y Rhyl 7 B8
Rhyn 106 B7
Ridleywood 73 C3
Rossett 68 B7
Roughhill 51 E1
Rowton 53 E5
Ruabon / Rhiwabon 86 B4
Ruthin / Rhuthun 141 A5

S
Saighton 53 E1
St Asaph / Llanelwy 16 C1
St George / Llansan-Siôr 14 B4
St Martin's 106 F5
St Martin's Moor 106 D4
Saith Ffynnon 20 B7
Saltney 51 D6

Sandycroft 40 B2
Sandy Lane 99 C5
Saughall 41 B8
Sealand 40 E6
Selattyn 114 F8
Shocklach 83 D7
Shocklach Green 83 C7
Shotton 39 B5
Shotwick 31 B4
Singret 67 C4
Sodylt Bank 97 C4
Sontley 80 A2
Soughton / Sychdyn 37 B2
Southsea 72 A4
Spon Green 48 D3
Stanley Green 113 C3
Street Dinas 97 A1
Street Lydan 100 C4
Stretton 76 F6
Stryt-cae-rhedyn 57 E6
Stryt-Issa 85 D8
Stryt-yr-hwch 80 B1
Summerhill 66 C1
Sydallt 66 C3

T
Tafarn-y-Gelyn 55 B8
Tai-nant 78 A2
Talacre 5 B6
Tallarn Green / Tallwrn Green 90 E5
Talwrn LL11 ....71 D4
Talwrn LL14 ....78 E4
Tanlan 5 B2
Tanlan Banks 5 A3
Tanyfron 71 E5
Tan-y-fron LL16 ....118 E7
Tarts Hill 100 C2

Tatham 85 F5
The Chequer 102 C6
The Dunks 73 C1
The Nant 71 D2
The Roe 16 A2
The Smelt 71 B3
The Wauns 72 E8
The Wern 71 B2
Threapwood 90 F7
Three Fingers 101 A8
Top Talwrn 71 C4
Top-y-rhos 57 C2
Towyn 6 B3
Trefnant 117 C5
Tregeiriog 138 F8
Trelawnyd 10 A4
Trelogan 10 F5
Tremeirchion 117 F8
Tre-Mostyn 11 A4
Trench 109 B8
Tre'r-llan 132 C4
Treuddyn 57 C1
Trevalyn 68 D6
Trevor 84 F1
Trevor Uchaf 84 A2
Two Mills 31 E8
Tynewydd 1 E4
Tyn-y-bwlch 128 A1
Tynymorfa 4 D5

U
Upper Hengoed 105 D1
Upper Threapwood 90 F7
Upper Wigginton 107 B4
Upton 42 D6
Upton Heath 42 F8

V
Vicarscross 43 E2

W
Waen 119 C5
Waen Aberwheeler 32 A7
Wallington 89 E7
Welshampton 110 D2
Welsh End 113 A4
Wepre 38 D2
Wern 105 B2
Wern-y-gaer 35 F6
Westminster Park 52 B6
Weston Rhyn 105 D4
Whelston 22 A5
Whitewell 102 D7
Whitford / Chwitffordd 11 F1
Whixall 113 B2
Wigginton 107 B4
Windmill 26 A3
Wolverley 115 E3
Woodbank 31 F6
Worthenbury 82 F1
Wrexham / Wrecsam 145 B2
Wynnville 86 B6

Y
Ysceifiog 25 A3

Index of streets, important buildings and places of interest

187 – Arr

1875 Bakers Ct CH1, CH3 ....144 C3

A
Aarons Rd LL11 ....72 C5
Abbey Cl LL13 ....74 E2
Abbey Ct
Denbigh / Dinbych LL16 ....140 E4
Greenfield / Maes-Glas CH8 ....21 C7
Abbeydale Cl / Clos Abbeydale LL13 ....73 F3
Abbey Dr LL19 ....4 C3
Abbey Farm Cvn Pk LL20 ....131 C3
Abbey Farm Mus & Visitor Ctr* CH8 ....21 C7
Abbeyford Cvn Pk LL22 ....6 A4
Abbey Gate Sch CH2 ....144 A3
Abbeygate Wlk LL13 ....89 A7
Abbey Gdns LL13 ....89 A7
Abbey Gn CH1 ....144 A3
Abbey Rd Rhuddlan LL18 ....15 F8
Wrexham / Wrecsam LL13 ....74 E1
Wrexham / Wrecsam LL13 ....81 E8
Abbey Rd / Ffordd Abaty [2] LL16 ....140 D4
Abbey Rd / Ffordd yr Abaty LL20 ....143 B6
Abbey Sq CH1 ....144 B3
Abbey St Chester CH1 ....144 B3
Rhyl / Y Rhyl LL18 ....7 A7
Abbey View Cvn Pk CH8 ....4 C4
Abbey View Trad Est CH8 ....21 D8
Abbots Cl CH6 ....22 C2
Abbots Cl CH2 ....42 C4
Abbot's Dr CH2 ....42 C4
Abbot's Grange CH2 ....144 A4
Abbots Knoll CH2 ....42 C4
Abbots Lane CP Sch CH4 ....59 A7
Abbot's Nook CH2 ....144 A4
Abbots Pk CH2 ....42 C4
Abbot St / Stryt Yrabad LL11 ....145 B2
Abbots Way LL13 ....89 A8
Abbots Wlk CH8 ....21 C5
Abbottsford Dr CH4 ....58 F7
Abbotts La CH4 ....59 A7
Abenbury Rd LL13 ....80 E7
Abenbury Way LL13 ....74 D2
Aber-Adda LL20 ....143 D4
Aber Clwyd LL18 ....6 E6
Aberconway Rd LL19 ....3 C2
Aber Cres CH7 ....37 B5
Aber Ct LL19 ....8 F8
Aberdaron Dr CH1 ....41 E3

Aberderfyn Rd
Johnstown LL14 ....79 A2
Rhosllanerchrugog LL14 ....78 F2
Abergele Rd / Ffordd Abergele LL18 ....15 B8
Aber Las CH6 ....28 B4
Aberllanerch Dr CH7 ....48 A6
Abermorddu CP Sch LL12 ....66 B6
Aber Park Ind Est CH6 ....27 F7
Aber Pk Ind Est CH6 ....28 A7
Aber Rd Flint / Y Fflint CH6 ....27 F7
Prestatyn LL19 ....3 B3
Aberteirw Cotts LL20 ....135 B2
Aber View CH5 ....38 C8
Abingdon Cres [4] CH4 ....51 F6
Abraham's La / Lon Abram [3] LL16 ....140 C3
Acacia Cl CH7 ....47 A3
Acacia Ct / Llys Acasia LL12 ....67 A5
Accar-y-Forwyn LL16 ....140 B3
Acorn Bsns Pk CH6 ....27 F7
Acorn Cl / Llys Derw CH7 ....48 E4
Acresfield Prim Sch CH2 ....42 F8
Acres La CH7 ....43 A8
Acton Gate LL11 ....73 B4
Acton Gdns LL12 ....73 C4
Acton Park Inf Sch LL12 ....73 C5
Acton Park Jun Sch LL12 ....73 C5
Acton Park Way LL12 ....73 B4
Acton Rd LL11 ....145 C4
Adder Hill CH3 ....53 B7
Adderley Bank / Glan-y-wiber [3] LL12 ....73 B7
Adelaide Rd CH1 ....41 D4
Adele Ave LL19 ....2 D2
Admiral's Wlk LL18 ....7 F1
Advance Pk CH14 ....85 C1
Adwy La LL11 ....71 E3
Adwy Wynt CH6 ....28 B4
Ael Y Bryn Brymbo LL11 ....65 E1
Denbigh / Dinbych LL16 ....140 C2
Ael Y Bryn CH7 ....46 E6
Ael-y-Bryn Nercwys CH7 ....56 E6
Wrexham / Wrecsam LL11 ....73 B5
Ael-y-Ffynnon CH8 ....21 A5
Aerial Rd LL12 ....66 F5
Afondale CH6 ....27 F6
Afoneitha Rd / Ffordd Afoneitha LL14 ....85 D7
Afon Glas LL20 ....143 B6
Afon Terr LL14 ....86 A7
Afon View CH5 ....38 C8
Afon Wen LL20 ....135 F5
Afonwen Craft and Antique Ctr* LL14 ....24 C3
Afon yr Rhos LL14 ....78 D1
Agden House La SY13 ....93 A5
Agenora CH5 ....38 C8
Ainsdale Cl CH7 ....48 A5
Ainsdale Dro LL12 ....73 E5

Airfield View CH4 ....50 B6
Air View Cvn Camp CH8 ....5 A6
Albany Terr LL11 ....145 B4
Albert Ave CH6 ....28 C5
Albert Gr LL14 ....86 B5
Albert Pl CH5 ....38 F8
Albert Rd LL16 ....140 D4
Albert's Ave LL11 ....65 E1
Albert St Chester CH1 ....144 C3
Leeswood / Coed Llai CH7 ....57 F5
Rhyl / Y Rhyl LL18 ....7 C7
Albert Terr [1] LL16 ....140 D4
Albion Mews CH1 ....144 B2
Albion Pl CH1 ....144 B1
Albion St CH1 ....144 B2
Alder Ave CH5 ....39 B3
Alderberry Rd CH5 ....48 F7
Alder Cl LL11 ....72 F8
Alder Ct LL18 ....7 F8
Alder Gr CH2 ....43 B4
Aldergrove Pl LL11 ....71 B4
Alderley Pl LL11 ....41 E6
Alderney Ho CH2 ....43 B4
Alders La SY13 ....112 D1
Aldford Rd CH2 ....42 F6
Aldford Sch CH3 ....62 F3
Aldford Way LL12 ....73 D4
Aled LL14 ....85 E4
Aled Ave LL18 ....7 C6
Aled Cres CH6 ....27 F4
Aled Gdns LL18 ....6 C5
Aled Terr LL16 ....118 C8
Aled Way CH4 ....51 D5
Alexander Ho [6] LL12 ....72 C3
Alexandra Ct / Llys Alexandra CH7 ....48 C4
Alexandra Dr LL19 ....8 E8
Alexandra Rd
Rhyl / Y Rhyl LL18 ....1 C5
Wrexham / Wrecsam LL13 ....145 A1
Alexandra Rd / Ffordd Alecsandra CH7 ....47 A4
Alexandra Sch LL12 ....145 C3
Alexandra St CH5 ....39 B6
Alkington Rd SY13 ....103 F6
Allans Cl CH5 ....39 C5
Allerton Cl CH4 ....49 B1
Allington Cres LL12 ....67 D1
Allington Dr LL13 ....73 E1
Allington Pl CH4 ....52 E7
Allitts Pk LL18 ....7 D6
All Saints' CE Inf Sch CH2 ....43 A3
All Saints Prim Sch LL12 ....67 D2
Alltami Rd Alltami CH7 ....47 F7
Buckley / Bwcle CH7 ....48 A6
Allt Bryn-Fotty CH7 ....63 C5
Allt Copperas / Copperas Hill LL14 ....85 D7
Allt Eisteddfod LL11 ....70 D5

Allt Goch
Flint / Y Fflint CH6 ....28 A6
Trefnant LL17 ....117 B6
Allt-Goch La CH6, CH7 ....28 B2
Allt Madiera / Madiera Hill LL13 ....145 B1
Allt Ty Gwyn / Vinegar Hill LL14 ....78 E3
Allt y Badi LL20 ....143 C2
Allt Y Ddol / Meadow Rise LL12 ....67 B5
Allt y Dref / Town Hill [9] LL13 ....145 B2
Allt y Ficeroy / Vicarage Hill [8] LL13 ....145 B2
Allt Y Golch CH8 ....20 D6
Allt Y Graig LL18 ....8 F5
Allt y Gwernant LL20 ....143 D1
Allt y Gwter / Gutter Hill LL14 ....78 F1
Allt-y-Plas CH8 ....26 D5
Allt Yr Eithin / Thornhill Dr LL14 ....79 E8
Allt Y Twr / Tower Hill LL14 ....85 A2
Alma Rd Froncysyllte LL20 ....94 F7
[2] Llangollen Rural LL20 ....95 A7
Alma St CH2 ....42 F2
Almond Dr [7] SY12 ....109 A2
Almond Gr LL13 ....73 D2
Almond Way LL12 ....59 B2
Almshouses [3] LL14 ....86 A4
Alpraham Cres CH4 ....42 E6
Alun Cl CH7 ....37 F4
Alun Cres CH4 ....52 A6
Alun Sch CH7 ....46 F3
Alvis Rd CH5 ....40 B3
Alwen LL11 ....85 E3
Alwen Ave CH7 ....47 E5
Alwen Dr Bagillt CH6 ....22 B3
Connah's Quay CH5 ....38 E6
Alwen Terr LL21 ....123 C3
Alwyn Cl CH7 ....46 E6
Alwyn Gdns CH2 ....42 F8
Alyn Cl LL11 ....73 B7
Alyn Cres / Cilgant Alun LL12 ....66 B7
Alyndale LL12 ....59 B4
Alyndale Ave CH7 ....47 F8
Alyndale Rd Saltney CH4 ....51 D6
Wrexham / Wrecsam LL12 ....73 B5
Alyn Dr Penyffordd CH4 ....59 A6
Rossett LL12 ....68 B7
Alyn Fields LL12 ....59 A1
Alyn Ind Est LL12 ....66 D3
Alyn Mdw CH7 ....46 F5
Alyn Pk CH5 ....48 F8
Alyn Rd CH7 ....48 A5
Alyn St CH7 ....47 A5
Alyn Terr CH7 ....58 B5

Alyn Waters Ctry Pk / Parc Gwledig Dyfroedd Alun* LL11 ....66 D1
Amanda Gr LL14 ....79 C6
Ambleside CH2 ....43 A6
Ambleside Cl CH5 ....38 C7
Ambrose Terr CH7 ....47 A4
Andrew Cres CH4 ....144 C1
Anfield Cl CH5 ....38 D4
Anglesey Cl LL12 ....73 E4
Annefield Pk / Parc Annefield LL12 ....67 E2
Anne's Way CH4 ....144 C1
Ansell Rd LL13 ....73 E4
Antelope Ind Pk CH7 ....35 F2
Anthony Eden Dr LL13 ....80 E8
Anvil Pottery* LL16 ....120 F6
Apex Ctr LL13 ....81 C6
Appleby Dr CH5 ....39 C2
Appleton Rd CH2 ....42 E6
Applewood Cl / Clos y Pren Afal LL13 ....80 B7
Appleyards La CH4 ....52 E7
Aquarium Cres LL18 ....7 A7
Aquarium St LL18 ....7 A7
Aragon Gn CH1 ....41 E6
Aran Cl CH7 ....47 E6
Aran Rd LL12 ....73 C2
Archers Gn LL19 ....2 E2
Archers Way CH1 ....42 A2
Archer's Way LL13 ....73 C2
Archimedes Ctr LL13 ....72 E2
Archway CH7 ....47 A3
Arderne Ho CH2 ....42 F7
Arenig Cl LL11 ....72 D5
Arenig Rd LL13 ....73 E1
Arfon Ave LL19 ....2 B1
Arfon Cl LL18 ....7 B6
Arfryn LL11 ....72 B4
Argoed Brymbo LL11 ....71 E8
Kinmel Bay / Bae Cinmel LL18 ....6 D3
Argoed Ave CH7 ....47 C7
Argoed High Sch / Ysgol Uwchradd Argoed CH7 ....47 E6
Argoed La LL13 ....88 C1
Argoed Rd / Ffordd Argoed CH7 ....48 B5
Argoed View CH7 ....47 C7
Argyle St / Stryt Argyle [3] LL11 ....145 B2
Argyll Ave CH4 ....52 A7
Arkle Ct [3] CH3 ....43 B2
Arley Cl CH2 ....42 F6
Arley Rd / Ffordd Arley [1] LL13 ....73 B7
Arllwyn LL11 ....70 F8
Arnhem Way CH3 ....53 B5
Arnold Gdns LL18 ....6 C5
Arnold Gr CH5 ....38 F7
Arnold's Cres CH4 ....50 A3
Arosfa Cres LL20 ....143 F4
Arradon Ct CH2 ....42 E5

Arran Dr LL18 ....7 D5
Arrowcroft Rd CH3 .....43 F5
Arthur St CH1 ....42 A2
Artillery Row LL18 .....14 E4
Ascot Dr LL18 ....7 D5
Ashbourne Ave LL11 ....72 D8
Ashburn Way LL13 .....80 D7
Ashby Pl CH2 ....144 C4
Ash Cl
  Weston Rhyn SY10 ...105 D4
  Wrexham / Wrecsam LL11 .72 C8
Ash Ct LL18 ....7 E7
Ash Dr CH7 ....48 B6
Ashfield Cres Blacon CH1 .41 D5
  Connah's Quay CH5 ...39 D2
Ashfield Rd 3 CH5 ....39 B6
Ashfield Rd / Maes yr Onnen
  LL11 ....145 A4
Ash Gr Acrefair LL14 ..85 D3
  Bagillt CH6 ....22 E1
  Chester CH4 ....52 B5
  4 Chirk / Y Waun LL14 ..95 E3
  Connah's Quay CH5 ...39 B6
  Kinmel Bay / Bae Cinmel
  LL18 ....6 D5
  Llay LL12 ....67 B4
  Mold / Yr Wyddgrug CH7 .46 E5
  Mynydd Isa CH7 .....47 E5
  Prestatyn LL19 .....3 B2
  Wrexham / Wrecsam LL13 .73 D2
Ash Grove / Llwyn Onn
  CH7 ....57 F5
Ash Hay La CH2 ....43 C8
Ash La CH5 ....39 D1
Ashlands Rd SY10 ......105 D4
Ashlar Ct CH5 ....39 C1
Ash Lawn Ct CH2 ......42 C4
Ashlea Cl CH5 ....39 D2
Ashleigh Cl CH4 ....51 E6
Ashly Ct / Cwrt Ashly
  LL17 ....16 A1
Ashmount Ent Pk CH6 ..27 F6
Ashmount Ind Ctr CH6 ..28 A7
Ashmuir Cl CH1 ....41 E3
Ash Rd (North) LL13 ...74 D1
Ash Rd S LL13 ....81 E8
Ash Rd (South) LL13 ...74 D1
Ash View Alltami CH7 ..47 F8
  Connah's Quay CH5 ...39 A4
Ashwood Ct CH2 ....43 A3
Asiatic Cotts CH5 ......40 B3
Aspen Cl CH5 ....38 D7
Aspen Ct SY10 ....105 D4
Aspen Gr
  Kinmel Bay / Bae Cinmel
  LL18 ....6 D5
  Saughall CH1 ....41 B7
Aspen Grange SY10 ....105 D4
Aspen Way CH2 ....43 B4
Aspen Wlk LL18 ....7 F8
Assembly Rd LL11 .....71 C3
Astley Ct LL18 ....6 D6
Aston Gr LL12 ....73 C2
Aston Hill CH5 ....39 A4
Aston Mead CH5 ......39 B3
Aston Park Rd
  Connah's Quay CH5 ...39 A4
  Connah's Quay CH5 ...39 A4
Aston Rd CH5 ....39 C4
Athrofa Gogledd Ddwyrain
Cymru / North East Wales
Inst of H Ed The LL11 .145 A4
Atis Croft CH6 ....28 C5
Atlea LL11 ....72 C3
Auckland Rd CH1 ......41 D4
Auden Cl CH5 ....48 E7
Audley Cres CH4 ......52 E6
Aughton Way CH4 .....50 D4
Augusta Cl CH1 ....41 D5
Augusta Dr / Rhoda Augusta
  LL13 ....73 F2
Aurelius Ho 4 LL11 ...72 D7
Austen Cl CH5 ....48 E8
Australia St / Heol Awstralia
  14 LL14 ....78 E2
Avalon Ct / Cwrt Afallon
  LL13 ....80 B7
Avenue The
  Hawarden / Penarlâg CH5 .49 C8
  Mold / Yr Wyddgrug CH7 .47 A4
  Prestatyn LL19 .....3 C2
  Prestatyn LL19 .....9 B8
Avon Cl LL12 ....73 C4
Avon Ct
  Connah's Quay CH5 ...38 D6
  Mold / Yr Wyddgrug CH7 .47 A3
Avondale Cres / Clignant
  Avondale 2 LL12 ...73 B7
Avondale Dr LL18 .....7 F7
Avondale Gr LL12 .....73 E5
Avondale Rd CH7 .....48 D4
Avonlea Cl CH4 ....51 E4
Awelfryn LL14 ....85 D7
Awelon LL22 ....6 B3
Awelon Mor LL19 .....2 F3
Awel-y-Mor CH8 ......21 D5

B

Babbage Rd CH5 ......40 A4
Bache Ave CH2 ....42 C5
Bache Dr CH2 ....42 C5
Bachefield Ave CH3 ...53 A6
Bache Hall Ct CH2 ....42 C5
Bache Hall Est CH2 ...42 C5
Bachelor's Ct CH3 ....53 A8
Bachelor's La CH3 ....53 A8

Bache Mill Rd LL20 ...143 D4
Bache Sta CH2 ....42 D5
Back Chapel St SY10 .138 A1
Back La SY14 ....90 E7
Back Queen St CH1 ..144 B3
Back Row / Lon Gefn 11
  LL16 ....140 C3
Bader Cl LL13 ....73 F5
Badgers Cl CH3 ......53 E7
Badgers Rise / Bryn-y-Broch
  CH5 ....38 D5
Bagillt Rd LL18 ......21 E7
Bailey Bridge Cl CH2 .42 D4
Bakery Fields LL11 ...72 B5
Bala Ave CH5 ....21 E7
Bala Rd LL13 ....73 E1
Ballater Cres CH3 ....43 B2
Ballerat Cl CH1 ......41 D4
Balmoral Cl
  Flint / Y Fflint CH6 ...27 E6
  Wrexham / Wrecsam LL11 .73 A4
Balmoral Gr 2 LL18 ..7 A6
Balmoral Pk CH1 .....42 B3
Balmoral Rd / Fordd
  Balmoral LL11 .....73 A4
Banastre Ave LL19 ...3 A2
Bangor Cres LL19 ....8 F8
Bangor-on-Dee race course
  ....88 D6
Bangor Rd Johnstown LL14 86 B8
  Overton / Owrtyn LL13 .88 E2
Bank Cl CH2 ....42 E5
Bank La CH7 ....48 F6
Bank Pl CH8 ....21 B4
Bank Rd CH5 ....29 D1
Bank Row CH7 ....48 D3
Banks Rd CH5 ....39 D1
Bank St LL11 ....72 A4
Bank St / Stryd y Banc 1
  LL13 ....145 C2
Bank St / Stryd y Bonc
  LL14 ....78 E2
Bank Top Ind Est SY11 .106 C5
Bank Villas CH7 .....46 F5
Bannel La
  Buckley / Bwcle CH4, CH7 .48 E3
  Penymynydd CH4, CH5 .49 A3
Baptist Row CH7 .....48 F5
Baptist St / Stryd y
  Bedyddwyr 12 LL14 ..78 E2
Baristow Cl CH2 ....144 B4
Barkby Ave LL19 ....3 B4
Barker's La
  Wrexham / Wrecsam LL12,
  LL13 ....73 D6
  Wrexham / Wrecsam LL13 .73 F6
Barker's Lane Prim Sch
  ....73 D6
Barker's Well La / Ffynnon
  Barcer LL16 ....140 C3
Barkhill Rd CH3 .....43 B3
Barley Croft CH3 ....53 A7
Barmouth Cl CH5 ....38 D7
Barnefelde La LL12 ..67 F7
Barnes Cl CH1 ......41 F6
Barnfield Cl 2 SY13 ..103 A8
Barnfield / Maes Yr Ysgubor
  LL13 ....145 C1
Barnston Ct CH3 ....69 C2
Barnwood Dr CH4 ...51 F6
Barnyard The 39 B3
Barons Cl CH6 ......28 A6
Barons Ct CH3 ......42 C4
Barons Rd LL13 .....73 C1
Barony Way CH4 ....51 E4
Barrel Well Hill CH2 .42 F1
Barretts Hill LL11 ...66 F1
Barrfield Cl 2 LL18 ..7 F2
Barrfield Rd / Fordd
  Barrfield 5 LL18 ...7 F7
Barry Rd N 9 LL18 ...7 A6
Barry Rd S LL18 ....7 A6
Bars The CH1, CH3 ..144 C2
Barter Ct LL13 ......80 C7
Barter Rd LL13 .....80 C7
Bartholomew Way CH4 .52 C6
Bartlet Ct CH5 ......39 F6
Barton Cl LL13 ......80 B6
Barton Rd CH3 .....69 F1
Basingwerk Ave CH8 .21 C8
Bastion Cl LL19 .....3 A3
Bastion Gdns LL19 ..3 A3
Bastion Rd LL19 ....3 A3
Bathfields Cres 1 SY13 103 E7
Bath St CH1 ....144 C2
Bath St / Stryd Y Baddon 3
  LL18 ....7 B8
Bay Trad Est LL18 ...6 D5
Baytree Cl SY11 ....106 F6
Beach Ave LL19 ....3 B3
Beach Cl Prestatyn LL19 .3 A4
  Talacre CH8 ....4 A5
Beach Rd E LL19 ...3 A4
Beach Rd W LL19 ..2 F4
Beacon Rd LL11 ....72 D6
Beacon Rd / Fordd y Bannau
  1 LL11 ....72 C3
Beaconsfield Rd 7 CH5 .39 A6
Beaconsfield St CH4 .144 C2
Beacon's Hill / Rhiw'r
  Bigwn LL16 ....140 C3
Beaumaris Cl CH7 ..48 C6
Beaumaris Rd CH5 ..38 C7
Beaumont Cl CH4 ...51 E6
Beaver Cl CH4 .....51 E5
Becketts La CH7 ....48 A3

Beckett's La CH3 ....53 B8
Bedford St LL18 .....7 B7
Bedford Way CH7 ...46 E5
Bedward Row CH1 ..144 A2
Bedwell Cl / Clos Bedwell
  LL14 ....86 B6
Bedwell Cres LL13 ..81 D3
Bedwell Rd LL13 ...81 C4
Bedwyr Ct / Cwrt Bedwyr
  LL13 ....80 B7
Bee Bank LL20 .....94 F7
Beech Ave Gresford LL12 .67 E2
  Rhyl / Y Rhyl LL18 ..7 D8
  Wrexham / Wrecsam LL11 .72 F8
Beech Ave / Stryt y Doctor
  ....78 E1
Beech Cl SY13 .....101 B4
Beechcroft Cl CH6 ..22 B3
Beech Dr
  18 Ellesmere SY12 ..109 A2
  Mold / Yr Wyddgrug CH7 .46 E5
Beeches The Chester CH2 .43 A6
  Ewloe CH5 ....48 F7
  Holywell / Treffynnon CH8 .21 B2
  Hope / Yr Hôb LL12 ..59 B2
  Whitchurch SY13 ....93 F1
  Wrexham / Wrecsam
  LL12 ....145 C4
Beech Gdns LL13 ...145 C1
Beech Gr Bagillt CH6 .22 E1
  Chester CH2 ....43 A3
  Ellesmere SY12 ....109 A2
  Mynydd Isa CH7 ....47 E5
Beech La LL12 .....67 F4
Beechlands LL12 ...73 C3
Beechlands Ave CH3 .43 A1
Beechley Rd LL13 ..145 C1
Beechmuir CH1 .....41 E3
Beech Rd
  Connah's Quay CH5 ..39 A3
  Drury CH7 ....48 F5
Beech St LL11 ......72 C8
Beech Terr LL14 ....86 A5
Beech Tree Ave LL11 .67 A3
Beechtree Rd / Fordd
  Ffawydden CH7 ....48 B5
Beechway CH2 .....42 C6
Beechwood Ave CH5 .38 D7
Beechwood Cl CH7 .46 E6
Beechwood Rd
  Rhyl / Y Rhyl LL18 ..1 C5
  Saltney CH4 ....51 E5
Beeston Rd
  Broughton CH4 ....50 B3
  Higher Kinnerton CH4 .60 A7
Beeston Terr LL13 ..73 E2
Beeston View CH4 ..52 E7
Belfry Cl / Clos y Clochdy
  LL13 ....73 F4
Belgrave Ave CH4 ..51 E6
Belgrave Cl CH4 ....61 A6
Belgrave Ct LL12 ...67 F3
Belgrave Inf Sch CH4 .52 B5
Belgrave Pl CH4 ...144 B1
Belgrave Rd CH3 ...53 B8
Belgrave Rd / Fordd
  Belgrave LL13 .....145 B1
Belgrave St CH1 ....144 C3
Bellard Dr CH2 .....43 A4
Bella Vista CH4 ....49 A1
Bell Ct LL13 ....80 C7
Bellevue Ct / Llys
  Tremhyfryd LL13 ...145 B1
Bellevue La CH3 ....43 E4
Bellevue Rd LL13 ...145 B2
Belle Vue Terr CH4 .59 A8
Bells Way LL13 ....80 E5
Belmont Ave CH5 ..38 F6
Belmont Ct CH7 ....48 C6
Belmont Dr CH4 ...51 C6
Belmont Rd LL13 ..145 B1
Belton Cl SY13 ....103 E7
Belton Rd SY13 ...103 E7
Belvedere Cl CH3 ..39 D5
Belvedere Dr Blacon CH1 .41 E4
  Wrexham / Wrecsam LL11 .72 E2
Belvedere The LL11 .70 E7
Benjamin Rd LL13 ..80 C8
Benllech Cl CH5 ....38 C7
Bennett's La
  Connah's Quay CH5 ..39 C1
  Higher Kinnerton CH4 .60 A7
Bennett's Rd LL13 ..72 B8
Bennett's Row CH6 ..28 D4
Bennion's Rd LL13 ..145 C1
Bently Ave LL11 ...72 D8
Benton Dr CH2 .....42 C4
Bents Rd / Fordd Bents
  LL14 ....78 F3
Berkley Dr CH4 ....52 E6
Berllan Ave LL18 ...7 E1
Berllan Cl SY10 ...105 E5
Berllan La CH8 .....4 E3
Bernard Rd LL13 ...73 C1
Bernfels Ct LL14 ...78 F2
Bernsdale Cl CH5 ..38 C7
Berse Gdns / Gerddi'r Berse
  11 LL11 ....72 C3
Berse La / Lon Berse
  Rhostyllen LL14 ...79 C8
  Wrexham / Wrecsam LL11 .72 D2
Berse Rd LL11 .....72 D2
Bersham Ent Ctr / Parc
  Menter Bersham LL14 .79 C5
Bersham Ironworks &
Heritage Ctr★ LL14 ..79 C7

Bersham Rd
  Wrexham / Wrecsam
  LL13, LL14 ....145 A1
  Wrexham / Wrecsam LL13,
  LL14 ....79 D8
  Wrexham / Wrecsam, New
  Broughton LL11 ...72 B3
Berthlog CH8 ....10 F4
Bertie Rd LL13 .....73 C1
Berwyn LL14 ....79 B1
Berwyn Ave
  Penyffordd CH4 ....59 A6
  Weston Rhyn SY10 .105 E6
Berwyn Cl Bryn-y-baal CH7 47 E6
  Buckley / Bwcle CH7 .48 C4
  Marchwiel LL13 ....80 E4
Berwyn Cres
  Kinmel Bay / Bae Cinmel
  LL18 ....6 E6
  Prestatyn LL19 ....2 E3
Berwyn Dr Marchwiel LL13 80 E5
  St. Martin's SY11 ..106 E5
Berwyn Rd LL13 ...143 B6
Berwyn St Carrog LL21 .129 F2
  Llangollen LL20 ...143 C4
  Llangynog SY10 ...136 F1
Berwyn Sta★ LL20 ..131 B2
Berwyn St / Heol-y-Berwyn
  LL21 ....132 D4
Berwyn View LL13 ..73 E1
Bethania Rd / Fordd
  Bethania LL13 .....85 B3
Bethel Pl CH5 ......38 E8
Bethesda St LL11 ...4 A4
Bettws Gwerfil Goch Sch
  LL21 ....128 D5
Betws Ave LL18 ....6 E6
Beverley Cl LL13 ..80 F7
Beverley Dr LL19 ..2 E2
Bewley Cl CH4 ....53 A7
Bickerton Dr LL11 ..72 D6
Bickleywood Dr LL13 .73 D3
Bidston Cl CH2 ....42 D5
Bieston Cl LL13 ...73 D6
Bilberry Cl CH4 ...49 A1
Birch Cl CH7 ......48 C4
Birch Croft CH5 ...39 E2
Birch Cl 6 CH5 ...38 D8
Birch Ct / Llys Bedw
  CH7 ....57 F5
Birch Dr LL12 .....67 F2
Birches The CH4 ..50 B3
Birchfield Cres CH5 .39 B3
Birch Gr Prestatyn LL19 .9 B8
  Rhyl / Y Rhyl LL18 ..7 F8
Birch Heath La CH3 .53 F8
Birch Hill LL20 ...143 E4
Birch La
  Maelor South LL13 .99 D8
  Overton / Owrtyn LL13 .89 C1
Birchmuir CH1 .....41 E3
Birch Rd Chester CH4 .51 F5
  Ellesmere SY12 ...109 C2
Birch Ridge CH6 ...27 E5
Birch Rise CH2 ....42 D6
  Connah's Quay CH5 .39 B1
Birch St LL13 .....145 C1
Birch Terr LL20 ...143 C1
Birch Tree Ct LL11 .72 B5
Birch Tree Cl CH2 ..144 C4
Birchwood CH7 ...79 D7
Birkdale Ave CH7 .48 A5
Birkdale Rd LL13 ..73 F4
Bishops' Blue Coat CE High
  Sch The CH3 .....53 A7
Bishops Cl CH4 ...50 C4
Bishopsfield Ct CH2 .42 F3
Bishops Gate CH2 ..43 A3
Bishop St CH2 .....42 F3
Bishops Wlk LL17 ..16 B1
Bishop's Wlk / Heol Esgob
  LL20 ....143 D5
Bishopswood Rd LL19 .9 B8
Bistre Ave CH7 ....48 B4
Bistre Cl CH7 .....48 A5
Black Brook CH7 ..37 A1
Blackbrook Ave CH5 .39 C2
Blackbrook Dr / Lon
  Blackwood LL14 ...86 B5
Black Diamond St CH1 .144 B4
Blacklane Rd LL13 ..72 A8
Blackley Hall LL12 ..67 A1
Blackthorn Cl
  Broughton CH4 ....50 B3
  Huntington CH3 ...53 A5
  Marford LL12 ......67 F2
Blackwood Rd LL20 .84 C3
Blacon Ave CH1 ...42 A5
Blacon Hall Jun Sch CH1 41 E5
Blacon High Sch CH1 .41 E5
Blacon Inf Sch CH1 ..41 E5
Blacon Point Rd CH1 .41 E3
Blaencoed CH8 ....21 C2
Blaen Wern
  Denbigh / Dinbych LL16 .140 F2
  Gwernymynydd CH7 .46 B2
Blaen-y-Coed LL16 ..140 B3
Blake Cl CH7 ......41 F6
Blantern Rd CH4 ...60 C7
Blantern Way LL13 ..73 E4
Blast Rd LL11 .....71 E8
Blenheim Cl CH5 ..39 A1
Blenheim Ho CH1 ..42 B3
Blessed Edward Jones RC
  Sch LL18 ....7 D6

Bluebell Cl CH3 ....53 B6
Blue Bell Est LL11 ..73 B7
Blue Bell La LL11, LL12 ..73 B7
Bodafon LL16 ......120 F5
Bodannerch Dr LL18 ..7 C8
Bodawen LL15 .....121 D5
Bodelwyddan Ave LL18 .6 E5
Bodelwyddan Castle★
  LL22 ....14 F2
Bodfari Prim Sch LL16 .23 A1
Bodfari Rd LL16 ...117 D5
Bodfor St / Stryd Bodfor 7
  LL18 ....7 B7
Bod Hamer LL18 ...14 A7
Bodhyfryd Mostyn CH8 .12 B4
  Wrexham / Wrecsam
  LL12, LL13 ....145 C3
Bod Idris LL11 .....71 E8
Bod Llewelyn LL18 .7 F6
Bodlondeb CH6 ....28 B4
Bodlyn LL14 ....85 D4
Bod Nant 4 LL16 ..140 B3
Bodnant Ave LL19 ..3 C3
Bodnant Gr CH5 ...38 D6
Bodnant Inf Sch LL19 .3 B3
Bodnant Jun Sch LL19 .3 B3
Bod Offa Dr CH7 ...47 F4
Bodrhyddan Ave / Rhodfa
  Bodrhyddan LL18 ..7 F7
Bodrhyddan Hall★ LL18 .8 D2
Bodtegwel Terr LL22 .14 A6
Bodwyn Pk / Parc Bodwyn
  LL12 ....67 E2
Bodylltyn Terr LL14 .85 D2
Bold Pl CH1 ....144 B3
Bold Sq CH1 ......144 C3
Bolesworth Rd CH2 ..42 F6
Boleyn Cl CH1 .....41 E6
Bolingbroke Hts CH6 ..28 A7
Bollam Cl CH5 .....38 C8
Bolland's Ct CH1 ..144 A2
Bonc Ddu LL14 ....78 F2
Bonc Ddu / North Rd
  LL14 ....78 F2
Bonc Wen LL14 ...78 F2
Borderbrook Sch
  Drury Lane LL13 ...92 D3
  Tallarn Green / Tallwrn Green
  SY14 ....90 F5
Border Ret Pk LL13 ..73 C1
Borders Ind Pk The / Parc
  Diwydiannol Y Ffin CH4 51 C7
Border Way 43 C1
Borough Gr CH4 ...28 B6
Borras Hall La LL13 ..74 C6
Borras Park Inf Sch LL12 73 E4
Borras Park Jun Sch
  LL12 ....73 E4
Borras Park Rd LL12 ..73 E4
Borras Rd Llan-y-pwll LL13 74 C8
  Wrexham / Wrecsam, Borras
  LL13 ....73 F6
  Wrexham / Wrecsam, Rhosnesni
  LL12 ....73 D3
Borthyn LL15 .....141 B5
Borthyn Prim Sch LL15 141 B5
Boston Gate LL13 ..73 E1
Bosworth Gr LL19 ..3 C3
Bottom Rd LL11 ...72 C8
Bottoms La CH4 ...52 F8
Boughton CH3 .....42 F2
Boughton Ave LL18 ..7 D4
Boughton Hall Ave CH3 .43 A1
Boughton Hall Dr CH3 .43 A1
Boughton Heath Prim Sch
  CH3 ....43 A1
Boughton Lodge 2 CH3 .43 A1
Boulevard The
  Broughton CH4 ....50 C3
  Prestatyn LL19 ....2 C1
  Rhyl / Y Rhyl LL18 ..7 D8
Boundary La Chester CH4 .51 E6
  Threapwood CH4 ..90 E8
Bouverie St CH1 ...144 A4
Bowen's La LL11 ...85 B1
Bowers Rd LL14 ...85 A4
Bowers Villas 8 LL16 ..140 B3
Bowery The CH1 ...40 D4
Bowkers La SY13 ..102 D5
Bowlers Ct 1 CH5 ..39 B6
Box La LL12 ....73 C5
Boxmoor Ct CH4 ..52 A5
Boydell Way CH4 ..61 A6
Bracken Cl CH4 ...50 C4
Bracken Ct / Llys Rhedyn
  LL11 ....71 E2
Brackendale Rd CH5 .39 D4
Bracken Rise 3 SY12 .109 A3
Brackens The CH7 ..48 A3
Brackenwood Cl LL14 .79 D7
Bradeley Gn La SY13 ..93 F6
Bradford St CH4 ...52 D7
Bradley Farm La SY14 .93 C7
Bradley Rd LL13 ..145 A2
Bradshaw Ave CH4 ..51 B7
Braeside CH5 .....39 C2
Braeside / Ochr Y Bryn
  LL13 ....80 E7
Brae The LL19 ....9 A6
Brake Rd Brymbo LL11 ..71 D8
  Wrexham / Wrecsam LL11 .72 B8
Bramble Cl
  Buckley / Bwcle CH7 .48 C3
  Chester CH3 ......53 A7
  Marford LL12 ......67 F2

Brambles The
Connah's Quay CH5 . . . . .39 B6
5 Wrexham / Wrecsam
LL11 . . . . .72 B4
Bramley La
Higher Kinnerton CH4 . . . . .59 D7
Penymynydd CH4 . . . . . .49 E1
Bramley Way CH5 . . . . . .48 F8
Bran LL14 . . . . .85 D4
Brandie Brook LL14 . . . . .86 A8
Brandie Cotts LL14 . . . . . .85 F8
Brandon Ct 2 LL18 . . . . . .7 C8
Brandon Gr LL12 . . . . . . .68 B7
Bray Rd CH4 . . . . .51 F6
Breamar Cl CH3 . . . . .43 C3
Breck Cl LL13 . . . . .80 E4
Brecon Cl LL12 . . . . .73 E4
Breeze Hill CH5 . . . . .38 F7
Brennus Pl CH1 . . . . . . .144 A3
Brentwood Rd CH1 . . . . . .41 E5
Breton Cl CH2 . . . . .42 E5
Bretton Ct Mews CH4 . . . .50 A3
Bretton Dr CH4 . . . . .50 B3
Bretton La CH4 . . . . .50 F5
Bretton Rd CH4 . . . . .50 E4
Brewery La CH3 . . . . .69 E3
Brewery Pl LL13 . . . . . . .145 B2
Briar Cl LL13 . . . . .81 D3
Briar Dr CH7 . . . . .48 C4
Briarswood LL11 . . . . .72 F6
Briarswood Ct CH1 . . . . .144 B5
Brickbarn Cl CH7 . . . . . . .48 B5
Brickfields CH7 . . . . .43 F2
Brickfields CH7 . . . . .48 D4
Brick Kiln Gate CH7 . . . . .18 C2
Bridge Bsns Pk LL18 . . . . . .7 B6
Bridge Ct Chester CH2 . . . .43 A2
3 Wrexham / Wrecsam
LL11 . . . . .72 A4
Bridge Dr CH3 . . . . .53 D7
Bridge End Mews LL12 . . .66 C8
Bridgegate Rd LL18 . . . . . . .7 E8
Bridgeman Rd CH1 . . . . . .41 E3
Bridge Pl CH1 . . . . .144 B1
Bridge Rd LL13 . . . . .81 D7
Bridge Rd N LL13 . . . . . . .81 E8
Bridge Rd S LL13 . . . . . . .81 E8
Bridge Road / Ffordd Y Bont
LL19 . . . . .3 A3
Bridge St Chester CH1 . . .144 B2
Connah's Quay CH5 . . . . . .39 A7
21 Denbigh / Dinbych
LL16 . . . . .140 C3
Holt LL13 . . . . .69 E1
Llangollen LL20 . . . . . . .143 D5
Mold / Yr Wyddgrug CH7 . . .47 A5
Penycae LL14 . . . . .85 B7
7 Rhyl / Y Rhyl LL18 . . . . . .7 A6
Ruabon / Rhiwabon LL14 . .86 A4
Saltney CH4 . . . . .51 D7
Wrexham / Wrecsam LL13 . .72 A4
Wrexham / Wrecsam, Southsea
LL11 . . . . .72 A4
Bridge St Row E CH1 . . . .144 B2
Bridge St Row W CH1 . . .144 B2
Bridge St / Stryd Y Bont
LL21 . . . . .142 D4
Bridge St / Stryt Y Bont
LL14 . . . . .85 D8
Bridge Terr CH3 . . . . .43 B2
Bridge View CH5 . . . . . . .39 F7
Bridgewater Dr CH3 . . . . . .43 C2
Bridgewater Mews / Cwrt
Bridgewater LL13 . . . . . . .73 A7
Bridgeway Ctr The LL13 . . . .81 D7
Bridgeway E LL13 . . . . . . .81 C6
Bridgeway W LL13 . . . . . .81 C6
Brighton Rd / Ffordd
Brighton LL18 . . . . .7 C7
Brighton Terr CH6 . . . . . . .21 F6
Bright St LL13 . . . . .145 A2
Brig-Y-Don LL19 . . . . .2 D2
Brisbane Rd CH1 . . . . . . .41 C4
Bristol Cl CH1 . . . . .41 C4
Britannia Rd CH7 . . . . . . .58 A4
Broadacre Cl CH6 . . . . . . .22 C2
Broad La LL12 . . . . .68 C8
Broadmead CH3 . . . . .43 C2
Broad Oak Ave CH4 . . . . . .50 A3
Broad Oak Cl CH5 . . . . . . .38 D6
Broadoaks LL12 . . . . .68 C8
Broad St / Stryt Lydan 11
LL14 . . . . .78 E2
Broadway
Connah's Quay CH5 . . . . . .38 E6
Ewloe CH5 . . . . .38 E5
Broadway E CH2 . . . . .42 E5
Broadway The LL19 . . . . . . .2 E1
Broadway W CH2 . . . . . . .42 D5
Bro Afallon LL16 . . . . . . .140 C4
Bro Alun CH7 . . . . .46 F5
Bro Alyn CH7 . . . . .58 B5
Bro Awelon LL14 . . . . .85 B7
Bro Berllan 1 LL18 . . . . . . .7 F1
Bro Cloiori LL15 . . . . . . .125 C3
Bro Clwyd LL15 . . . . .121 C3
Bro Clywedog LL15 . . . . .121 C3
Bro-Ddewi LL20 . . . . .135 F8
Bro Deg Flint / Y Fflint CH6 27 F5
Rhyl / Y Rhyl LL18 . . . . .7 F6
Ruthin / Rhuthin LL15 . . . .141 E3
Bro Dinam LL21 . . . . .132 D4
Bro Gwerfyl LL21 . . . . . . .128 C3
Bro Gwilym
Cefn-mawr LL14 . . . . .85 B1

Bro Gwilym *continued*
Cefn-mawr LL14 . . . . .95 B8
Bro Hafryn LL21 . . . . . . .142 C5
Bro Havard LL21 . . . . .16 A1
Bro Helyg LL21 . . . . .132 D3
Bro Lleweni LL16 . . . . .32 B7
Bromfield Ave LL12 . . . . . .67 A4
Bromfield Cl CH7 . . . . . . .47 A3
Bromfield Gr LL12 . . . . . .145 C4
Bromfield La CH7 . . . . . . .47 A3
Bromfield Pk CH7 . . . . . . .47 A3
Bromfield St LL14 . . . . . . .78 F1
Bronallt Cefn-y-Bedd LL12 66 C3
Leeswood / Coedllai CH7 . . .58 A5
Bronallt LL12 . . . . .85 E7
Bron Alyn LL12 . . . . .67 B3
Bronant
Lixwm / Licswm CH8 . . . . .25 E2
Trefnant LL16 . . . . .117 C5
Bron Castell LL16 . . . . . .140 B2
Broncoed Bsns Pk CH7 . . . .47 A2
Broncoed Ind Est CH7 . . . . .46 F2
Broncoed La CH7 . . . . .46 F3
Broncoed Pk CH7 . . . . . . .47 A3
Bron Deg 8 F2
Brondyffryn LL17 . . . . . . .117 B6
Bronhallt Est LL16 . . . . . .119 D7
Bron Haul Bagillt CH6 . . . .21 F5
Dyserth LL18 . . . . .9 A3
Rhyl / Y Rhyl LL18 . . . . . . .7 F7
Trelawnyd LL18 . . . . .9 F4
Bronington Pk SY13 . . . . .102 B3
Bronington VA Prim,Sch
SY13 . . . . .102 B2
Bronllan LL16 . . . . .116 F3
Bron Llwyn CH6 . . . . .28 B4
Bronte Gr CH5 . . . . .48 E8
Bronwen Ave LL18 . . . . . . .6 D5
Bronwylfa Rd
Rhostyllen LL14 . . . . .79 A6
Wrexham / Wrecsam LL14 . .78 F5
Bronwylfa Sq LL17 . . . . . .16 B1
Bron-y-clwyd LL15 . . . . . .126 B6
Bron-y-Coed LL13 . . . . . . .80 A6
Bron-y-Crest 1 LL16 . . . . .140 B3
Bron-y-Dre LL13 . . . . .79 F7
Bron Y Gamlas LL20 . . . . . .85 A1
Bronygarth Rd SY10 . . . . .105 C4
Bron Y Nant CH7 . . . . . . .47 A4
Bron-y-nant LL13 . . . . . . .145 A3
Bron-yr-Efail LL12 . . . . . . .73 B6
Bron-yr-Eglwys CH7 . . . . .47 C5
Bron-y-Wern CH6 . . . . . . .22 C2
Brook Ave / Rhodfa Nant
LL22 . . . . .6 B2
Brook Cl LL13 . . . . .80 E6
Brook Ct CH1 . . . . .42 B3
Brookdale Ave
Connah's Quay CH5 . . . . . .38 C6
Flint / Y Fflint CH6 . . . . . .27 F5
Brookdale Pl CH1 . . . . . .144 B3
Brookdale Rd LL18 . . . . . . .7 D7
Brooke Ave CH2 . . . . .42 F8
Brooke Cl CH5 . . . . .48 E8
Brookes Ave
Broughton CH4 . . . . .50 B3
Rhyl / Y Rhyl LL18 . . . . . . .7 B5
Brookfield LL13 . . . . .103 E8
Brookfield Cl SY10 . . . . . .105 D4
Brookfield Dr CH2 . . . . . . .42 E4
Brookfields SY10 . . . . . . .105 C4
Brookhill Way CH7 . . . . . .48 B7
Brook La Broughton CH5 . . .50 C7
Chester CH2 . . . . .42 E4
Hanmer SY13 . . . . .100 F5
Brooklands Camp LL18 . . . . .2 B1
Brookleigh Ave CH5 . . . . . .39 D2
Brook Park Ave LL19 . . . . . .3 B3
Brook Rd CH5 . . . . .39 A6
Brookside Chester CH3 . . . .53 A8
Garden City CH5 . . . . .39 E7
Northop Hall CH7 . . . . . . .37 F4
Brookside Cres CH7 . . . . . .37 F4
Brookside Terr CH2 . . . . .144 C4
Brook St
Buckley / Bwcle CH7 . . . . .48 D4
Chester CH1 . . . . .144 B3
Llanarmon-yn-Ial CH7 . . . .127 B7
Llangollen LL20 . . . . .143 D4
Northop / Llan-eurgain CH7 37 A5
Rhosymedre LL14 . . . . . . .85 D2
Brook St / Glan Yr Afon
LL13 . . . . .145 B2
Brook St / Heol-yr-Afon
LL14 . . . . .78 D1
Brook St / Heol yr Afon
LL14 . . . . .78 E1
Brook Street Bridge
CH1, CH2 . . . . .144 C4
Brook St / Stryd-y-Nant 21
CH7 . . . . .46 F4
Brook Terr CH7 . . . . .46 E5
Broomfield Ind Est CH7 . . . .47 A3
Broom Gr LL13 . . . . .73 D2
Broomhill La / Lon Brombil
15 LL16 . . . . .140 C3
Broughton Cres SY14 . . . . .83 A1
Broughton Hall Rd CH4 . . .50 C4
Broughton Inf Sch CH4 . . . .50 C4
Broughton Jun Sch CH4 . . . .50 C4
Broughton Mills Rd CH4 . . .50 F6
Broughton Rd LL11 . . . . . .72 A5
Broughton Sh Pk CH4 . . . . .50 E4
Bro Wen LL14 . . . . .140 F3
Browning Cl CH1 . . . . .41 F6
Brownlow Cres 1 SY12 . . .109 B3
Brownlow Pk 2 SY12 . . . .109 B2
Brownlow Rd SY12 . . . . . .109 B2

Browns Holiday Pk LL22 . . .6 A3
Brown's La
Cefn-Mawr LL14 . . . . .85 C2
Chester CH4 . . . . .52 C7
Brow The LL11 . . . . .72 B7
Broxton Rd LL13 . . . . .73 D2
Broxton Terr 2 LL11 . . . . . .73 A5
Brunswick Rd CH7 . . . . . . .48 C4
Brunswood Ave CH6 . . . . . .27 E5
Brushwood Ave CH6 . . . . . .27 E5
Bryan Gr CH7 . . . . .47 B5
Brymau Four Est CH4 . . . . .51 D7
Brymau One Est CH4 . . . . .51 E7
Brymau Three Est CH4 . . . .51 D7
Brymau Two Est CH4 . . . . .51 E7
Brymbo Rd
Bwlchgwyn LL11 . . . . .71 C7
Tanyfron LL11 . . . . .71 E6
Bryn Aber Bagillt CH6 . . . .22 C2
Holywell / Treffynnon CH8 . .21 A5
Bryn Aelwyd Ucha CH8 . . .20 D6
Bryn Afon
Greenfield / Maes-Glas CH8 21 B7
Penycae LL14 . . . . .85 D7
Rhuddlan LL18 . . . . .7 E2
Brynafon Cl SY10 . . . . . . .106 B1
Bryn-a-Glyn LL11 . . . . . . .72 F4
Bryn Arthur LL17 . . . . . . .16 B2
Bryn Artro Ave CH7 . . . . . .55 B8
Bryn Aur Caerwys CH7 . . . .24 C7
Lloc CH8 . . . . .19 F6
Bryn Ave Johnstown LL14 . .79 A1
Kinmel Bay / Bae Cinmel
LL18 . . . . .6 E6
Rhyl / Y Rhyl LL18 . . . . .7 E8
Bryn Awel Gwaenysgor LL18 9 C7
Pentre Halkyn CH8 . . . . . .26 D6
Wrexham / Wrecsam LL11 . .72 B8
Bryn Awel Ct 1 LL11 . . . . . .72 D7
Bryn Awelon
BuckleyBuckley / Bwcle CH7 47 F4
Buckley / Bwcle CH7 . . . . .48 A4
Cyffylliog LL15 . . . . .124 F8
Eryrys CH7 . . . . .127 C8
Gronant LL19 . . . . .4 A3
Mold / Yr Wyddgrug CH7 . . .47 A6
Bryn Barns LL14 . . . . .87 A1
Bryn Barug CH7 . . . . .58 B6
Bryn Cae Pl CH5 . . . . .38 E8
Bryn-Celyn SY10 . . . . . . .139 C3
Bryn Celyn Nannerch CH7 . .34 C7
Wrexham / Wrecsam LL11 . .72 A8
Bryn Cerrig CH8 . . . . .25 D3
Bryn Clwyd CH7 . . . . .47 D6
Bryn Clyd CH7 . . . . .58 A4
Bryn Clywedog LL11 . . . . .71 C3
Bryn Coch LL15 . . . . .141 D5
Bryn Coch Cres CH7 . . . . .46 E3
Bryn Coch La / Lon Bryn
Coch CH7 . . . . .46 F3
Bryn Coch Uchaf / Upper
Bryn Coed
St Asaph / Llanelwy LL17 . .16 B2
Wrexham / Wrecsam CH7 . .72 C7
Bryn Coed Pk LL18 . . . . . . .7 E6
Bryn-Coed-Wepre CH5 . . . .38 C4
Bryn-Cres LL18 . . . . .15 F8
Bryn Ct LL19 . . . . .8 F8
Bryn Cwnin Rd LL19 . . . . . .7 F5
Bryn Dedwydd
Bodelwyddan LL18 . . . . . .14 F4
Denbigh / Dinbych LL16 . . .140 C3
Nannerch CH7 . . . . .34 D7
Bryn Derw
Cefn-y-Bedd LL12 . . . . . . .66 C3
Flint / Y Fflint CH6 . . . . . .28 B4
Bryn Derwen CH7 . . . . . . .47 E4
Bryn Deva Com Prim Sch
CH5 . . . . .38 D8
Bryn Dr CH5 . . . . .39 C2
Bryndraw Terr LL13 . . . . .145 B2
Bryn Dr / Rhodfa'r Bryn
LL11 . . . . .71 D3
Bryn Dyffryn CH8 . . . . . . .20 F6
Bryn Dyrys CH6 . . . . .22 C2
Bryn Eglwys CH6 . . . . .28 A1
Bryn Eglwys Rd LL13 . . . . .73 E1
Bryn Eitha LL14 . . . . .85 C7
Bryn Eithen CH7 . . . . .55 A7
Bryn Eithin
Connah's Quay CH5 . . . . . .38 C5
Gwernymynydd CH7 . . . . .46 A1
Pentre Halkyn CH8 . . . . . .26 D5
Bryneithin Ave LL19 . . . . . . .3 B2
Bryn Elian Gr LL18 . . . . . . .6 E3
Bryn Elwern LL21 . . . . . . .129 B5
Bryn Elwy LL17 . . . . .117 B8
Bryn Eryl
Ruthin / Rhuthin LL15 . . . .141 D5
Trevor LL20 . . . . .84 F1
Bryn Estyn Ave 1 SY13 . . .103 E8
Bryn Estyn Ct LL13 . . . . . .74 A3
Bryn Estyn Rd
Llan-y-pwll LL13 . . . . .74 B3
Wrexham / Wrecsam LL13 . .73 F3
Bryn Felin CH8 . . . . .26 D4
Brynffynnon Terr
24 Denbigh / Dinbych
LL16 . . . . .140 C3
Holywell / Treffynnon CH8 . .20 D5
Brynffynon Terr LL14 . . . . .85 B2
Brynford Prim Sch CH8 . . . .20 F1
Brynford Rd
Holywell / Treffynnon CH8 . .21 B3
Pentre Halkyn CH8 . . . . . .26 D6

Brynford St CH8 . . . . .21 B4
Bryn Garmon CH7 . . . . . . .46 F5
Bryn Garth
Bagillt / Dinbych LL16 . . . .140 A3
Pen-y-ffordd CH8 . . . . . . .11 C8
Bryn Glas
Flint / Y Fflint CH6 . . . . . .27 F4
Pentre-celyn LL15 . . . . . .126 C5
Rhosllanerchrugog LL14 . . .78 D1
Ruthin / Rhuthin LL15 . . . .141 D4
Wrexham / Wrecsam LL11 . .72 C7
Bryn Gobaith LL17 . . . . . .16 B2
Bryn Goleu LL11 . . . . .72 B5
Bryn Gollen CH7 . . . . .35 E3
Bryn Goodman LL15 . . . . .141 D6
Bryn Gr LL13 . . . . .73 E2
Bryn Gryffydd LL12 . . . . . .73 D5
Bryn Gwenfro LL11 . . . . . .71 F5
Bryn Gwyn CH6 . . . . .28 B4
Bryn-Gwyn La CH7 . . . . . . .38 A5
Bryn Hadydd Sch LL18 . . . . .7 E8
Bryn Hafod Rhuddlan LL18 . .7 F2
Wrexham / Wrecsam LL13 . .80 C8
Bryn Haul
4 Ruthin / Rhuthin LL15 . .141 D5
Wrexham / Wrecsam LL11 . .72 F7
Bryn Hedd LL11 . . . . .72 B4
Brynhedydd Bay LL18 . . . . . .1 C5
Brynhedydd Cl LL18 . . . . . . .1 C5
Brynhedydd Rd LL18 . . . . . .1 C5
Bryn Helig CH6 . . . . .28 B5
Bryn Heulog Acrefair LL14 85 B3
Cefn-Mawr LL14 . . . . .85 C2
Mold / Yr Wyddgrug CH7 . . .46 E4
Ysceifiog CH8 . . . . .25 A4
Bryn Hilyn La CH7 . . . . . . .47 A3
Brynhyfryd LL14 . . . . .79 A2
Bryn Hyfryd
Coedpoeth LL11 . . . . .71 B4
Connah's Quay CH5 . . . . . .38 C6
Dyserth LL18 . . . . .8 F3
Soughton / Sychdyn CH7 . . .37 A1
Trefnant LL16 . . . . .117 C5
Brynhyfryd Ave LL18 . . . . . .7 C7
Bryn Hyfryd / Mount
Pleasant 10 LL14 . . . . . . .78 F2
Bryn Ibod LL17 . . . . .117 D7
Brynisa Rd LL13 . . . . .72 B5
Bryn Issa Ho LL13 . . . . . .145 B2
Bryn La Hanmer SY13 . . . .100 B6
New Brighton CH7 . . . . . . .47 C7
Wrexham / Wrecsam LL13 . .74 F2
Wrexham / Wrecsam LL11 . .81 F7
Bryn Llan LL16 . . . . .120 E6
Brynllys LL19 . . . . .9 A6
Bryn-Llys 9 LL18 . . . . .7 F7
Brynllys E LL19 . . . . .9 A6
Brynllys W LL19 . . . . .9 A6
Bryn Llywelyn LL21 . . . . . .142 D3
Brynmally Pk LL11 . . . . . . .72 A8
Bryn Mawr CH7 . . . . .48 B4
Bryn Mawr Rd CH8 . . . . . .21 B5
Bryn Mor Gronant LL19 . . . .4 B3
Pen-y-ffordd CH8 . . . . . . .11 C8
Brynmor Ave LL18 . . . . .7 D6
Bryn Mor Dr CH6 . . . . .27 F5
Bryn Morfa LL18 . . . . .14 F5
Bryn Mwsogl / Moss Hill
LL11 . . . . .72 B8
Bryn Nebo LL11 . . . . .70 E7
Bryn Noddfa CH7 . . . . .46 E5
Bryn Offa Johnstown LL14 . .79 A2
Mynydd Isa CH7 . . . . .47 C4
Bryn Onnen
Denbigh / Dinbych LL16 . . .140 C3
Flint / Y Fflint CH6 . . . . . .28 B4
Bryn Parc LL19 . . . . .4 B2
Bryn Pl LL12 . . . . .67 B3
Bryn Rd Brymbo LL11 . . . . .71 E6
Buckley / Bwcle CH7 . . . . .48 A6
Connah's Quay CH5 . . . . . .38 D8
Flint / Y Fflint CH6 . . . . . .28 A5
Mynydd Isa CH7 . . . . .47 D5
Towyn LL22 . . . . .6 A4
Wrexham / Wrecsam LL11 . .72 A8
Bryn Refail LL21 . . . . .130 C6
Bryn Rhedyn LL11 . . . . . . .72 B4
Bryn Rhosyn
Pantymwyn CH7 . . . . .45 D6
St Asaph / Llanelwy LL17 . .16 A1
Bryn Rhyd CH7 . . . . .37 A5
Bryn Rodyn CH7 . . . . .47 B4
Bryn Seion LL16 . . . . .140 B3
Bryn Seion La CH7 . . . . . . .37 A1
Bryn Siriol
23 Denbigh / Dinbych
LL16 . . . . .140 C3
Flint / Y Fflint CH6 . . . . . .28 C5
Bryn Siriol / Pleasant Mount
LL11 . . . . .71 C4
Bryn St LL14 . . . . .86 A5
Bryn Stanley LL16 . . . . . . .140 B2
Bryn Tabor / Tabor Hill
LL11 . . . . .71 C3
Bryn Teg
Denbigh / Dinbych LL16 . . .140 C3
Holywell / Treffynnon CH8 . .21 D5
6 Prestatyn LL19 . . . . .3 B2
Soughton / Sychdyn CH7 . . .37 A1
Towyn LL22 . . . . .6 B3
Brynteg Cres LL11 . . . . . . .72 B5
Bryntegla LL11 . . . . .127 B3
Bryn Terr Acrefair LL14 . . . .85 B3
Ruabon / Rhiwabon LL14 . .86 A5
Bryn The CH6 . . . . .27 F5

Bryntirion CH7 . . . . .57 F6
Bryn Tirion Henllan LL16 . .116 F3
Lixwm / Licswm CH8 . . . . .25 E3
Rhewl-Mostyn CH8 . . . . . .12 B5
Bryntirion Ave
Prestatyn LL19 . . . . .3 B1
Rhyl / Y Rhyl LL18 . . . . . . .7 D8
Bryntirion Cl LL19 . . . . .3 B1
Bryntirion Dr LL19 . . . . .3 B1
Bryntirion Rd CH6 . . . . . . .22 C1
Bryntirion Terr
Denbigh / Dinbych LL16 . . .140 D4
Llangollen LL20 . . . . .143 D4
Ruabon / Rhiwabon LL14 . .86 A5
Bryn Utca LL11 . . . . .72 F6
Bryn View LL14 . . . . .86 A5
Bryn Way LL14 . . . . .86 B6
Brynwood Dr CH7 . . . . . . .48 B3
Bryn-y-Baal Rd CH7 . . . . . .47 D6
Bryn-y-Barcot LL14 . . . . . .85 C7
Bryn-y-Broch / Badgers Rise
CH5 . . . . .38 D5
Bryn-y-Cabanau Rd LL13 80 C7
Bryn-y-Coed
Holywell / Treffynnon CH8 . .21 B6
Penycae LL14 . . . . .85 C7
Brynydd LL14 . . . . .78 F2
Bryn-y-Felin Dyserth LL18 . .8 F3
Holywell / Treffynnon CH8 . .21 B6
Brynyffynnon LL11 . . . . . .145 B2
Bryn-y-Ffynnon LL11 . . . . .71 E8
Brynyffynnon Rd / Ffordd
Brynffynnon LL11 . . . . . . .85 C7
Bryn-y-Foel CH7 . . . . .36 A6
Bryn y Gaer Rd / Ffordd Bryn
y Gaer LL11 . . . . .72 B7
Bryn-y-Garn Rd / Ffordd
Bryn-y-Garn LL16 . . . . . .116 F3
Bryn-y-Grog LL13 . . . . .80 D6
Bryn-y-Grog Hill LL13 . . . . .80 D7
Bryn-y-Gwynt
Holywell / Treffynnon CH8 . .21 C5
Pentre Halkyn CH8 . . . . . .26 E5
Bryn Yorkin LL11 . . . . .66 A7
Bryn Yorkin La LL12 . . . . . .66 A7
Bryn-Yorkin Rd LL12 . . . . . .66 A6
Bryn-yr-Onnen LL11 . . . . . .72 B5
Bryn Yr Ysgol CH7 . . . . . . .57 C1
Bryn-y-Wern LL11 . . . . . . .71 C3
Buarth Coed Aeron /
Woodberry Cl LL11 . . . . . .79 E8
Buckingham Ave CH3 . . . . .43 B2
Buckingham Rd LL11 . . . . .73 A5
Buckley Ave LL18 . . . . .7 A6
Buckley Southdown Com
Prim Sch CH7 . . . . .48 A5
Buckley Sta CH7 . . . . .48 F3
Buck Rd LL13 . . . . .74 D7
Buddugfa / Victory Pl
LL12 . . . . .67 B3
Bulkeley St CH3 . . . . .43 A1
Bullcroft Cl SY14 . . . . .83 D7
Bull La CH3 . . . . .140 C3
Bumper's La CH1 . . . . .41 F1
Bunce St CH1 . . . . .144 A1
Burganey Ct CH4 . . . . .61 D2
Burgedin Terr 4 LL18 . . . . . .7 E1
Burgess Dr CH1 . . . . .41 A5
Burgess La LL13 . . . . .99 C7
Burges St CH2 . . . . .42 F3
Burkit St LL14 . . . . .79 C6
Burlington Cres LL18 . . . . . .7 D6
Burlington Dr LL19 . . . . .2 E1
Burnham Gdns LL13 . . . . . .73 E1
Burnham Rd CH4 . . . . .51 F6
Burns Cl CH5 . . . . .48 E7
Burns Dr LL18 . . . . .1 D5
Burns Way CH1 . . . . .41 E6
Burntwood Cl CH7 . . . . . . .48 C6
Burntwood Rd CH7 . . . . . . .48 C6
Burton Cl LL12 . . . . .68 A7
Burton Dr
Higher Kinnerton CH4 . . . . .59 F7
Wrexham / Wrecsam LL12 . .73 B6
Burton Hall Rd LL12 . . . . . .60 D1
Burton Rd Blacon CH1 . . . .41 E5
Rossett LL12 . . . . .67 F2
Burton Rise LL12 . . . . .67 E2
Burton Terr / Teras Burton
LL14 . . . . .85 B3
Bury St LL13 . . . . .145 C1
Bush Rd CH3 . . . . .53 E7
Butchers Row / Rhes y
Cigydd 5 LL18 . . . . .78 E1
Butcher St / Stryt y Cigydd
10 LL14 . . . . .78 E2
Butler Hill LL20 . . . . .143 D4
Butler St CH5 . . . . .39 B5
Butterbache Rd CH3 . . . . . .53 A6
Butterbur Cl CH3 . . . . .53 A6
Buttermere Cl CH5 . . . . . . .38 C7
Butterton Rd LL18 . . . . .7 A7
Buxton Ct 2 LL18 . . . . .7 B6
Buxton La CH8 . . . . .20 C4
Bwgan-Ddu La LL13 . . . . . .80 D1
Bwlchgwyn Prim Sch
LL11 . . . . .70 F7
Bwlch Oernant / Horseshoe
Pass LL20 . . . . .131 A6
Bwlch Y Ddeufryn CH7 . . . .45 E6
Bye Pass The CH3 . . . . . . .43 E2
Byre Units LL13 . . . . .72 E2
Byron Cl Blacon CH1 . . . . .41 F6
Connah's Quay CH5 . . . . . .38 D5
Ewloe CH5 . . . . .48 E8
Byron St LL18 . . . . .10 A4
Bythom Cl CH3 . . . . .53 E7
By-Way The LL14 . . . . .85 A2

C

Cable Ct CH5 38 E8
Cable St CH5 38 E8
Cader Ave LL18 6 D4
Cader Dinmael LL21 128 A3
Cadnant Ave LL19 3 B4
Cadnant Cl CH1 41 D3
Cadnant Ct CH4 50 D5
Cadnant Dr CH6 22 B3
Cadney La SY13 111 C3
Cadole Rd CH7 45 F5
Cadwalader LL18 6 E4
Cae Adar La LL11 70 F6
Cae Bach Llandrillo LL21 132 D4
Llansannan LL16 118 C8
Cae Bedw LL14 85 B3
Cae Berwyn CH7 37 B1
Cae Blodau LL18 6 D4
Cae Bracty CH7 46 F4
Cae Bryn Garth LL20 84 D2
St Asaph / Llanelwy LL17 16 B1
Cae Bychan CH6 28 B4
Cae Castan LL15 141 D4
Cae-Coch La LL14 85 C2
Cae Coed LL21 142 C3
Cae Daniel LL14 85 E8
Cae Dderwen / Oakleigh LL14 85 D7
Cae Delyn CH7 24 B7
Cae Derw
Flint / Y Fflint CH6 28 B5
Pentre Halkyn CH8 26 D6
Cae Derwen CH7 55 B6
Cae-Dyah La LL13 88 E1
Cae Eithn CH8 25 D4
Cae Fawnog CH4 59 A7
Cae Ffynnon LL21 142 C3
Cae Fron LL16 140 C4
Cae Gabriel LL14 85 D8
Cae Glas Coedpoeth LL11 71 C3
Mold / Yr Wyddgrug CH7 46 D3
Soughton / Sychdyn CH7 37 B1
Trefnant LL16 117 C5
Cae-Glo Cefn-Mawr LL14 85 C2
Wrexham / Wrecsam LL11 72 F4
Cae-Glo La LL14 85 B3
Caegoody La SY12 108 F4
Caego Terr LL11 72 C3
Cae Gruffydd LL18 7 F7
Cae-gwilym La LL14 95 B8
Cae-Gwilym La / Lon-Cae-Gwilym LL14 85 B1
Cae Gwynedd CH8 21 B7
Cae Haf CH7 38 A4
Cae Hafod LL20 135 C4
Cae Helyg CH8 26 D6
Cae Hir Flint / Y Fflint CH6 28 B5
Mold / Yr Wyddgrug CH7 46 D4
Cae Isa CH7 47 C8
Cae Isaf LL11 71 F5
Cae Llys Cl CH5 38 C5
Cae Masarn CH8 26 D5
Cae-Mefus CH8 21 A4
Cae Merfyn LL11 71 E5
Cae Mor LL22 6 A3
Cae Mynach CH7 64 C8
Cae Onner LL22 116 C8
Cae Pedr LL17 117 E7
Cae Pentre LL11 72 B6
Cae-Pen-Ty Rd LL12 66 A3
Cae Petit CH6 28 B5
Cae Plas Teg LL20 135 C4
Caer Castell LL13 75 D8
Caer Efail Bwlchgwyn LL11 70 E7
Pentre-celyn LL15 126 C5
Caer Eglwys LL14 78 E2
Caer Estyn LL12 66 E8
Cae'r Felin LL16 120 F5
Cae'r Felin / Millfields LL11 72 B3
Cae'r Ffynnon
Bagillt CH6 21 F5
Rhosesmor CH7 36 A5
Cae'r Fron CH8 21 B3
Cae'r Goenaint LL16 119 D7
Cae'r Gog CH7 45 C6
Caergwrle Sta LL12 66 B7
Caer Haf LL11 66 B1
Cae Rhug La CH7 45 E6
Cae Richard / School Rd LL14 78 D2
Caer Llan LL14 86 A4
Caerllew LL13 69 E1
Caer-Mul CH7 45 F5
Cae'r Nant LL19 3 B3
Caernarvon Cl CH5 39 B5
Caernarvon Rd LL12 73 E4
Caernarvon Terr 3 LL14 78 F2
Cae'r Odyn CH7 127 C8
Caer Onnen CH8 26 D6
Caerphilly Rd CH7 48 C6
Cae'r Rhos CH7 36 A5
Cae'r Ysgol LL20 135 C4
Caesar Ave CH6 28 C5
Cae Seren LL15 141 C5
Cae Shon LL17 117 B6
Cae Uchaf LL18 7 D8
Cae-y-Dderwen CH8 21 B7
Caia Gdns LL13 80 C8
Caia Rd LL13 145 C2
Cairndale Ave CH5 38 D7
Cairns Cres CH1 41 D4
Cairnton Cres CH8 21 D2
Caldbeck Cres CH5 38 C7
Caldecott Cres 2 SY13 103 E7
Caldlas Cl CH5 38 C4
Caldy Ave CH5 38 D6
Caldy Cl CH2 42 D5
Caldy Valley Rd CH3 53 B7
Calthorpe Dr LL19 9 B8
Camberley Cres LL12 73 C3
Camberley Dr LL12 73 C3
Cambria Ave SY12 109 A2
Cambrian Ave CH3 43 B2
Cambrian Bsns Pk CH7 47 B2
Cambrian Cl
Connah's Quay CH5 38 E7
Mold / Yr Wyddgrug CH7 47 A2
Cambrian Dr LL19 9 B8
Cambrian Ind Est LL13 145 C1
Cambrian Pl LL13 145 C1
Cambrian Rd CH1 42 B2
Cambrian Terr LL20 135 C4
Cambrian Way CH5 39 A2
Cambrian Wlk LL18 7 F5
Cambridge Rd CH2 42 F5
Cambridge Sq LL11 73 B6
Camfa'r Cwn / College St LL13 145 B2
Cam o'r Afon LL20 135 C4
Campbell Cl LL12 68 B7
Campbell St / Stryt y Cambeliaid 3 LL14 78 E2
Campion Cl CH3 53 A6
Camrose Cl CH5 38 C4
Canadian Ave CH2 43 A3
Canal Side CH1 144 C3
Canal St CH1 144 A3
Canal Wood Ind Est LL14 105 C8
Canberra Way CH1 41 D4
Canning St CH1 144 A3
Cannon Way CH4 59 F6

Canolfan = centre

Canolfan Ambrose Lloyd Ctr 15 CH7 46 F4
Canolfan Fusnes Clwydfro Bsns Ctr LL15 141 C6
Canol Y Bryn CH7 47 E6
Canol-y-Dre LL15 141 C6
Canon Dr CH6 22 C1
Canterbury Dr LL19 8 F8
Canterbury Rd CH1 41 F5
Canton Garage Ind Est CH8 21 E6
Capeland Cl CH4 51 E5
Capenhurst La CH1 31 F7
Capper's Hill LL11 72 C5
Caradoc Rd LL19 3 B3
Caradog Terr LL17 16 A1
Carden Park Way / Ffordd Carden Park 3 LL13 73 E3
Carden Rd LL11 72 B8
Cardiff Way LL19 8 F8
Cardigan Rd LL12 73 E4
Carlines Ave
Connah's Quay CH5 39 A2
Ewloe CH5 38 F2
Carlisle Ave LL18 1 E5
Carlisle Rd CH1 41 E5
Carlson Dr LL11 73 B6
Carlton Ave CH4 51 D6
Carlton Cl CH2 43 E8
Carlton Dr / Lon Carlton LL11 72 D8
Carlton Grange LL11 145 B3
Carlton Ho LL12 66 B7
Carlton Pl CH2 43 A4
Carlton Villas LL13 145 B1
Carlton Way LL18 7 E5
Carmel Cl CH1 41 D3
Carmel Rd CH8 20 C6
Carnoustie Cl / Rhodfa Carnoustie 6 LL13 73 F3
Caroline Ho CH1 41 E6
Carreg Heilin La / Ffordd Carreg Heilin LL18 8 F4
Carrick Rd CH4 52 B7
Carrog Sta★ LL21 129 F2
Carter St CH1 144 C3
Carthagena La LL12 67 E1
Cartmel Cl / Clos Cartmel 4 LL13 80 D7
Carton Rd CH7 47 D4
Cartref LL11 72 B6
Cassandra Ct 10 LL19 3 B2
Castell Alun High Sch LL12 59 B2
Castell Dinas Bran★ LL20 143 E7
Castle Cl Broughton CH4 50 B6
Pulford CH4 61 D2
Wrexham / Wrecsam LL11 73 A5
Castle Cres LL14 105 D8
Castle Croft Rd CH4 52 B5
Castle Ct LL13 75 E8
Castle Dr CH1 144 B1
Castle Dyke St CH6 28 B7
Castle Grange / Plas Y Castell LL12 66 B7
Castle Hill
Denbigh / Dinbych LL16 140 C2
Pulford CH4 61 C2
Castle Hill St CH5 39 B4
Castle La LL16 140 C2
Castlemere Cl CH4 50 A3
Castle Mews LL13 75 E8
Castle Park Ave CH5 38 C5
Castle Pk / Parc Y Castell LL15 141 D3
Castle Rd CH6 28 B7
Castle Rd / Ffordd Y Castell LL14 105 D7
Castle Rd / Heol Y Castell LL11 71 D3
Castle Rise CH5 49 D8
Castle St Caergwrle LL12 66 B7
Chester CH1 144 B1
Flint / Y Fflint CH6 28 B7
Holt LL13 75 D8
Castle St / Ffordd-y-Castell LL18 7 E1
Castle St / Heol y Castell LL20 143 D5
Castle St / Stryd-y-Castell LL15 141 C5
Castle St / Stryt y Castell 4 LL14 78 F2
Castletown La CH3 76 D2
Castletown Rd LL11 72 B7
Castle View / Golygfa'r Castell LL16 140 D4
Castle Way CH4 61 A6
Cathcart Gn CH3 43 F5
Cathedral Church of Christ & the Blessed Virgin Mary★ CH1 144 B2
Cathedral Wlk LL17 16 B1
Catheralls Ind Est CH7 48 B7
Catherine Ave LL19 2 D2
Catherine Ct CH5 50 B6
Catherine Dr CH5 39 A2
Catherine St CH1 42 B2
Catholic High Sch The CH4 52 D6
Caughall Rd CH2 42 E8
Cavalier Dr CH1 41 E6
Cavendish Cl LL12 67 F3
Cavendish Rd CH4 52 B6
Cavendish Sq LL12 73 C6
Cawdor Dr CH3 43 A2
Caxton Pl LL11 145 B3
CC Bsns Pk LL18 6 D3
Cecil St CH3 43 A1
Cedar Ave
Connah's Quay CH5 29 C1
6 Ellesmere SY12 109 A3
Garden City CH5 40 A7
Rhyl / Y Rhyl LL18 7 E7
Cedar Cl
Connah's Quay CH5 40 A7
Marford LL12 67 F2
St. Martin's SY11 106 E5
Wrexham / Wrecsam, Acton LL12 73 D5
Wrexham / Wrecsam, Bradley LL11 72 F8
Cedar Cl / Clos Cedrwydden CH7 48 B5
Cedar Ct 4 CH5 38 D8
Cedar Dr Chester CH2 43 B4
Wrexham / Wrecsam LL11 72 C8
Cedar Gdns CH5 39 A3
Cedar Gr Chester CH2 43 B4
Mold / Yr Wyddgrug CH7 46 E5
Cedar Mews CH1 41 E4
Cedar Mews / Heol y Cedrwydd LL11 72 C8
Cedar Pk CH3 43 C2
Cedars The LL15 121 D5
Cedars The / Y Cedrwydd CH7 47 E4
Cefna Cl CH5 38 C5
Cefn Berain LL16 116 C4
Cefn Bychan Rd CH7 45 C5
Cefndre LL13 80 E8
Cefndy Rd LL18 7 C6
Cefndy Road Employment Pk LL18 7 C5
Cefn La Bagillt CH6, CH8 26 F8
Bwlchgwyn LL11 70 F7
Holywell / Treffynnon CH6, CH8 21 E1
Cefn Mairwen LL17 116 E6
Cefn Parc LL14 85 C8
Cefn Rd Bwlchgwyn LL11 71 A8
Connah's Quay CH5 38 D8
Wrexham / Wrecsam LL13 81 A6
Wrexham / Wrecsam, Llwyn-Onn LL13 80 E7
Wrexham / Wrecsam, Pentre Broughton LL11 72 A7
Cefn Rd / Ffordd Cefn LL13 73 E2
Cefn-y-Bedd Sta LL12 66 C5
Cefn-y-Gwrych LL19 9 A7
Cegidog Ave LL11 65 C3
Ceg-Y-Ffordd LL19 2 D2
Ceiriog Cl LL14 105 D8
Ceiriog Jun Sch LL14 95 E1
Ceiriog Rd LL13 73 E1
Ceiriog Terrace Rd LL20 135 C5
Celandine Cl CH3 53 A7
Celmar Gr LL14 79 C6
Celtic Ind Est LL11 72 B8
Celtic St CH5 39 A7
Celyn Ave CH5 38 E7
Celyn Cl Carmel CH8 20 C6
Wrexham / Wrecsam LL11 72 D6
Celyn Cres CH4 51 D5
Celyn Dr LL12 66 A8
Celyn La CH8 20 C6
Celyn Pk CH8 20 C6
Celyn Pl LL11 71 E3
Cement Pl CH1 144 B3
Cemetery Rd / Ffordd y Fynwent LL14 78 E1
Cemetery Rd / Heol Y Fynwent LL11 71 C3
Cemlyn Cl CH1 41 E3
Centenary Rd LL13 79 E8
Central Arc 2 LL13 145 C2
Central Ave Prestatyn LL19 3 A2
Wrexham / Wrecsam LL12 73 C4
Central Dr CH5 39 B4
Central Prec CH7 48 B4
Central Rd LL13 145 A3
Central Trad Est CH4 51 E7
Ceri Ave LL19 2 D2
Cerney Rd LL11 72 A8
Cerrig St LL15 141 A4
Cestrian St CH5 38 F8
Chain Maker's Row CH4 51 E7
Challinor St CH3 43 A1
Chambers La CH7 47 D5
Chancel Dr CH6 22 C1
Chandos Cl CH4 52 E6
Chanticleer Cl LL13 73 D3
Chantry Ct CH1 41 E2
Chapel Cotts LL12 67 D2
Chapel Ct
Connah's Quay CH5 38 E8
Ruabon / Rhiwabon LL14 86 B2
1 Wrexham / Wrecsam LL11 72 A4
Chapel House La CH64 31 A7
Chapel La
Bronington SY13 102 B1
Chester CH3 43 A1
Chirk / Y Waun LL14 95 E1
Ellesmere Rural SY12 108 C5
Holt LL13 75 D8
Rossett LL12 68 C7
Saighton CH3 53 E1
Threapwood SY14 90 E8
Whixall SY4 112 B1
Woodbank CH1 31 E8
Chapel La / Lon Y Capel LL12 67 B6
Chapel Lodge CH1 144 C3
Chapel Mews
Ffynnongroyw CH8 5 D1
Wrexham / Wrecsam LL11 72 E7
Chapel Pl LL16 140 C3
Chapel Rd Prestatyn LL19 2 F3
Wrexham / Wrecsam LL11 72 C3
Chapel Row CH8 5 D1
Chapel St
3 Cefn-mawr LL14 95 D8
Chester CH3 144 C3
Connah's Quay CH5 38 E8
Corwen LL21 142 D4
Holt LL13 75 D8
Penycae LL14 85 B7
Rhosllanerchrugog LL14 78 F1
Rhostyllen LL14 79 C6
Trefnant LL16 117 C5
Trelawnyd LL18 10 A4
Wrexham / Wrecsam LL13 145 B1
Chapel St / Heol-y-Capel CH7 24 B6
Chapel St / Heol y Capel LL20 143 D4
Chapel St / Lon Swan 7 LL16 140 C3
Chapel St / Lon Y Capel 1 CH6 28 A6
Chapel St / Stryd Y Capel LL14 85 B3
Chapel St / Stryd-y-Capel
18 Mold / Yr Wyddgrug CH7 46 F4
Rhosymedre LL14 85 C2
Chapel St / Stryt y Capel LL14 78 F2
Chapel Terr Bagillt CH6 22 B3
Gronant LL19 4 B3
Leeswood / Coed Llai CH7 57 F5
Rhosllanerchrugog LL14 78 F1
Rhostyllen LL14 79 C7
Chapel View SY13 111 C3
Charles Ave LL20 84 F1
Charles Cres CH4 144 C1
Charles Dr CH6 28 B5
Charles Rd CH2 42 C8
Charles Rd / Ffordd Siarl CH7 58 A4
Charles St Chester CH1 144 B3
Chester, Hoole Park CH2 42 F3
Chirk / Y Waun LL14 95 E2
1 Johnstown LL14 79 A1
Mold / Yr Wyddgrug CH7 46 F2
Charles St / Stryt Siarl LL13 145 C2
Charleston Ave LL19 2 C1
Charlesville Rd LL18 6 E5
Charlotte Ct CH1 144 B3
Charlotte St CH1 42 B2
Charlton Ct CH2 43 A4
Charmleys La 2 CH5 39 B6
Charnell's Well / Ffynnon Charnell 2 LL16 140 C3
Charterhall Dr CH2 42 F2
Chaser Ct CH1 41 F3
Chase The CH4 59 F7
Chatsworth Cl LL19 9 B8
Chatsworth Dr
Chester CH2 43 A5
Wrexham / Wrecsam LL11 72 D6
Chatsworth Gdns / Gerddi Chatsworth LL12 73 B7
Chatsworth Ho CH1 42 B3
Chatsworth Rd LL18 7 B6
Chaucer Cl Blacon CH1 41 E6
Ewloe CH5 48 E7
Chelford Cl CH1 41 F1
Chelford Mews 4 CH3 43 B2
Chelston Ave LL13 73 D6
Cheltenham Ave LL18 7 E7
Chemistry SY13 103 D7
Chemistry La CH5 39 E4
Cheriton Cl CH5 38 C4
Cherry Cl LL19 2 B1
Cherry Dale Rd CH4 50 A3
Cherry Dr
Ellesmere SY12 109 A2
Mynydd Isa CH7 47 D6
Cherry Field / Maes Ceirios LL11 72 C4
Cherry Gdns CH3 43 A1
Cherry Grove Prim Sch CH3 43 A1
Cherry Grove Rd CH3 43 A1
Cherry Hill Dr LL12 73 E5
Cherry Orchard Rd CH4 49 E5
Cherry Orch / Y Berllan Geirios LL13 75 D8
Cherry Rd CH3 43 A1
Cherry Tree Dr SY11 106 F6
Cherry Tree Rd LL11 66 F1
Cherry Tree Wlk LL18 7 E7
Chesham St CH1 144 C3
Cheshire La CH7 48 B6
Cheshire Military Mus★ CH1 144 A1
Cheshire View
Brymbo LL11 65 D1
Chester CH4 52 E7
Wrexham / Wrecsam LL13 73 D2
Chester Aerospace Pk CH4 50 B6
Chester Ave SY13 103 E8
Chester Ave / Rhodfa Caer LL18 6 D4
Chesterbank Bsns Pk CH4 51 D7
Chester Bsns Pk CH4 52 B3
Chester Cl
Connah's Quay CH5 39 B6
Prestatyn LL19 2 F1
Chester Classic The CH1 144 B3
Chester FC (Deva Stadium) CH1 41 E1
Chester race course CH1 88 D6
Chester Rd
Broughton CH4, CH5 50 D5
Buckley / Bwcle CH7 48 E4
Churton CH3 69 F6
Connah's Quay CH6 29 A3
Gresford LL12 67 D2
Hawarden / Penarlâg CH5 49 B4
Huntington CH3 53 A6
Mold / Yr Wyddgrug CH7 47 A4
Oakenholt CH6 28 D5
Penymynydd CH4 49 B1
Rossett LL12 68 B7
Saltney CH4 51 C6
Sandycroft CH5 40 A2
Whitchurch SY13 93 E1
Whitchurch Urban SY13 93 C2
Wrexham / Wrecsam, Little Acton LL12 73 B6
Chester Rd (East)
Connah's Quay, Pentre CH5 39 E4
Connah's Quay, Queensferry CH5 39 D5
Chester Rd / Ffordd Caer
Wrexham / Wrecsam, Garden Village LL11, LL12 73 B5
Wrexham / Wrecsam LL11 145 C4
Chester Rd (West) CH5 39 B6
Chester Ret Pk CH1 42 A3
Chester St Chester CH4 51 F7
Rhyl / Y Rhyl LL18 7 C8
St Asaph / Llanelwy LL17 16 C1
Chester Sta CH1 144 C3
Chester St / Heol Caer CH6 28 B7
Chester St / Stryd Gaer CH7 46 F4
Chester St / Stryt Caer LL13 145 C3
Chesterton Ave CH5 48 E8
Chesterton Ct CH2 42 D4
Chester Toy & Doll Mus★ CH1 144 B2
Chester Way LL13 89 A7
Chester West Employment Pk CH1 41 E2
Chester Zoological Gdns★ CH2 42 D8
Chestnut Ave
Ellesmere Rural SY12 108 B6
Gwersyllt LL11 66 C1
Wrexham / Wrecsam LL12 73 C4
Chestnut Cl Chester CH2 43 A3
Flint / Y Fflint CH6 27 F5
Gresford LL12 67 E2
Soughton / Sychdyn CH7 47 A8
Whitchurch SY13 103 F6
Chestnut Cotts LL14 86 A5
Chestnut Cres CH5 48 F7
Chestnut Ct
7 Connah's Quay CH5 38 D8
Rhyl / Y Rhyl LL18 7 E8
Chestnut Ct / Cwrt Castanwydd LL11 72 C7

Chestnut Gr CH5 . . . . .39 C2
Chestnut Rd
  Mold / Yr Wyddgrug CH7 . . .46 D4
  Wrexham / Wrecsam LL11 . .72 F8
Chetwyn Ct LL12 . . . . .67 E3
Cheviot Cl LL11 . . . . .72 C6
Chevron Cl CH1 . . . . .41 E4
Chevron Hey CH1 . . . . .41 E4
Chevrons Ct / Llys Ceibren
  CH5 . . . . .39 B5
Chevrons Rd CH5 . . . . .39 C4
Chevrons Way CH5 . . . . . . .39 D6
Cheyney Rd CH1 . . . . .42 B3
Chichester Ct CH1 . . . . . .144 A3
Chichester Dr LL19 . . . . .2 F1
Chichester St CH1 . . . . . . .144 A3
Chiltern Ct Chester CH4 . . .52 B5
  Connah's Quay CH5 . . . . . .38 D6
  Wrexham / Wrecsam LL11 . .72 D6
Chirk Castle ★ LL14 . . . . . .94 F1
Chirk Castle (NT) ★ LL14 . .95 A1
Chirk Cl CH2 . . . . .42 F6
Chirk Com Hospl LL14 . . . .95 F3
Chirk Rd LL14 . . . . .105 E7
Chirk Sta LL14 . . . . .105 C8
Christina Ave LL19 . . . . .2 C1
Christleton High Sch
  CH3 . . . . .53 F7
Christleton Prim Sch
  CH3 . . . . .53 E8
Christleton Rd CH3 . . . . . .43 A1
Christleton Sports Ctr
  CH3 . . . . .53 F8
Church Ave LL13 . . . . .88 F7
Church Cl
  Buckley / Bwcle CH7 . . . . .48 C6
  Greenfield / Maes-Glas CH8 21 C8
  Northop Hall CH7 . . . . .37 F4
  St. Martin's SY11 . . . . . . .106 E5
Church College Cl CH1 . . . .42 B3
Church Cotts
  Hawarden / Penarlâg CH5 . .49 D8
  Penyffordd CH4 . . . . .59 A7
Church Croft CH4 . . . . .61 A6
Church Ct CH3 . . . . .69 E4
Church Gn LL12 . . . . .67 D3
Church Hall Cl CH1 . . . . . . .41 E4
Church Hill
  Connah's Quay CH5 . . . . . .38 E8
  5 Ellesmere SY12 . . . . . .109 C2
Churchill Cl CH5 . . . . .49 A8
Churchill Dr LL13 . . . . .73 E1
Church La Aldford CH3 . . . .62 F3
  Chester CH2 . . . . .42 D7
  Ellesmere Rural SY12 . . . .108 A6
  Ewloe CH5 . . . . .38 F3
  Farndon CH3 . . . . .69 E1
  Guilden Sutton CH3 . . . . . .43 B3
  Gwernaffield / Y-Waun CH7 .45 F6
  Hawarden / Penarlâg CH5 . .49 D8
  Mold / Yr Wyddgrug CH7 . . .46 F5
  Prestatyn LL19 . . . . .3 B2
  St. Martin's SY11 . . . . . . .106 E5
  Whixall SY13 . . . . .113 B2
Church Mdw CH7 . . . . .35 E2
Church Rd Broughton CH4 . .50 C4
  Buckley / Bwcle CH7 . . . . .48 C5
  Connah's Quay CH5 . . . . . .38 E8
  Eccleston CH4 . . . . .52 E2
  Minera LL11 . . . . .71 A4
  Northop / Llan-eurgain CH7 .37 A8
  Saughall CH1 . . . . .41 A8
  Shocklach CH3 . . . . .76 C1
  Worthenbury LL13 . . . . . . .82 F1
  Wrexham / Wrecsam, Brynteg
  LL11 . . . . .72 B5
  Wrexham / Wrecsam, Southsea
  LL11 . . . . .72 A4
Churchside Wlk CH4 . . . . . .51 F7
Church St Chester CH1 . . .144 B4
  Chirk / Y Waun LL14 . . . . .105 F6
  Connah's Quay CH5 . . . . . .29 C1
  Ellesmere SY12 . . . . .109 C2
  Farndon LL13 . . . . .69 E2
  Llangollen LL20 . . . . .143 D4
  Llangynog SY10 . . . . .136 F1
  Llanrhaeadr-ym-Mochnant
  SY10 . . . . .138 A1
  Penycae LL14 . . . . .85 B7
  Rhostyllen LL14 . . . . .79 C6
  Rhuddlan LL18 . . . . .8 C3
  Ruabon / Rhiwabon LL14 . . .86 A4
  St George / Llansan-Sior
  LL22 . . . . .14 A4
Church St / Heol-yr-Eglwys
  CH6 . . . . .A6
Church St / Stryd yr Eglwys
  LL16 . . . . .116 F2
Church St / Stryd-yr-Eglwys
  LL14 . . . . .85 C2
Church St / Stryd Yr Eglwys
  2 Rhuddlan LL18 . . . . .7 B8
  Wrexham / Wrecsam LL11 . .72 D8
Church St / Stryt y Gof 4
  LL14 . . . . .78 E1
Church St / Stryt Yr Eglws 3
  LL13 . . . . .145 C2
Church Terr CH8 . . . . .26 B2
Church View
  Bodelwyddan LL18 . . . . . .14 F4
  Brymbo LL11 . . . . .65 E1
  Connah's Quay CH5 . . . . . .39 F3
  Llangynog SY10 . . . . .136 F1
  Marchwiel LL13 . . . . .80 F4
  Wrexham / Wrecsam LL11 . .72 A7

Church View Ct LL13 . . . .80 F4
Church View / Golyfgar
  Eglwys 13 LL14 . . . . .86 A4
Church Walks LL19 . . . . . . .3 B2
Churchward Cl CH2 . . . . . .42 D4
Church Way CH1 . . . . .41 E5
Church Wlk Bagillt CH6 . . .22 C2
  Broughton CH4 . . . . .50 C5
Church Wlks
  Christleton CH3 . . . . .53 E8
  Ruthin / Rhuthin LL15 . . . .141 C5
Churton Dr LL13 . . . . .73 C2
Churton Rd Chester CH3 . .43 A2
  Farndon CH3 . . . . .69 E2
  Rhyl / Y Rhyl LL18 . . . . .7 C8
Churton St CH3 . . . . .43 A2
Chwarel Wynne Slate Mine &
  Mus ★ LL20 . . . . .135 B4
Chweched Rhodfa / Sixth
  Ave LL12 . . . . .67 A4
Cilcain Rd CH7 . . . . .45 B7
Cilcen LL11 . . . . .72 C8
Cilcen Gr LL12 . . . . .145 C4
Cilcoed LL14 . . . . .95 E3
Cilfan CH6 . . . . .27 F6
Cilgant Alun / Alyn Cres
  LL12 . . . . .66 B7
Cilgant Eglwys Wen LL18 . 15 A4
Cilgant Sant Mellion / St
  Mellion Cres 5 LL13 . . . . .73 F3
Cilgant St Andrews / St
  Andrews Cres 5 LL13 . . . .73 E3
Cilgant Yr Eithin / Gorse
  Cres LL12 . . . . .67 F2
Cilgwyn LL15 . . . . .121 C3
Cil Y Bont LL19 . . . . .3 B3
Cil Y Coed / Edge Of The
  Woods 10 LL14 . . . . .86 A4
Cinder Cl CH3 . . . . .43 F5
Cinder La CH3 . . . . .43 F5
Circle The
  Kinmel Bay / Bae Cinmel
  LL18 . . . . .6 C5
  Prestatyn LL19 . . . . .3 C2
Circular Dr Chester CH4 . . .51 F4
  Ewloe CH5 . . . . .38 E2
City Apartments CH1 . . . .144 C3
City Rd CH1 . . . . .144 C3
City Walls Rd CH1 . . . . . . .144 A2
Clair Ave CH5 . . . . .40 A3
Clappers La LL12 . . . . .67 D2
Clare Ave CH2 . . . . .43 A3
Clare Ho CH1 . . . . .41 E6
Claremont Ave CH6 . . . . . .39 F6
Claremont Cotts 2 LL11 .72 D8
Clarence Ave CH3 . . . . . . .43 B2
Clarence Rd / Ffordd
  Clarence LL11 . . . . .73 A4
Clarence St CH5 . . . . .39 A5
Clarendon Ave LL11 . . . . . .72 F4
Clarendon Cl CH4 . . . . . . .52 E6
Clarke Rd LL12 . . . . .73 D4
Clarke St / Stryt Clarke
  LL14 . . . . .78 F2
Clawdd Offa LL11 . . . . . . .79 A2
Clawdd Poncen LL21 . . . .142 C5
Clay La CH5 . . . . .39 C4
Claypit La LL12 . . . . .67 F3
Claypit Rd CH4 . . . . .52 B5
Claypits La CH3 . . . . .53 F5
Clayton Ct CH7 . . . . .46 E4
Clayton Dr LL19 . . . . .9 B8
Clayton Rd Brymbo LL11 . .71 F8
  Mold / Yr Wyddgrug CH7 . . .46 F4
  Wrexham / Wrecsam LL11 . .72 A8
Cleaver Rd CH1 . . . . .41 E4
Cledwen Dr CH7 . . . . .47 E5
Cledwen Rd CH4 . . . . .50 D5
Cleggs Cl CH3 . . . . .53 B7
Clement Dr LL18 . . . . .7 F6
Clement Ho 5 LL11 . . . . .72 C3
Cleveland Gr CH5 . . . . . . .39 E6
Cleveland St LL14 . . . . . . .86 A5
Cleves Cl CH1 . . . . .41 D6
Clifford Dr CH4 . . . . .51 F5
Clifton Ave LL18 . . . . .7 D7
Clifton Cl LL13 . . . . .80 D7
Clifton Dr CH1 . . . . .41 E3
Clifton Gr LL18 . . . . .7 D7
Clifton Park Ave CH5 . . . . .38 D8
Clifton Park Rd LL18 . . . . . .7 D8
Clifton Terr 3 LL16 . . . . .140 D4
Clignant Avondale /
  Avondale Cres 2 LL12 . .73 B7
Clive Ave LL19 . . . . .2 C2
Cliveden Rd CH4 . . . . .51 F5
Clivedon Rd CH5 . . . . .38 D6
Clocaenog Sch LL15 . . . .125 C5
Clos Abbeydale / Abbeydale
  Cl LL13 . . . . .73 F3
Clos Aberconwy LL19 . . . . .3 D2
Clos Ascot LL13 . . . . .80 F7
Clos Bedwell / Bedwell Cl
  LL14 . . . . .86 B6
Clos Bodnant LL19 . . . . . . .3 B3
Clos Cartmel / Cartmel Cl 4
  LL13 . . . . .80 D7
Clos Cedrwydden / Cedar Cl
  CH7 . . . . .48 B5
Clos Celynnen / Holly Cl
  CH7 . . . . .48 B5
Clos Coed CH5 . . . . .39 B1
Clos Coed Ywen / Yew Tree
  Cl LL14 . . . . .16 B2
Clos Deganwy LL18 . . . . . .14 F4
Clos Derw / Oak Cl LL17 . 16 B2
Clos Dinas Bran LL18 . . . .14 F4
Clos Dinbych LL18 . . . . . . .14 F4

Clos Dol-y-Coed LL19 . . . .8 E8
Clos Efrog / York Cl
  LL13 . . . . .80 F7
Close The
  Connah's Quay CH5 . . . . . .39 B1
  Greenfield / Maes-Glas CH8 21 C8
  Mold / Yr Wyddgrug CH7 . . .46 E3
  Prestatyn LL19 . . . . .3 C2
  Saughall CH1 . . . . .41 A8
Clos Ffordorddisa LL19 . . . . .3 B1
Clos Fontwell / Fontwell Cl
  LL13 . . . . .80 E7
Clos Gladstone LL18 . . . . .7 D8
Clos Glanaber / Glan Aber Cl
  LL11 . . . . .72 E6
Clos Gwaun Deau LL19 . . .2 F2
Clos Gwynant / Whitebrook
  Cl LL14 . . . . .86 B5
Clos Highgrove / Highgrove
  Cl 1 LL14 . . . . .79 C6
Clos Kelso / Kelso Cl
  LL13 . . . . .80 E7
Clos Kensington /
  Kensington Cl 3 LL14 . . . .79 C6
Clos Lincoln / Lincoln Cl 2
  LL13 . . . . .73 E4
Clos Lindisfarne /
  Lindisfarne Cl LL14 . . . . . .86 A4
Clos Lindum / Lindum Cl
  CH7 . . . . .47 C7
Clos Llywellyn LL11 . . . . . .71 C4
Clos Meadway / Meadway Cl
  LL11 . . . . .72 E8
Clos Meithrin / Nursery Cl
  LL19 . . . . .3 A2
Clos Morfudd LL11 . . . . . . .7 F6
Clos Muirfield / Muirfield Cl
  7 LL14 . . . . .73 F3
Clos Nant Emral / Emral
  Brook LL14 . . . . .86 B5
Clos Newbury / Newbury Cl
  LL13 . . . . .80 E7
Clos Pry Copyn LL19 . . . . .2 F2
Clos Ryder / Ryder Cl 2
  LL13 . . . . .73 E3
Clos Sandringham /
  Sandringham Cl 4
  LL14 . . . . .79 C6
Clos Sedgefield / Sedgefield
  Cl LL13 . . . . .80 F7
Clos Teg Fan LL18 . . . . . . .7 F6
Clos Tir Griffin / Tir Griffin
  Cl LL20 . . . . .84 E2
Clos Treftadaeth / Heritage
  Cl 2 LL14 . . . . .79 C6
Clos Woburn / Woburn Cl 6
  LL13 . . . . .73 E3
Clos-y-Berllan LL18 . . . . . .7 F2
Clos y Capel CH7 . . . . . . .48 C5
Clos y Clochdy / Belfry Cl
  LL13 . . . . .80 F7
Clos Y Criafol / Rowan Cl
  LL12 . . . . .67 A5
Clos Y Dur / Steel Cl
  LL11 . . . . .71 F8
Clos Y Fasarnen / Maple Cl
  LL12 . . . . .67 F2
Clos Y Ffwrnais / Furnace Cl
  LL11 . . . . .71 F8
Clos Y Fron / Vron Cl
  LL11 . . . . .71 F8
Clos Y Gelli / Hazelwood Cl
  CH5 . . . . .38 D5
Clos y Gweundia /
  Heathwood Cl 2 LL11 . .72 D6
Clos Y Meillion CH5 . . . . . .48 F8
Clos Y Meryw / Juniper Cl
  LL12 . . . . .67 F2
Clos Y Pererin / Pilgrims Cl
  CH7 . . . . .37 A5
Clos y Plasau / Plassey Cl
  LL13 . . . . .73 F4
Clos Y Plasty / Manor Cl
  LL12 . . . . .66 F4
Clos y Pren Afal / Applewood
  Cl LL13 . . . . .80 B7
Clos Yr Allt / Hill Cl 2
  LL14 . . . . .85 C7
Clos y Rhaglaw / Regent Cl
  3 LL11 . . . . .72 D6
Clos Yr Ucheldir / Highlands
  Cl 6 LL18 . . . . .7 F2
Clos Y Stem / Steam Cl
  LL11 . . . . .71 F8
Clos Ystrad LL13 . . . . .80 A7
Clover La CH4 . . . . .51 F5
Clover Pl CH4 . . . . .51 F5
Cloy Ct LL13 . . . . .89 A6
Cloy La Overton LL13 . . . . .98 F6
  Overton / Owrtyn LL13 . . . .89 B3
Clwyd Ave
  Greenfield / Maes-Glas
  CH8 . . . . .21 D6
  Mynydd Isa CH7 . . . . .47 E4
  Rhyl / Y Rhyl LL18 . . . . .7 B6
Clwyd Ave / Rhodfa Clwyd
  Denbigh / Dinbych LL16 . .140 E3
  Dyserth LL18 . . . . .8 F1
  Prestatyn LL19 . . . . .3 B2
  Rhuddlan LL18 . . . . .8 C3
Clwyd Bank LL18 . . . . .6 E5
Clwyd Cl CH4 . . . . .50 B6
Clwyd Cres CH7 . . . . .47 C7
Clwyd Ct Prestatyn LL19 . . .8 F8
  Wrexham / Wrecsam LL11 . .72 F5
Clwyd Forest Trail ★ CH7 .54 E7
Clwyd Gdns LL18 . . . . .6 C5
Clwyd Gr CH7 . . . . .48 A4

Clwydian Ave LL17 . . . . .117 B6
Clwydian Park Ave LL17 117 B6
Clwydian Park Cres
  LL17 . . . . .117 B6
Clwydian Park View
  LL17 . . . . .117 B6
Clwyd Pk LL18 . . . . .6 E3
Clwyd Ret Pk LL18 . . . . . . .7 E4
Clwyd St CH5 . . . . .39 B4
Clwyd St / Heol Clwyd
  9 Rhyl / Y Rhyl LL18 . . . . .7 B7
  Ruthin / Rhuthin LL15 . . . .141 C5
Clwyd Wen LL13 . . . . .80 C8
Clydesdale Rd CH7 . . . . . .48 F5
Clydfan CH8 . . . . .20 C6
Clywedog Cl 1 LL14 . . . . .72 D6
Clywedog Rd E LL13 . . . . .81 C7
Clywedog Rd N LL13 . . . . .81 C8
Clywedog Rd S LL13 . . . . .81 C7
Coachhouse Mews LL15 . .126 C8
Coatings By Pass Rd CH5 29 F2
Coatings Two CH5 . . . . . . .29 E2
Cobblers La / Lon Y Cryddion
  LL12 . . . . .67 A8
Cobbles The CH4 . . . . .52 D7
Cobblestone Ct CH2 . . . . .43 E8
Cobden Rd LL13 . . . . .145 A2
Cobham Cl LL13 . . . . .80 B6
Cockbank La LL13 . . . . . . .87 E8
Coed Aben LL13 . . . . .80 E8
Coed Aben Rd LL13 . . . . . .81 D8
Coed Afon LL20 . . . . .143 E4
Coed Ave LL18 . . . . .6 F2
Coed Bach CH7 . . . . .27 F5
Coed Efa La LL11 . . . . . . .72 B4
Coed Mawr Cvn Site CH7 45 D7
Coed Mor CH8 . . . . .11 C8
Coed Mor Dr LL19 . . . . .3 B1
Coed Onn Rd CH6 . . . . . . .28 B4
Coed Richard LL14 . . . . . .85 C3
Coed Terfin CH7 . . . . .49 A2
Coed-y-Bryn LL13 . . . . . . .80 E7
Coedyfelin Cl LL11 . . . . . . .71 F8
Coedyfelin Rd LL11 . . . . . .65 F1
Coed-y-Ffynnon LL13 . . . . .80 A7
Coed-y-Fron CH8 . . . . .21 A4
Coed-y-Glyn Terr LL20 . . .135 C4
Coed-y-Graig LL14 . . . . . . .85 E2
Coed Y Graig CH4 . . . . . . .49 A2
Coed-y-Nant
  Penycae LL14 . . . . .85 D7
  Wrexham / Wrecsam LL13 .80 A6
Coetiau Postol / Vicarage La
  LL18 . . . . .7 E1
Colchester Sq CH4 . . . . . .51 F5

Coleg = college

Coleg Garddwriaeth Cymru /
  Welsh Coll of Horticulture
  CH7 . . . . .36 F6
Coleg Glannau Dyfrdwy /
  Deeside Coll of F Ed
  CH5 . . . . .29 C2
Coleg Ial / Yale Coll
  LL12 . . . . .145 B3
Coleg Llysfasi LL15 . . . . .126 C3
Coleg Y Groes / The College
  LL21 . . . . .142 D3
Coleg Y Rhyl Coll LL18 . . . .7 C5
Colehill Pl CH5 . . . . .29 C1
Colemere St LL13 . . . . . . .145 B1
Coleridge Cl CH1 . . . . .42 A5
Coleshill Lea CH6 . . . . . . .28 A7
Coleshill Rd CH6 . . . . .22 D1
Coleshill St
  Flint / Y Fflint CH6 . . . . . . .28 A6
  Holywell / Treffynnon CH8 . .21 B4
Colin Dr LL18 . . . . .7 F6
Colinwood Ave CH4 . . . . . .50 B3
College Gn CH4 . . . . .52 D5
College Hill LL11 . . . . .71 F5
College of Law (Christleton
  Hall) CH3 . . . . .53 D8
College St / Camfa'r Cwn
  LL21 . . . . .142 D3
College View CH5 . . . . . . .29 C1
Colliers La LL14 . . . . .47 E4
Colliery La CH5 . . . . .39 D3
Colliery Rd
  Chirk / Y Waun LL14 . . . . .95 F1
  Wrexham / Wrecsam LL11 . .72 F4
  Wrexham / Wrecsam, Southsea
  LL11 . . . . .72 A4
Collins Ct LL13 . . . . .80 C7
Colomendy LL15 . . . . .124 F8
Colomendy Ind Est / Ystad
  Ddiwdiannol Colomendy
  LL16 . . . . .140 D5
Colson Ct CH2 . . . . .144 A4
Coltsfoot Cl CH3 . . . . .53 B5
Columbine Cl CH3 . . . . . . .53 A6
Colwyn Rd LL13 . . . . .73 C1
Commonhall St CH1 . . . . .144 A2
Commonwood Rd LL13 . . .74 F7
Compton Pl CH4 . . . . .52 A6
Concorde Row CH5 . . . . . .73 E5
Conery La SY13 . . . . .102 D2
Congleton Rd CH4 . . . . . . .50 C4
Conifers The LL12 . . . . . . .67 E3
Coniston Cl CH5 . . . . .38 C6
Coniston Dr LL19 . . . . .2 F5
Coniston Rd CH2 . . . . .42 F5
Connah's Quay High Sch
  CH5 . . . . .29 C1

Connah's Quay Rd CH7 . .37 D5
Connaught Ave 9 CH5 . .39 B6
Conningsby Ct LL13 . . . . .73 F4
Conniston Dr CH7 . . . . . . .48 D5
Connor Cres LL13 . . . . . . .80 C8
Constitution Hill CH7 . . . . .58 B5
Conway Ave CH7 . . . . .48 D3
Conway Cl Caergwrle LL12 66 A7
  Flint / Y Fflint CH6 . . . . . . .27 F4
  Saltney CH4 . . . . .51 D5
  Wrexham / Wrecsam LL11 . .72 E8
Conway Ct 5 LL18 . . . . . . .7 E1
Conway Dr LL13 . . . . .73 E1
Conway St LL18 . . . . .7 C8
Cooks La SY13 . . . . .93 D6
Coopers Cl LL13 . . . . .73 D3
Cooper's Croft CH3 . . . . . .53 A7
Coopers Field 3 SY11 . .106 F7
Coopers La SY11 . . . . . . .106 F6
Cooper's La CH5 . . . . .29 D1
Copes La SY12 . . . . .110 D3
Copeswood Cl CH4 . . . . . .50 C3
Coppack Cl CH5 . . . . .38 C5
Coppafield Cl CH7 . . . . . . .48 D4
Coppa View CH7 . . . . .48 C4
Copperas Hill / Allt Copperas
  LL14 . . . . .85 D7
Copper Beach Cl CH4 . . . .50 C3
Coppergate The CH5 . . . . .39 C1
Coppice La SY13 . . . . . . .113 E5
Coppice The CH5 . . . . .38 F2
Coppins Cl CH3 . . . . .43 A2
Copse The Ewloe CH5 . . . .48 F8
  Rossett LL12 . . . . .68 A7
Corbett Ave CH8 . . . . .5 A5
Corkscrew La LL14 . . . . . .79 B3
Cornish Cl LL13 . . . . .80 B6
Cornist Dr CH6 . . . . .27 F6
Cornist La CH6 . . . . .27 D6
Cornist Park Prim Sch
  CH6 . . . . .27 E6
Cornist Rd CH6 . . . . .27 F6
Cornwall Rd Chester CH2 . .42 F7
  Connah's Quay CH5 . . . . . .39 B4
Cornwall St CH1 . . . . .144 B4
Coronation Cl LL18 . . . . . .14 E4
Coronation Cotts 1 LL11 72 B4
Coronation Dr LL14 . . . . . .95 E2
Coronation Rd
  Broughton CH4 . . . . .50 B3
  Wrexham / Wrecsam LL11 . .72 C3
Coronation St
  Cefn-Mawr LL14 . . . . .85 C1
  Cefn-mawr LL14 . . . . .95 C8
  Chester CH4 . . . . .51 F7
Coronation Terr
  Caergwrle LL12 . . . . .66 B7
  2 Wrexham / Wrecsam
  LL11 . . . . .72 C3
Corporation St CH6 . . . . . .28 B7
Corun Y Bryn CH5 . . . . . . .38 C5
Corwen Cl CH5 . . . . .38 C6
Corwen Rd
  Penyffordd CH4 . . . . .59 A7
  Pontybodkin CH7 . . . . .58 B4
Corwen Rd / Fforrdd Corwen
  LL15 . . . . .141 C3
Corwen Way CH4 . . . . .59 A7
Cosy Nook CH7 . . . . .37 A5
Cotebrook Dr CH2 . . . . . . .42 E7
Cotes Pl CH1 . . . . .41 E3
Cotgreaves Cl CH4 . . . . . .52 B5
Cotswold Cl CH2 . . . . .42 F6
Cottage Cl LL12 . . . . .68 C8
Cottage Fields SY11 . . . . .106 F6
Cottage Gdns CH7 . . . . . . .48 D4
Cottage La
  Connah's Quay CH5 . . . . . .39 D2
  St. Martin's SY11 . . . . . . .106 F6
Cottage Rd CH4 . . . . .52 B5
Cotterill Cl CH5 . . . . .38 D5
Council Houses
  Wrexham / Wrecsam, Moss
  LL11 . . . . .72 A8
  Wrexham / Wrecsam,
  Pentre Broughton LL11 . . .72 A7
Council St / Stryd Y Cyngor
  LL12 . . . . .67 B3
Council Terr LL18 . . . . .7 C6
Countess Ct CH1 . . . . .42 B5
Countess of Chester Hospl
  CH2 . . . . .42 B6
Countess Way CH2 . . . . . .42 C5
County Dr LL18 . . . . .7 D8
County Rd CH7 . . . . .58 A4
Court Dr CH5 . . . . .38 C8
Courtland Dr CH5 . . . . . . .39 A3
Courtney Rd CH4 . . . . .51 E5
Courtyard The CH5 . . . . . .39 C6
Cousens Way CH1 . . . . . . .42 B4
Coventry Dr LL18 . . . . .7 C7
Coventry Gr LL19 . . . . .2 E2
Cowhey Cl CH4 . . . . .52 B5
Cox La / Lon Cox LL12 . . .68 B5
Crabwall Pl CH1 . . . . .41 F5
Craigle 15 LL14 . . . . .78 E2
Craig Melyd LL19 . . . . .9 A6
Craigmillar Rd LL12 . . . . .145 C3
Craig Way LL12 . . . . .73 C4
Craithie Rd CH3 . . . . .43 A2
Cramer Ct LL18 . . . . .7 B6
Cranbrook Cl CH5 . . . . . . .38 E6

Crane La LL14 .85 B1
Crane St LL14 .85 B1
Crane The LL14 .85 B1
Cranford Ct CH4 .52 A5
Cranford Rd LL13 .73 D2
Cranleigh Cres CH1 .42 B4
Crathie Pl LL11 .73 A4
Crawford's Wlk CH2 .42 F3
Crecas La CH8 .20 E5
Crescent Cl LL13 .73 C1
Crescent Ct 2 LL18 .7 B7
Crescent Rd
Rhyl / Y Rhyl LL18 .7 B7
Wrexham / Wrecsam LL13 .73 C1
Crescent Sq 16 LL18 .7 B7
Crescent The Chester CH2 42 D4
Rhyl / Y Rhyl LL18 .7 C7
Crescent The / Y Cilgant LL21 .142 C3
Crewe Hill La CH3 .76 A6
Crewe La CH3 .69 F1
Crewe La S CH3 .76 A7
Crewe St CH1 .144 C3
Crib-y-Gwynt CH8 .10 F4
Crib Yr Argau / Moss Valley Brow LL11 .72 C4
Criccieth Cl CH7 .48 C7
Criftins CE Prim Sch SY12 .108 B5
Crippa Ave LL11 .72 B4
Crispin La LL11 .145 A4
Cristionnydd La / Lon Cristionnydd LL14 .85 C6
Cristionydd LL14 .85 C7
Croes Atti La CH6 .28 C5
Croesfoel Ind Est LL14 .79 C6
Croes-Hir SY10 .139 C2
Croeshowell Hill LL12 .67 D6
Croeshowell La LL12 .67 D7
Croesnewydd Rd LL13 .72 E2
Croes Stryt SY10 .138 C1
Croft Ave CH5 .38 E6
Crofters Pk CH5 .40 A3
Crofters Way
Connah's Quay CH5 .39 E2
Saughall CH1 .40 F8
Croft La CH4 .61 A7
Crofts The CH3 .69 F1
Croft The Chester CH2 .42 D5
Connah's Quay CH5 .39 B3
Crogen 6 LL14 .95 E3
Cromar Cres LL12 .68 C8
Crompton Cl CH4 .59 F7
Cromwell Ave CH7 .48 A6
Cromwell Cl
Hawarden / Penarlâg CH5 .38 F1
Penyffordd CH4 .59 A8
Crook St CH1 .144 A2
Crosfield CH8 .21 B7
Cross Foxes LL22 .116 C8
Cross Gn CH2 .42 E6
Cross Hey CH4 .144 C1
Cross Keys CH7 .36 B6
Cross Keys Pl 1 LL14 .85 C1
Cross La Llangollen LL20 .143 D4
Wrexham / Wrecsam LL11 .72 A6
Cross Lanes SY12 .107 E6
Crossley Cres CH2 .43 B5
Cross Rds / Groesffyrdd CH8 .21 B4
Cross St Chester CH2 .42 F2
1 Ellesmere SY12 .109 C2
Holt LL13 .75 E8
Holywell / Treffynnon CH8 .21 B4
Rhuddlan LL18 .7 E1
Wrexham / Wrecsam LL11 145 B4
Wrexham / Wrecsam, New Broughton LL11 .72 B4
Cross The Holt LL13 .75 E8
7 Mold / Yr Wyddgrug CH7 .46 F4
Cross Tree Ct CH7 .48 D8
Crosstree La CH5 .49 D8
Cross Tree Rise CH5 .49 D8
Crossway CH5 .38 F2
Crossways Caergwrle LL12 66 B6
Connah's Quay, Big Mancot CH5 .39 E3
Connah's Quay, Shotton CH5 .39 B5
Penymynydd CH4 .49 A1
Wrexham / Wrecsam LL13 .73 C2
Crown Est CH8 .19 B5
Crown La / Lon Crown 9 LL16 .140 C3
Crown Pl LL12 .67 A3
Crown Sq 10 LL16 .140 C3
Crud-y-Castell LL16 .140 E2
Crud Y Gwynt 2 LL16 .140 B3
Crud-y-Gwynt CH7 .47 E4
Crud Yr Awel
Clawdd-newydd LL15 .125 C3
Denbigh / Dinbych LL16 .140 E4
Prestatyn LL19 .2 E1
Crugan Ave LL18 .6 D6
Culfan LL14 .78 D1
Cumberland La SY13 .113 C5
Cunliffe St
Mold / Yr Wyddgrug CH7 .46 F3
Wrexham / Wrecsam LL11 145 B4
Cunliffe Wlk LL11 .73 B5
Cunningham Ave LL13 .73 C2
Cuppin St CH1 .144 A2
Curzon Cl CH4 .52 B8
Curzon Pk N CH4 .52 B7
Curzon Pk S CH4 .52 B7
Curzon St CH4 .51 F7
Custom House Lane Cty Prim Sch CH5 .38 F7
Cwat Erwain CH4 .51 E7
Cwmalis Rd LL20 .94 E6
Cwm Arthur LL16 .140 F2
Cwm Cl CH7 .47 D4
Cwm Eithin
Denbigh / Dinbych LL16 .140 E4
Wrexham / Wrecsam LL12 .73 C7
Cwm Eithion CH6 .28 B4
Cwm Glas / Park St LL14 78 F1
Cwm Llewenni LL16 .140 F2
Cwm Rd / Ffordd-y-Cwm
Cwm LL18 .17 A8
Dyserth LL18 .8 F2
Cwrt Afallon / Avalon Ct LL13 .80 B7
Cwrt Ashly / Ashly Ct LL17 .16 A1
Cwrt Bedwyr / Bedwyr Ct LL13 .80 B7
Cwrt Berllan LL19 .8 E8
Cwrt Brenig CH7 .48 D4
Cwrt Bridgewater / Bridgewater Mews LL13 73 A7
Cwrt Bryn Y Pys 8 LL13 .98 C8
Cwrt Castanwydd / Chestnut Ct LL11 .72 C7
Cwrt Dowell LL19 .3 A2
Cwrt Leighton / Leighton Ct CH5 .38 E8
Cwrt Lytham / Lytham Ct 4 LL13 .73 F3
Cwrt Onnen CH5 .39 E2
Cwrt Pendragon / Pendragon Ct LL13 .80 B7
Cwrt Pentref / Village Ct 3 LL11 .73 B5
Cwrt Seion LL19 .9 A6
Cwrt-y-gwindy 1 LL18 .7 E1
Cwrt-y-Plas LL18 .8 E4
Cwr Y Gaer LL21 .142 C6
Cwttir La LL17 .15 E1
Cwybr Fawr LL18 .7 E3
Cygnet Cl SY12 .109 B3
Cylch-y-Nant / Nant Cl 1 LL18 .7 F2
Cyman Cl CH1 .41 D3
Cymau La LL11 .65 E4
Cymau Rd LL11 .65 D3
Cynlas
Kinmel Bay / Bae Cinmel LL18 .6 D3
Wrexham / Wrecsam LL11 .72 B4
Cynlas St / Stryt Cynlas 10 LL14 .78 E1
Cypress Gr LL18 .7 E8
Cysgodfa LL16 .140 D3
Cysgod-y-Graig LL16 .140 C3

D

Dafydd Cl CH7 .47 E6
Daisy Bank Cl LL14 .79 E8
Daisy Hill Rd CH7 .48 C4
Daisy La LL12 .68 E4
Daisy Rd LL11 .72 B5
Dalar Wen LL16 .140 F4
Dale Ct LL11 .72 C3
Dale Dr CH2 .42 D8
Dale Rd
Connah's Quay CH5 .39 A4
Wrexham / Wrecsam LL11 .72 C4
Daleside
BuckleyBuckley / Bwcle CH7 .47 F4
Chester CH2 .42 D8
Daleside Ave LL12 .73 E5
Dale St Chester CH3 .43 A1
Wrexham / Wrecsam LL13 .73 C1
Dalle Crucis Abbey★ LL20 .131 C3
Dalton Cl CH1 .41 E3
Dane Cl Chester CH4 .51 F5
Wrexham / Wrecsam LL11 .72 D6
Dane Gr CH2 .43 F8
Daneswood LL13 .80 F4
Daniel Ct CH5 .39 A7
Daniel Dr LL18 .7 F5
Daniell Way CH3 .53 A7
Daniel Owen Prec 5 CH7 .46 F4
Daniels Dr LL14 .86 B6
Darby Rd LL11 .72 B5
Dark La 3 LL13 .98 C8
Dark La / Lon Dywyll
Hope / Yr Hôb LL12 .66 F8
Llay LL12 .67 A7
Darland Cl LL12 .68 C8
Darland High Sch LL12 .68 C8
Darland La Darland LL12 .68 C8
Trevalyn LL12 .68 E7
Darland View LL12 .68 C8
Darwen Dr CH4 .49 B1
Darwen Terr 2 LL18 .7 F1
Darwin Rd CH1 .41 C4
Daulwyn Rd CH7 .48 E6
Davids Cl LL19 .3 A1
Davies Ave LL11 .71 E8
Davies Ct LL13 .80 C7
Davies's Cotts CH7 .47 F8
Davy Way / Ffordd Davy LL12 .66 E6
Dawn Cl CH7 .48 B3
Dawpool Cl CH2 .42 D5
Dawson Cl LL19 .3 A1
Dawson Cres LL19 .3 A1
Dawson Ct LL19 .3 A1
Dawson Dr Chester CH2 .144 A4
Prestatyn LL19 .3 A1
Daytona Dr CH7 .38 B4
Daywell Cres SY11 .106 A1
Ddol Awel CH7 .46 D4
Ddol Hir Cvn Pk LL20 .135 C3
Ddol Hyfryd LL19 .4 A3
Ddreiniog Rd CH8 .20 C6
Dean Cl LL13 .73 D4
Deanery Cl CH2 .42 C4
Dean Rd LL13 .73 E3
Dean's Ave CH5 .38 E7
Deansbury Cl CH6 .27 E6
Deans Cl Bagillt CH6 .22 C1
Chester CH2 .42 D6
Deans Pl CH5 .38 F7
Deans Way CH4 .60 A8
Dean's Wlk LL17 .16 A1
Dee Ave LL12 .73 C4
Dee Banks Chester CH3 .53 A8
Huntington CH3 .52 F7
Dee Banks Sch CH3 .53 A7
Dee Cotts CH6 .28 C6
Dee Cres CH3 .69 E2
Dee Ct LL13 .89 A8
Dee Fords Ave CH3 .43 A1
Dee Hills Pk CH3 .144 C2
Dee La Chester CH1, CH3 144 C2
Holt LL13 .75 D7
Llangollen LL20 .143 C5
Dee Mdws LL13 .75 D7
Dee Pk LL13 .75 D8
Dee Point Cty Inf Sch CH1 .41 D3
Dee Point Cty Jun Sch CH1 .41 D3
Dee Rd
Connah's Quay CH5 .38 F6
Garden City CH5 .39 F7
Talacre CH8 .5 A6
Dee Road Inf Sch CH5 .38 F7
Deeside LL13 .75 E8
Deeside Coll of F Ed / Coleg Glannau Dyfrdwy CH5 .29 B1
Deeside Com Hospl / Ysbyty Cymuned Glannau Dyfrdwy CH5 .39 B4
Deeside Cres CH1 .40 E5
Deeside Ent Ctr CH5 .39 B6
Deeside Halt★ LL21 .130 F1
Deeside Ind Pk / Parc Diwydiannol Glannau Dyfrdwy CH5 .30 E2
Deeside La CH1 .40 D4
Dee Valley Ct / Llys Dyffryn Dyfrdwy LL14 .85 B3
Dee View
Connah's Quay CH5 .39 C4
Ewloe CH5 .38 F2
Farndon CH3 .69 E2
Dee View Cotts CH8 .5 B1
Dee View Rd CH5 .29 E1
Deganwy Cl CH7 .48 C7
Degas Cl CH5 .38 C8
Deiniol Ave LL13 .80 F4
Deiniol Prim Sch LL13 .80 F4
Deiniol's Rd CH5 .39 E2
Delamere Ave
Buckley / Bwcle CH7 .48 D4
Wrexham / Wrecsam LL11 .72 D8
Delamere St CH1 .144 A3
Delfryn LL14 .85 D7
Dell The
Guilden Sutton CH3 .43 F5
Prestatyn LL19 .3 A1
Delph La / Lon Delph 17 LL14 .78 E2
Delph Rd LL14 .85 C4
Delta Ct CH4 .51 B6
Delves Wlk CH3 .53 B7
Delvine Dr CH2 .42 D6
Delyn LL14 .79 A2
Delyn Rd CH8 .21 C7
Demage La CH2 .42 D8
Demage La S CH2 .42 D7
Denbigh Castle★ LL16 .140 C2
Denbigh Circ LL18 .6 E3
Denbigh Cl
Buckley / Bwcle CH7 .48 C7
Wrexham / Wrecsam LL12 .73 E4
Denbigh Com Coll LL16 140 C3
Denbigh Friary (rems of)★ LL16 .140 D4
Denbigh High Sch LL16 140 D3
Denbigh Infmy LL16 .140 D3
Denbigh L Ctr★ LL16 .140 E3
Denbigh Mus & Liby★ LL16 .140 C3
Denbigh Rd
Mold / Yr Wyddgrug CH7 .46 E6
Ruthin / Rhuthin LL15 .141 B5
Denbigh Row CH8 .5 C1
Denbigh St Chester CH1 .42 B3
Henllan LL16 .116 F3
Denford Cl CH4 .50 C4
Denhall Cl CH2 .42 E5
Denmore Ave LL18 .1 E5
Denning Rd LL12 .73 D5
Dennis Ct 4 LL14 .86 A4
Dennis Dr CH4 .52 B5
Denson Dr CH5 .39 A2
Denstone Dr CH4 .52 A4
Denteth Dr CH1 .41 E5
Derby Rd Caergwrle LL12 .66 A8
Wrexham / Wrecsam LL13 .80 C8
Derby Terr CH8 .21 E7
Derby Villas LL13 .145 C1
Derfel Est LL16 .140 E8
Dergoed LL11 .72 B5
Deric Cl LL19 .2 C2
Derwen 1 LL14 .95 E3
Derwen Cl CH5 .38 E8
Derwen Ct LL13 .80 A7
Derwen Deg CH7 .58 A4
Derwen Dr LL18 .7 E4
Derwent Cl Prestatyn LL19 .2 F3
Wrexham / Wrecsam LL12 .73 B4
Derwent Cres LL12 .73 B4
Derwen Terr LL16 .23 A1
Derwent Rd CH2 .43 A5
Derwen Villas CH7 .46 F3
Deunant LL21 .129 B5
Deva Ave
Connah's Quay CH5 .38 D7
Holywell / Treffynnon CH8 .21 B5
Saltney CH4 .51 D6
Deva Bsns Pk CH5 .40 A8
Deva Cl CH6 .28 C5
Deva Cres LL18 .1 D5
Deva Ct CH2 .42 F2
Deva La CH2 .42 C6
Deva Link CH1 .42 A3
Deva Stad (Chester City FC) CH1 .41 E1
Deva Terr CH3 .144 C2
Deva Way LL13 .73 D1
Devon Cl
Connah's Quay CH5 .38 D6
Wrexham / Wrecsam LL11 .73 B6
Devon Rd CH2 .42 F5
Devonshire Pl CH4 .52 E7
Devonshire Rd CH4 .50 C4
Dewi Ave CH8 .21 A4
Diamond Cotts LL12 .67 D2
Diane Dr LL18 .7 D5
Dicksons Dr CH2 .42 D4
Didsbury Ave CH8 .5 A6
Dig La CH5 .49 D7
Diksmuide Dr SY12 .109 B3
Dinas LL14 .85 E3
Dinas Ave LL18 .6 C5
Dinas Cl CH1 .41 D3
Dinas Dr LL20 .143 F4
Dinbren Rd LL20 .143 C6
Dinghouse CH7 .48 E6
Dinghouse Wood CH7 .48 E6
Dingle Bank CH4 .52 C7
Dingle Pl LL12 .67 B3
Dingle Road / Ffordd Y Glyn CH7 .58 A5
Dirty Mile
Buckley / Bwcle CH7 .48 F4
Hawarden / Penarlâg CH5 .49 A4
Disraeli Cl CH5 .49 A8
Dixon's Ho CH3 .53 E8
Dobshill Hospl CH5 .49 A3
Dock Rd
Connah's Quay CH5 .38 F8
Connah's Quay CH5 .39 A8
Dock Road Workshops CH5 .39 A7
Dodds Ct CH5 .39 A4
Dodd's Dr CH5 .38 F7
Dodd's La
Lower Wych SY13, SY14 .92 E7
Wrexham / Wrecsam LL11 .72 E7
Dodleston CE Prim Sch CH4 .61 A7
Dodleston La CH4 .61 C3
Dog La
Ruthin / Rhuthin LL15 .141 C5
Threapwood SY14 .91 C7
Dol Acton LL11 .72 F5
Dol Awel CH5 .38 F1
Dolfechlas Rd CH7 .35 E3
Dolhendra SY10 .136 F1
Dol Mwyn LL11 .71 D3
Dolphin Ct CH4 .52 A7
Dol-y-Bont SY10 .138 A1
Dolydd LL15 .121 C3
Dolydd Bychain / Little Mdws LL11 .72 E8
Dolydd La Cefn-Mawr LL14 85 B1
1 Cefn-mawr LL14 .95 B8
Dolydd Rd Cefn-Mawr LL14 85 B1
Wrexham / Wrecsam LL13 .145 A2
Dol Y Pentre / Village Mdws 14 LL14 .86 A4
Donald Ave LL18 .7 D5
Donne Pl CH1 .41 F6
Donnington Way CH4 .51 F7
Doran LL14 .79 A1
Dorchester Cl LL18 .7 E4
Dorchester Rd CH4 .51 F5
Doren Ave LL18 .7 F5
Dorfold Way CH2 .42 E6
Dorin Park Sch CH2 .42 D6
Dorset Dr LL11 .73 B6
Dorset Pl CH2 .43 A5
Dorset Rd CH2 .42 F7
Douglas Pl CH4 .51 E6
Dover Rd CH4 .52 A6
Dovey Cl
Connah's Quay CH5 .38 D6
Flint / Y Fflint CH6 .27 F4
Downham Pl CH1 .41 E4
Downsfield Rd CH4 .52 A6
Downswood Ct CH2 .42 C4
Downswood Dr CH2 .42 C4
Dreflan CH7 .46 E5
Drift Cotts LL12 .61 C1
Drive A CH5 .31 A2
Drive B CH5 .31 A2
Drive C CH5 .31 A2
Drive D CH5 .31 A1
Drome Rd CH5 .31 A2
Drovers La / Lon-y-Porthmyn CH7 .24 B7
Druid Ho LL14 .85 D3
Drury Com Prim Sch CH7 48 F5
Drury La
Buckley / Bwcle CH7 .48 E5
Hawarden / Penarlâg CH5 .49 A5
Leeswood / Coed Llai CH7 .57 F5
Drury Lane Ind Est CH7 .48 E6
Drury New Rd CH7 .48 E5
Drws-y-Coed LL13 .80 A6
Dryden Cl CH5 .48 E8
Duchess Pl CH2 .144 A4
Duckers La CH5 .39 E2
Dudleston Pk SY12 .108 B7
Duffryn Cl CH7 .48 D4
Duke Rd / Ffordd y Dug LL14 .78 F1
Duke's Ct CH1 .144 B1
Duke's Field Dr CH7 .48 C5
Duke St Chester CH1 .144 B1
Chirk / Y Waun LL14 .95 E2
Flint / Y Fflint CH6 .28 A6
9 Ruabon / Rhiwabon LL14 .86 A4
Soughton / Sychdyn CH7 .37 B1
Duke St / Stryt y Dug
Rhosllanerchrugog LL14 .78 E1
1 Wrexham / Wrecsam LL11 .145 B2
Dukesway CH2 .42 E7
Duke Wlk 5 CH6 .28 A6
Dulas Ave / Rhodfa Dulas LL18 .6 D4
Dulas Ct CH2 .42 E8
Dulas Pk LL18 .6 D4
Dulverton Ave CH3 .43 C2
Dunale Villas 13 LL11 .72 C3
Dunbar Cl CH5 .29 D1
Dundas St CH5 .39 D5
Dunham Way CH2 .42 F6
Dunkeson's Cvn Camp LL19 .4 A4
Dunlin Ave CH5 .38 D8
Dunster Rd LL13 .81 E8
Durban Ave CH3 .53 D7
Durham Dr LL19 .2 F1
Durham Rd CH1 .41 F5
Durlston Dr LL19 .2 E1
Durrant Cl LL18 .7 E5
Dutton Rd LL13 .74 E1
Dwyfor Ave CH7 .47 D5
Dwyfor Ct LL19 .8 E8
Dyfed Dr CH5 .39 D4
Dyffryn LL15 .125 F5
Dyffryn Teg LL17 .17 C2
Dyke St LL11 .71 E8
Dylan Cl CH5 .48 E7
Dymock Pl LL13 .99 F4
Dyserth Hall Mews LL18 .8 E4
Dyserth Rd Blacon CH1 .41 D3
Rhuddlan LL18 .15 F8
Dyserth Rd / Ffordd Dyserth LL18, LL19 .8 C6
Dyserth Waterfall★ LL18 .8 F3

E

Eardswick Cl CH2 .144 B4
Earle's Cres CH5 .39 E3
Earle's Ct LL13 .145 B1
Earle St LL13 .145 B1
Earl Rd / Heol Yr Iarll 2 CH7 .46 F4
Earls Lea CH6 .28 A7
Earls Oak CH2 .42 D7
Earl's Port CH1 .42 B2
Earl St CH6 .28 A7
Earlston Ct CH3 .144 C2
Earlsway CH4 .52 A8
Earlswood Ave LL19 .2 C2
East Ave Prestatyn LL19 .3 C2
Ruabon / Rhiwabon LL14 .86 A5
Wrexham / Wrecsam LL11 .73 A4
East Cl Mynydd Isa CH7 .47 C4
Prestatyn LL19 .2 B2
Eastern Pathway CH4 .144 C1
Eastfield Ct LL13 .80 E7
Eastfields Gr CH1 .41 A8
Eastgate Row N CH1 .144 B2
Eastgate Row S CH1 .144 B2
Eastgate St CH1 .144 B2
East Gn CH5 .40 A6
Eastleigh Cl LL11 .73 A5
East Par LL18 .7 B8
East St LL20 .143 C5
East View
New Brighton CH7 .47 C7
Wrexham / Wrecsam LL11 .73 A7
Eastville Ave LL18 .1 E5
Eastwick La SY12 .98 E1
Eastwood Ct CH4 .50 B7
Eaton Ave Chester CH4 .52 D7
Connah's Quay CH5 .38 F6
Rhyl / Y Rhyl LL18 .1 E5
Eaton Cl Broughton CH4 .50 C4
Rossett LL12 .68 C7
Eaton Dr LL13 .73 E2
Eaton Gr CH4 .51 E6
Eaton Grange LL12 .67 F2
Eaton Mews CH4 .52 D7
Eaton Pl CH7 .58 A4
Eaton Rd CH4 .52 E4

Ebury Pl CH4 ....52 D7
Eccleston Ave CH4 ....52 D6
Eccleston CE Prim Sch CH4 ....52 E2
Eccleston Rd CH4 ....60 A7
Echo Cl CH4 ....51 E5
Eden Ave LL19 ....3 B2
Edgar Ct CH4 ....144 B1
Edgar Pl CH4 ....144 B1
Edgar's Terr 4 LL16 ....140 C3
Edgbaston Rd LL18 ....1 F5
Edge Gr CH2 ....42 F2
Edge of The Woods / Cil Y Coed 10 LL14 ....86 A4
Edgewood CH3 ....53 A8
Edinburgh Ave LL12 ....66 A8
Edinburgh Rd / Ffordd Caeredin LL11 ....73 A4
Edinburgh Way CH4 ....144 C1
Edison Ct LL13 ....72 E2
Edmund St CH7 ....46 F3
Edna St CH2 ....42 F3
Edward Henry St LL18 ....7 A7
Edward Rd CH8 ....11 E4
Edwards Ave LL11 ....71 E8
Edward's Holiday Camp LL22 ....6 A3
Edwards Rd CH4 ....52 A6
Edward St LL13 ....145 B1
Edwin Dr CH6 ....28 B5
Egerton Dr CH2 ....42 D5
Egerton Rd CH1 ....41 E5
Egerton St CH1 ....144 C3
Egerton Street Cty Inf Sch CH1 ....144 C3
Egerton St / Stryt Egerton LL11 ....145 B2
Egerton Wlk
Dodleston CH4 ....61 A7
Wrexham / Wrecsam LL11 ....73 B5
Eglwys Cl CH7 ....48 A4
Eglwysfan LL14 ....85 C2
Eighth Ave LL12 ....67 A4
Eilison Ct CH1 ....144 B3
Eirian Ave LL18 ....6 E4
Elder Cl LL12 ....67 F2
Elder Dr CH4 ....51 E5
Eldon Gr / Gelli Eldon LL14 ....79 D6
Eleri Cl LL18 ....7 D5
Eleventh Ave LL12 ....67 B4
Elfed Dr CH7 ....48 A5
Elfed High Sch CH7 ....48 B5
Elgin Cl CH3 ....43 B3
Elidie Cl CH5 ....38 C8
Eliot Cl CH5 ....48 E8
Elizabeth Cres CH4 ....144 C1
Elizabeth Ct CH5 ....38 D8
Elk View SY14 ....90 F5
Ellesmere Ave
Broughton CH4 ....50 D4
Chester CH2 ....42 D5
Ellesmere Bsns Pk SY12 ....108 F1
Ellesmere La LL13 ....99 F3
Ellesmere Prim Sch SY12 ....109 A2
Ellesmere Rd
Bronington SY13 ....102 E5
Mynydd Isa CH7 ....47 E4
St. Martin's SY11 ....106 E6
Ellice Way LL13 ....72 E2
Elliot Ho CH1 ....42 A5
Ellis Ave LL18 ....7 A6
Ellis St / Stryt Ellis 7 LL14 ....78 F2
Elmanoak Gr / Gelli Derllwy LL12 ....67 A5
Elm Ave
Connah's Quay CH5 ....38 E7
Flint / Y Fflint CH6 ....27 F6
Elm Cl 5 Ellesmere SY12 ....109 A3
Whitchurch SY13 ....103 F6
Elm Cotts LL11 ....72 C4
Elm Croft CH5 ....39 E2
Elm Ct LL12 ....68 A7
Elm Dr
Mold / Yr Wyddgrug CH7 ....46 E5
Northop Hall CH7 ....37 F4
Elm Gr
Buckley / Bwcle CH7 ....48 B3
Rhyl / Y Rhyl LL18 ....7 D8
Saltney CH4 ....51 E5
Wrexham / Wrecsam LL12 ....73 C4
Elm Grove Way LL12 ....73 C4
Elmir CH1 ....41 E3
Elm Rd
Connah's Quay CH5 ....39 A3
Wrexham / Wrecsam LL13 ....74 F1
Elm Sq CH4 ....51 F6
Elms The Ewloe CH5 ....48 F7
Tallarn Green / Tallwrn Green SY14 ....90 F5
Elmsway Dr LL19 ....3 B1
Elm Way CH5 ....38 E2
Elm Wlk CH7 ....47 E5
Elm Wlk / Rhodfa'r Llwyfen LL12 ....67 B4
Elmwood Ave CH2 ....42 F4
Elmwood Cl CH5 ....39 B4
Elson Rd SY12 ....108 F3
Elstree Ave CH3 ....43 B3
Elwy Ave / Rhodfa Elwy LL18 ....8 F1
Elwy Circ LL18 ....6 E4
Elwy Cl CH7 ....47 E5
Elwy Cres
Flint / Y Fflint CH6 ....27 F4
St Asaph / Llanelwy LL17 ....16 A1
Elwy Dr LL18 ....7 D8
Elwyn Dr LL13 ....80 F4
Elwy Parc LL16 ....117 C5
Elwy St LL18 ....7 B7
Elwy Terr LL17 ....16 B1
Embassy Cl CH1 ....41 C4
Emlyn Gr LL18 ....7 A7
Emmanuel Gr 2 LL14 ....95 C8
Empress Rd LL13 ....145 A1
Emral Brook / Clos Nant Emral LL14 ....86 B5
Emral Ct SY14 ....83 A1
Emral Park Cvn Pk LL13 ....89 F5
Encil-y-Creyr Cvn Pk CH7 ....24 C4
Enderby Rd CH1 ....144 A3
Endsleigh Cl CH2 ....42 E8
Endsleigh Gdns CH2 ....42 E8
Eneurys Rd LL11 ....73 B4
Engineer Pk CH5 ....40 A4
Engine Hill LL18 ....14 F2
Englefield Ave
Connah's Quay CH5 ....38 D7
Saltney CH4 ....51 D6
Englefield Cres CH7 ....47 D5
Englefield Dr CH6 ....28 C5
Englefield Rd CH8 ....21 C8
Epsom Way / Ffordd Epsom LL13 ....80 E7
Epworth Cl LL11 ....72 B8
Epworth Rd LL18 ....7 E4
Erddig Cl LL14 ....79 D6
Erddig Country Pk★ LL13 ....79 F5
Erddig Rd / Ffordd Erddig
Wrexham / Wrecsam LL13 ....79 F7
Wrexham / Wrecsam LL13 ....80 A7
Erith St CH7 ....58 A4
Erlas Gr LL13 ....73 E1
Erlas La
Wrexham / Wrecsam LL13 ....74 C2
Wrexham / Wrecsam LL13 ....81 C8
Erlas Park Rd LL13 ....73 F4
Ermine Rd CH2 ....144 C4
Ernest Parry Rd LL13 ....73 E2
Ernest St LL18 ....7 C6
Erw Deg Acrefair LL14 ....85 C3
Llangollen LL20 ....143 D3
Erw Fach CH7 ....47 D6
Erw Ffynnon CH7 ....64 B8
Erw Gaer LL11 ....72 A8
Erwgerrig LL14 ....78 E1
Erw Goch LL15 ....141 D4
Erw Goed CH7 ....47 D6
Erw Heulog / Sunnyacre 3 LL11 ....72 D6
Erw Lan LL17 ....16 A2
Erw Las Caerwys CH7 ....24 B6
Llandegla LL11 ....127 B2
Pwll-glas LL15 ....125 F5
Rhosllanerchrugog LL14 ....85 E8
Rhyl / Y Rhyl LL18 ....7 F6
Wrexham / Wrecsam LL12 ....73 C2
Erw Lwyd LL14 ....85 D8
Erw'r Fron CH7 ....46 B2
Erw'r Llan CH7 ....64 C8
Erw Salusbury LL16 ....140 F3
Erw Wen LL18 ....9 F4
Erw-wladys LL20 ....135 C5
Esless La / Lon Esless LL14 ....79 E7
Essex Cl LL11 ....73 B5
Essex Rd CH2 ....43 A5
Estuary View CH5 ....39 A2
Estyn Cl LL12 ....59 B1
Estyn Rd / Ffordd Estyn CH7 ....58 A4
Ethelda Dr CH2 ....43 A5
Etna Rd CH7 ....48 D6
Eton Pk LL18 ....7 E1
Etterick Pk CH3 ....43 A2
Eurgain Ave / Rhodfa Eurgain CH5 ....38 C6
Evansleigh Dr CH5 ....40 A3
Evans St CH6 ....28 A7
Eversley Cl LL18 ....7 F5
Eversley Ct Chester CH2 ....42 C4
Minera LL11 ....71 A4
Eversley Pk CH2 ....42 C4
Ewart St
Chirk / Y Waun LL14 ....95 E2
Saltney CH4 ....51 B7
Ewloe Barns Ind Est CH7 ....38 B1
Ewloe Castle★ CH5 ....38 D4
Ewloe Green Cty Prim Sch CH5 ....38 E1
Ewloe Pl CH7 ....48 B6
Ewood Gr LL11 ....72 E7
Exeter Cl LL19 ....2 E2
Exeter Pl CH1 ....41 F5
Expressway Bsns Pk CH5 ....39 E5
Exton Pk CH1 ....144 A4
Eyton CW Prim Sch LL13 ....87 B7
Eyton Gr LL13 ....87 B7
Eytonhall La LL13 ....88 A5

F

Facit Glen Ind Est CH4 ....51 F7
Factory Pl LL16 ....140 C3
Factory Rd CH5 ....40 A3
Fagl La LL12 ....59 A2
Faircroft Ct LL13 ....80 E7
Fairfield LL11 ....71 F8
Fairfield Ave
Ffynnongroyw CH8 ....5 C1
Rhyl / Y Rhyl LL18 ....7 C8
Fairfield Rd
Broughton CH4 ....50 B4
Chester CH2 ....43 A4
Connah's Quay CH5 ....39 D5
Drury CH7 ....48 F5
Fairfield St LL13 ....145 B1
Fairford Rd CH4 ....51 F6
Fairhaven CH8 ....21 D5
Fairholme Prep Sch LL17 ....16 B2
Fairlands Cres LL18 ....7 F1
Fairmeadow CH4 ....61 D2
Fairmount Rd / Ffordd Brynteg 4 LL13 ....73 E3
Fairoaks Cres / Y Doerwen Deg LL12 ....67 A5
Fairoaks Dr CH5 ....38 C6
Fairview Holt LL13 ....75 E8
Penyffordd CH4 ....58 F7
Fairview Ave LL19 ....3 A1
Fairview Cl CH7 ....24 B6
Fairview Cres LL19 ....3 A1
Fairview Gdns LL11 ....72 D6
Fairview / Trem Hyfryd LL14 ....79 C7
Fairway CH5 ....40 A2
Fairway Cl CH5 ....38 D5
Fairy Rd / Ffordd y Tylwyth Teg LL13 ....145 B1
Falcon Rd / Heol Hebog LL13 ....73 E2
Fammau View Dr CH4 ....49 A1
Farbailey Cl CH4 ....52 B5
Farfield Ave CH5 ....38 E7
Farm Cl CH7 ....48 B4
Farm Dr CH5 ....29 C1
Farmfield Cl CH5 ....39 B5
Farm House Mews 3 LL13 ....73 E4
Farm La LL11 ....71 F5
Farm Rd
Buckley / Bwcle CH7 ....48 B4
Garden City CH5 ....39 E7
Farmside LL12 ....73 D5
Farm View LL13 ....81 D3
Farmworld★ LL13 ....79 D2
Farndon Cl CH4 ....50 C4
Farndon Prim Sch CH3 ....69 E2
Farndon St LL13 ....145 C2
Farnsworth Ct LL18 ....1 D5
Farriers Wlk LL12 ....67 F3
Faulkners Cl CH4 ....60 A7
Faulkners La CH3 ....53 D8
Faulkner St CH2 ....42 F3
Feathers Lea CH6 ....28 A7
Feathers St CH6 ....28 A7
Fedwen Arian CH4 ....49 A2
Felin Dyfrdwy LL20 ....143 D5
Fellows La LL12 ....66 B8
Fennant Ct / Llys Fennant LL14 ....79 A2
Fennant Rd / Y Ffennant
Johnstown LL14 ....79 A2
Rhosllanerchrugog LL14 ....78 F2
Fenwick Dr LL13 ....73 E2
Ferguson Ave LL19 ....2 D3
Fern Ave / Rhodfda Rhedyn 7 LL19 ....3 B2
Fern Bank CH7 ....38 B4
Fern Cl Cross Lanes LL13 ....81 D3
Flint / Y Fflint CH6 ....27 F5
2 Rhyl / Y Rhyl LL18 ....7 F8
Fern Ct 3 CH5 ....38 D8
Ferndale LL13 ....73 D2
Ferndale Ave LL14 ....79 C6
Ferndale Cl CH4 ....49 B1
Ferndale Rise 6 LL11 ....72 D6
Fern Gr CH5 ....39 A3
Fernham Dr 3 LL13 ....73 C6
Fernhill Ave SY11 ....106 B1
Fernhill Rd CH1 ....41 E6
Fernlea Ct CH1 ....40 F8
Fernleigh Terr LL14 ....86 A5
Fernside Rd CH5 ....39 A4
Fern Way LL18 ....7 E8
Fern Wlk 1 LL18 ....7 F8
Ferry Bank / Glan Y Fferi CH5 ....39 E6
Ferry Cl CH5 ....40 A6
Ferry La CH1 ....41 C1
Festival Gdns★ LL19 ....2 D3
Fferm Llidiart Werdd / Greengate Farm LL11 ....71 C4

Ffordd = road, way

Ffordd Aber Mostyn CH8 ....12 C4
Rhuddlan LL18 ....7 E2
Ffordd Abergele / Abergele Rd LL18 ....15 B8
Ffordd Aelwyd CH8 ....20 D6
Ffordd Aeron LL11 ....71 C3
Ffordd Afoneitha / Afoneitha Rd LL14 ....85 D7
Ffordd Alafon LL12 ....73 D5
Ffordd Alecsandra / Alexandra Rd CH7 ....47 A4
Ffordd Aled
Denbigh / Dinbych LL16 ....140 E4
Wrexham / Wrecsam LL12 ....73 D6
Ffordd Almer 5 LL12 ....73 B7
Ffordd Alun LL12 ....73 D6
Ffordd Angharad CH7 ....24 B6
Ffordd Anwyl LL18 ....7 E8
Ffordd Argoed CH7 ....47 B5
Ffordd Argoed / Argoed Rd CH7 ....48 B5
Ffordd Arley / Arley Rd 1 LL12 ....73 B7
Ffordd Balmoral / Balmoral Rd LL11 ....73 A4
Ffordd Barrfield / Barrfield Rd 5 LL18 ....7 F2
Ffordd Belgrave / Belgrave Rd LL13 ....145 B1
Ffordd Bents / Bents Rd LL14 ....78 F3
Ffordd Bethania / Bethania Rd LL14 ....85 B3
Ffordd Beuno CH8 ....20 E6
Ffordd Brenig CH7 ....47 E5
Ffordd Brighton / Brighton Rd LL18 ....7 C7
Ffordd Brigog CH7 ....47 E4
Ffordd Bruton LL18 ....7 F6
Ffordd Bryn Estyn CH7 ....46 D4
Ffordd Brynffynnon / Brynyffynnon Rd LL14 ....85 C7
Ffordd Bryniau LL18, LL19 ....9 A5
Ffordd Bryn Madoc LL11 ....70 D5
Ffordd Bryn Melyd LL19 ....9 A6
Ffordd Brynteg / Fairmount Rd 4 LL13 ....73 E3
Ffordd Bryn y Gaer / Bryn y Gaer Rd LL11 ....72 B7
Ffordd Bryn-y-Garn / Bryn-y-Garn Rd LL16 ....116 F3
Ffordd Cae Felln LL19 ....8 E8
Ffordd Cae Glas LL18 ....7 F2
Ffordd Cae Glas / Greenfield Rd LL15 ....141 D6
Ffordd Cae Llwyn CH5 ....38 C5
Ffordd Cae Newydd CH7 ....56 C3
Ffordd Caer / Chester Rd
Wrexham / Wrecsam, Garden Village LL11, LL12 ....73 B5
Wrexham / Wrecsam LL11 ....145 C4
Ffordd Caeredin / Edinburgh Rd LL11 ....73 A4
Ffordd Calcoed CH8 ....20 C2
Ffordd Caledfryn LL16 ....140 E4
Ffordd Carden Pk / Carden Park Way 3 LL13 ....73 E3
Ffordd Carreg Heilin / Carreg Heilin La LL18 ....8 F4
Ffordd Carreg-y-Llech CH7 ....57 B2
Ffordd Cefn / Cefn Rd LL13 ....73 E2
Ffordd Celyn
Denbigh / Dinbych LL16 ....140 E5
Leeswood / Coed Llai CH7 ....57 F4
Soughton / Sychdyn CH7 ....37 B2
Ffordd Clarence / Clarence Rd LL11 ....73 A4
Ffordd Colomendy LL16 ....140 E5
Ffordd Coppy LL16 ....140 A4
Ffordd Corwen / Corwen Rd LL15 ....141 C1
Ffordd Craiglun LL18 ....6 F3
Ffordd Cunedda LL15 ....141 E5
Ffordd Cwm LL13 ....80 A6
Ffordd Cynan LL12 ....73 D5
Ffordd Davy / Davy Way LL12 ....66 E6
Ffordd Dawel CH7 ....37 A1
Ffordd Ddyfrdwy CH8 ....12 C4
Ffordd Derwen LL18 ....7 D5
Ffordd Derw / Oak Dr CH7 ....57 F5
Ffordd Derwyn CH4 ....58 F7
Ffordd Dewi LL18 ....7 F1
Ffordd Dolgoed CH7 ....46 E3
Ffordd Dwyfor CH8 ....21 B7
Ffordd Dyfed
Rhosllanerchrugog LL14 ....78 F1
Wrexham / Wrecsam LL12 ....73 D3
Ffordd Dylan LL12 ....73 C3
Ffordd Dyserth / Dyserth Rd LL18, LL19 ....8 C6
Ffordd Edern LL15 ....141 E5
Ffordd Edgeworth LL12 ....73 C3
Ffordd Edwin CH7 ....37 A5
Ffordd Eglwyswen / Whitchurch Rd
Denbigh / Dinbych LL16 ....117 E1
Llandyrnog LL16 ....121 A8
Ffordd Eisteddfod LL11 ....70 D6
Ffordd Elan
Rhyl / Y Rhyl LL18 ....7 F8
Wrexham / Wrecsam LL12 ....73 C5
Ffordd Eldon CH7 ....37 B2
Ffordd Elfed LL12 ....73 D3
Ffordd Elwy LL12 ....73 C5
Ffordd Epsom / Epsom Way LL13 ....80 E7
Ffordd Erddig / Erddig Rd
Wrexham / Wrecsam LL13 ....79 F7
Wrexham / Wrecsam LL13 ....80 A7
Ffordd Estyn LL11 ....73 B5
Ffordd Estyn / Estyn Rd CH7 ....58 A4
Ffordd Euron / Laburnum Way LL12 ....67 A5
Ffordd Faddon / Bath Rd LL13 ....145 B1
Ffordd Fawr / Main Rd LL11 ....72 F6
Ffordd Fer
Holywell / Treffynnon CH8 ....21 B5
Mynydd Isa CH7 ....47 D5
Ffordd Ffawydden / Beechtree Rd CH7 ....48 B5
Ffordd Ffrainc LL18 ....8 E2
Ffordd Ffrith LL19 ....2 F3
Ffordd Ffynnon
Carmel CH8 ....20 D6
Dyserth LL18 ....8 F1
Ewloe CH5 ....48 F8
Prestatyn LL19 ....8 F8
Rhuddlan LL18 ....7 E2
Ffordd Ffynnon / Well La LL18 ....9 C7
Ffordd Foel / Foel Rd LL18 ....9 A3
Ffordd Foster / Foster Rd LL11 ....145 C4
Ffordd Frondeg LL13 ....80 B6
Ffordd Ganol Rhuddlan LL18 ....7 F2
Soughton / Sychdyn CH7 ....37 B1
Ffordd Garmonydd LL12 ....73 B7
Ffordd Gelfft CH5 ....38 C6
Ffordd Gerwyn LL13 ....80 B6
Ffordd Glanrafon / Glanrafon Rd 25 CH7 ....46 F4
Ffordd Gledlom CH8 ....25 D3
Ffordd Glyn
Mold / Yr Wyddgrug CH7 ....46 D3
Wrexham / Wrecsam LL13 ....80 A6
Ffordd Glyndwr
Flint / Y Fflint CH6 ....28 B5
Nercwys CH7 ....56 B6
Northop / Llan-eurgain CH7 ....37 A5
Ffordd Goch LL16 ....121 C7
Ffordd Gogor LL16 ....118 C8
Ffordd Gryffydd LL12 ....66 F4
Ffordd Gwelfor CH8 ....20 D6
Ffordd Gwenllain LL12 ....67 B4
Ffordd Gwilym
Prestatyn LL19 ....8 F6
Wrexham / Wrecsam LL12 ....73 C4
Ffordd Gwynach LL15 ....141 D4
Ffordd Gwynedd
Northop / Llan-eurgain CH7 ....37 A5
Rhosllanerchrugog LL14 ....85 F8
Wrexham / Wrecsam LL11 ....73 A5
Ffordd Haearn CH4 ....59 A8
Ffordd Hafod / Hafod Rd CH7 ....46 A3
Ffordd Helygen Mair / Myrtle Rd LL12 ....67 F2
Ffordd Hendre
Prestatyn LL19 ....8 F6
Wrexham / Wrecsam LL13 ....80 B6
Ffordd Hengoed CH7 ....46 E3
Ffordd Hiraddug / Hiraddug Rd LL18 ....9 A3
Ffordd Hiraethog CH8 ....12 C4
Ffordd Holt / Holt Rd LL12 ....68 C7
Ffordd Hooson LL12 ....73 C3
Ffordd Idwal LL19 ....2 E3
Ffordd Ifor LL14 ....85 D7
Ffordd Iorwerth LL12 ....67 B4
Fforddisa LL19 ....3 A1
Ffordd Isaf LL11 ....70 D5
Ffordd Isaf Dinbych / Lower Denbigh Rd LL17 ....117 A8
Ffordd Isar Foel / Lower Foel Rd LL18 ....9 A2
Ffordd Jarvis LL12 ....73 C4
Ffordd Kayton 4 LL14 ....95 C8
Fforddlas LL19 ....3 C1
Ffordd Las Cymau LL11 ....65 F5
Denbigh / Dinbych LL16 ....140 C2
Penymynydd CH4 ....49 A1
Rhyl / Y Rhyl LL18 ....7 C6
Soughton / Sychdyn CH7 ....37 B1
Ffordd Lerry LL12 ....73 C6
Ffordd Llanarmon / Llanarmon Rd LL11 ....70 B7
Ffordd Llanarth CH5 ....38 C7
Ffordd Llanelwy / St Asaph Rd LL18 ....8 F2
Ffordd Llanerch LL14 ....85 D7
Ffordd Llaneurgain / Northop Rd CH6 ....28 A4
Ffordd Llanfynydd CH7, LL11 ....65 B7
Ffordd Llangollen / Llangollen Rd LL14, LL20 ....85 C3
Ffordd Llanrhydd / Llanrhydd Rd LL15 ....141 D5
Ffordd Llewelyn
Flint / Y Fflint CH6 ....28 B5
Nercwys CH7 ....56 E4
Ffordd Llidiart LL20 ....94 F7
Ffordd Llyn Goch LL18 ....9 C6
Ffordd Llys Nant / Nant Hall Rd LL19 ....3 B2
Ffordd Llywelyn LL12 ....73 C7
Ffordd Mabon LL12 ....66 F3
Ffordd Maddock LL12 ....67 A3
Ffordd Madoc LL12 ....73 C6
Ffordd Maelor LL12 ....73 C3
Ffordd Maesgwyn / Maesgwyn Rd LL11 ....145 A3
Ffordd Maeshafan CH7 ....55 F6
Ffordd Maes Mawr / Maes Mawr Road LL20 ....84 C3
Ffordd Maes Yr Haf LL19 ....2 E1
Ffordd Mailyn LL13 ....80 B6
Ffordd Marian LL19 ....4 B3
Ffordd Masarn / Sycamore Dr CH7 ....57 F5
Ffordd Meifod / Meifod Rd LL16 ....116 F3
Ffordd Meirionnydd LL11 ....72 F5
Ffordd Mellion CH5 ....38 C5

Ffordd Menai / Menai Way
5 LL11 ....72 D8
Ffordd Mon LL11 ....73 A5
Ffordd Montgomery /
Montgomery Rd LL13 .73 C1
Ffordd Morgan LL12 ....66 F3
Ffordd Morgan Llwyd
LL12 ....73 C7
Ffordd Morgannwg 7
LL11 ....73 A5
Ffordd Morley / Morley Rd
LL18 ....7 C7
Ffordd Morris LL15 ....7 F1
Ffordd Mwydodofa / Smelt
La LL11 ....71 B3
Ffordd Mynachlog /
Monastery Rd CH8 ....20 C4
Ffordd Mynydd Isa / Lower
Mountain Rd LL14 ....85 D8
Ffordd Myr y Parc / Park
Wall Rd LL11 ....72 E8
Ffordd Nant
Kinmel Bay / Bae Cinmel LL18 6 F3
Rhuddlan LL18 ....7 F2
Ffordd Nant-y-Gaer /
Nantygaer Rd LL12 ....85 A1
Ffordd Nercwys CH7 ....57 A1
Ffordd Neuadd CH8 ....20 D6
Ffordd Newydd
Connah's Quay CH5 ....38 C4
Denbigh / Dinbych LL16 ...140 C2
Gwynfryn LL11 ....70 D6
Mold / Yr Wyddgrug CH7 ..46 D3
St Asaph / Llanelwy LL17 ..117 A8
Ffordd Newydd Llai / Llay
New Rd
Llay LL12 ....67 A3
Wrexham / Wrecsam LL11 .72 F8
Ffordd Newydd / New Rd
Cefn-Mawr LL14, LL20 ....85 A1
Coedpoeth LL11 ....71 E3
Rhuddlan LL18 ....7 F1
Ffordd Offa
5 Cefn-mawr LL14 ....95 C8
Mynydd Isa CH7 ....47 D4
Rhosllanerchrugog LL14 ..85 F8
Rhyl / Y Rhyl LL18 ....7 F6
Ffordd Ogwen CH7 ....47 E5
Ffordd Onnen LL19 ....3 D3
Ffordd Owain
Brymbo LL11 ....71 E8
Wrexham / Wrecsam LL12 .73 C6
Ffordd Owen CH7 ....37 A6
Ffordd Pandarus CH8 ....12 C4
Ffordd Pant Gwyn CH5 ...38 C6
Ffordd Pantycelyn LL19 ..8 E8
Ffordd Pant Y Celyn LL19 .2 E1
Ffordd Pant-y-Ffordd
CH7 ....64 A7
Ffordd Parc Bodnant LL19 3 B3
Ffordd Parc Castell LL18 .14 F4
Ffordd Parc-y-Fron / Fron
Park Rd CH8 ....21 A4
Ffordd Pedrog LL13 ....73 D5
Ffordd Pel-y-Dryn CH5 ..48 F8
Ffordd Pendwll / Pendwll Rd
LL11 ....72 B8
Ffordd Pendyffryn LL19 ..3 B2
Ffordd Pennant
Mold / Yr Wyddgrug CH7 ..46 E6
Mostyn CH8 ....12 C4
Prestatyn LL19 ....8 F6
Ffordd Penrhwlfa LL19 ...8 F8
Ffordd Penrhwylfa LL19 ..8 F8
Ffordd Penri / Penry St 6
LL14 ....78 E2
Ffordd Pentre
Carmel CH8 ....20 D6
Johnstown LL14 ....79 A1
Mold / Yr Wyddgrug CH7 ..47 A4
Ffordd Pentre Bach 56 D8
Ffordd Pen Y Bryn 56 F6
Ffordd Pen Y Coed
.......117 C5
Ffordd Pen-y-gaer /
Pen-y-gaer Rd LL20 ....84 C2
Ffordd Pen Y Maes
LL16 ....117 C5
Ffordd Pen-y-Maes /
Pen-y-Maes Rd CH8 ...21 D5
Ffordd Percy / Percy Rd
LL13 ....80 B7
Ffordd Pigot / Pigot Rd 2
LL16 ....140 D3
Ffordd Plas Acton / Plas
Acton Rd LL11 ....73 A7
Ffordd Plas Bennion / Plas
Bennion Rd LL14 ....85 D5
Ffordd Plas Newydd
LL15 ....141 B4
Ffordd Plas Trefor / Trevor
Hall Rd LL20 ....84 D1
Ffordd Plas Ucha CH7 ...56 E3
Ffordd Powell LL11 ....72 C3
Ffordd Powys LL14 ....78 F1
Ffordd Rhiw Ial CH7 ...127 A7
Ffordd Rhosddu / Rhosddu
Rd
5 Wrexham / Wrecsam
LL11 ....145 B2
Wrexham / Wrecsam, Rhosddu
LL11 ....145 B4
Ffordd Rhufon LL15 ...141 D5
Ffordd Rhyl / Rhyl Rd
LL16 ....140 D4
Ffordd Richard Davies
LL17 ....116 E8

Ffordd Russell / Russell Rd
LL18 ....7 C8
Ffordd Sandringham /
Sandringham Rd LL13 .73 A4
Ffordd Sant Marc / St
Mark's Rd LL13 ....145 B2
Ffordd Siarl LL17 ....16 A1
Ffordd Siarl / Charles Rd
CH7 ....58 A4
Ffordd Smithfield /
Smithfield Dr LL13 ...75 D8
Ffordd Sonlli / Sontley Rd
LL13 ....80 A7
Ffordd Stanley / Stanley Rd
LL14 ....78 F2
Ffordd Sugn SY10 .....139 A5
Ffordd Talargoch
Dyserth LL18, LL19 ....8 F5
Prestatyn LL18 ....9 A7
Ffordd Talbot / Talbot Rd
LL13 ....145 B1
Ffordd Talwyrn LL13 ....56 E2
Ffordd Tanrallt LL19 ....9 A6
Ffordd Tegid Ewloe CH5 ..48 E8
Wrexham / Wrecsam LL13 ..73 D6
Ffordd Tegla LL13 ....73 D6
Ffordd Terfyn LL18 ....14 C5
Ffordd Thomas Gee
LL16 ....140 E4
Ffordd Tirion CH7 ....37 B1
Ffordd Top-y-Rhos CH7 ..57 C2
Ffordd Trefaldwyn 5
LL11 ....73 A5
Ffordd Treffynnon / Holywell
Rd CH7 ....24 B7
Ffordd Trefin LL12 ....73 D6
Ffordd Trelawnyd /
Newmarket Rd LL18 ...9 C4
Ffordd Trem Y Foel CH7 ..46 E3
Ffordd Tudor / Tudor Rd
LL13 ....80 B7
Ffordd Ty Cerrig LL21 ..142 C5
Ffordd Ty Newydd LL19 ..9 F6
Ffordd Tyn y Cestyll / Tyn y
Cestyll Road LL20 ....135 B4
Ffordd Uchaf LL11 ....70 D6
Ffordd Uchaf Foel / Upper
Foel Rd LL18 ....9 A2
Ffordd Victoria / Victoria Rd
12 CH7 ....46 F4
Ffordd Walwen CH8 ....25 E3
Ffordd Wellington /
Wellington Rd
Rhyl / Y Rhyl LL18 ....7 A7
Wrexham / Wrecsam LL13 145 B1
Ffordd Westbury / Westbury
Dr LL12 ....73 B7
Ffordd William Morgan
LL17 ....15 D1
Ffordd Windsor / Windsor
Rd LL18 ....78 E1
Ffordd Wyn LL19 ....4 A3
Ffordd Wynnstay / Wynnstay
Rd 5 LL15 ....141 D5
Ffordd y Abaty / Abbey Rd 2
LL16 ....140 D4
Ffordd y Bannau / Beacon Rd
1 LL11 ....72 D6
Ffordd-y-Berllan LL22 ...6 B2
Ffordd Y Blaenau CH7 ...64 A5
Ffordd-y-Bont
Coed Talon CH7 ....57 E2
Pontybodkin CH7 ....58 A3
Ffordd Y Bont / Bridge Rd
LL19 ....3 A3
Ffordd-y-Bryn / Mount Rd
LL17 ....16 B2
Ffordd Y Castell / Castle Rd
LL14 ....105 D7
Ffordd-y-Castell / Castle St
LL14 ....7 E1
Ffordd y Chwarel / Quarry
Road LL20 ....135 B4
Ffordd Y Crib Uchel / High
Ridge Dr LL14 ....79 E8
Ffordd-y-cwm / Cwm Rd
Cwm LL18 ....17 A8
Dyserth LL18 ....8 F2
Ffordd Y Dderwen / Oak Rd
2 LL14 ....78 F2
Ffordd y Ddol / Lea Rd
LL13 ....145 B2
Ffordd Y Ddraenen Wen /
Hawthorn Rd LL12 ...67 F2
Ffordd y Dug / Duke Rd
LL14 ....78 E1
Ffordd-y-Dyffryn / Vale Rd
1 LL16 ....140 D3
Ffordd Y Dyffryn / Valley
Way LL13 ....80 B7
Ffordd Y Felin Wynt /
Windmill Rd CH7 ....48 B5
Ffordd-y-Ffair / Smithfield
Rd LL14 ....140 B2
Ffordd-y-Ffynnon CH8 ..12 C4
Ffordd Y Ffynnon / Spring
Rd LL14 ....79 C6
Ffordd Y Fran CH6 ....28 B4
Ffordd y Fynwent / Cemetary
Rd LL14 ....78 E1
Ffordd-y-gaer LL11 ....72 F8
Ffordd Y Gardden / Gardden
Rd LL14 ....78 E2
Ffordd-y-Gilfach / Greek Rd
LL14 ....78 E2

Ffordd Y Gilrhos CH7 ....64 B8
Ffordd Y Glowyr / Miners Rd
LL12 ....66 F6
Ffordd Y Glyn CH8 ....21 B7
Ffordd Y Glyn / Dingle Rd
CH7 ....58 A5
Ffordd Y Goedwig / Forest
Rd LL12 ....67 B4
Ffordd Y Goedwig / Forest
Wlk CH7 ....48 E4
Ffordd Y Graig
Denbigh / Dinbych LL16 ...140 C4
Lixwm / Licswm CH8 ....25 E2
Rhes-y-cae CH8 ....26 B2
Ffordd-y-Graig / Rock Rd
LL14 ....85 A3
Ffordd-y-Llan CH7 ....44 F7
Ffordd Y Llan CH7 ....57 C1
Ffordd y Llyn / Pool Rd 8
LL14 ....80 E7
Ffordd-y-Pandy / Pandy La
LL18 ....9 A4
Ffordd Y Pentre CH7 ...56 E6
Ffordd Y Poplys / Poplar Rd
LL14 ....85 C7
Ffordd yr Abaty / Abbey Rd
LL20 ....143 B6
Ffordd Yr Argau / Moss
Valley Road LL12 ....72 C4
Ffordd-y-Rhaeadr /
Waterfall Rd LL18 ....8 F3
Ffordd Y Rhos CH7 ....64 A7
Ffordd Y Odyn CH7 ....64 A8
Ffordd-Yr-Orsaf / Station Rd
LL14 ....105 D8
Ffordd Yr Orsaf / Station Rd
Prestatyn LL19 ....3 A3
8 Ruabon / Rhiwabon
LL14 ....86 A4
Ruthin / Rhuthin LL15 ...141 D5
Ffordd-yr-Ucheldir /
Highland's Rd LL18 ....7 F2
Ffordd Yr Ysgol LL11 ...70 E5
Ffordd Yr Ysgol / School Rd
LL15 ....141 D5
Ffordd Ysgubor CH8 ....12 B4
Ffordd Ysgubor /
Gwaenynog Rd LL16 .140 A3
Ffordd Ystrad / Ystrad Rd
LL16 ....140 E2
Ffordd y Tylwyth Teg / Fairy
Rd LL13 ....145 B1
Ffordd y Tywysob / Princes
Rd 7 LL14 ....78 E1
Fforded Y Ffwrnais /
Furnace Rd LL12 ....66 A3
Fforrd Hirwaun LL19 ....8 E8
Ffridd Y Gog LL21 ....142 C5
Ffrwd Rd LL12 ....66 B4
Ffynnon Bach LL15 ...125 E1
Ffynnon Barcer / Barker's
Well La LL14 ....140 C3
Ffynnon Charnell /
Charnell's Well 2
LL16 ....140 C3
Ffynnongroew Rd LL18 ...7 B7
Ffynnon Nefydd LL16 ...116 B5
Ffynnon Nephal LL11 ....70 F7
Ffynnon Tegla LL11 ....127 B3
Field Cl CH6 ....27 F5
Field Farm La CH7 ....48 A6
Field Farm Rd CH7 ....48 A6
Fielding Cl CH5 ....48 E8
Field Pk CH5 ....38 D4
Fieldside CH5 ....39 C2
Field Terr CH6 ....21 F5
Field View
Connah's Quay CH5 ....39 E4
Wrexham / Wrecsam LL13 .73 C1
Fieldway CH2 ....42 E4
Fifth Ave
Flint / Y Fflint CH6 ....28 A4
Talacre CH8 ....5 A6
Fifth Ave / Pumed Rhodfa
LL12 ....67 A4
Filkin's La CH3 ....43 A1
Finchett Ct CH1 ....42 B3
Finchett Dr CH1 ....42 B3
Finney Cl LL11 ....72 F4
Firbeck Cl CH4 ....50 B3
Fir-Brook Ave CH5 ....38 F6
Firemans Sq CH1 .....144 B3
Fir Gr CH7 ....46 E5
Firgrove Cnr LL12 ....73 D5
Firs Sch CH2 ....42 E5
First Ave
Connah's Quay CH5 ....31 C4
Flint / Y Fflint CH6 ....28 A5
Pentre Maelor LL13 ....74 E1
Prestatyn LL19 ....2 F4
Wrexham / Wrecsam LL12 .72 C7
First Ave / Rhodfa Gyntaf
LL12 ....67 A4
Firs The
Mold / Yr Wyddgrug CH7 ..47 A2
Whitchurch SY13 ....103 F8
Fir Tree Ave CH4 ....52 B5
Firtree Cl 3 SY12 ....109 A2
Fir Tree La CH3 ....43 E2
Fir Tree Rd LL18 ....72 F8
Fir Trees Holiday Pk
CH1 ....41 C4
Fishermans' Rd CH5 ...38 F4
Fisher Rd CH1 ....41 E4
Five Ashes Rd CH4 ....52 B5
Five Crosses Ind Est LL11 71 B5

Flag La N CH2 ....42 E8
Flag La S CH2 ....42 E8
Flaxfield Cl CH8 ....20 E3
Flaxmere Dr CH3 ....53 B8
Fleming Dr LL11 ....72 F4
Flint Castle* CH6 ....28 B7
Flint Cottage Hospl CH6 .27 F6
Flint High Sch CH6 ....28 A4
Flintshire Retail Ctr CH6 .28 B7
Flint Sta CH6 ....28 B7
Florita Cl CH5 ....38 C8
Foel Gron / Voel Gron
CH6 ....22 C2
Foel Pk / Parc-y-Foel
LL18 ....8 F2
Foel Rd / Ffordd Foel
LL18 ....9 A3
Foel View Rd LL18 ....7 E6
Fontwell Cl / Clos Fontwell
LL13 ....80 E7
Foregate St CH1 ....144 B3
Forest Dr CH4 ....50 C3
Forest Pines / Pinwyddy
Goedwig 2 LL13 ....73 F3
Forest Rd / Ffordd Y
Goedwig LL12 ....67 B4
Forest St CH1 ....144 C2
Forest Wlk / Ffordd Y
Goedwig CH7 ....48 E4
Forge Cl LL12 ....72 A4
Forge Rd LL11 ....72 A4
Forge The / Yr Efail CH4 49 A1
Forge Way CH4 ....51 F4
Forresters Terr LL14 ....86 A5
Forum The CH1 ....144 A2
Foryd Rd CH8 ....0 D5
Foster Rd / Ffordd Foster
LL11 ....145 C2
Foundry Rd LL13 .....145 C2
Four Crosses
Llanferres CH7 ....55 B2
Nannerch CH7 ....34 F1
Trelogan CH8 ....10 E5
Fourth Ave
Connah's Quay CH5 ....30 E2
Flint / Y Fflint CH6 ....28 A5
Llay LL12 ....67 A4
Talacre CH8 ....5 A6
Fourth Rd LL13 ....74 E1
Fowler Rd CH1 ....41 D4
Foxcote Cl CH1 ....41 D5
Fox Cover CH3 ....43 F5
Fox Covert La CH2 ....43 B8
Foxes Cl CH5 ....39 E3
Foxes Wlk Chester CH3 ..53 A7
Higher Kinnerton CH4 .....59 F7
Foxglove Cl CH3 ....53 A6
Fox Lea CH1 ....41 A8
Foxwist Cl CH2 ....144 B4
Foxwood Dr LL14 ....79 E7
Foxwood Rise LL12 ....67 C4
Frances Ave
Rhyl / Y Rhyl LL18 ....7 D5
Wrexham / Wrecsam LL12 .73 B6
Francis Cl CH1 ....144 C3
Francis La Holt LL13 ....75 B6
Holt LL13 ....75 D7
Francis Rd LL11 ....72 B8
Francis Row CH8 ....5 D1
Francis St CH1 ....144 C3
Franklyn Ave LL19 ....2 C1
Fraser Ct CH4 ....52 D7
Fraser Dr CH7 ....48 A4
Frederick St
Johnstown LL14 ....79 A1
Rhyl / Y Rhyl LL18 ....7 A5
Friars Cl LL12 ....73 C6
Friars Ct CH5 ....49 C8
Friar's Ct LL13 ....88 F8
Friars Gate CH1 ....144 B2
Friars Mews LL13 ....89 A8
Frodsham St CH1 .....144 B3
Frog La Holt LL13 ....75 D8
Worthenbury LL13, SY14 ..83 B1
Worthenbury SY14 ....83 C2
Wrexham / Wrecsam LL13 .80 E7
Fron Bache LL20 ....143 C4
Fron Castell LL20 ....143 C4
Frondeg LL11 ....72 B5
Fron Deg Bagillt CH6 ....22 B4
Pantymwyn CH7 ....45 D2
Fron Deg Terr LL21 ...142 D3
Frongoed LL16 ....119 D5
Fron Haul
Ruthin / Rhuthin LL15 ...141 E5
St Asaph / Llanelwy LL17 ..16 C1
Fron Heulog
Coedpoeth LL11 ....71 E3
Hawarden / Penarlâg CH5 ..38 F1
Fronheulog Hill LL11 ...70 E7
Fron Heulog Terr CH7 ...56 D7
Fron Las Coedpoeth LL11 .71 C3
Holywell / Treffynnon CH8 .21 D5
Fron Park Rd / Ffordd
Parc-y-Fron CH8 ....21 A4
Fron Rd CH5 ....38 F7
Fulbrooke CH8 ....21 C8
Furnace Cl / Clos Y Ffwrnais
LL11 ....71 B4
Furnace Rd / Ffordd Y
Ffwrnais LL12 ....66 A3
Furne Rd CH1 ....41 E4

G

Gabriel Cl 4 LL13 ....73 E4
Gadlys La Bagillt CH6 ....22 B3
Bagillt, Gadlys CH6 ....22 A1
Gaer View LL21 ....142 C3
Gainford Ave CH5 ....38 D7
Gaingc Rd LL22 ....6 A4
Gainsborough Rd LL12 ..73 E5
Gala Cl CH4 ....50 C3
Galaxy Gr LL11 ....72 C5
Gamfa Wen CH8 ....5 A6
Gamford La LL12 ....68 D7
Gamlin St LL18 ....7 B7
Gamul Pl CH1 ....144 B1
Gardd Eirlys CH7 ....47 E4
Gardd Eithin CH7 ....38 A4
Gardden Ct LL14 ....78 F1
Gardden Ind Est LL14 ...86 A6
Gardden Rd / Ffordd y
Gardden LL11 ....78 F1
Gardden View LL11 ....86 A6
Gardd Estyn 1 LL11 ...73 B5
Gardd Francis LL14 ....85 C7
Gardd-y-Gwanwyn CH8 .38 A4
Garden City Ind Est CH5 .39 B6
Garden Ct Chester CH1 ..144 A3
Wrexham / Wrecsam LL13 .73 B5
Garden Hs The* LL13 ...97 E7
Garden La CH1 ....144 A3
Garden Rd LL11 ....145 B3
Garden Row CH8 ....12 D4
Gardens The Holt LL13 ..69 E1
Wrexham / Wrecsam
LL11 ....145 C3
Garden Terr
Chester, Boughton CH2 ...42 F2
Chester CH1 ....144 A3
Garden Village SY11 ...106 E6
Garden Way 3 CH5 ....39 A6
Gardner's Row CH6 ....28 D4
Gareth Cl LL8 ....7 D6
Garfield Terr LL16 .....140 D3
Garford Rd LL18 ....1 E5
Garner Rd LL13 ....73 D2
Garner's La SY13 .....113 C3
Garnett Ave LL18 ....7 B6
Garnett Dr LL19 ....2 B1
Garratt Cl CH5 ....38 E7
Garreg Lwyd LL21 .....129 B5
Garth Clarendon LL18 ...6 E3
Garth Dr CH2 ....42 C5
Garth Ganol CH6 ....28 B4
Garth La CH8 ....11 E8
Garth Morea LL18 ....6 E3
Garthorpe Ave CH5 ....38 E8
Garthorpe Cl CH5 ....38 E8
Garth Prim Sch LL20 ...84 D2
Garth Rd / Ffordd Y Garth
LL20 ....84 E2
Garwyn Ave LL19 ....8 F7
Gas La / Lon Nwy CH7 ...47 A4
Gas Works La 3 A2
Gatefield LL13 ....145 C1
Gate Rd Froncysyllte LL20 .94 F8
Llangollen Rural LL20 ....95 A7
Gatesheath Dr CH2 ....42 E7
Gateway LL12 ....73 B4
Gatewen Rd LL11 ....72 D3
Gatiau'r Stabl / Stablegates
LL11 ....79 A1
Gawer Pk CH2 ....42 C4
Gaymoore Cl CH2 .....144 A4
Gayton Cl Chester CH2 ..42 E5
Connah's Quay CH5 ....38 D6
Gegin La / Lon-y-Gegin
LL12 ....67 C5
Gegin Rd LL11 ....67 A5
Gele Ave / Rhodfa Gele 7
LL13 ....7 D8
Gelli Derllwy / Elmanoak Gr
LL12 ....67 A5
Gelli Dywod / Sandy Gr
CH7 ....46 E3
Gelli Eldon / Eldon Gr
LL14 ....79 D6
Gelli For LL18 ....7 F6
Gellifor Sch LL15 .....121 D5
Gelli Goodwood / Goodwood
Gr 3 LL13 ....80 D7
Gelli'r Gollan Ffrengig /
Walnut Gr LL12 ....67 A5
Gelli'r Pinwydd / Pine Gr
LL12 ....67 B4
Gell'r Eurmen / Linden Gr
LL12 ....67 A5
Gemig St LL17 ....16 B1
George Ave LL20 ....85 A1
George Kenyon Mews
CH4 ....51 E6
George St Chester CH1 ..144 A3
Chirk / Y Waun LL14 ....95 E2
Llangollen LL20 ....143 C5
Wrexham / Wrecsam LL11 145 B4
Gerald St / Stryt Gerallt
LL11 ....145 B3
Gerddi LL11 ....78 E2
Gerddi Chatsworth /
Chatsworth Gdns LL12 .73 B7
Gerddi Mair LL16 .....140 E4
Gerddi'r Berse / Berse Gdns
11 LL11 ....72 C3

Gerddi'r Pistyll / Spring Gdns LL11 ....145 B3
Gerddi Twr / Tower Gdns CH8 ....21 B4
Gerddi Sussex / Sussex Gdns 2 LL11 ....73 B5
Gernant
 Pentre Llanrhaeadr LL16 .120 F5
 Wrexham / Wrecsam LL13 .80 E8
Gerrards Ave CH3 ....43 A1
Ger-y-ddol LL20 ....143 C5
Ger-y-Llan CH7 ....46 B2
Ger y Nant
 Llangollen LL20 ....143 C4
 Rhosymedre LL14 ....85 D2
Ger-y-Pistyll CH7 ....56 E6
Geufron LL11 ....7 C7
Gibson St LL13 ....145 A2
Gilbert's La SY13 ....113 A1
Gillian Cl LL18 ....7 E5
Gillian Dr LL18 ....7 E5
Gipsy La Rhuddlan LL18 .15 B8
 Rhyl / Y Rhyl LL18 ....7 A1
Gladstone Ave CH1 ....42 B2
Gladstone Rd
 Broughton CH4 ....50 B3
 Chester CH1 ....42 B3
Gladstone St
 4 Connah's Quay CH5 ....39 A6
 Connah's Quay, Queensferry CH5 ....39 D5
 17 Mold / Yr Wyddgrug CH7 ....46 F4
Gladstone Terr CH5 ....39 F3
Gladstone Terr / Rhesdai Gladstone LL16 ....121 B8
Gladstone Way CH5 ....39 D2
Gladwyn Rd LL12 ....73 B6
Gladwyn Terr 3 LL11 ....72 B4
Glamis Cl LL13 ....43 A2
Glan Aber LL12 ....73 C3
Glan Aber Cl / Clos Glanaber LL11 ....72 E6
Glanaber Cl CH4 ....52 A7
Glan Aber Ct CH6 ....21 F5
Glan Aber Dr CH4 ....51 F7
Glan Aber Pk CH4 ....52 A7
Glanaber Trad Est LL18 ...7 A5
Glan Alun LL19 ....46 F4
Glandwr LL19 ....2 E2
Glandwr Cres LL18 ....6 E4
Glanffrwd Terr LL20 .....135 C4
Glan Ffyddion LL18 ....8 F3
Glan Garth LL12 ....73 C3
Glanglasfor 4 LL18 ....7 B7
Glan Gors
 Flint / Y Fflint CH6 ....28 B4
 Wrexham / Wrecsam LL13 .80 E8
Glan-Llyn Rd LL11 ....72 E8
Glan Mor LL19 ....3 A3
Glanrafon LL11 ....78 D1
Glanrafon Rd / Ffordd Glanrafon **25** CH7 .....46 F4
Glan Sarno CH8 ....21 B3
Glan Traeth LL19 ....3 A3
Glan-y-Don CH8 ....21 C6
Glan Y Fferi / Ferry Bank CH5 ....39 E6
Glan Y Gors LL19 ....2 F2
Glan-Y-Gors LL11 ....7 E5
Glan-y-Morfa Ct CH5 ....38 F7
Glan Y Morfa Ind Est LL18 7 A5
Glan Yr Afon / Brook St LL13 ....145 B2
Glan yr Afon Terr CH8 ...10 F8
Glan-yr-Afon Terr LL17 ..16 B1
Glan Yr Eglwys CH7 ....37 A6
Glan-y-wiber / Adderley Bank LL12 ....73 B7
Glascoed Ave LL18 ....6 C5
Glascoed Rd
 Bodelwyddan LL22 ....14 E1
 Ffrith LL11 ....65 B2
 St Asaph / Llanelwy LL17 .116 E8
Glascoed Way LL11 ....72 D6
Glasdir Ffynnongroyw CH8 ..5 B1
 Treuddyn CH7 ....57 B1
Glasdir Terr CH7 ....24 B6
Glasfryn Henllan LL16 .....116 F3
 Johnstown LL14 ....79 B1
 Ruthin / Rhuthin LL15 ....141 D4
Glasfryn Ave LL19 ....9 A7
Glasfryn Terr LL11 ....72 C3
Glas-Goed CH7 ....44 F7
Glasll Wyn CH5 ....39 B4
Glaslyn Acrefair LL14 ......85 E3
 Pwll-glas LL15 ....141 B3
Glas Meadow La LL16 ....140 B2
Glasolr / Greenways LL13 ....80 E6
Glassblobbery The★ LL21 ....128 C1
Glastonbury Ave CH2 .....42 F7
Gleggs Cl CH3 ....53 B7
Glen Avon LL12 ....73 C2
Glendale Ave CH5 ....39 F3
Glendale Bsns Pk CH5 ....40 A3
Glendale Pk CH5 ....40 A3
Glendower Ct 1 LL18 ....7 C8
Glendower Cvn Pk SY10 .136 F1
Glendower Pl SY13 ....101 B3
Gleneagles LL13 ....73 E3
Gleneagles Cl CH3 ....43 D5
Glenesk Ct CH5 ....39 F6
Glen Morfa LL22 ....6 B3

Glenside Cl CH1 ....41 D5
Glen The Blacon CH1 ......41 E5
 Marchwiel LL13 ....80 F4
Glen Way LL11 ....71 E5
Globe Way CH7 ....48 D7
Gloddaeth Cres CH8 ....12 A5
Gloddaeth Villas LL16 ....140 D5
Gloucester Ave 8 CH5 ....39 B6
Gloucester Dr LL11 ....72 E3
Gloucester St CH1 ....144 B4
Glovers Loom CH3 ....53 B7
Gloverstone Ct CH1 ......144 B1
Glyn Abbott Ave CH5 ......21 D5
Glyn Ave Prestatyn LL19 ...3 B2
 Rhyl / Y Rhyl LL18 ....7 E6
 Wrexham / Wrecsam LL13 .73 C5
Glyn Ave / Rhodfa Glyn **3** LL18 ....7 E5
Glyn Castell LL16 ....121 B5
Glyn Circ LL18 ....6 E4
Glyndwr Ct CH7 ....47 A3
Glyndwr Rd
 Gwernymynydd CH7 ....46 B1
 Nercwys CH7 ....56 B8
 Wrexham / Wrecsam LL12 .73 B5
Glyndwr Terr
 Carrog LL21 ....129 F2
 Corwen LL21 ....142 E3
Glyndyfrdwy Com Sch LL21 ....130 D1
Glyndyfrdwy Sta★ LL13 130 D1
Glynnedale Pk CH5 ....39 A1
Glynne St
 Connah's Quay, Queensferry CH5 ....39 D5
 Connah's Quay, Wepre CH5 .38 F7
Glynne Way CH5 ....49 D8
Glynteg CH7 ....46 F3
Glyon La LL11, LL12 ....65 F2
Goblin's La SY13 ....113 A1
Godre'r Coed
 Cynwyd LL21 ....132 F8
 Gwernymynydd CH7 ....46 B1
Godre'r Gaer LL21 ....142 C5
Godre'r Garn LL16 ....116 F3
Godre'r Graig LL16 ....116 B5
Godre'r Mynydd CH7 ......46 C2
Godre'r Waen CH6 ....28 A1
Godstall La CH1 ....144 B2
Gofer LL22 ....14 A7
Golden Gr LL18 ....7 D5
Golden Sands Holiday Camp LL18 ....6 C5
Golftyn Com Prim Sch CH5 ....38 D8
Golftyn Dr CH5 ....29 C1
Golftyn La
 Connah's Quay CH5 ....38 C8
 Connah's Quay CH7 ....38 B7
Golygfa'r Castell / Castle View CH5 ....140 D4
Golygfa'r Dyffryn / Vale View LL14 ....85 B3
Golygfar Eglwys / Church View **13** LL11 ....86 A4
Gonsley Cl CH2 ....144 B4
Goodwick Dr / Rhodfa Gwdig **1** LL13 ....80 D7
Goodwood Cl CH1 ....42 B2
Goodwood Gr CH5 ....38 A4
Goodwood Gr / Gelli Goodwood **3** LL13 .....80 D7
Goodwood Gr / Llwyn Goodwood CH7 ....57 F5
Gordon Ave Prestatyn LL19 .3 A1
 Rhyl / Y Rhyl LL18 ....7 A7
Gordon Terr CH7 ....47 A5
Gornel Ave CH5 ....38 E7
Gorphwysfa 1 LL11 ....72 C3
Gorphwysfa Ave LL19 ......3 A3
Gorse Cl CH4 ....49 B1
Gorse Cres / Cilgant Yr Eithin LL12 ....67 F2
Gorse Stacks CH1 ....144 B3
Gorse Way CH3 ....53 A6
Gors Rd LL22 ....6 B2
Gosforth Pl CH2 ....42 F3
Gosmore Rd CH7 ....47 C7
Goss St CH1 ....144 A2
Goulbourne Ave / Rhodfa Goulbourne **5** LL13 ...73 E4
Gourton Sq LL13 ....73 E4
Goya Cl CH5 ....38 C8
Grafton Mews CH2 ....144 B4
Graham Ave LL19 ....8 F7
Graham Dr LL18 ....7 D8
Graham Rd CH1 ....41 F3
Graig La LL13 ....89 A8
Graigwen Rd LL13 ....72 B6
Graig Yard Ind Est LL14 .140 C4
Granaries Bsns Pk CH8 ....4 F4
Granby Ct CH5 ....38 C8
Grange Ave
 Rhyl / Y Rhyl LL18 ....7 D7
 Wrexham / Wrecsam LL11 .73 C4
Grange Cl LL12 ....73 C4
Grange Ct Rhyl / Y Rhyl LL18 .7 E7
 Wrexham / Wrecsam LL11 .72 F4
Grange La CH8 ....20 E5
Grange Rd
 Bronington SY13 ....101 F3
 Chester CH2 ....42 D4
 Chester CH3 ....43 C2
 Connah's Quay CH5 ....39 B4
 Ellesmere Urban SY12 ....109 A4
 Llangollen LL20 ....143 D3
 Maelor South LL13 ....100 B2
 Rhyl / Y Rhyl LL18 ....7 D7

Grange Rd W CH3 ....43 C2
Grangeside CH2 ....42 D7
Grange Villas CH3 ....53 F6
Grango La / Lon Grango LL14 ....78 E2
Granston Cl CH5 ....38 C4
Grant Dr CH5 ....39 A4
Granville Rd CH1 ....42 B3
Grasmere Cl
 Connah's Quay CH5 ....38 C7
 Prestatyn LL19 ....2 F3
Grasmere Cres CH7 ....48 D6
Grasmere Rd CH7 ....42 F5
Grasmere Way 3 LL12 ....73 B6
Grays Rd CH7 ....47 D4
Greaves La LL14 ....90 E6
Greaves La E SY14 ....90 E7
Gredington Pk LL13 ....73 F4
Greek Rd / Fford-y-Gilfach LL14 ....78 E2
Greenacre Dr CH6 ....22 D2
Greenacre Rd CH4 ....51 F4
Greenacres Cvn Pk LL19 ...4 A4
Greenacres Farm Pk★ CH5 ....39 D3
Green Ave LL18 ....6 F4
Greenbank CH4 ....52 E6
Green Bank CH4 ....52 E6
Greenbank Dr CH6 ....27 F5
Greenbank Rd
 Chester CH2 ....43 A4
 Connah's Quay CH5 ....39 A5
Greenbank St LL13 ....145 C1
Greenbank Terr 6 LL16 140 C3
Green Cl LL18 ....85 D2
Green End Farm CH4 ....50 C2
Green Farm CH4 ....62 B2
Greenfield LL20 ....143 C5
Greenfield Ave CH4 ....60 A7
Greenfield Bsns Ctr CH8 .21 D8
Greenfield Bsns Pk CH8 ..21 E7
Greenfield Cres CH2 ....43 B5
Greenfield La CH2 ....43 B5
Greenfield / Maesglas LL11 ....145 B4
Greenfield Pl LL18 ....7 C7
Greenfield Prim Sch CH8 21 C7
Greenfield Rd
 Broughton CH4 ....50 C4
 Coedpoeth LL11 ....71 A4
 Greenfield / Maes-Glas CH8 21 C7
Greenfield Rd / Ffordd Cae Glas LL15 ....141 D6
Greenfields 2 SY13 ....103 F8
Greenfields La CH3 ....53 F5
Greenfields Rise SY13 ...103 E8
Greenfield St
 Holywell / Treffynnon CH8 .21 B5
 Rhyl / Y Rhyl LL18 ....7 C7
Greenfield Terr
 1 Wrexham / Wrecsam, Gwersyllt LL11 ....72 D8
 4 Wrexham / Wrecsam LL11 ....72 C3
Greenfield Valley Heritage Pk★ CH8 ....21 C6
Greenfield View LL13 ....81 D3
Greengate Farm / Fferm Llidiart Werdd LL11 ...71 C4
Greenhill Ave CH5 ....39 A1
Green La
 Bangor on Dee / Bangor-is-y-coed LL13 ....89 D6
 Chester CH3 ....43 B3
 Chester CH3 ....51 E4
 Chirk / Y Waun LL14 ....95 F3
 Connah's Quay CH5 ....39 B5
 Ewloe CH5 ....38 D2
 Higher Kinnerton CH4 ....60 B6
 Saughall CH1 ....41 C7
 Shocklach SY14 ....83 C7
 St. Martin's SY11 ....106 E5
 Whixall SY13 ....113 A1
Green La E CH5 ....40 D7
Green La / Lon Werdd LL20 ....143 C5
Green Lane Est
 Connah's Quay CH5 ....31 C1
 Sealand CH5 ....40 C8
Green Lanes LL19 ....2 B2
Green La W CH5 ....31 B3
Green La / Y Lon Las LL21 ....142 D4
Green Mdws
 Hawarden / Penarlâg CH5 .49 A8
 Wrexham / Wrecsam LL11 .72 C3
Green Pk
 Connah's Quay CH5 ....38 F7
 Penymynydd CH4 ....49 A1
 Wrexham / Wrecsam LL13 .79 F7
Green Rd LL11 ....65 F1
Green Side CH7 ....46 E4
Green St LL13 ....69 E1
Greensway CH4 ....52 A7
Green The Gresford LL12 .67 D3
 Higher Kinnerton CH4 ....60 B7
 Lixwm / Licswm CH8 ....25 D4
 Northop / Llan-eurgain CH7 37 A5
 Wrexham / Wrecsam LL13 .73 B6
Greenville Ave CH5 ....38 E2
Greenway CH3 ....69 C3
Greenways / Glasolr LL13 ....80 E6
Greenway St CH4 ....144 B1
Greenway The 11 SY12 ..109 A4
Greenway View LL12 ....67 D3

Greenwood Ave Chester CH4 ....52 D7
 2 Wrexham / Wrecsam LL13 ....72 D7
Grenadin Cl LL11 ....72 B5
Grenville Ave / Rhodfa Grenville **5** LL18 ....7 F1
Grenville Lo LL18 ....14 F4
Gresford Ave CH2 ....144 C4
Gresford Ind Pk LL13 .....73 B8
Gresford Pk LL12 ....67 D3
Gresford Rd
 Hope / Yr Hôb LL12 ....66 D8
 Llay LL12 ....67 C4
Grey Cl CH5 ....48 E8
Greyfriars 5 LL13 ....73 C6
Grey Friars CH1 ....144 A3
Greyhound Park Rd CH1 .42 A3
Greyhound Pk CH1 ....42 A3
Greystones LL11 ....145 C4
Greystones Rd CH3 ....43 C1
Greythorne Cl LL12 ....67 D3
Griffin Cl CH1 ....41 F6
Griffiths Ct CH5 ....39 A5
Griffiths Rd LL11 ....71 D3
Griffith's Rd / Heol Gryffudd LL11 ....71 D3
Griffiths Sq CH7 ....46 F5
Grindley Bank CH2 ....43 D4
Groesfan LL14 ....85 C7
Groesffordd
 Greenfield / Maes-Glas CH8 21 D8
 Tremeirchion LL17 ....117 F3
Groesffordd Nant-y-ci LL16 ....119 E4
Groesffyrdd / Cross Rds CH8 ....21 B3
Gronant Hill LL19 ....4 A3
Gronant Rd Prestatyn LL19 .3 C3
 Prestatyn LL19 ....3 E3
Gronant St LL18 ....7 A7
Groome Ave LL18 ....7 D5
Groomscroft CH5 ....39 B1
Groomsdale La CH5 ....49 B8
Grosvenor Ave CH7 ....47 E7
Grosvenor Cotts SY12 ...109 A3
Grosvenor Cres LL12 ......68 B7
Grosvenor Ct CH1 ....144 C2
Grosvenor Dr CH7 ....48 B5
Grosvenor Mus★ CH1 ...144 A1
Grosvenor Nuffield Hospl CH4 ....52 C6
Grosvenor Pk Rd CH1 ....144 C2
Grosvenor Pk Terr CH1, CH3 ....144 C2
Grosvenor Pl CH1 ....144 B1
Grosvenor Rd
 Chester CH4 ....52 C7
 Connah's Quay CH5 ....39 B5
 Prestatyn LL19 ....2 F3
 Rhyl / Y Rhyl LL18 ....7 D5
 Wrexham / Wrecsam LL11 145 C3
Grosvenor Sh Ctr The CH1 ....144 B2
Grosvenor St
 Chester CH1 ....144 A2
 Mold / Yr Wyddgrug CH7 ..46 F4
Grove Ave CH3 ....43 B3
Grove Gdns CH3 ....43 E2
Grove Lodge Cl LL11 ....145 C4
Grove Park Ave LL18 ....7 D8
Grove Park Rd LL11 ....145 B3
Grove Rd LL11 ....145 C4
Grove Rd / Lon Goch LL16 ....140 D3
Groves High Sch The LL12 ....145 C3
Groves The Chester CH1 144 B2
 Connah's Quay CH5 ....39 A7
 Gwersyllt LL11 ....66 C5
 Northop Hall CH7 ....37 F4
Grove Terr Marchwiel LL13 80 E5
 3 Rhuddlan LL18 ....7 F1
Grove The
 Holywell / Treffynnon CH8 .21 B3
 Marchwiel LL13 ....80 F4
 Prestatyn LL19 ....9 A6
 Rhyl / Y Rhyl LL18 ....7 C8
 Whitchurch SY13 ....93 F2
Guernsey Ho CH2 ....43 B5
Guilden Gn CH3 ....43 E4
Guilden Sutton CE Prim Sch CH3 ....43 E5
Guilden Sutton La CH3 ...43 D5
Guildford Cl 1 CH4 ....51 F6
Gun St LL12 ....68 B7
Gurnard Pl LL18 ....7 F1
Gutter Hill / Allt y Gwter LL18 ....78 F1
Gwaenynog Rd / Fffordd Ysgubor LL13 ....140 A3
Gwalia Caergwrle LL12 .....66 A8
 Johnstown LL14 ....79 B1
Gwalia Ave LL18 ....7 C6
Gwalia Rd Brymbo LL11 ...71 E8
 Wrexham / Wrecsam LL11 .72 A7
Gwalia Terr
 Rhosymedre LL14 ....85 C2
 Ruabon / Rhiwabon LL14 ..86 A5
Gwalia Villas LL16 ....140 C2
Gwel Afon CH8 ....20 F5
Gwelfryn LL19 ....3 A2
Gwellyn Ave CH5 ....6 E2
Gwel Y Mor LL19 ....4 B3
Gwel Y Mynydd CH7 ....48 A5
Gwenarth Dr CH8 ....7 E4
Gwenffrwd Rd CH8 ....21 A4

Gwenfra Cotts 4 LL11 ....72 A4
Gwenfro LL13 ....73 D1
Gwenfro Jun & Inf Sch LL11 ....80 D8
Gwenfro Units LL13 ....72 E2
Gwernaffield Rd CH7 ......46 E6
Gwern Gwalia LL21 ....128 C1
Gwern La LL11 ....66 D8
Gwern-y-Glyn CH7 ....58 A4
Gwernymynydd Sch CH7 .46 B2
Gwersyllt Jun Sch LL11 ..72 E7
Gwersyllt Sta LL11 ....72 D7
Gwindy St LL18 ....7 E1
Gwydyr Way LL13 ....80 B7
Gwylan Ave CH5 ....38 C8
Gwylfa Terr LL21 ....129 F2
Gwyndy Terr 2 LL18 ....7 E1
Gwynedd Dr CH6 ....28 A6
Gwynedd Prim Sch CH6 ..28 A6
Gwynfa LL11 ....72 C4
Gwynfan LL14 ....85 F8
Gwynfryn Ave LL18 ....7 B6
Gwytherin Ave LL22 ....6 A4
Gypsey Cnr SY13 ....92 E2
Gyrfa Macswell / Maxwell Dr CH7 ....57 F5
Gyrfa Seymour / Seymour Dr **6** LL18 ....7 F1

H

Hackett Ct LL13 ....80 C7
Haddon Cl 5 LL18 ....7 B6
Hadfield Cl CH5 ....38 D5
Hadley Cres LL18 ....7 D8
Hadrian Dr CH1 ....41 E6
Hafan Clwyd LL15 ....141 C5
Hafan Deg
 Holywell / Treffynnon CH8 .20 F6
 Mold / Yr Wyddgrug CH7 ..46 E3
 Treuddyn CH7 ....57 B1
Hafan Yr Ewyn LL18 ....6 E4
Hafan Yr Heli LL18 ....6 F4
Hafod CH6 ....27 F6
Hafod Ave LL18 ....6 F2
Hafod Cl Blacon CH1 ....41 D3
 Connah's Quay CH5 ....29 C1
Hafod Dr CH8 ....26 E5
Hafod Pk 1 CH5 ....38 D8
Hafod Rd / Parc Yr Hafod CH6 ....46 D4
Hafod Rd Prestatyn LL19 ...3 B3
 Rhostyllen LL13 ....79 D3
 Ruabon / Rhiwabon LL14 ..86 C8
Hafod Wen LL14 ....86 A8
Hafod-y-Bryn CH8 ....20 F1
Hafod-y-coed CH8 ....20 C6
Hafod Y Coed LL20 ....84 D2
Hafod-y-Ddol CH8 ....12 E3
Hafod-y-Glyn 3 LL14 ......79 A1
Hafod Y Mor LL19 ....3 B3
Hafod-y-Wern CH7 ....46 B2
Hafod y Wern Inf Sch LL13 ....73 D1
Hafod y Wern Jun Sch LL13 ....73 D1
Hafon Dirion LL18 ....7 A7
Haford Rd / Ffordd Hafod CH7 ....46 A3
Haig Rd LL13 ....145 C1
Halcog LL11 ....65 F1
Halghtonhall La LL13 ....89 F2
Halghton La
 Hanmer SY13 ....100 C8
 Pandy LL13 ....90 B2
Halkett Cl CH4 ....51 E5
Halkyn Hall CH8 ....26 D5
Halkyn Rd Chester CH2 ...144 C4
 Flint / Y Fflint CH6 ....27 F4
 Holywell / Treffynnon CH8 .21 C2
Halkyn St CH6 ....28 A6
Halkyn St / Heol Helygain CH8 ....21 B4
Halkyn Terr LL12 ....68 B7
Halkyn View CH5 ....38 D5
Hall Farm Pk★ LL18 ....15 D6
Hallfield Cl CH6 ....27 E4
Halla La CH5 ....38 E6
Hall La / Stryt-y-Plas LL14 ....78 C2
Hall Sq / Sgwar Y Neuadd **13** LL16 ....140 C3
Hall St LL20 ....143 C4
Hall St / Stryd Y Neuadd LL14 ....85 C7
Hall St / Stryt y Neuadd LL18 ....78 E2
Hall View LL11 ....72 C3
Hals Cl CH5 ....38 C8
Halstonwood Cl LL13 ......73 D3
Halton Rd CH2 ....42 F6
Hamdden Cl LL16 ....121 B8
Hamilton Ave CH5 ....40 A3
Hamilton Cl LL13 ....73 F4
Hamilton Pl CH1 ....144 A2
Hamilton Rd CH5 ....38 D8
Hamilton St CH2 ....42 F3
Hamlington Ave LL11 ......72 D6
Hammond Ct LL18 ....7 E5
Hammond Sch
 Chester CH2 ....144 A4
 Hoole Bank CH2 ....43 B7
Hampden Cl LL13 ....145 A1
Hampden Rd LL13 ....145 A1
Hampden Way LL14 ....85 E3

Hampshire Dr LL11 . . . . . . .73 B6
Hampson Ave LL13 . . . . . .80 C8
Hampsons Gr LL14 . . . . . . .86 B5
Hampton Ave CH5 . . . . . . .39 E4
Hampton Rd CH4 . . . . .51 F6
Hancock's La CH7 . . . . . . .48 A3
Handbridge CH4 . . . . . . .144 B1
Handford Rd CH2 . . . . .42 F6
Hand La / Yr Erw 1
LL14 . . . . .78 F2
Handsworth Cres LL18 . . . . .7 E6
Hankelow Cl CH2 . . . . . . .144 B4
Hanmer Cl
  Buckley / Bwcle CH7 . . . . .48 C3
  6 Overton LL13 . . . . .98 C8
Hanmer Prim Sch SY13 101 A4
Hanmer Terr CH6 . . . . .22 B4
Hanover Way LL13 . . . . . . .80 B7
Happy Days Holiday Camp
LL22 . . . . .6 B1
Harbbour Cl CH2 . . . . .42 E7
Harding Ave LL18 . . . . .15 F8
Harding Rd CH2 . . . . .42 B8
Hardwynn Dr LL19 . . . . .8 F6
Hardy Ave LL5 . . . . .1 D5
Harebell Cl CH3 . . . . .53 A6
Hare La CH3 . . . . .43 D3
Harington Cl CH2 . . . . .42 C8
Harington Rd CH2 . . . . .42 C8
Harlech Ave CH5 . . . . .38 D7
Harlech Cl CH7 . . . . .48 C7
Harlech Cres LL19 . . . . .2 F1
Haroldgate SY13 . . . . .93 F1
Harrison Dr LL18 . . . . .6 D5
Harrison Gr CH5 . . . . .40 A3
Harrison's Row LL20 . . . . . .84 D3
Harrowby Rd 1 CH7 . . . . . .46 F4
Hartford Mews 5 CH3 . . . . .43 B2
Hartford Way CH1 . . . . .42 A2
Harthill Rd CH1 . . . . .41 E6
Hartington St CH4 . . . . .52 E7
Hartley Cl CH4 . . . . .59 F7
Harwd Rd LL11 . . . . .71 F8
Harwoods Cl LL12 . . . . .68 D6
Harwood's La LL12 . . . . . . .68 C6
Haslin Cres CH3 . . . . .53 D7
Hatchmere Dr CH3 . . . . . . .53 B8
Hatherton Way CH2 . . . . .144 B4
Hatton Rd LL11 . . . . .41 E6
Haulfryn
  Ruthin / Rhuthin LL15 . . .141 D5
  Soughton / Sychdyn CH7 . .37 A1
Havard Way LL13 . . . . .73 E1
Haven The LL14 . . . . .78 F3
Hawarden Airport CH4,
CH5 . . . . .50 D7
Hawarden Bridge Sta
CH5 . . . . .39 C8
Hawarden Castle★ CH5 .49 D7
Hawarden Dr CH7 . . . . .48 F5
Hawarden High Sch CH5 39 A1
Hawarden Ind Pk CH4 . . . .50 B6
Hawarden Inf Sch CH5 . .49 D8
Hawarden Pk CH4 . . . . .50 B6
Hawarden Rd
  Caergwrle LL12 . . . . .66 B7
  Penymynydd CH4 . . . . . . .49 A1
Hawarden Sta CH5 . . . . . . .49 C8
Hawarden View CH7 . . . . . .48 E6
Hawarden Way CH5 . . . . . . .39 E3
Hawker Cl CH4 . . . . .50 C4
Hawkesbury Rd CH7 . . . . . .48 C5
Hawklane Cl CH5 . . . . .38 C6
Hawkstone Way / Rhodfa
Hawkstone 8 LL13 . . . . .73 F3
Hawthorn Ave
  Connah's Quay CH5 . . . . .39 B3
  Mold / Yr Wyddgrug CH7 . .46 E5
Hawthorn Cl
  Connah's Quay CH5 . . . . .39 B3
  2 St. Martin's SY11 . . . . .106 F6
Hawthorne Ave CH7 . . . . . .48 C4
Hawthorne Ave / Rhodfa'r
Doraenen Wen LL14 . . .85 C3
Hawthorne Cl SY13 . . . . . .113 C3
Hawthorne Way / Rhodfa
Hawthorne LL12 . . . . . . .66 F4
Hawthorn Rd Chester CH4 52 A6
  Christleton CH3 . . . . .53 E7
Hawthorn Rd / Ffordd Y
Ddraenen Wen LL12 . . .67 F2
Hawthorns The
  2 Ellesmere Urban SY12 .109 A3
  Wrexham / Wrecsam LL12 .73 C3
Hawthorn View CH5 . . . . . .40 A7
Haydn Cl LL18 . . . . .6 E5
Haydock Cl CH1 . . . . .42 B2
Haydock Cl / Llys Heidog
CH7 . . . . .57 F5
Haydock Rd LL13 . . . . .89 A8
Haydon Way CH5 . . . . .39 F6
Hayes Pk CH1 . . . . .144 A4
Hayfield Dr LL12 . . . . .67 F2
Haymakers Cl CH4 . . . . . . .51 F4
Haymakers Way CH1 . . . . . .41 A8
Haytor Rd LL11 . . . . .73 A4
Hazel Ave / Rhoda'f Gollen
LL11 . . . . .72 D7
Hazel Ct Flint / Y Fflint CH6 27 E5
  Rhyl / Y Rhyl LL18 . . . . . . .7 E8
Hazel Dr CH4 . . . . .49 B1
Hazel Gr Gwersyllt LL11 . . .72 D7
  Mold / Yr Wyddgrug CH7 . .46 E5
  Trevor LL20 . . . . .84 C1
  Wrexham / Wrecsam
  LL11 . . . . .145 C4
Hazel Rd CH4 . . . . .51 F5

Hazelwood Cl / Clos Y Gelli
CH5 . . . . .38 D5
Hazelwood Cres CH5 . . . . .48 F7
Headlands The CH1,
CH3 . . . . .144 C2
Health St 4 CH5 . . . . .39 B6
Heath Bank CH3 . . . . .43 D5
Heath Cl CH3 . . . . .53 B8
Heathcote Cl CH2 . . . . .42 C4
Heather Cres LL19 . . . . .8 F8
Heather Ct CH3 . . . . .53 A8
Heatherdale Cl LL11 . . . . . .72 D6
Heathfields CH2 . . . . .144 B4
Heath La CH3 . . . . .53 A8
Heath Rd CH2 . . . . .42 E7
Heath Terr CH2 . . . . .42 E8
Heber Mount LL13 . . . . . . .73 D2
Hedgeway Cl LL14 . . . . .79 D7
Heigad / Highgate 17
LL16 . . . . .140 C3
Heinzel Pk CH6 . . . . .27 F7
Helfa Bach 2 LL14 . . . . . . .95 E3
Hen Afon LL17 . . . . .117 F8
Hen-Afon Rd LL18 . . . . .7 E6
Henblas
  Flint Mountain CH6 . . . . . .28 A1
  Mold / Yr Wyddgrug CH7 . .46 E4
Henblas Rd LL14 . . . . .79 D6
Henblas Sq LL14 . . . . .145 C2
Henblas St / Stryt Henblast
LL13 . . . . .145 C2
Hendir CH6 . . . . .28 A1
Hendre-bach LL15 . . . . . .125 E1
Hendre Cl LL18 . . . . .7 F1
Hendre Cotts LL15 . . . . . .125 E1
Hendre Ct LL19 . . . . .3 B2
Hendy Rd
  Mold / Yr Wyddgrug CH7 . .46 C4
  Mold / Yr Wyddgrug CH7 . .46 E4
Hen Felin LL21 . . . . .132 D3
Henffordd
  Mold / Yr Wyddgrug CH7 . .46 F5
  Nercwys CH7 . . . . .56 D5
Hen Ffordd Bwlchgwyn / Old
Road Bwlchgwyn LL11 .70 D6
Hen Ffordd Mwynglawdd /
Old Road Minera LL11 . .71 A5
Hen Ffordd Rhuthun / Old
Ruthin Rd LL16 . . . . . . .120 E8
Hen Fuarth CH8 . . . . .21 B4
Hengoed / Old Wood
LL11 . . . . .72 C4
Henley Ave CH5 . . . . .38 F6
Henley Rd CH4 . . . . .51 F6
Henllan Pl / Llain Henllan 20
LL16 . . . . .140 C3
Henllan St / Stryd Henllan
LL16 . . . . .140 B3
Henlle Cl SY11 . . . . .105 F1
Henlle Gdns SY11 . . . . . .105 F1
Hen Lon LL16 . . . . .116 F3
Henrietta St CH5 . . . . .39 B6
Henry Pl CH4 . . . . .144 B4
Henry's Ave LL18 . . . . .7 E2
Henry St Rhostyllen LL14 . .79 D6
  Ruabon / Rhiwabon LL14 . .86 A5
Henry Taylor St CH6 . . . . . .28 B6
Henry Wood Ct CH4 . . . . . .51 E6
Henshall St CH1 . . . . .144 A4
Heol Abon LL20 . . . . .95 B8
Heol Afon LL17 . . . . .16 A1
Heol Awstralia / Australia St
14 LL14 . . . . .78 E2
Heol Bathafarn LL11 . . . . . .71 D3
Heol Bennion 5 LL20 . . . . .95 B8
Heol Berwyn 4 LL20 . . . . . .95 B8
Heol Bronwydd LL14 . . . . . .86 A8
Heol Bryniog LL11 . . . . .71 D3
Heol Cadfan LL11 . . . . .71 E3
Heol Caer / Chester St
CH6 . . . . .28 B7
Heol Camlas LL11 . . . . .72 C8
Heol Caradoc
  Coedpoeth LL11 . . . . .71 C4
  Rhosllanerchrugog LL11 . .78 D1
Heol Cefn LL11 . . . . .72 C8
Heol Cefnydd
  Cefn-Mawr LL14 . . . . .85 B1
  3 Cefn-mawr LL14 . . . . . .95 B8
Heol Celyn LL11 . . . . .71 E3
Heol Celyn LL17 . . . . .16 A1
Heol Clwyd / Clwyd St
9 Rhyl / Y Rhyl LL18 . . . . . .7 B7
  Ruthin / Rhuthin LL15 . . .141 C5
Heol Dafydd LL12 . . . . .73 C6
Heol Ddwr / Water St
CH7 . . . . .24 B6
Heol Ddyfrdwy LL14 . . . . . .86 A8
Heol Dinas LL12 . . . . .73 C5
Heol Dirion LL11 . . . . .71 D3
Heol Eifion LL14 . . . . .78 E1
Heol Esgob LL17 . . . . .15 F1
Heol Esgob / Bishop's Wlk
LL20 . . . . .143 D5
Heol Fammau LL17 . . . . . . .7 D6
Heol Fawr / High St
  Caerwys CH7 . . . . .24 B6
  Holywell / Treffynnon CH8 .21 B4
Heol Glanrafon LL11 . . . . . .71 E3
Heol Graigfab 2 LL14 . . . . .95 B8
Heol Gryffudd / Griffith's Rd
LL11 . . . . .71 D3
Heol Gwenallt LL11 . . . . . . .71 D3
Heol Gwynfa / Paradise St 11
LL18 . . . . .7 B7

Heol Hafod
  Coedpoeth LL11 . . . . .71 E3
  Johnstown LL14 . . . . .86 A8
Heol Hebog / Falcon Rd
LL13 . . . . .73 E2
Heol Helygain / Halykn St
CH8 . . . . .21 B4
Heol Helyg / Willow Rd
LL11 . . . . .71 C4
Heol Hendre LL18 . . . . .7 F1
Heol Horeb LL11 . . . . .71 C2
Heol Hyfryd LL11 . . . . .72 C8
Heol Hyfrydle LL11 . . . . . . .71 D3
Heol Isaf / Lower Rd
LL11 . . . . .71 C2
Heol Islwyn LL11 . . . . .71 E3
Heol Kenyon LL11 . . . . .86 A8
Heol Llanddewi LL12 . . . . . .73 C7
Heol Llanteg LL12 . . . . .73 C7
Heol Llawhaden 1 LL12 . . .73 C6
Heol Llewelyn LL11 . . . . . . .71 C3
Heol Llugwy / Llugwy Rd
LL11 . . . . .6 D4
Heol Llundain / London Rd
LL21 . . . . .142 D3
Heol Mabon LL14 . . . . .85 D7
Heol Maelor
  Coedpoeth LL11 . . . . .71 D3
  Johnstown LL14 . . . . .86 A8
Heol Mona LL11 . . . . .71 C4
Heol Offa Coedpoeth LL11 .71 B3
  Johnstown LL14 . . . . .86 A8
  Tanyfron LL11 . . . . .71 E5
Heol Orsaf LL14 . . . . .86 B8
Heol Pedr LL11 . . . . .72 C7
Heol Penally LL12 . . . . .73 C7
Heol Penderyst LL20 . . . . . .84 F1
Heol Pen-y-Bal / Pen-y-Ball
St CH8 . . . . .21 A4
Heol Penyfelin LL11 . . . . . . .72 C8
Heol Sussex / Sussex St 17
LL18 . . . . .7 B7
Heol Tywysog CH8 . . . . . . .26 E5
Heol Wen LL11 . . . . .71 E3
Heol-y-Berwyn / Berwyn St
LL21 . . . . .132 D4
Heol-y-Brenin
  Holywell / Treffynnon CH8 .21 B5
  Tremeirchion LL17 . . . . . .117 F7
Heol Y Brenin / King St
CH7 . . . . .46 F5
Heol-y-Brenin / King St
CH7 . . . . .47 A6
Heol-y-Bryn
  Flint / Y Fflint CH6 . . . . . .28 B4
  Penycae LL14 . . . . .85 D7
Heol y Bryn / Hill St
LL20 . . . . .143 D4
Heol-y-Capel / Chapel St
CH7 . . . . .24 B6
Heol y Capel / Chapel St
LL20 . . . . .143 D4
Heol Y Castell / Castle Rd
LL11 . . . . .71 D3
Heol y Castell / Castle St
LL20 . . . . .143 D5
Heol y Cedrwydd / Cedar
Mews LL11 . . . . .72 C8
Heol-y-Coed LL11 . . . . .72 C7
Heol-y-Cyngor LL14 . . . . . .86 B8
Heol-y-Dderwen CH7 . . . . . .57 F4
Heol-y-De / South St
CH7 . . . . .24 B6
Heol y Farchnad / Market St
LL20 . . . . .143 C5
Heol y Felin LL20 . . . . .78 D2
Heol-y-felin / Mill St
LL20 . . . . .143 D5
Heol-y-Fferm LL11 . . . . .72 C8
Heol-y-Ffynnon LL11 . . . . . .72 F8
Heol Y Frenhines / Queen St
LL18 . . . . .7 B7
Heol y Frenhines /
Queensway LL11 . . . . . .72 E8
Heol Y Fynwent / Cemetery
Rd LL11 . . . . .71 C3
Heol-y-Gelli LL11 . . . . .72 C7
Heol-y-Gogledd / North St
CH7 . . . . .24 B7
Heol Y Goron CH7 . . . . .57 F4
Heol-y-Llys 10 LL14 . . . . . . .7 F7
Heol-y-Mynydd / Mountain
St 2 LL11 . . . . .78 E2
Heol Y Nant / Nant Rd
LL11 . . . . .71 C2
Heol-y-Parc LL11 . . . . .72 E8
Heol Y Park / Park Rd
  Coedpoeth LL11 . . . . .71 C3
  Ruthin / Rhuthin LL15 . . .141 C5
Heol-yr-afon / Brook St
LL14 . . . . .78 D1
Heol yr Afon / Brook St
LL14 . . . . .78 E1
Heol Yr Efail / Smithy Rd
LL11 . . . . .71 D3
Heol-yr-Eglwys LL11 . . . . . .72 C7
Heol-yr-Eglwys / Church St
CH6 . . . . .28 A6
Heol Y Iarll / Earl Rd 2
CH7 . . . . .46 F5
Heol-y-Vro LL11 . . . . .71 D3
Heol-y-Waen LL11 . . . . .72 C8
Heol-y-Wal LL11 . . . . .66 E1
Herbert Jennings Ave
LL12 . . . . .73 C4
Hereford Pl CH1 . . . . .42 A5
Hereward Rd CH3 . . . . .43 B1

Heritage Cl / Clos
Treftadaeth 2 LL14 . . . .79 C6
Heritage Sq CH7 . . . . .64 B8
Hermitage LL20 . . . . .143 D4
Hermitage Ct CH1 . . . . .41 A8
Hermitage Dr LL13 . . . . . . .80 B7
Hermitage Rd CH1 . . . . . . .41 B7
Heronbrook 1 SY13 . . . . .103 E8
Heron Cl Broughton CH4 . .50 C4
  Ellesmere Urban SY12 . . .109 B3
  Farndon CH3 . . . . .69 F1
Heron Pl CH2 . . . . .144 B4
Herons Way CH4 . . . . .52 B3
Herriot Gr CH5 . . . . .38 E1
Heulfre Jun Sch LL16 . . . .140 A3
Heulfryn LL18 . . . . .78 E1
Heulfryn / Sunnyhill
LL11 . . . . .72 C5
Heulwen Cl LL12 . . . . .66 B8
Hewitt's La CH7 . . . . .48 A4
Hewitt St CH2 . . . . .42 F3
Hey La CH5 . . . . .38 E1
Heywoods The CH2 . . . . . . .42 C4
Hickmore Heys CH5 . . . . . .43 F5
Highbury Ave LL19 . . . . .3 B3
Highbury Cl LL19 . . . . .3 A3
Highbury Cres LL19 . . . . . . .3 A3
Highcliffe Ave CH1 . . . . . . .42 B4
Highcroft CH5 . . . . .39 A5
Highcroft The CH5 . . . . .38 C6
Higher Berse Rd LL11 . . . . .72 A3
Higher Cl CH5 . . . . .38 C7
Higher Common Cl CH7 . . .48 C6
Higher Common Rd CH7 48 C6
Higher Common Way
CH7 . . . . .48 C5
Higher Ferry CH1 . . . . .51 B8
Higher La / Lon Uchaf
LL12 . . . . .67 C6
Higher Shotton Farm
CH5 . . . . .39 A5
Highfield
  Hawarden / Penarlâg CH5 .49 C8
  Wrexham / Wrecsam LL11 .72 A8
Highfield Ave CH7 . . . . .47 E5
Highfield Com Prim Sch
CH1 . . . . .41 F4
Highfield Dr CH7 . . . . .48 C3
Highfield Pk LL13 . . . . .72 D8
Highfield Rd Bagillt CH6 . .22 C5
  Blacon CH1 . . . . .41 D5
  Wrexham / Wrecsam LL11 .72 D5
Highfields CH3 . . . . .92 A2
Highfields Ave SY13 . . . . .103 F6
Highfield Villas CH7 . . . . . .46 F3
Highgate / Heigad 17
LL16 . . . . .140 C3
Highgrove / Clos
Highgrove 1 LL14 . . . . .79 C6
Highland Ave CH7 . . . . .39 A3
Highlands Cl / Clos Yr
Ucheldir 6 LL18 . . . . . . .7 F2
Highland's Rd /
Ffordd-Yr-Ucheldir LL18 .7 E2
High Meadow Ct / Llys Maes
Ucha CH6 . . . . .27 F6
Highmere Dr CH5 . . . . .38 C7
Highmore Ct LL13 . . . . .80 C7
High Park Est CH7 . . . . . . .45 F5
High Pk CH5 . . . . .39 C1
High Ridge Dr / Ffordd Y
Crib Uchel LL14 . . . . . . .79 E8
High St Bagillt CH6 . . . . . . .22 C3
  Bangor on Dee / Bangor-is-y-coed
  LL13 . . . . .88 F7
  Brymbo LL11 . . . . .71 E8
  Caergwrle LL12 . . . . .66 A8
  Cefn-Mawr LL14 . . . . .85 B1
  Connah's Quay CH5 . . . . .39 A7
  3 Ellesmere SY12 . . . . . .109 C2
  Farndon CH3 . . . . .69 E2
  Ffrith LL11 . . . . .65 C3
  Gresford LL12 . . . . .67 D2
  Johnstown LL14 . . . . .79 A1
  Llandrillo LL21 . . . . .132 D4
  Northop / Llan-eurgain CH7 37 A5
  Overton LL13 . . . . .98 C8
  Rhostyllen LL14 . . . . .79 C6
  Rhosymedre LL14 . . . . . . .85 C2
  Rhuddlan LL18 . . . . .7 E1
  Ruabon / Rhiwabon LL14 . .86 A4
  Saltney LL14 . . . . .51 E7
  St Asaph / Llanelwy LL17 . .16 B1
  Trelawnyd LL18 . . . . .10 A4
  Weston Rhyn SY10 . . . . .105 C4
  Wrexham / Wrecsam, Gwersyllt
  LL11 . . . . .72 D8
  Wrexham / Wrecsam,
  Pentre Broughton LL11 . .72 A7
  Wrexham / Wrecsam, Southsea
  LL11 . . . . .72 A4
High St / Heol Fawr
  Caerwys CH7 . . . . .24 B6
  Holywell / Treffynnon CH8 .21 B4
High St / Stryd Fawr
  12 Denbigh / Dinbych
  LL16 . . . . .140 C3
  Mold / Yr Wyddgrug CH7 . .46 F5
  Prestatyn LL19 . . . . .3 B2
High St / Stryd Fawr
LL13 . . . . .145 C2
High St / Stryd Uchaf
LL20 . . . . .135 C2
High St / Stryd Fawr
  Dyserth LL18 . . . . .8 F1
  1 Rhyl / Y Rhyl LL18 . . . . . .7 B7
High St / Y Stryt Fawr
  Coedpoeth LL11 . . . . .71 C3

Ham – Hol 157

High St / Y Stryt Fawr
continued
  Rhosllanerchrugog LL14 . . .78 E2
Hightown Rd LL13 . . . . . .145 C2
Highvale CH5 . . . . .38 C7
Highway The CH5 . . . . .39 B1
Hilary Cl Chester CH3 . . . . .43 B1
  Denbigh / Dinbych LL16 . .140 E2
Hilbre Rd CH5 . . . . .38 D8
Hillary Gr CH7 . . . . .48 B4
Hillbury Rd LL13 . . . . .80 A7
Hill Cl / Clos Yr Allt 2
LL14 . . . . .85 C7
Hillcourt Ave CH6 . . . . .22 D1
Hill Cres SY12 . . . . .108 B7
Hill Crest
  Ellesmere Urban SY12 . . .109 C3
  Penley LL13 . . . . .99 E3
  Wrexham / Wrecsam LL13 .73 C2
Hillcrest Ct CH8 . . . . .14 F2
Hill Ct LL13 . . . . .80 C7
Hillewood Ave SY13 . . . . .103 F6
Hillfield Rd CH5 . . . . .39 B3
Hillock La CH2 . . . . .67 F2
Hill Pk SY12 . . . . .108 B6
Hill Rd CH4 . . . . .52 E2
Hillrise LL13 . . . . .80 C7
Hillsdown Dr CH5 . . . . .38 D5
Hillside
  Connah's Quay CH5 . . . . .39 C1
  Prestatyn LL19 . . . . .3 C1
  St Asaph / Llanelwy LL17 . .16 B1
Hillside Ave CH5 . . . . .38 D7
Hillside Cres
  Buckley / Bwcle CH7 . . . . .48 B3
  Mold / Yr Wyddgrug CH7 . .46 E6
Hillside Ct CH8 . . . . .21 B5
Hillside Rd Blacon CH1 . . . .41 E4
  Penymynydd CH4 . . . . . . .49 A1
Hillside Way CH6 . . . . .27 F5
Hills Lea CH6 . . . . .28 A7
Hill St Cefn-Mawr LL14 . . . .85 B1
  2 Cefn-mawr LL14 . . . . . .95 D8
  Rhostyllen LL14 . . . . .79 C6
  Wrexham / Wrecsam, Brynteg
  LL11 . . . . .72 B6
  Wrexham / Wrecsam,
  Summer Hill LL11 . . . . . .72 C8
Hill St / Heol y Bryn
LL20 . . . . .143 D4
Hill St / Penybryn LL21 142 D3
Hill St / Stryt Yr Allt
  1 Penycae LL14 . . . . .85 C7
  Rhosllanerchrugog LL14 . .78 E1
  Wrexham / Wrecsam LL11 145 B2
Hillsview Rd CH7 . . . . .48 B3
Hilltop Cl CH5 . . . . .38 E2
Hilltop Dr LL12 . . . . .67 F3
Hilltop Flats LL12 . . . . .67 F3
Hilltop Rd
  Guilden Sutton CH3 . . . . .43 F5
  Rhyl / Y Rhyl LL18 . . . . . . .7 E5
Hilltop View Rd LL12 . . . .73 D5
Hill View CH7 . . . . .47 D6
Hilton Cl LL11 . . . . .72 D8
Hilton Dr LL18 . . . . .1 E5
Hinsley Dr / Rhodfa Hinsley
LL13 . . . . .73 E4
Hiraddug Rd / Ffordd
Hiraddug LL18 . . . . .9 A3
HM Stanley Hospl LL17 .117 B8
Hobart Way CH1 . . . . .41 C3
Hob La CH3 . . . . .69 F5
Hoel Treffynnon / Holywell
St CH6 . . . . .28 A7
Hoel y Dderwen / Oak St
LL20 . . . . .143 D5
Hoel-y-plas LL14 . . . . .95 C3
Hoel-y-Wern CH7 . . . . .46 B2
Holbein Cl CH4 . . . . .52 E6
Holborn Cres LL11 . . . . . . .72 B5
Holkham The CH3 . . . . .43 B1
Holland Park Dr LL18 . . . . . .7 E6
Holland Rd LL11 . . . . .65 F1
Hollies The
  Buckley / Bwcle CH7 . . . . .48 C6
  St. Martin's SY11 . . . . . .106 E5
  7 Wrexham / Wrecsam
  LL13 . . . . .73 E3
Hollins La Ewloe CH5 . . . . .48 F7
  Whitchurch Rural SY13 . .103 D1
Hollowbrook Dr CH5 . . . . . .38 C6
Holly Bank Sch CH1 . . . . .144 A4
Hollybush Cl LL11 . . . . .72 F8
Hollybush La
  Maelor South LL13 . . . . . .99 E7
  Overton / Owrtyn LL13 . . .89 D2
  Overton / Owrtyn LL13 . . .89 D3
Hollybush Terr LL11 . . . . . .72 F8
Holly Cl
  Connah's Quay CH5 . . . . .29 C1
  1 Ellesmere SY12 . . . . . .109 A3
  Mickle Trafford CH2 . . . . . .43 F8
  Rhyl / Y Rhyl LL18 . . . . . . .7 E8
Holly Cl / Clos Celynnen
CH7 . . . . .48 B5
Holly Ct
  5 Connah's Quay CH5 . . .38 D8
  Gresford LL12 . . . . .67 D2
Holly Ct / Llys Celyn CH7 57 F5
Holly Dr
  Mold / Yr Wyddgrug CH7 . .46 E5
  Penymynydd CH4 . . . . . . .49 B1
Hollyfield LL12 . . . . .67 F3

Holly Gr
Connah's Quay CH5 . . . . . .39 B3
Wrexham / Wrecsam LL13 .73 D2
Holly Grange SY10 . . . .105 F5
Holly Wlks LL12 . . . . . .145 C4
Holme CH3 . . . . .53 E7
Holm Oak LL11 . . . . . . .145 B3
Holmwood Ave LL18 . . . . .7 E6
Holt Rd / Ffordd Holt
LL12 . . . . .68 C7
Holt Rd / Stryt Holt LL13 73 D3
Holt's Com Prim Sch
LL13 . . . . .75 C7
Holt St / Stryt Holt
LL13 . . . . .145 C2
Holway Ct CH8 . . . . .20 E6
Holway Rd CH8 . . . . .20 E6
Holy Grange CH5 . . . . . . .38 D7
Holyrood Cres LL11 . . . . .73 A4
Holyrood Way CH3 . . . . . .43 D2
Holy Tree Cl / Llys Celyn
CH5 . . . . .38 E1
Holywell Cottage Hospl /
Ysbyty Treffynnon CH8 .21 B4
Holywell Cres LL18 . . . . . .6 E3
Holywell High Sch CH8 . .21 C5
Holywell Leisure Ctr★
CH8 . . . . .21 B4
Holywell Rd Ewloe CH5 . .38 C2
Flint / Y Fflint CH6 . . . . .28 A7
St Asaph / Llanelwy LL17 .16 E2
Holywell Rd / Ffordd
Treffynnon CH7 . . . . . . .24 B7
Holywell St / Hoel
Treffynnon CH7 . . . . . . .28 A7
Homedee Ho CH1 . . . .144 A3
Homestead Ave SY11 . . .106 F6
Homestead La LL13 . . . . .72 E1
Homestead La / Lon
Homestead LL13, LL14 . .79 E8
Homestead The / Y Tyddyn
LL14 . . . . .79 E8
Honeysuckle Cl CH4 . . . .50 C3
Hoole Gdns CH2 . . . . . . .43 B3
Hoole Ho CH2 . . . . .43 B4
Hoole La CH2 . . . . .43 A3
Hoole Rd CH2 . . . . .42 F3
Hoole Way CH1 . . . . . . .144 B3
Hope Hall Dr LL12 . . . . . .59 C1
Hope Pl LL18 . . . . .7 B7
Hope Rd CH4 . . . . .50 B3
Hope St Caergwrle LL12 . .66 A8
Chester CH4 . . . . .51 F7
Wrexham / Wrecsam LL11 .72 D7
Hope Sta LL12 . . . . .59 B1
Hope St / Stryt Gobaith
LL14 . . . . .78 D2
Hope St / Stryt Yr Hob
LL11 . . . . .145 B2
Hope View Cotts LL12 . . .66 A7
Hornbeam Ave / Rhoffa'r
Teubren CH7 . . . . .48 E4
Hornesby Cl CH5 . . . . . . .38 C8
Horrocks Ct CH2 . . . . . . .42 E5
Horseshoe La SY12 . . . .108 D5
Horseshoe Pass★ LL20 .131 A6
Horseshoe Pass / Bwlch
Oernant LL20 . . . . .131 A6
Horseshoe Pass View
LL20 . . . . .143 D4
Horsley Dr LL12 . . . . . . .73 B6
Hoseley La LL12 . . . . . . .68 A2
Hospital Of St John
Almhouses CH1 . . . . . .144 A3
Hough Gn CH4 . . . . .52 B7
Housesteads Dr CH2 . . . .42 F3
Housman Cl CH1 . . . . . . .42 A5
Howard Rd CH4 . . . . .51 D6
Howards Cl CH4 . . . . . . .59 A8
Howard St CH5 . . . . .38 F7
Howell Ave / Rhodfa Hywel
❹ LL18 . . . . .7 F2
Howell Dr LL18 . . . . .7 F6
Howell's Sch LL16 . . . . .140 D2
Howe Rd LL18 . . . . .52 B7
HTM Bsns Pk LL18 . . . . .15 D8
Hudsons Hill LL14 . . . . . .68 A2
Hughe's Row LL14 . . . . . .85 C3
Hugh St CH4 . . . . .52 D7
Hullah La LL13 . . . . .73 D2
Hulleys Cl CH4 . . . . .49 B1
Hunters Croft CH4 . . . . . .59 F7
Hunters Mdw LL13 . . . . . .81 D3
Hunter St CH1 . . . . .144 A3
Hunters Way LL12 . . . . . .66 F4
Hunters Wlk
Chester CH1 . . . . .144 A2
Chester CH1 . . . . .144 A3
Huntington Com Prim Sch
CH3 . . . . .53 E4
Huntroyde Ave LL13 . . . .145 C1
Hunts Cl CH3 . . . . .43 B1
Huntsman's Cnr LL12 . . . .73 E5
Hurlbutt's Dr CH5 . . . . . .39 D6
Hurst Newton LL14 . . . . .79 E8
Hush Ho CH1 . . . . .144 A2
Huxleys La LL12 . . . . . . .59 B2
Hyfrydle LL18 . . . . .8 E3
Hylas La / Lon Hylas
LL18 . . . . .15 F8
Hywelfa LL11 . . . . .72 B5

I

Idwal LL14 . . . . .85 D3
Ifton Heath Prim Sch
SY11 . . . . .106 E7
Imperial Ave CH1 . . . . . .41 C4
Imperial Terr ❸ LL11 . . .72 C3
Ince Dr CH3 . . . . .69 F1
Ingham Cl CH3 . . . . .43 A1
Inglewood Villas LL12 . . .59 B1
Institute La CH7 . . . . . . .38 A4
Irene Ave LL11 . . . . .2 C1
Irving's Cres CH4 . . . . . .51 E6
Isabella Ct Ewloe CH5 . . .38 E7
Sealand CH4 . . . . .51 E6
Isfryn Rd E LL19 . . . . .9 A7
Isfryn Rd S LL19 . . . . .9 A7
Isglan Rd CH8 . . . . .20 E8
Island Green Sh Ctr
LL13 . . . . .145 B2
Islwyn Ave LL18 . . . . .7 D8
Is Terfyn LL17 . . . . .16 A1
Is-y-Mynydd CH7 . . . . . . .44 F7
Ithens Way LL13 . . . . . . .80 B6
Iver Cl CH2 . . . . .42 E7
Iver Rd CH2 . . . . .42 E7
Ivy Cl LL11 . . . . .73 A4
Ivy Cres CH7 . . . . .46 E5
Ivy Ct
❷ Connah's Quay CH5 . . .38 D8
Pulford CH4 . . . . .61 D2
Ivy Mews CH2 . . . . .43 A5

J

Jackson Ct CH4 . . . . .50 B7
Jaclyn Cl LL19 . . . . .2 C2
James Pk / Parc Iago
LL18 . . . . .8 F3
James Pl CH2 . . . . .42 F2
James St Chester CH1 . .144 B3
Rhostyllen LL14 . . . . . . .79 C6
Jamieson Cl CH3 . . . . . . .43 A2
Jarman Ave LL13 . . . . . .145 C1
Jarvis Way LL12 . . . . . . .73 C4
Jasmine Cres CH7 . . . . . .46 E5
Jasmine Ct LL11 . . . . . . .72 C4
Jefferson Rd CH5 . . . . . . .39 A4
Jeffreys Cl LL12 . . . . .73 C5
Jeffreys Rd LL12 . . . . . . .73 D5
Jeffreys Terr LL20 . . . . . .84 F1
Jesmond Rd CH1 . . . . . . .42 B2
JH Godwin Prim Sch
CH1 . . . . .41 D4
John's Ct LL12 . . . . .67 F7
John's Dr LL18 . . . . .14 F4
Johnsons Cl CH4 . . . . . . .52 B5
Johnson St / Yr Hobin Cast
LL14 . . . . .78 E2
John St
Chirk / Y Waun LL14 . . . .95 C8
Llangollen LL20 . . . . . .143 C4
Rhyl / Y Rhyl LL18 . . . . . .7 A7
Ruabon / Rhiwabon LL14 .86 A5
Wrexham / Wrecsam LL11 145 B1
Johnstown Inf Sch LL14 .79 A1
Johnstown Jun Sch LL14 79 A1
John Summers High Sch
CH5 . . . . .39 C5
Jonathan's Way CH1 . . . .41 E5
Jones St / Pentre Felin
LL14 . . . . .78 D1
Jubilee Ct CH7 . . . . .48 C4
Jubilee Dr CH8 . . . . .26 F1
Jubilee Rd
Buckley / Bwcle CH7 . . . .48 C4
Wrexham / Wrecsam
LL13 . . . . .145 A2
Jubilee St CH5 . . . . .39 B6
Jubilee Villas
Coedpoeth LL11 . . . . . . .71 D7
❿ Mold / Yr Wyddgrug
CH7 . . . . .46 F4
Julius Cl CH6 . . . . .28 C5
July Cotts CH4 . . . . .52 E2
Juniper Cl
Connah's Quay CH5 . . . . .38 D7
Wrexham / Wrecsam LL12 .73 D5
Juniper Cl / Clos Y Meryw
LL12 . . . . .67 F2
Juniper Ct CH2 . . . . .43 B4
Juniper Way LL18 . . . . . . .7 E8
Jupiter Dr CH7 . . . . .41 E2
Jutland Ave LL11 . . . . . . .72 D6

K

Karen Ct LL16 . . . . .140 F2
Kathen Ct LL12 . . . . .67 F2
Kaymaur Cl SY12 . . . . . .108 B6
Kearsley Ave CH5 . . . . . .39 A1
Kearsley Dr LL18 . . . . .7 F5
Keats Cl CH5 . . . . .48 F8
Keats Terr CH1 . . . . .42 A5
Keens Rd LL17 . . . . .16 A1
Kelso Cl / Clos Kelso
LL13 . . . . .80 E7
Kelsterton Ct CH5 . . . . . .29 C1
Kelsterton La
Connah's Quay CH6 . . . . .29 B1
Flint / Y Fflint CH6, CH7 . .38 A8
Kelsterton Rd
Connah's Quay CH5, CH6 . .29 C2
Flint / Y Fflint CH6 . . . . .29 A3
Kelvin Gr CH2 . . . . .42 E4

Kempton Cl CH1 . . . . . . .42 B2
Kendal Cl CH2 . . . . .43 A6
Kendall Way LL12 . . . . . .73 C6
Kendal Rd LL18 . . . . .6 E5
Kenfig Pl ❷ LL14 . . . . . .85 C1
Kenilworth Ho CH1 . . . .144 C3
Kennedy Ave CH1 . . . . . .43 A5
Kennedy Dr CH5 . . . . . . .39 D2
Kennington Cres CH5 . . . .39 D4
Kensington Ave CH5 . . . .39 A5
Kensington Cl CH4 . . . . . .52 A6
Kensington Cl / Clos
Kensington ❸ LL14 . . . .79 C6
Kensington Gn CH4 . . . . .51 F6
Kensington Gr / Llwyn
Kensington LL12 . . . . . . .73 C5
Kensington Rd CH4 . . . . .52 A6
Kenstone Ct CH7 . . . . . . .47 A4
Kent Ave CH5 . . . . .39 B5
Kent Cl CH4 . . . . .49 B1
Kent Dr LL11 . . . . .73 B6
Kent Gdns CH2 . . . . .42 F5
Kentigern Ct LL17 . . . . . .16 B1
Kent Rd Brymbo LL11 . . .71 F7
Chester CH2 . . . . .42 F5
Connah's Quay CH5 . . . . .38 D3
Wrexham / Wrecsam LL11 .72 A6
Kenyon Ave LL11 . . . . . . .73 B5
Kerfoot Ave LL18 . . . . .7 C6
Kerfoot's Cvn Camp LL22 .6 B4
Keristal Ave CH3 . . . . . . .53 A7
Kerry Pl LL12 . . . . .73 C2
Kestrel Cl CH5 . . . . .38 D5
Keswick Cl CH2 . . . . .43 A5
Ketlan Ct CH4 . . . . .51 E7
Ketland Cl CH5 . . . . .39 C6
Killins La CH5 . . . . .39 A5
Kilmorey Park Rd CH2 . . .42 F3
Kilmorey Pk CH2 . . . . . . .42 F4
Kilmorey Pk Ave CH2 . . .144 C4
Kiln Cl CH7 . . . . .48 A5
Kiln Cl / Lon Odyn CH6 . . .28 A6
Kiln La LL12 . . . . .59 C1
Kimberley Terr CH2 . . . . .42 F2
Kinard Dr CH4 . . . . .7 C8
King Edward Bldgs ❹
CH3 . . . . .43 A1
King Edward Dr CH6 . . . .28 A5
King Edward St CH5 . . . . .39 B6
Kingfisher Cl CH5 . . . . . .69 F1
Kingfisher Wlk SY11 . . . .109 B3
King George Ct LL11 . . . .70 E8
King George St CH5 . . . . .39 A6
Kings Ave
Flint / Y Fflint CH6 . . . . . .28 B6
Greenfield / Maes-Glas CH8 21 C7
Rhyl / Y Rhyl LL18 . . . . . . .7 B7
Kings' Ave / Rhodfa Brenin
❷ LL19 . . . . .3 B3
Kingsbury ❶ SY11 . . . .106 F7
Kingsbury Cl CH6 . . . . . . .27 E6
Kings Cl Chester CH4 . . .51 F5
Wrexham / Wrecsam LL13 .80 C7
King's Cres E CH3 . . . . . .43 A1
King's Cres W CH3 . . . . . .43 A1
Kings Croft CH5 . . . . .29 D1
Kingsfield Ct CH4 . . . . . .52 C5
Kings Lea Ho CH3 . . . . . .53 A8
Kingsley Ave LL18 . . . . . . .7 C6
Kingsley Gdns CH3 . . . . .53 B8
Kingsley Rd Chester CH3 . .53 B8
Garden City CH5 . . . . . . .39 F7
Kingsmead CH7 . . . . .42 C8
Kingsmills Rd LL13 . . . . .80 C8
Kings Oak Ct LL13 . . . . . .80 C7
Kings Sch CH5 . . . . .38 D8
King St Cefn-Mawr LL14 . .85 B2
Chester CH1 . . . . .144 A3
Leeswood / Coedllai CH7 . .58 A4
King St / Heol Y Brenin
CH7 . . . . .46 F5
King St / Heol-y-Brenin
CH7 . . . . .47 A6
Kingston Dr CH5 . . . . . . .38 D7
Kingston Rd ❻ LL18 . . . . .7 A7
Kingstown LL12 . . . . .73 C2
King St / Stryt y Brenin
LL11 . . . . .145 B3
King St / Stryt y Brenin ❻
LL11 . . . . .78 E1
Kingsway High Sch CH2 . .42 F5
Kingsway W CH2 . . . . . . .42 E4
Kingswood La CH3 . . . . . .41 C8
Kinmel Bay / Bae Cinmel
CH5 . . . . .6 E2
Kingsway High Sch CH2 . .42 F5
Kinmel Cl LL18 . . . . .6 D5
Kinmel Cres LL18 . . . . . . .6 C5
Kinmel Dr
Bodelwyddan LL18 . . . . .14 F3
Kinmel Bay / Bae Cinmel
CH5 . . . . .6 E2
Kinmel Park Ind Est LL18 14 F3
Kinmel St / Stryd Cilmael
LL18 . . . . .7 B7
Kinmel Terr ❶❺ LL18 . . . .7 B7
Kinmel Way / Maes Cinmel
LL22 . . . . .6 B3
Kinnerton Cl CH4 . . . . . .51 E5
Kinnerton Hts CH4 . . . . .60 A7
Kinnerton La
Higher Kinnerton CH4 . . .59 F8
Penymynydd CH4 . . . . . .49 E1

Kinnerton Rd CH4, LL12 . .59 D4
Kipling Cl CH5 . . . . .48 E8
Kipling Rd CH1 . . . . .41 F5
Kirby Ave LL19 . . . . .3 D3
Kirby Cl CH2 . . . . .42 D5
Kirkett Ave CH4 . . . . .59 F7
Kirkwood CH3 . . . . .43 A2
Kitchen St CH1 . . . . .42 B1
Knights Gn CH6 . . . . .28 B6
Knowle La CH7 . . . . .48 C5
Knowles Ave
Prestatyn LL19 . . . . .3 A1
Rhyl / Y Rhyl LL18 . . . . . . .1 E5
Knowles La SY12 . . . . . .111 B3
Knowl La CH5 . . . . .69 E5
Knowl The CH3 . . . . .69 F5
Knowsley Ave LL18 . . . . . .7 D7
Knutsford Way CH1 . . . . .41 F2
Kohima Cres CH3 . . . . . .53 B5
K.U.S. Ind Est CH5 . . . . . .50 A6
Kynaston Dr CH4 . . . . . . .51 C7
Kynaston Pl ❶ LL14 . . . .95 C8
Kynaston Rd LL19 . . . . . . .2 C2

L

Laburnam Cl SY11 . . . . .106 F6
Laburnam Dr ❻ SY12 . . .109 A2
Laburnam Cl LL12 . . . . . .67 B4
Laburnam Dr LL18 . . . . . . .7 E8
Laburnam Gr CH4 . . . . . .51 E6
Laburnam Way LL13 . . . .69 D1
Laburnam Way / Ffordd
Euron LL12 . . . . .67 A5
Laburnus Gr ❾ LL11 . . . .72 C3
Lache Hall Cres CH4 . . . .51 F4
Lache La
Chester, Roughill CH4 . . . .51 E3
Chester, Westminster Park
CH4 . . . . .52 B5
Roughhill CH4 . . . . .51 D1
Lache Park Ave CH4 . . . . .52 A6
Lache Prim Sch CH4 . . . .52 A5
Lady Bagot's Dr
Pentre Llanrhaeadr LL15 .120 F1
Ruthin / Rhuthin LL15 . . .121 A2
Lake Ave LL18 . . . . .7 A6
Lakelands Sch SY12 . . . .109 A1
Lakeside Bsns Village
CH5 . . . . .38 F1
Lakeside Cl
Buckley / Bwcle CH7 . . . .48 B7
Chester CH2 . . . . .42 F7
Gresford LL12 . . . . .67 D2
Lake View LL12 . . . . .73 D5
Lake View Terr LL12 . . . . .67 D2
Lakewood CH4 . . . . .52 B2
Lambpit St LL13 . . . . . . .145 C2
Lambpit St / Stryt Yr Lampit
CH4 . . . . .85 C7
Lamb's La CH7 . . . . .48 D4
Lancaster Dr CH3 . . . . . .43 B2
Lancaster Pk CH4 . . . . . .50 A8
Lancaster Terr LL14 . . . . .85 C3
Lane End LL13 . . . . .99 F4
Lane The SY13, SY14 . . . .91 C3
Langdale Ave
Buckley / Bwcle CH7 . . . .48 D5
Rhostyllen LL14 . . . . . . .79 C6
Langdon Ho CH4 . . . . . . .52 A7
Langford Cl LL13 . . . . . . .73 E3
Langford Cres CH7 . . . . . .47 F4
Langford Dr LL18 . . . . .6 D5
Langport Dr CH3 . . . . . . .43 C2
Lansbury Gr LL11 . . . . . . .72 B5
Lansdowne Rd CH5 . . . . .29 D1
Lansdown Dr CH4 . . . . . .50 B4
Larch Ave CH5 . . . . .39 B4
Larch Cl ❶ SY12 . . . . . .109 A2
Larch Dr LL18 . . . . .7 E8
Larches The CH5 . . . . . . .48 F7
Larchfields CH1 . . . . .41 A8
Larch Gr LL13 . . . . .73 D2
Larch Way CH4 . . . . .51 E6
Larchwood Rd LL12 . . . . .73 D5
Larkmount Rd LL18 . . . . . .7 E7
Larksfield Cl LL12 . . . . . .59 B3
Larkspur Cl CH4 . . . . . . .51 F4
Larne Dr CH4 . . . . .50 A4
Laurel Cl LL12 . . . . .67 F2
Laurel Ct LL18 . . . . .7 E8
Laurel Dr CH7 . . . . .48 C4
Laurel Gr Chester CH2 . . .43 A3
Johnstown LL14 . . . . . . .79 A1
Laurel Grove Mews LL22 . .6 B3
Laurels Ave LL13 . . . . . . .89 A4
Laurels Cl SY12 . . . . . . .109 B3
Laurels The LL12 . . . . . . .73 C4
Lavender Cl ❼ CH5 . . . . .39 B6
Lavister Gdns ❷ LL12 . . .73 B6
Lavister Wlks LL12 . . . . . .61 C1
Lawn Dr CH7 . . . . .42 D7
Lawn The LL18 . . . . .7 C8
Lawnt-y-Pentre CH6 . . . .28 A1
Lawrence St CH5 . . . . . . .40 A3
Laws Gdns CH3 . . . . .53 A8
Lawson Cl LL12 . . . . . . .145 C4
Law St CH2 . . . . .42 F3
Lawton Ho LL14 . . . . .86 A6
Lazy Acre Cvn Pk CH8 . . . .4 C4
Leaches Cl CH5 . . . . .39 E3
Leaches La CH5 . . . . .39 E3
Leadbrook Dr CH5 . . . . . .28 D3
Lead Mills / Melin Blwm
CH7 . . . . .47 A5

Lea Dr CH7 . . . . .48 C4
Leadworks La CH1 . . . . .144 C3
Leahurst Cl CH2 . . . . . . .42 F4
Leahurst Gdns CH2 . . . . .72 E8
Lea Rd / Ffordd y Ddol
LL13 . . . . .145 B2
Leaside Rd CH1 . . . . .41 E6
Ledsham La CH5 . . . . . . .49 B6
Leen La LL12 . . . . .144 B3
Lee St CH1 . . . . .144 C3
Leeswood Rd CH7 . . . . . .48 B4
Leete La CH7 . . . . .35 F2
Leete Pk CH7 . . . . .35 E3
Leicester La
Broughton CH4 . . . . .49 F2
Higher Kinnerton CH4 . . . .59 F8
Leicester Terr LL16 . . . .140 C2
Leighstone Ct CH4 . . . . .144 A4
Leighton Ct / Cwrt Leighton
CH5 . . . . .38 E8
Leonard Ave LL18 . . . . . . .7 E6
Leonard St CH1 . . . . .42 B3
Level Cotts CH5 . . . . .48 F8
Level Rd Ewloe CH5 . . . . .48 F8
Hawarden / Penarlâg CH5 .38 F1
Lewis Terr CH8 . . . . .5 D1
Lexham Green Cl CH7 . . .48 C4
Leyfield Ct CH4 . . . . .51 F5
Leyland Dr CH4 . . . . .51 C6
Lichfield Cl LL13 . . . . . . .73 F5
Lichfield Dr LL19 . . . . .2 E2
Lichfield Rd CH1 . . . . . . .41 F5
Lido Beach Cvn Pk LL19 . .2 F3
Lightfoot St CH2 . . . . . . .42 F2
Lighthouse Bsns Pk LL19 . .3 A3
Lilac Ave LL18 . . . . .7 E8
Lilac Dr CH4 . . . . .59 A8
Lilac Way LL12 . . . . .145 A6
Lime Cl
Connah's Quay CH5 . . . . .38 D7
❷ Ellesmere SY12 . . . . .109 A2
Lime Gr Chester CH2 . . . .43 A3
Saltney CH4 . . . . .51 D6
Lime St LL11 . . . . .65 D3
Limes The LL12 . . . . .68 F7
Lime Tree Dr CH3 . . . . . .69 F1
Lincoln Cl / Clos Lincoln ❷
LL13 . . . . .73 E4
Lincoln Dr CH2 . . . . .43 A5
Lincoln Rd Blacon CH1 . . .41 F5
Connah's Quay CH5 . . . . .39 C4
Lindale CH4 . . . . .38 C7
Linden Ave
Chirk / Y Waun LL14 . . . .95 E3
Connah's Quay CH5 . . . . .38 D7
Whitchurch SY13 . . . . . .103 F7
Wrexham / Wrecsam LL13 .80 C8
Linden Cl LL19 . . . . .3 C2
Linden Cl CH5 . . . . .38 D8
Linden Dr
Mold / Yr Wyddgrug CH7 . .46 D3
Prestatyn LL19 . . . . .3 C1
Linden Gr Chester CH2 . . .43 A4
Saltney CH4 . . . . .51 D6
Linden Gr / Gelli'r Eurmen
LL12 . . . . .67 A5
Linden Wlk LL19 . . . . .3 C2
Linderick Ave CH7 . . . . . .48 A5
Lindfield Dr LL13 . . . . . . .81 D3
Lindfields CH4 . . . . .51 F6
Lindisfarne Cl / Clos
Lindisfarne LL14 . . . . . .86 B6
Lindum Cl / Clos Lindum
CH7 . . . . .47 C7
Links Av / Rhodfa Dolennau
❹ LL18 . . . . .7 F1
Links The
Gwernaffield / Y-Waun CH7 .45 E5
Wrexham / Wrecsam LL13 .73 F4
Linksway CH2 . . . . .42 C7
Linley Ave LL14 . . . . .79 B1
Linley Pl LL11 . . . . .73 A6
Linthorpe Cl CH7 . . . . . . .48 C5
Linthorpe Gdns CH7 . . . .48 D4
Linthorpe Rd CH7 . . . . . .48 C5
Linwood Cl CH4 . . . . .49 B1
Lion La SY12 . . . . .99 C3
Lisburne Gr LL12 . . . . . . .73 D6
Little Abbey Gateway
CH1 . . . . .144 A3
Little Acton Dr LL12 . . . . .73 B5
Little Heath Rd
Chester CH3 . . . . .43 E1
Christleton CH3 . . . . .53 E1
Little Mdws / Dolydd Bychain
LL12 . . . . .72 B2
Little Mountain Ind Est
CH7 . . . . .48 E4
Little Mountain Rd CH7 . .48 F3
Little Paddock CH7 . . . . . .6 E2
Little Roodee CH5 . . . . . .50 B7
Little St John St CH1 . . .144 B2
Littleton La CH3 . . . . .43 E2
Liverpool Rd
Buckley / Bwcle CH7, CH5 .48 C7
Chester CH2 . . . . .42 C6
Ewloe CH5 . . . . .38 F2
Whitchurch SY13 . . . . . .103 F6
Liverpool Terr LL21 . . . .142 E3
Lixwm Cty Prim Sch CH8 25 D3
Llafar y Nant LL20 . . . . .135 C4
Llain Goch LL15 . . . . . . .141 B5
Llain Henllan / Henllan ❷❿
LL16 . . . . .140 C3
Llain Hiraethog LL16 . . . .118 C8
Llain Portland / Portland Pl
❶❽ LL16 . . . . .140 C3

Llanarmon Rd LL20 ....135 C4
Llanarmon Road / Fordd
  Llanarmon LL11 .....70 B7
Llanasa Rd LL19 ......4 C2
Llanbedr Hall LL15 ..121 F2
Llandaff Dr LL19 ......2 C1
Llanddulas Avenue / Rhodfa
  Llandulas 6 E3
Llandore Cl CH5 .....38 C4
Llandrillo Prim Sch
  LL21 .....132 C4
Llandrillo Rd LL21 ..132 F2
Llanerch Crossing LL17 .117 C4
Llanerch Hall LL17 ...117 C7
Llanfair St / Stryt Llanfair
  LL15 .....141 D4
Llanfynydd CP Sch LL11 .65 C6
Llangollen Com Hospl
  LL20 .....143 C5
Llangollen Motor Mus★
  LL20 .....143 B8
Llangollen Railway★
  LL21 .....130 B2
Llangollen Road / Fordd
  Llangollen LL14,LL20 ..85 C3
Llangollen Sta★ LL20 .143 C5
Llangollen Terr / Y Craig
  LL14 .....85 C2
Llannefydd Sch LL16 ..116 B5
Llanrhaeadr-ym-Mochnant
  CP Sch SY10 .....138 A1
Llanrhydd Rd / Fordd
  Llanrhydd LL15 .....141 D5
Llantysilio CW Sch LL20 131 A3
Llawr-y-Dyffryn LL15 .141 D5
Llay Ct LL12 .....67 A3
Llay Hall Ave / Rhodfa Plas
  Llai LL12 .....67 A4
Llay Ind Est (North) / Ystad
  Ddiwydiannol Llai (Gogledd)
  LL12 .....66 F6
Llay Ind Est (South) / Ystad
  Ddiwydiannol Llai (De)
  LL12 .....66 F5
Llay New Rd / Fordd
  Newydd Llai
  Llay LL12 .....67 A3
  Wrexham / Wrecsam LL11 .72 E6
Llay Pl Ave LL12 .....67 A4
Llay Rd Cefn-y-Bedd LL12 ..66 F4
  Rossett LL12 .....67 F6
Lleprog La CH6 .....27 B6
Llewellyn St CH5 .....39 A6
Llewelyn Ct Brymbo LL11 .65 F1
  Rhyl / Y Rhyl LL18 .....7 F6
Llewelyn Dr CH7 .....47 E6
Llewelyn Rd LL11 .....71 E5
Llewelyn's Est LL14 ..140 B2
Llidiart Annie LL20 ..131 A4
Llidiart-cae-hir LL20 .138 C5
Llindir St LL14 .....116 F3
Lloyd Ave LL16 .....140 B3
Lloyd Cl CH3 .....69 E2
Lloyd Pl CH1 .....41 E4
Lloyd's Cres LL11 .....11 E4
Lloyd's La / Lon Lloyd
  LL14 .....95 E1
Lloyd St CH6 .....28 B7
Lluesty Hospl / Ysbyty
  Lluesty CH8 .....21 B2
Llugwy Rd / Heol Llugwy
  LL18 .....6 D4
Llwybr-Hir CH7 .....18 E4
Llwybry y Fuwch LL20 .131 D4
Llwydiarth ① LL14 ....78 E2
Llwyn Aled LL18 .....21 A4
Llwyn Alun LL12 .....59 B1
Llwyn Bach CH7 .....46 D3
Llwyn Bach / The Small
  Woods ① LL14 .....86 A4
Llwyn Bedw CH7 .....45 F6
Llwyn Derw CH7 .....47 D6
Llwyn Eglwys LL12 .....59 B1
Llwyn Einion Rd LL14 ..78 C4
Llwyn Eithin CH7 .....46 E3
Llwyn Elwy LL17 .....16 A1
Llwyn Goodwood /
  Goodwood Gr CH7 ..57 F5
Llwyn Harlech LL14 ..14 F4
Llwyn Helig / Willow Gr
  CH7 .....48 B7
Llwyni Dr CH5 .....38 C5
Llwyn-Ifor La CH8 .....20 D8
Llwyn Kensington /
  Kensington Gr LL12 ..73 C5
Llwyn Mair ⑤ LL18 ..140 B3
Llwyn Menlli LL15 ....141 E4
Llwyn Mesen LL19 .....9 A6
Llwynon Cl CH7 .....47 E5
Llwyn Onn
  Flint Mountain CH6 ..28 B2
  Prestatyn LL18 .....9 D7
  St Asaph / Llanelwy LL17 .117 A8
Llwyn Onn / Ash Gr CH7 57 F5
Llwyn Onn La CH7 .....28 B2
Llwyn Rhuthun LL18 ..14 F4
Llwyn-y-Coed / Wood Gr
  CH7 .....57 F5
Llwyn-y-Rhos LL16 ..120 E7
Llygadog LL21 .....142 C5
Llyn Brenig Archaeological
  Trail★ LL16 .....123 E8
Llyn Brenig Visitor Ctr★
  LL21 .....123 C5
Llyndir La LL12 .....68 B8
Llys Acasia / Acacia Ct
  .....67 A5

Llys Aderyn Du LL18 ....8 A8
Llys Alafowlia LL16 ..140 E4
Llys Alard LL18 .....8 A7
Llys Alarch LL19 .....2 E3
Llys Alexandra / Alexandra
  Ct CH7 .....48 C4
Llys Alun Rhydymwyn CH7 .35 E3
  St Asaph / Llanelwy LL17 .117 A8
Llys Alwen LL18 .....7 F7
Llys Alyn
  Connah's Quay CH5 ..38 C4
  Wrexham / Wrecsam LL11 .72 D8
Llys Ambrose LL18 ....46 D3
Llys Ann CH7 .....58 A4
Llys Argoed CH7 .....47 D5
Llys Armon CH8 .....25 D2
Llys Arthur LL22 .....6 B3
Llys Awelon LL11 .....145 C4
Llys Bedw LL20 .....143 C4
Llys Bedw / Birch Ct
  CH7 .....57 F5
Llys Bedwen LL18 .....7 F6
Llys Ben CH7 .....38 A4
Llys Berllan CH7 .....47 F5
Llys Bodnant
  ① LL19 .....3 B2
  ③ Rhyl / Y Rhyl LL18 .....7 F7
Llys Bran LL19 .....2 E3
Llys Branwen LL18 .....6 D4
Llys Brenig Ewloe CH5 ..48 E8
  Rhyl / Y Rhyl LL18 .....7 F8
Llys Brunswick ① LL18 .7 C7
Llys Bryn Eglwys CH7 ..46 F5
Llys Buddug ③ LL19 ....3 B2
Llys Cadnant ⑦ LL18 ....7 F7
Llys Caer CH4 .....50 A3
Llys Cae'r Glo CH7 ....37 B1
Llys Canol CH8 .....21 B4
Llys Caradoc LL22 .....6 B3
Llys Caradog LL17 ....117 B6
Llys Catrin
  Denbigh / Dinbych LL16 .140 F3
  Rhyl / Y Rhyl LL18 .....7 F8
Llys Ceibren / Chevrons Ct
  CH5 .....39 B5
Llys Ceirios LL16 .....117 B6
Llys Celyn / Holly Ct CH7 57 F5
Llys Celyn / Holy Tree Cl
  CH5 .....38 E1
Llys Cerddin / Rowan Cl
  CH7 .....48 D4
Llys Cerrig LL17 .....117 B6
Llys Charles LL22 .....6 B3
Llys Clwyd
  Denbigh / Dinbych LL16 .140 F3
  St Asaph / Llanelwy LL17 .117 A8
Llys Colomen LL18 .....8 A7
Llys Cowlyd ⑥ LL18 ....7 F7
Llys Cregyn LL18 .....6 E6
Llys Cynan LL18 .....6 E6
Llys Cynffig LL18 .....6 E4
Llys Dafydd LL18 .....6 E4
Llys Daniel Owen CH7 ..46 E6
Llys David Lord LL13 ..145 A2
Llys Dedwydd
  Mynydd Isa CH7 .....47 D5
  Pentre Halkyn CH8 ..26 D6
  Rhyl / Y Rhyl LL18 .....7 F8
Llys Degwm CH7 .....57 C1
Llys Delyn ① LL18 .....7 F7
Llys Derw LL14 .....78 F2
Llys Derw / Acorn Cl
  CH7 .....48 E4
Llys Derwen
  Higher Kinnerton CH4 ..59 F8
  Mold / Yr Wyddgrug CH7 .47 A4
Llys Dewi Gronant LL19 ..4 A3
  Pen-y-ffordd CH8 .....11 C8
  Rhyl / Y Rhyl LL18 .....7 F8
Llys Dinas ② LL18 .....7 F7
Llys Dyffryn Dyfrdwy / Dee
  Valley Ct LL20 .....85 B3
Llys Edmund Prys LL15 .15 C1
Llys Edward Gronant LL19 ..4 B3
  Towyn LL22 .....6 B3
Llys Eglwys CH8 .....21 C7
Llys Eirlys LL18 .....7 F8
Llys Eithin CH7 .....38 A4
Llys Elinor LL18 .....6 E4
Llys Enfys
  Gwernymynydd CH7 ..46 A1
  Rhosesmor CH7 .....36 A5
Llys Eos LL18 .....8 A8
Llys Erw LL15 .....141 B6
Llysfaen Ave LL18 .....6 D5
Llys Famau LL15 .....141 A5
Llys Fammau
  Denbigh / Dinbych LL16 .140 F3
  Mynydd Isa CH7 .....47 D5
  Pantymwyn CH7 .....45 C6
Llys Fennant / Fennant Ct
  LL14 .....79 D4
Llys Glan Aber LL18 ....7 C6
Llys Glanrafon LL18 ....6 E6
Llys Glyndwr LL22 .....6 B3
Llys Golygfa'r Maes /
  Meadowview Ct CH5 ..49 B4
Llys Gwennol LL18 .....8 A8
Llys Gwilym LL16 .....120 F5
Llys Gwyddfid CH7 ....64 B8
Llys Gwylan LL18 .....8 A7
Llys Gwynant
  Bryn-y-baal CH7 .....47 E6
  Rhyl / Y Rhyl LL18 .....7 F7
Llys Gwyrdd LL11 .....71 F8
Llys Hafod ⑥ LL14 ....79 A1
Llys Heidog / Haydock Cl
  CH7 .....57 F5

Llys Helyg LL18 .....7 F8
Llys Helyg / Willow Cl
  CH7 .....48 C4
Llys Hendre LL18 .....7 F1
Llys Idris LL17 .....16 B1
Llys Iorwg CH7 .....46 F5
Llys Iwan LL18 .....4 A3
Llys John Dafis CH7 ...46 E6
Llys Llannerch LL17 ..117 B6
Llys Llewelyn LL22 .....6 B3
Llys Llydaw LL19 .....2 E3
Llys Madoc LL17 .....16 B2
Llys Maes Ucha / High
  Meadow Ct CH6 .....27 F6
Llys Mai CH7 .....48 A5
Llys Menden CH7 .....46 A5
Llys Mervyn CH7 .....46 E6
Llys Miaren ③ LL18 ....7 F8
Llys Morgan LL18 .....7 F6
Llys Mornant CH8 .....5 D1
Llys Mostyn LL18 .....10 A4
Llys Mymbr LL19 .....2 E3
Llys Nercwys CH7 ....47 A2
Llys Offa ⑤ LL19 .....3 B2
Llys Ogwen LL18 .....6 D4
Llys Owain LL12 .....66 F4
Llys Owen
  Ffynnongroyw CH8 .....5 D1
  Gronant LL19 .....4 A3
Llys Padarn Ewloe CH5 ..48 E8
  ④ Rhyl / Y Rhyl LL18 ....7 F8
Llys Pant Derw CH5 ..38 C6
Llys Pendefig LL18 ....6 D5
Llys Pendre CH7 .....24 B6
Llys Penuel ⑧ LL14 ...78 E2
Llys Pen-y-Cefndy LL18 ..7 D5
Llys Pen-y-Ffordd LL18 ..7 D5
Llys Pen-y-Glyn CH6 ..27 F1
Llys Peris ⑤ LL18 .....7 F7
Llys Pont-y-Felin CH7 ..47 A6
Llys Preswylfa CH7 ...46 E4
Llys Rhedyn / Bracken Ct
  LL11 .....71 E2
Llys Rhuddlan / Rhuddlan Ct
  ⑤ CH4 .....51 F6
Llys Robin Goch LL18 ....8 A7
Llys Sant Iago / St James Ct
  CH5 .....29 D1
Llys Sion LL18 .....7 F8
Llys Taf LL18 .....7 F7
Llys Teg LL17 .....117 C5
Llys Tegid LL18 .....7 F7
Llys Thomas Jones ①
  LL16 .....140 C3
Llys Tomas Sant / St Thomas
  Ct CH6 .....28 A1
Llys Tomos ⑥ CH5 ....39 B6
Llys Trahearne LL18 ....6 E6
Llys Tremhyfryd / Bellevue
  Ct LL13 .....145 B1
Llys Trewithan LL17 ...16 B2
Llys Tudela Cilnant CH7 .46 D4
Llys Tudor LL22 .....6 B3
Llys Tudur
  Denbigh / Dinbych LL16 .140 F2
  Rhyl / Y Rhyl LL18 .....7 F8
Llys Tywi LL18 .....7 F8
Llys Vyrnwy LL19 .....2 E3
Llys Wylfa CH7 .....47 D5
Llys-y-Barcty LL20 ....143 D4
Llys-y-Berllan
  Greenfield / Maes-Glas CH8 21 B7
  Ruthin / Rhuthin LL15 ..141 E4
Llys Y Castell LL18 .....6 F3
Llys Y Coed LL21 .....132 D3
Llys-y-Coed CH7 .....47 A2
Llys y Coed LL11 .....145 B4
Llys Y Faner LL18 .....140 E3
Llys-y-Felin LL16 .....16 B2
Llys Y Ffynnon LL16 ..140 A6
Llys Y Foel Dyserth LL18 ..8 F2
  Mold / Yr Wyddgrug CH7 .47 A3
Llys-y-Fron CH7 .....46 D4
Llys Y Gamog LL16 ..140 D3
Llys Y Garreg CH7 ....46 F3
Llys-y-Gerddi LL18 .....7 D5
Llys-y-Goron CH7 ....24 B7
Llys Y Grawys ⑥ LL16 .140 B3
Llys-y-Marchog LL18 ....6 E6
Llys-y-Mor CH8 .....20 D6
Llys-y-Nant
  Mold / Yr Wyddgrug CH7 .47 A3
  Pentre Halkyn CH8 ..26 E5
Llys-y-Pentre CH7 ....24 C4
Llys-yr-Awel CH7 .....47 A3
Llys Yr Efail
  Mold / Yr Wyddgrug CH7 .46 F4
  Wrexham / Wrecsam LL11 .72 A4
Llys Yr Erwain LL16 ..117 C5
Llys Yr Orsaf / Station Ct ⑤
  LL11 .....72 D7
Llys-yr-Wyddfa LL18 ....7 F8
Llys-y-Tywysog
  ⑧ Rhyl / Y Rhyl LL18 ....7 F8
Llys Y Wennol LL16 ..116 F3
Llys-y-wennol CH7 ...12 C2
Llys Y Wennol CH7 ...38 A4
Llys-y-Wern CH7 .....37 A1
Llys Y Wern CH7 .....57 B1
Lodge Gdns CH2 .....42 D6
Lodge Rd LL11 .....72 F4
Lodge Villas CH7 .....57 E1
Loggerheads Ctry Pk★
  CH7 .....45 D2

Lon Abram / Abraham's La
  ③ LL16 .....140 C3
Lon Aeron ⑥ LL18 ....7 F8
Lon Alun LL16 .....140 E5
Lon Alwen LL19 .....3 B2
Lon Bedw LL18 .....7 F8
Lon Berse / Berse La
  Rhostyllen LL14 .....79 C8
  Wrexham / Wrecsam LL11 .72 C1
Lon Blackwood / Blackbrook
  Dr LL14 .....86 B6
Lon Brombil / Broomhill La
  ⑮ LL18 .....140 C3
Lon Bryn Coch / Bryn Coch
  La CH7 .....46 D4
Lon Brynhyfryd LL15 ..141 E5
Lon Brynli LL19 .....2 E1
Lon Cadfan LL19 .....8 E8
Lon Cae Del Ewloe CH5 ..48 E8
  Mold / Yr Wyddgrug CH7 .46 D4
Lon Cae Glas LL15 ...121 C2
Lon Caerau LL16 .....140 E1
Lon Carlton / Carlton Dr
  LL11 .....72 D8
Lon Ceiriog
  Denbigh / Dinbych LL16 .140 E3
  Prestatyn LL19 .....8 E8
Lon Celyn CH5 .....38 D7
Lon Celynnen LL18 .....7 F7
Lon Cerys LL16 .....140 E5
Lon Cilan CH7 .....44 F8
Lon Copner LL18 .....7 F7
Lon Cox / Cox La LL12 ..68 B5
Lon Cristionnydd /
  Cristionnydd ① LL14 ..85 C6
Lon Crown / Crown La ⑨
  LL16 .....140 C3
Lon Cwybr LL18 .....7 E2
Lon Cynan LL19 .....2 E3
Lon Dderwen CH5 ....38 D7
Lon Delph / Delph La ⑰
  LL14 .....78 C2
Lon Delyn LL18 .....3 B3
Lon Derwen LL16 .....140 E2
Lon Derw / Oak La LL17 .16 B2
London Rd
  Soughton / Sychdyn CH7 .37 A1
  Trelawnyd LL18 .....10 A4
London Rd / Heol Llundain
  LL21 .....142 D3
Lon Dyffryn LL16 .....140 C2
Lon Dyfi LL19 .....2 D2
Lon Dyrpeg / Turnpike La
  LL12 .....67 F3
Lon Dywoddog / Sandy La
  LL12 .....67 F3
Lon Dywyll / Dark La
  Hope / Yr Hôb LL12 ..66 F8
  Llay LL12 .....67 A7
Lon Eglyn ④ LL18 .....7 F8
Lon Eirin LL22 .....6 B3
Lon Eirlys LL19 .....3 B3
Lon Elan LL19 .....8 F7
Lon Esless / Esless La
  LL14 .....79 E7
Lon Fammau LL16 .....140 E5
Lon Fawr LL15 .....141 B4
Long Acre Dr CH6 ....22 D4
Lon Ganol / Middle La
  LL16 .....140 C3
Longdale Dr CH5 .....41 C5
Lon Gefn / Back Row ⑪
  LL16 .....140 C3
Longfellow Ave CH5 ..48 E8
Longfield LL14 .....95 E1
Longfield Ave CH2 ....42 F7
Long La
  Bronington SY13 .....102 D4
  Chester CH2 .....42 F7
  Wrexham / Wrecsam LL11 .72 A6
Lon Glyn LL16 .....140 E5
Lon Goch / Grove Rd
  LL16 .....140 D3
Lon Goed CH8 .....20 E6
Lon Grango / Grango La
  LL14 .....78 E2
Lon Groes CH6 .....27 F6
Longueville LL13 .....80 A7
Longview Rd LL11 ....72 B7
Lon Gwernydd LL15 ..141 A7
Lon Gwynant CH5 .....48 D8
Lon Gwyndaf LL19 .....2 E1
Lon Hafren LL18 .....7 F1
Lon Hedyn LL18 .....7 E6
Lon Heulog LL18 .....6 D4
Lon Homestead / Homestead
  La LL13 .....79 D4
Lon Howell LL16 .....140 D3
Lon Hylas / Hylas La
  LL18 .....15 F8
Lon Isaf CH7 .....47 A4
Lon Islwyn LL19 .....8 E8
Lon Jack-Ffwrn LL16 ..116 F4
Lon Las LL16 .....116 F3
Lon Lelog ⑤ LL18 .....7 F8
Lon Llewelyn LL16 ..140 D3
Lon Lloyd / Lloyd's La
  LL14 .....95 E1
Lon Llwyni CH5 .....38 C5
Lon Mafon LL18 .....7 F8
Lon Menlli LL15 .....141 A5
Lon Nant LL16 .....140 F2
Lon Nwy / Gas La CH7 ..47 A6
Lon Odyn / Kiln Cl CH6 .28 A6
Lon Olwen LL18 .....6 D4

Lon Parc / Park St
  LL16 .....140 D3
Lon Parcwr LL15 .....141 C6
Lon Parcwr Bsns Pk
  LL15 .....141 C6
Lon Penrhyn / Penrhyn Dr
  LL11 .....72 B7
Lon Pentre / Pentre La
  LL12 .....67 B3
Lon Pont Y Capel / Pont Y
  Capel La LL12 .....67 B1
Lon Rhosyn ⑦ LL18 ....7 F8
Lonsdale Ct CH4 .....51 F4
Lon Shellbrook / Shellbrook
  Dr LL14 .....86 B6
Lon Speiriol-Isaf LL15 .141 D4
Lon Speiriol-Uchaf
  LL15 .....141 E4
Lon Swan / Chapel St ⑦
  LL16 .....140 C3
Lon Syr Herbert CH7 ..24 B6
Lon Taliesin LL19 .....2 E1
Lon Tilsli LL19 .....8 E8
Lon Tywysog LL16 ....140 F2
Lon Uchaf / Higher La
  LL12 .....67 C6
Lon Walker / Walkers La ⑤
  LL14 .....78 F4
Lon Wen LL18 .....7 F8
Lon Werdd / Green La
  LL20 .....143 C5
Lon Wynne LL16 .....140 E5
Lon-y-Berth CH7 .....46 D3
Lon Y Capel / Chapel La
  LL12 .....67 B6
Lon Y Capel / Chapel St ①
  CH6 .....28 A6
Lon Y Cryddion / Cobblers La
  LL12 .....67 A8
Lon y De / South La
  LL14 .....78 E2
Lon Y Fedw Arian LL16 .140 E4
Lon Y Felin / Mill La
  LL14 .....85 B1
Lon-y-Fron CH8 .....26 E5
Lon-y-Gegin / Gegin La
  LL12 .....67 C5
Lon Y Gelli LL16 .....140 E4
Lon-y-Gelli LL12 .....73 C7
Lon-y-Gog CH7 .....28 B1
Lon Y Mynydd CH8 ....20 D2
Lon-y-Parc CH7 .....46 E3
Lon-y-Pentref / Pentre La
  .....7 F2
Lon Y Plas CH6 .....27 F2
Lon-y-Porthmyn / Drovers
  La CH7 .....24 B7
Lon-y-Post / Post Office La
  LL16 .....140 C3
Lon Yr Orsaf CH7 .....47 A4
Lon Yr Ysgol CH7 .....24 B6
Lon yr Ysgol / School La
  LL14 .....78 F2
Lon Ystrad LL18 .....7 F7
Lon y Wern / Wern La ⑪
  LL14 .....78 E1
Lord St CH3 .....69 E2
Lord St / Stryt Yr Arglwydd
  ② LL11 .....145 B2
Lorne St Chester CH1 ..144 A3
  Wrexham / Wrecsam LL11 145 B3
Lothian Pk LL17 .....16 B1
Louise St CH1 .....144 A3
Love La
  Denbigh / Dinbych LL16 .140 C2
  Mold / Yr Wyddgrug CH7 .46 F5
Love St CH1 .....144 A2
Lower Aston Hall La CH5 39 B2
Lower Bank Terr LL18 ..10 A4
Lower Bridge St CH1 ..144 B1
Lower Brook St LL13 ..29 D1
Lower Dee Mill Exhibition
  Ctr★ LL20 .....143 D5
Lower Dee View Rd CH8 .21 C7
Lower Denbigh Rd / Fordd
  Isaf Dinbych LL17 ....117 A8
Lower Field Rd CH4 ...52 A5
Lower Mill Dr LL12 ....72 C3
Lower Minster LL12 ...73 C6
Lower Mountain La LL12 52 D6
Lower Mountain Rd CH4 .59 B6
Lower Mountain Rd / Fordd
  Mynydd Isa LL14 .....85 D8
Lower Mumforth St CH6 .28 B2
Lower Park Rd CH4 ...144 C2
Lower Rd / Heol Isaf
  LL11 .....71 C2
Lower St LL17 .....16 B1
Lower Sydney St CH6 ..28 B7
Lowther Ct LL18 .....6 E3
Lowther St LL18 .....15 A4
Lucerne Cl CH3 .....53 B6
Ludlow Cl LL13 .....89 C4
Ludlow Rd
  Bangor on Dee / Bangor-is-y-coed
  LL13 .....89 A8
  Blacon CH1 .....42 A5
Ludwell Cl CH4 .....52 B6
Luke St LL17 .....16 B1
Lumley Pl CH1 .....144 B2
Lumley Rd CH2 .....42 C4
Lupin Dr CH3 .....53 B6
Lyme Gr CH7 .....48 D4
Lyndale Gr LL12 .....73 C5
Lyndon Dr LL18 .....6 E3

Lyneal La SY12 ....**110** D2
Lynfield Cl CH5 ....**38** D7
Lynton Cl CH4 ....**51** F6
Lynton Pl CH4 ....**50** B4
Lynton Wlk LL18 ....**7** D8
Lynwood Dr LL18 ....**7** D8
Lynwood Rd CH1 ....**41** F5
Lyon St CH1 ....**144** B3
Lyons Holiday Pk LL18 .....**2** A1
Lyons Yd (Cvn Site) CH5 .**39** E4
Lytham Ct / Cwrt Lytham **4**
LL13 ....**73** F3

M

Machynlleth Way CH5 ......**38** C6
McKeown Cl CH5 ....**38** C5
Madeley Cl CH4 ....**50** C4
Madiera Hill / Allt Madiera
LL13 ....**145** B1
Madras Sch LL13 ....**99** E4
Madryn Ave LL18 ....**7** E7
Maelor Ave / Rhodfa Maelor
LL14 ....**85** D8
Maelor Cl
Buckley / Bwcle CH7 ....**48** C3
Wrexham / Wrecsam LL11 .**72** B7
Maelor Ct LL13 ....**88** C1
Maelor Pl LL14 ....**86** A4
Maelor Rd LL14 ....**79** A1
Maelor Sch LL13 ....**7** F6
Maelor Terr Acrefair LL14 .**85** B3
Wrexham / Wrecsam LL11 .**72** F6
Maelor View Brymbo LL11 .**65** E1
Marchwiel LL13 ....**80** F4
Maengwyn Ave CH5 ....**38** C7
Maesafallen LL21 ....**142** E5
Maes Afon CH6 ....**27** F6
Maes Alarch CH8 ....**12** A5
Maes Alaw
Flint / Y Fflint CH6 .....**28** B5
Rhuddlan LL18 ....**7** E1
Maes Aled LL16 ....**118** C8
Maes Alyn LL11 ....**72** F6
Maes Annedd LL21 ....**125** A1
Maes Arthur **2** LL18 ......**7** F6
Maes Bache LL20 ....**143** D3
Maes Bedwen LL18 ....**7** E2
Maes Bodlonfa CH7 ......**46** E4
Maes Brenin LL13 ....**81** C7
Maes Bryn Melyd LL18 .....**7** F6
Maes Caenog LL15 ....**125** C5
Maes Cantaba LL15 ......**141** E4
Maes Cefndy LL18 ....**7** D6
Maes Ceirios / Cherry Field
LL11 ....**72** C4
Maes Celyn
Llanbedr Dyffryn Clwyd
LL15 ....**121** F2
Northop / Llan-eurgain CH7 **36** F6
Wrexham / Wrecsam LL13 .**80** A7
Maes Cibyn LL12 ....**66** B6
Maes Cinmel / Kinmel Way
LL22 ....**6** B3
Maes Clwyd
Llandyrnog LL16 ....**121** B7
Rhyl / Y Rhyl LL18 ....**7** F6
Maes Collen LL20 ....**143** D4
Maes Creiniog LL16 ......**118** C8
Maes Cwm **4** LL18 ....**7** F6
Maes Cynfaen CH8 ....**20** E2
Maes Derw LL15 ....**121** C3
Maes Derwen
Llanbedr Dyffryn Clwyd
LL15 ....**121** F2
Rhuddlan LL18 ....**7** E2
St Asaph / Llanelwy LL17 ..**16** B2
Maes Derwydd LL14 ......**85** C3
Maes Dolwen
Henllan LL16 ....**116** B5
Ruthin / Rhuthin LL15 ...**141** B5
Maes Emlen LL11 ....**72** B5
Maes Emlyn
Pen-y-ffordd CH8 ....**11** C8
Rhyl / Y Rhyl LL18 ....**7** C8
Maes Enion LL14 ....**78** D2
Maes Esgob LL18 ....**8** E3
Maes Famau **1** LL18 ......**7** F6
Maes Ffordd LL18 ....**7** E1
Maes Ffynnon LL15 ......**141** B5
Maes Gaer **5** LL18 ....**7** E1
Maes Garmon CH7 ....**127** A7
Maes Glan LL14 ....**78** D1
Maes Glas Dyserth LL18 ....**8** E3
Ewloe CH5 ....**48** F8
Flint / Y Fflint CH6 ......**27** F6
Prestatyn LL19 ....**3** B3
Treuddyn CH7 ....**57** C1
Wrexham / Wrecsam
LL13 ....**145** A1
Maesglas Ave LL16 ......**140** B3
Maesglas / Greenfield
LL11 ....**145** B4
Maes Glyndwr CH7 ....**57** C1
Maes Gogor LL16 ....**118** C8
Maes Gruffydd
Soughton / Sychdyn CH7 ..**37** A1
Trefnant LL16 ....**117** C5
Maes Grug LL14 ....**78** F2
Maes Grugoer LL16 ......**118** F6
Maes Gwalia CH7 ....**37** B1
Maes Gwelfor CH8 ....**26** D6
Maes Gwern CH7 ....**46** F2
Maesgwyn LL18 ....**6** D3

Maes Gwyn
Flint / Y Fflint CH6 ......**28** C5
Llanarmon-yn-Ial CH7 ....**63** A5
Maes Gwynfryn CH8 ....**4** E3
Maesgwyn Rd / Ffordd
Maesgwyn LL11 ....**145** A3
Maes Gynnan CH7 ....**127** A7
Maes Hafal LL15 ....**121** D5
Maes Hafod LL15 ....**141** B5
Maes Hedydd LL18 ....**7** E7
Maes Helyg LL18 ....**7** E1
Maes Hir LL21 ....**132** D4
Maes Hiraddug LL18 ....**9** A3
Maes Hyfryd
Coedpoeth LL11 ....**71** E3
Cynwyd LL21 ....**132** F8
Maes-Hyfryd **7** LL16 ...**140** B3
Maes Hyfryd LL18 ....**8** E3
Maes-Hyfryd CH6 ....**28** A5
Maes Hyfryd
Pentre-celyn LL15 ....**126** C5
Ruthin / Rhuthin LL15 ...**141** D6
St Asaph / Llanelwy LL17 ..**16** B2
Wrexham / Wrecsam LL11 .**72** F6
Maes Ial CH7 ....**127** A7
Maes Isaf Johnstown LL14 .**79** A1
Rhyl / Y Rhyl LL18 ....**7** F6
Maes Llan
Gwernaffield / Y-Waun CH7 .**45** F6
Llanarmon-yn-Ial CH7 ....**127** A7
Llandyrnog LL16 ....**121** B8
Maes Llewelyn
Rhyl / Y Rhyl LL18 ....**7** E6
Treuddyn CH7 ....**57** C1
Maes Lliwen LL16 ....**119** D5
Maesllwyn Cl SY13 ......**102** A4
Maesllwyn La SY13 ......**101** F4
Maes Lygan LL18 ....**26** E5
Maes Madoc LL14 ....**85** C3
Maes Madog LL20 ....**135** F5
Maes Maenefa LL18 ....**7** F6
Maes Mathonwy LL16 ...**140** B3
Maesmawr Rd LL20 ......**143** F4
Maes Mawr Rd / Ffordd
Maes Mawr LL20 ......**84** C3
Maes Meillion LL11 ....**71** A4
Maes Menlli
Rhyl / Y Rhyl LL18 ....**7** E6
Ruthin / Rhuthin LL15 ...**141** E4
Maes-Meredydd LL20 ...**135** F5
Maes Meugan LL15 ......**141** E4
Maes Meurig LL19 ....**8** F7
Maesmor Cotts LL21 .....**128** B3
Maes Offa LL18 ....**10** E2
Maes Onnen LL18 ....**7** E2
Maesowain LL21 ....**130** C1
Maes Owen
Bodelwyddan LL18 ....**14** E4
Mold / Yr Wyddgrug CH7 ..**46** E6
Maes Pengwern LL20 ....**143** D4
Maes Rathbone LL17 ......**16** D3
Maes Rhosyn
Rhuddlan LL18 ....**7** E2
Towyn LL22 ....**6** A2
Maes Rhydwen CH8 ......**11** F1
Maes Robert LL17 ....**116** E6
Maes Sadwrn LL16 ......**116** F3
Maes Stanley LL18 ....**14** E4
Maestag **6** LL11 ....**72** D8
Maesteg Cymau LL11 .....**65** E4
Gwynfryn LL11 ....**70** D5
Wrexham / Wrecsam LL11 .**72** B5
Maes Teg
Flint / Y Fflint CH6 ......**28** A4
Llandegla LL11 ....**127** B3
Penycae LL14 ....**85** C8
Trefnant LL16 ....**117** C5
Maes Tegid LL19 ....**3** A1
Maes Telford LL20 ....**84** F2
Maes Tomos LL13 ....**80** A7
Maes Tyddyn LL11 ....**71** D3
Maes Tyrnog LL16 ....**121** B7
Maes Uchaf CH5 ....**38** C4
Maes Walwen CH6 ....**21** E6
Maes Wepre CH5 ....**38** C5
Maes Y Blanhigfa / The
Nurseries CH6 ....**27** F5
Maes-y-Bryn Rhuddlan LL18 **7** F2
Trelogan CH8 ....**10** F4
Maes-y-Capel LL11 ....**71** C3
Maes-y-Coed
Flint / Y Fflint CH6 ......**27** F6
Saltney CH4 ....**51** E6
Wrexham / Wrecsam LL11 .**72** E7
Maes Y Coed Rd LL16 ...**140** D4
Maes-y-Coed Terr CH7 ...**24** B4
Maes y Dderwen SY10 ...**138** A1
Maes Y Delyn LL15 ......**124** F8
Maes-Y-Don Dr LL18 ....**1** D5
Maes-y-Dre CH7 ....**24** C7
Maes Y Dre LL16 ....**140** B3
Maes-y-dre Gronant LL19 ...**4** A3
Mold / Yr Wyddgrug CH7 ..**46** E6
Maes-y-Dre Ave CH6 .....**28** B5
Maesydre Rd LL12 ......**145** C4
Maes-y-Dyffryn CH8 .....**21** C7
Maes-y-Efail LL16 ....**116** F3
Maes y Fedwen LL21 ....**130** C1
Maes-y-Fedwen Arian
LL17 ....**117** A8
Maes-y-felin LL16 ....**120** F5
Maesyffynnon Rd LL11 ...**70** E5
Maes-y-Ficerdy LL14 ......**78** F1
Maes-y-Foel LL18 ....**8** F3
Maes-y-Gog LL18 ....**8** A4
Maes-y-Gornel LL14 ......**78** D3
Maes Y Goron LL16 .....**140** B3
Maes-y-Graig LL16 ....**23** B1

Maes-y-Groes LL19 ....**3** B2
Maes-y-Gwanwyn LL14 ...**79** C5
Maes-y-Lan La LL14 ......**86** B4
Maes-y-Llan LL21 ....**129** F2
Maes y Llan
Llansilin SY10 ....**139** D1
Towyn LL22 ....**6** A4
Maes-y-Llan Rd LL15 ....**141** F4
Maes-y-Llys LL18 ....**8** E3
Maes Y March CH7 ....**46** E5
Maes Y Meillion CH7 .....**57** F4
Maes-y-Nant LL14 ....**85** B7
Maes Y Parc **3** LL18 ......**7** F6
Maes Y Plwm CH8 ....**20** E6
Maes-yr-Afon CH8 ....**21** D5
Maes Yr Efail LL21 ......**129** B5
Maes-yr-Eglwys LL16 ....**140** B3
Maes-yr-Haf
Mold / Yr Wyddgrug CH7 ..**46** E4
4 Wrexham / Wrecsam
LL12 ....**73** B7
Maes-yr-Hafod LL21 .....**122** D1
Maes Yr Haul CH7 ....**46** E3
Maes Yr Odyn CH8 ....**21** B4
Maes yr Onnen / Ashfield Rd
LL14 ....**145** A4
Maes Yr Ysgol
Chirk / Y Waun LL14 .....**95** E1
Flint / Y Fflint CH6 ......**27** F6
Maes Yr Ysgubor / Barnfield
LL13 ....**145** A4
Maes-y-waen LL21 ....**129** E2
Maesywern LL20 ....**135** E4
Maes-y-wern CH7 ....**46** B2
Mafryn LL20 ....**84** C3
Magazine La CH7, CH5 ....**38** C2
Magnolia Cl
Wrexham / Wrecsam LL11 ..**7** E7
Magnolia Dr **9** SY12 ...**109** A2
Main Rd Broughton CH4 ...**50** B4
Higher Kinnerton CH4 ....**59** F6
Soughton / Sychdyn CH7 ..**37** A1
Main Rd / Ffordd Fawr
LL11 ....**72** F6
Mainwaring Dr CH4 ......**51** C7
Mairion Terr CH8 ....**5** D1
Mais-Einion LL21 ....**138** F8
Maitland Way CH1 ....**41** D4
Makepeace Cl CH3 ....**43** C3
Mallard Ct CH2 ....**42** F7
Mallory Wlk CH4 ....**61** A7
Mallow Cl CH3 ....**53** A6
Mall The
16 Mold / Yr Wyddgrug
CH7 ....**46** F4
Prestatyn LL19 ....**3** A4
Malt Ho The CH7 ....**37** C6
Maltkiln La
Whitchurch Rural SY13 ...**113** E7
Whixall SY13 ....**112** C2
Malvern Dr LL11 ....**72** D6
Malvern Rd CH1 ....**42** A5
Manbry Cl CH5 ....**38** C7
Mancot La CH5 ....**39** D3
Mancot Royal Cl CH5 ....**39** D3
Mancot Way CH5 ....**39** B7
Manley Ct CH5 ....**39** B7
Manley Rd Coedpoeth LL11 **71** C3
Wrexham / Wrecsam LL13 .**73** C1
Manning La S CH2 ....**43** A5
Mannings La CH2 ....**43** B6
Mannings La S CH2 ......**43** A5
Manod Rd LL11 ....**9** A7
Manor Cl Broughton CH5 ..**50** C7
Prestatyn LL19 ....**3** C1
Manor Cl / Clos Y Plasty
LL12 ....**66** F4
Manor Cres CH4 ....**50** C8
Manor Dr Bagillt CH6 .....**22** E1
Buckley / Bwcle CH7 .....**48** C4
Chester CH3 ....**43** C1
Manor Farm Cl CH2 ......**43** F8
Manor Farm Ct CH5 .....**50** B7
Manor Gr LL11 ....**72** E7
Manor House National
Nature Reserve Base★
SY13 ....**112** C1
Manor Ind Est CH6 ......**22** D2
Manor La Broughton CH5 ..**50** B7
Marford LL12 ....**68** B6
Manor Pk Broughton CH4 ..**50** B7
Soughton / Sychdyn CH7 ..**37** A1
Manor Pk / Park Manor
CH6 ....**22** E1
Manor Rd Chester CH4 ...**52** B5
Sealand CH5 ....**40** A6
Manor Way LL18 ....**6** E5
Mansfield Ave CH5 ....**48** F8
Maple Ave
4 Ellesmere SY12 ....**109** A3
Rhyl / Y Rhyl LL18 ....**7** A3
Wrexham / Wrecsam LL12 .**73** C2
Maple Cl / Clos Y Fasarnen
LL12 ....**67** F2
Maple Cres CH5 ....**48** F7
Maple Dr LL14 ....**85** C3
Maple Gr Chester CH2 ....**43** B4
Saltney CH4 ....**51** D5
Maplewood Gr LL14 ......**41** B8
Maplewood Ave CH5 .....**39** F5
Marble Church★ LL18 .....**15** A3
Marble Church Gr LL18 ...**15** A4
Marbury Ave CH7 ....**48** C3
Marbury Rd CH3 ....**43** C2
Marcella Cres LL13 ....**81** A4
Marcella's Ct LL16 ......**140** F2
Marchnad y Bobl / The
Peoples Mkt LL13 ......**145** C2
Mare Hey La CH5 ....**38** E1

Mareilian Ave LL12 ....**68** A2
Marford Hill LL12 ....**68** A4
Marford Hts LL12 ....**67** F5
Marian CH6 ....**28** A5
Marian Dr CH3 ....**53** B8
Marina Dr Chester CH2 ...**42** E7
Connah's Quay CH5 .....**39** B6
Marine Dr LL18 ....**1** D5
Marine Flats CH3 ....**53** E7
Marine Par LL18 ....**1** D5
Marine Rd LL19 ....**3** B3
Marine Rd E LL19 ....**3** C4
Marine Rd LL19 ....**2** D2
Marion Rd LL14 ....**41** C8
Mark Cl CH2 ....**42** F2
Market Sq CH1 ....**144** A2
Market Sq / Y Farchnad
CH6 ....**28** A7
Market St
6 Ellesmere SY12 ......**109** B2
Llanrhaeadr-ym-Mochnant
SY10 ....**138** A1
Market St / Heol y Farchnad
LL20 ....**143** C5
Market St / Stryd Y
Farchnad 5 LL18 ....**7** B7
Market St / Stryt y Farchnad
2 Rhosllanerchrugog LL14 .**78** E1
Ruthin / Rhuthin LL15 ...**141** C5
Wrexham / Wrecsam
LL13 ....**145** C2
Marlborough Ave
Ewloe CH5 ....**48** F8
Hawarden / Penarlâg CH5 ..**49** A8
Marlborough Cl **1** CH3 ..**43** B2
Marlborough Gr CH4 ......**6** F5
Marlborough Rd LL13 ....**81** F8
Marlbrook CH5 ....**85** D3
Marl Croft CH3 ....**53** B7
Marleston Ct CH4 ....**51** E1
Marley Way CH4 ....**51** C7
Marl Heys CH7 ....**42** E7
Marlow Ave CH2 ....**42** F7
Marlowe Ave CH5 ....**38** F6
Marlowe Cl CH1 ....**42** A5
Marlowe Terr **22** CH7 ...**46** F4
Marlston Ave CH4 ....**52** A6
Marlwood Pl CH4 ....**50** A3
Marnel Dr CH5 ....**39** E4
Marsh Cres LL12 ....**73** C3
Marsh La CH6 ....**28** B7
Marsh Rd Rhuddlan LL18 ..**15** D8
Rhuddlan LL18 ....**7** B6
Rhyl / Y Rhyl LL18 ....**7** B6
Marsh View CH5 ....**39** A7
Marsland Cl SY11 ....**107** A6
Martin Cl CH2 ....**42** A8
Martin Rd CH2 ....**42** C8
Marton Rd CH4 ....**50** A3
Masefield Dr CH1 ....**41** E6
Mason Ave LL13 ....**145** C4
Mason St CH2 ....**144** A3
Matthais Rd CH2 ....**72** B7
Matthew Cl CH2 ....**42** F2
Maude St
Connah's Quay CH5 .....**38** F7
Rhyl / Y Rhyl LL18 ....**7** A7
Mawddwy Ave LL11 .....**145** B4
Maxwell Ave CH5 ....**39** E3
Maxwell Cl
Buckley / Bwcle CH7 .....**48** C5
Gresford LL12 ....**67** D1
Maxwell Dr / Gyrfa Macswell
CH7 ....**57** F5
Maybury Ave LL20 ....**135** C4
Maydor Ave CH4 ....**51** C7
Mayfeild Gr LL18 ....**7** E8
Mayfield Ct LL12 ....**67** A3
Mayfield Dr CH7 ....**47** F4
Mayfield Mews CH7 .....**48** A5
Mayfield Rd CH1 ....**41** D5
Mayflower Dr / Rhodfa
Blodyn Mai LL12 ....**67** F2
May Terr LL11 ....**16** B1
Maytree Ave CH3 ....**43** B2
Mayville Ave LL11 ....**145** B4
Mayville Ave / Rhodfa
Mayville LL12 ....**67** A3
Meadow Ave CH7 ....**48** E6
Meadow-Bank CH6 ....**27** F5
Meadowbrook Cl LL13 ....**81** D3
Meadow Cl CH3 ....**69** F1
Meadow Cl / Y Dolydd
LL14 ....**79** E7
Meadow Cres LL12 ......**66** A8
Meadowcroft
Cross Lanes LL13 ....**81** D3
Higher Kinnerton CH4 ....**60** A7
3 Whitchurch Urban
SY13 ....**103** E8
Meadow Ct LL12 ....**6** B2
Meadow Field Rd CH4 ....**52** A5
Meadow La CH3 ....**53** A5
Meadow Lea LL13 ....**73** C1
Meadow Pl **4** CH7 ......**46** F4
Meadow Rd CH4 ....**50** C4
Meadow Rise CH4 ......**59** A7
Meadow Rise / Allt Y Ddol
LL12 ....**67** B5
Meadowside
Connah's Quay CH5 .....**39** A1
Mold / Yr Wyddgrug CH7 ..**46** E6
Meadowside Mews CH1 ..**42** B4
Meadows La
Chester CH4 ....**144** C1
Prestatyn LL19 ....**9** A8
Saughall CH1 ....**41** A8
Meadowslea Hospl CH4 ...**59** A6

Meadows Pl CH4 ....**52** E7
Meadows The
Connah's Quay CH5 .....**39** B5
Flint / Y Fflint CH6 ......**28** A6
Prestatyn LL19 ....**9** A8
Wrexham / Wrecsam LL11 .**72** D6
Meadows View LL12 ......**67** F2
Meadowsway CH2 ....**42** D8
Meadow View
Buckley / Bwcle CH7 .....**48** F3
Sealand CH5 ....**40** A6
Tanyfron LL11 ....**71** E5
Meadowview Ct / Llys
Golygfa'r Maes CH5 .....**49** B4
Meadow View Rd SY13 ..**103** F7
Meadway Cl / Clos Meadway
LL11 ....**72** E8
Mechanics' La CH5 ......**39** E4
Medea Dr LL11 ....**1** D5
Medlar Cl CH4 ....**51** F5
Meg's La CH7 ....**48** C3
Meifod LL16 ....**116** F3
Meifod Pl LL15 ....**145** B1
Meifod Rd / Ffordd Meifod
LL16 ....**116** F3
Melbourne Rd Blacon CH1 **41** D4
Buckley / Bwcle CH7 .....**48** B4
Melbreck Ave CH5 ....**39** A1
Melford Pl CH5 ....**38** D4
Meliden Rd LL19 ....**9** A7
Melin Blwm / Lead Mills
CH7 ....**47** A5
Melin-y-Dre CH8 ....**21** B7
Melkridge Cl CH2 ....**43** A3
Melling's La **8** LL16 ....**140** C3
Melrose Ave Chester CH3 .**43** B2
Connah's Quay CH5 .....**39** B4
Melverly Dr CH1 ....**41** C4
Melwood Cl CH4 ....**49** A1
Melyd Ave Johnstown LL14 **79** A1
Prestatyn LL19 ....**9** A8
Menai Ave LL18 ....**7** B6
Menai Rd LL13 ....**73** E1
Menai Way / Ffordd Menai
5 LL11 ....**72** D6
Mendip Cl LL11 ....**72** D6
Mercer Way CH4 ....**51** F6
Mercia Dr CH7 ....**47** D5
Mercier Dr LL18 ....**1** D5
Mercury Ct CH1 ....**41** E2
Mercury Units LL18 ....**6** D2
Mere Cres LL13 ....**73** E5
Merecroft **1** CH3 ....**43** A1
Meredith Cl LL18 ....**7** D6
Meredith Cres LL18 ....**7** D6
Meredith St LL11 ....**145** A1
Meres Visitor Ctr★
SY12 ....**109** D2
Merfyn Way LL18 ....**7** F6
Merion Cl LL18 ....**7** D5
Merlin Ct **7** LL14 ....**79** A1
Merlin Rd LL12 ....**73** C6
Merlin St **5** LL14 ....**79** A1
Merllyn LL17 ....**117** E7
Merllyn Ave CH5 ....**38** D7
Merllyn La CH6 ....**22** C3
Merllyn Prim Sch CH6 ....**22** C2
Merllyn Rd LL18 ....**7** E7
Merton Dr CH4 ....**52** A4
Merton House Sch CH2 ...**42** C4
Merton Pl LL18 ....**7** E4
Mertyn La CH8 ....**20** D7
Methodist Hill **4** LL20 ...**95** A7
Methven Dr LL11 ....**2** C2
Meynell Pl CH1 ....**42** A5
Michaels Rd LL18 ....**7** E5
Micklegate CH2 ....**43** E8
Mickle Trafford Village Sch
CH2 ....**43** E8
Middlecroft CH3 ....**43** C5
Middle La Aldford CH3 ....**62** F3
Hope / Yr Hôb CH4, LL12 ..**59** D4
Middle La / Lon Ganol
LL16 ....**140** C3
Middle Rd LL11 ....**71** C2
Middle Row CH6 ....**22** C2
Middle St LL14 ....**95** C8
Midlothian Ho CH1 .....**144** C3
Milborne Dr CH2 ....**42** E5
Mile Barn Rd LL13 ....**73** E5
Milford St CH7 ....**46** F5
Millais Cl CH5 ....**38** C8
Millars Ct **9** LL14 ......**79** A1
Millbank Rd LL13 ....**7** C7
Millbrook La CH3 ....**53** F1
Millbrook Rise LL13 .....**89** A4
Millbrook Rd LL13 ......**80** C7
Mill Cl CH2 ....**42** D6
Mill Cotts CH3 ....**53** D8
Mill Court CH6 ....**28** C5
Mill Ct **7** LL13 ....**98** C8
Millers Ct CH7 ....**48** B5
Mill Field Cl CH3 ....**69** F2
Mill La CH3 ....**53** F1
Millfields / Cae'r Felin
LL11 ....**72** B3
Mill La Bronington SY13 ..**102** A4
Buckley / Bwcle CH7 .....**48** B5
Chester CH2 ....**42** D6
Connah's Quay CH5 .....**39** A6
Henllan LL16 ....**116** F3
Penycae LL14 ....**85** C7
Mill Lane / Lon Y Felin
LL14 ....**85** B1
Mill Rd SY13 ....**102** A5
Mill St Chester CH4 ....**144** B1
Corwen LL21 ....**142** D3

Mill St *continued*
Ruthin / Rhuthin LL15 ... 141 C5
St Asaph / Llanelwy LL17 ... 16 B2
Mill St / Heol-y-Felin LL20 ... 143 D5
Millstone Pk CH4 ... 59 A8
Mill Terr Bersham LL14 ... 79 B7
Caerwys CH7 ... 24 C3
Rhydymwyn CH7 ... 35 C4
Mill View Prim Sch CH2 ... 42 E6
Mill View Rd CH5 ... 39 A6
Millwood Rise 9 LL13 ... 98 C8
Milmor Way LL19 ... 2 E2
Milton Rd CH1 ... 41 F6
Milton St CH1 ... 144 B3
Minafon LL13 ... 80 E8
Min Awel CH6 ... 28 B4
Minera Hall Rd LL11 ... 71 B4
Minera Lead Mines & Ctry Pk★ LL11 ... 71 B2
Minera Prim Sch LL11 ... 71 A4
Minera Rd LL11 ... 65 E2
Miners Rd / Ffordd Y Glowyr LL12 ... 66 F6
Minerva Ave CH1 ... 41 E2
Minerva Ct CH1 ... 41 E2
Minffordd Fields CH7 ... 46 B2
Minshalls Croft LL14 ... 85 B1
Min y Brenig LL21 ... 123 D3
Min-y-Clwyd LL21 ... 128 D7
Min-y-Coed LL20 ... 143 E4
Min-y-Graig Ave LL11 ... 71 E8
Min-y-Grug LL11 ... 71 A4
Min Y Morfa LL19 ... 2 F2
Min-y-Morfa LL22 ... 6 B3
Min-yr-Aber LL11 ... 72 F8
Min-yr-Afon LL15 ... 141 C5
Min-y-Rhos LL21 ... 130 C6
Mirral View CH8 ... 12 B5
Moel Famau Country Park★ LL16 ... 121 F6
Moel Fammau Rd CH7 ... 47 C7
Moel Ganol
Mold / Yr Wyddgrug CH7 ... 46 D4
Mynydd Isa CH7 ... 47 D5
Moel Gron CH7 ... 47 D5
Moel Parc CH6 ... 28 B4
Moel View Dr CH7 ... 37 F4
Moel View Rd
Buckley / Bwcle CH7 ... 48 B3
Gronant LL19 ... 4 A4
Mynydd Isa CH7 ... 47 E4
Moelwyn Ave E LL18 ... 6 E5
Moelwyn Ave N LL18 ... 6 D6
Moelwyn Ave W LL18 ... 6 D5
Moelwyn Cl CH7 ... 47 E6
Mold Bsns Pk
Mold / Yr Wyddgrug CH7 ... 46 F2
Mold / Yr Wyddgrug CH7 ... 47 A2
Mold Com Hospl / Ysbyty Cymunedol Y Wyddgrug CH7 ... 46 E5
Mold Ind Est CH7 ... 47 A2
Mold Mus & Art Gall★ CH7 ... 46 F4
Mold Rd Alltami CH7, CH5 ... 38 B1
Broughton CH4 ... 50 A3
Buckley / Bwcle CH7 ... 48 A5
Caergwrle LL12 ... 59 A1
Cefn-y-Bedd LL12 ... 66 C2
Connah's Quay CH5, CH7 ... 38 D6
Ewloe CH5 ... 38 E1
Mynydd Isa CH7 ... 47 D4
Ruthin / Rhuthin LL15 ... 141 E5
Wrexham / Wrecsam, Gwersyllt LL11 ... 72 D6
Wrexham / Wrecsam LL11 ... 145 A4
Mold Road Est LL11 ... 72 D7
Moldsdale Rd CH7 ... 47 A4
Mold Way CH5 ... 38 E2
Molineaux Rd LL18 ... 1 E5
Monastery Road / Ffordd Mynachlog CH8 ... 20 C4
Mona Terr LL18 ... 7 C7
Monet Cl CH5 ... 38 C8
Monger Rd LL13 ... 80 C7
Monmouth Gr LL19 ... 2 E2
Monmouth Rd LL12 ... 73 E4
Montgomery Rd / Ffordd Montgomery LL13 ... 73 C1
Montrose Ct CH4 ... 51 F7
Montrose Gdns LL13 ... 73 E2
Montrose Terr LL12 ... 67 D2
Monza Cl
Buckley / Bwcle CH7 ... 47 F4
Northop Hall CH7 ... 38 B4
Moor Ave CH8 ... 20 E6
Moor Cres CH4 ... 50 D1
Moor Croft CH7 ... 47 D7
Moorcroft Ave CH3 ... 43 B1
Moorcroft Cres CH3 ... 43 C4
Moorcroft Mews CH4 ... 51 C5
Moorefields CH7 ... 48 C4
Moorfield Ct CH5 ... 39 B3
Moorfield Rd CH5 ... 39 B3
Moorfields CH8 ... 20 F6
Moorhead Cl LL13 ... 73 D2
Moorhouse Cl CH2 ... 42 D5
Moorings The CH3 ... 53 E7
Moor La
Connah's Quay CH5 ... 39 F1
Hawarden / Penarlâg CH5 ... 49 E8
Higher Kinnerton CH4 ... 60 D8
Holywell / Treffynnon CH8 ... 20 F6
Lower Kinnerton CH4 ... 60 C6
Moorland Ave LL13 ... 73 D2
Moors La SY11 ... 106 D4
Moreton Ave LL14 ... 86 A8
Moreton Bsns Pk SY10 ... 105 E5
Moreton Hall Sch SY10 ... 105 F4
Moreton St LL14 ... 79 A1
Morfa Ave LL18 ... 6 C4
Morfa Bach LL18 ... 7 C7
Morfa Cl LL19 ... 2 E1
Morfa Clwyd Bsns Ctr LL18 ... 7 B6
Morfa L Ctr★ LL22 ... 6 C4
Morfa View LL18 ... 14 F4
Morgan Ave LL11 ... 73 A4
Morgan Cl CH1 ... 41 F6
Morgan Rd LL19 ... 2 D2
Morlan Pk LL18 ... 7 B8
Morley Ave CH5 ... 38 E6
Morley Cl CH2 ... 43 F8
Morley Rd LL19 ... 3 B3
Morley Rd / Ffordd Morley LL18 ... 7 C7
Mornant Ave
Ffynnongroyw CH8 ... 5 D1
Prestatyn LL19 ... 3 B4
Mornington Cres CH7 ... 48 E5
Morris Ave LL19 ... 2 D2
Morse Ho LL11 ... 71 E8
Mortlake Cres CH3 ... 43 A1
Morton Rd CH1 ... 41 E4
Mortons Hoilday Camp LL22 ... 6 A4
Morton Wiew LL13 ... 86 E8
Moses Ct CH1 ... 144 C3
Moss Bank CH2 ... 42 C4
Moss Gn LL12 ... 68 C7
Moss Gr CH4 ... 51 D6
Moss Hill / Bryn Mwsogl LL11 ... 72 B8
Moss La
Bronington SY13 ... 102 B3
Ellesmere Rural SY12 ... 108 C6
Hanmer SY13 ... 101 C2
Mossley Ct CH5 ... 49 C8
Moss Rd LL11 ... 72 B7
Moss Valley Brow / Crib Yr Argau LL11 ... 72 C4
Moss Valley Road / Ffordd Yr Argau LL11 ... 72 C4
Moston Rd CH2 ... 42 D8
Mostyn Ave LL19 ... 3 C2
Mostyn Pl CH1 ... 41 E6
Mostyn Rd Coedpoeth LL11 ... 71 C1
Gronant LL19 ... 4 A3
Mostyn St CH5 ... 39 B6
Mounds Cvn Pk CH8 ... 4 D4
Mountain Cl LL12 ... 59 B2
Mountain Lane Com Prim Sch CH7 ... 48 C5
Mountain St / Heol-y-Mynydd 2 LL14 ... 78 E2
Mountain View
Brymbo LL11 ... 65 E1
Hope / Yr Hôb LL12 ... 59 B2
Saltney CH4 ... 51 E6
Trevalyn LL12 ... 68 D6
4 Wrexham / Wrecsam LL11 ... 73 A5
Mountain View Ave CH7 ... 47 E5
Mountain View Cl CH5 ... 38 D4
Mount Bradford La SY11 ... 107 A7
Mount Cl CH7 ... 47 D4
Mountfield Rd CH5 ... 39 B3
Mount Fields LL13 ... 89 A8
Mount Hill LL11 ... 71 F8
Mount Ida Rd LL19 ... 3 C1
Mount Isa Dr / Rhodfa Mount Isa LL11 ... 71 F8
Mount Pl CH2 ... 42 F2
Mount Pleasant
Cefn-Mawr LL14 ... 85 C1
22 Denbigh / Dinbych LL16 ... 140 C3
2 Ruabon / Rhiwabon LL14 ... 86 A4
Mount Pleasant Ave CH6 ... 28 A5
Mount Pleasant / Bryn Hyfryd 1 LL14 ... 78 F2
Mount Pleasant Rd CH7 ... 48 D6
Mount Pleasent CH4 ... 51 F7
Mount Rd LL18 ... 7 C7
Mount Road / Ffordd-Y-Bryn LL17 ... 16 B2
Mount St Rhostyllen LL14 ... 79 C6
Ruthin / Rhuthin LL15 ... 141 C5
Wrexham / Wrecsam LL13 ... 145 C2
Mount Tabor Cl CH4 ... 49 B2
Mount Terr LL21 ... 142 D3
Mount The Chester CH3 ... 42 F1
Holywell / Treffynnon CH8 ... 21 C2
Wrexham / Wrecsam LL12 ... 73 C2
Mount Wlk 8 CH6 ... 28 A6
Mount Zion LL11 ... 65 D1
Muirfield Cl / Clos Muirfield 7 LL13 ... 73 F3
Muirfield Rd CH7 ... 48 A5
Muir Rd CH1 ... 41 E3
Mulberry Ave 5 SY12 ... 109 A2
Mulsford Ct LL13 ... 90 A8
Mulsford La LL13, SY14 ... 90 B7
Mumforth Wlk 3 CH6 ... 28 A6
Music Hall Pass CH1 ... 144 B2
Musley La LL13 ... 98 D6
Muspratt Wlk 7 CH6 ... 28 A6
Mwrog St LL15 ... 141 B4
Mwyn Ffordd LL11 ... 71 A4
Myddelton Ave / Rhoddfa Miltwn LL16 ... 140 B2
Mynydd Isa Jun Sch CH7 ... 47 D6
Myrica Gr CH2 ... 43 B3
Myrtle Ave CH4 ... 60 A7
Myrtle Gr CH2 ... 43 B3
Myrtle La CH8 ... 21 C4
Myrtle Rd CH7 ... 47 F5
Myrtle Rd / Ffordd Helygen Mair LL12 ... 67 F2
Mytton Pk LL16 ... 140 E3

N

Nannerch Prim Sch CH7 ... 34 D8
Nant Alyn Rd CH7 ... 35 E2
Nant Cl / Cylch-y-Nant 1 LL18 ... 7 F2
Nant Ddu Rd LL22 ... 14 A5
Nant-Ddu Terr LL22 ... 14 A6
Nant Derw CH7 ... 46 D4
Nant Dr LL19 ... 3 C3
Nant Eos CH8 ... 20 F6
Nant Erw LL16 ... 117 C5
Nant Garmon CH7 ... 46 E4
Nant Glyd LL16 ... 121 B8
Nant Glyn
Buckley / Bwcle CH7 ... 48 B3
Rhosymedre LL14 ... 85 D2
Nant Hall Rd / Ffordd Llys Nant LL19 ... 3 B2
Nant Lais LL11 ... 71 B4
Nant Mawr Cres CH7 ... 48 A4
Nant Mawr Ct CH7 ... 48 A3
Nant Mawr Rd CH7 ... 48 A3
Nant Mill★ LL11 ... 71 D1
Nant Rd Bagillt CH6, CH8 ... 27 A6
Bwlchgwyn LL11 ... 70 D7
Connah's Quay CH5 ... 38 D8
Nant Rd / Heol Y Nant LL11 ... 71 C2
Nant View Ct CH7 ... 48 A3
Nant Y Coed CH8 ... 21 C5
Nant-y-Coed CH7 ... 46 E3
Nant Y Crai La LL19 ... 4 A2
Nant-y-Faenol Rd LL18 ... 15 D4
Nantygaer Rd / Ffordd Nant-y-Gaer LL12 ... 67 B4
Nant Y Garth Pass LL15 ... 126 E2
Nant-y-Glyn CH6 ... 22 B3
Nant-y-Gro LL19 ... 4 B3
Nant-y-Patrick LL17 ... 117 B6
Nantyr Rd LL20 ... 135 B4
Naomi Cl CH1 ... 41 D5
Napier Rd CH2 ... 42 C8
Napier Sq LL13 ... 80 C8
Narrow La Brynford CH8 ... 20 E2
Gresford LL12 ... 67 E2
Trevalyn LL12 ... 68 E6
Nayland Ave LL12 ... 67 F2
Nebo Hill LL11 ... 70 E7
Nefod La SY11 ... 106 B6
Nefyn Cl CH5 ... 38 C7
Nelson St Chester CH1 ... 144 C3
Connah's Quay CH5 ... 39 B6
Wrexham / Wrecsam LL13 ... 80 C8
Nelson Terr 5 LL11 ... 72 A4
Nercwys Prim Sch CH7 ... 56 F5
Nescott Terr LL20 ... 135 C4
Neston Dr CH2 ... 42 E5
Neston View CH6 ... 22 C2
Netley Rd LL18 ... 7 B6
Neuadd Pantwn / Panton Hall 19 LL16 ... 140 C3
Neville Cres LL12 ... 145 C4
Neville Dr CH3 ... 43 B1
Neville Rd CH3 ... 43 B1
Nevin Rd CH1 ... 41 D3
Newbridge Rd LL14 ... 95 C8
Newbrigg Rd 4 LL12 ... 73 B6
Newbrighton Rd CH7 ... 47 B8
New Brighton Rd
Bagillt CH6 ... 21 F5
Soughton / Sychdyn CH7 ... 37 B1
Newbury Cl / Clos Newbury LL13 ... 80 E7
Newbury Rd CH4 ... 51 F6
Newby Wlk CH5 ... 38 C8
New Crane Bank CH1 ... 42 B1
New Crane St CH1 ... 42 B1
Newell Dr LL14 ... 86 A6
Newgate St CH1 ... 144 B2
Newhall Ct CH2 ... 42 E6
New Hall La SY13 ... 102 B4
Newhall Rd CH2 ... 42 F6
New Hall Rd LL14 ... 86 B6
New High St LL14 ... 86 A5
New Home Farm Cotts CH64 ... 31 A7
New House Ave / Rhodfa Ty Newydd LL12 ... 67 A3
New Inn Terr LL21 ... 130 D1
New La CH3 ... 69 F6
Newmarket Rd / Ffordd Trelawnyd LL18 ... 9 C4
Newmarket Rise / Rhiw Newmarket LL13 ... 80 E7
New Park Rd CH5 ... 39 A3
Newport Cl LL13 ... 80 E7
Newquay Dr / Rhodfa Ceinewydd 2 LL13 ... 80 D7
New Rd Brymbo LL11 ... 71 F7
Glyn Ceiriog LL20 ... 135 C4
Gwespyr CH8 ... 4 E2
Hanmer SY13 ... 101 B2
Holywell / Treffynnon CH8 ... 21 A5
Wrexham / Wrecsam, Brynteg LL11 ... 72 B6
Wrexham / Wrecsam LL11 ... 73 A4
New Rd *continued*
Wrexham / Wrecsam, New Broughton LL11 ... 72 C3
Wrexham / Wrecsam, Pentre Broughton LL11 ... 72 A7
Wrexham / Wrecsam, Southsea LL11 ... 72 B4
Wrexham / Wrecsam, Summer Hill LL11 ... 72 C8
New Rd / Ffordd Newydd
Cefn-Mawr LL14, LL20 ... 85 A1
Coedpoeth LL11 ... 71 E3
Rhuddlan LL18 ... 7 F1
New Roskell Sq CH6 ... 28 B7
Newry Ct CH2 ... 42 D4
Newry Pk CH2 ... 42 D4
Newry Pk E CH2 ... 42 D4
New St CH5 ... 38 F7
New St / Stryd Newydd CH7 ... 46 F4
New St / Stryt Newydd 9 LL14 ... 78 E2
Newthorne Pl LL19 ... 3 B3
Newthorn Pl CH7 ... 48 B4
Newton Cl CH7 ... 37 F4
Newton Dr CH7 ... 48 F5
Newton Hall Ct CH2 ... 42 F5
Newton Hall Dr CH2 ... 42 F5
Newton La CH2 ... 42 F4
Newton Lodge LL13 ... 145 B1
Newton Park View CH2 ... 42 D4
Newton Prim Sch CH2 ... 42 E4
Newton St LL13 ... 80 C8
Newtown LL12 ... 67 D2
Newtown CE Prim Sch SY4 ... 115 F4
Newtown Cl CH1 ... 144 B3
New Union St 8 CH5 ... 38 D8
Nicholas Ct CH1 ... 144 A2
Nicholas St CH1 ... 144 A2
Nicholas St Mews CH1 ... 144 A2
Nickolson Cl CH2 ... 43 F8
Nield Ct CH2 ... 42 D7
Nightingale Cl CH3 ... 69 F1
Ninth Ave LL12 ... 67 A4
No. 156 CH1 ... 144 C2
Nook La SY13 ... 101 F1
Nook The Chester CH2 ... 42 E4
Connah's Quay CH5 ... 39 D2
Guilden Sutton CH3 ... 43 C4
Saltney CH4 ... 51 E6
Norbreck Dr LL18 ... 7 F5
Norfolk Ave 8 LL19 ... 3 B2
Norfolk Rd Chester CH2 ... 42 F4
Wrexham / Wrecsam LL12 ... 73 D5
Norham Ct LL11 ... 72 B8
Norley Dr CH3 ... 43 C1
Normanby Dr CH5 ... 38 D6
Norman Dr Prestatyn LL19 ... 3 D2
Rhyl / Y Rhyl LL18 ... 7 C7
Norman Rd LL13 ... 80 B7
Norman St CH5 ... 39 B5
Norman Way CH1 ... 41 E5
Norparc LL16 ... 140 C5
Norris Rd CH1 ... 41 E5
Norse Cl LL11 ... 72 D6
North Ave Prestatyn LL19 ... 3 A2
Rhyl / Y Rhyl LL18 ... 7 A7
Ruabon / Rhiwabon LL14 ... 86 A6
North Dr LL18 ... 7 E5
North East Wales Inst of H Ed The / Athrofa Gogledd Ddwyrain Cymru LL11 ... 145 A4
North East Wales Sch of Art LL13 ... 145 B3
Northern Pathway CH4 ... 144 C1
Northern Terr LL21 ... 142 D3
Northgate Ave CH2 ... 144 B4
Northgate Row CH1 ... 144 B2
Northgate St CH1 ... 144 A3
North Gn CH5 ... 40 A6
Northleigh Gr LL11 ... 73 A5
Northop Cl CH5 ... 38 D5
Northop Hall Cty Prim Sch CH7 ... 38 A4
Northop Rd CH7 ... 37 A5
Northop Rd / Ffordd Llaneurgain CH6 ... 28 A4
North Rd
Connah's Quay CH5 ... 29 F2
Holywell / Treffynnon CH8 ... 21 B4
North Rd / Bonc Ddu LL14 ... 78 F2
North St Chester CH3 ... 43 A1
Connah's Quay CH5 ... 39 C5
Saltney CH4 ... 51 B7
Sandycroft CH5 ... 40 A3
North St / Heol-y-Gogledd CH7 ... 24 B7
Northway CH4 ... 52 A7
Northwood LL12 ... 73 D5
Norton Ave Prestatyn LL19 ... 3 A3
Saltney CH4 ... 51 D6
Norton Rd CH3 ... 43 C2
Norwood Dr CH4 ... 52 B6
Nuns Rd CH1 ... 144 A1
Nurseries The
Chirk / Y Waun LL14 ... 95 E1
Cymau LL11 ... 65 E4
Gresford LL12 ... 67 E2
Nurseries The / Maes Y Blanhigfa CH6 ... 27 F5
Nursery Cl / Clos Meithrin LL19 ... 3 A2

O

Oak Alyn Ct LL12 ... 66 C3
Oak Ave LL13 ... 99 F3
Oak Bank La CH2 ... 43 C6
Oak Cl Connah's Quay CH5 ... 38 C7
Gwersyllt LL11 ... 66 F1
Weston Rhyn SY10 ... 105 D4
Wrexham / Wrecsam LL11 ... 72 C8
Oak Cl / Clos Derw LL17 ... 16 B2
Oakcroft LL14 ... 105 D8
Oakdale 9 LL14 ... 78 F2
Oakdale Cl CH4 ... 50 B3
Oakdene LL13 ... 81 D3
Oak Dr
Buckley / Bwcle CH7 ... 48 B7
10 Ellesmere SY12 ... 109 A2
Higher Kinnerton CH4 ... 60 A7
Whitchurch SY13 ... 103 F6
Wrexham / Wrecsam LL12 ... 73 C4
Oak Dr / Ffordd Derw CH7 ... 57 F5
Oak Dr / Rhodfa'r Ddermen LL12 ... 67 F2
Oakenholt La CH6 ... 28 F1
Oakfield Garth LL20 ... 84 D2
Wrexham / Wrecsam LL13 ... 80 C7
Oakfield Ave CH2 ... 42 E8
Oakfield Cl SY11 ... 107 A6
Oakfield Cotts LL12 ... 67 D2
Oakfield Cvn Pk LL18 ... 6 C4
Oakfield Dr CH2 ... 42 E8
Oakfield Pk Home Est LL12 ... 67 A5
Oakfield Rd Blacon CH1 ... 41 D4
Buckley / Bwcle CH7 ... 48 C4
Connah's Quay CH5 ... 39 A1
Oak Gr CH6 ... 22 D1
Oak Hill Dr LL19 ... 3 B1
Oak Hill La LL19 ... 3 B1
Oakhurst LL13 ... 73 E3
Oak La / Lon Derw LL17 ... 16 B2
Oakland Ave LL18 ... 7 A6
Oaklands CH3 ... 43 F4
Oaklands Ave LL13 ... 73 D4
Oaklands Rd LL14 ... 105 E6
Oaklea LL18 ... 6 E3
Oaklea Ave CH2 ... 42 F4
Oaklea Ct LL18 ... 7 E6
Oakleigh / Cae Dderwen LL14 ... 85 D7
Oakley Rd CH5 ... 39 E2
Oak Mdws LL11 ... 71 E5
Oakmere Dr CH3 ... 53 B8
Oak Pk / Parc Derwen CH7 ... 57 F5
Oak Rd Acrefair LL14 ... 85 D3
Chester CH4 ... 51 F5
Wrexham / Wrecsam LL13 ... 82 A7
Oak Rd / Ffordd y Dderwen 2 LL14 ... 78 F2
Oaks Dr The CH2 ... 42 D7
Oaks The Ewloe CH5 ... 48 F7
Penycae LL14 ... 85 D8
Oak St / Hoel y Dderwen LL20 ... 143 D5
Oak Tree Ave / Rhodfa'r Dderwen LL12 ... 67 A4
Oaktree Bsns Pk CH7 ... 47 B2
Oak Tree Cl
Buckley / Bwcle CH7 ... 48 C5
Connah's Quay CH5 ... 39 A4
Oaktree Ct CH2 ... 43 A3
Oak Villas CH7 ... 57 F5
Oakville Ave LL18 ... 1 E5
Oakwood Cl CH7 ... 46 E6
Oakwood Ct LL14 ... 79 D7
Oakwood Pk / Parc Coed Derw LL13 ... 99 F4
Oakwood Rd LL18 ... 7 E8
Oakwood Villas CH5 ... 38 E6
Ochr-y-Bryn LL16 ... 116 F3
Ochr Y Bryn LL19 ... 9 A6
Och'r-y-Bryn CH8 ... 26 F2
Ochr Y Bryn / Braeside LL13 ... 80 E7
Ochr-y-Foel CH7 ... 127 C8
Ochr Y Waen CH7 ... 48 A6
Odeon Bldg CH1 ... 144 A3
Offa LL14 ... 95 E3
Offa Ct 4 LL14 ... 79 A1
Offa St Brymbo LL11 ... 65 E1
Johnstown LL14 ... 79 A1
Ogwen LL14 ... 85 D3
Ogwen Ave LL18 ... 6 F5
Old Aston Hill CH5 ... 39 A3
Old Bank La CH7 ... 48 B3
Old Carriage Yd The LL12 ... 68 A5
Oldcastle La SY14 ... 90 E8
Old Chads La SY13 ... 93 C8
Old Chester Rd Ewloe CH5 ... 38 F2
Holywell / Treffynnon CH8 ... 21 B3
Old Chirk Rd SY11 ... 105 F1
Old Farm Cotts CH1 ... 40 E3
Old Farm Rd LL14 ... 79 D7
Oldfield Cres CH4 ... 51 F5
Oldfield Dr CH3 ... 43 C2
Oldfield Prim Sch CH3 ... 43 C3
Old Foryd Rd LL18 ... 6 E6
Old Gaol Gall★ LL15 ... 141 C5
Old Gardens The / Yr Hen Erddi 1 LL13 ... 73 E3

Oldgate Rd LL19 ....2 C2
Old George The CH1 ..144 B3
Old Golf Rd LL18 ....1 D5
Old Hall Cl LL14 ....79 D7
Old Hall Gdns CH2 ...144 C4
Old Hall Pk CH3 ....43 F5
Old Hall Pl CH1 ....144 A2
Old Hall Rd CH5 ....39 A1
Old La CH4 ....61 E2
Old Liverpool Rd CH5 ..38 E1
Old London Rd
  Bagillt CH6 ....22 B2
  Bagillt CH6 ....22 D1
  Flint / Y Fflint CH6 ...27 F6
Old Mdw Ct LL12 ....67 A5
Old Mill Ct CH2 ....42 B6
Old Mold Rd Ewloe CH5 ..38 F2
  Wrexham / Wrecsam LL12 ..73 D7
Old Orchard The / Yr Hen
  Berllan CH5 ....49 D8
Old Palace The LL17 ...16 B1
Old Paper Mill La CH6 ..28 E3
Old Pearl La CH3 ....43 B1
Old Quay CH8 ....21 C7
Old Rd LL20 ....135 D4
Old Road Bwlchgwyn / Hen
  Ffordd Bwlchgwyn LL11 70 D6
Old Road Minera / Hen
  Ffordd Mwynglawdd
  LL11 ....71 A5
Old Ruthin Rd / Hen Ffordd
  Rhuthun LL16 ....120 E8
Old Sch Mews ▌1▐ LL13 ..98 C8
Old School Cl
  Caergwrle LL12 ....66 C6
  Ruabon / Rhiwabon LL14 ..85 F5
Old Seals Way CH1 .....42 A3
Old Smelt Rd LL11 .....71 B4
Old Vicarage Cvn Pk The
  CH8 ....11 B8
Old Walls LL16 ....16 A2
Old Woman's La CH3 ...53 D7
Old Wood / Hengoed
  LL11 ....72 C4
Old Wrexham Rd
  Chester CH4 ....52 C7
  Gresford LL12 ....67 D1
  Wrexham / Wrecsam LL12 ..73 D8
Olinda St LL18 ....7 C8
Olivia Dr LL18 ....1 D5
Onslow Rd CH1 ....41 D4
'On The Air', The
  Broadcasting Mus & Vintage
  Sound Shop ★ CH1 ..144 B2
Orchard Cl
  Buckley / Bwcle CH7 ...48 B4
  Chester CH2 ....42 D5
  Connah's Quay CH5 ....39 D3
Orchard Croft CH3 .....43 E5
Orchard Ct
  ▌3▐ Chester CH4 ......43 A1
  Gresford LL12 ....67 D2
Orchard Gdns LL11 ....73 B5
Orchard Gr CH3 ....69 F1
Orchard St CH1 ....144 A3
Orchards The
  Connah's Quay CH5 ....38 C4
  Leeswood / Coedllai LL14 ..58 A4
  Saltney CH4 ....51 D6
  Wrexham / Wrecsam LL13 ..80 D7
Orchard The Chester CH3 ..53 A8
  Rossett LL12 ....68 B7
Orchard View LL12 .....67 D2
Orchard Way
  Garden City CH5 ......39 F7
  Mold / Yr Wyddgrug CH7 ..46 E6
Orchid Cl CH3 ....53 B6
Orhcards The LL13 ....75 D8
Oriel Ho CH2 ....42 C4
Orme View Dr LL19 .....9 B8
Ormonde Rd CH2 ......42 C4
Ormonde St CH1 ......144 C3
Orton Gr ▌10▐ LL18 .....7 A6
Osborne Cl LL11 ......73 A4
Osborne Gr ▌3▐ LL18 ...7 A6
Osborne Rd LL11 ......73 A4
Osborne St / Stryt Osborne
  ▌3▐ LL14 ....78 E1
Osbourne Ct CH5 ......38 E1
Osprey Ct CH4 ....144 A4
Oswald Way LL12 ......73 C3
Oswestry Rd ▌12▐ SY12 ..109 A2
Oulton Ave CH2 ....42 E7
Oulton Pl CH1 ....144 B3
Oval The LL14 ....81 C7
Overdale Ave CH7 .....47 E4
Overlea Cres CH5 .....39 C2
Overlea Dr CH5 ....39 C2
Overleigh Ct CH4 .....52 D7
Overleigh Dr
  Buckley / Bwcle CH7 47 F5
  Wrexham / Wrecsam LL13 ..73 E4
Overleigh Rd CH4 .....52 C7
Overleigh St Mary's CE Prim
  Sch CH4 ....52 D6
Overleigh Terr CH4 ....52 C7
Overton Ave LL19 ......2 F2
Overton Cl CH7 ....48 C4
Overton Rd
  Bangor on Dee / Bangor-is-y-coed
  LL13 ....88 F7
  St. Martin's SY11 ....106 E6
Overton Way LL12 .....73 C4
Overwood La CH1 .....41 C4

Owain Glyndwr LL18 ....6 E4
Owain Gwynedd LL18 ...6 E4
Owen Cl Blacon CH1 ...41 E6
  Rhyl / Y Rhyl LL18 .....7 D5
Owen's Holiday Camp
  LL22 ....6 A3
Owens St / Stryt Owen
  LL14 ....78 D2
Owens Terr LL15 ....26 B6
Owen Terr LL15 ....5 B6
Oxford Gr ▌13▐ LL18 ....7 B7
Oxford Rd CH4 ....51 F6
Oxford St LL13 ....73 C1

P

Padarn Cl CH4 ....51 D5
Paddock Cl LL14 ......79 D7
Paddock Rd CH4 ......52 E1
Paddock Row LL14 ....86 A4
Paddocks The LL11 ...71 E3
Paddock The Chester CH4 52 B7
  Connah's Quay CH5 ...39 D2
  Cross Lanes LL13 .....81 D3
  Prestatyn LL19 ....9 A7
  St Asaph / Llanelwy LL17 ..16 B1
Paddock Way
  Gwernymynydd CH7 ...46 B1
  Higher Kinnerton CH4 ..60 A7
Padeswood Dr CH7 ...48 C2
Padeswood Rd N CH7 ..48 B4
Padeswood Rd S CH7 ..48 B2
Palace Ave LL14 ....7 A7
Palace Cl CH6 ....27 E6
Palatine Cl CH1 ......41 D6
Palgrave Cl CH1 ......42 A5
Palins Holiday Camp 6 C4
Palmeira Gdns LL19 ...3 B1
Palmer St LL13 ....73 C1
Palmerston Cres CH5 ..48 F8
Palmerstone Cl CH1 ...42 B4
Pandy La LL11 ....70 B6
Pandy La / Ffordd-y-Pandy
  LL11 ....9 A4
Pandy Ind Est CH5 ....73 A7
Panorama Wlk Garth LL20 84 A2
  Llangollen LL20 ......143 E8
Pantasaph Franciscan
  Friary ★ CH8 ....20 C5
Pant Glas
  Bodelwyddan LL17 ....15 F2
  Ruthin / Rhuthin LL15 ..141 D6
  Soughton / Sychdyn CH7 ..37 A1
Pant Hill LL14 ....85 E8
Pant Isa CH7 ....37 A1
Pant La
  Ellesmere Rural SY12 ..97 E4
  Gresford LL12 ....67 E3
Pant Olwen LL12 ....67 E3
Panton Hall / Neuadd
  Pantwn ▌19▐ LL14 ...140 C3
Panton Pl Chester CH2 ..42 F3
  Holywell / Treffynnon CH8 ..21 B4
Panton Rd CH2 ....42 F3
Pant Ucha CH7 ....37 A1
Pant-y-Ffrith CH7 .....35 F8
Pant Y Fownog Dr CH7 ..47 F4
Paper Mill Cotts CH6 ..28 E3
Paper Mill La CH6 .....28 E3
Parade St LL20 ......143 C5
Parade The CH1 ......41 E4
Paradise CH4 ....144 B1
Paradise La CH5 ......48 F8
Paradise St / Heol Gwynfa ▌11▐
  LL18 ....7 B7
Parc Aberconwy LL19 ...3 D2
Parc Alafowlia LL16 ..140 E4
Parc Alun CH7 ....47 A5
Parc Annefield / Annefield
  Pk LL12 ....67 E2
Parc-Bach LL16 ......140 E3
Parc Bach LL16 ......117 C5
Parc Bodwyn / Bodwyn Pk
  LL12 ....67 E2
Parc Bron Deg LL12 ...67 E2
Parc Bryn Castell CH5 ..38 C4
Parc Bychan LL11 ....73 A5
Parc Capel LL11 ......25 D3
Parc Clwyd LL16 ....140 F2
Parc Coed Derw / Oakwood
  Pk LL13 ....99 F4
Parc Cwn Pk CH7 ...127 B6
Parc Derwen LL16 ...140 E7
Parc Derwen / Oak Pk
  CH7 ....57 F5
Parc Diwydiannol Glannau
  Dyfrdwy / Deeside Ind Pk
  CH5 ....30 C2
Parc Diwydiannol Y Ffin /
  Borders Ind Pk The
  CH4 ....51 C7
Parc Dyffryn LL19 .....3 A2
Parc Edith LL18 ....7 E1
Parc Elen LL18 ....6 E3
Parc Esmor LL18 ......7 D8
Parc Ffordlas LL18 .....7 C6
Parc Gorsedd CH8 ...20 A6
Parc Gwelfor LL18 ....8 F4
Parc Gwledig Dyfroedd Alun
  / Alyn Waters Ctry Pk ★
  LL11 ....66 D1
Parc Hafod CH7 ......24 B7
Parc Hendy CH7 ......46 D4
Parc Hiraddug LL18 ....8 F3
Parc Hyde LL18 ....6 E3

Parc Iago / James Pk
  LL18 ....8 F3
Parc Ial / Yale Park
  LL11 ....145 A3
Parc Issa CH7 ....47 E6
Parc Luned LL18 ......6 E3
Parc Menter Bersham /
  Bersham Ent Ctr LL14 ..79 C5
Parc Morfa LL18 ....6 D4
Parc Offa LL18 ....10 A4
Parc Talardy / Talardy Pk
  LL17 ....16 A2
Parc Terr LL11 ....129 F2
Parc Tref Y Nant /
  Tref-y-nant Pk LL14 ...85 A2
Parc Tudur / Tudor Pk
  LL18 ....6 F3
Parc Y Castell LL22 ...6 C2
Parc Y Castell / Castle Pk
  LL11 ....141 A4
Parc-y-Dre Rd LL15 ..141 B5
Parc-y-Foel / Foel Pk
  LL18 ....8 F2
Parc-y-Llan Cilcain CH7 ..44 F7
  Henllan LL16 ....116 F3
Llanfair Dyffryn Clwyd
  LL15 ....126 B6
Parc-y-Lleng LL18 .....7 E1
Parc / Y Parc The LL15 ..141 B5
Parc Yr Hafod / Hafod Pk
  CH7 ....46 D4
Park Ave
  Bodelwyddan LL17 ....14 E4
  Carmel CH8 ....20 E6
  Connah's Quay, Mancot Royal
  CH5 ....39 D2
  Connah's Quay, Shotton
  CH5 ....39 C6
  Flint / Y Fflint CH6 ...28 B6
  Higher Kinnerton CH4 ..59 F7
  Kinmel Bay / Bae Cinmel
  LL18 ....6 E4
  Llangollen LL20 .....143 F4
  Mold / Yr Wyddgrug CH7 ..46 E5
  Mynydd Isa CH7 ......47 D5
  Saltney CH4 ....51 E6
  Wrexham / Wrecsam LL12 ..73 C3
Park Cres Carmel CH8 ..20 D6
  Penyffordd CH4 ......59 A7
Park Ct Chester CH1 ..144 C3
Park Dr Carmel CH8 ...20 D6
  Chester CH2 ....43 A4
  Rhyl / Y Rhyl LL18 .....7 D7
Park Dr S CH2 ....43 A4
Parkend Wlk LL14 ....79 C7
Parker Dr CH3 ....69 E1
Parker Dr S CH3 ......69 F1
Parkers Cl LL11 ....73 A4
Parker's Row CH3 ....69 F6
Parkfield LL12 ....67 D3
Parkfield Rd CH4 .....50 C3
Parkgate Ct CH1 .....42 B4
Parkgate Rd Blacon CH1 ..42 A6
  Woodbank CH1 ....31 E7
Park Gr Caerwys CH7 ..24 C6
  Connah's Quay CH5 ...38 F6
Park Hall Rd CH8 .....21 C7
Park Hill Ave LL11 ....72 D8
Parkhill Rd CH5 ......39 A7
Park House Mews ▌14▐
  CH7 ....46 F4
Park Jun & Inf Sch LL12 67 A4
Park La
  Holywell / Treffynnon CH8 ..21 B4
  Marford LL12 ....68 C2
  Penyffordd CH4 ......59 A7
  Pulford CH4 ....61 E5
Parklands CH7 ....55 B6
Parklands Wlk / Rhodfa'r
  Parc ▌15▐ LL14 ....86 A4
Parkleigh Ct LL12 ....73 C2
Park Manor / Manor Pk
  CH6 ....22 E1
Park Mews LL14 ......78 F1
Park Rd Bagillt CH6 ...22 C1
  Buckley / Bwcle CH7 ..48 C5
  Carmel CH8 ....20 D6
  Cefn-mawr LL14 ......95 C8
  Llay LL12 / LL11 ......67 A2
  Rhosllanerchrugog LL14 ..78 F3
  Rhosymedre LL14 .....85 D2
  Tanyfron LL11 ....71 F5
  Whitchurch SY13 ....103 F7
Park Rd / Heol Y Park
  Coedpoeth LL11 ......71 C3
  Ruthin / Rhuthin LL15 ..141 C5
Park Rd W CH4 ....52 A7
Parkside
  Buckley / Bwcle CH7 ..48 B5
  Overton / Owrtyn LL13 ..88 C1
Parkside Ave / Rhodfa Ger Y
  Parc CH5 ....38 C6
Park St Chester CH1 ..144 B2
  Johnstown LL14 ......79 A1
  Llanrhaeadr-ym-Mochnant
  SY10 ....138 A1
  Ruabon / Rhiwabon LL14 ..86 A4
  Wrexham / Wrecsam LL11 145 B4
Park St / Cwm Glas LL14 78 F1
Parks The
  Connah's Quay CH5 ...38 C6
  Tanyfron LL11 ....71 F5
Park St / Lon Parc
  LL16 ....140 D3
Park The CH3 ....53 E8
Park The / Y Parc 46 F4

Park View Caerwys CH7 ..24 C3
  Drury CH7 ....47 F5
  Northop / Llan-eurgain CH7 37 C5
  Rossett LL12 ....68 C8
Parkview Ct CH5 ......49 C8
Park View / Trem y Parc
  LL14 ....78 F1
Park Villas ▌13▐ CH7 ..47 F5
Park W CH1 ....41 E2
Park Wall Rd / Ffordd Myr y
  Parc LL11 ....72 E8
Parkway
  Connah's Quay CH5 ...30 E1
  Mold / Yr Wyddgrug CH7 ..46 F4
Parkway Bsns Ctr CH5 ..30 E1
Park Wlk
  Buckley / Bwcle CH7 ..48 C5
  Chester CH2 ....42 E4
Parliament St LL18 .....7 E1
Parry's Cotts CH5 .....38 B1
Parsonage Cl LL12 ...67 D2
Parsons La CH2 ....42 B7
Pastures The CH4 ....59 A7
Patagonia Ave LL18 ...7 E1
Patrick Ave LL18 ......7 E5
Patten Cl CH5 ....48 E8
Pavilions The CH4 ....52 B3
Peace Field CH3 ......53 B7
Peake's La LL16 ......140 C3
Pearlings The LL15 ...43 B1
Pearl La Chester CH3 ..43 C1
  Littleton CH3 ....43 D1
Pearson St / Stryt Pearson
  ▌7▐ LL14 ....78 E2
Pear Tree Cl CH5 .....39 A4
Peartree La SY13 ....100 D7
Pear Tree La CH2 .....42 F6
Pear Tree Way CH2 ...42 F6
Peckforton Way CH2 ..42 F6
Peel Cl ▌5▐ LL13 .....98 C8
Peel St LL13 ....145 A2
Peel Terr CH1 ....144 C3
Peever Ct SY12 .....108 B7
Pemba Dr CH7 ....48 C5
Pemberton Rd CH5 ...39 D4
Pemberton Rd LL14 ..144 A3
Pembroke Cl Chester CH4 52 E6
  Connah's Quay CH5 ...39 D4
Pembroke Rd LL12 ...73 E4
Pembry Rise CH5 .....38 C8
Penarlag Cty Prim Sch
  CH5 ....39 A2
Pencoed CH5 ....85 A1
Penda's Pk LL13 .....99 F4
Penderyn Way LL12 ...67 A3
Pendine Way LL11 ...72 D6
Pendragon Ct / Cwrt
  Pendragon LL13 .....80 B7
Pendre Ave Prestatyn LL19 ..3 A4
  Rhyl / Y Rhyl LL18 .....7 E6
Pendwll Rd / Ffordd Pendwll
  LL11 ....72 B8
Penfold Hey CH2 .....42 D7
Penfold Way CH4 .....61 A7
Pengwern LL20 ......143 D3
Pengwern Hall Coll LL18 15 D6
Pengwladys Ave CH5 ..38 D5
Penisaf Ave LL22 ......6 A3
Penisardre Rd LL18 ...3 A2
Penlan LL11 ....79 A1
Pen Lan LL22 ....6 A3
Penlan Dr CH5 ....39 C2
Penley Ave LL19 ......2 E2
Penley Hospl LL13 ....99 F5
Penllan LL11 ....9 A6
Pen Llan LL11 ....127 D3
Penllwyn LL14 ....79 B1
Pen Lon CH6 ....21 F6
Penmon Cl CH1 ......41 D3
Pennant Flats ▌3▐ LL16 ..140 D3
Pennant Gr LL11 ......3 B3
Pennant St CH7 ......38 F7
Penny Bank Cl CH4 ...50 A3
Penrallt LL11 ....72 A8
Penrho CH8 ....12 D3
Penrhos LL11 ....72 C8
Pen-rhos LL21 ......130 C6
Penrhos Ct CH5 ......38 C4
Penrhyn
  Holywell / Treffynnon CH8 ..21 D5
  Marchwiel LL13 ......80 E4
Penrhyn Dr / Lon Penrhyn
  LL14 ....95 E6
Penry St / Fforddd Penri ▌6▐
  LL14 ....78 E2
Pensby Ave CH2 ......42 D5
Pent Cotts LL12 ......67 F3
Pentland LL14 ....43 A2
Pentre-Bychan Rd LL14 ..79 A5
Pentre Church in Wales
  Controlled Prim Sch
  LL14 ....95 E6
Pentredwr LL14 ......78 E2
Pentre Felin LL13 ...145 B2
Pentre Felin / Jones St
  LL14 ....78 D1
Pentre Fron Rd LL11 ..71 C4
Pentre Gwyn LL13 ....80 E7
Pentre Hill CH6 ......27 F1
Pentre Ind Est CH5 ...39 F4
Pentre La
  Buckley / Bwcle CH7 ..48 A6
  Gronant LL19 ....4 B1
Pentre La / Lon Pentre
  LL12 ....67 B3

Pentre La / Lon-y-Pentref
  LL18 ....7 F2
Pentre Nant La LL13 ..88 A8
Pentre Rd CH8 ....26 F4
Pentre St LL13 ....67 B3
Pen Tywyn LL19 ....2 F2
Pen-y-Ball Hill 21 A4
Pen-y-Ball St / Heol
  Pen-y-Bal CH8 ....21 A4
Pen-y-Bont
  Cefn-Mawr LL20 ......85 A1
  ▌3▐ Rhuddlan LL18 ....7 E1
Penybryn LL12 ....67 B3
Pen Y Bryn LL21 ....142 C3
Pen-y-Bryn
  Flint / Y Fflint CH6 ...28 B4
  Hope / Yr Hôb LL12 ...59 B2
  Mold / Yr Wyddgrug CH7 ..46 E4
  Soughton / Sychdyn CH7 ..37 A1
  Wrexham / Wrecsam LL13 145 B1
Penybryn / Hill St LL21 142 B1
Penycae Ave LL11 ...106 A1
Penycae Cl SY10 ....106 A1
Penycae Inf Sch LL14 ..85 D7
Penycae Jun Sch LL14 ..85 D7
Pen-y-Cefndy LL18 ....7 D5
Penycefn Rd CH7 .....24 B6
Pen-y-Coed CH7 .....34 D7
Pen-y-Coed Rd CH7 ..48 C6
Pen-y-Felin Rd CH7 ..34 C8
Penyffordd Jun Sch CH4 59 A8
Penyffordd / Picton Rd
  CH8 ....5 B1
Pen-y ffordd Sta CH4 ..58 F7
Penyfron Rd CH7 .....45 D7
Pen-y-gaer Rd / Ffordd
  Pen-y-gaer LL20 .....84 C2
Pen-y-Garreg Cl CH7 ..47 E5
Pen-y-Gelli LL15 ....125 C8
Penygelli Ave LL11 ...71 D2
Penygelli Prim Sch LL11 71 D3
Penygelli Rd LL11 ....71 D2
Pen-y-Glyn CH6 ......22 B3
Penygraig LL14 ....78 E1
Pen Y Graig LL16 ....140 B3
Pen-y-Graig Rd LL11 ..71 E4
Pen Y Llan St LL13 ...38 D8
Pen-y-Llan St LL13 ...98 C8
Pen-y-Llyn LL11 ......72 E7
Pen-y-Llys LL18 ....7 E1
Pen-y-Ion LL11 ......47 C4
Penymaes CH7 ....47 D5
Pen Y Maes CH7 .....48 A4
Pen-y-Maes Prestatyn LL19 ..9 A6
  Ruthin / Rhuthin LL15 141 D3
Penymaes Ave LL14 ..145 C4
Pen-y-Maes Ave LL18 ..7 E5
Pen-y-Maes Gdns CH5 ..21 C4
Pen-y-Maes Rd / Ffordd
  Pen-y-Maes CH7 .....21 D5
Penymynydd Rd CH4 ..49 A1
Pen-y-Nant CH6 .....22 B3
Penypalmant Rd LL11 ..71 A5
Pen y Parc Bglws CH7 ..36 A8
Pen-y-Pentre CH7 .....37 B1
Pen-yr-allt LL21 .....130 C1
Pen Y Waun LL14 .....95 E1
Pen-y-Wern LL14 .....78 F1
Peoples Mkt The / Marchnad
  y Bobl LL14 ....145 C2
Pepper St Chester CH1 ..144 B2
  Christleton CH3 ......53 D8
Percival Cl CH2 ....42 C8
Percival Rd CH2 ......42 C8
Percy Rd Chester CH4 ..52 C7
  Wrexham / Wrecsam LL13 145 B1
Percy Rd / Ffordd Percy
  LL13 ....80 B7
Peris LL14 ....85 D3
Peris Ave LL22 ....6 A4
Perrins Wlk ▌2▐ CH6 ..28 A6
Perry Rd SY10 ....106 B1
Perry View SY10 ....106 B1
Perth-y-Terfyn Inf Sch
  CH8 ....21 B4
Peters Cl LL19 ....9 A8
Peter St / Stryt Pedr
  LL14 ....78 E2
Petit Cl LL12 ....66 B5
Philips Cl LL12 ....73 D4
Philip's Rd LL11 .....72 D6
Philip St CH5 ....40 A2
Phillips Rd CH1 ......41 D3
Phillip St CH2 ....42 F3
Phoenix St CH5 ......40 A3
Pickering St CH2 ....144 C4
Pickmere Dr CH3 .....53 B8
Picton Gorse La CH2 ..43 B7
Picton / Picton Rd 5 A1
Picton Rd / Penyffordd
  CH8 ....5 B1
Picton Rd / Picton CH8 ..5 A1
Picton Rd (Picton) CH8 ..11 B8
Pierce's Sq LL13 ....145 B2
Pierce St CH5 ....39 D5
Piercy Ave LL13 ......80 F4
Pierpoint La CH1 ....144 B2
Pigeon House La LL12 ..59 A2
Pigeon La SY13 .....100 C6
Pigot Rd / Ffordd Pigod ▌2▐
  LL16 ....140 D3
Pikey La Gresford LL12 ..67 D1
  Wrexham / Wrecsam LL12 ..73 D8
Pilgrims Cl / Clos y Pererini
  CH7 ....37 A5
Pilgrim Way LL13 .....81 C6
Pillar of Eliseg ★ LL20 ..131 C3

Pine Cl
8 Ellesmere SY12 . . . . . .109 A2
Gwersyllt LL11 . . . . .66 C1
Wrexham / Wrecsam, Bradley LL11 . . . . .72 F8
Pine Crest CH6 . . . . .27 E5
Pine Gdns CH2 . . . . .42 C6
Pine Gr Chester CH2 . . . . .43 B4
Mynydd Isa CH7 . . . . .47 E5
Pine Gr / Gelli'r Pinwydd LL12 . . . . .67 B4
Pines The Ewloe CH5 . . . . .48 F7
Wrexham / Wrecsam LL12 . . . . .145 C4
Pine Tree Cl CH4 . . . . .50 C3
Pinewood Ave CH5 . . . . . . .38 E7
Pinewood Cl LL14 . . . . . . .79 D7
Pinewood Rd CH7 . . . . . . .48 F5
Pinfold Ct CH4 . . . . .52 E6
Pinfold Ind Est CH7 . . . . .48 B7
Pinfold La
Buckley / Bwcle CH7 . . . . .48 A8
Chester CH4 . . . . .52 D6
Chester CH4 . . . . .52 E7
Ellesmere SY12 . . . . .109 C2
Llay LL12 . . . . .66 F5
Northop Hall CH7 . . . . . . .38 A2
Northop Hall CH7 . . . . . . .38 B3
Pinfold The LL13 . . . . .75 D8
Pinfold Workshops
Buckley / Bwcle CH7 . . . . . .48 B7
Rhyl / Y Rhyl LL18 . . . . .7 C5
Pingot Croft CH3 . . . . .53 B7
Pinwyddy Goedwig / Forest Pines 2 LL13 . . . . .73 F3
Pipers Ct CH2 . . . . .43 B4
Pipers La Chester CH2 . . . .43 B4
Puddington CH64 . . . . .31 A8
Pippins Cl CH5 . . . . .39 A6
Pisgah Hill LL11 . . . . .72 B7
Pistyll CH8 . . . . .21 C2
Pistyll Hill LL12 . . . . .68 A3
Pistyll Rhaeadr★ SY10 .137 B4
Pitmans La CH5 . . . . .39 C1
Plas Acton Cl LL12 . . . . . .73 B7
Plas Acton Prec LL11 . . . .73 B7
Plas Acton Rd / Ffordd Plas Acton LL11 . . . . .73 A7
Plas Alyn LL11 . . . . .72 C7
Plas Angharad LL14 . . . . .79 D7
Plas Ave LL19 . . . . .3 B2
Plas Bach LL18 . . . . .6 E5
Plas Bennion Rd / Ffordd Plas Bennion LL14 . . . . .85 D5
Plas Coch Rd LL11 . . . . . .72 F4
Plas Cyril LL18 . . . . .7 C6
Plas Darland LL11 . . . . .145 C4
Plas Dur LL11 . . . . .71 F8
Plas Foryd LL18 . . . . .6 E6
Plas Gorphwysfa LL19 . . . .3 A3
Plas Gwyn LL12 . . . . .73 C3
Plas Hafan LL14 . . . . .79 A1
Plas Howell LL11 . . . . .71 D2
Plas Isaf LL14 . . . . .85 D2
Plas Kynaston La LL14 . . .85 C1
Plas Madoc 2 LL13 . . . . .98 C8
Plas Maen Dr LL12 . . . . . .66 B4
Plas Newton La CH2 . . . . .42 F5
Plas Newydd Dr LL19 . . . . .2 D2
Plas Newydd (Mus)★ LL20 . . . . .143 D4
Plas Rd LL18 . . . . .7 E7
Plassey Cl / Clos y Plasau LL13 . . . . .73 F4
Plassey Ct LL13 . . . . .89 A7
Plassey Gdns LL13 . . . . . .89 A7
Plas Teg LL11 . . . . .127 B3
Plastirion LL22 . . . . .6 A3
Plas Tirion LL14 . . . . .79 A1
Plastirion Ave LL19 . . . . . . .3 C2
Plastirion Ct 3 LL18 . . . . .7 C8
Plastirion Dr LL19 . . . . .3 C2
Plastirion Pk LL22 . . . . .6 A3
Plas Uchaf Ave LL19 . . . . . .3 B1
Plas-y-Brenin
Rhuddlan LL18 . . . . .7 F1
12 Rhyl / Y Rhyl LL18 . . . . . . .7 B7
Plas-y-Bwl LL12 . . . . .66 A7
Plas Y Castell / Castle Grange LL12 . . . . .66 B7
Plas-yn-Llan LL20 . . . . .143 D4
Plas-yn-Rhos CH4 . . . . . .58 F7
Platt La Penyffordd CH4 . . .59 B6
Whixall SY13 . . . . .113 B5
Pleasant La LL11 . . . . .65 E1
Pleasant Mount / Bryn Siriol LL11 . . . . .71 C4
Pleasant View
Froncysyllte LL20 . . . . .94 F7
Penymynydd CH4 . . . . .49 B1
Weston Rhyn SY10 . . . . . .105 C4
Wrexham / Wrecsam, Moss LL11 . . . . .72 A8
Wrexham / Wrecsam, Pentre Broughton LL11 . . .72 B6
Pleasant View Camp LL18 . . . . .15 F8
Pleasant Villas 12 LL11 . . .72 C3
Plemstall Cl CH2 . . . . .43 F8
Plough La Christleton CH3 .53 F7
Connah's Quay CH5 . . . . . .39 B4
Plover Cl CH3 . . . . .69 F1
Plumley Cl CH3 . . . . .43 C1
Plum Terr CH1 . . . . .144 A3
Plymouth St CH5 . . . . .39 A6
Point of Ayr Cvn Pk CH8 . .4 F6
Point of Ayr Gas Terminal Visitor Ctr★ CH8 . . . . .4 F4
Pont Adam LL14 . . . . .85 F5
Pont Adam Cres LL14 . . . .85 F4
Pont Pentre CH7 . . . . .47 B4
Pont Wen LL13 . . . . .80 C8
Pont-y-Bedol LL16 . . . . . .120 F5
Pontybodkin Hill CH7 . . .58 A3
Pont-y-Brenig Nature Trail★ LL16 . . . . .123 C8
Pont-y-Capel La LL12 . . .67 C2
Pont Y Capel La / Lon Pont Y Capel LL12 . . . . .67 B1
Pontydd LL22 . . . . .6 A3
Pont-yr-Afon LL14 . . . . . .85 C7
Poolmouth Rd LL11 . . . . .72 C5
Pool Rd / Ffordd y Llyn 8 LL14 . . . . .78 F2
Poplar Ave CH5 . . . . .39 B4
Poplar Ave / Rhodfa'r Poplys
Gresford LL12 . . . . .67 E3
8 Rhosllanerchrugog LL14 .78 E1
Poplar Cl Coedpoeth LL11 .71 D2
Connah's Quay CH5 . . . . . . .38 E6
3 Whitchurch SY13 . . . . . .103 E7
Poplar Dr LL12 . . . . .67 F2
Poplar Gr Ewloe CH5 . . . . .38 E2
Prestatyn LL19 . . . . .2 F3
Poplar Rd Chester CH4 . . . .51 F5
Rhostyllen LL14 . . . . .79 C6
Wrexham / Wrecsam LL13 145 B1
Poplar Rd / Ffordd Y Poplys LL14 . . . . .85 C7
Poplar Row / Rhes Y Poplys LL12 . . . . .67 F7
Poplars Dr LL18 . . . . .7 D6
Poplars The CH5 . . . . .48 F7
Poppy Field Dr CH4 . . . . .59 A8
Porch La LL12 . . . . .66 A8
Portal Ave LL13 . . . . .73 C2
Porters Croft CH3 . . . . . . .43 F5
Porth-y-cwm LL20 . . . . .138 D7
Porth-y-Dre LL15 . . . . . . .141 B5
Porth-y-Llys LL18 . . . . .7 F7
Porth-ysgaden LL20 . . . .143 D4
Porth-y-Waen LL16 . . . . . .32 B7
Portland Pl / Llain Portland 18 LL16 . . . . .140 C3
Post Office La
Pantasaph CH8 . . . . .20 C4
Pantymwyn CH7 . . . . .45 D6
Wem Rural SY13 . . . . .113 C1
Post Office La / Lon-y-Post LL16 . . . . .140 C3
Post Office Terr LL16 . . .117 C5
Potters Way CH7 . . . . .48 A5
Pottery Cotts CH5 . . . . . . .38 C1
Powell Rd
Buckley / Bwcle CH7 . . . . .48 A3
Wrexham / Wrecsam LL12 . . . . .145 C3
Powell's Orch CH4 . . . . . .52 C7
Powys Cl
Buckley / Bwcle CH7 . . . . .48 C6
Connah's Quay CH5 . . . . . .39 D4
Poyser St LL13 . . . . .145 B1
Precinct Way The CH7 . . .48 B4
Preeshenlle La SY10 . . .106 B2
Pren Ave CH7 . . . . .47 E4
Prenton Pl CH4 . . . . .52 E7
Prescot St CH2 . . . . .42 F3
Prestatyn High Sch
Prestatyn LL19 . . . . .9 A8
Prestatyn LL19 . . . . .3 A1
Prestatyn Hillside Nature Reserve★ LL19 . . . . .9 B8
Prestatyn Nova Ctr★ LL19 .2 F4
Prestatyn Rd LL19 . . . . .3 D3
Prestatyn Sta LL19 . . . . . . .3 A3
Presthaven Sands Holiday Camp LL19 . . . . .4 B5
Preston Rd LL13 . . . . .74 D1
Pretoria St CH4 . . . . .52 D7
Price's La LL11 . . . . .145 B4
Price's Row 8 CH7 . . . . . .46 F4
Primrose Cl
Huntington CH3 . . . . .53 A6
Northop Hall CH7 . . . . .38 B4
Primrose Hill
Connah's Quay CH5 . . . . . . .38 F8
St George / Llansan-Sior LL22 . . . . .14 B4
Primrose St CH5 . . . . .38 E8
Primrose Way LL11 . . . .145 A3
Prince Charles Rd LL13 . .73 D1
Prince Edward Ave LL18 . .7 C7
Prince Of Wales Ave
Flint / Y Fflint CH6 . . . . .28 B5
Holywell / Treffynnon CH8 .21 C5
Prince of Wales Ct
Buckley / Bwcle CH7 . . . . .48 D4
Wrexham / Wrecsam LL11 .72 C8
Princes Ave Chester CH1 144 C3
Prestatyn LL19 . . . . .9 A8
Princes Cl 1 LL11 . . . . . . .73 A5
Princes Dr CH6 . . . . .28 B5
Princes Pk LL18 . . . . .15 F8
Princes Rd LL18 . . . . .7 F1
Princes Rd / Ffordd y Tywysob 7 LL14 . . . . . . .78 E1
Princess Ave
Buckley / Bwcle CH7 . . . . . .48 B4
Chirk / Y Waun LL14 . . . . . .95 E2
Princess Elizabeth Ave LL18 . . . . .7 D8
Princess St Chester CH1 .144 A2
Llangollen LL20 . . . . .143 C5
Wrexham / Wrecsam LL13 . . . . .145 A1
Princes St
Flint / Y Fflint CH6 . . . . . . .28 B6
Rhyl / Y Rhyl LL18 . . . . .7 B7
Prince's St CH5 . . . . .38 E7
Prince William Ave CH5 .40 B3
Prince William Ct CH5 . .39 A1
Prince William Gdns CH5 39 E2
Priors Cl CH5 . . . . .39 A4
Prior St / Stryd Y Prior LL15 . . . . .141 C5
Priory Cl Chester CH2 . . . .42 C4
Penyffordd CH4 . . . . .59 A7
Priory La LL19 . . . . .3 B2
Priory Pl CH1 . . . . .144 B2
Priory St / Stryt y Priordy 7 LL11 . . . . .145 B2
Privy La LL16 . . . . .140 F4
Proffit Terr CH8 . . . . .4 E3
Promenade LL19 . . . . .3 A4
Promenade The LL18 . . . . .6 C5
Promised Land La CH3 . .53 E5
Prospect Cl CH5 . . . . .39 A2
Prospect Dr LL11 . . . . . . .71 D4
Prospect Terr LL12 . . . . . .66 C5
Provan Way CH1 . . . . .41 D5
Providence Ct CH8 . . . . . .21 D7
Puddington La CH64 . . . . .30 E8
Puddle La SY11 . . . . .106 E5
Pulford Ct CH4 . . . . .61 D2
Pulford La CH4 . . . . .61 A6
Pulford Rd CH1 . . . . .41 E5
Pumed Rhodfa / Fifth Ave LL12 . . . . .67 A4
Pump La CH3 . . . . .69 F5
Purbeck Ave LL19 . . . . .2 E2
Purser La SY14 . . . . .83 E4
Pwll Glas CH7 . . . . .46 E5
Pwll-glas Terr LL15 . . . . .125 F5
Pwll-y-Bont LL19 . . . . .8 F7
Pwll-y-Grawys LL16 . . . .140 B3
Pwll Y Hwyaden CH6 . . . .28 B4
Pyecroft St CH4 . . . . .52 D7

Q

Quadrant The CH1 . . . . . .41 E2
Quakers Way LL13 . . . . . .69 E1
Quarry Ave CH3 . . . . .69 F1
Quarry Bank LL16 . . . . . . .23 B1
Quarry Brow LL12 . . . . . . .67 F3
Quarry Cl Chester CH4 . . . .52 C7
Northop Hall CH7 . . . . .37 F4
Quarry Hill CH3 . . . . .69 F1
Quarry La Christleton CH3 .53 E7
Connah's Quay CH5 . . . . . .38 E6
Quarry Rd LL11 . . . . .72 B6
Quarry Rd / Ffordd y Chwarel LL20 . . . . .135 B4
Quay Bsns Pk CH5 . . . . . . .38 E8
Quay La CH5 . . . . .38 E8
Quay Morfa CH5 . . . . .38 F8
Quay St LL18 . . . . .6 F6
Queens Ave CH6 . . . . .28 B5
Queen's Ave
Chester CH1 . . . . .144 C3
Connah's Quay CH5 . . . . . .38 D8
Sandycroft CH5 . . . . .40 A3
Queensbury Dr CH6 . . . . .27 F6
Queens Cres CH2 . . . . . . .42 E7
Queens Ct LL19 . . . . .3 A3
Queens Dr CH7 . . . . .48 B4
Queen's Dr CH4 . . . . . . .144 C1
Queens Ferry Cty Prim Sch CH5 . . . . .39 C5
Queensferry Ind Est CH5 39 E4
Queen's La CH7 . . . . .47 B3
Queens Park High Sch CH4 . . . . .144 B1
Queen's Park Ho CH4 . . .144 B1
Queen's Park Rd CH4 . .144 B1
Queen's Park View CH4 . . . . .144 B1
Queens Pk CH7 . . . . .46 E5
Queens Pl CH1 . . . . .144 B3
Queens Rd CH3 . . . . .43 B3
Queen's Rd Brymbo LL11 . .71 F8
Chester CH1 . . . . .144 C3
Garden City CH5 . . . . .39 F7
Greenfield / Maes-Glas CH8 21 C8
Queen's Sch (Lower) The CH2 . . . . .42 C4
Queen's Sch The CH1 . .144 A2
Queen's Sq LL14 . . . . . . .85 C2
Queens Sq / Sgwar y Frenhines 4 LL11 . . . . .145 B2
Queen St Cefn-Mawr LL14 .85 B1
Chester CH1 . . . . .144 B2
Connah's Quay CH5 . . . . . .39 D5
Flint / Y Fflint CH6 . . . . . . .28 B6
Leeswood / Coedllai CH7 . .58 A4
Llangollen LL20 . . . . .143 E4
Ruabon / Rhiwabon LL14 . . .86 A5
Treuddyn CH7 . . . . .64 B8
Queens Terr LL12 . . . . . . .66 C4
Queen St / Heol Y Frenhines LL18 . . . . .7 B7
Queen St / Stryt y Frenhines 9 LL14 . . . . .78 E1
Queen St / Stryt y Syfwr 6 LL11 . . . . .145 B2
Queensway Chester CH2 . .42 F5
Connah's Quay CH5 . . . . . .39 A6
Hope / Yr Hôb LL12 . . . . . .66 C8
Prestatyn LL19 . . . . .3 B2
Wrexham / Wrecsam LL13 .80 D8
Queen's Way CH4 . . . . . . .50 B4
Queensway / Heol y Frenhines LL11 . . . . .72 E8
Queensway Ind Est LL13 .80 D8
Queensway Terr LL13 . . .80 C8
Queen's Wlk LL18 . . . . .7 C8
Quinta Terr LL14 . . . . . . .105 D5

R

Race Course The (Wrexham FC) LL11 . . . . .145 A4
Rachel Dr LL18 . . . . .7 F5
Rackery La LL12 . . . . .66 F7
Rack La SY13 . . . . .112 F1
Radford Cl CH5 . . . . .39 A7
Radnor Cl CH5 . . . . .39 D4
Radnor Dr CH4 . . . . .52 A4
Raewood Ave Ewloe CH5 . .48 F8
Hawarden / Penarlâg CH5 .49 A8
Raikes La
Mold / Yr Wyddgrug CH7 . . .46 F8
Soughton / Sychdyn CH7 . .47 A7
Railway Rd Brymbo LL11 . .71 F8
Wrexham / Wrecsam LL11 .72 F4
Railway Terr Bodfari LL16 .23 B1
Caergwrle LL12 . . . . .66 B8
Caerwys CH7 . . . . .24 C3
Connah's Quay CH5 . . . . . . .38 E8
Corwen LL21 . . . . .142 D3
Padeswood CH7 . . . . .48 B1
Rhosymedre LL14 . . . . .85 C2
Ruabon / Rhiwabon LL14 . . .86 A4
Sandycroft CH5 . . . . .40 B3
Trefnant LL16 . . . . .117 C5
Railway Terr / Rhes Y Rhailffordd 2 LL15 . . .141 D5
Rake La Broughton CH5 . . .50 A8
Eccleston CH4 . . . . .52 C1
Hawarden / Penarlâg CH5 . .49 F7
Rake Way CH1 . . . . .41 A8
Ramsden Ct CH4 . . . . .51 F4
Range Rd LL13 . . . . .80 C7
Ranscombe Cres 2 LL13 .73 C6
Ranwonath Ct CH2 . . . . .144 B4
Raven Sq CH6 . . . . .28 A7
Rawson Rd CH1 . . . . .41 E3
Raymond St CH1 . . . . . . .144 A3
Raynham Ave LL12 . . . . . .67 E2
Rayon Rd CH8 . . . . .21 D7
Record St LL15 . . . . .141 C5
Rector Drew Sch CH5 . . .49 D8
Rectors La CH5 . . . . .39 F4
Rectory Cl Farndon CH3 . .69 E1
Flint / Y Fflint CH6 . . . . . . .28 A5
Rectory Cl / Rheithordy Clos CH8 . . . . .25 A4
Rectory La
Hawarden / Penarlâg CH5 .49 D8
Llanferres CH7 . . . . .55 B6
Red Dragon Cvn Pk LL12 66 C5
Red Grouse Ctry Pk★ CH7 . . . . .63 C2
Red Hall Ave CH5 . . . . . . .38 F7
Red Hall La LL13 . . . . .98 F3
Red Hall Prec CH5 . . . . . .38 D7
Red Hill LL17 . . . . .16 B2
Redhill Rd CH4 . . . . .51 F6
Red Hos CH7 . . . . .46 D7
Redland Cl Chester CH4 . . .52 A7
Gresford LL12 . . . . .67 E3
Redland Ho CH4 . . . . .52 B7
Red Lion Cotts LL13 . . . . .80 D7
Red Lion Sq LL14 . . . . . . .85 B2
Red Rd CH7 . . . . .48 B6
Red St CH8 . . . . .12 B5
Redwither Ind Complex LL13 . . . . .74 E1
Redwither La
Marchwiel LL13 . . . . .81 B8
Wrexham / Wrecsam LL13 .81 C5
Redwither Rd LL13 . . . . . .81 E7
Redwood Cl Holt LL13 . . . .75 D8
Saltney CH4 . . . . .51 E6
Redwood Dr LL18 . . . . .7 E8
Reece Cl CH2 . . . . .43 E8
Rees Ave LL18 . . . . .7 D8
Reeves Rd CH3 . . . . .53 B8
Regency Ct CH2 . . . . .43 E8
Regent Cl / Clos y Rhaglaw 3 LL11 . . . . .72 D8
Regent Rd LL18 . . . . .7 D8
Regents Cl CH3 . . . . .43 B2
Regent St LL20 . . . . .143 D4
Regent St / Stryt y Rhaglaw LL11 . . . . .145 A3
Renfrew Cl LL11 . . . . .72 C7
Reservoir Terr CH2 . . . . . .42 F2
Rest The 3 LL14 . . . . .95 C8
Revells Cl SY12 . . . . .108 C6
Reynolds Rd CH6 . . . . .22 E1
Rheithordy Clos / Rectory Cl CH8 . . . . .25 A4
Rhes Bryn Teg CH8 . . . . . .11 B8
Rhesdai Gladstone / Gladstone Terr LL16 . . .121 B8
Rhes Thomas / Thomas Row CH6 . . . . .22 B4
Rhes-y-Cae Sch CH8 . . . . .26 C3
Rhes y Cigydd / Butchers Row 5 LL14 . . . . .78 E1
Rhes y Deml / Temple Row 4 LL13 . . . . .145 C2
Rhes Y Poplys / Poplar Row LL12 . . . . .67 F7
Rhes Y Rhailffordd / Railway Terr 2 LL15 . . . . .141 D5
Rhewl Fawr Rd CH8 . . . . .11 C8
Rhewl La SY10 . . . . .106 B1
Rhewl Sch LL15 . . . . .121 B3
Rhiw Newmarket / Newmarket Rise LL13 . .80 E7
Rhiw'r Bigwn / Beacon's Hill LL16 . . . . .140 C3
Rhoda Augusta / Augusta Dr LL13 . . . . .73 F3
Rhoda'f Gollen / Hazel Ave LL11 . . . . .72 D7
Rhoddfa Miltwn / Middleton Ave LL16 . . . . .140 B2
Rhoddfa Plas Coed 8 LL18 . . . . .7 F7
Rhodfa Anwyl LL18 . . . . . . .7 E2
Rhodfa Arthur LL18 . . . . . . .9 F4
Rhodfa Bedwen LL19 . . . . .3 D3
Rhodfa Blodyn Mai / Mayflower Dr LL12 . . . . .67 F2
Rhodfa Bodrhyddan / Bodrhyddan Ave LL18 . . . .7 F1
Rhodfa Brenin / King's Ave 2 LL19 . . . . .3 B2
Rhodfa Caer / Chester Ave LL18 . . . . .6 D4
Rhodfa Canolblas (Avenue) LL18 . . . . .14 E4
Rhodfa Carnoustie / Carnoustie Cl 6 LL13 . .73 F3
Rhodfa Ceinewydd / Newquay Dr 2 LL13 . . .80 D7
Rhodfa Celyn LL19 . . . . . . .3 D3
Rhodfa Cilcain CH7 . . . . .46 D3
Rhodfa Clwyd LL17 . . . . .117 B6
Rhodfa Clwyd / Clwyd Ave
Denbigh / Dinbych LL16 . . .140 E3
Dyserth LL18 . . . . .8 F1
Prestatyn LL19 . . . . .3 B2
Rhuddlan LL18 . . . . .7 E2
Rhodfa Conwy LL18 . . . . . .8 F4
Rhodfa Conwy / Conwy Ave 7 LL18 . . . . .7 F1
Rhodfa Criccieth LL18 . . .14 F4
Rhodfa Ddeg / Tenth Ave LL12 . . . . .67 A3
Rhodfa Derwen LL19 . . . . .3 D3
Rhodfa Dolennau / Links Ave 4 LL18 . . . . .7 F1
Rhodfa Dulas / Dulas Ave LL18 . . . . .6 D4
Rhodfa Elgwern LL16 . . .140 E4
Rhodfa Elwy / Elwy Ave LL18 . . . . .8 F1
Rhodfa Eurgain / Eurgain Ave CH5 . . . . .38 C6
Rhodfa Ffordd Las / Ridgeway Ave LL12 . . . . .67 F4
Rhodfa Ganol
Johnstown LL14 . . . . .79 A1
Prestatyn LL19 . . . . .8 F6
Rhodfa Gele / Gele Ave 7 LL11 . . . . .72 D8
Rhodfa Ger Y Parc / Parkside Ave CH5 . . . .38 C6
Rhodfa Glenys LL17 . . . . .16 B2
Rhodfa Glyn / Glyn Ave 3 LL18 . . . . .7 F2
Rhodfa Gofer LL18 . . . . . . .8 F4
Rhodfa Gop LL18 . . . . .10 A4
Rhodfa Gorllewin / West Par LL18 . . . . .7 A7
Rhodfa Goulbourne / Goulbourne Ave 5 LL13 73 E4
Rhodfa Graig LL19 . . . . . . .8 F6
Rhodfa Grenville / Grenville Ave 5 LL18 . . . . .7 F1
Rhodfa Gwdig / Goodwick Dr 1 LL13 . . . . .80 D7
Rhodfa Gwilym LL17 . . .117 B6
Rhodfa Gyntaf / First Ave LL12 . . . . .67 A4
Rhodfa Hawkstone / Hawkstone Way 8 LL13 73 F3
Rhodfa Hawthorne / Hawthorn Way LL12 . . .66 F4
Rhodfa Heilyn LL18 . . . . . . .8 F4
Rhodfa Helyd / Willow Wlk CH7 . . . . .57 F5
Rhodfa Hendre LL19 . . . . . . .8 F6
Rhodfa Hinsley / Hinsley Dr LL13 . . . . .73 E4
Rhodfa Hywell / Howell Ave 4 LL18 . . . . .7 F2
Rhodfa Kempton LL13 . . .80 F7
Rhodfa Llanddulas / Llanddulas Avenue LL18 .6 E3
Rhodfa Maelor / Maelor Ave LL14 . . . . .85 D8
Rhodfa Maen Gwyn LL18 . .7 F6
Rhodfa Maes Hir LL18 . . . .7 F6
Rhodfa Mayville / Mayville Ave LL12 . . . . .67 A3
Rhodfa Mount Isa / Mount Isa Dr LL11 . . . . .71 F8
Rhodfa Mynydd CH7 . . . .46 E3
Rhodfa Nant / Brook Ave LL22 . . . . .6 B2
Rhodfa Padarn LL19 . . . . . .2 D3
Rhodfa Pedr LL18 . . . . .8 F4
Rhodfa Plas LL19 . . . . .8 F6
Rhodfa Plas Llai / Llay Hall Ave LL12 . . . . .67 A4
Rhodfa'r Bryn / Bryn Dr LL11 . . . . .71 D3

164 Rho – San

Rhodfa'r Ddermen / Oak Dr LL12 ... 67 F2
Rhodfa'r Dderwen / Oak Tree Ave LL12 ... 67 A4
Rhodfa'r Doraenen Wen / Hawthorne Ave LL14 ... 85 C3
Rhodfa'r Garn LL12 ... 67 B4
Rhodfar Gelli / Spinney Wlk 12 LL14 ... 86 A4
Rhodfa Rhedyn / Fern Ave 7 LL19 ... 3 B2
Rhodfa'r Llwyfen / Elm Wlk LL12 ... 67 B4
Rhodfa Ronald / Ronaldsway LL18 ... 14 F4
Rhodfa'r Orsaf / Station Wlk LL15 ... 141 D5
Rhodfa'r Parc / Parklands Wlk 15 LL14 ... 86 A4
Rhodfa'r Poplys / Poplar Ave
Gresford LL12 ... 67 E3
8 Rhosllanerchrugog LL14 ... 78 E1
Rhodfa'r Sycamowyddens / Sycamore Dr LL12 ... 67 F3
Rhodfa'r Wyddfa / Snowdon Dr LL11 ... 73 B5
Rhodfa Sandy / Sandy Way 1 LL13 ... 73 F4
Rhodfa Sian LL18 ... 8 F2
Rhodfa Taunton LL13 ... 80 F7
Rhodfa Teyrn LL19 ... 2 E3
Rhodfa Thomas / Thomas Ave LL18 ... 8 F2
Rhodfa Thornhurst / Thornhurst Dr 3 LL13 ... 73 F3
Rhodfa Ty Newydd / New House Ave LL12 ... 67 A3
Rhodfa Victoria / Victoria Ave 4 LL19 ... 3 B2
Rhodfa Wenlo CH8 ... 21 B7
Rhodfa Westwood / Westwood Dr 1 LL13 ... 73 F3
Rhodfa Wilkinson / Wilkinson Dr LL14 ... 79 C6
Rhodfa Wyn LL19 ... 2 E3
Rhoffa'r Teubren / Hornbeam Ave CH7 ... 48 E4
Rhone Ct CH3 ... 53 A8
Rhos Ave CH4 ... 58 F7
Rhos Berse Rd LL11 ... 71 E2
Rhosddu Ind Est LL11 ... 72 F6
Rhosddu Prim Schs LL11 ... 145 B4
Rhosddu Rd / Ffordd Rhosddu
5 Wrexham / Wrecsam LL11 ... 145 B2
Wrexham / Wrecsam, Rhosddu LL11 ... 145 B4
Rhos Estyn La LL12 ... 59 B3
Rhos Helyg
Llandrillo LL21 ... 132 D3
Treuddyn CH7 ... 64 B8
Rhoslan CH8 ... 21 C5
Rhos Llan LL21 ... 132 D3
Rhosnesni La LL12 ... 73 C3
Rhos Rd CH4 ... 58 F7
Rhosrhedyn La LL11 ... 72 B4
Rhosrobin Rd LL11 ... 72 F6
Rhos St Sch LL15 ... 141 D5
Rhos St / Stryt Y Rhos LL15 ... 141 D5
Rhostyllen Com Prim Sch LL14 ... 79 C6
Rhoswen CH6 ... 28 B4
Rhoswydd / Rosewood LL11 ... 72 C4
Rhosymedre Inf Sch LL14 ... 85 D3
Rhosymedre Jun Sch LL14 ... 85 D3
Rhos-y-wern 3 LL15 ... 141 D5
Rhuddlan Castle★ LL18 ... 15 E8
Rhuddlan Ct / Llys Rhuddlan 5 CH4 ... 51 F6
Rhuddlan Rd Blacon CH1 ... 41 D3
Buckley / Bwcle CH7 ... 48 C7
Rhyl / Y Rhyl LL18 ... 7 E5
St George / Llansan-Sior LL22 ... 14 C7
Rhyd Broughton La LL13 ... 72 E2
Rhyddyn Hill LL12 ... 66 C7
Rhyd Galeo SY11 ... 106 A1
Rhyd Osber CH7 ... 57 F2
Rhydwen Cl LL18 ... 7 B5
Rhydwen Dr LL18 ... 7 B6
Rhyd Y Byll LL15 ... 121 B3
Rhydymwyn Rd CH7 ... 45 F7
Rhyl Coast Rd
Prestatyn LL18 ... 2 A1
Rhyl / Y Rhyl LL18 ... 1 E5
Rhyl High Sch LL18 ... 7 D7
Rhyl Rd LL18 ... 7 F1
Rhyl Rd / Ffordd Rhyl LL16 ... 140 D4
Rhyl Sta LL18 ... 7 B7
Rhyn La SY11 ... 96 C1
Rhyn Pk Sch SY11 ... 106 C5
Rhys Ave LL18 ... 6 C5
Richard Hts CH6 ... 28 A7
Richards Croft CH3 ... 53 A7
Richmond Cres CH3 ... 43 C2
Richmond Gdns 3 LL14 ... 95 E3
Richmond Mews CH2 ... 42 F2
Richmond Rd
Connah's Quay CH5 ... 38 F6
Wrexham / Wrecsam LL12 ... 73 C6
Ridgehill Dr CH6 ... 22 B3
Ridgeway Ave LL18 ... 1 E5
Ridgeway Cl CH5 ... 38 D6
Ridgeway La / Rhodfa Ffordd Las LL12 ... 67 F4
Ridgeway The
Connah's Quay CH5 ... 39 B1
Holywell / Treffynnon CH8 ... 21 C1
Marchwiel LL13 ... 80 F4
Northop Hall CH7 ... 37 F4
Ridings The CH1 ... 41 B8
Ridley View LL13 ... 73 E1
Ridley Wood Cl LL13 ... 80 B6
Ridley Wood Ind Complex LL13 ... 74 F2
Ridley Wood Rd LL13 ... 75 A3
Ring Rd Chester CH3 ... 43 C3
Connah's Quay CH5 ... 29 E2
Riverbank CH6 ... 21 E5
River Cl LL13 ... 80 D7
Riverdale LL13 ... 80 E7
River La Chester CH4 ... 52 C7
Farndon CH3 ... 69 E2
Saltney CH4 ... 51 E7
River Rd CH5 ... 29 F1
Riverside Bsns Pk LL12 ... 66 C3
Riverside Cl LL18 ... 6 E5
Riverside Ct
Huntington CH3 ... 52 F7
Pontblyddyn CH7 ... 58 B6
Riverside Pk
Connah's Quay CH5 ... 38 E8
Garden City CH5 ... 39 F6
Riversleigh Ct LL12 ... 59 B1
Riversmead CH3 ... 53 A6
River St LL18 ... 7 A7
River View Bagillt CH6 ... 21 F5
Connah's Quay CH5 ... 38 D8
Rivulet Rd LL13 ... 145 C1
Roberts Croft LL12 ... 66 B7
Roberts La / Stryt Fechan 5 LL14 ... 78 E2
Robert's Rd LL11 ... 72 B6
Roberts Terr Acrefair LL14 ... 85 B3
Coedpoeth LL11 ... 71 C2
Robert's Terr CH1 ... 42 B1
Robin Cl SY12 ... 109 B3
Robin Hood Holiday Camp LL18 ... 2 A1
Robinsons Croft CH3 ... 53 B7
Rochester Dr LL19 ... 2 F1
Rockcliffe CH7 ... 47 D6
Rock Cotts CH5 ... 29 D1
Rock Hill LL14 ... 85 C1
Rock Hos CH8 ... 5 D1
Rock La
Caergwrle, Caer-Estyn LL12 ... 66 D7
Caergwrle LL12 ... 66 A8
Cefn-Mawr LL14 ... 85 B2
Chester CH2 ... 144 A4
Hanmer LL13 ... 100 B8
Rocklife La CH6 ... 29 A3
Rock Pl Cefn-Mawr LL14 ... 85 B1
Coedpoeth LL11 ... 71 D2
Rock Rd CH5 ... 29 E1
Rock Rd / Ffordd-y-Graig LL14 ... 85 C2
Rock View CH7 ... 55 E7
Rockwood Rd LL11 ... 72 B5
Rodens Cl LL12 ... 68 C7
Roebourne Rise CH1 ... 41 D4
Roe Parc LL17 ... 16 A2
Roe The LL17 ... 16 A2
Rofft Sch The LL12 ... 67 F3
Roft Cl LL11 ... 72 D6
Rogers La LL11 ... 72 C6
Roland Ave LL18 ... 6 D6
Roman Dr CH1 ... 41 D6
Romans Way CH6 ... 22 D1
Roman Way
Buckley / Bwcle CH7 ... 48 B4
Whitchurch SY13 ... 103 F8
Ronaldsway LL18 ... 7 D5
Ronaldsway / Rhodfa Ronald LL18 ... 14 F4
Rookery The CH4 ... 50 B3
Rosebine View 6 LL11 ... 72 D7
Rosedale Gdns LL18 ... 7 F5
Rosedene Cl CH2 ... 42 E8
Rose Gr LL13 ... 73 E3
Rose Grange LL11 ... 72 B4
Rosehill CH8 ... 21 B4
Rose Hill Trelawnyd LL18 ... 10 B4
Wrexham / Wrecsam LL11 ... 72 B5
Rose Hill Ct CH5 ... 38 F7
Rosehill Rd LL18 ... 7 E5
Rose La CH7 ... 47 E3
Roselands Ct LL12 ... 61 C1
Rosemary Cl CH4 ... 50 C3
Rosemary Cres LL14 ... 79 D6
Rosemary La LL12 ... 67 E8
Rosemary Wlk 6 CH6 ... 28 A6
Rosemount Ave LL18 ... 6 D6
Roseview Cres / Trem-y-Rhosyn LL18 ... 6 E5
Roseway LL12 ... 67 E7
Rose Way LL11 ... 71 E5
Rosewood Ave
Chester CH2 ... 42 D5
Wrexham / Wrecsam LL13 ... 73 D2
Rosewood Gr Drury CH7 ... 48 F5
Saughall CH1 ... 41 B8
Rosewood / Rhoswydd LL11 ... 72 C4
Rosse Ave LL14 ... 79 B1
Rossett Bsns Village LL12 ... 61 B1
Rossett Pk LL12 ... 61 C1
Rossett Rd Holt LL13 ... 69 A1
Trevalyn LL13 ... 68 E5
Rossett Way LL12 ... 73 B6
Rosslyn Cl CH5 ... 40 A2
Rosslyn Rd CH3 ... 43 B3
Rothesay Cl LL11 ... 73 A4
Rothesay Rd CH4 ... 52 A7
Roughlyn Cres CH4 ... 51 E1
Roundel Cl LL13 ... 73 E5
Round Hill Mdw CH3 ... 53 B7
Roundwood Ave LL19 ... 8 F7
Rowan Cl 4 SY12 ... 109 A2
Rowan Cl / Clos Y Criafol LL12 ... 67 A5
Rowan Cl / Llys Cerddin CH7 ... 48 D4
Rowan Dr LL18 ... 7 F5
Rowan Gr CH5 ... 29 C1
Rowan Pk CH3 ... 53 E7
Rowan Pl CH2 ... 43 B4
Rowan Rd CH5 ... 39 A3
Rowans The CH4 ... 50 B3
Rowcliffe Ave CH4 ... 52 A4
Rowden Cres 6 CH5 ... 39 A6
Rowden St CH5 ... 39 A6
Rowe La
Maelor South SY12 ... 111 A4
Welshampton & Lyneal SY12 ... 110 F4
Rowena Ct CH2 ... 42 F3
Rowlands Rd LL11 ... 72 B7
Rowley's Dr CH5 ... 39 C6
Rowleys Pk CH5 ... 39 C6
Rowton Bridge Rd CH3 ... 53 E7
Rowton La CH3 ... 53 F6
Royal Alexandra General Hospl LL18 ... 1 C5
Royal Ct CH5 ... 38 E8
Royal Dr CH6 ... 27 E7
Royal International Pav★ LL20 ... 143 C5
Royal Welch Ave LL18 ... 14 F4
Roy Ave LL19 ... 2 B2
Royden Gdns LL13 ... 73 E1
Royton Cl LL13 ... 80 B6
Ruabon Rd
Ruabon / Rhiwabon LL14 ... 86 A7
Wrexham / Wrecsam LL13 ... 145 A1
Wrexham / Wrecsam LL13 ... 79 F7
Ruabon Sta LL14 ... 86 A4
Rubery Way LL13 ... 80 D8
Ruby Hos CH7 ... 35 F4
Ruby Terr LL17 ... 16 B1
Rufus Ct CH1 ... 144 A3
Rumney Cl CH5 ... 38 C4
Rushfield Rd CH4 ... 52 B5
Rushmere La CH3 ... 62 F3
Rushton Dr CH2 ... 42 E7
Russell Ct LL18 ... 7 C8
Russell Dr LL19 ... 2 D2
Russell Gdns LL18 ... 7 C8
Russell Gr LL12 ... 73 C3
Russell Rd / Ffordd Russell LL18 ... 7 C8
Russell St Cefn-Mawr LL14 ... 85 B2
Chester CH1, CH3 ... 144 C3
Ruthin Cl CH7 ... 48 C6
Ruthin Craft Ctr★ LL15 ... 141 D6
Ruthin Hospl LL15 ... 141 D5
Ruthin Rd Bwlchgwyn LL11 ... 70 D7
Denbigh / Dinbych LL16 ... 120 E8
Minera LL11 ... 71 B5
Mold / Yr Wyddgrug CH7 ... 46 D3
Wrexham / Wrecsam LL11, LL13 ... 72 E1
Ruthin Sch LL15 ... 141 E6
Rutland Ct CH5 ... 38 E6
Rutland Pl CH2 ... 43 A5
Rutland Rd LL13 ... 80 C8
Rydal Ct LL13 ... 73 D3
Rydal Dr CH7 ... 48 D6
Rydal Gr CH4 ... 52 A6
Ryder Cl / Clos Ryder 2 LL13 ... 73 E3
Ryeland St CH5 ... 39 B7

S

Saighton CE Prim Sch CH3 ... 53 E1
Saighton La CH3 ... 53 F2
St Albans Hts LL11 ... 71 F5
St Alban's Rd LL11 ... 71 F5
St Alban's View LL11 ... 71 E5
St Alkmond Mdw 3 SY13 ... 103 F8
St Andrews Cl CH5 ... 49 C8
St Andrews Cres / Cilgant St Andrews 5 LL13 ... 73 E3
St Andrews Dr LL19 ... 3 A1
St Andrew's Dr CH7 ... 48 A5
St Andrews Wlk CH2 ... 43 F8
St Anne's Ave LL19 ... 8 E8
St Anne's RC Prim Sch LL13 ... 73 E1
St Anne St CH1 ... 144 B3
St Ann's St LL18 ... 7 C7
St Anthony's RC Prim Sch CH4 ... 51 E6
St Asaph Ave
Kinmel Bay / Bae Cinmel LL18 ... 6 E3
Towyn LL22 ... 14 E8
St Asaph Bsns Pk
Bodelwyddan LL17 ... 15 D1
St Asaph / Llanelwy LL17 ... 116 E8
St Asaph Cath★ LL17 ... 16 B1
St Asaph Dr LL19 ... 8 F8
St Asaph L Ctr★ LL17 ... 16 C1
St Asaph Rd
Bodelwyddan LL18 ... 14 C5
Lloc CH8 ... 19 F6
Rhuddlan LL18 ... 15 E6
St George / Llansan-Sior LL22 ... 14 A5
Trefnant LL17 ... 117 B6
St Asaph Rd / Ffordd Llanelwy LL18 ... 8 F2
St Asaph Sch LL17 ... 16 C1
St Asaph St LL18 ... 7 C8
St Barbara's Ave LL18 ... 14 E4
St Bartholomews Ct CH5 ... 40 E6
St Brelade's Dr LL19 ... 3 A1
St Bridgets Ct CH4 ... 52 B6
St Brigid's Sch LL16 ... 140 E6
St Catherines' Cl CH6 ... 28 A6
St Chad's Rd CH1 ... 41 F4
St Chads Way LL19 ... 9 A8
St Christophers Cl CH2 ... 42 D8
St Christophers Sch / Ysgol Sant Christopher LL13 ... 80 B7
St Clare's RC Prim Sch CH4 ... 52 A5
St Cynfarch's Ave LL12 ... 59 B1
St Davids Cl CH6 ... 28 B4
St David's Cl
Buckley / Bwcle CH7 ... 48 A6
Ewloe CH5 ... 38 F2
St Davids Cres LL12 ... 67 A3
St David's Cres LL13 ... 73 C2
St Davids' Ct LL13 ... 73 D3
St David's Dr
Connah's Quay, Golftyn CH5 ... 38 E7
Connah's Quay, Shotton CH5 ... 39 B6
St David's High Sch CH4 ... 51 C6
St David's High Sch / Ysgol Dewi Sant LL13 ... 73 D3
St David's La
Denbigh / Dinbych LL16 ... 140 D3
Mold / Yr Wyddgrug CH7 ... 47 A5
St David's RC Sch CH7 ... 47 A5
St Davids' Ret Pk CH4 ... 51 D7
St David's Sq LL18 ... 7 C6
St David's Terr CH4 ... 51 C6
St David's Wlk 6 CH7 ... 46 F4
St Elmo's Dr LL19 ... 3 B1
St Ethelwold's Prim Sch CH5 ... 39 B4
St Ethelwold's St CH5 ... 39 B4
St George Prim Sch LL22 ... 14 A4
St Georges Cres LL18 ... 7 D8
St George's Cres
Chester CH4 ... 144 C1
Wrexham / Wrecsam LL13 ... 145 C2
St Georges Dr LL19 ... 3 A1
St George's Rd LL22 ... 14 A4
St Giles Cres LL13 ... 73 C1
St Giles Inf Sch LL13 ... 145 B1
St Giles Jun Sch LL13 ... 145 B1
St Giles Way / Ffordd San Silyn LL13 ... 145 C1
St Helens Pl 8 LL18 ... 7 B7
St Hilary's Terr LL16 ... 140 C2
St Ives Pk CH5 ... 40 A3
St Ives Way CH5 ... 40 A3
St James Ave CH2 ... 42 F7
St James Cl CH5 ... 49 C8
St James Ct LL11 ... 145 B4
St James Ct / Llys Sant Iago CH5 ... 29 D1
St James Dr LL19 ... 3 A1
St James's CE Jun Sch CH2 ... 43 A2
St James St CH1 ... 144 B3
St Johns Cl
Hawarden / Penarlâg CH5 ... 49 C8
Penymynydd CH4 ... 49 B2
St John's Cl
Buckley / Bwcle CH7 ... 48 B5
4 Ellesmere SY12 ... 109 C2
St Johns Ct CH1 ... 144 B2
St John's Ct LL13 ... 80 C8
St John's Hill SY12 ... 109 C2
St Johns Pk CH7 ... 35 E2
St John's Rd CH4 ... 144 C1
St John's Rear Rd CH4 ... 144 C1
St John's St LL13 ... 80 C8
St John St CH1 ... 144 B2
St Joseph's RC High Sch LL13 ... 80 A7
St Margaret's Ave LL19 ... 8 E8
St Margaret's Dr LL18 ... 7 D6
St Margaret's Row LL18 ... 14 F4
St Margaret Way LL12 ... 73 B4
St Mark's Ave CH5 ... 38 D7
St Marks Rd CH4 ... 51 F6
St Mark's Rd / Ffordd Sant Marc LL11 ... 145 B2
St Marks Terr LL13 ... 73 E1
St Martins Mews LL12 ... 67 A4
St Martin's Rd SY10 ... 106 C3
St Martin's Way CH1 ... 144 A3
St Mary's Ave LL13 ... 98 C8
St Mary's Camping Site LL19 ... 4 B3
St Mary's CE Inf Sch CH2 ... 42 E7
St Marys Cl CH7 ... 37 F4
St Mary's Cl LL14 ... 105 E8
St Mary's Ct LL18 ... 7 C8
St Mary's Dr
Northop Hall CH7 ... 37 F4
Rhyl / Y Rhyl LL18 ... 7 D5
St Mary's Hill CH1 ... 144 B1
St Mary's Mews CH7 ... 46 F5
St Marys Prim Sch LL11 ... 65 E1
St Mary's Prim Sch LL14 ... 86 A4
St Mary's RC Prim Sch CH6 ... 28 B5
St Mary's RC Sch LL13 ... 145 B2
St Mary's Rd CH4 ... 61 A7
St Mary's Way CH4 ... 50 C5
St Mellion Cres / Cilgant Sant Mellion 5 LL13 ... 73 F3
St Mellor's Rd CH7 ... 48 A5
St Michaels Cl
Ruabon / Rhiwabon LL14 ... 86 A5
Welshampton & Lyneal SY12 ... 110 C2
St Michael's Cl CH7 ... 24 B7
St Michaels Cvn Pk LL22 ... 6 B3
St Michael's Dr CH7 ... 24 C7
St Michael's Gn SY12 ... 110 C2
St Olave St CH1 ... 144 B1
St Oswalds Way CH1, CH2 ... 144 B3
St Pauls Cl CH5 ... 49 C8
St Paul's Inf Sch CH3 ... 144 C3
St Paul's Prim Sch LL13 ... 82 B8
St Peters CW Prim Sch LL12 ... 68 C7
St Peter's Est CH8 ... 21 C4
St Peter's Pk CH7 ... 37 A6
St Peter's Sq LL15 ... 141 C5
St Peters Way CH2 ... 43 F8
St Richard Gwyn RC High Sch CH6 ... 28 B5
St Theresa's RC Prim Sch CH1 ... 41 F5
St Thomas Ct / Llys Tomas Sant CH6 ... 28 A1
St Thomas of Canterbury Blue Coat CE Jun Sch CH1 ... 144 A4
St Thomas's Pathway CH1 ... 144 B2
St Werburgh's & St Columba's RC Prim Sch CH2 ... 42 F2
St Werburgh St CH1 ... 144 B2
St Winefrides RC Sch LL17 ... 16 A1
St Winefride's RC Sch CH8 ... 21 A5
St Winefride's Well★ CH8 ... 21 B5
Saith-Aelwyd Pk CH8 ... 20 D6
Salem Rd LL11 ... 71 C3
Salisbury Ave CH4 ... 51 E6
Salisbury Cl LL13 ... 145 C1
Salisbury Dr LL19 ... 2 F1
Salisbury Rd LL13 ... 145 C1
Salisbury St Chester CH1 ... 42 B3
Connah's Quay CH5 ... 39 B7
Salop Rd Overton LL13 ... 98 C7
Wrexham / Wrecsam LL13 ... 145 C1
Salter's La CH2 ... 43 C8
Saltney Bsns Ctr CH4 ... 51 F7
Saltney Ferry Prim Sch CH4 ... 51 B6
Saltney Ferry Rd CH4 ... 51 B7
Saltney Terr CH4 ... 51 B7
Salusbury St CH6 ... 28 B7
Samuel St CH1 ... 144 C3
Sandbank Rd LL22 ... 6 A4
Sandfield Pl 6 LL18 ... 7 A6
Sandhurst Rd LL19 ... 2 E2
Sandiway LL19 ... 2 C2
Sandon Rd CH2 ... 42 E4
Sandown Cl LL13 ... 89 A8
Sandown Ct CH5 ... 39 B4
Sandown Rd
Bangor on Dee / Bangor-is-y-coed LL13 ... 89 A8
Connah's Quay CH5 ... 39 A4
Sandown Terr CH3 ... 42 F1
Sandpiper Ct CH4 ... 52 B2
Sandpiper Way CH4 ... 52 B3
Sandringham Ave
Chester CH3 ... 43 A2
Rhyl / Y Rhyl LL18 ... 7 A6
Sandringham Cl / Clos Sandringham 4 LL14 ... 79 C6
Sandringham Rd / Ffordd Sandringham LL11 ... 73 A4
Sandrock Rd
Christleton CH3 ... 53 E7
Marford LL12 ... 67 F3
Sandway Rd LL11 ... 73 A4
Sandwood Ave CH4 ... 50 B3
Sandy Bay Holiday Camp LL22 ... 6 A4
Sandycroft Cty Prim Sch CH5 ... 39 E3
Sandy Gr / Gelli Dywod CH7 ... 46 E3
Sandy La Bagillt CH6 ... 22 A3
Bagillt, Gadlys CH6 ... 22 A2
Chester CH3 ... 43 A1
Ellesmere Urban SY12 ... 109 C1
Garden City CH5 ... 39 F7
Hope / Yr Hôb CH4, LL12 ... 59 E3
Llan-y-pwll LL13 ... 74 B4

Sandy La continued

Prestatyn LL19 . . . . .3 A3
Saighton CH3 . . . . .53 C3
Saltney CH4 . . . . .51 D6
Threapwood SY14 . . . . .90 E8
Sandy La / Lon Dywoddog
LL12 . . . . .67 F3
Sandy Lane Bsns Pk LL19 .3 A2
Sandy Way
Connah's Quay CH5 . . . . . .38 C6
Ewloe CH5 . . . . .39 A1
Sandy Way / Rhodfa Sandy
1 LL13 . . . . .73 F4
San Remo Ave LL22 . . . . .6 A4
San Remo Chalet Pk LL22 .6 A4
Sark Ho CH2 . . . . .43 B4
Sarl Williams Ct CH1 . . .144 A4
Sarn Bank Rd SY14 . . . . . .90 E6
Sarn La Caergwrle LL12 . .66 B8
Hope / Yr Hôb LL12 . . . . . .59 B1
Sarn Rd SY14 . . . . .90 D8
Saronia Ct **9** LL19 . . . . . . .3 B2
Saughall Rd CH1 . . . . .41 B3
Saunders Way LL18 . . . . .7 D5
Savage St LL14 . . . . .78 E2
Saxon Rd LL11 . . . . .72 D6
Saxon St LL13 . . . . .145 C1
Saxon Way CH1 . . . . .41 E6
Scholars Cl CH4 . . . . .51 E6
School Cotts LL13 . . . . .80 F4
School Hill LL12 . . . . .67 D2
School La Aldford CH3 . . . .62 F2
Bronington SY13 . . . . .102 B3
Coedpoeth LL11 . . . . .71 D3
Coed Talon CH7 . . . . .57 F2
Flint Mountain CH6 . . . . . .28 A1
Gobowen SY11 . . . . .106 A1
Greenfield / Maes-Glas CH8 21 C7
Guilden Sutton CH3 . . . . . .43 E5
3 Llangollen Rural LL20 . .95 A7
Mickle Trafford CH2 . . . . . .43 E8
Overton LL13 . . . . .98 C8
St. Martin's SY11 . . . . . . .106 F7
6 Wrexham / Wrecsam
LL11 . . . . .72 B4
School La / Lon yr Ysgol
LL14 . . . . .78 F2
School Mews
Bangor on Dee / Bangor-is-y-coed
LL13 . . . . .88 F8
Rhostyllen LL14 . . . . .79 C6
School Rd LL12 . . . . .67 A4
School Rd / Cae Richard
LL14 . . . . .78 D2
School Rd / Fford Yr Ysgol
LL15 . . . . .141 C5
School Row CH8 . . . . .5 C1
School St Chester CH2 . . . .42 F3
Rhostyllen LL14 . . . . .79 C6
School St / Stryd yr Ysgol
LL16 . . . . .116 F3
School St / Stryt y Weirglodd
LL14 . . . . .78 D2
School Terr CH7 . . . . .56 F5
Scotch Row CH5 . . . . .39 E2
Scot Ho LL15 . . . . .141 C4
Scotland St SY12 . . . . . . .109 B2
Scots Rd CH5 . . . . .39 D2
Scotts Cl LL13 . . . . .80 F4
Seabank Dr LL19 . . . . .2 E2
Seabank Rd LL18 . . . . .7 A6
Seahill Rd CH1 . . . . .40 F8
Sealand Ave
Garden City CH5 . . . . .39 F7
Holywell / Treffynnon CH8 .21 C4
Sealand Cty Prim Sch
CH5 . . . . .39 E6
Sealand Ind Est CH1 . . . . .41 F2
Sealand Rd Blacon CH1 . . .41 C3
Chester CH1 . . . . .42 A2
Sealand Trad Pk CH1 . . . . .41 F2
Sea Life Ctr★ LL18 . . . . . . .7 B8
Sea Rd LL19 . . . . .2 F3
Seathwaite Way CH5 . . . . .38 C6
Sea View Ct LL18 . . . . .6 C5
Sea View Cvn Pk CH8 . . . . .4 D3
Sea View Terr CH8 . . . . . . .20 F5
Seaville St CH3 . . . . .144 C3
Sebring Ave CH7 . . . . .38 B4
Second Ave
Connah's Quay CH5 . . . . . .30 F3
Flint / Y Fflint CH6 . . . . . . .28 A5
Llay LL12 . . . . .67 A4
Prestatyn LL19 . . . . .2 F4
Wrexham / Wrecsam,
Gwersyllt LL11 . . . . .72 D7
Wrexham / Wrecsam LL14 .74 E1
Sedgefield Cl / Clos
Sedgefield LL13 . . . . .80 F7
Sedgefield Rd CH1 . . . . . . .42 B2
Sedum Cl CH3 . . . . .53 A6
Sefton Rd CH2 . . . . .43 A4
Selattyn CE Prim Sch
SY10 . . . . .114 F8
Selkirk Dr CH4 . . . . .52 A7
Selkirk Rd CH4 . . . . .52 A7
Seller St CH1 . . . . .144 C3
Selsdon Cl CH4 . . . . .48 A5
Selsdon Ct CH4 . . . . .52 C7
Sens Cl CH1 . . . . .144 A2
Serenity La CH5 . . . . .49 B4
Serpentine The CH4 . . . . . .52 B7
Sevenacre Cl CH6 . . . . .22 D2
Seven Sisters Rd LL19 . . . . .3 A3
Seventh Ave LL12 . . . . .67 A4
Seymour Dr / Gyrfa Seymour
6 LL18 . . . . .7 F1

Sgwar y Frenhines / Queens
Sq **4** LL11 . . . . .145 B2
Sgwar Y Neuadd / Hall Sq 13
LL16 . . . . .140 C3
Shaftesbury Ave CH3 . . . . .43 C2
Shaftesbury Dr CH6 . . . . . .27 E6
Shaftsbury Ave LL11 . . . . .72 D6
Shakespeare Ave CH5 . . . .48 F7
Shannon Cl CH4 . . . . .51 E5
Sharps Dr SY13 . . . . .103 F7
Shaun Cl LL18 . . . . .7 E5
Shaun Dr LL18 . . . . .7 E5
Shavington Ave CH2 . . . . . .42 F4
Shaw Cl CH5 . . . . .48 E8
Shed La CH3 . . . . .43 B2
Sheldon Ave CH3 . . . . .43 B2
Shellbrook Dr / Lon
Shellbrook LL14 . . . . .86 B6
Shelley Cl CH5 . . . . .48 E8
Shelley Rd CH1 . . . . .41 F6
Shepherds Bush LL11 . . . . .71 A5
Shepherd's La
Chester CH2 . . . . .42 D5
Chirk / Y Waun LL14 . . . . .105 C3
Shepherds Rd LL13 . . . . . . .74 E6
Sherbourne Ave
Chester CH4 . . . . .52 B5
Wrexham / Wrecsam LL11 .72 E8
Sheridan Ave CH5 . . . . .48 E8
Sheringham Cl CH4 . . . . . . .51 E5
Sherrymill Hill SY13 . . . . .103 F8
Sherwell Ave LL13 . . . . . . .73 C6
Sherwood Ave LL18 . . . . . . .2 B1
Sherwood Ct LL18 . . . . .1 D5
Sherwood Dr LL18 . . . . .1 D5
Sherwood Rd CH1 . . . . .41 E5
Shields Ct LL13 . . . . .80 C7
Shipbrook Rd CH2 . . . . .42 F6
Shipgate St CH1 . . . . .144 B1
Shipgate The CH1 . . . . . . .144 B1
Shire View CH7 . . . . .46 F5
Shocklach Oviatt CE Prim
Sch SY14 . . . . .83 C7
Shocklach Rd CH4 . . . . .42 F6
Sholing Dr LL18 . . . . .7 F8
Shone's La LL12 . . . . .67 A3
Shordley Cl LL12 . . . . .68 C7
Shordley Rd LL12 . . . . .59 E2
Shore Rd LL19 . . . . .4 A4
Short La 1 LL14 . . . . .95 D8
Shotton Inf Sch CH5 . . . . . .39 B6
Shotton La
Connah's Quay, Higher Shotton
CH5 . . . . .39 A4
Connah's Quay, Shotton
CH5 . . . . .39 B5
Shotton Sta CH5 . . . . .39 B6
Shotton View CH5 . . . . .39 A3
Shotwick La CH1 . . . . .31 D6
Shotwick Rd CH5 . . . . .30 F3
Shrewsbury Way CH4 . . . . .51 F6
Sibbersfield La CH3 . . . . . .69 F4
Sibell St CH1 . . . . .144 C3
Siddeley Cl CH4 . . . . .50 C4
Sidney St / Stryt Sidney
LL14 . . . . .78 D2
Signal Ct CH2 . . . . .42 F7
Silverbirch Croft CH4 . . . . .50 B3
Silver Birch Cvn Pk CH8 . . .4 D4
Silverbirch Dr LL12 . . . . . . .67 C2
Silver Birch Way CH4 . . . . .59 A8
Silverdale Ave CH7 . . . . . . .48 F5
Silverdale Terr LL17 . . . . . .16 B1
Silvermuir CH1 . . . . .41 E3
Silverstone Dr CH7 . . . . . . .47 F4
Simonstone Rd CH4 . . . . . .50 D4
Simpson Rd CH2 . . . . .42 C8
Simpsons Way CH4 . . . . . . .50 B3
Sisson St LL18 . . . . .7 C7
Sixth Ave
Connah's Quay CH5 . . . . . .30 E1
Flint / Y Fflint CH6 . . . . . . .28 A5
Sixth Ave / Chweched
Rhodfa LL12 . . . . .67 A4
Skip's La CH3 . . . . .53 F7
Slack La CH3 . . . . .49 B5
Smallbrook Rd LL13 . . . . .103 E7
Small Woods The / Llwyn
Bach **11** LL14 . . . . .86 A4
Smelt La / Fford
Mwyddofa LL11 . . . . .71 B3
Smelt Rd LL11 . . . . .71 B3
Smithfield Dr / Fford
Smithfield LL13 . . . . .75 D8
Smithfield Rd LL13 . . . . . . .73 C1
Smithfield Rd /
Fford-y-Ffair LL16 . . .140 B2
Smithfield St LL13 . . . . .75 D8
Smith St / Stryt yr Efail 1
LL14 . . . . .78 E1
Smithy Cl 1 LL13 . . . . .73 B6
Smithy Cotts LL13 . . . . .80 F4
Smithy Ct Christleton CH3 .53 E7
8 Wrexham / Wrecsam
LL13 . . . . .73 E3
Smithy La Ewloe CH5 . . . . .38 C1
Northop Hall CH7 . . . . .37 F5
Pentre Bychan LL14 . . . . . .79 A4
Wrexham / Wrecsam LL12 .73 B6
Smithy Pathway CH4 . . . . .51 F4
Smithy Rd LL11 . . . . .72 A4
Smithy Rd / Heol Yr Efail
LL11 . . . . .71 D3
Smithy The Chester CH2 . . .42 E8
Rossett LL12 . . . . .68 B7
Smokey La
Bronington SY13 . . . . .102 B7
Drury Lane SY13 . . . . .92 A1

Snowdon Ave
Bryn-y-baal CH7 . . . . .47 E6
Connah's Quay CH5 . . . . . .38 D7
Snowdon Cres CH4 . . . . . . .52 A5
Snowdon Dr LL14 . . . . .79 B1
Snowdon Dr / Rhodfa'r
Wyddfa LL11 . . . . .73 B5
Soar Chapel 7 LL11 . . . . .72 C3
Somerford Rd CH4 . . . . .50 C4
Somerset Rd CH2 . . . . .42 F5
Somerset St CH1 . . . . . . .144 B4
Sontley Hill LL13 . . . . .80 B5
Sontley Rd LL13 . . . . .80 A3
Sontley Rd / Fford Sonlli
LL13 . . . . .80 A7
Sorrel Cl CH3 . . . . .53 A6
Soughton Hall★ CH7 . . . . .37 B3
Souter's La CH1 . . . . . . .144 B2
South Arc 5 LL13 . . . . . .145 C2
South Ave Chester CH2 . . .144 C4
Prestatyn LL19 . . . . .3 A1
Rhyl / Y Rhyl LL18 . . . . .7 A6
South Bank Chester CH2 . . .42 C6
Connah's Quay CH5 . . . . . .39 B4
South Crescent Rd CH4 144 C1
South Dr LL18 . . . . .7 E4
South Fields Cl CH7 . . . . . .48 A5
South Gn CH5 . . . . .40 A6
South Kinmel St / Stryd
Cilmael **14** LL18 . . . . .7 B7
South La CH7 . . . . .48 A5
South La / Lon y De
LL14 . . . . .78 E2
Southlands Rd LL18 . . . . . . .6 E6
Southleigh Dr LL11 . . . . . . .73 A4
South Meadow Cl LL19 . . . .2 F2
Southsea Rd LL11 . . . . .72 A4
South St CH3 . . . . .43 A1
South St / Heol-y-De
CH7 . . . . .24 B6
South View
Buckley / Bwcle CH7 . . . . .48 C3
Chester CH4 . . . . .52 D7
Christleton CH3 . . . . .53 F7
Wrexham / Wrecsam LL11 .73 A7
South View Rd LL18 . . . . . .42 B2
South Way CH1 . . . . .41 F4
Sovereign Way LL11 . . . . . .41 E2
Sparks Cl CH3 . . . . .53 B7
Spectrum Ind Pk LL13 . . . .81 E7
Speed's Way CH3 . . . . .69 E2
Speedwell Cl CH3 . . . . .53 B5
Spencer Trad Est LL16 . . .140 D4
Spenser Cl CH5 . . . . .48 E8
Spinney The
Gwynfryn LL11 . . . . .70 E6
Marford LL12 . . . . .67 F5
Spinney Wlk / Rhodfar Gelli
12 LL14 . . . . .86 A4
Spital Wlk CH2 . . . . .42 F2
Spon Gn CH7 . . . . .48 D3
Sportsman Terr CH7 . . . . . .24 C4
Spring Bank CH8 . . . . .21 B6
Spring Dale CH5 . . . . .39 A1
Springfield
Hawarden / Penarlâg CH5 .49 C8
Wrexham / Wrecsam LL11 145 B4
Springfield Cl
Connah's Quay CH5 . . . . . .38 C6
Flint / Y Fflint CH6 . . . . . . .27 F5
Higher Kinnerton CH4 . . . . .60 A7
Springfield Cl LL12 . . . . . . .67 D2
Springfield Ct / Llys Maes Y
Ffynnon CH4 . . . . .60 A8
Springfield Dr CH7 . . . . . . .47 F4
Springfield La LL12 . . . . . . .67 E4
Springfield Pk LL13 . . . . . . .98 C7
Springfields
Holywell / Treffynnon CH8 .21 C4
Mickle Trafford CH2 . . . . . .43 E8
Spring Gdns / Gerddi'r
Pistyll LL11 . . . . .145 B3
Spring Rd LL11 . . . . .145 B3
Spring Rd / Fford Y
Ffynnon LL11 . . . . .79 C6
Spring St CH5 . . . . .39 A7
Springwood Cl CH1 . . . . . . .41 C4
Spruce Ave LL18 . . . . .7 E8
Spruce Cl 7 SY12 . . . . . .109 A3
Square The
Christleton CH3 . . . . .53 E8
Corwen LL21 . . . . .142 D4
Cynwyd LL21 . . . . .132 F8
Kinmel Bay / Bae Cinmel
LL18 . . . . .6 D5
Kinmel Bay / Bae Cinmel
LL18 . . . . .6 C5
Trefnant LL16 . . . . .117 C5
Stable Cott CH7 . . . . .57 C7
Stablegates / Gatiau'r Stabl
LL14 . . . . .79 A1
Stabler Cres LL13 . . . . .73 A5
Stables Rd LL11 . . . . .72 B8
Stables The CH3 . . . . .43 F5
Stadium Way CH1 . . . . .42 B3
Stafford Park Holiday Camp
LL18 . . . . .7 B6
Stafford Rd LL13 . . . . .39 F7
Stag Cotts LL16 . . . . .117 C5
Stags Leap SY13 . . . . . . .103 E8
Stainton Gr CH5 . . . . .38 C8
Stamford Ct CH3 . . . . .43 C2
Stamford Rd CH1 . . . . .41 E6
Stamford Way
Ewloe CH5 . . . . .38 C3
Holywell / Treffynnon CH8 .21 C2
Stancliffe Ave LL12 . . . . . . .68 A2
Standard Rd CH7 . . . . .48 D6

Stanham Cl 6 SY12 . . . .109 B2
Stanham Dr SY12 . . . . . . .109 B2
Stanley Est CH7 . . . . .48 A4
Stanley Gr LL14 . . . . .86 B5
Stanley Park Ave LL18 . . . . .7 E6
Stanley Park Ct CH4 . . . . . .51 E5
Stanley Park Dr CH4 . . . . . .51 E5
Stanley Pk LL17 . . . . .16 A1
Stanley Pl Chester CH1 . .144 A2
Connah's Quay CH5 . . . . . .39 A5
Stanley Place Mews
CH1 . . . . .144 A2
Stanley Rd CH7 . . . . .48 A4
Stanley Rd / Fford Stanley
LL14 . . . . .78 F2
Stanley St Chester CH1 . .144 A2
19 Mold / Yr Wyddgrug
CH7 . . . . .46 F4
Wrexham / Wrecsam
LL13 . . . . .145 C1
Stanley Terr LL14 . . . . . . .140 C2
Stanmore St LL18 . . . . .7 A6
Stannage La CH3 . . . . .69 F5
Stansty Chain Rd LL11 . . . .72 E5
Stansty Cl LL11 . . . . .72 F4
Stansty Dr LL11 . . . . .72 F4
Stansty Lodge La LL11 . . . .72 E5
Stansty Rd LL11 . . . . .72 F4
Stanton Dr CH2 . . . . .42 D5
Starkey La
Northop / Llan-eurgain CH7 37 B8
Northop / Llan-eurgain CH7 37 B8
Starkey Rd CH7 . . . . .37 D6
Starling Cl CH3 . . . . .69 F1
Station App LL11 . . . . .145 A3
Station Ave LL14 . . . . .105 D8
Station Cotts CH4 . . . . .40 F7
Station Ct / Llys Yr Orsaf 5
LL11 . . . . .72 D7
Station La
Guilden Sutton CH3 . . . . . .43 F7
Hawarden / Penarlâg CH5 .49 C8
Station Rd Bagillt CH6 . . .22 C3
Bangor on Dee / Bangor-is-y-coed
LL13 . . . . .89 A8
Chester CH4 . . . . .144 C1
Connah's Quay CH5 . . . . . .39 D5
Denbigh / Dinbych LL16 . .140 D3
Greenfield / Maes-Glas
CH8 . . . . .21 B8
Hawarden / Penarlâg CH5 .49 C8
Holywell / Treffynnon CH8 .21 B5
Marchwiel LL13 . . . . .80 F4
Overton LL13 . . . . .98 C8
Rhostyllen LL14 . . . . .79 C6
Rhuddlan LL18 . . . . .15 C6
Rossett LL12 . . . . .68 A7
Sandycroft CH5 . . . . .40 A2
Talacre CH8 . . . . .4 F4
Trevor LL20 . . . . .85 A1
Weston Rhyn SY10 . . . . . .105 D4
Wrexham / Wrecsam LL11 .72 A8
Station Rd / Fford-Yr-Orsaf
LL14 . . . . .105 D8
Station Rd / Fford Yr Orsaf
8 Ruabon / Rhiwabon
LL14 . . . . .86 A4
1 Ruthin / Rhuthin LL15 .141 D5
Station Road / Fford Yr
Orsaf LL19 . . . . .3 A3
Station View CH2 . . . . .42 F7
Station Way CH4 . . . . .51 E5
Station Wlk / Rhodfa'r Orsaf
1 LL15 . . . . .141 D5
Steam Cl / Clos Y Stem
LL11 . . . . .71 F8
Steam Mill St CH1, CH3 .144 C3
Stearns Cl LL11 . . . . .42 A5
Stearns Ho CH1 . . . . .42 A5
Steel Cl / Clos Y Dur
LL11 . . . . .71 F8
Steele St CH1 . . . . .144 B2
Stephen Gray Rd CH7 . . . . .47 B3
Stephen Rd LL13 . . . . .2 C2
Stephens La LL14 . . . . .78 D2
Steven Ct CH3 . . . . .144 C3
Stile End CH2 . . . . .43 F8
Stirling Ave LL11 . . . . .73 A5
Stirling Cl CH3 . . . . .43 A2
Stocks Ave 5 CH3 . . . . . .43 A1
Stocks La Chester CH3 . . . .43 A1
Welshampton & Lyneal
SY12 . . . . .110 B5
Stoneby Dr LL19 . . . . .3 C1
Stone Croft CH3 . . . . .53 B7
Stoneleigh Cl CH5 . . . . .39 F6
Stone Pl CH2 . . . . .42 F3
Stone Row Caergwrle LL12 66 B6
Cefn-y-Bedd LL12 . . . . . . .66 C5
Mynydd Isa CH7 . . . . .47 E2
New Brighton CH7 . . . . . . .47 C7
Stones Holiday Camp
LL22 . . . . .6 A4
Stonewalls LL12 . . . . .67 F7
Straight Mile
Eccleston CH4 . . . . .61 F5
Llay LL12 . . . . .67 C6
Strand Cl CH8 . . . . .21 B5
Strand Cres CH8 . . . . .21 B5
Strand La CH8 . . . . .21 B5
Strand Pk CH8 . . . . .21 B4
Strand Wlk CH8 . . . . .21 B5
Stratford Cl LL12 . . . . .73 C4
Stratford Rd CH1 . . . . .41 E4
Strawberry Fields CH3 . . . .53 B7
Street The CH2 . . . . .43 D8
Stretton Cl LL13 . . . . .80 B6

San – Str **165**

Strickland St CH5 . . . . .39 B5
Striga Bank SY13 . . . . . . .101 B4
Striga La SY13 . . . . .101 B4
Stringer's La LL12, CH4 . . .60 B4
Stryd Bodfor / Bodfor St 1
LL18 . . . . .7 B7
Stryd Cilmael / Kinmel St
LL18 . . . . .7 B7
Stryd Cilmael / South Kinmel
St 14 LL18 . . . . .7 B7
Stryd Fawr / High St
12 Denbigh / Dinbych
LL16 . . . . .140 C3
Mold / Yr Wyddgrug CH7 . .46 F5
Prestatyn LL19 . . . . .3 B2
Stryd Gaer / Chester St
CH7 . . . . .46 F4
Stryd Henardd CH7 . . . . . .46 F4
Stryd Henllan / Henllan St
LL16 . . . . .140 B3
Stryd Newydd / New St
CH7 . . . . .46 F4
Stryd Wrecsam / Wrexham
St CH7 . . . . .46 F4
Stryd Y Baddon / Bath St 3
LL18 . . . . .7 B8
Stryd Y Bont / Bridge St
LL21 . . . . .142 D4
Stryd Y Brython LL15 . . .141 E5
Stryd Y Capel / Chapel St
LL14 . . . . .85 B3
Stryd-y-Capel / Chapel St
18 Mold / Yr Wyddgrug
CH7 . . . . .46 F4
Rhosymedre LL14 . . . . .85 C2
Stryd-y-Castell / Castle St
LL15 . . . . .141 C5
Stryd Y Cyngor / Council St
LL12 . . . . .67 B3
Stryd y Dwr / Water St
5 Denbigh / Dinbych
LL16 . . . . .140 C3
Rhyl / Y Rhyl LL18 . . . . .7 B7
Stryd-y-Dyffryn / Vale St
LL16 . . . . .140 C3
Stryd Y Farchnad / Market
St 5 LL18 . . . . .7 B7
Stryd-y-Ffynnon / Well St
LL15 . . . . .141 D5
Stryd-y-Nant / Brook St 21
CH7 . . . . .46 F4
Stryd Y Neuadd / Hall St
LL14 . . . . .85 C7
Stryd Y Prior / Prior St
LL15 . . . . .141 C5
Stryd yr Eglwys / Church St
LL16 . . . . .116 F3
Stryd-yr-Eglwys / Church St
LL14 . . . . .85 C2
Stryd Y Eglwys / Church St
2 Rhyl / Y Rhyl LL18 . . . . .7 B8
Wrexham / Wrecsam LL11 .72 D8
Stryd yr Ysgol / School St
LL16 . . . . .116 F3
Stryt Argyle / Argyle St 3
LL11 . . . . .145 B2
Stryt Caer / Chester St
LL13 . . . . .145 C3
Stryt Clarke / Clarke St
LL14 . . . . .78 F2
Stryt Cynlas / Cynlas St 10
LL14 . . . . .78 E1
Stryt Efrog / Yorke St
LL13 . . . . .145 C2
Stryt Egerton / Egerton St
LL11 . . . . .145 B2
Stryt Ellis / Ellis St 7
LL14 . . . . .78 F2
Stryt Fawr / High St
LL13 . . . . .145 C2
Stryt Fechan / Roberts La 5
LL14 . . . . .78 E2
Stryt Fictoria / Victoria St 12
LL14 . . . . .78 E1
Stryt Gerallt / Gerald St
LL11 . . . . .145 B3
Stryt Gobaith / Hope St
LL14 . . . . .78 D2
Stryt Henblast / Henblas St
LL13 . . . . .145 C2
Stryt Holt / Holt Rd 73 D3
Stryt Holt / Holt St
LL13 . . . . .145 C2
Stryt Isa LL12 . . . . .59 B2
Stryt Isaf
Hope / Yr Hôb CH4, LL12 . .59 A4
Penyffordd CH4 . . . . .58 F5
Stryt-Issa LL14 . . . . .85 D8
Stryt Las LL14 . . . . .85 F8
Stryt Llanfair / Llanfair St
LL15 . . . . .141 D4
Stryt Lydan / Broad St 11
LL14 . . . . .78 E2
Stryt Maelor LL11 . . . . . . .70 E8
Stryt Newydd / New St 9
LL12 . . . . .78 E2
Stryt Osborne / Osborne St
3 LL14 . . . . .78 E1
Stryt Owen / Owens St
LL14 . . . . .78 D2
Stryt Pearson / Pearson St
7 LL14 . . . . .78 E2
Stryt Pedr / Peter St
LL14 . . . . .78 E2
Stryt Pentre LL20 . . . . . .135 E3

Stryt Siarl / Charles St LL13 .....145 C2
Stryt Sidney / Sidney St LL14 .....78 D2
Stryt Trefor / Trevor St LL13 .....145 B1
Stryt Twtil / Tuttle St LL13 .....145 C2
Stryt Uchaf / High St LL20 .....135 C4
Stryt William / William St 6 LL14 .....78 F2
Stryt y Banc / Bank St 1 LL13 .....145 C2
Stryt y Bedyddwyr / Baptist St 12 LL14 .....78 E2
Stryt y Bonc / Bank St LL14 .....78 E2
Stryt Y Bont / Bridge St LL20 .....85 D8
Stryt y Brenin / King St LL11 .....145 B3
Stryt y Brenln / King St 6 LL14 .....78 E1
Strytybydden LL11 .....72 C2
Stryt y Cambeliaid / Campbell St 3 LL14 .....78 E2
Stryt y Capel / Chapel St LL14 .....78 F2
Stryt y Castell / Castle St 4 LL14 .....78 F2
Stryt y Cigydd / Butcher St 10 LL14 .....78 E2
Stryt y Doctor / Beech Ave LL14 .....78 E1
Stryt y Dug / Duke St
  Rhosllanerchrugog LL14 .....78 A1
  1 Wrexham / Wrecsam LL11 .....145 B2
Stryt y Farchnad / Market St
  2 Rhosllanerchrugog LL14 .....78 E1
  Ruthin / Rhuthin LL15 .....141 C5
  Wrexham / Wrecsam LL13 .....145 C2
Stryt y Frenhines / Queen St 9 LL14 .....78 E1
Stryt y Gof / Church St 4 LL14 .....78 E1
Stryt y Neuadd / Hall St LL14 .....78 E2
Stryt-y-plas / Hall La LL14 .....78 C2
Stryt y Priordy / Priory St 7 LL11 .....145 B2
Stryt Yrabad / Abbot St LL11 .....145 B2
Stryt yr Alarch / Swan St 4 LL14 .....78 E2
Stryt Yr Allt / Hill St
  1 Penycae LL14 .....85 C7
  Rhosllanerchrugog LL14 .....78 E1
  Wrexham / Wrecsam LL11 145 B2
Stryt Yr Arglwydd / Lord St LL13 .....145 B2
Stryt yr Efail / Smith St 2 LL14 .....78 E1
Stryt Yr Eglws / Church St 3 LL13 .....145 C2
Stryt y Rhaglaw / Regent St LL11 .....145 A3
Stryt Yr Hob / Hope St LL11 .....145 B2
Stryt Y Rhos / Rhos St LL15 .....141 D5
Stryt Yr Lampit / Lambpit St LL14 .....85 C7
Stryt Y Scweiar LL11, ...71 C2
Stryt y Syfwr / Queen St 6 LL11 .....145 B2
Stryt Y Veri LL11 .....95 B6
Stryt y Weirglodd / School St LL14 .....78 D2
Stuart Cl CH3 .....43 C3
Stuart Pl CH1 .....144 B3
Stuart St LL13 .....80 B7
Stuart Way LL13 .....80 B7
Stubbs Pl CH1 .....41 E3
Sturges Wlk 4 LL11 .....72 B4
Sudbury Cl 4 LL18 .....7 D6
Suffolk Ho CH1 .....144 C3
Sullivan's Rise CH5 .....38 E8
Summerdale Rd CH5 .....39 A4
Summerfield Cl CH4 .....50 A3
Summerfield Rd CH3 .....43 F5
Summerfields LL14 .....79 D7
Summerhill Rd LL14 .....78 D7
Summersville Cl CH5 .....38 D7
Sumner Rd CH1 .....41 E4
Sumpter Pathway CH2 .....42 F3
Sunbury Cres 3 CH4 .....51 F6
Sun Centre ★ LL18 .....1 C5
Sundawn Ave CH8 .....21 C4
Sundorne 4 LL13 .....98 C8
Sun La LL13 .....82 C5
Sunningdale CH7 .....48 A6
Sunningdale Cl LL13 .....73 F4
Sunnside Cl CH6 .....21 F5
Sunnyacre / Erw Heulog 1 LL11 .....72 D6
Sunnyhill / Heulfryn LL11 .....72 C5
Sunny Ridge CH7 .....46 E6
Sunnyridge Ave LL12 .....67 F4

Sunny Sands Holiday Pk LL19 .....4 A4
Sunnyside Bagillt CH6 .....21 F5
  Connah's Quay CH5 .....39 E2
Sunnyvale Holiday Camp LL18 .....6 E6
Sunny View LL11 .....72 C7
Sunny Villas LL12 .....68 A7
Sun Valley Cvn Pk LL18 .....7 F2
Surrey Rd CH2 .....43 A5
Susan Gr LL19 .....2 F2
Sussex Gdns / Gerddi Sussex 2 LL11 .....73 B5
Sussex La LL18 .....7 B7
Sussex Rd CH2 .....42 F4
Sussex St / Heol Sussex 17 LL18 .....8 B7
Sussex Way CH4 .....42 F4
Sutherland Way CH3 .....43 B3
Sutton Cl
  Connah's Quay CH5 .....38 C5
  Mickle Trafford CH2 .....43 F8
Sutton Dr Chester CH2 .....42 E5
  Wrexham / Wrecsam LL13 .....73 E2
Swain Ave CH7 .....48 D3
Swallowfields Farndon CH3 .....69 E2
  Ffrith LL11 .....65 D3
Swan Hill SY12 .....109 C3
Swan La CH7 .....46 C1
Swan Mere Pk SY12 .....109 C3
Swan St / Stryt yr Alarch 4 LL14 .....78 E2
Swan Wlk 4 CH6 .....28 A6
Swinchiard La CH6 .....28 A6
Swinchiard Wlk CH6 .....28 A6
Swinleys Hey CH3 .....53 A7
Swn Y Dail LL18 .....14 F4
Swn-y-Gwynt CH6 .....28 B4
Swn-y-Nant CH7 .....46 F3
Sycamore Ave CH5 .....38 E7
Sycamore Cl Ewloe CH5 .....48 F7
  3 St. Martin's SY11 .....106 F6
Sycamore Cres 7 Ellesmere SY12 .....109 C2
  Prestatyn LL19 .....3 B1
Sycamore Dr Chester CH4 .....51 F6
  5 Chirk / Y Waun LL14 .....95 E3
Sycamore Dr / Ffordd Masarn CH7 .....57 F5
Sycamore Dr / Rhodfa'r Sycamowyddens LL12 .....67 F3
Sycamore Gr Broughton CH4 .....50 B3
  Rhyl / Y Rhyl LL18 .....7 D8
Sycamore Rd LL13 .....73 E2
Sycamore Terr CH8 .....21 C8
Sycamore Villas 8 CH7 .....46 F4
Sydenham Ave CH5 .....6 F6
Sydney Hall Ct CH5 .....38 C5
Sydney Rd CH1 .....42 B3
Sydney St CH6 .....28 A6
Sydney Wlk CH6 .....28 A6
Sylvan Mews CH1 .....41 E6
Sylvester Ct LL13 .....80 C7

T
Tabernacle St CH7 .....48 B4
Tabor Hill / Bryn Tabor LL11 .....71 C3
Tai Capel 3 LL11 .....72 D7
Tai-clawdd 6 LL14 .....86 A4
Tai Gwynedd LL14 .....85 B2
Tai Nestig CH7 .....45 F6
Tai Newydd LL20 .....135 C5
Tai-newyddion LL11 .....131 B7
Tai Owain LL11 .....71 E8
Tair Felin LL17 .....16 B2
Tai Tudors CH7 .....45 D6
Talacre Beach Cvn Pk CH8 .....5 A6
Talardy Pk / Parc Talardy LL17 .....16 A2
Talargoch Trad Est LL18 .....8 F5
Talbot Cl LL13 .....145 B1
Talbot Dr CH8 .....5 A6
Talbot Rd / Ffordd Talbot LL13 .....145 B1
Talbot St Chester CH1 .....144 B4
  Ellesmere SY12 .....109 C2
Talfryn Cl CH5 .....29 D1
Talgarreg Dr CH5 .....38 C4
Taliesin Ave CH5 .....39 A6
Taliesin Cl LL13 .....80 F5
Taliesin Jun Sch CH5 .....39 A5
Talton Cres LL19 .....3 C1
Talton Cl LL19 .....3 C2
Talwrn Rd LL11 .....71 D4
Tanat Way LL13 .....73 E1
Tanrallt Ave LL18 .....6 F2
Tanrallt Rd CH8 .....4 E2
Tanrallt Terr LL19 .....2 F3
Tan'rallt Terr LL20 .....143 E4
Tanybryn LL20 .....135 F4
Tan-y-Bryn Buckley / Bwcle CH7 .....48 A6
  Caergwrle LL12 .....73 D7
  Greenfield / Maes-Glas CH8 21 C8
Tan Y Bryn Llanbedr Dyffryn Clwyd LL15 .....121 F2
  Pwll-glas LL15 .....125 F5
  Rhosllanerchrugog LL14 .....85 E8

Tan-y-Bryn Soughton / Sychdyn CH7 .....37 A1
  St Asaph / Llanelwy LL17 .....16 A1
  Wrexham / Wrecsam LL13 .....73 E1
Tan-y-Cae CH7 .....34 D7
Tan-y-Castell LL15 .....141 C5
Tanyclawdd LL14 .....79 A1
Tan y Clogwyn LL16 .....119 D7
Tanycoed LL20 .....143 E3
Tan-y-Coed Carmel CH8 .....20 D6
  Johnstown LL14 .....79 A2
  Mold / Yr Wyddgrug CH7 .....46 E4
  Soughton / Sychdyn CH7 .....37 A1
Tan Y Coed LL13 .....80 E7
Tan-y-Ddol LL20 .....143 C5
Tan-y-Felin CH7 .....21 B7
Tan-y-fforest LL18 .....17 A7
Tanyfron Prim Sch LL11 .....7 F5
Tanyfron Rd Tanyfron LL11 .....71 F5
  Wrexham / Wrecsam LL11 .....72 A5
Tan-y-Geraint LL20 .....143 C5
Tan-y-Graig CH7 .....46 D4
Tan-y-Gwalia LL16 .....140 C2
Tan Y Lloc La CH8 .....19 E6
Tan-y-Maes LL19 .....4 B2
Tan-y-Marian Cl LL19 .....4 B2
Tan y Plas LL13 .....143 C4
Tan-yr-Allt LL12 .....66 C3
Tan-Yr-Eglwys LL18 .....7 E1
Tan-Yr-Eglwys Rd LL18 .....7 E1
Tan-yr-Hafod CH7 .....45 F5
Tan-y-Rhos CH7 .....56 E6
Tan-yr-Ysgol CH7 .....37 A1
Tan Y 'sgubor LL16 .....140 B3
Tapley Ave LL12 .....73 D4
Tarleton St LL13 .....7 C8
Tarporley Rd SY13 .....93 F2
Tarquin Dr LL18 .....7 F5
Tarvin Rd
  Chester, Boughton CH3 .....43 A2
  Chester, Vicarscross CH3 .....43 A2
Tatham Rd LL14 .....85 F5
Tatton Cl CH4 .....51 E5
Taylors View CH5 .....39 B5
Taynton Cl CH5 .....38 C7
Teal Dr SY12 .....109 B3
Tecwyn Dr CH5 .....38 C8
Tegfan Johnstown LL14 .....79 A1
  Rhosllanerchrugog LL14 .....85 F8
Tegfan Ct LL12 .....66 B8
Tegid LL14 .....85 D3
Tegid Way CH4 .....51 D5
Telford Ave Trevor LL20 .....84 F1
  Weston Rhyn LL14 .....105 E6
Telford Way CH4 .....51 F6
Temperance Rd LL11 .....72 A4
Temple Bar Sq 14 LL16 .....140 C3
Temple Row / Rhes y Deml 4 LL13 .....145 C2
Temple Vale LL11 .....85 B1
Tennyson Wlk CH1 .....42 A5
Tenters La LL13 .....145 B1
Tenters Sq LL13 .....145 B1
Tenth Ave Connah's Quay CH5 .....30 D3
  Connah's Quay CH5 .....30 E3
Tenth Ave / Rhodfa Ddeg LL12 .....67 A3
Teras Burton / Burton Terr LL14 .....85 B3
Terence Ave LL18 .....7 B6
Terfyn LL11 .....79 A2
Terfyn Cotts LL18 .....14 C5
Terfyn Pella Ave LL18 .....2 B2
Terfyn Pella Camp LL18 .....2 B1
Terrace Cotts LL13 .....73 E2
Terrace La CH4 .....59 B7
Terrig Cres CH7 .....48 B4
Terrig St CH5 .....39 B4
Terrig Way LL11 .....72 D6
Terr The LL21 .....142 D4
Tewkesbury Cl CH2 .....42 F7
Thackeray Dr CH3 .....43 C3
Thimble La SY11 .....106 F6
Third Ave Connah's Quay CH5 .....30 F1
  Flint / Y Fflint CH6 .....28 A5
  Llay LL12 .....67 A4
  Prestatyn LL19 .....2 F4
  Talacre CH8 .....5 A6
  Wrexham / Wrecsam LL11 .....72 C7
Thirlmere Cl LL11 .....72 E8
Thirlmere Rd CH2 .....43 A5
Thisledown Cl LL14 .....79 D7
Thomas Ave CH5 .....48 E8
Thomas Ave / Rhodfa Thomas LL18 .....8 F2
Thomas Brassey Cl CH2 .....144 C4
Thomas Cl Blacon CH1 .....41 F6
  Mickle Trafford CH2 .....43 F8
Thomas Cotts CH5 .....39 A1
Thomas Ct LL13 .....80 C7
Thomas Ho CH1 .....42 A5
Thomas Row / Rhes Thomas CH6 .....22 B4
Thomas St CH6 .....28 B7
Thompson Dr SY13 .....103 E7
Thornberry Cl CH1 .....41 B8
Thornfield Ave CH5 .....38 F6
Thornfields CH5 .....39 A4
Thornhill Cl CH4 .....51 D5
Thornhill Dr / Allt Yr Eithin LL14 .....79 E8
Thorn Ho CH4 .....52 A5
Thornhurst Dr / Rhodfa Thornhurst 3 LL13 .....73 F3

Thornleigh LL13 .....73 E3
Thornleigh Dr LL12 .....67 F2
Thornley Ave LL18 .....7 E6
Thornton Cl 3 LL18 .....7 B6
Thornton Dr CH2 .....42 D5
Thorpe St LL13 .....7 C7
Threos Cl CH5 .....38 C4
Thurston Rd CH4 .....51 E5
Tilers Cl CH7 .....48 B5
Timberfields Rd CH1 .....41 A8
Tintern Ave CH2 .....42 F6
Tip La LL19 .....2 F1
Tir Griffin Cl / Clos Tir Griffin LL20 .....84 E2
Tir Llwyd Ent Pk LL18 .....6 D2
Tir Llwyd Ind Est LL18 .....6 D1
Tir Wat CH7 .....47 E4
Titian Cl CH5 .....38 C8
Tivaton Cl CH5 .....38 D6
Tiverton Cl CH2 .....42 F5
Tn y Dre LL13 .....73 D2
Toft Cl CH4 .....51 E5
Toll Bar Rd CH3 .....53 C8
Tollemache Terr CH2 .....42 F2
Tomkinson St CH2 .....144 C4
Tomlins Terr CH1 .....41 E5
Toogood Cl CH2 .....43 F8
Top Rd Coedpoeth LL11 .....71 A2
  Wrexham / Wrecsam LL11 .....72 C8
Totland Gr CH2 .....42 E4
Tower Ct LL18 .....7 D5
Tower Gdns LL18 .....7 D5
Tower Gdns / Gerddir Twr CH8 .....21 B4
Tower Hill LL20, LL14 .....84 E3
Tower Hill / Allt Y Twr LL14 .....85 A2
Tower Rd Chester CH1 .....42 B2
  Llangollen LL20 .....143 C6
Towers Way CH4 .....59 A8
Tower View Acrefair LL14 .....85 B3
  Wrexham / Wrecsam LL13 .....73 D2
Townfield Ave CH3 .....69 E2
Townfield La Blacon CH1 .....41 F8
  Farndon CH3 .....69 D2
Town Hill / Allt y Dref 9 LL13 .....145 B2
Townsend Ave LL12 .....73 E5
Towyn Cl LL19 .....2 E1
Towyn Jun Sch LL18 .....6 C4
Towyn Rd LL22 .....6 B4
Towyn Way E LL22 .....6 C2
Towyn Way W LL22 .....6 B4
Trafalgar Ct LL13 .....80 B7
Trafford St CH1 .....144 B3
Tram La CH7 .....48 C5
Tram Rd CH7 .....48 C6
Tramway St CH1 .....144 C3
Trebor Ave CH6 .....22 C1
Tre Borth LL19 .....3 A3
Treborth Rd CH1 .....41 D3
Treetops Ct LL18 .....7 F1
Tree Tops Cvn Pk CH8 .....5 A2
Trefnant Ave LL18 .....6 E4
Trefoil Cl CH3 .....53 B6
Trefor Ave LL18 .....6 E5
Tref-y-nant Pk / Parc Tref Y Nant LL14 .....85 A2
Tregele Cl CH1 .....41 D3
Trehearn Dr LL14 .....7 D8
Trehowell Ave SY10 .....105 D5
Trelawny Ave CH6 .....28 B6
Trelawnyd VP Sch LL18 .....9 F4
Trelawny Sq CH6 .....28 A7
Trelech CH5 .....38 C4
Trellewelyn Cl LL18 .....7 E6
Trellewelyn Rd LL18 .....7 E6
Trem Afon CH7 .....47 D5
Trem Cinmel LL22 .....6 B3
Trem Dolydd LL14 .....85 B1
Trem Elwy LL18 .....6 E5
Trem Eryri LL11 .....73 A5
Trem Hyfryd / Fairview LL14 .....79 C7
Trem Menlli LL15 .....141 E4
Trem-y-Berwyn LL14 .....85 D7
Trem-y-Bont LL18 .....6 E5
Trem y Castell LL14 .....143 D4
Trem-y-Castell LL22 .....6 A2
Trem Y Coed LL15 .....125 C3
Trem y Dyffryn LL16 .....140 D4
Trem-y-Dyffryn CH7 .....6 F3
Trem-y-Ffair LL18 .....6 E5
Trem-y-Foel LL21 .....130 C6
Trem Y Foel LL21 .....132 F3
Trem-y-Foel
  Rhes-y-cae CH8 .....26 B2
  Ruthin / Rhuthin LL15 .....141 A5
  Soughton / Sychdyn CH7 .....47 A8
Trem-y-Foryd LL18 .....6 D3
Trem-y-Gardden LL14 .....85 E7
Trem-y-Geulan LL18 .....6 D3
Trem-y-Gwernant LL14 .....143 E3
Trem-y-Mynydd LL11 .....71 A4
Trem y Nant LL14 .....72 B7
Trem-y-Nant LL18 .....80 A6
Trem y Parc / Park View LL14 .....78 F1
Trem-yr-Afon LL18 .....6 E5
Trem-yr-Edlwys LL14 .....105 E8
Trem-yr-Eglwys LL13 .....80 A7
Trem-yr-Harbwr LL18 .....6 E5
Trem-yr-Rhosyn / Roseview Cres LL18 .....6 E5
Trem Yr Ysgol LL20 .....143 E3
Trevalyn Hall View LL12 ..68 C7

Trevalyn Hospl LL12 .....68 B5
Trevalyn Way LL12 .....68 C7
Trevenna Way LL13 .....73 C2
Trevor Ave Rhostyllen LL14 .....79 C6
  Rhuddlan LL18 .....7 F2
  St. Martin's SY11 .....106 E5
Trevor Hall Rd / Ffordd Plas Trefor LL20 .....84 D1
Trevor Rd Chirk / Y Waun LL14 .....105 E8
  Llangollen LL20 .....143 F5
  Prestatyn LL19 .....3 A3
Trevor Sq LL20 .....143 D5
Trevor St / Stryt Trefor LL13 .....145 B1
Trewen LL13 .....140 E3
Treweryn Cl LL12 .....66 F3
Trewythen Cotts LL12 .....67 E2
Trewythen Pk LL12 .....67 E2
Triangle The 1 LL13 .....73 E4
Trident Way LL13 .....73 E5
Trimpley Ct 5 SY12 .....109 B2
Trimpley St SY12 .....109 B2
Trinity Cl LL14 .....79 C6
Trinity Ct 10 LL18 .....7 B7
Trinity Rd CH8 .....21 C8
Trinity St Chester CH1 .....144 A2
  Rhostyllen LL14 .....79 C6
  Wrexham / Wrecsam LL13 .....145 B3
Tri-thy Needlecraft Ctr ★ CH7 .....58 B2
Troedle 16 LL14 .....78 E2
Troed Y Fenlli LL15 .....121 F2
Troed Y Rhiw
  16 Denbigh / Dinbych LL16 .....140 C3
  Ruthin / Rhuthin LL15 .....141 C5
Trofryn LL14 .....85 D7
Troon Cl LL13 .....73 F4
Tros-yr-Aber CH8 .....21 B7
Trueman's Ct CH5 .....49 C8
Trueman's Way
  Connah's Quay CH5 .....39 C1
  Hawarden / Penarlâg CH5 .....49 C8
Trum-yr-hydref CH7 .....38 A4
Tryweryn Pl LL13 .....73 E1
Tudor Ave Flint / Y Fflint CH6 .....28 A4
  Prestatyn LL19 .....3 C2
  Rhostyllen LL14 .....79 C6
  Rhyl / Y Rhyl LL18 .....7 D6
Tudor Cl Connah's Quay CH5 .....39 B5
  Holywell / Treffynnon CH8 .....21 A4
  Northop Hall CH7 .....37 F4
Tudor Ct Hope / Yr Hôb LL12 .....59 A2
  Johnstown LL14 .....79 A1
  9 Mold / Yr Wyddgrug CH7 .....46 F4
Tudor Dr LL13 .....99 E3
Tudor Gdn CH1 .....41 E6
Tudor Gr LL18 .....6 D5
Tudor Park / Parc Tudur LL18 .....6 F3
Tudor Rd / Ffordd Tudor LL13 .....80 B7
Tudor's Ave LL11 .....72 D8
Tudor St LL11 .....71 C2
Tudor Way CH3 .....53 A7
Turnberry Avenue (Rhodfa Turnberry) LL13 .....73 F3
Turner Cl 7 LL13 .....73 E4
Turner Ho LL11 .....86 B6
Turning St LL13 .....88 C1
Turnpike La / Lon Dyrpeg LL12 .....67 F3
Tuscan Way CH5 .....38 E8
Tushingham Cl CH3 .....53 B7
Tuttle St / Stryt Twtil LL13 .....145 C2
Twain Cl CH5 .....48 E8
Twenty Hos LL11 .....70 F7
Twining Hill LL13 .....87 C3
Two Mile Ind Est LL11 .....72 B6

Ty = house
Ty Cerrig Dr LL20 .....66 A7
Ty-Coch St LL16 .....116 F3
Tyddyn Mesham CH6 .....22 D2
Tyddyn St CH7 .....47 A4
Ty Gwlfa LL19 .....3 A3
Ty Gwyn LL14 .....78 E2
Ty Gwyn La LL11 .....73 A6
Ty Hooson LL14 .....78 D3
Ty Mawr Ctry Pk ★ LL20 .....95 C7
Tyn Dwr Rd LL20 .....143 F4
Ty Newydd Ct 5 LL14 .....86 A4
Tynewydd Rd LL18 .....7 E8
Ty-newydd Terr LL18 .....7 E7
Ty'n-Llan CH7 .....55 B6
Tynno Uchaf La LL20 .....84 C2
Tyn Twll La CH6 .....21 F4
Tyn-y-Celyn Dr LL20 .....143 A4
Tyn y Cestyll Rd / Ffordd Tyn y Cestyll LL20 .....135 B4
Ty'n-y-coed LL15 .....125 D8
Ty'n-y-llidiart Ind Est LL11 .....142 C6
Ty'n-y-Parc LL15 .....141 B5
Ty'n-y-eithin Cvn Pk LL16 .....140 E5
Ty Rheil Ffordd LL11 .....65 F1
Ty Rhosydd LL14 .....78 D2
Tyr Llwyn LL14 .....78 D3
Ty'r Pk LL11 .....145 B4

Ty Wesley **13** LL14 ......78 E2
Tywyn Ganol LL11 ....2 F2
Tywyn Isaf LL19 ....2 F3

U

Ullswater Cres CH2 .....43 A6
Ullswater Rd CH7 ....48 D6
Unedau Busnes Llys
  Edeyrnion Bsns Units
  LL21 ....142 E4
Union Rd LL11 ....145 B3
Union St CH1 ....144 C2
Union Terr CH1 ....144 B3
Union Wlk CH1 ....144 B2
University College Chester
  CH1 ....144 A4
Uplands Ave CH5 ....38 E5
Upper Aston Hall La CH5 39 B1
Upper Bryn Coch / Bryn
  Coch Uchaf CH7 ....46 D3
Upper Bryn Rd **9** CH5 ..38 D8
Upper Bryntirion Dr LL19 .3 B1
Upper Cambrian Rd CH1 42 B2
Upper Clwyd St LL15 ...141 C5
Upper Denbigh Rd LL17 117 B8
Upper Downing Rd CH8 ..11 F1
Upper Foel Rd / Ffordd
  Uchaf Foel LL18 ....9 A2
Upper Northgate St
  CH1 ....144 A3
Upper River Bank CH6 ...21 E6
Upton Dr CH2 ....42 F6
Upton La CH2 ....42 C6
Upton Manor Cty Jun Sch
  CH2 ....42 D7
Upton Pk CH2 ....42 E8
Upton Westlea Prim Sch
  CH2 ....42 D6
Uwchydre LL21 ....142 C3
Uwch-y-Dre CH7 ....46 B2
Uwch-y-Mor CH8 ....26 D5
Uwch-y-Nant CH7 ....47 D5

V

Vale Ave CH5 ....48 F7
Vale Cl CH4 ....50 C3
Vale Dr CH7 ....47 D4
Vale Pk
  Denbigh / Dinbych LL16 .140 D5
  Rhyl / Y Rhyl LL18 .....7 C6
Vale Rd LL18 ....7 C6
Vale Rd / Ffordd-y-Dyffryn
  1 LL16 ....140 D3
Vale Road Bridge LL18 ...7 C7
Vale St / Stryd-y-Dyffryn
  LL16 ....140 D3
Vale View Llay LL12 .....67 B3
  Wrexham / Wrecsam LL11 72 B5
Vale View / Golygfa'r
  Dyffryn LL14 ....85 B3
Vale View Terr LL18 .....7 C7
Valley Ct LL11 ....72 B6
Valley Dr CH2 ....42 C5
Valley Rd LL11 ....65 C3
Valley View LL20 ....135 D4
Valley Way / Ffordd Y
  Dyffryn CH7 ....80 B7
Vaughan Cl LL19 ....3 A1
Vaughans La CH3 ....53 A8
Vaughan St **3** LL18 ....7 B7
Vaughan Way CH5 ....38 D5
Vauxhall Ind Est LL14 ...86 A7
Venable's Rd CH1 ....41 F4
Venerable Edward Morgan
  RC Prim Sch CH5 ......39 A5
Vermeer Cl CH5 ....38 C8
Vernay Gn CH4 ....52 B5
Vernon Cl Rhostyllen LL14 .79 C6
  Saughall CH1 ....41 A8
Vernon Rd CH1 ....42 B2
Vernon St LL11 ....145 B3
Vetches The CH3 ....43 F5
Vezey St **1** CH7 ......7 C7
Vicarage Cl
  Bodelwyddan LL18 ......15 A4
  Guilden Sutton CH3 ....43 F5
  Wrexham / Wrecsam LL11 .72 C8
Vicarage Dr CH6 ....22 C1
Vicarage Fields LL14 ....86 B4
Vicarage Hill Minera LL11 .71 A4
  Rhostyllen LL14 ....79 C6
Vicarage Hill / Allt y Ficeroy
  8 LL13 ....145 B2
Vicarage La Gresford LL12 67 E1
  Weston Rhyn SY10 ....105 D4
Vicarage La / Coetiau Postol
  LL18 ....7 E1
Vicarage Rd Bagillt CH6 ..22 C2
  Brymbo LL11 ....65 F2
  Chester CH2 ....42 F3
  Llangollen LL20 ......143 C4
Vicars Cross Ct **2** CH3 .43 F3
Vicars Cross Rd CH3 ....43 C2
Vicar's La CH1 ....144 B2
Vickers Cl CH5 ....39 C3
Victoria Ave
  Buckley / Bwcle CH7 ...48 C5
  2 Johnstown LL14 ..79 A1
  Rhyl / Y Rhyl LL18 ....7 A6
Victoria Ave / Rhodfa
  Victoria **4** LL19 ....3 B2
Victoria Bsns Pk LL18 ...7 C6

Victoria Cres
  Chester CH2 ....144 A4
  Chester, Queen's Park
  CH4 ....144 C1
  5 Connah's Quay CH5 .39 A6
  Pontybodkin CH7 ....58 A3
Victoria Ct CH2 ....144 A4
Victoria Inf Sch
  Chester CH1 ....144 A4
  Wrexham / Wrecsam
  LL13 ....145 A1
Victoria Jun Sch LL13 ..145 A1
Victoria La LL11 ....2 F3
Victorian Sch & Mus★
  LL20 ....143 C5
Victoria Park Ave LL19 ...2 F3
Victoria Pathway CH4 ..144 C1
Victoria Pl Chester CH1 ..144 B3
  Holywell / Treffynnon CH8 .21 B4
Victoria Rd Bagillt CH6 ..21 F5
  Buckley / Bwcle CH7 ...48 C5
  Chester CH1, CH2 .....144 B3
  Chester CH2 ....144 A4
  Coedpoeth LL11 ....71 C3
  Connah's Quay CH5 ....39 A6
  Mold / Yr Wyddgrug CH7 .47 A4
  Prestatyn LL19 ....2 E3
  Rhyl / Y Rhyl LL18 .....7 C6
  Saltney CH4 ....51 D6
  Wrexham / Wrecsam, Brynteg
  LL11 ....72 B5
  Wrexham / Wrecsam
  LL13 ....145 A1
Victoria Rd / Ffordd Victoria
  12 CH7 ....46 F4
Victoria Rd W LL19 ......2 C2
Victoria St SY12 ....109 B2
Victoria St / Stryt Fictoria **12**
  LL14 ....78 E1
Victoria Terr
  Corwen LL21 ....142 E3
  Mold / Yr Wyddgrug CH7 .47 A5
Victory Ct CH7 ....47 A4
Victory Pl / Buddugfa
  LL12 ....67 B3
Viking Cl LL11 ....72 D6
Viking Way CH5 ....38 D8
Village Ct / Cwrt Pentref **3**
  LL11 ....73 B5
Village Mdws / Dol Y Pentre
  14 LL14 ....86 A4
Village Rd Christleton CH3 .53 E8
  Nannerch CH7 ....34 D7
Village The
  Bodelwyddan LL18 ......15 A4
  Llandegla LL11 ....127 B3
Village Walks LL12 ......68 A5
Villa Rd CH5 ....40 B7
Villiers St LL13 ....145 A2
Vincent Cl LL18 ....7 C8
Vincent Dr CH4 ....52 C6
Vincent St LL14 ....86 A5
Vinegar Hill / Allt Ty Gwyn
  LL14 ....78 E3
Viola Ave LL18 ....7 E3
Violet Gr LL18 ....7 F6
Virginia Dr CH1 ....41 C4
Voel Gron / Foel Gron
  CH6 ....22 C2
Volunteer St CH1 ......144 B2
Vounog Hill CH4 ....59 A7
Vownog CH7 ....37 A2
Vownog Newydd CH7 ....37 B2
Vron Cl / Clos Y Fron
  LL11 ....71 F8
Vulcan Cotts **2** LL11 ..72 B4
Vyrnwy Cl LL11 ....72 D5
Vyrnwy Rd CH4 ....51 D6
Vyrnwy Way LL13 ....73 E1

Warren Cres CH7 ....48 F4
Warren Dr Broughton CH4 .50 A3
  Prestatyn LL19 ....3 C4
Warren Hall Ct CH7 .....49 E2
Warren Rd Prestatyn LL19 .3 B3
  Rhyl / Y Rhyl LL18 .....7 A6
Warrenwood Rd LL12 .....73 D4
Warren Workshops The
  LL12 ....66 E5
Warrington Rd CH2 ......43 E7
Warwick Ave LL13 ....80 C8
Warwick Rd CH1 ....41 F5
Washington Ct LL18 .....7 C7
Washington Dr CH5 .....39 A2
Waterfall Rd /
  Ffordd-y-Rhaeadr LL18 ..8 F3
Waterfall St SY10 .....138 A1
Watergate Rd CH1 .....144 A2
Watergate Sq CH1 .....144 A2
Watergate St
  Chester CH1 ....144 A2
  2 Ellesmere SY12 ..109 C2
Waterloo Cl LL13 ....80 B7
Waterloo Rd CH2 ....42 C4
Waters Edge CH1 ....42 B2
Waterside LL13 ....103 F8
Waters Reams CH3 ......53 B8
Water St
  CH7 ....46 F4
Water St / Heol Ddwr
  CH7 ....24 B6
Water St / Stryd Y Dwr
  5 Denbigh / Dinbych
  LL16 ....140 C3
  Rhyl / Y Rhyl LL18 .....7 B7
Water Tower (Mus)★
  CH1 ....42 B2
Water Tower St CH1 ...144 A3
Watertower View CH2 ...42 F2
Watery La LL13 ....82 B2
Watery Rd LL13 ....145 A2
Watkin St CH5 ....40 A3
Watling Cres CH4 ......52 E7
Watling Ct CH3 ....43 C2
Wats Dyke LL12 ....66 F4
Wat's Dyke Ave CH7 ....47 D5
Wat's Dyke Ave CH8 ....21 B5
Wat's Dyke Prim Sch
  LL11 ....73 A5
Wat's Dyke View **1**
  LL14 ....86 B6
Wat's Dyke Way
  Soughton / Sychdyn CH7 .37 B1
  Wrexham / Wrecsam LL11 .73 B1
Watson's Ct CH4 ....50 C3
Wat's Rd CH4 ....59 A7
Watts Ct CH7 ....47 F4
Waun-y-Llyn Ctry Pk★
  LL11 ....58 C1
Wavell Ave LL13 ....73 C1
Wavells Way CH3 ....53 B5
Waverley Cres LL12 .....68 C8
Waverley Terr CH2 ......42 E4
Wavertree Rd CH4 ......41 C5
Wayside Ct CH2 ....43 F8
Weale Ct LL13 ....80 C7
Wealstone Ct CH2 ......42 E5
Weal Stone La CH2 .....42 E6
Weaver Ave LL18 ....7 E6
Weaver Gr CH4 ....43 F8
Weavers La LL18 ....8 F3
Weavert St CH1 ....144 A2
Weaverton Dr LL11 ......7 E5
Webster Cl CH4 ....50 C3
Wedgewood Hts CH8 ....20 F5
Wedgwood Rd CH5 ......39 B3
Weighbridge Rd
  Connah's Quay CH5 ....30 B4
  Connah's Quay CH5 ....30 C5
Welland Dr CH5 ....38 D6
Wellfield SY13 ....93 F1
Well House Dr CH4 .....49 B1
Wellington Cl CH5 ......48 F8
Wellington Ho **5** CH5 .39 B6
Wellington Pl CH1 .....144 B3
Wellington Rd CH4 .....50 B4
Wellington Rd / Ffordd
  Wellington
  Rhyl / Y Rhyl LL18 .....7 A7
  Wrexham / Wrecsam LL13 145 B1
Wellington St CH5 ......39 B6
Wellington Terr **8** LL18 .7 A6
Well La CH2 ....42 E5
  Ffynnongroyw CH8 ......5 D1
Well La / Ffordd Ffynnon
  LL18 ....9 C7
Well Pl LL13 ....145 B2
Wells Cl
  Mickle Trafford CH2 ...43 F8
  Prestatyn LL19 ....2 E1
Well St
  BuckleyBuckley / Bwcle CH7 47 F3
  Buckley / Bwcle CH7 ...48 A4
  Cefn-Mawr LL14 ....85 C1
  Holywell / Treffynnon CH8 .21 B4
  Holywell / Treffynnon CH8 .21 B5
  Trelawnyd LL18 ....10 A4
  Treuddyn CH7 ....57 C2
Well St / Stryd-y-Ffynnon
  LL15 ....141 D5
Wellswood Rd LL13 .....73 C6
Welshampton CE Prim Sch
  SY12 ....110 C3
Welsh Coll of Horticulture /
  Coleg Garddwriaeth Cymru
  ....36 F6
Welsh Rd CH1 ....31 C6

Welsh Road Cotts CH1 ...31 D8
Wem Moss Nature Reserve★
  SY13 ....111 E1
Wemyss Rd CH1 ....41 D6
Wendover Ave LL22 ......6 D3
Wenfryn Cl LL20 ....85 A2
Wenlock Cres CH5 ......39 E3
Wenlock Way CH4 ......51 F6
Wentworth Cl CH7 ......48 A6
Wentworth Rise LL13 ...73 F4
Wepre Ct CH5 ....39 E3
Wepre Dr CH5 ....39 A7
Wepre Hall Cres CH5 ...38 E6
Wepre La CH5 ....38 D4
Wepre Cty Prim Sch CH5 38 D4
Wepre Park Visitor Ctr★
  CH5 ....38 E5
Wepre Pk★ CH5 ....38 E5
  Connah's Quay CH5 ....38 F6
Wern LL14 ....95 D3
Wern Ave CH6 ....22 C2
Wernfadog LL20 ....135 F5
Wernfechan LL15 ......141 D5
Wern Ganol LL15 ......141 D6
Wern Isaf LL15 ....141 D6
Wern La / Lon y Wern **11**
  LL14 ....78 C1
Wern Las LL14 ....85 F8
Wern Rd LL14 ....143 D5
Wern Ucha CH6 ....22 B2
Wern Uchaf LL15 ......141 D6
Wesley Rd LL11 ....70 E7
Wesley St CH5 ....38 F8
West Ave LL19 ....3 C2
West Bank CH2 ....42 C4
West Bank Rd LL12 .....66 F5
Westbourne Ave LL18 ....7 A6
Westbourne Cres CH7 ...48 A4
Westbourne Ctr **5** LL18 .7 A6
Westbourne Dr LL14 ....79 D6
Westbourne Rd CH1 .....42 A4
Westbrook Ave **4** SY13 103 F8
Westbrook Dr CH7 ......48 C3
Westbury Dr CH7 ....48 E4
Westbury Dr / Ffordd
  Westbury
  Westbury LL12 ....73 B7
Westbury Way LL14 .....51 F6
West Cheshire Coll
  (Handbridge Ctr) CH4 ..52 D7
West Circ LL13 ....73 C2
West Cl LL13 ....2 B2
Westdale Ct LL18 ....7 F1
West Dr CH1 ....21 A4
Westend Ct LL13 ....75 D8
West End Terr **1** LL14 .86 A4
Western App CH2 ....42 E4
Western Ave CH1 ....41 D4
Western Ct CH2 ....42 E4
Western View LL11 .....73 A4
Western Villas **6** LL11 .72 A4
Westfield Cl CH7 ....52 B7
Westfield Cres LL13 ....80 E7
Westfield Dr CH4 ......58 F7
Westfield Rd LL18 ......7 D7
West Gr LL14 ....79 C6
West Kinmel St LL18 ....7 B7
Westleigh Way **8** LL11 .73 A5
West Lorne St CH1 ....144 A3
Westminster Ave
  Chester CH4 ....52 B6
  Rhyl / Y Rhyl LL18 .....7 E6
Westminster Cl LL12 ..145 C4
Westminster Cres CH5 ..39 C5
Westminster Dr
  Gresford LL12 ....67 F2
  Wrexham / Wrecsam
  LL12 ....145 C4
Westminster Gn CH4 ...52 D7
Westminster Rd
  Broughton CH4 ....50 B3
  Chester CH2 ....42 F3
  Wrexham / Wrecsam LL11 .72 B7
Westminster Terr CH4 ..52 C7
Weston Cl CH5 ....39 F6
Weston Ct LL18 ....1 E5
Weston Dr LL11 ....72 F4
Weston Gr CH2 ....42 E7
Weston Rd
  Rhyl / Y Rhyl LL18 .....7 B6
  Wrexham / Wrecsam LL11 .72 C3
Weston Rhyn Prim Sch
  SY10 ....105 D5
Weston View **8** LL11 ..72 C5
West Par / Rhodfa Gorllewin
  LL18 ....5 A6
West Rd CH8 ....21 A4
West St Chester CH2 ...144 A4
  Llangollen LL20 ......143 C5
  Rhyl / Y Rhyl LL18 .....7 A6
  Wrexham / Wrecsam
  LL11 ....145 A4
Westune SY13 ....103 F6
West View
  Buckley / Bwcle CH7 ...48 C3
  Mold / Yr Wyddgrug CH7 .46 F4
  Penyffordd CH4 ....59 A6
  3 Wrexham / Wrecsam
  LL11 ....73 A5
West View Dr CH7 ......47 C4
Westway CH5 ....39 E2
West Way Penley LL13 ..99 E3
  Rossett LL12 ....68 C7
Westwood Com Prim Sch
  CH7 ....48 B4
Westwood Dr / Rhodfa
  Westwood **1** LL13 ...73 F3
Wetherby Cl CH1 ....42 B2
Wetreins La SY14, CH3 ..76 D6

Weybourne Cl CH4 ......51 E5
Whaddon Dr CH4 ....51 F4
Whaley Ct CH1 ....41 A8
Whalley's Way LL14 .....85 D3
Wharfdale Ave CH5 .....38 D6
Wharf Hill LL20 ....143 D5
Wharf Rd SY12 ....109 B2
Wheat CH1 ....72 C6
Wheatsheaf La LL11 ....72 D7
Wheatsheaf Mews LL11 .72 D7
Wheldon Cl CH2 ....42 E8
Whipcord La CH1 ....42 A3
Whitby Ave CH2 ....42 D5
Whitchurch Rd
  Bangor on Dee / Bangor-is-y-coed
  LL13 ....89 D3
  Chester CH3 ....43 B1
  Christleton CH3 ....53 E7
Whitchurch Rd / Ffordd
  Eglwyswen
  Denbigh / Dinbych LL16 .117 E1
  Denbigh / Dinbych LL16 .120 F8
Whitebrook Cl / Clos
  Gwynant LL14 ....86 B5
Whitecroft Cl CH5 .....38 C7
White Farm Rd CH4 .....48 A7
Whitefield Terr CH6 ....22 C2
Whitefriars **4** LL12 ...73 C6
White Friars CH1 .....144 A2
Whitegate Fields LL13 ..69 D1
Whitegate Ind Complex
  LL13 ....80 D8
Whitegate Rd LL13 .....80 C8
White La CH3 ....53 D8
White Lion Cl LL11 .....72 C8
White Oaks LL11 ....70 F7
White Oaks Dr CH7 .....38 A4
White Rose Cl LL19 .....3 A3
White Rose Sh Ctr The
  LL18 ....7 B8
Whites Mdw CH3 ....53 A7
Whiteway Dr LL12 ......67 E3
White Way Gr CH5 .....39 F6
Whitewell Rd SY13 ....102 C8
Whitford St CH8 ....21 A4
Whitland Way LL13 .....80 E7
Whitrock Rd CH4 ......49 B1
Whittle Cl CH5 ....40 A3
Whitton Dr CH2 ....42 E5
Whixall CE Prim Sch
  SY13 ....112 E3
Wicker La CH3 ....43 F5
Wiend The CH1 ....42 D4
Wigdale Row CH5 ......49 C8
Wigdale The CH5 ....49 C8
Wilding Bsns Pk CH3 ...43 C4
Wilkinson Dr / Rhodfa
  Wilkinson LL14 ....79 C6
Willan Rd CH1 ....41 D4
Willeymoor La LL13 ....93 D7
Williams Cl Chester CH2 .42 C4
  Penymynydd CH4 ......49 B1
  Ruabon / Rhiwabon LL14 .86 B5
Williams Pl CH8 ....5 C1
Williams St LL18 ....7 C7
William St Chester CH1 144 B3
  Chester, Hoole Park CH2 .42 F3
William St / Stryt William **6**
  LL14 ....78 F2
Williams Way LL12 .....68 B7
Willow Ave LL11 ....66 C8
Willoway Rd CH3 ....43 B2
Willow Cl Chester CH7 ..42 D8
  1 St. Martin's SY11 106 F6
Willow Cl / Llys Helyg
  CH7 ....48 E4
Willow Cres Chester CH2 .43 A4
  Connah's Quay CH5 ....38 E7
  3 Ellesmere SY12 ..109 B2
  Ewloe CH5 ....48 F8
Willow Ct
  Bangor on Dee / Bangor-is-y-coed
  LL13 ....89 A8
  Connah's Quay CH5 ....29 D1
  Higher Kinnerton CH4 ..60 A7
  Rhyl / Y Rhyl LL18 .....7 E8
  Wrexham / Wrecsam LL13 .73 E3
Willow Dr Blacon CH1 ...41 D5
  Flint / Y Fflint CH6 ....27 E5
  Llay LL12 ....67 B4
  Marford LL12 ....67 F2
Willowfield CH8 ....26 E5
Willow Gr Chester CH2 ..43 B4
  Talacre CH8 ....5 A6
Willow Gr / Llwyn Helyg
  CH7 ....48 B7
Willowherb Cl CH3 .....53 B6
Willow La CH5 ....39 E4
Willow Lea Cl **4** LL11 .72 D6
Willow Pk CH5 ....39 D4
Willow Rd CH4 ....51 F6
Willow Rd / Heol Helyg
  LL11 ....71 C4
Willow St
  Ellesmere SY12 ....109 B2
  Llangollen LL20 ......143 C4
  Overton LL13 ....98 C8
Willows The Prestatyn LL19 **2** D2
  Wrexham / Wrecsam
  LL12 ....145 C4
Willow The CH7 ....48 B7
Willow Way CH4 ....50 B3
Willow Wlk / Rhodfa Helyg
  CH7 ....57 F5
Wilson Ave LL13 ....73 C2

168 Wil – Zio

Wilson Ho 10 LL11 ......72 C3
Wilton Rd CH5 ....39 D2
Winchester Dr LL19 ......2 F1
Winchester Sq CH4 .....51 F5
Winchester Way LL12 ...67 E3
Windermere Ave
  Chester CH2 ....43 A6
  Connah's Quay CH5 ....38 F7
Windermere Dr LL19 ......2 F3
Windermere Rd LL12 ...73 C6
Windmill Cl
  Buckley / Bwcle CH7 ....48 B5
  Holywell / Treffynnon CH8 .21 C4
Windmill La CH3 ....53 D8
Windmill Rd / Ffordd Y Felin
  Wynt CH7 ....48 B5
Windmill Rise CH2 ......42 D7
Windrush Cl LL13 ....80 C7
Windsor Ave
  Caergwrle LL12 ....66 A8
  10 Connah's Quay, Shotton
  CH5 ....39 B6
  Connah's Quay, Wepre CH5 .38 F6
Windsor Ct Chester CH1 .144 B1
  1 Rhyl / Y Rhyl LL18 ....7 B7
Windsor Dr
  Broughton CH4 ....50 A3
  Flint / Y Fflint CH6 .....27 F6
  Wrexham / Wrecsam LL11 .72 E3
Windsor Gr LL18 ....6 D5
Windsor Pk CH8 ....20 D6
Windsor Rd Chester CH4 .51 F6
  Wrexham / Wrecsam LL11 .72 C3
Windsor Rd / Ffordd
  Windsor LL14 ....78 E1
Windsor St 6 LL18 ....7 B7
Winkup's Camp LL22 .....6 F2
Winkwell Dr CH4 ....52 A5
Winnard Ave LL18 ....7 A6
Winscombe Dr CH4 .....43 C2
Winsford Way CH1 ....41 F2
Winston Ct CH2 ....43 A5
Wirral View
  Connah's Quay CH5 ....38 D7
  Ewloe CH5 ....39 B2
Withy Croft CH3 ....53 B7
Witter Pl CH1 ....144 C3
Woburn Cl / Clos Woburn 6
  LL13 ....73 E3
Woburn Dr CH2 ....42 F7
Wold Ct CH5 ....49 C8
Woodall Ave CH4 ....51 E6
Woodbank La CH1 ......31 D5
Woodbank Rd CH5 .....38 E6
Woodberry Cl / Buarth Coed
  Aeron LL14 ....79 E8
Woodbine Cotts CH7 ...37 F4
Woodbury 2 SY11 ....106 F7
Wood Croft
  Buckley / Bwcle CH7 ....48 E6
  Guilden Sutton CH3 ....43 F4
Woodfield Ave CH6 .....28 B6
Woodfield Cl
  Broughton CH4 ....50 A3
  Connah's Quay CH5 ....38 E6
Woodfield Gr CH2 ......43 B5
Woodfield Ho CH2 .....43 A5
Woodfield Prim Sch CH2 43 A5
Woodfields 53 E7
Wood Gn CH7 ....47 B4
Wood Gr / Llwyn-y-Coed
  CH7 ....57 F5
Woodhouse La LL13 ....80 D3
Wood La Broughton CH4 .50 B4
  Hawarden / Penarlâg CH5 .38 F1
  Holywell / Treffynnon CH8 .21 D5
  Penyffordd CH4 ....59 A8
Woodland LL11 ....72 E7
Woodland Cotts CH8 .....5 C1
Woodland Cres 2 CH5 .39 A6
Woodland Ct 27 F5
Woodland Dr
  Flint / Y Fflint CH6 .....27 F5
  Greenfield / Maes-Glas CH8 21 B7
Woodland Gr
  Wrexham / Wrecsam,
  Gwersyllt Hill LL11 .....72 C7
  Wrexham / Wrecsam, Rhosnesni
  LL13 ....73 E3
Woodland Rd LL11 .....72 A8
Woodlands Ave CH1 ....42 B4
Woodlands Cl CH7 .....47 A4
Woodlands Ct CH5 .....39 C8
Woodlands Cvn Pk CH8 .4 D4
Woodlands Dr
  Chester CH2 ....42 E4
  Ewloe CH5 ....48 F7

Woodlands Gr 5 LL20 ...95 A7
Woodlands Hall Cvn Pk
  LL15 ....125 D8
Woodlands La CH3 .....43 A2
Woodlands Rd
  Chester CH4 ....52 A7
  Huntington CH3 ....53 A6
  Llangollen Rural LL20 ...95 A7
  Marford LL12 ....67 F3
  Mold / Yr Wyddgrug CH7 .47 B4
Woodland St CH5 ......39 A6
Woodlands The CH5 ....49 A4
Woodlea Ave CH2 ......42 F7
Wood Memorial Sch CH4 51 F6
Wood Rd LL18 ....7 A6
Woodridge Ave LL12 ...67 F3
Woodside Ave LL18 .....6 C5
Woodside Cl CH5 ......39 A1
Woodside Ct Chester CH2 42 C4
  Rhostyllen LL14 ....79 D7
Woodside Gdns LL18 ....7 D5
Woodside Rd CH1 .....41 C5
Wood St CH5 ....40 A2
Wood Ville CH5 ....39 D2
Worcester Dr LL19 ......2 F1
Worcester Pl CH1 ......42 A4
Worcester Rd LL11 ....89 A8
Wordsworth Cl CH5 ....48 B5
Wordsworth Cres CH1 ..42 A5
Wordsworth Mews CH1 .42 A5
Wordsworth Sq CH1 ...42 A5
Worsley Ave
  Johnstown LL14 ....79 A1
  Saughall CH1 ....41 A8
Worthington Ct CH2 ...42 D4
Wrekin Way CH4 ....51 F6
Wrexham Central Sta
  LL13 ....145 B2
Wrexham FC (The Race
  course) LL11 ....145 A4
Wrexham General Sta
  LL11 ....145 A3
Wrexham Ind Est / Ystad
  Ddiwydiannol Wrecsam
  ....81 E7
Wrexham Rd
  Caergwrle LL12 ....66 B6
  Chester CH4 ....52 B4
  Holt LL13 ....75 B7
  Holt LL13 ....75 D8
  Hope / Yr Hôb CH4, LL12 .59 B4
  Johnstown LL14 ....79 A3
  Marchwiel LL13 ....80 F4
  Mold / Yr Wyddgrug CH7 .47 A2
  Overton LL13 ....98 C8
  Overton / Owrtyn LL13 ..88 B1
  Penyffordd CH4 ....59 A6
  Pulford CH4 ....61 E5
  Rhostyllen LL14 ....79 D6
  Roughhill CH4 ....51 F1
  Ruthin / Rhuthin LL15 .141 D3
  4 Whitchurch LL13 ...103 E2
  Whitchurch Urban SY13 .103 B7
  Worthenbury SY14 .....83 C1
  Wrexham / Wrecsam LL11 72 E5
Wrexham St / Stryd
  Wrecsam CH7 ....46 F4
Wrexham Tech Pk LL13 .72 E2
Wroxham Ct CH2 ....144 B4
Wycliffe Ct CH2 ....43 A2
Wylfa Ave CH7 ....47 C4
Wyndham Dr LL12 .....66 B5
Wyndham Gdns LL13 ...73 E1
Wyndham Rd LL11 .....41 C4
Wynn Ave
  Ruabon / Rhiwabon LL14 .86 B5
  Wrexham / Wrecsam LL11 .73 A4
Wynne Cl LL18 ....15 F8
Wynne's Parc Cotts
  LL16 ....140 F2
Wynnhall Terr LL14 ....85 D6
Wynnstay Ave LL13 ....73 D2
Wynnstay Cres LL14 ...79 C6
Wynnstay Ct
  Ruabon / Rhiwabon LL14 .86 A5
  Ruabon / Rhiwabon, Rhosymadoc
  LL14 ....86 B2
Wynnstay La LL12 .....68 A2
Wynnstay Mews 7 LL14 .86 A4
Wynnstay Rd CH4 .....50 C4
Wynnstay Rd / Ffordd
  Wynnstay 5 LL14 ....141 D5
Wynnstay Technology Pk
  LL14 ....85 E4

Y

Yale Coll / Coleg Ial
  LL12 ....145 B3

Yale Gr LL12 ....145 C4
Yale Park / Parc Ial
  LL11 ....145 A3
Yale Private Hospl / Ysbyty
  Ial LL12 ....72 E2
Yale St LL14 ....78 F1
Yardington 5 SY13 ...103 F8
Yarrow Cl CH4 ....50 C3
Yarwood Dr LL13 ......73 C6
Yew Tree Cl CH4 ......50 C3
Yew Tree Cl / Clos Coed
  Ywen LL17 ....16 B2
Yew Tree Ct LL12 .....67 D3
Y Farchnad / Market Sq
  CH6 ....28 A7
Y Ffennant / Fennant Rd
  Johnstown LL14 ....79 A2
  Rhoslanerchrugog LL14 .78 F2
Y Ffrith LL18 ....7 D8
Y Fron LL14 ....79 A1
Y Gamer LL20 ....135 C5
Ygerddi CH8 ....12 C4
Y Gilfach LL16 ....140 D4
Y-Gesail LL14 ....86 B8
Y Gilfach CH7 ....46 F3
Y Gorlan Pwll-glas LL15 .125 F5
  Rhyl / Y Rhyl LL18 ......7 C8
Y Llys LL15 ....121 F2
Y Lon Las / Green La
  LL21 ....142 C6
Y Maes
  Denbigh / Dinbych LL16 .140 E4
  Glyn Ceiriog LL20 .....135 C5
Y Nant CH8 ....12 B5
Yonne The CH1 ......144 A2
York Ave CH5 ....39 B5
York Cl LL19 ....2 F1
York Cl / Clos Efrog
  LL13 ....80 F7
York Dr CH2 ....43 E8
Yorke Ave LL13 ....80 E5
Yorke Cl LL13 ....81 A4
Yorke St / Stryt Efrog
  LL13 ....145 C2
York Rd CH5 ....29 C1
York St CH1 ....144 B3
Yowley Rd CH5 ....38 F2
Y Parc LL17 ....16 A1
Y Parc / Park The
  Mold / Yr Wyddgrug CH7 .46 F4
  Ruthin / Rhuthin LL15 ..141 B5
Yr Efail / The Forge CH4 49 A1
Yr Erw / Hand La 1
  LL14 ....78 F2
Yr Helfa LL14 ....95 E3
Yr Hen Berllan / The Old
  Orch LL14 ....49 D8
Yr Hen Erddi / Old Gardens
  The 1 LL13 ....73 E3
Yr Hobin Cast / Johnson St
  LL14 ....78 E2
Y Rhos LL14 ....85 C2
Yr Ochr LL20 ....94 F7
Yr Ydlan CH7 ....47 D6

Ysbyty = hospital

Ysbyty Cymuned Glannau
  Dyfrdwy / Deeside Com
  Hospl CH5 ....39 B4
Ysbyty Cymunedol Y
  Wyddgrug / Mold Com
  Hospl CH7 ....46 E5
Ysbyty Glan Clwyd (Hospl)
  LL18 ....15 A5
Ysbyty Ial / Yale Private
  Hospl LL12 ....72 E2
Ysbyty Lluesty / Lluesty
  Hospl CH8 ....21 B2
Ysbyty Maelor Wrecsam /
  Wrexham Maelor Hospl
  LL13 ....145 A2

Ysbyty Treffynnon / Holywell
  Cottage Hospl CH8 ....21 B4

Ysgol = school

Ysgol Acrefair LL14 ....85 B3
Ysgol Belmont CH7 ....48 B6
Ysgol Bodhyfryd LL13 ..80 B7
Ysgol Bro Aled Llansannan
  LL16 ....118 C8
Ysgol Bro Carmel CH8 ..20 C6
Ysgol Bro Cinmeirch
  LL16 ....120 F6
Ysgol Bro Cynllaith
  SY10 ....139 D3
Ysgol Bro Famau-Llanarmon
  Unit CH7 ....127 B7
Ysgol Bro Famau-Llanferres
  Unit CH7 ....55 B6
Ysgol Bro
  Fammau-Graianrhyd Unit
  CH7 ....63 C5
Ysgol Bryn Alyn High Sch
  LL11 ....72 C8
Ysgol Bryn Clwyd LL16 .121 B8
Ysgol Bryn Coch CH7 ..46 F4
Ysgol Bryn Collen LL20 .143 E3
Ysgol Bryn Garth CH8 ..11 C8
Ysgol Bryn Golau Sch
  LL11 ....72 D7
Ysgol Bryn Gwalia CH7 .46 E4
Ysgol Brynhyfryd LL15 .141 E5
Ysgol Bryn Offa
  Wrexham / Wrecsam LL13 .72 C1
  Wrexham / Wrecsam LL13 .73 C1
Ysgol Bryn Pennant CH8 12 C4
Ysgol Bryn Tabor LL11 ..71 C3
Ysgol Caer Drewyn
  LL21 ....142 C6
Ysgol Cefn Meiriadog
  LL22 ....116 D8
Ysgol Croes Atti CH4 ...28 B6
Ysgol Cyffylliog LL15 ..125 A8
Ysgol Cynddelw LL20 ..135 C5
Ysgol Delyn CH7 ......46 F4
Ysgol Derwen CH4 .....60 A7
Ysgol Derwenfa CH7 ...58 A4
Ysgol Dewi Sant LL18 ...7 E5
Ysgol Dewi Sant / St David's
  High Sch LL13 ....73 D3
Ysgol Dinas Bran LL20 .143 D5
Ysgol Dinmael LL21 ...128 A3
Ysgol Dyffran Iâl CH7 ..127 B3
Ysgol Emmanuel LL18 ...7 E5
Ysgol Esgob Morgan
  LL17 ....16 A2
Ysgol Frongoch LL16 ..140 D4
Ysgol Glan Aber CH6 ...21 F5
Ysgol Glanrafon CH7 ...46 F3
Ysgol Gronant LL19 .....4 B3
Ysgol Gwaenysg LL16 .140 A3
Ysgol Gwenffrwd CH8 ..21 A5
Ysgol Gymraeg Mornant
  CH8 ....4 F1
Ysgol Gynradd Carrog
  LL21 ....129 F2
Ysgol Gynradd Eglwys Crist
  LL18 ....73 E3
Ysgol Gynradd Gwyddelwern
  LL21 ....129 B5
Ysgol Gynradd Henllan
  LL16 ....116 F3
Ysgol Gynradd Llawrybetws
  LL21 ....128 C1
Ysgol Gynradd Pentrecelyn
  LL15 ....126 C3
Ysgol Gynradd Rhydgaled
  LL16 ....119 C7
Ysgol Gynradd Trelogan
  CH8 ....10 F4
Ysgol Hiraddug LL18 .....8 F2
Ysgol Hooson LL14 ....78 D2
Ysgol Llanarmon Dyffryn
  Ceiriog LL20 ....138 D7
Ysgol Llywelyn LL18 .....7 E6
Ysgol Maes Edwin CH6 .28 A1
Ysgol Maes Garmon CH7 46 F3
Ysgol Maes Hyfryd LL21 132 F8
Ysgol Maes-y-Llan LL14 .86 B4
Ysgol Mair RC Sch LL18 .7 D6
Ysgol Melyd LL19 ....8 F6
Ysgol Min-y-Ddol LL14 .85 C1
Ysgol Morgan Llwyd Sch
  LL13 ....73 E2
Ysgol Owen Jones Prim
  CH7 ....37 A6
Ysgol Parc Y Llan CH7 .64 C8
Ysgol Pen Barras LL15 .141 D5
Ysgol Penmorfa LL19 ...3 A1

Ysgol Penrhyn LL11 ....72 B4
Ysgol Plas Brondyffryn
  Denbigh / Dinbych LL16 .140 D3
  Denbigh / Dinbych LL16 .140 E2
Ysgol Plas Coch LL11 ..72 F4
Ysgol Powys LL11 .....72 E7
Ysgol Reoledig Llanbedr
  LL15 ....121 E3
Ysgol Reoledig Llanfair
  Dyffryn Clwyd LL15 ..126 B6
Ysgol Rhiwabon LL14 ..85 F4
Ysgol Rhos Helyg CH7 .36 A8
Ysgol Sant Christopher / St
  Christophers Sch LL13 .80 B7
Ysgol Sant Dunawd LL13 89 A7
Ysgol Sychdyn Prim CH7 37 A1
Ysgol Terrig CH7 ......64 C8
Ysgol Tir Morfa
  Rhuddlan LL18 ....7 F2
  Rhyl / Y Rhyl LL18 ......7 D5
Ysgol Trefnant LL16 ...117 C5
Ysgol Tremeirchion
  LL17 ....117 F8
Ysgol Twm o'r Nant
  LL16 ....140 D4
Ysgol Uwchradd Argoed /
  Argoed High Sch CH7 .47 E6
Ysgol Uwchradd Glan Clwyd
  LL17 ....16 C1
Ysgol-y-bryn CH5 .....39 A5
Ysgol y Castell LL18 ...15 F8
Ysgol Y Ddol CH7 .....35 E3
Ysgol-y-Drindod Jun Sch
  LL11 ....72 D7
Ysgol y Faenol LL18 ...14 E4
Ysgol Y Foel CH7 .....44 F7
Ysgol Y Foryd LL18 .....6 D4
Ysgol-y-Fron Jun Sch
  CH8 ....21 B4
Ysgol y Gaer LL11 .....72 E7
Ysgol-Y-Grango LL14 ..78 E2
Ysgol Y Llan, Whitford
  ....11 F1
Ysgol Y Llys LL17 ......9 A8
Ysgol-y-Parc LL16 ....140 E3
Ysgol Y Ponciau LL14 ..78 F2
Ysgol Yr Esgob CH7 ...24 B6
Ysgol Y Rhos LL14 ....78 D2
Ysgol Y Waun CH7 ....45 E6
Ysgol-y-Wern LL14 ....78 E1
Ysgubor Newydd La LL17 17 E3
Ysgubor-wen LL16 ....140 F3

Ystad = estate

Ystad Ddiwydiannol
  Colomendy / Colomendy
  Ind Est LL16 ....140 D5
Ystad Ddiwydiannol Coppi
  Ind Est LL14 ....78 D2
Ystad Ddiwydiannol Llai (De)
  / Llay Ind Est (South)
  LL12 ....66 F5
Ystad Ddiwydiannol Llai
  (Gogledd) / Llay Ind Est
  (North) LL12 ....66 F6
Ystad Ddiwydiannol Wrecsam
  / Wrexham Ind Est LL13 81 E8
Ystad Ddiwydianol Corwen
  (Ind Est) LL21 ....142 C6
Ystrad Rd / Ffordd Ystrad
  LL16 ....140 E2
Y Stryd Fawr / High St
  Dyserth LL18 ....8 F3
  1 Rhyl / Y Rhyl LL18 ....7 B8
Y Stryt Fawr / High St
  Coedpoeth LL11 ....71 C3
  Rhoslanerchrugog LL14 .78 E2
Y Tyddyn / The Homestead
  LL14 ....79 E8
Y Waen Flint Mountain CH6 28 A1
  Gwernaffield / Y-Waun CH7 .45 E6
Y Weirglodd LL16 .....140 E4
Y Werddon LL13 ......145 B2
Y Wern LL13 ....80 D8

Z

Zion Cotts 2 LL11 ....72 A4
Zion St LL14 ....85 B2